AN INTRODUCTION TO
PHILOSOPHY
THROUGH LITERATURE

ROBERT C. BALDWIN

PROFESSOR OF PHILOSOPHY AND HEAD OF
THE DEPARTMENT OF PHILOSOPHY
THE UNIVERSITY OF CONNECTICUT

JAMES A. S. McPEEK

PROFESSOR OF ENGLISH
THE UNIVERSITY OF CONNECTICUT

THE RONALD PRESS COMPANY , NEW YORK

6

Library of Congress Catalog Card Number: 50-8252

PRINTED IN THE UNITED STATES OF AMERICA

C.B.S.
6 3⁰
9-13-61 ᵇ ᵖ ᵐ
9-18-61 a ᵏᵛ

To

K. G. McP. and C. R. B.

I bring a branch of Evin's apple-tree,
In shape like those you know:
Twigs of white silver are upon it,
Buds of crystal with blossoms.

—*The Voyage of Bran*

PREFACE

This book is intended to introduce students to philosophy through the medium of selections from good literature. Our experience in teaching convinces us that this approach holds more rewarding possibilities than any other. The student has selected for him, and the instructor has at hand, material challenging endless discussion, leading toward exploration and discovery and comparison on the individual's own initiative. The method itself, which involves classroom analysis and discussion and reviewing by the instructor, is at least as old as Socrates. That Berkeley and Descartes knew it is clear from their writings. Many of our best radio forums of today likewise illustrate its value. Method and material both are designed to give freshness to the study of philosophy, to make the reader more richly aware of the relation between philosophy and experience, and to help him develop the habit of looking for philosophical values in his general reading.

The value of this approach to philosophy is recognized in the constant literary allusions that enliven the pages of our more stimulating introductory textbooks. Indications of a trend may be seen in the steady increase in the number of courses in philosophy in literature that have become accepted parts of college curricula. Signs yet more favorable to our intention may be observed in the emphasis of philosophers like Santayana and Edman and Katherine Gilbert on literary values and of authors like T. S. Eliot, W. H. Auden, and Thomas Mann on philosophic thought, an emphasis which has at times made it happily impossible to distinguish between philosopher and poet.

The selections chosen are drawn from much of the best literature of ideas, including the writings of many leading philosophers. More than a hundred authors are represented, nearly half of them contemporary. As more fully explained in "A Letter to the Reader" and the separate chapter introductions, the selections in each chapter are organized around one of the major philosophical themes, with the final passages in each chapter often affording a natural transition to the topic of the next.

This book, while oriented to the needs of the beginner in philosophy, does not address him as though he were isolated in a specialized department of knowledge. For this reason we hope that it will appeal to general readers who wish to relate what they read to universal human interests. For the same reason teachers in general education and the humanities may find this volume precisely suited to their needs. Students in junior and teachers colleges and technical and engineering schools should profit from the use here of forms of speech close to the concreteness of their familiar thinking, while being introduced to the great problems and points of view of philosophy.

When we turn to thank those who have helped us, we find that our first and largest obligation is to those authors whose writings compose our subject matter. In the early formative stages of the book we benefited from the valuable guidance and encouragement of Professor Arthur E. Murphy of Cornell University. In the long task of preparing the manuscript for printing, we have profited more than can be estimated from the friendly interest, competence, and editorial skill of our colleague Newton L. Carroll and of Mrs. Newton L. Carroll. Finally we are indebted to many teachers—preeminent among them George Lyman Kittredge, John Livingston Lowes, Fernand Baldensperger, Andrew Campbell Armstrong, Cornelius F. Krusé, and Charles A. Bennett—teachers who planted in our minds the conviction that literature reflects life and that the proper study of philosophy can never be less than a living experience.

R. C. B.
J. A. S. McP.

Storrs, Connecticut
May, 1950

ACKNOWLEDGMENTS

Grateful acknowledgment is made to the following persons and publishers who have freely granted permission to quote from works written or controlled by them:

IRWIN EDMAN, for "Eternity," in Chapter 1.

MRS. MARY DARRAH FINE, for "Time" by Bhartrihari, translated by Paul Elmer More, published in *Century of Indian Epigrams*, edited by Paul Elmer More, in Chapter 7.

HARVARD UNIVERSITY PRESS, for "Letter to William James," reprinted by permission of the publishers from *The Thought and Character of William James, Briefer Version*, by Ralph Barton Perry, copyright 1948 by the Harvard University Press, in Chapter 15; and for excerpts reprinted by permission of the publishers from *Three Philosophical Poets* by George Santayana, copyright, 1910, 1935, by Harvard University Press, Cambridge, Massachusetts, in "A Letter to the Reader."

RUTH LECHLITNER (MRS. PAUL COREY), for "Snowflakes" in Chapter 2.

LUDWIG LEWISOHN, for "The Thought Eternal," reprinted from *Goethe: The Story of a Man* (New York: Farrar, Straus & Co., Inc., 1949), copyright, Ludwig Lewisohn, in Chapter 1.

ARCHIBALD MACLEISH, for excerpts from his "Humanism and the Belief in Man," published in *The Atlantic Monthly* for November, 1944, in Chapter 14.

OHIO STATE UNIVERSITY PRESS, for excerpts from *Emerson and Beyond* by William Yerington, copyright, 1929, by Ohio State University Press, in Chapter 14.

CHARLOTTE ROSS, for "Lines Written After Class in Philosophy 100," in Chapter 13.

The Spectator, for "Passing Thought," by Neville de Caun, published in their issue for November 19, 1948, in Chapter 12.

SATURDAY REVIEW ASSOCIATES, INC., for "Transient" by Don Marquis in *Saturday Review of Literature*, IX (Oct. 22, 1932), in Chapter 5.

YALE UNIVERSITY PRESS, for "God Finite and Infinite," from *Belief Unbound* by William Pepperell Montague, copyright, 1930, Yale University Press, in Chapter 4.

We wish to thank also the following authors, publishers, and others for their permission to reprint selections from copyrighted works in this volume:

RICHARD ALDINGTON, for the following selections from *Candide and Other Romances* by Voltaire, translated by Richard Aldington (London: Routledge and Kegan Paul, Ltd.): excerpts from *Candide*, in Chapters 7, 8, 9, 12, 15; excerpts from *Lord Chesterfield's Ears*, in Chapters 1 and 11; and an excerpt from *Babouc's Vision*, in Chapter 8.

GEORGE ALLEN & UNWIN, LTD., for excerpts from *The Meaning of Good* (1906) by G. Lowes Dickinson, in Chapter 6; excerpts from *Twilight of the Idols* by Friedrich Nietzsche, translated by A. M. Ludovici, in Chapter 2; "A Free Man's Worship" from *Mysticism and Logic* (1929) by Bertrand Russell, in Chapter 13; and excerpts from "The Harm That Good Men Do" in *Sceptical Essays* (1928), in Chapter 3. (See further acknowledgment with the selections from Bertrand Russell on pages 105 and 502.)

ANDERSON HOUSE, for excerpts from *Key Largo* by Maxwell Anderson, copyright, 1939, by Maxwell Anderson, in Chapters 3 and 14.

The Atlantic Monthly, for an excerpt from "Invisible Kingdom" by Freda Bond, published in their issue for July, 1934, in Chapter 11; and for an excerpt from "Humanism and the Belief in Man" by Archibald MacLeish, published in their issue for November, 1944, in Chapter 14.

CAMBRIDGE UNIVERSITY PRESS, for excerpts from the Introduction and from "Pointer Readings" in *The Nature of the Physical World* by Sir Arthur Stanley Eddington, copyright, 1928, by The Macmillan Co., in Chapter 10; and for "The Broom," "The Calm After the Storm," "To Count Pepoli," "To Himself," "Night Song," and "Sappho's Last Song" from *The Poems of Leopardi* (1923), translated by G. L. Bickersteth, in Chapters 5, 7, and 12.

JONATHAN CAPE, LIMITED, for an excerpt from *The Way of All Flesh* by Samuel Butler, by permission of the publishers and the Executors of Samuel Butler, in Chapter 3; and for excerpts from *A Portrait of the Artist as a Young Man* by James Joyce, by permission of the publishers and the Executors of James Joyce, in Chapter 2.

CHATTO & WINDUS, for "The Cicadas" from *The Cicadas and Other Poems* (1931) and "First Philosopher's Song" from *Leda* (1920) by Aldous Huxley, in Chapters 8 and 13. (See further acknowledgments with the poems on pages 344 and 502.)

THE CLARENDON PRESS, Oxford, for an excerpt from "To a Socialist in London" from Robert Bridges' *Poetical Works* by permission of the Clarendon Press, Oxford, in Chapter 13.

CLARKE, IRWIN & CO., LTD., as Canadian agents, for "First Philosopher's Song" from *Leda* (1920) by Aldous Huxley, in Chapter 13.

DODD, MEAD & CO. INC., for "Heaven," reprinted from *The Collected Poems of Rupert Brooke,* copyright, 1915, by Dodd, Mead & Co., Inc., in Chapter 4; for excerpts from *Heretics* by G. K. Chesterton, copyright, 1905, and used by permission of Dodd, Mead & Co., Inc., in Chapter 1; and for excerpts from *Thaïs* (1925) by Anatole France, used by permission of Dodd, Mead & Co., Inc., in Chapter 10.

FABER & FABER, LTD., for "Musée des Beaux Arts" from *The Collected Poetry of W. H. Auden,* copyright, 1945, by W. H. Auden, in Chapter 2; "Animula" from *Collected Poems, 1909-1935* by T. S. Eliot, in Chapter 11 (see further acknowledgment with the poem on page 430); "Snow" and "Plurality" from *Poems 1925-1940* (1940) by Louis MacNeice, in Chapter 11; and "I think continually" from *Poems* by Stephen Spender, in Chapter 5.

HARVARD UNIVERSITY PRESS, for excerpts from Lucretius, *De Rerum Natura,* translated by W. H. D. Rouse, copyright, 1937, by Harvard University Press, in "A Letter to the Reader;" and for excerpts from *Sophocles* (2 vols.), translated by F. Storr, copyright, 1928-1929, by Harvard University Press, in Chapters 3 and 9: *both reprinted by permission of the publishers from the Loeb Classical Library editions.*

WILLIAM HEINEMANN, LTD., for excerpts from the following novels by Fyodor Dostoevsky, translated by Constance Garnett: *The Brothers Karamazov* in Chapter 6; *The Possessed* in Chapter 9; *White Nights and Other Stories,* in Chapters 3 and 9; and for excerpts from *Of Human Bondage* by W. Somerset Maugham, in Chapters 1, 2, 3, 4, 7, and 9. (See further acknowledgments with the selections from Maugham, pages 24, 76, 79, 83, 153, 283, 368.)

THE HOGARTH PRESS, LTD., for excerpts from *Duino Elegies* (1939) by Rainer Maria Rilke, in Chapter 10. (See further acknowledgment with the poems on page 403.)

THE HOGARTH PRESS, LTD., for "The Third Elegy" and "The Fourth Elegy" (in part) from *Duino Elegies* by Rainer Maria Rilke, translated by J. B. Leishman and Stephen Spender, in Chapter 10. (See further acknowledgment with the selections, page 403.)

HENRY HOLT & CO. INC., for "The Bear," in Chapter 1; for "The Strong Are Saying Nothing," in Chapter 5; and for excerpts from *A Masque of Reason,* in Chapter 6: all from *The Complete Poems of Robert Frost,* reproduced by permission of Henry Holt & Co., Inc., copyright, 1928, 1936, 1945, 1949; also for an excerpt from *Ethics,* Revised Edition, by John Dewey and James Tufts, by permission of Henry Holt & Co., Inc. copyright, 1908, 1932.

HOUGHTON MIFFLIN CO., for "Lines for an Interment" from *Poems, 1924-1933* by Archibald MacLeish, copyright 1925, 1926, 1928, 1932, 1933, by Archibald MacLeish, in Chapter 3; and for excerpts from "The Improbability of Freedom" in *The Problem of Freedom* by George Herbert Palmer, copyright, 1911, by Houghton Mifflin Co., in Chapter 9: *both reprinted by permission of and arrangement with Houghton Mifflin Co., the authorized publishers.*

MONSIGNOR RONALD KNOX, for his limerick beginning, "There was a young man," in Chapter 10.

LONGMANS, GREEN & CO., INC., for excerpts from the following: "Survival and Immortality" and "Our Present Discontents" in *Outspoken Essays* by Dean William Ralph Inge, copyright, 1919, by Longmans, Green & Co., Inc., in Chapters 5 and 14; "The Will to Believe"

ACKNOWLEDGMENTS

and "The Dilemma of Determinism" in *Essays on Faith and Morals* by William James, copyright, 1943, by Longmans, Green & Co., Inc., in Chapters 4 and 9; "What Pragmatism Means" in *Pragmatism* by William James, copyright, 1931, by Longmans, Green & Co., Inc., in Chapter 15; and *Varieties of Religious Experience* by William James, copyright, 1928, by Longmans, Green & Co., Inc., in Chapter 15.

THE MACMILLAN CO., for "The Virgin Mother" from *Selected Poems by A. E.* (George William Russell), copyright, 1935, by The Macmillan Co., in Chapter 13; Introduction by Arthur James Balfour from *Science, Religion and Reality,* ed. Joseph Needham, copyright, 1925, by The Macmillan Co., in Chapter 11; excerpts from "Theories of Knowledge" in *Democracy and Education* by John Dewey, copyright, 1925, by The Macmillan Co., in Chapter 15; "The Convergence of the Twain," "The Darkling Thrush," "God's Funeral," "Nature's Questioning," "New Year's Eve," "The Overworld" (in *The Dynasts*), and "The Subalterns" from *Collected Poems* by Thomas Hardy, copyright, 1925, by The Macmillan Co., in Chapters 1, 8, 9, and 12; "Not that the stars" and "There is no God" from *Lollingdon Downs and Other Poems* by John Masefield, copyright, 1917, by The Macmillan Co., in Chapter 14; excerpts from "Man Against the Sky" in *Man Against the Sky: A Book of Poems* by Edwin Arlington Robinson, copyright, 1916, by Edwin Arlington Robinson, in Chapter 7; "The Whisperer" and "Optimist" from *Insurrections* by James Stephens, copyright, 1909, by The Macmillan Co., in Chapters 4 and 8; "Wisdom" from *Love Songs* by Sara Teasdale, copyright, 1917, by The Macmillan Co., in Chapter 7; excerpts from "Religion and Science" in *Science and the Modern World* by Alfred North Whitehead, copyright, 1925, by The Macmillan Co., in Chapter 10; and excerpts from *The Tragic Sense of Life* by Miguel de Unamuno (translated by J. E. Crawford Flitch), in Chapters 1, 3, 6, and 10; *all used with the permission of The Macmillan Co.*

MACMILLAN & CO. LTD., for "The Virgin Mother" from *Collected Poems of A. E.* (George William Russell), London, 1920, by permission of Mr. Diarmuid Russell and Macmillan & Co., Ltd., in Chapter 13.

HAROLD MATSON, for excerpts from "From Feathers to Iron," "The Magnetic Mountain," and "Transitional Poem" in *Collected Poems, 1935* by C. Day Lewis in Chapters 4 and 15.

W. SOMERSET MAUGHAM, for excerpts from his *Of Human Bondage,* in Chapters 1, 2, 3, 4, 7, and 9.

McCLELLAND AND STEWART, LTD., for "Heaven," from *The Collected Poems of Rupert Brooke,* in Chapter 4.

NEW DIRECTIONS, for "All will grow great" and "Already ripening barberries grow red" from *Poems from the Book of Hours* by Rainer Maria Rilke, translated by Babette Deutsch, copyright, 1941, by New Directions, in Chapters 1 and 14; "The Heavy Bear" from *In Dreams Begin Responsibilities* by Delmore Schwartz, copyright, 1938, by New Directions, in Chapter 11; and "The 13th, 19th, & 20th Centuries" from *Paradox in the Circle* by Theodore Spencer, copyright, 1941, by New Directions, in Chapter 1.

ALFRED NOYES, for excerpts from *The Unknown God* (Sheed and Ward, New York, 1940), copyrighted by Alfred Noyes, in Chapter 6.

OXFORD UNIVERSITY PRESS, for "Carrion Comfort," "No Worst," "Nondum," "Pied Beauty," "Spring and Fall," and "The Times Are Nightfall" from *Poems of Gerard Manley Hopkins,* ed. W. H. Gardner, 3d edition, copyright, 1948, by Oxford University Press, reprinted by permission of the poet's family and the publishers, in Chapters 4, 7, 8, and 11; also for an excerpt from *Symposium* from *The Dialogues of Plato,* translated by Benjamin Jowett (Oxford University Press), in Chapter 2.

RANDOM HOUSE, INC., for the following selections: "Musée des Beaux Arts" and "The Labyrinth" from *The Collected Poetry of W. H. Auden,* copyright, 1945, by W. H. Auden in Chapters 2 and 10; "Invasion" (in part), "The Inhumanist" (in part), and "The King of Beasts" from *The Double Axe and Other Poems* by Robinson Jeffers, copyright, 1948, by Robinson Jeffers, in Chapters 2, 4, and 6; "Credo" from *Roan Stallion, Tamar and Other Poems* by Robinson Jeffers, copyright, 1935, by Modern Library; copyright, 1925, by Boni & Liveright, in Chapter 10; "The Giant's Ring" from *The Selected Poetry of Robinson*

Jeffers, copyright, 1938, by Robinson Jeffers, in Chapter 5; "Plurality" and "Snow" from *Poems, 1925-1940* by Louis MacNeice, copyright, 1937, 1939, 1940 by Louis MacNeice, in Chapter 11; "I Think Continually of Those Who Were Truly Great" from *Poems* by Stephen Spender, copyright, 1934, by Modern Library, in Chapter 5: *all reprinted by permission of Random House, Inc.*

THE VIKING PRESS, INC., for excerpts from "Intimations of Philosophy" from *Philosopher's Holiday* by Irwin Edman, copyright, 1938, by Irwin Edman, in Chapter 1; and for excerpts from *A Portrait of the Artist as a Young Man* by James Joyce, included in *The Portable James Joyce*, copyright, 1916, by B. W. Huebsch, 1944, by Nora Joyce, in Chapter 2: *both reprinted by permission of The Viking Press, Inc., New York.*

MRS. G. P. WELLS, for an excerpt from *New Worlds for Old* by H. G. Wells (New York: The Macmillan Co., 1911), reprinted by permission of the Executors of the late Mr. H. G. Wells, in Chapter 14.

ANN WOLFE, for "The Teacher" (in part) from *Requiem* (London: Ernest Benn, Ltd., 1927) and "The Uncourageous Violet" from *This Blind Rose* (London: Victor Gollancz, Ltd., 1928), by Humbert Wolfe, in Chapters 5 and 14.

Certain other permissions are acknowledged in footnotes in the text, as required by individual contractual arrangements.

CONTENTS

CONTENTS

CHAPTER 2

CHAPTER 5

CONTENTS

CHAPTER 10

CHAPTER 11

CHAPTER 12

OF TIME AND CHANGE 441

CHAPTER 13

CHAPTER 14

AN INTRODUCTION TO PHILOSOPHY THROUGH LITERATURE

A LETTER TO THE READER

This book is based on the theory that a valid nonacademic approach to philosophy is possible and that such an approach can be found in the everyday reading of cultivated persons. It is confidently offered as a solution to the main difficulties confronting both teacher and student in introductory courses in philosophy. These difficulties—the students' preconception of philosophy as a subject specialized and remote from experience and the abstruseness of the usual text with the barbed-wire entanglements of its jargon —have long been deplored. Careful observation over several years of the eager response of students to illustrations of philosophical ideas from the pages of literature has led us to believe that these difficulties for the beginner can be minimized by this approach.

Basically, of course, these difficulties resolve themselves into one—the problem of communication. Philosophy, embracing all experience, cannot usefully be aloof from it, however rapt in detachment. It is a common charge, generally admitted by the offenders, that philosophers talk about experience in a way that causes the beginning student (and some older minds) to feel lost in a wilderness of abstractions, without vision of the promised land. Professor Marten ten Hoor expresses the prevalent conviction when he says, "I believe it to be an incontrovertible and inexcusable fact that many philosophers as a class have themselves unnecessarily reduced their actual and potential influence by their regrettable language habits. No discipline has so varied, so confused, and so unstable a vocabulary."

It is clear that, at least for the beginning student, it would be helpful if philosophy might be expressed, so far as possible, in a more representational idiom—the language of perception, the language of metaphor, words that image reality. Students will take hold of ideas once they are attracted to them. First they must see and feel them. Metaphors are not decorations in language but windows that let in light. In interpreting his thought to the student, the philosopher is always more effective, and not less accurate or adequate, when he resorts to metaphor; and whenever he resorts to metaphor, he is, for the moment, a poet. The ideal interpreter of the universe will be the philosopher-poet or the poet-philosopher.

This is not to belittle—as if one could!—the scientific pretensions of philosophy, which are also large and important. There are many aspects of truth and reality that, though not unpoetical in themselves, can hardly find expression except in abstruse intricate reasoning and formulas, and we hope to prepare the way for these. But philosophy is not and should

3

not be regarded as science. In its broad meaning, of course, it includes both science and poetry; but in so far as the subject matter of poetry is, as Professor John Crowe Ransom has called it, "the World's Body," philosophy is manifestly closer to poetry in its interests than to science. Science may supply its findings and its method, in part, to philosophy, but apart from its poetic vision, its power of interpreting the findings of science richly and meaningfully, philosophy would be (as indeed some think it ought to be) nothing but science. Poetry—and by poetry we mean the crystallization of experience in significant form (in prose or verse)—is the very substance of philosophy. It either interprets truth and reality or is truth and reality, so far as we can humanly know it.

This is another way of saying that the truths that philosophy and poetry seek are one, as Whitehead intimates: "Philosophy is the endeavor to find a conventional phraseology for the vivid suggestiveness of the poet." And Santayana insists on the essentially poetic nature of philosophic insight:

> . . . the vision of philosophy is sublime. The order it reveals in the world is something beautiful, tragic, sympathetic to the mind, and just what every poet, on a small or on a large scale, is always trying to catch.
>
> In philosophy itself investigation and reasoning are only preparatory and servile parts, means to an end. They terminate in insight, or what in the noblest sense of the word may be called *theory, θεωρία,*—a steady contemplation of all things in their order and worth. Such contemplation is imaginative. No one can reach it who has not enlarged his mind and tamed his heart. A philosopher who attains it is, for the moment, a poet; and a poet who turns his practised and passionate imagination on the order of all things, or on anything in the light of the whole, is for that moment a philosopher. . . .
>
> It is the acme of life to understand life. The height of poetry is to speak the language of the gods.

It will be grasped at once that in this text we are primarily concerned with poetry of idea rather than poetry of things or *pure poetry,* as George Moore names it. Despite a modern tendency to depreciate poetry of idea and to exalt poetry untainted by the didactic, it remains true that taste for the best poetry of idea is still good taste. What is more important for the educator, many people are naturally drawn to this type of poetry. With most people who have any taste for philosophic reflection it is their earliest and latest liking in literature.

If it is charged that we are trying to sugar-coat abstractions to make them more agreeable, we are delighted that our intention is so palpable. Our apologist is Lucretius:

> I love to approach virgin springs and there to drink; I love to pluck fresh flowers, and to seek an illustrious chaplet for my head from fields whence ere this the Muses have crowned the brows of none: first because my teaching is of high matters, and I proceed to unloose the mind from the close knots of religion; next because the subject is so dark and the lines I write so clear, as

I touch all with the Muses' grace.   For even this seems not to be out of place;
but as with children, when physicians try to administer rank wormwood, they
first touch the rims about the cups with the sweet yellow fluid of honey, that
unthinking childhood may be deluded as far as the lips, and meanwhile that they
may drink up the bitter juice of wormwood, and though beguiled be not
betrayed, but rather by such means be restored and gain health, so now do I:
since this doctrine commonly seems somewhat harsh to those who have not
used it, and the people shrink back from it, I have chosen to set forth my
doctrine to you in sweet-speaking Pierian song, and as it were to touch it with
the Muses' delicious honey, if perchance in such a way I might engage
your mind in my verses, while you are learning to see in what shape is framed
the whole nature of things.

—*De Rerum Natura*, W. H. D. Rouse, tr., I, 927-50.

It is freely admitted that poetry (and good literature in general) illustrating
philosophical concepts rarely exists in a free state.   It is as often as not a
glittering conglomerate, a composite of many things which may impede or
deflect the attention of the searcher after truth.   But life also is such a
composite, and poetry is the convenient mirror of life.   The sheath of things,
the rubbled hull that rough things wear, which hides the good that philosophy is seeking, invites probing and analysis.   One sees the object by these
characteristics.   Spirit must be invested by flesh before we can think of
spirit.   No miner ever wittingly turned away from rich gold ore because of
the problem of refining it.   Philosophers have the philosopher's stone.
Through this examination of life as it is, one can guard against a tight and
artificial schematization, and still have the pleasure of a growing sense of
order.

Occasionally, to the impatient mind (most of us are in too much of a
hurry), an ambiguity in a poem will interpose a difficulty that may appear as
formidable as the abstruseness of unregenerate professional jargon; but
there is a difference in quality in these two obstacles.   Poetic ambiguity,
instead of being a dead end of linguistic confusion, may be of a sort that
will induce rich invention in students' minds.   It is certain that students
take genuine pleasure in attempting to discover in a poem the right meaning
out of several possible meanings.   And the exercise is invaluable, so long
as it is wisely directed and controlled by the instructor.

For that matter, except as form and content serve for ease, it has not been
our intention to produce an easy text in philosophy, but rather one that
will stimulate and inspire.   The process suggested is one of induction into
philosophy, a gradual, almost genial leading into its problems, a process by
which the student grows more and more keenly interested in its ramifications
until he finds himself welcoming the subtlest complexities of abstract
thought.   If the process can lead him personally to make a richer interpretation of such abstract thought, so much the better.   Sir Philip Sidney's un-
forgettable good sense comes to mind:

> , . . the philosopher . . . replenisheth the memory with many infallible grounds of wisdom, which, notwithstanding lie dark before the imaginative and judging power, if they be not illuminated or figured forth by the speaking picture of poesy . . . [the poet] doth not only show the way, but giveth so sweet a prospect into the way, as will entice any man to enter into it: Nay, he doth as if your journey should lie through a fair vineyard, at the very first, give you a cluster of grapes, that full of that taste, you may long to pass further.   He beginneth not with obscure definitions, which must blur the margin with interpretations, and load the memory with doubtfulness; but he cometh to you with words set in delightful proportion, either accompanied with or prepared for the well enchanted skill of music, and with a tale, which holdeth children from play, and old men from the chimney corner. . . .

In this vineyard the student may discover the fundamental ideas of philosophy for himself in private study, or in class discussion, with the instructor as a guide, supplementing and otherwise qualifying his thought as occasion arises.

It cannot be too strongly emphasized to the student that the introductions to each chapter are not offered as substitutes for the readings themselves. The only reason for these brief sketches is to guide the general reader from theme to theme.   For the most part, the authors of the readings speak with requisite clarity for themselves: they are the text of this book.   The student will come to understand and remember true literature for its double worth; and the instructor will find himself adequate to any problem that it develops. We believe that the instructor should encourage the student first to interpret the philosophical values of the readings for himself, then, in class discussion, to measure his ideas with those of his classmates.   The instructor, restored by this procedure to his rightful place of importance in the classroom, will act as moderator, and finally help the student to an effective understanding and synthesis of the various concepts, supplying theoretic formulations and historical notes when desirable.

In making our selections we have kept in mind, so far as was feasible, three criteria: clarity, vividness, and effectiveness of expression.   But we have not hesitated to prefer the rich opacity of some good philosophical poetry (whenever it was available) to the transparency of verse of obvious meaning.   And it should be thought strange if there were none among those known as philosophers who had proved capable of genuine literary merit. The reader will be reminded again, as he notes the absence of many authors whose names appear in histories of philosophy, that this is a book of selections.   A book of this size could not begin to include all the good literary statements on these problems, and we have been forced to omit, for one reason or another, many selections as valuable as those presented.   A further apology to all our authors: each selection must be interpreted in isolation from context.   At no time do we imply that the meaning of the passage represents necessarily the author's definitive position.   A discerning reader will quickly observe, for instance, that some of our favorite authors are quoted on both sides of an issue. We are introducing an argument or thesis and not a man. Furthermore we have followed the conventions of American usage where variations of spelling and punctuation have little or no relation to an author's thought. The few exceptions are indicated by footnotes.

The plan of the text is designed to appeal to the student as well as the general reader. The text opens with a chapter introducing the reader to the great questions of philosophy, thus giving him a pretaste of the various philosophical categories. Then we begin the study of specific problems with an inquiry into the nature of aesthetic values, a subject reasonably familiar to the student and richly provocative. The major issues raised here lead naturally to the question of the status of ethical values. In succession follow chapters on religious values, immortality, the problem of evil, pessimism, optimism, fate and freedom, the problem of knowledge, the one and the many, time and change, naturalism, humanism, and pragmatism. So far as possible, we have organized the reading in the successive chapters so that the final passages in each make an easy transition to the opening of the next subject. The readings in each chapter follow a coherent and instructive development, as will be gathered from the readings themselves and from the introductions to the chapters. This scheme has necessitated at times a piecemeal presentation of various works like the *Rubaiyat* and *In Memoriam,* an apparent fracturing of great works not so deplorable as some would sentimentally represent it to be: Many of the fragments make natural units in themselves, often better units than the complete work. At times we offer several different versions of the same concept, partly for the sake of emphasis, and partly because we believe the instructor will welcome variety.

Here, then, are some good literary expressions of perennially important human reactions to features of life and the world. The competent instructor and the thoughtful reader will be able to take these as points of departure from which to go on to more detailed studies in philosophy. There may be much or little of this more detailed study included in the introductory course. We hold that it is supremely important that the student be left finally with a grateful sense of enlightening experience. Thus this book is meant to serve as an introduction both to more advanced studies (it does not claim to be more than a good beginning) and to the formulation of a "philosophy of life" which can be made to include much of the civilizing effect of the humane approach that trusts the poets and others to describe and interpret the moods and reflections that are everyman's.

CHAPTER 1

THE GREAT QUESTIONS

Let no one delay to study philosophy while he is young, and when he is old let him not become weary of the study; for no man can ever find the time unsuitable or too late to study the health of his soul. And he who asserts either that it is not yet time to philosophize, or that the hour is passed, is like a man who should say that the time is not yet come to be happy, or that it is too late. So that both young and old should study philosophy, the one in order that, when he is old, he may be young in good things through the pleasing recollection of the past, and the other in order that he may be at the same time both young and old, in consequence of his absence of fear for the future.

—Epicurus, Letter to Menaeceus, C. D. Yonge, tr.

From the time when our first ancestors "grabbed at stone, discerning a new use," man has been trying to decipher the meanings of things, to read the language of sea, sun, and stars and unlock the mysteries of Time and Being. To ponder these riddles of existence is instinctive with man, as much a part of his nature as seeing or feeling. Indeed, it is his concern with these eternal questions that identifies man as man.

Hardy, Pascal, Unamuno, and Santayana articulate some of these questions: Why am I here? Who put me here? Is there some high purpose in the Universe? Why does an omnipotent God license evil? What will become of me? In "The Bear," Frost gently rebukes man's self-consciousness in the face of such problems: man becomes more than slightly ridiculous as he lumbers back and forth in his cramped world, swinging between Plato and Aristotle. But this urbane amusement at man's predicament is unusual. Matthew Arnold ("Buried Life") finds that love and love only may furnish us an answer. Through human love we come in touch with hidden truth. A yet nobler answer is offered by Traherne, who finds the resolution of our problems in divine love. Clough carries this religious fervor so far as to feel it necessary to renounce philosophy and its perplexities—or is he merely vexed with his inability to arrive at answers satisfying his reason? Tennyson, in the passage from *Maud*, turns to philosophy as a refuge in itself from the ugliness of inexplicable evil—a view that arbitrarily limits the scope of philosophy.

Everyone takes an attitude of some sort toward these great questions: One may be a Peter Bell, indifferent to hidden meanings in a flower, agree with Voltaire (*Lord Chesterfield's Ears*) in seeing (in one mood) a universe artfully conceived with levers and pulleys, sympathize with Hamlet gloomily reading the common lot of man in the skull of Yorick, or wonder with Aiken how rocks can think of hyacinths.

And meditation on these problems suggests codes of behavior. In *Of Human Bondage,* Philip, stirred by the timeless sorrow in the Elgin Marbles, arrives at what seems to him the ideal pattern for living, the simple pattern of the normal life. This marks his healthy emergence out of the defiant indulgence recommended by Omar (*Rubaiyat,* XXVI-XXXV). Walter Pater finds that consideration of these questions enriches life, intensifies experience; it should be our aim to "burn always with this hard gemlike flame." Wordsworth, troubled by the increasing preoccupation with science in modern thought, asks, Why should expanded knowledge bring a dwindling of souls? This increase in knowledge and the toll it takes in doubt are reflected in *Heretics* (Chesterton), "Eternity" (Edman), "The 13th, the 19th, the 20th Centuries, or, Ptolemy, Newton, Einstein" (Theodore Spencer), and "Empty Shells" (Logan Pearsall Smith). But the heart still fights against the head. These several points of view reflect almost as many separate kinds of philosophy, each of which is exemplified in the chapters following. Some of these types are playfully suggested or openly named by Smith and Edman.

Finally, what is the value of philosophy to us? This question can best be answered by the student after he has studied what the poets and philosophers have to say in the pages ahead. It is only the part of maturity to give heed to Rilke's profound warning, and to acknowledge the great invitation of Marcus Aurelius. One must believe with Goethe that everyone is the better for contemplating the great questions:

> If man think the thought eternal
> He is ever fair and great.

NATURE'S QUESTIONING

THOMAS HARDY

> When I look forth at dawning, pool,
>   Field, flock, and lonely tree,
>   All seem to gaze at me
> Like chastened children sitting silent in a school;
>
> Their faces dulled, constrained, and worn,
>   As though the master's ways
>   Through the long teaching days
> Had cowed them till their early zest was overborne.
>
> Upon them stirs in lippings mere
>   (As if once clear in call,
>   But now scarce breathed at all)—
> "We wonder, ever wonder, why we find us here!

"Has some Vast Imbecility,
  Mighty to build and blend,
  But impotent to tend,
Framed us in jest, and left us now to hazardry?

"Or come we of an Automaton
  Unconscious of our pains?...
  Or are we live remains
Of Godhead dying downwards, brain and eye now gone?

"Or is it that some high Plan betides,
  As yet not understood,
  Of Evil stormed by Good,
We the Forlorn Hope over which Achievement strides?"

Thus things around. No answerer I...
  Meanwhile the winds, and rains,
  And Earth's old glooms and pains
Are still the same, and Life and Death are neighbors nigh.

FROM PENSÉES

BLAISE PASCAL

692

When I see the blindness and the wretchedness of man, when I regard the whole silent universe, and man without light, left to himself, and, as it were, lost in this corner of the universe, without knowing who has put him there, what he has come to do, what will become of him at death, and incapable of all knowledge, I become terrified, like a man who should be carried in his sleep to a dreadful desert island, and should awake without knowing where he is, and without means of escape. And thereupon I wonder how people in a condition so wretched do not fall into despair. I see other persons around me of a like nature. I ask them if they are better informed than I am. They tell me that they are not. And thereupon these wretched and lost beings, having looked around them, and seen some pleasing objects, have given and attached themselves to them. For my own part, I have not been able to attach myself to them, and, considering how strongly it appears that there is something else than what I see, I have examined whether this God has not left some sign of Himself....

205

When I consider the short duration of my life, swallowed up in the eternity before and after, the little space which I fill, and even can see, engulfed in the infinite immensity of spaces of which I am ignorant, and which know me not, I am frightened, and am astonished at being here rather than there; for there is no reason why here rather than there, why now rather than then. Who has put me here? By whose order and direction have this place and time been allotted to me? *Memoria hospitis unius diei praetereuntis.*

206

The eternal silence of these infinite spaces frightens me.

207

How many kingdoms know us not?

208

Why is my knowledge limited? Why my stature? Why my life to one hundred years rather than to a thousand? What reason has nature had for giving me such, and for choosing this number rather than another in the infinity of those from which there is no more reason to choose one than another, trying nothing else?

209

Art thou less a slave by being loved and favored by thy master? Thou art indeed well off, slave. Thy master favors thee; he will soon beat thee.

210

The last act is tragic, however happy all the rest of the play is; at the last a little earth is thrown upon our head, and that is the end for ever.

213

Between us and heaven or hell there is only life, which is the frailest thing in the world.

217

An heir finds the title-deeds of his house. Will he say, "Perhaps they are forged" and neglect to examine them?

347

Man is but a reed, the most feeble thing in nature; but he is a thinking reed. The entire universe need not arm itself to crush him. A vapor, a drop of water suffices to kill him. But, if the universe were to crush him, man would still be more noble than that which killed him, because he knows that he dies and the advantage which the universe has over him; the universe knows nothing of this.

All our dignity consists, then, in thought. By it we must elevate ourselves, and not by space and time which we cannot fill. Let us endeavor, then, to think well; this is the principle of morality.

(W. F. Trotter, tr.)

FROM THE STARTING-POINT

In *The Tragic Sense of Life*

MIGUEL DE UNAMUNO

And now, why does man philosophize?—that is to say, why does he investigate the first causes and ultimate ends of things? Why does he seek the disinterested truth? For to say that all men have a natural tendency to know is true; but wherefore?

Philosophers seek a theoretic or ideal starting-point for their human work, the work of philosophizing; but they are not usually concerned to seek the practical and real starting-point, the purpose. What is the object in making philosophy, in thinking it and then expounding it to one's fellows? What does the philosopher seek in it and with it? The truth for the truth's own sake? The truth, in order that we may subject our conduct to it and determine our spiritual attitude towards life and the universe conformably with it?

Philosophy is a product of the humanity of each philosopher, and each philosopher is a man of flesh and bone who addresses himself to other men of flesh and bone like himself. And, let him do what he will, he philosophizes not with the reason only, but with the will, with the feelings, with the flesh and with the bones, with the whole soul and the whole body. It is the man that philosophizes.

I do not wish here to use the word "I" in connection with philosophizing, lest the impersonal "I" should be understood in place of the man that philosophizes; for this concrete, circumscribed "I," this "I" of flesh and bone, that suffers from tooth-ache and finds life insupportable if death is the annihilation of the personal consciousness, must not be confounded with that other counterfeit "I," the theoretical "I" which Fichte smuggled into philosophy, nor yet with the Unique, also theoretical, of Max Stirner. It is better to say "we," understanding, however, the "we" who are circumscribed in space.

Knowledge for the sake of knowledge! Truth for truth's sake! This is inhuman. And if we say that theoretical philosophy addresses itself to practical philosophy, truth to goodness, science to ethics, I will ask: And to what end is goodness? Is it, perhaps an end in itself? Good is simply that which contributes to the preservation, perpetuation, and enrichment of consciousness. Goodness addresses itself to man, to the maintenance and perfection of human society which is composed of men. And to what end is this? "So act that your action may be a pattern to all men," Kant tells us. That is well, but wherefore? We must needs seek for a wherefore.

In the starting-point of all philosophy, in the real starting-point, the practical not the theoretical, there is a wherefore. The philosopher philosophizes for something more than for the sake of philosophizing. *Primum vivere, deinde philosophari,* says the old Latin adage; and as the philosopher is a man before he is a philosopher, he must needs live before he can philosophize, and, in fact, he philosophizes in order to live. And usually he philosophizes either in order to resign himself to life, or to seek some finality in it, or to distract himself and forget his griefs, or for pastime and amusement. A good illustration of this last case is to be found in that terrible Athenian ironist, Socrates, of whom Xenophon relates in his *Memorabilia* that he discovered to Theodata, the courtesan, the wiles that she ought to make use of in order to lure lovers to her house so aptly, that she begged him to act as her companion in the chase, συνθηρατής, her pimp, in a word. And philosophy is wont, in fact, not infrequently to convert itself into a kind of art of spiritual pimping. And sometimes into an opiate for lulling sorrows to sleep.

I take at random a book of metaphysics, the first that comes to my hand, *Time and Space, a Metaphysical Essay,* by Shadworth H. Hodgson. I open it, and in the fifth paragraph of the first chapter of the first part I read:

"Metaphysics is, properly speaking, not a science but a philosophy—that is, it is a science whose end is in itself, in the gratification and education of the minds which carry it on, not in external purpose, such as the founding of any art conducive to the welfare of life." Let us examine this. We see that metaphysics is not, properly speaking, a science—that is, it is a science whose end is in itself. And this science, which, properly speaking, is not a science, has its end in itself, in the gratification and education of the minds that cultivate it. But what are we to understand? Is its end in itself or is it to gratify and educate the minds that cultivate it? Either the one or the other! Hodgson afterwards adds that the end of metaphysics is not any external purpose, such as that of founding an art conducive to the welfare of life. But is not the gratification of the mind of him who culti- vates philosophy part of the well-being of his life? Let the reader consider this passage of the English metaphysician and tell me if it is not a tissue of contra- dictions.

Such a contradiction is inevitable when an attempt is made to define humanly this theory of science, of knowledge, whose end is in itself, of knowing for the sake of knowing, of attaining truth for the sake of truth. Science exists only in per- sonal consciousness and thanks to it; astronomy, mathematics, have no other reality than that which they possess as knowledge in the minds of those who study and cultivate them. And if some day all personal consciousness must come to an end on the earth; if some day the human spirit must return to the nothingness—that is to say, to the absolute unconsciousness—from whence it sprang; and if there shall no more be any spirit that can avail itself of all our accumulated knowledge—then to what end is this knowledge? For we must not lose sight of the fact that the problem of the personal immortality of the soul involves the future of the whole human species.

This series of contradictions into which the Englishman falls in his desire to ex- plain the theory of a science whose end is in itself, is easily understood when it is remembered that it is an Englishman who speaks, and that the Englishman is be- fore everything else a man. Perhaps a German specialist, a philosopher who had made philosophy his specialty, who had first murdered his humanity and then buried it in his philosophy, would be better able to explain this theory of a science whose end is in itself and of knowledge for the sake of knowledge.

Take the man Spinoza, that Portuguese Jew exiled in Holland; read his *Ethic* as a despairing elegiac poem, which in fact it is, and tell me if you do not hear, be- neath the disemburdened and seemingly serene propositions *more geometrico,* the lugubrious echo of the prophetic psalms. It is not the philosophy of resignation but of despair. And when he wrote that the free man thinks of nothing less than of death, and that his wisdom consists in meditating not on death but on life— *homo liber de nulla re minus quam de morte cogitat et eius sapientia non mortis, sed vitae meditatio est (Ethic,* Part IV., Prop. LXVII.)—when he wrote that, he felt, as we all feel, that we are slaves, and he did in fact think about death, and he wrote it in a vain endeavor to free himself from this thought. Nor in writing Proposition XLII. of Part V., that "happiness is not the reward of virtue but virtue itself," did he feel, one may be sure, what he wrote. For this is usually the reason why men philosophize—in order to convince themselves, even though they fail in the attempt. And this desire of convincing oneself—that is to say, this desire of doing violence to one's own human nature—is the real starting-point of not a few philosophies.

Whence do I come and whence comes the world in which and by which I live? Whither do I go and whither goes everything that environs me? What does it all mean? Such are the questions that man asks as soon as he frees himself from the brutalizing necessity of laboring for his material sustenance. And if we look closely, we shall see that beneath these questions lies the wish to know not so much the "why" as the "wherefore," not the cause but the end. Cicero's definition of philoso- phy is well known—"the knowledge of things divine and human and of the causes in which these things are contained," *rerum divinarum et humanarum, causarumque quibus hae res continentur;* but in reality these causes are, for us, ends. And what is the Supreme Cause, God, but the Supreme End? The "why" interests us only in view of the "wherefore." We wish to know whence we came only in order the better to be able to ascertain whither we are going.

This Ciceronian definition, which is the Stoic definition, is also found in that formidable intellectualist, Clement of Alexandria, who was canonized by the Catholic Church, and he expounds it in the fifth chapter of the first of his *Stromata*. But this same Christian philosopher—Christian?—in the twenty-second chapter of his fourth *Stroma* tells us that for the gnostic—that is to say, the intellectual—knowledge, *gnosis*, ought to suffice, and he adds: "I will dare aver that it is not because he wishes to be saved that he, who devotes himself to knowledge for the sake of the divine science itself, chooses knowledge. For the exertion of the intellect by exercise is prolonged to a perpetual exertion. And the perpetual exertion of the intellect is the essence of an intelligent being, which results from an uninterrupted process of admixture, and remains eternal contemplation, a living substance. Could we, then, suppose anyone proposing to the gnostic whether he would choose the knowledge of God or everlasting salvation, and if these, which are entirely identical, were separable, he would without the least hesitation choose the knowledge of God?" May He, may God Himself, whom we long to enjoy and possess eternally, deliver us from this Clementine gnosticism or intellectualism!

Why do I wish to know whence I come and whither I go, whence comes and whither goes everything that environs me, and what is the meaning of it all? For I do not wish to die utterly, and I wish to know whether I am to die or not definitely. If I do not die, what is my destiny? and if I die, then nothing has any meaning for me. And there are three solutions: (a) I know that I shall die utterly, and then irremediable despair, or (b) I know that I shall not die utterly, and then resignation, or (c) I cannot know either one or the other, and then resignation in despair or despair in resignation, a desperate resignation or a resigned despair, and hence conflict.

"It is best," some reader will say, "not to concern yourself with what cannot be known." But is it possible? In his very beautiful poem, *The Ancient Sage*, Tennyson said:

> "Thou canst not prove the Nameless, O my son,
> Nor canst thou prove the world thou movest in,
> Thou canst not prove that thou art body alone,
> Thou canst not prove that thou art spirit alone,
> Nor canst thou prove that thou art both in one:
> Nor canst thou prove thou art immortal, no,
> Nor yet that thou art mortal—nay, my son,
> Thou canst not prove that I, who speak with thee,
> Am not thyself in converse with thyself,
> For nothing worthy proving can be proven,
> Nor yet disproven: wherefore thou be wise,
> Cleave ever to the sunnier side of doubt,
> Cling to Faith beyond the forms of Faith!"

Yes, perhaps, as the Sage says, "nothing worthy proving can be proven, nor yet disproven"; but can we restrain that instinct which urges man to wish to know, and above all to wish to know the things which may conduce to life, to eternal life? Eternal life, not eternal knowledge, as the Alexandrian gnostic said. For living is one thing and knowing is another; and, as we shall see, perhaps there is such an opposition between the two that we may say that everything vital is antirational, not merely irrational, and that everything rational is antivital.   And this is the basis of the tragic sense of life.

(J. E. Crawford Flitch, tr.)

CAPE COD *

GEORGE SANTAYANA

The low sandy beach and the thin scrub pine,
The wide reach of bay and the long sky line,—
   O, I am far from home!

The salt, salt smell of the thick sea air,
And the smooth round stones that the ebbtides wear,—
   When will the good ship come?

The wretched stumps all charred and burned,
And the deep soft rut where the cartwheel turned,—
   Why is the world so old?

The lapping wave, and the broad gray sky
Where the cawing crows and the slow gulls fly,—
   Where are the dead untold?

The thin, slant willows by the flooded bog,
The huge stranded hulk and the floating log,—
   Sorrow with life began!

And among the dark pines, and along the flat shore,
O the wind, and the wind, for evermore!
   What will become of man?

THE BEAR

ROBERT FROST

The bear puts both arms around the tree above her
And draws it down as if it were a lover
And its choke cherries lips to kiss good-bye,
Then lets it snap back upright in the sky.
Her next step rocks a boulder on the wall
(She's making her cross-country in the fall).
Her great weight creaks the barbed-wire in its staples
As she flings over and off down through the maples,
Leaving on one wire tooth a lock of hair.
Such is the uncaged progress of the bear.
The world has room to make a bear feel free;
The universe seems cramped to you and me.
Man acts more like the poor bear in a cage
That all day fights a nervous inward rage,

His mood rejecting all his mind suggests.
He paces back and forth and never rests
The toe-nail click and shuffle of his feet,
The telescope at one end of his beat,
And at the other end the microscope,
Two instruments of nearly equal hope,
And in conjunction giving quite a spread.
Or if he rests from scientific tread,
'Tis only to sit back and sway his head
Through ninety odd degrees of arc, it seems,
Between two metaphysical extremes.
He sits back on his fundamental butt
With lifted snout and eyes (if any) shut,
(He almost looks religious but he's not),
And back and forth he sways from cheek to cheek,
At one extreme agreeing with one Greek,
At the other agreeing with another Greek
Which may be thought, but only so to speak.
A baggy figure, equally pathetic
When sedentary and when peripatetic.

THE BURIED LIFE

MATTHEW ARNOLD

Light flows our war of mocking words, and yet,
Behold, with tears my eyes are wet.
I feel a nameless sadness o'er me roll.
Yes, yes, we know that we can jest,
We know, we know that we can smile;
But there's a something in this breast
To which thy light words bring no rest,
And thy gay smiles no anodyne.
Give me thy hand, and hush awhile,
And turn those limpid eyes on mine,
And let me read there, love, thy inmost soul.

Alas, is even love too weak
To unlock the heart and let it speak?
Are even lovers powerless to reveal
To one another what indeed they feel?
I knew the mass of men conceal'd
Their thoughts, for fear that if reveal'd
They would by other men be met
With blank indifference, or with blame reprov'd;
I knew they liv'd and mov'd
Trick'd in disguises alien to the rest
Of men, and alien to themselves—and yet
The same heart beats in every human breast!
But we, my love—does a like spell benumb
Our hearts—our voices?—must we too be dumb?

Ah, well for us, if even we,
Even for a moment, can get free
Our heart, and have our lips unchain'd;
For that which seals them hath been deep ordain'd.

Fate, which foresaw
How frivolous a baby man would be,
By what distractions he would be possess'd
How he would pour himself in every strife,
And well-nigh change his own identity;
That it might keep from his capricious play
His genuine self, and force him to obey
Even in his own despite, his being's law,
Bade, through the deep recesses of our breast
The unregarded river of our life
Pursue with indiscernible flow its way;
And that we should not see
The buried stream, and seem to be
Eddying about in blind uncertainty,
Though driving on with it eternally.

But often in the world's most crowded streets,
But often, in the din of strife,
There rises an unspeakable desire
After the knowledge of our buried life,
A thirst to spend our fire and restless force
In tracking out our true, original course;
A longing to inquire
Into the mystery of this heart that beats
So wild, so deep in us, to know
Whence our thoughts come and where they go.
And many a man in his own breast then delves,
But deep enough, alas, none ever mines:
And we have been on many thousand lines,
And we have shown on each talent and power,
But hardly have we, for one little hour,
Been on our own line, have we been ourselves;
Hardly had skill to utter one of all
The nameless feelings that course through our breast,
But they course on forever unexpress'd.
And long we try in vain to speak and act
Our hidden self, and what we say and do
Is eloquent, is well—but 'tis not true:
And then we will no more be rack'd
With inward striving, and demand
Of all the thousand nothings of the hour
Their stupefying power;
Ah yes, and they benumb us at our call:
Yet still, from time to time, vague and forlorn,
From the soul's subterranean depth upborne

As from an infinitely distant land,
Come airs, and floating echoes, and convey
A melancholy into all our day.

Only—but this is rare—
When a beloved hand is laid in ours,
When jaded with the rush and glare
Of the interminable hours,
Our eyes can in another's eyes read clear,
When our world-deafen'd ear
Is by the tones of a loved voice caress'd,
A bolt is shot back somewhere in our breast
And a lost pulse of feeling stirs again;
The eye sinks inward, and the heart lies plain,
And what we mean, we say, and what we would, we know.
A man becomes aware of his life's flow
And hears its winding murmur, and he sees
The meadows where it glides, the sun, the breeze.

And there arrives a lull in the hot race
Wherein he doth for ever chase
That flying and elusive shadow, Rest.
An air of coolness plays upon his face,
And an unwonted calm pervades his breast.
And then he thinks he knows
The Hills where his life rose,
And the Sea where it goes.

THE SALUTATION

THOMAS TRAHERNE

I
These little limbs,
These eyes and hands which here I find,
These rosy cheeks wherewith my life begins,
Where have ye been?   behind
What curtain were ye from me hid so long,
Where was, in what abyss, my speaking tongue?

II
When silent I
So many thousand, thousand years
Beneath the dust did in a chaos lie,
How could I smiles or tears,
Or lips or hands or eyes or ears perceive?
Welcome ye treasures which I now receive.

III
I that so long
Was nothing from eternity,
Did little think such joys as ear or tongue
To celebrate or see:

Such sounds to hear, such hands to feel, such feet,
Beneath the skies on such a ground to meet.

IV

New burnisht joys!
Which yellow gold and pearl excel!
Such sacred treasures are the limbs in boys,
    In which a soul doth dwell;
Their organized joints and azure veins
More wealth include than all the world contains.

V

From dust I rise,
    And out of nothing now awake;
These brighter regions which salute mine eyes,
    A gift from God I take.
The earth, the seas, the light, the day, the skies,
The sun and stars are mine; if those I prize.

VI

Long time before
    I in my mother's womb was born,
A God preparing did this glorious store,
    The world, for me adorn.
Into this Eden so divine and fair,
So wide and bright, I come His son and heir.

VII

A stranger here
    Strange things doth meet, strange glories see;
Strange treasures lodg'd in this fair world appear,
    Strange all and new to me;
But that they mine should be, who nothing was,
That strangest is of all, yet brought to pass.

IN A LECTURE-ROOM

ARTHUR HUGH CLOUGH

Away, haunt thou not me,
Thou vain Philosophy!
Little hast thou bestead,
Save to perplex the head,
And leave the spirit dead.
Unto thy broken cisterns wherefore go,
While from the secret treasure-depths below,
Fed by the skiey shower,
And clouds that sink and rest on hill-tops high,
Wisdom at once, and Power,
Are welling, bubbling forth, unseen, incessantly!
Why labor at the dull mechanic oar,
When the fresh breeze is blowing,
And the strong current flowing,
Right onward to the Eternal Shore?

MAUD, V-IX

ALFRED LORD TENNYSON

We are puppets, Man in his pride, and Beauty fair in her flower;
Do we move ourselves, or are moved by an unseen hand at a game
That pushes us off from the board, and others ever succeed?
Ah yet, we cannot be kind to each other here for an hour;
We whisper, and hint, and chuckle, and grin at a brother's shame;
However we brave it out, we men are a little breed.

A monstrous eft was of old the lord and master of earth,
For him did his high sun flame, and his river billowing ran,
And he felt himself in his force to be Nature's crowning race.
As nine months go to the shaping an infant ripe for his birth,
So many a million of ages have gone to the making of man:
He now is first, but is he the last? is he not too base?

The man of science himself is fonder of glory, and vain,
An eye well-practiced in nature, a spirit bounded and poor;
The passionate heart of the poet is whirl'd into folly and vice.
I would not marvel at either, but keep a temperate brain;
For not to desire or admire, if a man could learn it, were more
Than to walk all day like the sultan of old in a garden of spice.

For the drift of the Maker is dark, and Isis hid by the veil.
Who knows the ways of the world, how God will bring them about?
Our planet is one, the suns are many, the world is wide.
Shall I weep if a Poland fall? shall I shriek if a Hungary fail?
Or an infant civilization be ruled with rod or with knout?
I have not made the world, and He that made it will guide.

Be mine a philosopher's life in the quiet woodland ways,
Where if I cannot be gay let a passionless peace be my lot,
Far-off from the clamor of liars belied in the hubbub of lies;
From the long-neck'd geese of the world that are ever hissing dispraise
Because their natures are little, and, whether he heed it or not,
Where each man walks with his head in a cloud of poisonous flies.

FROM PETER BELL, Part First

WILLIAM WORDSWORTH

"He roved among the vales and streams,
In the green wood and hollow dell;
They were his dwellings night and day,—
But Nature ne'er could find the way
Into the heart of Peter Bell.

"In vain, through every changeful year,
Did Nature lead him as before;
A primrose by a river's brim
A yellow primrose was to him,
And it was nothing more."

FROM LORD CHESTERFIELD'S EARS, Chapter 2

VOLTAIRE

After many observations of Nature, made with my five senses, telescopes and microscopes, I said to Mr Sidrac one day:

"They make fun of us; there is no such thing as Nature, everything is art; it is by an admirable art that all the planets dance regularly around the sun, while the sun turns round upon himself. Obviously some one as learned as the Royal Society of London must have arranged things in such a way that the square of the revolutions of each planet is always proportionate to the cube root of their distance from their center; and a man must be a sorcerer to guess it.

"The ebb and flow of our Thames seem to me the constant result of an art not less profound and not less difficult to understand.

"Animals, vegetables, minerals, all seem to me arranged with weight, measure, number and movement; everything is a spring, a lever, a pulley, a hydraulic machine, a chemical laboratory, from the blade of grass to the oak, from the flea to man, from a grain of sand to our clouds.

"Certainly, there is nothing but art, and Nature is a delusion."

"You are right," replied Mr Sidrac, "but you are not the first in the field; that has already been said by a dreamer on the other side of the Channel, but nobody has paid any attention to him."

(Richard Aldington, tr.)

HAMLET, V, i, 202-37

WILLIAM SHAKESPEARE

HAMLET: Let me see.— (*Takes the skull.*) Alas! poor Yorick. I knew him, Horatio; a fellow of infinite jest, of most excellent fancy; he hath borne me on his back a thousand times; and now, how abhorred in my imagination it is! my gorge rises at it. Here hung those lips that I have kissed I know not how oft. Where be your gibes now? your gambols? your songs? your flashes of merriment, that were wont to set the table on a roar? Not one now, to mock your own grinning? quite chapfallen? Now get you to my lady's chamber, and tell her, let her paint an inch thick, to this favor she must come; make her laugh at that. Prithee, Horatio, tell me one thing.
HORATIO: What's that, my lord?
HAMLET: Dost thou think Alexander looked o' this fashion i' the earth?
HORATIO: E'en so.
HAMLET: And smelt so? pah!

(*Puts down the skull.*)

HORATIO: E'en so, my lord.

HAMLET: To what base uses we may return, Horatio! Why may not imagination
trace the noble dust of Alexander, till he find it stopping a bung-hole?

HORATIO: 'Twere to consider too curiously, to consider so.

HAMLET: No, faith, not a jot; but to follow him thither with modesty enough, and
likelihood to lead it; as thus: Alexander died, Alexander was buried, Alexander
returneth into dust; the dust is earth; of earth we make loam, and why of that
loam, whereto he was converted, might they not stop a beer-barrel?

> Imperious Caesar, dead and turn'd to clay,
> Might stop a hole to keep the wind away:
> O! that that earth, which kept the world in awe,
> Should patch a wall to expel the winter's flaw.

TIME IN THE ROCK, LII *

CONRAD AIKEN

But how it came from earth this little white
this waxen edge this that is sharp and white
this that is mortal and bright the petals bent
and all so curved as if for lovers meant
and why the earth unfolded in this shape
as coldly as words from the warm mouth escape

Or what it is that made the blood so speak
or what it was it wanted that made this
breath of curled air this hyacinth this word
this that is deeply seen profoundly heard
miracle of quick device
from fire and ice

Or why the snail puts out a horn to see
or the brave heart puts up a hand to take
or why the mind, as if to agonize,
will close, a century ahead, its eyes—
a hundred years put on the clock
its own mortality to mock—

Christ come, Confucius come, and tell us why
the mind delights before its death to die
embracing nothing as a lover might
in a terrific ecstasy of night—
and tell us why the hyacinth is sprung
from the world's dull tongue.

Did death so dream of life, is this its dream?
does the rock think of flowers in its sleep?
Then words and flowers are only thoughts of stone
unconscious of the joy it thinks upon;
and we ourselves are only the rock's words
stammered in a dark dream of men and birds.

FROM OF HUMAN BONDAGE, Chapter 106 *

W. SOMERSET MAUGHAM

. . . Philip's heart sank as he thought of the lost years. He walked on mechanically, not noticing where he went, and realized suddenly, with a movement of irrita-
tion, that instead of turning down the Haymarket he had sauntered along Shaftesbury
Avenue. It bored him to retrace his steps; and besides, with that news, he did not
want to read, he wanted to sit alone and think. He made up his mind to go to the
British Museum. Solitude was now his only luxury. Since he had been at Lynn's he
had often gone there and sat in front of the groups from the Parthenon; and, not deliberately thinking, had allowed their divine masses to rest his troubled soul. But this
afternoon they had nothing to say to him, and after a few minutes, impatiently, he
wandered out of the room. There were too many people, provincials with foolish
faces, foreigners poring over guide-books; their hideousness besmirched the everlasting
masterpieces, their restlessness troubled the god's immortal repose. He went into another room and here there was hardly anyone. Philip sat down wearily. His nerves
were on edge. He could not get the people out of his mind. Sometimes at Lynn's
they affected him in the same way, and he looked at them file past him with horror;
they were so ugly and there was such meanness in their faces, it was terrifying; their features were distorted with paltry desires, and you felt they were strange to any ideas of
beauty. They had furtive eyes and weak chins. There was no wickedness in
them, but only pettiness and vulgarity. Their humor was a low facetiousness.
Sometimes he found himself looking at them to see what animal they resembled
(he tried not to, for it quickly became an obsession), and he saw in them all the
sheep or the horse or the fox or the goat. Human beings filled him with disgust.

But presently the influence of the place descended upon him. He felt quieter.
He began to look absently at the tombstones with which the room was lined. They
were the work of Athenian stone masons of the fourth and fifth centuries before
Christ, and they were very simple, work of no great talent but with the exquisite
spirit of Athens upon them; time had mellowed the marble to the color of honey,
so that unconsciously one thought of the bees of Hymettus, and softened their
outlines. Some represented a nude figure, seated on a bench, some the departure
of the dead from those who loved him, and some the dead clasping hands with one
who remained behind. On all was the tragic word farewell; that and nothing more.
Their simplicity was infinitely touching. Friend parted from friend, the son from
his mother, and the restraint made the survivor's grief more poignant. It was so
long, long ago, and century upon century had passed over that unhappiness; for
two thousand years those who wept had been dust as those they wept for. Yet the
woe was alive still, and it filled Philip's heart so that he felt compassion spring up
in it, and he said:

"Poor things, poor things."

And it came to him that the gaping sight-seers and the fat strangers with their
guide-books, and all those mean, common people who thronged the shop, with their
trivial desires and vulgar cares, were mortal and must die. They too loved and
must part from those they loved, the son from his mother, the wife from her
husband; and perhaps it was more tragic because their lives were ugly and sordid,
and they knew nothing that gave beauty to the world. There was one stone which
was very beautiful, a bas relief of two young men holding each other's hand; and
the reticence of line, the simplicity, made one like to think that the sculptor here

had been touched with a genuine emotion. It was an exquisite memorial to that than which the world offers but one thing more precious, to a friendship; and as Philip looked at it, he felt the tears come to his eyes. He thought of Hayward and his eager admiration for him when first they met, and how disillusion had come and then indifference, till nothing held them together but habit and old memories. It was one of the queer things of life that you saw a person every day for months and were so intimate with him that you could not imagine existence without him; then separation came, and everything went on in the same way, and the companion who had seemed essential proved unnecessary. Your life proceeded and you did not even miss him. Philip thought of those early days in Heidelberg when Hayward, capable of great things, had been full of enthusiasm for the future, and how, little by little, achieving nothing, he had resigned himself to failure. Now he was dead. His death had been as futile as his life. He died ingloriously, of a stupid disease, failing once more, even at the end, to accomplish anything. It was just the same now as if he had never lived.

Philip asked himself desperately what was the use of living at all. It all seemed inane. It was the same with Cronshaw: it was quite unimportant that he had lived; he was dead and forgotten, his book of poems sold in remainder by secondhand booksellers; his life seemed to have served nothing except to give a pushing journalist occasion to write an article in a review. And Philip cried out in his soul: "What is the use of it?"

The effort was so incommensurate with the result. The bright hopes of youth had to be paid for at such a bitter price of disillusionment. Pain and disease and unhappiness weighed down the scale so heavily. What did it all mean? He thought of his own life, the high hopes with which he had entered upon it, the limitations which his body forced upon him, his friendlessness, and the lack of affection which had surrounded his youth. He did not know that he had ever done anything but what seemed best to do, and what a cropper he had come! Other men, with no more advantages than he, succeeded, and others again, with many more, failed. It seemed pure chance. The rain fell alike upon the just and upon the unjust, and for nothing was there a why and a wherefore.

Thinking of Cronshaw, Philip remembered the Persian rug which he had given him, telling him that it offered an answer to his question upon the meaning of life; and suddenly the answer occurred to him: he chuckled: now that he had it, it was like one of the puzzles which you worry over till you are shown the solution and then cannot imagine how it could ever have escaped you. The answer was obvious. Life had no meaning. On the earth, satellite of a star speeding through space, living things had arisen under the influence of conditions which were part of the planet's history; and as there had been a beginning of life upon it, so, under the influence of other conditions, there would be an end: man, no more significant than other forms of life, had come not as the climax of creation but as a physical reaction to the environment. Philip remembered the story of the Eastern King who, desiring to know the history of man, was brought by a sage five hundred volumes; busy with affairs of state, he bade him go and condense it; in twenty years the sage returned and his history now was in no more than fifty volumes, but the King, too old then to read so many ponderous tomes, bade him go and shorten it once more; twenty years passed again and the sage, old and gray, brought a single book in which was the knowledge the King had sought; but the King lay on his death-bed, and he had no time to read even that; and then the sage gave him the history of man in a single line; it was this: he was born, he suffered, and he died. There was no meaning in life, and man by living served no end. It was immaterial whether he was born or not born, whether he lived or ceased to live. Life was insignificant and death without consequence. Philip exulted, as he had exulted in his boyhood when the weight of a belief in God was lifted from his shoulders: it seemed to him that the last burden of responsibility was taken from him; and for the first time he was utterly free. His insignificance was turned to power, and he felt himself suddenly equal with the cruel fate which had seemed to persecute him; for, if life was meaningless, the world was robbed of its cruelty. What he did or left undone did not matter. Failure was unimportant and success amounted to nothing. He was the most inconsiderable creature in that swarming mass of mankind which for a brief space occupied the surface of the earth; and he was almighty because he had wrenched from chaos the secret of its nothingness. Thoughts came tumbling over one another in Philip's eager fancy, and he took long breaths of joyous satisfaction. He felt inclined to leap and sing. He had not been so happy for months.

"Oh life," he cried in his heart, "Oh life, where is thy sting?"

For the same uprush of fancy which had shown him with all the force of mathematical demonstration that life had no meaning, brought with it another idea; and that was why Cronshaw, he imagined, had given him the Persian rug. As the weaver elaborated his pattern for no end but the pleasure of his aesthetic sense, so might a man live his life, or if one was forced to believe that his actions were outside his choosing, so might a man look at his life, that it made a pattern. There was as little need to do this as there was use. It was merely something he did for his own pleasure. Out of the manifold events of his life, his deeds, his feelings, his thoughts, he might make a design, regular, elaborate, complicated, or beautiful; and though it might be no more than an illusion that he had the power of selection, though it might be no more than a fantastic legerdemain in which appearances were interwoven with moonbeams, that did not matter: it seemed, and so to him it was. In the vast warp of life (a river arising from no spring and flowing endlessly to no sea), with the background to his fancies that there was no meaning and that nothing was important, a man might get a personal satisfaction in selecting the various strands that worked out the pattern. There was one pattern, the most obvious, perfect, and beautiful, in which a man was born, grew to manhood, married, produced children, toiled for his bread, and died; but there were others, intricate and wonderful, in which happiness did not enter and in which success was not attempted; and in them might be discovered a more troubling grace. Some lives, and Hayward's was among them, the blind indifference of chance cut off while the design was still imperfect; and then the solace was comfortable that it did not matter; other lives, such as Cronshaw's, offered a pattern which was difficult to follow: the point of view had to be shifted and old standards had to be altered before one could understand that such a life was its own justification. Philip thought that in throwing over the desire for happiness he was casting aside the last of his illusions. His life had seemed horrible when it was measured by its happiness, but now he seemed to gather strength as he realized that it might be measured by something else. Happiness mattered as little as pain. They came in, both of them, as all the other details of his life came in, to the elaboration of the design. He seemed for an instant to stand above the accidents of his existence, and he felt that they could not affect him again as they had done before. Whatever happened to him now would be one more motive to add to the complexity of the pattern, and when the end approached he would rejoice in its completion. It would be a work of art, and it would be none the less beautiful because he alone knew of its existence, and with his death it would at once cease to be.

Philip was happy.

32317

RUBAIYAT, XXVI-XXXV
OMAR KHAYYAM

XXVI

Why, all the Saints and Sages who discuss'd
Of the Two Worlds so wisely—they are thrust
   Like foolish Prophets forth; their Words to Scorn
Are scatter'd, and their Mouths are stopt with Dust.

XXVII

Myself when young did eagerly frequent
Doctor and Saint, and heard great argument
   About it and about: but evermore
Came out by the same door where in I went.

XXVIII

With them the seed of Wisdom did I sow,
And with mine own hand wrought to make it grow;
   And this was all the Harvest that I reap'd—
"I came like Water, and like Wind I go."

XXIX

Into this Universe, and *Why* not knowing
Nor *Whence,* like Water willy-nilly flowing;
   And out of it, as Wind along the Waste,
I know not *Whither,* willy-nilly blowing.

XXX

What, without asking, hither hurried *Whence?*
And, without asking, *Whither* hurried hence!
   Oh, many a Cup of this forbidden Wine
Must drown the memory of that insolence!

XXXI

Up from Earth's Center through the Seventh Gate
I rose, and on the Throne of Saturn sate,
   And many a Knot unravel'd by the Road;
But not the Master-knot of Human Fate.

XXXII

There was the Door to which I found no Key;
There was the Veil through which I might not see:
   Some little talk awhile of ME and THEE
There was—and then no more of THEE and ME.

XXXIII

Earth could not answer; nor the Seas that mourn
In flowing Purple, of their Lord forlorn;
   Nor rolling Heaven, with all his Signs reveal'd
And hidden by the sleeve of Night and Morn.

XXXIV

Then of the THEE IN ME who works behind
The Veil, I lifted up my hands to find
   A lamp amid the Darkness; and I heard,
As from Without—"THE ME WITHIN THEE BLIND!"

XXXV

Then to the Lip of this poor earthen Urn
I lean'd, the Secret of my Life to learn:
   And Lip to Lip it murmur'd—"While you live,
Drink!—for, once dead, you never shall return."

(Edward Fitzgerald, tr.)

FROM THE RENAISSANCE: CONCLUSION

WALTER PATER

To regard all things and principles of things as inconstant modes or fashions has more and more become the tendency of modern thought. Let us begin with that which is without—our physical life. Fix upon it in one of its more exquisite intervals, the moment, for instance, of delicious recoil from the flood of water in summer heat. What is the whole physical life in that moment but a combination of natural elements to which science gives their names? But those elements, phosphorus and lime and delicate fibers, are present not in the human body alone: we detect them in places most remote from it. Our physical life is a perpetual motion of them—the passage of the blood, the waste and repairing of the lenses of the eye, the modification of the tissues of the brain under every ray of light and sound—processes which science reduces to simpler and more elementary forces. Like the elements of which we are composed, the action of these forces extends beyond us: it rusts iron and ripens corn. Far out on every side of us those elements are broadcast, driven in many currents; and birth and gesture and death and the springing of violets from the grave are but a few out of ten thousand resultant combinations. That clear, perpetual outline of face and limb is but an image of ours, under which we group them—a design in a web, the actual threads of which pass out beyond it. This at least of flamelike our life has, that it is but the concurrence, renewed from moment to moment, of forces parting sooner or later on their ways.

Or if we begin with the inward world of thought and feeling, the whirlpool is still more rapid, the flame more eager and devouring. There it is no longer the gradual darkening of the eye, the gradual fading of color from the wall—movements of the shore-side, where the water flows down indeed, though in apparent rest—but the race of the mid-stream, a drift of momentary acts of sight and passion and thought. At first sight experience seems to bury us under a flood of external objects, pressing upon us with a sharp and importunate reality, calling us out of ourselves in a thousand forms of action. But when reflection begins to play upon those objects they are dissipated under its influence; the cohesive force seems suspended like some trick of magic; each object is loosed into a group of impressions—color, odor, texture—in the mind of the observer. And if we continue to dwell in thought on this world, not of objects in the solidity with which language invests them, but of impressions, unstable, flickering, inconsistent, which burn and are extinguished with our consciousness of them, it contracts still further: the whole scope of observation is dwarfed into the narrow chamber of the individual mind. Experience, already reduced to a group of impressions, is ringed round for each one of us by that thick wall of personality through which no real voice has ever pierced on its way to us, or from us to that which we can only conjecture to be without. Every one of those impressions is the impression of the individual in his isolation, each mind keeping as a solitary prisoner its own dream of a world.

Analysis goes a step further still, and assures us that those impressions of the individual mind to which, for each one of us, experience dwindles down, are in perpetual flight; that each of them is limited by time, and that as time is infinitely divisible, each of them is infinitely divisible also; all that is actual in it being a single moment, gone while we try to apprehend it, of which it may ever be more truly said that it has ceased to be than that it is. To such a tremulous wisp constantly re-forming itself on the stream, to a single sharp impression, with a sense in it, a relic more or less fleeting, of such moments gone by, what is real in our life fines itself down. It is with this movement, with the passage and dissolution of impressions, images, sensations, that analysis leaves off—that continual vanishing away, that strange, perpetual weaving and unweaving of ourselves.

Philosophiren, says Novalis, *ist dephlegmatisiren vivificiren*. The service of philosophy, of speculative culture, towards the human spirit, is to rouse, to startle it to a life of constant and eager observation. Every moment some form grows perfect in hand or face; some tone on the hills or the sea is choicer than the rest; some mood of passion or insight or intellectual excitement is irresistibly real and attractive to us,—for that moment only. Not the fruit of experience, but experience itself, is the end. A counted number of pulses only is given to us of a variegated, dramatic life. How may we see in them all that is to be seen in them by the finest senses? How shall we pass most swiftly from point to point, and be present always at the focus where the greatest number of vital forces unite in their purest energy?

To burn always with this hard, gemlike flame, to maintain this ecstasy, is success in life. In a sense it might even be said that our failure is to form habits: for, after all, habit is relative to a stereotyped world, and meantime it is only the roughness of the eye that makes any two persons, things, situations, seem alike. While all melts under our feet, we may well grasp at any exquisite passion, or any contribution to knowledge that seems by a lifted horizon to set the spirit free for a moment, or any stirring of the senses, strange dyes, strange colors, and curious odors, or work of the artist's hands, or the face of one's friend. Not to discriminate every moment some passionate attitude in those about us, and in the very brilliancy of their gifts some tragic dividing of forces on their ways, is, on this short day of frost and sun, to sleep before evening. With this sense of the splendor of our experience and of its awful brevity, gathering all we are into one desperate effort to see and touch, we shall hardly have time to make theories about the things we see and touch. What we have to do is to be for ever curiously testing new opinions and courting new impressions, never acquiescing in a facile orthodoxy of Comte, or of Hegel, or of our own. Philosophical theories or ideas, as points of view, instruments of criticism, may help us to gather up what might otherwise pass unregarded by us. "Philosophy is the microscope of thought." The theory or idea or system which requires of us the sacrifice of any part of this experience, in consideration of some interest into which we cannot enter, or some abstract theory we have not identified with ourselves, or of what is only conventional, has no real claim upon us.

One of the most beautiful passages of Rousseau is that in the sixth book of the *Confessions*, where he describes the awakening in him of the literary sense. An undefinable taint of death had clung always about him, and now in early manhood he believed himself smitten by mortal disease. He asked himself how he might make as much as possible of the interval that remained; and he was not biassed by anything in his previous life when he decided that it must be by intellectual excitement, which he found just then in the clear, fresh writings of Voltaire. Well! we are all *condamnés*, as Victor Hugo says: we are all under sentence of death but with a sort of indefinite reprieve—*les hommes sont tous condamnés à mort avec des sursis indéfinis:* we have an interval, and then our place knows us no more. Some spend this interval in listlessness, some in high passions, the wisest, at least among "the children of this world," in art and song. For our one chance lies in expanding that interval, in getting as many pulsations as possible into the given time. Great passions may give us this quickened sense of life, ecstasy and sorrow of love, the various forms of enthusiastic activity, disinterested or otherwise, which come naturally to many of us. Only be sure it is passion—that it does yield you this fruit of a quickened, multiplied consciousness. Of such wisdom, the poetic passion, the desire of beauty, the love of art for its own sake, has most. For art comes to you proposing frankly to give nothing but the highest quality to your moments as they pass, and simply for those moments' sake.

FROM DESPONDENCY CORRECTED

In *The Excursion (IV)*

WILLIAM WORDSWORTH

This answer followed.—"You have turned my thoughts
Upon our brave Progenitors, who rose
Against idolatry with warlike mind,
And shrunk from vain observances, to lurk
In woods, and dwell under impending rocks
Ill-sheltered, and oft wanting fire and food;
Why?—for this very reason that they felt,
And did acknowledge, wheresoe'er they moved,
A spiritual presence, oft-times misconceived,
But still a high dependence, a divine
Bounty and government, that filled their hearts
With joy, and gratitude, and fear, and love;
And from their fervent lips drew hymns of praise,
That through the desert rang. Though favored less,
Far less, than these, yet such, in their degree,
Were those bewildered Pagans of old time.
Beyond their own poor natures and above
They looked; were humbly thankful for the good
Which the warm sun solicited, and earth
Bestowed; were gladsome,—and their moral sense
They fortified with reverence for the Gods;
And they had hopes that overstepped the Grave.
"Now, shall our great Discoverers," he exclaimed,
Raising his voice triumphantly, "obtain
From sense and reason, less than these obtained,
Though far misled? Shall men for whom our age
Unbaffled powers of vision hath prepared,
To explore the world without and world within,
Be joyless as the blind? Ambitious spirits—
Whom earth, at this late season, hath produced
To regulate the moving spheres, and weigh

The planets in the hollow of their hand;
And they who rather dive than soar, whose pains
Have solved the elements, or analyzed
The thinking principle—shall they in fact
Prove a degraded Race? and what avails
Renown, if their presumption make them such?
Oh! there is laughter at their work in heaven!
Inquire of ancient Wisdom; go, demand
Of mighty Nature, if 't was ever meant
That we should pry far off yet be unraised;
That we should pore, and dwindle as we pore,
Viewing all objects unremittingly
In disconnection dead and spiritless;
And still dividing, and dividing still,
Break down all grandeur, still unsatisfied
With the perverse attempt, while littleness
May yet become more little; waging thus
And impious warfare with the very life
Of our souls!
    "And if indeed there be
An all-pervading Spirit, upon whom
Our dark foundations rest, could he design
That this magnificent effect of power,
The earth we tread, the sky that we behold
By day, and all the pomp which night reveals;
That these—and that superior mystery
Our vital frame, so fearfully devised,
And the dread soul within it—should exist
Only to be examined, pondered, searched,
Probed, vexed, and criticized?   Accuse me not
Of arrogance, unknown Wanderer as I am,
If, having walked with Nature threescore years,
And offered, far as frailty would allow,
My heart a daily sacrifice to Truth,
I now affirm of Nature and of Truth,
Whom I have served, that their DIVINITY
Revolts, offended at the ways of men
Swayed by such motives, to such ends employed;
Philosophers, who, though the human soul
Be of a thousand faculties composed,
And twice ten thousand interests, do yet prize
This soul, and the transcendent universe,
No more than as a mirror that reflects
To proud Self-love her own intelligence;
That one, poor, finite object, in the abyss
Of infinite Being, twinkling restlessly!"

FROM INTRODUCTORY REMARKS ON THE IMPORTANCE
OF ORTHODOXY

In *Heretics*

GILBERT K. CHESTERTON

Nothing more strangely indicates an enormous and silent evil of modern society than the extraordinary use which is made nowadays of the word "orthodox." In former days the heretic was proud of not being a heretic. It was the kingdoms of the world and the police and the judges who were heretics. He was orthodox. He had no pride in having rebelled against them; they had rebelled against him. The armies with their cruel security, the kings with their cold faces, the decorous processes of State, the reasonable processes of law—all these like sheep had gone astray. The man was proud of being orthodox, was proud of being right. If he stood alone in a howling wilderness he was more than a man; he was a church. He was the center of the universe; it was round him that the stars swung. All the tortures torn out of forgotten hells could not make him admit that he was heretical. But a few modern phrases have made him boast of it. He says, with a conscious laugh, "I suppose I am very heretical," and looks round for applause. The word "heresy" not only means no longer being wrong; it practically means being clear-headed and courageous. The word "orthodoxy" not only no longer means being right; it practically means being wrong. All this can mean one thing, and one thing only. It means that people care less for whether they are philosophically right. For obviously a man ought to confess himself crazy before he confesses himself heretical. The Bohemian, with a red tie, ought to pique himself on his orthodoxy. The dynamiter, laying a bomb, ought to feel that, whatever else he is, at least he is orthodox.

It is foolish, generally speaking, for a philosopher to set fire to another philosopher in Smithfield Market because they do not agree in their theory of the universe. That was done very frequently in the last decadence of the Middle Ages, and it failed altogether in its object. But there is one thing that is infinitely more absurd and unpractical than burning a man for his philosophy. This is the habit of saying that his philosophy does not matter, and this is done universally in the twentieth century, in the decadence of the great revolutionary period. General theories are everywhere contemned; the doctrine of the Rights of Man is dismissed with the doctrine of the Fall of Man. Atheism itself is too theological for us today. Revolution itself is too much of a system; liberty itself is too much of a restraint. We will have no generalizations. Mr. Bernard Shaw has put the view in a perfect epigram: "The golden rule is that there is no golden rule." We are more and more to discuss details in art, politics, literature. A man's opinion on tramcars matters; his opinion on Botticelli matters; his opinion on all things does not matter. He may turn over and explore a million objects, but he must not find that strange object, the universe; for if he does he will have a religion, and be lost. Everything matters—except everything.

Examples are scarcely needed of this total levity on the subject of cosmic philosophy. Examples are scarcely needed to show that, whatever else we think of as affecting practical affairs, we do not think it matters whether a man is a pessimist or an optimist, a Cartesian or a Hegelian, a materialist or a spiritualist. Let me, however, take a random instance. At any innocent tea-table we may easily hear a man say, "Life is not worth living." We regard it as we regard the statement that it is a fine day; nobody thinks that it can possibly have any serious effect on the man or on the world. And yet if that utterance were really believed, the world would stand on its head. Murderers would be given medals for saving men from life; firemen would be denounced for keeping men from death; poisons would be used as medicines; doctors would be called in when people were well; the Royal Humane Society would be rooted out like a horde of assassins. Yet we never speculate as to whether the conversational pessimist will strengthen or disorganize society; for we are convinced that theories do not matter.

This was certainly not the idea of those who introduced our freedom. When the old Liberals removed the gags from all the heresies, their idea was that religious and philosophical discoveries might thus be made. Their view was that cosmic truth was so important that every one ought to bear independent testimony. The modern idea is that cosmic truth is so unimportant that it cannot matter what any one says. The former freed inquiry as men loose a noble hound; the latter frees inquiry as men fling back into the sea a fish unfit for eating. Never has there been so little discussion about the nature of men as now, when, for the first time, any one can discuss it. The old restriction meant that only the orthodox were allowed to discuss religion. Modern liberty means that nobody is allowed to discuss it. Good taste, the last and vilest of human superstitions, has succeeded in the silencing us where all the rest have failed. Sixty years ago it was bad taste to be an avowed atheist. Then came the Bradlaughites, the last religious men, the last men who cared about God; but they could not alter it. It is still bad taste to be an avowed atheist. But their agony has achieved just this—that now it is equally bad taste to be an avowed Christian. Emancipation has only locked the saint in the same tower of silence as the heresiarch. Then we talk about Lord Anglesey and the weather, and call it the complete liberty of all the creeds.

But there are some people, nevertheless—and I am one of them—who think that the most practical and important thing about a man is still his view of the universe. We think that for a landlady considering a lodger, it is important to know his income, but still more important to know his philosophy. We think that for a general about to fight an enemy, it is important to know the enemy's numbers, but still more important to know the enemy's philosophy. We think the question is not whether the theory of the cosmos affects matters, but whether, in the long run, anything else affects them. In the fifteenth century men cross-examined and tormented a man because he preached some immoral attitude; in the nineteenth century we feted and flattered Oscar Wilde because he preached such an attitude, and then broke his heart in penal servitude because he carried it out. It may be a question which of the two methods was the more cruel; there can be no kind of question which was the more ludicrous. The age of the Inquisition has not at least the disgrace of having produced a society which made an idol of the very same man for preaching the very same things which it made him a convict for practicing.

Now, in our time, philosophy or religion, our theory, that is, about ultimate things, has been driven out, more or less simultaneously, from two fields which it used to occupy. General ideals used to dominate literature. They have been driven out by the cry of "art for art's sake." General ideals used to dominate politics. They have been driven out by the cry of "efficiency," which may roughly be translated as "politics for politics' sake." Persistently for the last twenty years the ideals of order or liberty have dwindled in our books; the ambitions of wit and eloquence have dwindled in our parliaments. Literature has purposely become less political; politics have purposely become less literary. General theories of the relation of things have thus been extruded from both; and we are in a position to ask,

"What have we gained or lost by this extrusion? Is literature better, is politics better, for having discarded the moralist and the philosopher?"

ETERNITY

IRWIN EDMAN

I know there is no meaning in the mist
That wraps in gray these mountain girdled shores,
Nor in these loud black waves once moonlight kissed,
I fear no threat in their untimely roar.
I cannot read a language in the surge
Of breakers; there is no immortal sign
In midnight winds; I hear no Demi-urge
Hiss in the storm, nor think the wind divine.
I am too lessoned in the changeless law
Behind the beauty of this cloud-banked gloom,
To mark in it with simple trembling awe,
God's reckless accents of avenging doom.
   Yet while thus Reason routs these dreams and fears,
   Eternity keeps thundering in my ears.

THE 13TH, THE 19TH, THE 20TH CENTURIES
or, PTOLEMY, NEWTON, EINSTEIN

THEODORE SPENCER

When the sun went round the earth, I said:
A noble thing is man.
I said when the sun went round the earth:
A formidable thing is man.
(The heart kept fighting against the head
All that time and is steadily fighting.)

When the earth went round the sun, I said:
A small thing is man.
I said when the earth went round the sun:
Pity poor man.
(The head kept fighting against the heart
All that time and is steadily fighting.)

When the sun went round the stars, I said:
Nothing at all is man.
I said when the sun went round the stars:
Forget this man.
(The heart kept fighting against the head
All that time and is steadily fighting.)

EMPTY SHELLS *
LOGAN PEARSALL SMITH

They lie like empty sea-shells on the shores of Time, the old worlds which the spirit of man once built for his habitation, and then abandoned. Those little earth-centered, heaven-encrusted universes of the Greeks and Hebrews seem quaint enough for us, who have formed, thought by thought from within, the immense modern Cosmos in which we live—the great Creation of granite, planned in such immeasurable proportions, and moved by so pitiless a mechanism, that it sometimes appalls even its own creators. The rush of the great rotating Sun daunts us; to think to the distance of the fixed stars cracks our brains.

But if the ephemeral Being who has imagined these eternal spheres and spaces must dwell almost as an alien in their icy vastness, yet what a splendor lights up for him and dazzles in those great halls! Anything less limitless would be now a prison; and he even dares to think beyond their boundaries, to surmise that he may one day outgrow this Mausoleum, and cast from him the material Creation as an integument too narrow for his insolent Mind.

FROM LAST WORDS *
LOGAN PEARSALL SMITH

I got up with Stoic fortitude of mind in the cold this morning; but afterwards, in my hot bath, I joined the school of Epicurus. I was a Materialist at breakfast; after it an Idealist, as I smoked my first cigarette and turned the world to transcendental vapor. But when I began to read the *Times,* I had no doubt of the existence of an external world.

So all the morning and all the afternoon opinions kept flowing into and out of the receptacle of my mind; till by the time the enormous day was over, it had been filled by most of the widely-known Theories of Existence, and emptied of them.

This long speculation of life, this thinking and syllogizing that always goes on inside me, this running over and over of hypothesis and surmise and supposition—one day this infinite Argument will have ended, the debate will be for ever over, I shall have come to an indisputable conclusion, and my brain will be at rest.

FROM INTIMATIONS OF PHILOSOPHY IN EARLY CHILDHOOD
In *Philosopher's Holiday*
IRWIN EDMAN

It is possible, I suspect, for most people at all interested in philosophy to put their finger on the time and the book that first introduced them to the "subject." Philosophy in my own mind will always be associated with Bakewell's *Source Book in Ancient Philosophy,* which contains fragments remaining from the early Greeks: Thales, Anaximander, Heraclitus, and Empedocles. The names themselves sounded like incantations. I had an early impression (from which I have not yet recov-

* From *All Trivia* by Logan Pearsall Smith, copyright, 1945, by Harcourt, Brace & Company, Inc.

ered) that Greek philosophers in the Ionian Peninsula for some strange reason *wrote* in fragments. As a freshman, too, I vaguely had the idea that Bakewell had with his own hands gathered together these fragments at Yale, or had composed them there, and that the learned professor was himself somehow the source of Greek philosophy. I shall also associate my first bookish relations with philosophy with that great gray volume, translated from unintelligible German into formidable English: Paulsen's *Introduction to Philosophy*. There I gathered that philosophy consisted of an astounding number of isms, with innumerable sub-isms, and that somewhere in that ismatic jungle lay the Truth. Finally, by myself, outside of class, I discovered the little yellow book in the Home University Library, J. A. Thomson's *Introduction to Science,* which opened up the various branches of knowledge and their interrelations and made me feel that with sufficient time and diligence I could become one of the masters—in outline—of all that was to be known.

But there is a moment, or kind of moment, harder to identify. It occurs usually, I suspect, before one knows what the word "philosophy" is, or when one vaguely associates the word "philosophical" with Red Indians burning in stubborn and dignified fortitude at the stake, or with a man watching the ruins and embers of his house, or hearing of the death or elopement of his wife, with grave serenity. Some experience, some word, or some odd fancy crossing one's inexperienced mind—and one is in the presence of, and feels, the delicious, puzzling incitement (without knowing either phrase) of philosophical issues and ultimate things. I have friends who occasionally report instances of such early speculative awakening in their small children, and I know that, from John Locke down, the baby has been a favorite illustration of philosophers—the baby putting together the color and sound and taste and smell and feel of an orange and saying: "Lo! it is an object, it is an orange!"

Being childless, I have only the smallest stock of illustrations of this philosophical awakening among children, though I gather from my friends that their infant sons are all metaphysicians. I know, for instance, that Ian, aged nine, reads Gibbon, and I hear from his father that his mind is as skeptical and circumspect as that of Hume. I did once take a walk with a child who asked suddenly: "Who made the world?" For the sake of brevity I replied: "God." "Who made God?" was the next question. To reply that God was a First Cause, the Uncreated Creator of all things seemed a stiff dose for a child and would only bring on further questions. I said I would tell him later. But for the awakening of the philosophical impulse in children I can only refer to one autobiographical instance, and I shall try to keep out of my remembrance such sophisticated gloss as a later education in philosophy gave me. I am convinced, as I look back, that all the great issues, Freedom and Determinism, God, Immortality, the reality of the external world, and the nature of reality itself, are first stumbled upon when one is very young. I can even imagine that some day a psychiatrist will prove that speculative interests are early childhood fixations and that the metaphysician is an infant trailing clouds of inglorious complexes from the nursery.

Time is certainly the pet theme of much contemporary thought, and I had as certainly not read the modern physicists or Einstein's early work at the age of thirteen. But it was then, if I remember, that I myself first hit upon that perplexity, current in philosophy since Plato defined Time as the moving picture of eternity, a phrase itself puzzle enough. I remember one day coming to my older sister and saying I was bothered about Time. She was, as she is still, full of sound sense and human perception and has never allowed herself to be distracted by nonsense, however elaborate and imposing. She is a philosopher free from cobwebs.

"What do you mean," she said, "you are bothered by time?"

"Well," I said, "take today, for instance. It's really here right now, this very minute, for instance, isn't it?"

"Yes, of course," she said, and turned back to the piano on which she was playing one-half of Beethoven's *Fifth Symphony* arranged for four hands.

"But wait a minute," I said, "tomorrow today will be yesterday, won't it? It will be gone. And tomorrow is not here yet, and it really *isn't* at all. It's all very puzzling. What *is* Time?"

"Time for you to go to bed," she said briskly and, refusing to be entangled any further in aerie irrelevance and childishness, she turned back again to the Andante.

I did go to bed, but I did not sleep. For I was obsessed by the awful unreality of something I had hitherto taken for granted. There was, I mused, last summer on the Jersey coast—the long summer afternoons, the tang of the salt spray as the breakers broke round one as one waded into the surf, the agreeable burning warmth of the sun as one basked on the beach. But *that* was last summer, and it no longer was. It was, I suddenly realized with awe, the Past. But what was the Past? And where was it? And now and here, as I lay in bed this winter evening in a New York apartment, listening to my sister playing the piano, Time itself moved on, and tomorrow this dreaming about the past would be the Past, too. It made me feel uneasy. I got no further before I fell asleep.

I thought about it often in the next weeks. Thought is too systematic a word for what I actually did, I am sure. I did not try to solve the problem. I displayed no precocious dialectic virtuosity. I "thought" about it in that I felt about it seriously. I repeatedly had a sense of the dreamlike though intense quality of time past and remembered, the odd unreality of time sure to come but not yet here, the wavering evanescence of the present. Or, as I put it to myself, yesterday is gone; today is going, always going; tomorrow is coming but it *hasn't* come. I used to try to explain it all to people, to the Negro elevator boy, particularly; he seemed to be the only one who would listen, though he said: "You shouldn't worry yo' head about that!" I don't think I found out until five or six years later that I was far from the only one who had been bemused and bepuzzled by the theme. I had a secret feeling that there was something special, private, and abnormal about being worried about such things, just as a child may go on a long time thinking he is the only one bemused and bepuzzled by sex.

But Time was not the only philosophical problem of which I had an early intimation. I was to learn at college, by way of Paulsen's book, of something called the epistemological problem. How do we *know*, and how do we know that we know? I was to learn of metaphysics, the attempt to define scrupulously what was really real. But epistemology and metaphysics came by anticipation into my ken long before I knew the words or the professional arguments about them, or knew that there were grown men who spent their whole lives debating such issues and were paid by universities for doing so and for teaching others how to do it. I cannot lay claim myself to having hit upon the intimations of these things. It was Julian L., now, I am told, a much sought after pediatrist in New York, who was the agent to bring epistemology and metaphysics (though he, too, did not know the words) to my fourteen-year-old attention from out of his fourteen-year-old observation. The fact he pointed at, I discovered much later, is time and again used as a conventional illustration in philosophical treatises.

It was in the mountains on the afternoon of a hot July day. We had been talking drowsily under a tree by the side of a brook. I was almost asleep. Julian was stirring a stick in the water.

"The stick looks broken, doesn't it?" he said.

I looked up vaguely. "Yes; what of it?" I said. I sometimes shared my sister's realism.

"But it isn't; that's only the shadow in the water; it's *unreal,*" said Julian. He lapsed into silence, still stirring the stick. "But there's a *real* shadow," he said; "the shadow itself is *real,* all right."

"Yes," I said. "I'm going to sleep for a while."

Julian's remark made little immediate impression. The reality of a shadow, the unreality of a broken stick did not seem to matter very much amid this sunlight on this summer green. But days later, walking by the brook again with Julian and happening to stir a stick in it myself, my friend's comments of the other day suddenly came back with unexpected cogency and vividness into my mind.

"The shadow in a way *is* real," I suddenly said to Julian. Then two fourteen-year-old epistemologists, sitting by a mountain stream, wrestled dialectically, within the limits of their abilities, with the Real and the Unreal, how we knew anything really, and whether seeing was believing. I soon wearied of the controversy—as I have often done since. The whole problem, I somehow felt even then, was artificial, as I now think I have sound reasons for believing it to be. But the theme haunted me, and often that summer I reverted to it. Dreams, too, were like shadows, and the things one remembered were like dreams. I tried, without success even by my own fourteen-year-old standards, to write a poem about it. Indeed, even now it seems to me that the whole matter is a better theme for poetry than inquiry, and is poetic in its origins and fruits rather than primarily a genuine problem for analysis. The net effect for the time being was to make me a solitary solipsist—how I should have loved the words had I known them!—and I would pretend for as long as I could, till I was too hungry or too tired, that our house, my bed, the meat and milk and eggs at supper, the other summer visitors, Julian himself, were merely shadows or dreams in my mind, and that I myself perhaps was a dream. I seem to remember my mother found me particularly and annoyingly absent-minded the next week or two. It was fun to treat the world round about me as apparitions to my understanding and imagination. Many years later Santayana invented for such dreams, such passing appearances, such momentary objects of intuition, the term "essences." I had not realized until I began to recall these early explorations of epistemology that I had come upon essences long ago.

It was through Julian, too, at the same time, that I first began to think about Freedom and Determinism, Fate and Chance, Necessity and Accident, though, of course, not remotely in those terms. My friend and I used to discuss occasionally the accident that had brought us together in a friendship that, we were certain, would never end. It was a lucky accident, we decided. But the very luck of it, we redecided, *proved* that it was something more than luck; that it *could* not have been an accident. For look, we unanimously agreed, our parents, who had not known each other, must first have decided to come to the same place and, all unknown to each other, to rent houses directly opposite each other. It was not an accident. It was an inevitable chain; it was *intended.* It was Fate. And it was part of Fate, we warmly agreed, that we should be friends for ever. Fate and Freedom, these are the familiar preoccupations of theologians from St. Paul and St. Augustine down. So are death and immortality. Many philosophical conceptions, I was to learn later, have their origins in the mind of the child and the mind of the savage.

There is a whole library about primitive conceptions of the soul.   The appearance of dead men in dreams, if I remember, is supposed to lead the primitive warrior to believe that his dead friends and enemies live in another world.   I cannot say that I can recall having been concerned very early with the nature of the soul or the problem of immortality.   Nor early to have brooded upon death.   Death was what happened to *old* people, people in their forties and fifties or seventies; to people's grandparents, not to anybody one really knew or played with.   The death of a boy in our group—Herbert, the fat, good-natured, not very literary member of our Benjamin Franklin Club—first gave me pause and led me to think of the quite incredible fact of death.   When older people died, it was as if they had simply gone off or moved away.   And in any case one had never known them very well, and adults, besides, did strange things.   But Herbert, the liveliest of all, simply gone, stretched out in a coffin and carried away and buried!   It was far more upsetting than when Mr. S., the father of one of my friends, died.   That was sad and sudden.   He came home from a trip, had pneumonia; they brought an oxygen tent for him to breathe in, and three days later he was gone.   But *he* was bald-headed and had always seemed incredibly old; he was fifty.   It seemed odd not to see him emerge at the aristocratically late hour of a quarter to nine and in his top hat leisurely set off for the local rather than the urgent express train on the Elevated.   His son, my chum, wore a black tie and mourning-band and was not allowed to go to the theater and acquired for a while a special dignity and importance.   But that was different. The death of one of us, a contemporary, was another matter.   The very young believe not in immortal life, but in eternal life here on earth; it struck me as incredible that anyone, any young person, should really die, simply cease to be.   And yet I am convinced that one's adult philosophical opinions are formed in embryo very early, if one is going to have them at all.   For it never seemed to me that my friend was living as an angel in some other world.   He had ceased simply to be. Death was the end, and there both the incredibility and the sadness of it lay. Death, like birth, was a fact of existence, as inevitable and as natural.   I vaguely felt that as a child; I definitely think that now.

But the intimations of immortality that Wordsworth speaks of have, of course, nothing to do with an after-life.   They have to do with a sense of something "far more deeply interfused," a presence of something permeatingly beautiful in the crass or exquisite surface of things.   Like every child I felt, especially, I think, in the art of music, an adumbration of something acute in its poignancy and intensity, yet other-worldly in its distance from ordinary objects.   It doesn't matter much that it was nothing more musically profound than "Angel's Serenade" or *Kammenoi Ostrov* or the *Tannhäuser* Bacchanale that gave me this sense, or that it seldom came from anything commonly called real.   If it did not come from music, it came from poetry, and the poetry, too, did not have to be too profound.

"ALREADY RIPENING BARBERRIES GROW RED"

In *The Book of Hours*

RAINER MARIA RILKE

Already ripening barberries grow red,
the aging asters scarce breathe in their bed.
Who is not rich, with summer nearly done,
will never have a self that is his own.

Who is unable now to close his eyes,
certain that many visages within
wait slumbering until night shall begin
and in the darkness of his soul will rise,
is like an aged man whose strength is gone.

Nothing will touch him in the days to come,
and each event will cheat him and betray,
even you, my God.   And you are like a stone,
that draws him to a lower depth each day.

(Babette Deutsch, tr.)

FROM MEDITATIONS, II, xv

MARCUS AURELIUS

The time of a man's life is as a point; the substance of it ever flowing, the sense obscure; and the whole composition of the body tending to corruption. His soul is restless, fortune uncertain, and fame doubtful; to be brief, as a stream so are all things belonging to the body; as a dream, or as a smoke, so are all that belong unto the soul. Our life is a warfare, and a mere pilgrimage. Fame after life is no better than oblivion. What is it then that will adhere and follow? Only one thing, philosophy. And philosophy doth consist in this, for a man to preserve that spirit which is within him, from all manner of contumelies and injuries, and above all pains or pleasures; never to do anything either rashly, or feignedly, or hypo-critically; wholly to depend from himself, and his own proper actions: all things that happen unto him to embrace contentedly, as coming from Him from whom he himself also came; and above all things, with all meekness and a calm cheerful-ness, to expect death, as being nothing else but the resolution of those elements, of which every creature is composed. And if the elements themselves suffer nothing by this their perpetual conversion of one into another, that dissolution, and altera-tion, which is so common unto all, why should it be feared by any? Is not this according to nature? But nothing that is according to nature can be evil.

(Meric Casaubon, tr.)

THE THOUGHT ETERNAL

JOHANN WOLFGANG von GOETHE

Whether day my spirit's yearning
Unto far, blue hills has led,
Or the night lit all the burning
Constellations at my head—
Hours of light or hours nocturnal
Do I praise our mortal fate:
If man think the thought eternal
He is ever fair and great.

(Ludwig Lewisohn, tr.)

CHAPTER 2

THE MEANING OF BEAUTY

> . . . I believe that the beauty and nothing
> else is what things are formed for.   Certainly the world
> Was not constructed for happiness nor love nor wisdom.
> No, nor for pain, hatred and folly.   All these
> Have their seasons; and in the long year they balance
> each other, they cancel out.   But the beauty stands.
> —Robinson Jeffers, "Invasion."

"All architecture is what you do to it when you look upon it," Whitman boldly remarks.

"No," Edna St. Vincent Millay replies, "Let all who prate of Beauty hold their peace, And lay them prone upon the earth and cease To ponder on themselves."   Beauty is not subjective: it is absolute order.   But in "Snow-flakes" we are reminded that even beauty fears perfection.

Does man discover values, or does he make them by giving his approval? We look upon Beauty, and it is there, we feel.   But the voice of our sophistication recalls the axioms: "There is nothing either good or bad, but thinking makes it so."   "There is no disputing about tastes."   At the most, as Emerson says in "Each and All," beauty is to be found only in its own natural matrix.   "All are needed by each one, Nothing is fair or good alone." It *is* to be found there, however, and there is little we do dispute about more than about taste.

Santayana comes to our aid in this impasse and lifts the debate to the next level of analysis.   "Taste" needs criticism.   There is good taste and bad taste and "dogmatism in matters of taste has the same status as dogmatism in other spheres."   There is really no need for the notorious diversities of taste to lead to conflict; they do so only when their "basis or their function has been forgotten, and each has claimed a right to assert itself exclusively." Thus without abandoning the irreducibly subjective one may yet not forsake the ideal.

"What is beauty, saith my sufferings, then?" Christopher Marlowe asks. Something indeed more than can be said.   Browning calls to mind the miracle of the creation of beauty: the one point where man can be like the very "finger of God"—"That out of three sounds he frame, not a fourth sound, but a star."   Nietzsche gives a new turn and emphasis to the notion of the relativity of beauty.   " 'Beauty in itself,' " he says, ". . . is not even a concept." Man inevitably creates beauty in his own image. "A species has no other alternative than to say 'yea' to itself alone."

Joyce and Santayana again attempt definitions, although it would be closer to the mark to say that, for the former, beauty has no *meaning*, though the true and the beautiful are akin. The latter's shrewdly qualified subjectivism also serves as an introduction for the absolutism of Plato and his disciple Edmund Spenser.

Auden's discernment of the detachment of the Old Masters opens the discussion of the problem of the relationship of aesthetical and moral values. Friedrich Schiller shows how man, out of the superabundance of his energies, comes to create beauty in "aesthetical play." Man finds that "free pleasure comes to take a place among his wants and the useless soon becomes the best part of his joys. . . . Beauty alone confers happiness on all."

The "Ode on a Grecian Urn" testifies to the permanence of beauty in the scheme of things. The moral problem is also clearly before us: Plato warns us that poetry may cost more than it comes to. Banish the poets from the state: they are likely to do more harm than good. But his mistrust of the poets finds an answer in Shelley's incomparable defense of poetry: "Poetry is the record of the best and happiest moments of the happiest and best minds."

Wilde and Nietzsche point up the issue. To Wilde, who deplores the "decay of lying," Art finds her own perfection within. We shall not ask for her truth or goodness. But is it an answer to Plato to add the paradox that "it is none the less true that Life imitates art far more than Art imitates life"? Nietzsche, strange and late ally of Plato, succinctly observes that "art for art's sake" really means, "Let morality go to the devil!" "Veracity first of all," cries Emerson, "And forever." "Beauty rests on necessities." To Ruskin it is evident that not only morality but religion as well are mutually and inextricably involved in and with aesthetic taste. Art does and must have a meaning outside the naked experience. Three great nineteenth century evangelists thus concur in making art and beauty parts of the conduct of life.

Somerset Maugham, in a passage reminiscent of Wilde, utterly repudiates this Victorian insistence that great art cannot exist without a moral element. (Ruskin is not a name ever to be mentioned again in "decent society"!) The tranquil voice of Santayana is heard again; an intimation of sweet reasonableness in a distinction nicely drawn between judgments moral and aesthetic. Finally, out of and away from the heat of debate, Maugham presents another chapter in the spiritual biography of Philip Carey, who, as he brooded upon an El Greco, "felt strangely that he was on the threshold of some new discovery in life." May it not be that a discerning mind can find a philosophy of life itself by the path of aesthetic contemplation? "He was always seeking for a meaning in life, and here it seemed to him that a meaning was offered."

FROM CAROL OF OCCUPATIONS

WALT WHITMAN

List close, my scholars dear!
All doctrines, all politics and civilization, exurge from you;
All sculpture and monuments, and anything inscribed anywhere,
    are tallied in you;
The gist of histories and statistics as far back as the records
    reach, is in you this hour, and myths and tales the same;
If you were not breathing and walking here, where would they
    all be?
The most renown'd poems would be ashes, orations and plays would
    be vacuums.

All architecture is what you do to it when you look upon it;
(Did you think it was in the white or gray stone? or the lines
    of the arches and cornices?)

All music is what awakes from you when you are reminded by the
    instruments;
It is not the violins and the cornets—it is not the oboe nor
    the beating drums, nor the score of the baritone singer
    singing his sweet romanza—nor that of the men's chorus,
    nor that of the women's chorus,
It is nearer and farther than they.

"EUCLID ALONE HAS LOOKED ON BEAUTY BARE" *

EDNA ST. VINCENT MILLAY

Euclid alone has looked on Beauty bare.
Let all who prate of Beauty hold their peace,
And lay them prone upon the earth and cease
To ponder on themselves, the while they stare
At nothing, intricately drawn nowhere
In shapes of shifting lineage; let geese
Gabble and hiss, but heroes seek release
From dusty bondage into luminous air.
O blinding hour, O holy, terrible day,
When first the shaft into his vision shone
Of light anatomized!   Euclid alone
Has looked on Beauty bare.   Fortunate they
Who, though once only and then but far away,
Have heard her massive sandal set on stone.

* From *The Harp-Weaver and Other Poems*, published by Harper & Bros., copyright, 1920, 1928, by Edna St. Vincent Millay.

SNOWFLAKES

RUTH LECHLITNER

Shaped in some infinite Euclidian dream,
These crystal hexagons are the minute
And perfect variations of a theme
Called life: symmetrical and absolute.

But if we knew why even beauty fears
Perfection, we should better understand
Why order dies and logic disappears
In the warm hollow of the naked hand.

EACH AND ALL

RALPH WALDO EMERSON

Little thinks, in the field, yon red-cloaked clown,
Of thee, from the hill-top looking down;
And the heifer, that lows in the upland farm,
Far-heard, lows not thine ear to charm;
The sexton, tolling the bell at noon,
Dreams not that great Napoleon
Stops his horse, and lists with delight,
Whilst his files sweep round yon Alpine height;
Nor knowest thou what argument
Thy life to thy neighbor's creed has lent:
All are needed by each one,
Nothing is fair or good alone.

I thought the sparrow's note from heaven,
Singing at dawn on the alder bough;
I brought him home in his nest at even;—
He sings the song, but it pleases not now;
For I did not bring home the river and sky;
He sang to my ear; they sang to my eye.
The delicate shells lay on the shore;
The bubbles of the latest wave
Fresh pearls to their enamel gave;
And the bellowing of the savage sea
Greeted their safe escape to me;
I wiped away the weeds and foam,
And fetched my sea-born treasures home;
But the poor, unsightly, noisome things
Had left their beauty on the shore
With the sun, and the sand, and the wild uproar.

The lover watched his graceful maid
As 'mid the virgin train she strayed,
Nor knew her beauty's best attire
Was woven still by the snow-white quire;

At last she came to his hermitage,
Like the bird from the woodlands to the cage,—
The gay enchantment was undone,
A gentle wife, but fairy none.

Then I said, "I covet Truth;
Beauty is unripe childhood's cheat,—
I leave it behind with the games of youth."
As I spoke, beneath my feet
The ground-pine curled its pretty wreath,
Running over the club-moss burrs;
I inhaled the violet's breath;
Around me stood the oaks and firs;
Pine-cones and acorns lay on the ground;
Above me soared the eternal sky,
Full of light and of deity;
Again I saw, again I heard,
The rolling river, the morning bird;—
Beauty through my senses stole,
I yielded myself to the perfect whole.

FROM THE CRITERION OF TASTE *

In *Reason in Art*

GEORGE SANTAYANA

Dogmatism in matters of taste has the same status as dogmatism in other spheres. It is initially justified by sincerity, being a systematic expression of a man's preferences; but it becomes absurd when its basis in a particular disposition is ignored and it pretends to have an absolute or metaphysical scope. Reason, with the order which in every region it imposes on life, is grounded on an animal nature and has no other function than to serve the same; and it fails to exercise its office quite as much when it oversteps its bounds and forgets whom it is serving as when it neglects some part of its legitimate province and serves its master imperfectly, without considering all his interests.

Dialectic, logic, and morals lose their authority and become inept if they trespass upon the realm of physics and try to disclose existences; while physics is a mere idea in the realm of poetic meditation. So the notorious diversities which human taste exhibits do not become conflicts, and raise no moral problem, until their basis or their function has been forgotten, and each has claimed a right to assert itself exclusively. This claim is altogether absurd, and we might fail to understand how so preposterous an attitude could be assumed by anybody did we not remember that every young animal thinks himself absolute, and that dogmatism in the thinker is only the speculative side of greed and courage in the brute. The brute cannot surrender his appetites nor abdicate his primary right to dominate his environment. What experience and reason may teach him is merely how to make his self-assertion well balanced and successful. In the same way taste is bound to maintain its preferences but free to rationalize them. After a man has compared his feelings with

* Reprinted from *The Life of Reason: Reason in Art* by George Santayana; copyright, 1934, by Charles Scribner's Sons; used by permission of the publishers.

the no less legitimate feelings of other creatures, he can reassert his own with more complete authority, since now he is aware of their necessary ground in his nature, and of their affinities with whatever other interests his nature enables him to recognize in others and to coordinate with his own.

A criterion of taste is, therefore, nothing but taste itself in its more deliberate and circumspect form. Reflection refines particular sentiments by bringing them into sympathy with all rational life. There is consequently the greatest possible difference in authority between taste and taste, and while delight in drums and eagle's feathers is perfectly genuine and has no cause to blush for itself, it cannot be compared in scope or representative value with delight in a symphony or an epic. The very instinct that is satisfied by beauty prefers one beauty to another; and we have only to question and purge our aesthetic feelings in order to obtain our criterion of taste. This criterion will be natural, personal, autonomous; a circumstance that will give it authority over our own judgment—which is all moral science is concerned about—and will extend its authority over other minds also, in so far as their constitution is similar to ours. In that measure what is a genuine instance of reason in us, others will recognize for a genuine expression of reason in themselves also.

Aesthetic feeling, in different people, may make up a different fraction of life and vary greatly in volume. The more nearly insensible a man is the more incompetent he becomes to proclaim the values which sensibility might have. To beauty men are habitually insensible, even while they are awake and rationally active. Tomes of aesthetic criticism hang on a few moments of real delight and intuition. It is in rare and scattered instants that beauty smiles even on her adorers, who are reduced for habitual comfort to remembering her past favors. An aesthetic glow may pervade experience, but that circumstance is seldom remarked; it figures only as an influence working subterraneously on thoughts and judgments which in themselves take a cognitive or practical direction. Only when the aesthetic ingredient becomes predominant do we exclaim, How beautiful! Ordinarily the pleasures which formal perception gives remain an undistinguished part of our comfort or curiosity.

Taste is formed in those moments when aesthetic emotion is massive and distinct; preferences then grown conscious, judgments then put into words will reverberate through calmer hours; they will constitute prejudices, habits of apperception, secret standards for all other beauties. A period of life in which such intuitions have been frequent may amass tastes and ideals sufficient for the rest of our days. Youth in these matters governs maturity, and while men may develop their early impressions more systematically and find confirmations of them in various quarters, they will seldom look at the world afresh or use new categories in deciphering it. Half our standards come from our first masters, and the other half from our first loves. Never being so deeply stirred again, we remain persuaded that no objects save those we then discovered can have a true sublimity. These high-water marks of aesthetic life may easily be reached under tutelage. It may be some eloquent appreciations read in a book, or some preference expressed by a gifted friend, that may have revealed unsuspected beauties in art or nature; and then, since our own perception was vicarious and obviously inferior in volume to that which our mentor possessed, we shall take his judgments for our criterion, since they were the source and exemplar of all our own. Thus the volume and intensity of some appreciations, especially when nothing of the kind has preceded, makes them authoritative over our subsequent judgments. On those warm moments hang all our cold systematic opinions; and while the latter fill our days and shape our careers it is only the former that are crucial and alive.

. . . Good taste is indeed nothing but a name for those appreciations which the swelling incidents of life recall and reinforce. Good taste is that taste which is a good possession, a friend to the whole man. It must not alienate him from anything except to ally him to something greater and more fertile in satisfactions. It will not suffer him to dote on things, however seductive, which rob him of some nobler companionship. To have a foretaste of such a loss, and to reject instinctively whatever will cause it, is the very essence of refinement. Good taste comes, therefore, from experience, in the best sense of that word; it comes from having united in one's memory and character the fruit of many diverse undertakings. Mere taste is apt to be bad taste, since it regards nothing but a chance feeling. Every man who pursues an art may be presumed to have some sensibility; the question is whether he has breeding, too, and whether what he stops at is not, in the end, vulgar and offensive. Chance feeling needs to fortify itself with reasons and to find its level in the great world. When it has added fitness to its sincerity, beneficence to its passion, it will have acquired a right to live. Violence and self-justification will not pass muster in a moral society, for vipers possess both, and must nevertheless be stamped out. Citizenship is conferred only on creatures with human and cooperative instincts. A civilized imagination has to understand and to serve the world.

TAMBURLAINE THE GREAT, Part I, V, ii, 97-110

CHRISTOPHER MARLOWE

What is beauty, saith my sufferings, then?
If all the pens that ever poets held
Had fed the feeling of their masters' thoughts,
And every sweetness that inspired their hearts,
Their minds, and muses on admirèd themes;
If all the heavenly quintessence they still
From their immortal flowers of poesy,
Wherein, as in a mirror, we perceive
The highest reaches of a human wit;
If these had made one poem's period,
And all combined in beauty's worthiness,
Yet should there hover in their restless heads
One thought, one grace, one wonder, at the least,
Which into words no virtue can digest.

from ABT VOGLER

ROBERT BROWNING

But here is the finger of God, a flash of the will that can,
 Existent behind all laws, that made them and, lo, they are!
And I know not if, save in this, such gift be allowed to man,
 That out of three sounds he frame, not a fourth sound, but a star.
Consider it well: each tone of our scale in itself is naught;

It is everywhere in the world—loud, soft, and all is said:
Give it to me to use! I mix it with two in my thought:
And, there! Ye have heard and seen: consider and bow the head!

BEAUTIFUL AND UGLY

From "Skirmishes in a War with the Age" (§§ 19, 20), in
The Twilight of the Idols

FRIEDRICH NIETZSCHE

§ 19

Beautiful and Ugly: Nothing is more relative, let us say, more restricted, than our sense of the beautiful. He who would try to divorce it from the delight man finds in his fellows, would immediately lose his footing. "Beauty in itself," is simply a word, it is not even a concept. In the beautiful, man postulates himself as the standard of perfection; in exceptional cases he worships himself as that standard. A species has no other alternative than to say "yea" to itself alone, in this way. Its lowest instinct, the instinct of self-preservation and self-expansion, still radiates in such sublimities. Man imagines the world itself to be overflowing with beauty, —he forgets that he is the cause of it all. He alone has endowed it with beauty. Alas! and only with human all-too-human beauty! Truth to tell, man reflects himself in things, he thinks everything beautiful that throws his own image back at him. The judgment "beautiful" is the "vanity of his species." . . . A little demon of suspicion may well whisper into the skeptic's ear: is the world really beautified simply because man thinks it beautiful? He has only humanized it— that is all. But nothing, absolutely nothing proves to us that it is precisely man who is the proper model of beauty. Who knows what sort of figure he would cut in the eyes of a higher judge of taste? He might seem a little *outré*? perhaps even somewhat amusing? perhaps a trifle arbitrary? "O Dionysus, thou divine one, why dost thou pull mine ears?" Ariadne asks on one occasion of her philosophic lover, during one of those famous conversations on the island of Naxos. "I find a sort of humor in thine ears, Ariadne: why are they not a little longer?"

§ 20

Nothing is beautiful; man alone is beautiful: all aesthetic rests on this piece of ingenuousness, it is the first axiom of this science. And now let us straightway add the second to it: nothing is ugly save the degenerate man,—within these two first principles the realm of aesthetic judgments is confined. From the physiological standpoint, everything ugly weakens and depresses man. It reminds him of decay, danger, impotence; he literally loses strength in its presence. The effect of ugliness may be gauged by the dynamometer. Whenever man's spirits are downcast, it is a sign that he scents the proximity of something "ugly." His feeling of power, his will to power, his courage and his pride—these things collapse at the sight of what is ugly, and rise at the sight of what is beautiful. In both cases an inference is drawn; the premises to which are stored with extraordinary abundance in the instincts. Ugliness is understood to signify a hint and a symptom of degeneration: that which reminds us however remotely of degeneracy, impels us to the judgment "ugly." Every sign of exhaustion, of gravity, of age, of fatigue; every kind of constraint, such as cramp, or paralysis; and above all the smells, colors and forms associated with decomposition and putrefaction, however much they may have been attenuated into symbols,—all these things provoke the same reaction which is the judgment "ugly." A certain hatred expresses itself here: what is it that man hates? Without a doubt it is the *decline of his type*. In this regard his hatred springs from the deepest instincts of the race: there is horror, caution, profundity and far-reaching vision in this hatred,—it is the most profound hatred that exists. On its account alone Art is profound.

(Anthony M. Ludovici, tr.)

FROM A PORTRAIT OF THE ARTIST AS A YOUNG MAN
Chapter V *

JAMES JOYCE

After a pause Stephen began:
—Aristotle has not defined pity and terror. I have. I say . . . —
Lynch halted and said bluntly:
—Stop! I won't listen! I am sick. I was out last night on a yellow drunk with Horan and Goggins.—
Stephen went on:
—Pity is the feeling which arrests the mind in the presence of whatsoever is grave and constant in human sufferings and unites it with the human sufferer. Terror is the feeling which arrests the mind in the presence of whatsoever is grave and constant in human sufferings and unites it with the secret cause.—
—Repeat—said Lynch.
Stephen repeated the definitions slowly.
—A girl got into a hansom a few days ago—he went on—in London. She was on her way to meet her mother whom she had not seen for many years. At the corner of a street the shaft of a lorry shivered the window of the hansom in the shape of a star. A long fine needle of the shivered glass pierced her heart. She died on the instant. The reporter called it a tragic death. It is not. It is remote from terror and pity according to the terms of my definitions.
—The tragic emotion, in fact, is a face looking two ways, towards terror and towards pity, both of which are phases of it. You see I use the word *arrest*. I mean that the tragic emotion is static. Or rather the dramatic emotion is. The feelings excited by improper art are kinetic, desire or loathing. Desire urges us to possess, to go to something; loathing urges us to abandon, to go from something. The arts which excite them, pornographical or didactic, are therefore improper arts. The esthetic emotion (I used the general term) is therefore static. The mind is arrested and raised above desire and loathing.—
. . . —The desire and loathing excited by improper esthetic means are really not esthetic emotions not only because they are kinetic in character but also because they are not more than physical. Our flesh shrinks from what it dreads and responds to the stimulus of what it desires by a purely reflex action of the nervous system. Our eyelid closes before we are aware that the fly is about to enter our eye.—

* The author's preferences in spelling and punctuation have been preserved.

—Not always—said Lynch critically.

—In the same way—said Stephen—your flesh responded to the stimulus of a naked statue but it was, I say, simply a reflex action of the nerves. Beauty expressed by the artist cannot awaken in us an emotion which is kinetic or a sensation which is purely physical. It awakens, or ought to awaken, or induces, or ought to induce, an esthetic stasis, an ideal pity or an ideal terror, a stasis called forth, prolonged and at last dissolved by what I call the rhythm of beauty.—

—What is that exactly?—asked Lynch.

—Rhythm—said Stephen—is the first formal esthetic relation of part to part in any esthetic whole or of an esthetic whole to its part or parts or of any part to the esthetic whole of which it is a part.—

—If that is rhythm—said Lynch—let me hear what you call beauty: and, please remember, though I did eat a cake of cowdung once, that I admire only beauty.—

Stephen raised his cap as if in greeting. Then, blushing slightly, he laid his hand on Lynch's thick tweed sleeve.

—We are right—he said—and the others are wrong. To speak of these things and to try to understand their nature and, having understood it, to try slowly and humbly and constantly to express, to press out again, from the gross earth or what it brings forth, from sound and shape and color which are the prison gates of our soul, an image of the beauty we have come to understand—that is art.—

They had reached the canal bridge and, turning from their course, went on by the trees. A crude grey light, mirrored in the sluggish water, and a smell of wet branches over their heads seemed to war against the course of Stephen's thought.

—But you have not answered my question—said Lynch—What is art? What is the beauty it expresses?—

—That was the first definition I gave you, you sleepy-headed wretch—said Stephen —when I began to try to think out the matter for myself. Do you remember the night? Cranly lost his temper and began to talk about Wicklow bacon.—

—I remember—said Lynch. —He told us about them flaming fat devils of pigs.—

—Art—said Stephen—is the human disposition of sensible or intelligible matter for an esthetic end. You remember the pigs and forgot that. You are a distressing pair, you and Cranly.—

Lynch made a grimace at the raw grey sky and said:

—If I am to listen to your esthetic philosophy give me at least another cigarette. I don't care about it. I don't even care about women. Damn you and damn everything. I want a job of five hundred a year. You can't get me one.—

Stephen handed him the packet of cigarettes. Lynch took the last one that remained, saying simply:

—Proceed!—

—Aquinas—said Stephen—says that is beautiful the apprehension of which pleases.—

Lynch nodded.

—I remember that—he said—*Pulcra sunt quæ visa placent.*—

—He uses the word *visa*—said Stephen—to cover esthetic apprehensions of all kinds, whether through sight or hearing or through any other avenue of apprehension. This word, though it is vague, is clear enough to keep away good and evil, which excite desire and loathing. It means certainly a stasis and not a kinesis. How about the true? It produces also a stasis of the mind. You would not write your name in pencil across the hypothenuse of a rightangled triangle.—

—No,—said Lynch—give me the hypothenuse of the Venus of Praxiteles.—

—Static therefore—said Stephen—Plato, I believe, said that beauty is the splendor of truth. I don't think that it has a meaning but the true and the beautiful are akin. Truth is beheld by the intellect which is appeased by the most satisfying relations of the intelligible: beauty is beheld by the imagination which is appeased by the most satisfying relations of the sensible. The first step in the direction of truth is to understand the frame and scope of the intellect itself, to comprehend the act itself of intellection. Aristotle's entire system of philosophy rests upon his book of psychology and that, I think, rests on his statement that the same attribute cannot at the same time and in the same connection belong to and not belong to the same subject. The first step in the direction of beauty is to understand the frame and scope of the imagination, to comprehend the act itself of esthetic apprehension. Is that clear?—

—But what is beauty?—asked Lynch impatiently. —Out with another definition. Something we see and like! Is that the best you and Aquinas can do?—

—Let us take woman—said Stephen.

—Let us take her!—said Lynch fervently.

—The Greek, the Turk, the Chinese, the Copt, the Hottentot—said Stephen—all admire a different type of female beauty. That seems to be a maze out of which we cannot escape. I see, however, two ways out. One is this hypothesis: that every physical quality admired by men in women is in direct connection with the manifold functions of women for the propagation of the species. It may be so. The world, it seems, is drearier than even you, Lynch, imagined. For my part I dislike that way out. It leads to eugenics rather than to esthetic. It leads you out of the maze into a new gaudy lecture room where MacCann, with one hand on *The Origin of Species* and the other hand on the New Testament, tells you that you admired the great flanks of Venus because you felt that she would bear you burly offspring and admired her great breasts because you felt that she would give good milk to her children and yours.—

. . . —This hypothesis—Stephen repeated—is the other way out: that, though the same object may not seem beautiful to all people, all people who admire a beautiful object find in it certain relations which satisfy and coincide with the stages themselves of all esthetic apprehension. These relations of the sensible, visible to you through one form and to me through another, must be therefore the necessary qualities of beauty. Now, we can return to our old friend Saint Thomas for another pennyworth of wisdom.—

Lynch laughed.

—It amuses me vastly—he said—to hear you quoting him time after time like a jolly round friar. Are you laughing in your sleeve?—

—MacAlister—answered Stephen—would call my esthetic theory applied Aquinas. So far as this side of esthetic philosophy extends Aquinas will carry me all along the line. When we come to the phenomena of artistic conception, artistic gestation and artistic reproduction, I require a new terminology and a new personal experience.—

. . . They turned their faces towards Merrion Square and went on for a little in silence.

—To finish what I was saying about beauty—said Stephen—the most satisfying relations of the sensible must therefore correspond to the necessary phases of artistic apprehension. Find these and you find the qualities of universal beauty. Aquinas says: *Ad pulcritudinem tria requiruntur integritas, consonantia, claritas.* I translate it so: *Three things are needed for beauty, wholeness, harmony and radiance.*

Do these correspond to the phases of apprehension? Are you following?—

—Of course, I am—said Lynch. —If you think I have an excrementitious intelligence run after Donovan and ask him to listen to you.—

Stephen pointed to a basket which a butcher's boy had slung inverted on his head.

—Look at that basket—he said.

—I see it—said Lynch.

—In order to see that basket—said Stephen—your mind first of all separates the basket from the rest of the visible universe which is not the basket. The first phase of apprehension is a bounding line drawn about the object to be apprehended. An esthetic image is presented to us either in space or in time. What is audible is presented in time, what is visible is presented in space. But temporal or spatial, the esthetic image is first luminously apprehended as selfbounded and selfcontained upon the immeasurable background of space or time which is not it. You apprehended it as *one* thing. You see it as one whole. You apprehend its wholeness. That is *integritas.*—

—Bull's eye!—said Lynch, laughing—Go on.—

—Then—said Stephen—you pass from point to point, led by its formal lines; you apprehend it as balanced part against part within its limits; you feel the rhythm of its structure. In other words, the synthesis of immediate perception is followed by the analysis of apprehension. Having first felt that it is *one* thing you feel now that it is a *thing.* You apprehend it as complex, multiple, divisible, separable, made up of its parts, the result of its parts and their sum, harmonious. That is *consonantia.*

—Bull's eye again!—said Lynch wittily.—Tell me now what is *claritas* and you win the cigar.—

—The connotation of the word—Stephen said—is rather vague. Aquinas uses a term which seems to be inexact. It baffled me for a long time. It would lead you to believe that he had in mind symbolism or idealism, the supreme quality of beauty being a light from some other world, the idea of which the matter was but the shadow, the reality of which it was but the symbol. I thought he might mean that *claritas* was the artistic discovery and representation of the divine purpose in anything or a force of generalization which would make the esthetic image a universal one, make it outshine its proper conditions. But that is literary talk. I understand it so. When you have apprehended that basket as one thing and have then analyzed it according to its form and apprehended it as a thing you make the only synthesis which is logically and esthetically permissible. You see that it is that thing which it is and no other thing. The radiance of which he speaks is the scholastic *quidditas,* the *whatness* of a thing. This supreme quality is felt by the artist when the esthetic image is first conceived in his imagination. The mind in that mysterious instant Shelley likened beautifully to a fading coal. The instant wherein that supreme quality of beauty, the clear radiance of the esthetic image, is apprehended luminously by the mind which has been arrested by its wholeness and fascinated by its harmony is the luminous silent stasis of aesthetic pleasure, a spiritual state very like to that cardiac condition which the Italian physiologist Luigi Galvani, using a phrase almost as beautiful as Shelley's, called the enchantment of the heart.—

Stephen paused and, though his companion did not speak, felt that his words had called up around them a thought-enchanted silence.

THE DEFINITION OF BEAUTY *

In *The Sense of Beauty* (§ 11)

GEORGE SANTAYANA

We have now reached our definition of beauty, which, in the terms of our successive analysis and narrowing of the conception, is value positive, intrinsic, and objectified. Or, in less technical language, Beauty is pleasure regarded as the quality of a thing.

This definition is intended to sum up a variety of distinctions and identifications which should perhaps be here more explicitly set down. Beauty is a value, that is, it is not a perception of a matter of fact or of a relation: it is an emotion, an affection of our volitional and appreciative nature. An object cannot be beautiful if it can give pleasure to nobody: a beauty to which all men were forever indifferent is a contradiction in terms.

In the second place, this value is positive, it is the sense of the presence of something good, or (in the case of ugliness) of its absence. It is never the perception of a positive evil, it is never a negative value. That we are endowed with the sense of beauty is a pure gain which brings no evil with it. When the ugly ceases to be amusing or merely uninteresting and becomes disgusting, it becomes indeed a positive evil: but a moral and practical, not an aesthetic one. In aesthetics that saying is true—often so disingenuous in ethics—that evil is nothing but the absence of good: for even the tedium and vulgarity of an existence without beauty is not itself ugly so much as lamentable and degrading. The absence of aesthetic goods is a moral evil: the aesthetic evil is merely relative, and means less of aesthetic good than was expected at the place and time. No form in itself gives pain, although some forms give pain by causing a shock of surprise even when they are really beautiful: as if a mother found a fine bull pup in her child's cradle, when her pain would not be aesthetic in its nature.

Further, this pleasure must not be in the consequence of the utility of the object or event, but in its immediate perception; in other words, beauty is an ultimate good, something that gives satisfaction to a natural function, to some fundamental need or capacity of our minds. Beauty is therefore a positive value that is intrinsic; it is a pleasure. These two circumstances sufficiently separate the sphere of aesthetics from that of ethics. Moral values are generally negative, and always remote. Morality has to do with the avoidance of evil and the pursuit of good: aesthetics only with enjoyment.

Finally, the pleasures of sense are distinguished from the perception of beauty, as sensation in general is distinguished from perception; by the objectification of the elements and their appearance as qualities rather of things than of consciousness. The passage from sensation to perception is gradual, and the path may be sometimes retraced: so it is with beauty and the pleasures of sensation. There is no sharp line between them, but it depends upon the degree of objectivity my feeling has attained at the moment whether I say "It pleases me," or "It is beautiful." If I am self-conscious and critical, I shall probably use one phrase; if I am impulsive and susceptible, the other. The more remote, interwoven, and inextricable the pleasure is, the more objective it will appear; and the union of two pleasures often makes one beauty. In Shakespeare's LIVth sonnet are these words:

* Reprinted from *The Sense of Beauty* by George Santayana; copyright, 1896, by Charles Scribner's Sons; used by permission of the publishers.

"O how much more doth beauty beauteous seem
By that sweet ornament which truth doth give!
The rose looks fair, but fairer we it deem
For that sweet odor which doth in it live.
The canker-blooms have full as deep a dye
As the perfumèd tincture of the roses,
Hang on such thorns, and play as wantonly
When summer's breath their maskèd buds discloses.
But, for their beauty only is their show,
They live unwooed and unrespected fade;
Die to themselves. Sweet roses do not so:
Of their sweet deaths are sweetest odors made."

One added ornament, we see, turns the deep dye, which was but show and mere sensation before, into an element of beauty and reality; and as truth is here the coöperation of perceptions, so beauty is the coöperation of pleasures. If color, form, and motion are hardly beautiful without the sweetness of the odor, how much more necessary would they be for the sweetness itself to become a beauty! If we had the perfume in a flask, no one would think of calling it beautiful: it would give us too detached and controllable a sensation. There would be no object in which it could be easily incorporated. But let it float from the garden, and it will add another sensuous charm to objects simultaneously recognized, and help to make them beautiful. Thus beauty is constituted by the objectification of pleasure. It is pleasure objectified.

FROM LAST WORDS OF DIOTIMA

In *Symposium*

PLATO

[DIOTIMA:] "For he who would proceed aright in this matter should begin in youth to visit beautiful forms; and first, if he be guided by his instructor aright, to love one such form only—out of that he should create fair thoughts; and soon he will of himself perceive that the beauty of one form is akin to the beauty of another; and then if beauty of form in general is his pursuit, how foolish would he be not to recognize that the beauty in every form is one and the same! And when he perceives this he will abate his violent love of the one, which he will despise and deem a small thing, and will become a lover of all beautiful forms; in the next stage he will consider that the beauty of the mind is more honorable than the beauty of the outward form. So that if a virtuous soul have but a little comeliness, he will be content to love and tend him, and will search out and bring to the birth thoughts which may improve the young, until he is compelled to contemplate and see the beauty of institutions and laws, and to understand that the beauty of them all is of one family, and that personal beauty is a trifle; and after laws and institutions he will go on to the sciences, that he may see their beauty, being not like a servant in love with the beauty of one youth or man or institution, himself a slave mean and narrow-minded, but drawing towards and contemplating the vast sea of beauty, he will create many fair and noble thoughts and notions in boundless love of wisdom; until on that shore he grows and waxes strong, and at last the vision is revealed to him of a single science, which is the science of beauty everywhere. To this I will proceed; please to give me your very best attention:

"He who has been instructed thus far in the things of love, and who has learned to see the beautiful in due order and succession, when he comes towards the end will suddenly perceive a nature of wondrous beauty (and this, Socrates, is the final cause of all our former toils)—a nature which in the first place is everlasting, not growing and decaying, or waxing and waning; secondly, not fair in one point of view and foul in another, or at one time or in one relation or at one place fair, at another time or in another relation or at another place foul, as if fair to some and foul to others, or in the likeness of a face or hands or any other part of the bodily frame, or in any form of speech or knowledge, or existing in any other being, as for example, in an animal, or in heaven, or in earth, or in any other place; but beauty absolute, separate, simple, and everlasting, which without diminution and without increase, or any change, is imparted to the ever-growing and perishing beauties of all other things. He who from these ascending under the influence of true love, begins to perceive that beauty, is not far from the end. And the true order of going, or being led by another, to the things of love, is to begin from the beauties of earth and mount upwards for the sake of that other beauty, using these as steps only, and from one going on to two, and from two to all fair forms, and from fair forms to fair practices, and from fair practices to fair notions, until from fair notions he arrives at the notion of absolute beauty, and at last knows what the essence of beauty is.

"This, my dear Socrates," said the stranger of Mantineia, "is that life above all others which man should live, in the contemplation of beauty absolute; a beauty which if you once beheld, you would see not to be after the measure of gold, and garments, and fair boys and youths, whose presence now entrances you; and you and many a one would be content to live seeing them only and conversing with them without meat or drink, if that were possible—you only want to look at them and to be with them. But what if man had eyes to see the true beauty—the divine beauty, I mean, pure and clear and unalloyed, not clogged with the pollutions of mortality and all the colors and vanities of human life—thither looking, and holding converse with the true beauty simple and divine? Remember how in that communion only, beholding beauty with the eye of the mind, he will be enabled to bring forth, not images of beauty, but realities (for he has hold not of an image but of a reality), and bringing forth and nourishing true virtue to become the friend of God and be immortal, if mortal man may. Would that be an ignoble life?"

(Benjamin Jowett, tr.)

FROM AN HYMN IN HONOR OF BEAUTY

EDMUND SPENSER

What time this world's great workmaster did cast
To make all things, such as we now behold,
It seems that he before his eyes had placed
A goodly pattern, to whose perfect mold
He fashioned them as comely as he could;
That now so fair and seemly they appear,
As nought may be amended any where.

That wondrous Pattern wheresoe'er it be,
Whether in earth laid up in secret store,
Or else in heaven, that no man may it see

With sinful eyes, for fear it to deflower,
Is perfect Beauty which all men adore,
Whose face and feature doth so much excel
All mortal sense, that none the same may tell.

Thereof as every earthly thing partakes,
Or more or less by influence divine,
So it more fair accordingly it makes,
And the gross matter of this earthly mine.
Which clotheth it, thereafter doth refine,
Doing away the dross which dims the light
Of that fair beam, which therein is empight.

For through infusion of celestial power,
The duller earth it quickeneth with delight,
And life-full spirits privily doth pour
Through all the parts, that to the looker's sight
They seem to please.   That is thy sovereign might,
O Cyprian Queen, which flowing from the beam
Of thy bright star, thou into them dost stream.

That is the thing which giveth pleasant grace
To all things fair, that kindleth lively fire,
Light of thy lamp, which shining in the face,
Thence to the soul darts amorous desire,
And robs the hearts of those which it admire,
Therewith thou pointest thy Son's poisoned arrow,
That wounds the life, and wastes the inmost marrow.

How vainly then do idle wits invent,
That beauty is nought else but mixture made
Of colors fair, and goodly temperament
Of pure complexions, that shall quickly fade
And pass away, like to a summer's shade,
Or that it is but comely composition
Of parts well measured, with meet disposition.

Hath white and red in it such wondrous power,
That it can pierce through th' eyes unto the heart,
And therein stir such rage and restless stour,
As nought but death can stint his dolors smart?
Or can proportion of the outward part,
Move such affection in the inward mind,
That it can rob both sense and reason blind?

Why do not then the blossoms of the field,
Which are arrayed with much more orient hue,
And to the sense most dainty odors yield,
Work like impression in the looker's view?
Or why do not fair pictures like power shew,
In which ofttimes, we Nature see of Art
Excelled, in perfect limning every part.

But ah, believe me, there is more than so
That works such wonders in the minds of men.
I that have often proved, too well it know;
And who so list the like assays to ken,
Shall find by trial, and confess it then,
That Beauty is not, as fond men misdeem,
An outward show of things, that only seem.

For that same goodly hue of white and red,
With which the cheeks are sprinkled, shall decay,
And those sweet rosy leaves so fairly spread
Upon the lips, shall fade and fall away
To that they were, even to corrupted clay.
That golden wire, those sparkling stars so bright
Shall turn to dust, and lose their goodly light.

But that fair lamp, from whose celestial ray
That light proceeds, which kindleth lovers' fire
Shall never be extinguished nor decay
But when the vital spirits do expire,
Unto her native planet shall retire,
For it is heavenly born and can not die,
Being a parcel of the purest sky.

MUSÉE DES BEAUX ARTS

W. H. AUDEN

About suffering they were never wrong,
The Old Masters: how well they understood
Its human position; how it takes place
While someone else is eating or opening a window or just walking dully
    along;
How, when the aged are reverently, passionately waiting
For the miraculous birth, there always must be
Children who did not specially want it to happen, skating
On a pond at the edge of the wood:
They never forgot
That even the dreadful martyrdom must run its course
Anyhow in a corner, some untidy spot
Where the dogs go on with their doggy life and the torturer's horse
Scratches its innocent behind on a tree.

In Breughel's *Icarus,* for instance: how everything turns away
Quite leisurely from the disaster; the ploughman may
Have heard the splash, the forsaken cry,
But for him it was not an important failure; the sun shone
As it had to on the white legs disappearing into the green
Water; and the expensive delicate ship that must have seen
Something amazing, a boy falling out of the sky,
Had somewhere to get to and sailed calmly on.

LETTERS UPON THE AESTHETICAL EDUCATION OF MAN, XXVII

FRIEDRICH von SCHILLER

Do not fear for reality and truth. Even if the elevated idea of aesthetic appearance became general, it would not become so, as long as man remains so little cultivated as to abuse it; and if it became general, this would result from a culture that would prevent all abuse of it. The pursuit of independent appearance requires more power of abstraction, freedom of heart, and energy of will than man requires to shut himself up in reality; and he must have left the latter behind him if he wishes to attain to aesthetic appearance. Therefore a man would calculate very badly who took the road of the ideal to save himself that of reality. Thus reality would not have much to fear from appearance, as we understand it; but, on the other hand, appearance would have more to fear from reality. Chained to matter, man uses appearance for his purposes before he allows it a proper personality in the art of the ideal: to come to that point a complete revolution must take place in his mode of feeling, otherwise he would not be even on the way to the ideal. Consequently, when we find in man the signs of a pure and disinterested esteem, we can infer that this revolution has taken place in his nature, and that humanity has really begun in him. Signs of this kind are found even in the first and rude attempts that he makes to embellish his existence, even at the risk of making it worse in its material conditions. As soon as he begins to prefer form to substance and to risk reality for appearance (known by him to be such), the barriers of animal life fall, and he finds himself on a track that has no end.

Not satisfied with the needs of nature, he demands the superfluous. First, only the superfluous of matter, to secure his enjoyment beyond the present necessity; but afterwards he wishes a superabundance in matter, an aesthetical supplement to satisfy the impulse for the formal, to extend enjoyment beyond necessity. By piling up provisions simply for a future use, and anticipating their enjoyment in the imagination, he outsteps the limits of the present moment, but not those of time in general. He enjoys more; he does not enjoy differently. But as soon as he makes form enter into his enjoyment, and he keeps in view the forms of the objects which satisfy his desires, he has not only increased his pleasure in extent and intensity, but he has also ennobled it in mode and species.

No doubt nature has given more than is necessary to unreasoning beings; she has caused a gleam of freedom to shine even in the darkness of animal life. When the lion is not tormented by hunger, and when no wild beast challenges him to fight, his unemployed energy creates an object for himself; full of ardor, he fills the re-echoing desert with his terrible roars, and his exuberant force rejoices in itself, showing itself without an object. The insect flits about rejoicing in life in the sunlight, and it is certainly not the cry of want that makes itself heard in the melodious song of the bird; there is undeniably freedom in these movements, though it is not emancipation from want in general, but from a determinate external necessity.

The animal *works*, when a privation is the motor of its activity, and it *plays* when the plenitude of force is this motor, when an exuberant life is excited to action. Even in inanimate nature a luxury of strength and a latitude of determination are shown, which in this material sense might be styled play. The tree produces numberless germs that are abortive without developing, and it sends forth more roots, branches and leaves, organs of nutrition, than are used for the preservation of the species. Whatever this tree restores to the elements of its exuberant life, without using it, or enjoying it, may be expended by life in free and joyful movements. It is thus that nature offers, in her material sphere, a sort of prelude to the limitless, and that even there she suppresses partially the chains from which she will be completely emancipated in the realm of form. The constraint of superabundance or *physical play,* answers as a transition from the constraint of necessity, or of *physical seriousness,* to aesthetical play; and before shaking off, in the supreme freedom of the beautiful, the yoke of any special aim, nature already approaches, at least remotely, this independence, by the *free movement* which is itself its own end and means.

The imagination, like the bodily organs, has in man its free movement and its material play, a play in which, without any reference to form, it simply takes pleasure in its arbitrary power and in the absence of all hindrance. These plays of fancy, inasmuch as form is not mixed up with them, and because a free succession of images makes all their charm, though confined to man, belong exclusively to animal life, and only prove one thing—that he is delivered from all external sensuous constraint—without our being entitled to infer that there is in it an independent plastic force.

From this play of *free association* of ideas, which is still quite material in nature and is explained by simple natural laws, the imagination, by making the attempt of creating a free form, passes at length at a jump to the aesthetic play: I say at one leap, for quite a new force enters into action here; for here, for the first time, the legislative mind is mixed with the acts of a blind instinct, subjects the arbitrary march of the imagination to its eternal and immutable unity, causes its independent permanence to enter in that which is transitory, and its infinity in the sensuous. Nevertheless, as long as rude nature, which knows of no other law than running incessantly from change to change, will yet retain too much strength, it will oppose itself by its different caprices to this necessity; by its agitation to this permanence; by its manifold needs to this independence, and by its insatiability to this sublime simplicity. It will be also troublesome to recognize the instinct of play in its first trials, seeing that the sensuous impulsion, with its capricious humor and its violent appetites, constantly crosses. It is on that account that we see the taste, still coarse, seize that which is new and startling, the disordered, the adventurous and the strange, the violent and the savage, and fly from nothing so much as from calm and simplicity. It invents grotesque figures, it likes rapid transitions, luxurious forms, sharply marked changes, acute tones, a pathetic song. That which man calls beautiful at this time, is that which excites him, that which gives him matter; but that which excites him to give his personality to the object, that which gives matter to a *possible plastic operation,* for otherwise it would not be the beautiful for him. A remarkable change has therefore taken place in the form of his judgments; he searches for these objects, not because they affect him, but because they furnish him with the occasion of acting; they please him, not because they answer to a want, but because they satisfy a law, which speaks in his breast, although quite low as yet.

Soon it will not be sufficient for things to please him; he will wish to please: in the first place, it is true, only by that which belongs to him; afterwards by that which he is. That which he possesses, that which he produces, ought not merely to bear any more the traces of servitude, nor to mark out the end, simply and scrupulously, by the form. Independently of the use to which it is destined, the object ought also to reflect the enlightened intelligence which imagines it, the hand which shaped it with affection, the mind free and serene which chose it and exposed it to view. Now, the ancient German searches for more *magnificent* furs, for more *splendid* antlers of the stag, for more elegant drinking horns; and the Caledonian chooses the prettiest shells for his festivals. The arms themselves ought to be no longer only objects of terror, but also of pleasure; and the skilfully worked scabbard will not attract less attention than the homicidal edge of the sword. The instinct of play, not satisfied with bringing into the sphere of the necessary an aesthetic superabundance for the future more free, is at last completely emancipated from the bonds of duty, and the beautiful becomes of itself an object of man's exertions. He adorns himself. The free pleasure comes to take a place among his wants, and the useless soon becomes the best part of his joys. Form, which from the outside gradually approaches him, in his dwelling, his furniture, his clothing, begins at last to take possession of the man himself, to transform him, at first exteriorly, and afterwards in the interior. The disordered leaps of joy become the dance, the formless gesture is changed into an amiable and harmonious pantomime, the confused accents of feeling are developed, and begin to obey measure and adapt themselves to song. When, like the flight of cranes, the Trojan army rushes on to the field of battle with thrilling cries, the Greek army approaches in silence and with a noble and measured step. On the one side we see but the exuberance of a blind force, on the other the triumph of form and the simple majesty of law.

Now, a nobler necessity binds the two sexes mutually, and the interests of the heart contribute in rendering durable an alliance which was at first capricious and changing like the desire that knits it. Delivered from the heavy fetters of desire, the eye, now calmer, attends to the form, the soul contemplates the soul, and the interested exchange of pleasure becomes a generous exchange of mutual inclination. Desire enlarges and rises to love, in proportion as it sees humanity dawn in its object; and, despising the vile triumphs gained by the senses, man tries to win a nobler victory over the will. The necessity of pleasing subjects the powerful nature to the gentle laws of taste; pleasure may be stolen, but love must be a gift. To obtain this higher recompense it is only through the form and not through matter that it can carry on the contest. It must cease to act on feeling as a force, to appear in the intelligence as a simple phenomenon; it must respect liberty, as it is liberty it wishes to please. The beautiful reconciles the contrast of different natures in its simplest and purest expression. It also reconciles the eternal contrast of the two sexes, in the whole complex framework of society, or at all events it seeks to do so; and, taking as its model the free alliance it has knit between manly strength and womanly gentleness, it strives to place in harmony, in the moral world, all the elements of gentleness and of violence. Now, at length, weakness becomes sacred, and an unbridled strength disgraces; the injustice of nature is corrected by the generosity of chivalrous manners. The being whom no power can make tremble, is disarmed by the amiable blush of modesty, and tears extinguish a vengeance that blood could not have quenched. Hatred itself hears the delicate voice of honor, the conqueror's sword spares the disarmed enemy, and a hospitable hearth smokes for the stranger on the dreaded hill-side where murder alone awaited him before.

In the midst of the formidable realm of forces, and of the sacred empire of laws, the aesthetic impulse of form creates by degrees a third and a joyous realm, that of play and of the appearance, where she emancipates man from fetters, in all his relations, and from all that is named constraint, whether physical or moral.

If in the dynamic state of rights men mutually move and come into collision as forces, in the moral (ethical) state of duties, man opposes to man the majesty of the laws, and chains down his will. In this realm of the beautiful or the aesthetic state, man ought to appear to man only as a form, and an object of free play. To give freedom through freedom is the fundamental law of this realm.

The dynamic state can only make society simply possible by subduing nature through nature; the moral (ethical) state can only make it morally necessary by submitting the will of the individual to the general will. The aesthetic state alone can make it real, because it carries out the will of all through the nature of the individual. If necessity alone forces man to enter into society, and if his reason engraves on his soul social principles, it is beauty only that can give him a social *character;* taste alone brings harmony into society, because it creates harmony in the individual. All other forms of perception divide the man, because they are based exclusively either in the sensuous or in the spiritual part of his being. It is only the perception of beauty that makes of him an entirety, because it demands the coöperation of his two natures. All other forms of communication divide society, because they apply exclusively either to the receptivity or to the private activity of its members, and therefore to what distinguishes men one from the other. The aesthetic communication alone unites society, because it applies to what is common to all its members. We only enjoy the pleasures of sense as individuals, without the nature of the race in us sharing in it; accordingly, we cannot generalize our individual pleasures, because we cannot generalize our individuality. We enjoy the pleasures of knowledge as a race, dropping the individual in our judgment; but we cannot generalize the pleasures of the understanding, because we cannot eliminate individuality from the judgments of others as we do from our own. Beauty alone can we enjoy both as individuals and as a race, that is, as representing a race. Good appertaining to sense can only make one person happy, because it is founded on inclination, which is always exclusive; and it can only make a man partially happy, because his real personality does not share in it. Absolute good can only render a man happy conditionally, for truth is only the reward of abnegation, and a pure heart alone has faith in a pure will. Beauty alone confers happiness on all, and under its influence every being forgets that he is limited.

Taste does not suffer any superior or absolute authority, and the sway of beauty is extended over appearance. It extends up to the seat of reason's supremacy, suppressing all that is material. It extends down to where sensuous impulse rules with blind compulsion, and form is undeveloped. Taste ever maintains its power on these remote borders, where legislation is taken from it. Particular desires must renounce their egotism, and the agreeable, otherwise tempting the senses, must in matters of taste adorn the mind with the attractions of grace.

Duty and stern necessity must change their forbidding tone, only excused by resistance, and do homage to nature by a nobler trust in her. Taste leads our knowledge from the mysteries of science into the open expanse of common sense, and changes a narrow scholasticism into the common property of the human race. Here the highest genius must leave its particular elevation, and make itself familiar to the comprehension even of a child. Strength must let the Graces bind it, and the arbitrary lion must yield to the reins of love. For this purpose taste throws a veil over physical necessity, offending a free mind by its coarse nudity, and dissimulating our degrading parentage with matter by a delightful illusion of freedom. Mercenary art itself rises from the dust; and the bondage of the bodily, at its magic touch, falls off from the inanimate and animate. In the aesthetic state the most slavish tool is a free citizen, having the same rights as the noblest; and the intellect which shapes the mass to its intent must consult it concerning its destination. Consequently in the realm of aesthetic appearance, the idea of equality is realized, which the political zealot would gladly see carried out socially. It has often been said that perfect politeness is only found near a throne. If thus restricted in the material, man has, as elsewhere appears, to find compensation in the ideal world.

Does such a state of beauty in appearance exist, and where? It must be in every finely harmonized soul; but as a fact, only in select circles, like the pure ideal of the church and state—in circles where manners are not formed by the empty imitations of the foreign, but by the very beauty of Nature; where man passes through all sorts of complications in all simplicity and innocence, neither forced to trench on another's freedom to preserve his own, nor to show grace at the cost of dignity.

(Translator unknown)

ODE ON A GRECIAN URN

JOHN KEATS

Thou still unravished bride of quietness,
 Thou foster-child of silence and slow time,
Sylvan historian, who canst thus express
 A flowery tale more sweetly than our rhyme:
What leaf-fringed legend haunts about thy shape
 Of deities or mortals, or of both,
  In Tempe or the dales of Arcady?
What men or gods are these? What maidens loth?
What mad pursuit? What struggle to escape?
  What pipes and timbrels? What wild ecstasy?

Heard melodies are sweet, but those unheard
 Are sweeter; therefore, ye soft pipes, play on;
Not to the sensual ear, but, more endeared,
 Pipe to the spirit ditties of no tone:
Fair youth, beneath the trees, thou canst not leave
 Thy song, nor ever can those trees be bare;
  Bold Lover, never, never canst thou kiss,
Though winning near the goal—yet, do not grieve;
  She cannot fade, though thou has not thy bliss,
 For ever wilt thou love, and she be fair!

Ah, happy, happy boughs! that cannot shed
 Your leaves, nor ever bid the Spring adieu;
And, happy melodist, unwearièd,
 For ever piping songs for ever new;
More happy love! more happy, happy love!
 For ever warm and still to be enjoyed,
  For ever panting, and for ever young;
All breathing human passion far above,
  That leaves a heart high-sorrowful and cloyed,
 A burning forehead, and a parching tongue.

Who are these coming to the sacrifice?
To what green altar, O mysterious priest,
Lead'st thou that heifer lowing at the skies,
And all her silken flanks with garlands dressed?
What little town by river or sea shore,
Or mountain-built with peaceful citadel,
Is emptied of this folk, this pious morn?
And, little town, thy streets for evermore
Will silent be; and not a soul to tell
Why thou art desolate, can e'er return.

O Attic shape! Fair attitude! with brede
Of marble men and maidens over wrought,
With forest branches and the trodden weed;
Thou, silent form, dost tease us out of thought
As doth eternity: Cold Pastoral!
When old age shall this generation waste,
Thou shalt remain, in midst of other woe
Than ours, a friend to man, to whom thou say'st,
"Beauty is truth, truth beauty,"—that is all
Ye know on earth, and all ye need to know.

FROM THE REPUBLIC, X *

PLATO

SOCRATES: Well, that is my point when I say that the copying arts damage the mind. They produce something far from true and deal with something in us which is far from knowledge and no friend to it for any healthy purpose. And this is true not only with vision but with verses. So don't let us keep only to this parallel with painting but turn to see if that part of the mind with which poetry in fact deals is good or bad.

GLAUCON: Certainly.

SOCRATES: Poetry copies men: acting either under force or of their own free will; seeing themselves in the outcome to have done well or ill; and, in all this, feeling grief or joy. Is there something in addition?

GLAUCON: Nothing.

SOCRATES: Is a man of one mind with himself in all this? Or is there division and fighting with himself—as there was when in vision he had opposite opinions at the same time about the same things. But we came to agreement on that before. Our souls at any one time are attacked by endless opposite views. There was one thing, however, we didn't say then which has to be said now.

GLAUCON: What is it?

SOCRATES: We said then, I believe, that a good man who is guided by reason will take such blows of fate as the loss of a son or anything very dear to him less hard than other people.

GLAUCON: Certainly.

SOCRATES: Will he feel no grief or—that being impossible—will he be temperate in his grief?

GLAUCON: The last is truer.

* Reprinted from *The Republic of Plato* by I. A. Richards by permission of W. W. Norton & Company, Inc. Copyright, 1942, bv W. W. Norton & Company.

SOCRATES: Will he keep down his grief more when he [604] is under the eyes of his equals or when he is by himself?

GLAUCON: He will be much more self-controlled when he is on view.

SOCRATES: By himself he will cry out, as I see him, in ways which if another heard him would put him to shame, and he'll do things he would not have anyone see him doing. Reason and law urge him to keep down this grief, while the feeling itself forces him to give way to it. So, because there are two opposite impulses in such a man at the same time about the same thing, we say there are two things in him. One of them is ready to be guided by the law which, I take it, says that it is best to keep quiet as far as possible when griefs come and not to cry out, because we are not certain what is good and what is evil in such things, and to take them hard does not make them any better. Reason says that nothing in man's existence is to be taken so seriously, and our grief keeps us back from the very thing we need as quickly as possible in such times.

GLAUCON: What is that?

SOCRATES: To take thought on the event; and, as we order our play by the way the cards fall, to see how to order our acts, in view of what has come about, in the ways reason points to as the best. Don't let us be like children when they have had a fall, and go on crying out with a hand on the place. Look after the wound first and pick up what has had a fall, and make grief give place to medical help.

GLAUCON: That would certainly be the best way.

SOCRATES: And what is best in us is willing to be guided by reason?

GLAUCON: Clearly.

SOCRATES: And the part which goes over our grief in memory and never has enough of lamenting is unreasoning and useless and feeble-spirited?

GLAUCON: Yes, we will say so.

SOCRATES: Now the part which grieves may be copied in numberless different ways, while the reasoning temperate condition, always nearly the same, is hard to copy or to take in when copied—especially by the masses of very different people who go to the play. That whole way of [605] living is strange to them. The copying poet is not naturally turned toward this best thing in the soul, nor is his art framed to please it, for he has to get the praises of the public. So he gives himself up to the sort of man who cries out in changeful ways as something not so hard to copy. And in doing so he plants an evil government within every soul. He pleases its foolish part. But still we have not come to our chief point against poetry. Its power to make even the better sort worse is the thing most to be feared.

GLAUCON: It would be, if poetry could do that.

SOCRATES: Hear and take thought. The very best of us, hearing Homer or one of the other tragic poets copying some great man in grief, running on and on in his outcries, or wounding himself in his pain, have feelings of pleasure and let our hearts go out to the picture. We give ourselves up to it and praise, as a great poet, whoever makes us do this most.

GLAUCON: We do.

SOCRATES: But in our own lives, when some grief comes upon us, we take pride in the opposite behavior, in our power to keep quiet and take it with courage, believing that this is a man's part and that the other we were praising in the play is a woman's. Are we right to praise so what we would be ashamed of in ourselves?

GLAUCON: By Zeus, no. There is no reason in that!

SOCRATES: There is if you look at it this way.

GLAUCON: Which way?

SOCRATES: In our own grief there is that in the soul which [606] is kept back by force, which by its very nature is in need of tears and lamentations as an outlet. This is what the poets please and delight in us. And what is best in us, having never had a right education or even training, lets down its guard over this grieving part because here we are looking on at the grief of others. But what we take pleasure in when we see it in others will have its effect on ourselves; after feasting our feelings of pity there it is hard to keep them down in our own grief. Few are able to see that.

GLAUCON: Most true.

SOCRATES: And the same is true of the causes of laughter, with comedies, or in private talk. When you take the greatest pleasure in things so low that you would be full of shame about them if they were yours, you are doing just what you do at the tragedy. Sometimes you let yourself go so far that before you know it you become a clown yourself in private. And so, again, with the desires of sex, and with anger and all the other passions and desires and pains and pleasures of the soul that go along with all our acts. The effect of such poetry is the same. It waters and cares for these feelings when what we have to do is dry them up. It makes into our rulers the very things which have to be ruled, if we are to become better and happier men.

GLAUCON: I may not say no.

SOCRATES: Then, Glaucon, when the praisers of Homer say that he gave Hellas its education, and that if a man is to guide and better his behavior he will do well to give himself up to reading Homer, and that we are to order [607] our lives by his teaching, we may love and honor these people—as doing their very best—and agree that Homer is the highest and first of all tragic poets; but let us keep true to our belief that only hymns to the gods and praises of good men may be allowed in our state. For if you let in this honey-sweet music, pleasure and pain, not law, will be its lords.

GLAUCON: Most true.

SOCRATES: So—to make an end of this—we had good cause to send this Muse out of our state. For reason ordered so. And let us say again, if she protests against us as rough and unlettered, that there has been an old quarrel between poetry and philosophy of which the signs are everywhere. But if poetry has good arguments for a place in a well-ordered state, why then with joy we will let her in, for we ourselves well know the delights she offers. Only we may not sin against what we believe to be true.

(I. A. Richards, tr.)

FROM A DEFENSE OF POETRY

PERCY BYSSHE SHELLEY

Poetry is indeed something divine. It is at once the center and circumference of knowledge; it is that which comprehends all science, and that to which all science must be referred. It is at the same time the root and blossom of all other systems of thought; it is that from which all spring, and that which adorns all; and that which if blighted, denies the fruit and the seed, and withholds from the barren world the nourishment and the succession of the scions of the tree of life. It is the perfect and consummate surface and bloom of all things; it is as the odor and the color of the rose to the texture of the elements which compose it, as the form and splendor of unfaded beauty to the secrets of anatomy and corruption. What were virtue, love, patriotism, friendship,—what were the scenery of this beautiful universe which we inhabit; what were our consolations on this side of the grave— and what were our aspirations beyond it, if poetry did not ascend to bring light and fire from those eternal regions where the owl-winged faculty of calculation dare not ever soar? Poetry is not like reasoning, a power to be exerted according to the determination of the will. A man cannot say, "I will compose poetry." The greatest poet even cannot say it; for the mind in creation is as a fading coal, which some invisible influence, like an inconstant wind, awakens to transitory brightness; this power arises from within, like the color of a flower which fades and changes as it is developed, and the conscious portions of our nature are unprophetic either of its approach or its departure. Could this influence be durable in its original purity and force, it is impossible to predict the greatness of the results; but when composition begins, inspiration is already on the decline, and the most glorious poetry that has ever been communicated to the world is probably a feeble shadow of the original conceptions of the poet. I appeal to the greatest poets of the present day, whether it is not an error to assert that the finest passages of poetry are produced by labor and study. The toil and the delay recommended by critics, can be justly interpreted to mean no more than a careful observation of the inspired moments, and an artificial connection of the spaces between their suggestions, by the intertexture of conventional expressions; a necessity only imposed by the limitedness of the poetical faculty itself: for Milton conceived the Paradise Lost as a whole before he executed it in portions. We have his own authority also for the muse having "dictated" to him the "unpremeditated song." And let this be an answer to those who would allege the fifty-six various readings of the first line of the Orlando Furioso. Compositions so produced are to poetry what mosaic is to painting. The instinct and intuition of the poetical faculty is still more observable in the plastic and pictorial arts; a great statue or picture grows under the power of the artist as a child in the mother's womb; and the very mind which directs the hands in formation, is incapable of accounting to itself for the origin, the gradations, or the media of the process.

Poetry is the record of the best and happiest moments of the happiest and best minds. We are aware of evanescent visitations of thought and feeling, sometimes associated with place or person, sometimes regarding our own mind alone, and always arising unforeseen and departing unbidden, but elevating and delightful beyond all expression: so that even in the desire and regret they leave, there cannot but be pleasure, participating as it does in the nature of its object. It is as it were the interpenetration of a diviner nature through our own; but its footsteps are like those of a wind over the sea, which the morning calm erases, and whose traces remain only, as on the wrinkled sand which paves it. These and corresponding conditions of being are experienced principally by those of the most delicate sensibility and the most enlarged imagination; and the state of mind produced by them is at war with every base desire. The enthusiasm of virtue, love, patriotism, and friendship, is essentially linked with such emotions; and whilst they last, self appears as what it is, an atom to a universe. Poets are not only subject to these experiences as spirits of the most refined organization, but they can color all that they combine with the evanescent hues of this aetherial world; a word, a trait in the representation of a scene or a passion, will touch the enchanted chord, and reanimate, in those who have ever experienced these emotions, the sleeping, the cold, the buried image of the past. Poetry thus makes immortal all that is best and most beautiful in the world; it arrests the vanishing apparitions which haunt the interlunations of life, and veiling them, or in language or in form, sends them forth among mankind, bearing sweet news of kindred joy to those with whom their sisters abide—abide, because there is no portal of expression from the caverns of the spirit which they inhabit into the universe of things. Poetry redeems from decay the visitations of the divinity in man.

Poetry turns all things to loveliness; it exalts the beauty of that which is most beautiful, and it adds beauty to that which is most deformed; it marries exultation and horror, grief and pleasure, eternity and change; it subdues to union, under its light yoke, all irreconcilable things. It transmutes all that it touches, and every form moving within the radiance of its presence is changed by wondrous sympathy to an incarnation of the spirit which it breathes: its secret alchemy turns to potable gold the poisonous waters which flow from death through life; it strips the veil of familiarity from the world, and lays bare the naked and sleeping beauty, which is the spirit of its forms.

FROM THE DECAY OF LYING

OSCAR WILDE

CYRIL: What do you mean by saying that Nature is always behind the age?

VIVIAN: Well, perhaps that is rather cryptic. What I mean is this. If we take Nature to mean natural simple instinct as opposed to self-conscious culture, the work produced under this influence is always old-fashioned, antiquated, and out of date. One touch of Nature may make the whole world kin, but two touches of Nature will destroy any work of Art. If, on the other hand, we regard Nature as the collection of phenomena external to man, people only discover in her what they bring to her. She has no suggestions of her own. Wordsworth went to the lakes, but he was never a lake poet. He found in stones the sermons he had already hidden there. He went moralizing about the district, but his good work was produced when he returned, not to Nature but to poetry. Poetry gave him "Laodamia," and the fine sonnets, and the great Ode, such as it is. Nature gave him "Martha Ray" and "Peter Bell," and the address to Mr. Wilkinson's spade.

CYRIL: I think that view might be questioned. I am rather inclined to believe in the "impulse from a vernal wood," though, of course, the artistic value of such an impulse depends entirely on the kind of temperament that receives it, so that the return to Nature would come to mean simply the advance to a great personality. You would agree with that, I fancy. However, proceed with your article.

VIVIAN: (reading): "Art begins with abstract decoration, with purely imaginative and pleasurable work dealing with what is unreal and nonexistent. This is the first stage. Then Life becomes fascinated with this new wonder, and asks to be admitted into the charmed circle. Art takes life as part of her rough material, recreates it, and refashions it in fresh forms, is absolutely indifferent to fact, invents, imagines, dreams, and keeps between herself and reality the impenetrable barrier of beautiful style, of decorative or ideal treatment. The third stage is when Life gets the upper hand, and drives Art out into the wilderness. This is the true decadence, and it is from this that we are now suffering.

" . . . wherever we have returned to Life and Nature, our work has always become vulgar, common, and uninteresting. Modern tapestry, with its aërial effects, its elaborate perspective, its broad expanses of waste sky, its faithful and laborious realism, has no beauty whatsoever. The pictorial glass of Germany is absolutely detestable. We are beginning to weave possible carpets in England, but only because we have returned to the method and spirit of the East. Our rugs and carpets of twenty years ago, with their solemn depressing truths, their inane worship of Nature, their sordid reproductions of visible objects, have become, even to the Philistine, a source of laughter. A cultured Mahommedan once remarked to us, 'You Christians are so occupied in misinterpreting the fourth commandment that you have never thought of making an artistic application of the second.' He was perfectly right, and the whole truth of the matter is this: The proper school to learn art in is not Life but Art. . . .

"Art finds her own perfection within, and not outside of, herself. She is not to be judged by any external standard of resemblance. She is a veil, rather than a mirror. She has flowers that no forests know of, birds that no woodland possesses. She makes and unmakes many worlds, and can draw the moon from heaven with a scarlet thread. Hers are the 'forms more real than living man,' and hers the great archetypes of which things that have existence are but unfinished copies. Nature has, in her eyes, no laws, no uniformity. She can work miracles at her will, and when she calls monsters from the deep they come. She can bid the almond tree blossom in winter, and send the snow upon the ripe cornfield. At her word the frost lays its silver finger on the burning mouth of June, and the winged lions creep out from the hollows of the Lydian hills. The dryads peer from the thicket as she passes by, and the brown fauns smile strangely at her when she comes near them. She has hawk-faced gods that worship her, and the centaurs gallop at her side. . . ."

Paradox though it may seem—and paradoxes are always dangerous things— it is none the less true that Life imitates art far more than Art imitates life. We have all seen in our own day in England how a certain curious and fascinating type of beauty, invented and emphasized by two imaginative painters, has so influenced Life that whenever one goes to a private view or to an artistic salon one sees, here the mystic eyes of Rossetti's dream, the long ivory throat, the strange square-cut jaw, the loosened shadowy hair that he so ardently loved, there the sweet maidenhood of "The Golden Stair," the blossom-like mouth and weary loveliness of the "Laus Amoris," the passion-pale face of Andromeda, the thin hands and lithe beauty of the Vivien in "Merlin's Dream." And it has always been so. A great artist invents a type, and Life tries to copy it, to reproduce it in a popular form, like an enterprising publisher. Neither Holbein nor Vandyck found in England what they have given us. They brought their types with them, and Life with her keen imitative faculty set herself to supply the master with models. The Greeks, with their quick artistic instinct, understood this, and set in the bride's chamber the statue of Hermes or of Apollo, that she might bear children as lovely as the works of art that she looked at in her rapture or her pain. They knew that Life gains from Art not merely spirituality, depth of thought and feeling, soul-turmoil or soul-peace, but that she can form herself on the very lines and colors of art, and can reproduce the dignity of Phidias as well as the grace of Praxiteles. Hence came their objection to realism. They disliked it on purely social grounds. They felt that it inevitably makes people ugly, and they were perfectly right. We try to improve the conditions of the race by means of good air, free sunlight, wholesome water, and hideous bare buildings for the better housing of the lower orders. But these things merely produce health, they do not produce beauty. For this, Art is required, and the true disciples of the great artist are not his studio-imitators, but those who become like his works of art, be they plastic as in Greek days, or pictorial as in modern times; in a word, Life is Art's best, Art's only pupil. . . .

CYRIL: The theory is certainly a very curious one, but to make it complete you must show that Nature, no less than Life, is an imitation of Art. Are you prepared to prove that?

VIVIAN: My dear fellow, I am prepared to prove anything.

CYRIL: Nature follows the landscape painter then, and takes her effects from him?

VIVIAN: Certainly. Where, if not from the Impressionists, do we get those wonderful brown fogs that come creeping down our streets, blurring the gas-lamps and changing the houses into monstrous shadows? To whom, if not to them and their master, do we owe the lovely silver mists that brood over our river, and turn to faint forms of fading grace, curved bridge and swaying barge? The extraordinary change that has taken place in the climate of London during the last ten years is entirely due to this particular school of Art. You smile. Consider the matter from a scientific or a metaphysical point of view, and you will find that I am right. For what is Nature? Nature is no great mother who has borne us. She is our creation. It is in our brain that she quickens to life. Things are because we see them, and what we see, and how we see it, depends on the Arts that have influenced us. To look at a thing is very different from seeing a thing. One does not see anything until one sees its beauty. Then, and then only, does it come into existence. At present, people see fogs, not because there are fogs, but because poets and painters have taught them the mysterious loveliness of such effects. There may have been fogs for centuries in London. I dare say there were. But no one saw them, and so we do not know anything about them. They did not exist till Art had invented them. Now, it must be admitted, fogs are carried to excess. They have become the mere mannerism of a clique, and the exaggerated realism of their method gives dull people bronchitis. Where the cultured catch an effect, the uncultured catch cold. And so, let us be humane, and invite Art to turn her wonderful eyes elsewhere. She has done so already, indeed. That white quivering sunlight that one sees now in France, with its strange blotches of mauve, and its restless violet shadows, is her latest fancy, and, on the whole, Nature reproduces it quite admirably. Where she used to give us Corots and Daubignys, she gives us now exquisite Monets and entrancing Pissaros. Indeed, there are moments, rare, it is true, but still to be observed from time to time, when Nature becomes absolutely modern. Of course she is not always to be relied upon. The fact is that she is in this unfortunate position: Art creates an incomparable and unique effect, and, having done so, passes on to other things. Nature, upon the other hand, forgetting that imitation can be made the sincerest form of insult, keeps on repeating this effect until we all become absolutely wearied of it. Nobody of any real culture, for instance, ever talks nowadays about the beauty of a sunset. Sunsets are quite old-fashioned. They belong to the time when Turner was the last note in art. To admire them is a distinct sign of provincialism of temperament. Upon the other hand they go on. Yesterday evening Mrs. Arundel insisted on my going to the window, and looking at the glorious sky, as she called it. Of course I had to look at it. She is one of those absurdly pretty Philistines, to whom one can deny nothing. And what was it? It was simply a very second-rate Turner, a Turner of a bad period, with all the painter's worst faults exaggerated and over-emphasized. . . .

The final revelation is that Lying, the telling of beautiful untrue things, is the proper aim of Art. But of this I think I have spoken at sufficient length. And now let us go out on the terrace, where "droops the milk-white peacock like a ghost," while the evening star "washes the dusk with silver." At twilight nature becomes a wonderfully suggestive effect, and is not without loveliness, though perhaps its chief use is to illustrate quotations from the poets. Come! We have talked long enough.

L'ART POUR L'ART

From "Skirmishes in a War with the Age" (§ 24), in
The Twilight of the Idols

FRIEDRICH NIETZSCHE

L'Art pour l'Art.—The struggle against a purpose in art is always a struggle against the moral tendency in art, against its subordination to morality. *L'art pour l'art* means, "let morality go to the devil!"—But even this hostility betrays the preponderating power of the moral prejudice. If art is deprived of the purpose of preaching morality and of improving mankind, it does not by any means follow that art is absolutely pointless, purposeless, senseless, in short *l'art pour l'art*—a snake which bites its own tail. "No purpose at all is better than a moral purpose!"—thus does pure passion speak. A psychologist, on the other hand, puts the question: what does all art do? does it not praise? does it not glorify? does it not select? does it not bring things into prominence? In all this it strengthens or weakens certain valuations. Is this only a secondary matter? an accident? something in which the artist's instinct has no share? Or is it not rather the very prerequisite which enables the artist to accomplish something? . . . Is his most fundamental instinct concerned with art? Is it not rather concerned with the purpose of art, with life? with a certain desirable kind of life? Art is the great stimulus to life: how can it be regarded as purposeless, as pointless, as *l'art pour l'art.*—There still remains one question to be answered: Art also reveals much that is ugly, hard and questionable in life,—does it not thus seem to make life intolerable?—And, as a matter of fact, there have been philosophers who have ascribed this function to art. According to Schopenhauer's doctrine, the general object of art was to "free one from the Will"; and what he honored as the great utility of tragedy, was that it "made people more resigned."—But this, as I have already shown, is a pessimistic standpoint; it is the "evil eye": the artist himself must be appealed to. What is it that the soul of the tragic artist communicates to others? Is it not precisely his fearless attitude towards that which is terrible and questionable? This attitude is in itself a highly desirable one; he who has once experienced it honors it above everything else. He communicates it. He must communicate, provided he is an artist and a genius in the art of communication. A courageous and free spirit, in the presence of a mighty foe, in the presence of a sublime misfortune, and face to face with a problem that inspires horror—this is the triumphant attitude which the tragic artist selects and which he glorifies. The martial elements in our soul celebrate their Saturnalia in tragedy; he who is used to suffering, he who looks out for suffering, the heroic man, extols his existence by means of tragedy,—to him alone does the tragic artist offer this cup of sweetest cruelty.—

(Anthony M. Ludovici, tr.)

FROM BEAUTY

RALPH WALDO EMERSON

The question of Beauty takes us out of surfaces to thinking of the foundations of things. Goethe said, "The beautiful is a manifestation of secret laws of Nature which, but for this appearance, had been forever concealed from us." And the working of this deep instinct makes all the excitement—much of it superficial and absurd enough—about works of art, which leads armies of vain travelers every year to Italy, Greece, and Egypt. Every man values every acquisition he makes in the science of beauty, above his possessions. The most useful man in the most useful world, so long as only commodity was served, would remain unsatisfied. But as fast as he sees beauty, life acquires a very high value.

I am warned by the ill fate of many philosophers not to attempt a definition of Beauty. I will rather enumerate a few of its qualities. We ascribe beauty to that which is simple; which has no superfluous parts; which exactly answers its end; which stands related to all things; which is the mean of many extremes. It is the most enduring quality, and the most ascending quality. We say love is blind, and the figure of Cupid is drawn with a bandage round his eyes. Blind: yes, because he does not see what he does not like; but the sharpest-sighted hunter in the universe is Love, for finding what he seeks, and only that; and the mythologists tell us that Vulcan was painted lame and Cupid blind, to call attention to the fact that one was all limbs, and the other all eyes. In the true mythology Love is an immortal child, and Beauty leads him as a guide: nor can we express a deeper sense than when we say, Beauty is the pilot of the young soul.

Beyond their sensuous delight, the forms and colors of Nature have a new charm for us in our perception that not one ornament was added for ornament, but each is a sign of some better health or more excellent action. Elegance of form in bird or beast, or in the human figure, marks some excellence of structure: or, beauty is only an invitation from what belongs to us. 'T is a law of botany that in plants the same virtues follow the same forms. It is a rule of largest application, true in a plant, true in a loaf of bread, that in the construction of any fabric or organism any real increase of fitness to its end is an increase of beauty.

The lesson taught by the study of Greek and of Gothic art, of antique and of Pre-Raphaelite painting, was worth all the research,—namely, that all beauty must be organic; that outside embellishment is deformity. It is the soundness of the bones that ultimates itself in a peach-bloom complexion; health of constitution that makes the sparkle and the power of the eye. 'T is the adjustment of the size and of the joining of the sockets of the skeleton that gives grace of outline and the finer grace of movement. The cat and the deer cannot move or sit inelegantly. The dancing-master can never teach a badly built man to walk well. The tint of the flower proceeds from its root, and the lusters of the sea-shell begin with its existence. Hence our taste in building rejects paint, and all shifts, and shows the original grain of the wood: refuses pilasters and columns that support nothing, and allows the real supporters of the house honestly to show themselves. Every necessary or organic action pleases the beholder. A man leading a horse to water, a farmer sowing seed, the labors of haymakers in the field, the carpenter building a ship, the smith at his forge, or whatever useful labor, is becoming to the wise eye. But if it is done to be seen, it is mean. How beautiful are ships on the sea! but ships in the theater,—or ships kept for picturesque effect on Virginia Water by George IV and men hired to stand in fitting costumes at a penny an hour! What a difference in effect between a battalion of troops marching to action, and one of our independent companies on a holiday! In the midst of a military show and a festal procession gay with banners, I saw a boy seize an old tin pan that lay rusting under a wall, and poising it on the top of a stick, he set it turning and made it describe the most elegant imaginable curves, and drew away attention from the decorated procession by this startling beauty.

Another text from the mythologists. The Greeks fabled that Venus was born of the foam of the sea. Nothing interests us which is stark or bounded, but only what streams with life, what is in act or endeavor to reach somewhat beyond. The pleasure a palace or a temple gives the eye is, that an order and method has been communicated to stones, so that they speak and geometrize, become tender or sublime with expression. Beauty is the moment of transition, as if the form were just ready to flow into other forms. Any fixedness, heaping, or concentration on one feature,—a long nose, a sharp chin, a hump-back,—is the reverse of the flowing, and therefore deformed. Beautiful as is the symmetry of any form, if the form can move we seek a more excellent symmetry. The interruption of equilibrium stimulates the eye to desire the restoration of symmetry, and to watch the steps through which it is attained. This is the charm of running water, sea-waves, the flight of birds and the locomotion of animals. This is the theory of dancing, to recover continually in changes the lost equilibrium, not by abrupt and angular but by gradual and curving movements. . . .

One more text from the mythologists is to the same purpose,—*Beauty rides on a lion*. Beauty rests on necessities. The line of beauty is the result of perfect economy. The cell of the bee is built at that angle which gives the most strength with the least wax; the bone or the quill of the bird gives the most alar strength with the least weight. "It is the purgation of superfluities," said Michael Angelo. There is not a particle to spare in natural structures. There is a compelling reason in the uses of the plant for every novelty of color or form; and our art saves material by more skilful arrangement, and reaches beauty by taking every superfluous ounce that can be spared from a wall, and keeping all its strength in the poetry of columns. In rhetoric, this art of omission is a chief secret of power, and, in general, it is proof of high culture to say the greatest matters in the simplest way.

Veracity first of all, and forever. *Rien de beau que le vrai*. In all design, art lies in making your object prominent, but there is a prior art in choosing objects that are prominent. The fine arts have nothing casual, but spring from the instincts of the nations that created them.

Beauty is the quality which makes to endure. In a house that I know, I have noticed a block of spermaceti lying about closets and mantel-pieces, for twenty years together, simply because the tallow-man gave it the form of a rabbit; and I suppose it may continue to be lugged about unchanged for a century. Let an artist scrawl a few lines or figures on the back of a letter, and that scrap of paper is rescued from danger, is put in portfolio, is framed and glazed, and, in proportion to the beauty of the lines drawn, will be kept for centuries. Burns writes a copy of verses and sends them to a newspaper, and the human race take charge of them that they shall not perish.

As the flute is heard farther than the cart, see how surely a beautiful form strikes the fancy of men, and is copied and reproduced without end. How many copies are there of the Belvedere Apollo, the Venus, the Psyche, the Warwick Vase, the Parthenon and the Temple of Vesta? These are objects of tenderness to all. In our cities an ugly building is soon removed and is never repeated, but any beautiful building is copied and improved upon, so that all masons and carpenters work to repeat and preserve the agreeable forms, whilst the ugly ones die out. . . .

A beautiful person among the Greeks was thought to betray by this sign some secret favor of the immortal gods; and we can pardon pride, when a woman possesses such a figure that wherever she stands or moves or leaves a shadow on the wall, or sits for a portrait to the artist, she confers a favor on the world. And yet— it is not beauty that inspires the deepest passion. Beauty without grace is the hook without the bait. Beauty, without expression, tires. Abbé Ménage said of the President Le Bailleul that "he was fit for nothing but to sit for his portrait." A Greek epigram intimates that the force of love is not shown by the courting of beauty, but when the like desire is inflamed for one who is ill-favored. And petulant old gentlemen, who have chanced to suffer some intolerable weariness from pretty people, or who have seen cut flowers to some profusion, or who see, after a world of pains have been successfully taken for the costume, how the least mistake in sentiment takes all the beauty out of your clothes,—affirm that the secret of ugliness consists not in irregularity, but in being uninteresting.

We love any forms, however ugly, from which great qualities shine. If command, eloquence, art or invention exist in the most deformed person, all the accidents that usually displease, please, and raise esteem and wonder higher. . . .

All high beauty has a moral element in it, and I find the antique sculpture as ethical as Marcus Antoninus; and the beauty ever in proportion to the depth of thought. Gross and obscure natures, however decorated, seem impure shambles; but character gives splendor to youth and awe to wrinkled skin and gray hairs. An adorer of truth we cannot choose but obey, and the woman who has shared with us the moral sentiment,—her locks must appear to us sublime. Thus there is a climbing scale of culture, from the first agreeable sensation which a sparkling gem or a scarlet stain affords the eye, up through fair outlines and details of the landscape, features of the human face and form, signs and tokens of thought and character in manners, up to the ineffable mysteries of the intellect. Wherever we begin, thither our steps tend: an ascent from the joy of a horse in his trappings, up to the perception of Newton that the globe on which we ride is only a larger apple falling from a larger tree; up to the perception of Plato that globe and universe are rude and early expressions of an all-dissolving Unity,—the first stair on the scale to the temple of the Mind.

from TRAFFIC

JOHN RUSKIN

Taste is not only a part and an index of morality—it is the ONLY morality. The first, and last, and closest trial question to any living creature is, "What do you like?" Tell me what you like, and I'll tell you what you are. Go out into the street, and ask the first man or woman you meet, what their "taste" is, and if they answer candidly, you know them, body and soul. "You, my friend in the rags, with the unsteady gait, what do you like?" "A pipe and a quartern of gin." I know you. "You, good woman, with the quick step and tidy bonnet, what do you like?" "A swept hearth and a clean tea-table, and my husband opposite me, and a baby at my breast." Good, I know you also. "You, little girl with the golden hair and the soft eyes, what do you like?" "My canary, and a run among the wood hyacinths." "You, little boy with the dirty hands and the low forehead, what do you like?" "A shy at the sparrows, and a game at pitch-farthing." Good; we know them all now. What more need we ask?

"Nay," perhaps you answer: "we need rather to ask what these people and children do, than what they like. If they *do* right, it is no matter that they like what is wrong; and if they *do* wrong, it is no matter that they like what is right. Doing is the great thing; and it does not matter that the man likes drinking, so that he does not drink; nor that the little girl likes to be kind to her canary, if she will not learn her lessons; nor that the little boy likes throwing stones at the sparrows, if he goes to the Sunday school." Indeed, for a short time, and in a provisional sense, this is true. For if, resolutely, people do what is right, in time they come to like doing it. But they only are in a right moral state when they *have* come to like doing it; and as long as they don't like it, they are still in a vicious state. The man is not in health of body who is always thirsting for the bottle in the cupboard, though he bravely bears his thirst; but the man who heartily enjoys water in the morning and wine in the evening, each in its proper quantity and time. And the entire object of true education is to make people not merely *do* the right things, but *enjoy* the right things—not merely industrious, but to love industry—not merely learned, but to love knowledge—not merely pure, but to love purity—not merely just, but to hunger and thirst after justice.

But you may answer or think, "Is the liking for outside ornaments,—for pictures, or statues, or furniture, or architecture,—a moral quality?" Yes, most surely, if a rightly set liking. Taste for *any* pictures or statues is not a moral quality, but taste for good ones is. Only here again we have to define the word "good." I don't mean by "good," clever—or learned—or difficult in the doing. Take a picture by Teniers, of sots quarrelling over their dice: it is an entirely clever picture; so clever that nothing in its kind has ever been done equal to it; but it is also an entirely base and evil picture. It is an expression of delight in the prolonged contemplation of a vile thing, and delight in that is an "unmannered," or "immoral" quality. It is "bad taste" in the profoundest sense—it is the taste of the devils. On the other hand, a picture of Titian's, or a Greek statue, or a Greek coin, or a Turner landscape, expresses delight in the perpetual contemplation of a good and perfect thing. That is an entirely moral quality—it is the taste of the angels. And all delight in art, and all love of it, resolve themselves into simple love of that which deserves love. That deserving is the quality which we call "loveliness"—(we ought to have an opposite word, hateliness, to be said of the things which deserve to be hated); and it is not an indifferent nor optional thing whether we love this or that; but it is just the vital function of all our being. What we *like* determines what we *are*, and is the sign of what we are; and to teach taste is inevitably to form character. As I was thinking over this, in walking up Fleet Street the other day, my eye caught the title of a book standing open in a bookseller's window. It was—"On the necessity of the diffusion of taste among all classes." "Ah," I thought to myself, "my classifying friend, when you have diffused your taste, where will your classes be? The man who likes what you like, belongs to the same class with you, I think. Inevitably so. You may put him to other work if you choose; but, by the condition you have brought him into, he will dislike the other work as much as you would yourself. You get hold of a scavenger, or a costermonger, who enjoyed the Newgate Calendar for literature, and 'Pop goes the Weasel' for music. You think you can make him like Dante and Beethoven? I wish you joy of your lessons; but if you do, you have made a gentleman of him:—he won't like to go back to his costermongering."

And so completely and unexceptionally is this so, that, if I had time tonight, I could show you that a nation cannot be affected by any vice, or weakness, without expressing it, legibly, and for ever, either in bad art, or by want of art; and that there is no national virtue, small or great, which is not manifestly expressed in all the art which circumstances enable the people possessing that virtue to produce. Take, for instance, your great English virtue of enduring and patient courage. You have at present in England only one art of any consequence—that is, iron-working. You know thoroughly well how to cast and hammer iron. Now, do you think in those masses of lava which you build volcanic cones to melt, and which you forge at the mouths of the Infernos you have created; do you think, on those iron plates, your courage and endurance are not written for ever—not merely with an iron pen, but on iron parchment? . . .

I hope, now, that there is no risk of your misunderstanding me when I come to the gist of what I want to say tonight—when I repeat, that every great national architecture has been the result and exponent of a great national religion. You can't have bits of it here, bits there—you must have it everywhere, or nowhere. It is not the monopoly of a clerical company—it is not the exponent of a theological dogma—it is not the hieroglyphic writing of an initiated priesthood; it is the manly language of a people inspired by resolute and common purpose, and rendering resolute and common fidelity to the legible laws of an undoubted God.

. . . Your Greek worshiped Wisdom, and built you the Parthenon—the Virgin's temple. The Mediaeval worshiped Consolation, and built you Virgin temples alsc —but to our Lady of Salvation. Then the Revivalist worshiped beauty, of a sort, and built you Versailles, and the Vatican. Now, lastly, will you tell me what *we* worship, and what *we* build?

You know we are speaking always of the real, active, continual, national worship; that by which men act while they live; not that which they talk of when they die. Now, we have, indeed, a nominal religion, to which we pay tithes of property, and sevenths of time; but we have also a practical and earnest religion, to which we devote nine-tenths of our property and six-sevenths of our time. And we dispute a great deal about the nominal religion; but we are all unanimous about this practical one, of which I think you will admit that the ruling goddess may be best generally described as the "Goddess of Getting-on," or "Britannia of the Market." The Athenians had an "Athena Agoraia," or Minerva of the Market; but she was a subordinate type of their goddess, while our Britannia Agoraia is the principal type of ours. And all your great architectural works, are, of course, built to her. It is long since you built a great cathedral; and how you would laugh at me, if I pro-posed building a cathedral on the top of one of these hills of yours, taking it for an Acropolis! But your railroad mounds, prolonged masses of Acropolis; your rail-road stations, vaster than the Parthenon, and innumerable; your chimneys, how much more mighty and costly than cathedral spires! your harbor-piers; your ware-houses; your exchanges!—all these are built to your great Goddess of "Getting-on;" and she has formed, and will continue to form, your architecture, as long as you worship her; and it is quite vain to ask me to tell you how to build to *her;* you know far better than I.

. . . Continue to make that forbidden deity your principal one, and soon no more art, no more science, no more pleasure will be possible. Catastrophe will come; or worse than catastrophe, slow moldering and withering into Hades. But if you can fix some conception of a true human state of life to be striven for—life for all men as for yourselves—if you can determine some honest and simple order of existence; following those trodden ways of wisdom, which are pleasantness, and seeking her quiet and withdrawn paths, which are peace;—then, and so sanctifying wealth into "commonwealth," all your art, your literature, your daily labors, your domestic affection, and citizen's duty, will join and increase into one magnificent harmony. You will know then how to build, well enough; you will build with stone well, but with flesh better; temples not made with hands, but riveted of hearts; and that kind of marble, crimson-veined, is indeed eternal.

FROM OF HUMAN BONDAGE, Chapter 41 *

W. SOMERSET MAUGHAM

There was another American at the table. He was dressed like those fine fellows whom Philip had seen that afternoon in the Luxembourg. He had a handsome face, thin, ascetic, with dark eyes; he wore his fantastic garb with the dashing air of a buccaneer. He had a vast quantity of dark hair which fell constantly over his eyes, and his most frequent gesture was to throw back his head dramatically to get some long wisp out of the way. He began to talk of the *Olympia* by Manet, which then hung in the Luxembourg.

"I stood in front of it for an hour today, and I tell you it's not a good picture."

Lawson put down his knife and fork. His green eyes flashed fire, he gasped with rage; but he could be seen imposing calm upon himself.

"It's very interesting to hear the mind of the untutored savage," he said. "Will you tell us why it isn't a good picture?"

Before the American could answer someone else broke in vehemently.

"D'you mean to say you can look at the painting of that flesh and say it's not good?"

"I don't say that. I think the right breast is very well painted."

"The right breast be damned," shouted Lawson. "The whole thing's a miracle of painting."

He began to describe in detail the beauties of the picture, but at this table at Gravier's they who spoke at length spoke for their own edification. No one listened to him. The American interrupted angrily.

"You don't mean to say you think the head's good?"

Lawson, white with passion now, began to defend the head; but Clutton, who had been sitting in silence with a look on his face of good-humored scorn, broke in.

"Give him the head. We don't want the head. It doesn't affect the picture."

"All right, I'll give you the head," cried Lawson. "Take the head and be damned to you."

"What about the black line?" cried the American, triumphantly pushing back a wisp of hair which nearly fell in his soup. "You don't see a black line round objects in nature."

"Oh, God, send down fire from heaven to consume the blasphemer," said Lawson. "What has nature got to do with it? No one knows what's in nature and what isn't! The world sees nature through the eyes of the artist. Why, for centuries it saw horses jumping a fence with all their legs extended, and by Heaven, sir, they were extended. It saw shadows black until Monet discovered they were colored, and by Heaven, sir, they were black. If we choose to surround objects with a black line, the world will see the black line, and there will be a black line; and if we paint grass red and cows blue, it'll see them red and blue, and, by Heaven, they will be red and blue."

"To hell with art," murmured Flanagan. "I want to get ginny."

Lawson took no notice of the interruption.

* From *Of Human Bondage* by W. Somerset Maugham. Copyright, 1917, by Doubleday & Company, Inc.

"Now look here, when *Olympia* was shown at the Salon, Zola—amid the jeers of the philistines and the hisses of the *pompiers*, the academicians, and the public, Zola said: 'I look forward to the day when Manet's picture will hang in the Louvre opposite the *Odalisque* of Ingres, and it will not be the *Odalisque* which will gain by comparison.' It'll be there. Every day I see the time grow nearer. In ten years the *Olympia* will be in the Louvre."

"Never," shouted the American, using both hands now with a sudden desperate attempt to get his hair once for all out of the way. "In ten years that picture will be dead. It's only a fashion of the moment. No picture can live that hasn't got something which that picture misses by a million miles."

"And what is that?"

"Great art can't exist without a moral element."

"Oh God!" cried Lawson furiously. "I knew it was that. He wants morality." He joined his hands and held them towards heaven in supplication. "Oh, Christopher Columbus, Christopher Columbus, what did you do when you discovered America?"

"Ruskin says . . ."

But before he could add another word, Clutton rapped with the handle of his knife imperiously on the table.

"Gentlemen," he said in a stern voice, and his huge nose positively wrinkled with passion, "a name has been mentioned which I never thought to hear again in decent society. Freedom of speech is all very well, but we must observe the limits of common propriety. You may talk of Bouguereau if you will: there is a cheerful disgustingness in the sound which excites laughter; but let us not sully our chaste lips with the names of J. Ruskin, G. F. Watts, or E. B. Jones."

"Who was Ruskin anyway?" asked Flanagan.

"He was one of the great Victorians. He was a master of English style."

"Ruskin's style—a thing of shreds and purple patches," said Lawson. "Besides, damn the Great Victorians. Whenever I open a paper and see Death of a Great Victorian, I thank Heaven there's one more of them gone. Their only talent was longevity, and no artist should be allowed to live after he's forty; by then a man has done his best work, all he does after that is repetition. Don't you think it was the greatest luck in the world for them that Keats, Shelley, Bonnington, and Byron died early? What a genius we should think Swinburne if he had perished on the day the first series of *Poems and Ballads* was published!"

The suggestion pleased, for no one at the table was more than twenty-four, and they threw themselves upon it with gusto. They were unanimous for once. They elaborated. Someone proposed a vast bonfire made out of the works of the Forty Academicians into which the Great Victorians might be hurled on their fortieth birthday. The idea was received with acclamation. Carlyle and Ruskin, Tennyson, Browning, G. F. Watts, E. B. Jones, Dickens, Thackeray, they were hurried into the flames; Mr. Gladstone, John Bright, and Cobden; there was a moment's discussion about George Meredith, but Matthew Arnold and Emerson were given up cheerfully. At last came Walter Pater.

"Not Walter Pater," murmured Philip.

Lawson stared at him for a moment with his green eyes and then nodded.

"You're quite right, Walter Pater is the only justification for Mona Lisa."

CONTRAST BETWEEN MORAL AND AESTHETIC VALUES *

In *The Sense of Beauty* (§ 3)

GEORGE SANTAYANA

The relation between aesthetic and moral judgments, between the spheres of the beautiful and the good, is close, but the distinction between them is important. One factor of this distinction is that while aesthetic judgments are mainly positive, that is, perceptions of good, moral judgments are mainly and fundamentally negative, or perceptions of evil. Another factor of the distinction is that whereas, in the perception of beauty, our judgment is necessarily intrinsic and based on the character of the immediate experience, and never consciously on the idea of an eventual utility in the object, judgments about moral worth, on the contrary, are always based, when they are positive, upon the consciousness of benefits probably involved. Both these distinctions need some elucidation.

Hedonistic ethics have always had to struggle against the moral sense of mankind. Earnest minds, that feel the weight and dignity of life, rebel against the assertion that the aim of right conduct is enjoyment. Pleasure usually appears to them as a temptation, and they sometimes go so far as to make avoidance of it a virtue. The truth is that morality is not mainly concerned with the attainment of pleasure; it is rather concerned, in all its deeper and more authoritative maxims, with the prevention of suffering. There is something artificial in the deliberate pursuit of pleasure; there is something absurd in the obligation to enjoy oneself. We feel no duty in that direction; we take to enjoyment naturally enough after the work of life is done, and the freedom and spontaneity of our pleasures are what is most essential to them.

The sad business of life is rather to escape certain dreadful evils to which our nature exposes us,—death, hunger, disease, weariness, isolation, and contempt. By the awful authority of these things, which stand like spectres behind every moral injunction, conscience in reality speaks, and a mind which they have duly impressed cannot but feel, by contrast, the hopeless triviality of the search for pleasure. It cannot but feel that a life abandoned to amusement and to changing impulses must run unawares into fatal dangers. The moment, however, that society emerges from the early pressure of the environment and is tolerably secure against primary evils, morality grows lax. The forms that life will further assume are not to be imposed by moral authority, but are determined by the genius of the race, the opportunities of the moment, and the tastes and resources of individual minds. The reign of duty gives place to the reign of freedom, and the law and the covenant to the dispensation of grace.

The appreciation of beauty and its embodiment in the arts are activities which belong to our holiday life, when we are redeemed for the moment from the shadow of evil and the slavery to fear, and are following the bent of our nature where it chooses to lead us. The values, then, with which we here deal are positive; they were negative in the sphere of morality. The ugly is hardly an exception, because it is not the cause of any real pain. In itself it is rather a source of amusement. If its suggestions are vitally repulsive, its presence becomes a real evil towards which we assume a practical and moral attitude. And, correspondingly, the pleasant is never, as we have seen, the object of a truly moral injunction.

FROM OF HUMAN BONDAGE, Chapter 88 *

W. SOMERSET MAUGHAM

"Do you know El Greco?" he asked.

"Oh, I remember one of the men in Paris was awfully impressed by him."

"El Greco was the painter of Toledo. Betty couldn't find the photograph I wanted to show you. It's a picture that El Greco painted of the city he loved, and it's truer than any photograph. Come and sit at the table."

Philip dragged his chair forward, and Athelny set the photograph before him. He looked at it curiously, for a long time, in silence. He stretched out his hand for other photographs, and Athelny passed them to him. He had never before seen the work of that enigmatic master; and at the first glance he was bothered by the arbitrary drawing: the figures were extraordinarily elongated; the heads were very small; the attitudes were extravagant. This was not realism, and yet, and yet even in the photographs you had the impression of a troubling reality. Athelny was describing eagerly, with vivid phrases, but Philip only heard vaguely what he said. He was puzzled. He was curiously moved. These pictures seemed to offer some meaning to him, but he did not know what the meaning was. There were portraits of men with large, melancholy eyes which seemed to say you knew not what; there were long monks in the Franciscan habit or in the Dominican, with distraught faces, making gestures whose sense escaped you; there was an Assumption of the Virgin; there was a Crucifixion in which the painter by some magic of feeling had been able to suggest that the flesh of Christ's dead body was not human flesh only but divine; and there was an Ascension in which the Saviour seemed to surge up towards the empyrean and yet to stand upon the air as steadily as though it were solid ground: the uplifted arms of the Apostles, the sweep of their draperies, their ecstatic gestures, gave an impression of exultation and of holy joy. The background of nearly all was the sky by night, the dark night of the soul, with wild clouds swept by strange winds of hell and lit luridly by an uneasy moon.

"I've seen that sky in Toledo over and over again," said Athelny. "I have an idea that when first El Greco came to the city it was by such a night, and it made so vehement an impression upon him that he could never get away from it."

Philip remembered how Clutton had been affected by this strange master, whose work he now saw for the first time. He thought that Clutton was the most interesting of all the people he had known in Paris. His sardonic manner, his hostile aloofness, had made it difficult to know him; but it seemed to Philip, looking back, that there had been in him a tragic force, which sought vainly to express itself in painting. He was a man of unusual character, mystical after the fashion of a time that had no leaning to mysticism, who was impatient with life because he found himself unable to say the things which the obscure impulses of his heart suggested. His intellect was not fashioned to the uses of the spirit. It was not surprising that he felt a deep sympathy with the Greek who had devised a new technique to express the yearnings of his soul. Philip looked again at the series of portraits of Spanish gentlemen, with ruffles and pointed beards, their faces pale against the sober black of their clothes and the darkness of the background. El Greco was the painter of the soul; and these gentlemen, wan and wasted, not by exhaustion but by restraint, with their tortured minds, seem to walk unaware of the beauty of the world; for their eyes look only in their hearts, and they are dazzled by the glory of the unseen.

No painter has shown more pitilessly that the world is but a place of passage. The souls of the men he painted speak their strange longings through their eyes: their senses are miraculously acute, not for sounds and odors and color, but for the very subtle sensations of the soul. The noble walks with the monkish heart within him, and his eyes see things which saints in their cells see too, and he is unastounded. His lips are not lips that smile.

Philip, silent still, returned to the photograph of Toledo, which seemed to him the most arresting picture of them all. He could not take his eyes off it. He felt strangely that he was on the threshold of some new discovery in life. He was tremulous with a sense of adventure. He thought for an instant of the love that had consumed him: love seemed very trivial beside the excitement which now leaped in his heart. The picture he looked at was a long one, with houses crowded upon a hill; in one corner a boy was holding a large map of the town; in another was a classical figure representing the river Tagus; and in the sky was the Virgin surrounded by angels. It was a landscape alien to all Philip's notions, for he had lived in circles that worshiped exact realism; and yet here again, strangely to himself, he felt a reality greater than any achieved by the masters in whose steps humbly he had sought to walk. He heard Athelny say that the representation was so precise that when the citizens of Toledo came to look at the picture they recognized their houses. The painter had painted exactly what he saw, but he had seen with the eyes of the spirit. There was something unearthly in that city of pale gray. It was a city of the soul seen by a wan light that was neither that of night nor day. It stood on a green hill, but of a green not of this world, and it was surrounded by massive walls and bastions to be stormed by no machines or engines of man's invention, but by prayer and fasting, by contrite sighs and by mortifications of the flesh. It was a stronghold of God. Those gray houses were made of no stone known to masons, there was something terrifying in their aspect, and you did not know what men might live in them. You might walk through the streets and be unamazed to find them all deserted, and yet not empty; for you felt a presence invisible and yet manifest to every inner sense. It was a mystical city in which the imagination faltered like one who steps out of the light into darkness; the soul walked naked to and fro, knowing the unknowable, and conscious strangely of experience, intimate but inexpressible, of the absolute. And without surprise, in that blue sky, real with a reality that not the eye but the soul confesses, with its rack of light clouds driven by strange breezes, like the cries and the sighs of lost souls, you saw the Blessed Virgin with a gown of red and a cloak of blue, surrounded by winged angels. Philip felt that the inhabitants of that city would have seen the apparition without astonishment, reverent and thankful, and have gone their ways.

Athelny spoke of the mystical writers of Spain, of Teresa de Avila, San Juan de la Cruz, Fray Diego de Leon; in all of them was that passion for the unseen which Philip felt in the pictures of El Greco: they seemed to have the power to touch the incorporeal and see the invisible. They were Spaniards of their age, in whom were tremulous all the mighty exploits of a great nation: their fancies were rich with the glories of America and the green islands of the Caribbean Sea; in their veins was the power that had come from age-long battling with the Moor; they were proud, for they were masters of the world; and they felt in themselves the wide distances, the tawny wastes, the snow-capped mountains of Castile, the sunshine and the blue sky, and the flowering plains of Andalusia. Life was passionate and manifold, and because it offered so much they felt a restless yearning for something more; because they were human they were unsatisfied; and they threw this eager vitality of theirs into a vehement striving after the ineffable. Athelny was not displeased to find someone to whom he could read the translations with which for some time he had amused his leisure; and in his fine, vibrating voice he recited the canticle of the Soul and Christ her lover, the lovely poem which begins with the words *en una noche oscura,* and the *noche serena* of Fray Luis de Leon. He had translated them quite simply, not without skill, and he had found words which at all events suggested the rough-hewn grandeur of the original. The pictures of El Greco explained them, and they explained the pictures.

Philip had cultivated a certain disdain for idealism. He had always had a passion for life, and the idealism he had come across seemed to him for the most part a cowardly shrinking from it. The idealist withdrew himself, because he could not suffer the jostling of the human crowd; he had not the strength to fight and so called the battle vulgar; he was vain, and since his fellows would not take him at his own estimate, consoled himself with despising his fellows. For Philip his type was Hayward, fair, languid, too fat now and rather bald, still cherishing the remains of his good looks and still delicately proposing to do exquisite things in the uncertain future; and at the back of this were whiskey and vulgar amours of the street. It was in reaction from what Hayward represented that Philip clamored for life as it stood; sordidness, vice, deformity, did not offend him; he declared that he wanted man in his nakedness; and he rubbed his hands when an instance came before him of meanness, cruelty, selfishness, or lust: that was the real thing. In Paris he had learned that there was neither ugliness nor beauty, but only truth: the search after beauty was sentimental. Had he not painted an advertisement of *chocolat Menier* in a landscape in order to escape from the tyranny of prettiness?

But here he seemed to divine something new. He had been coming to it, all hesitating, for some time, but only now was conscious of the fact; he felt himself on the brink of a discovery. He felt vaguely that here was something better than the realism which he had adored; but certainly it was not the bloodless idealism which stepped aside from life in weakness; it was too strong; it was virile; it accepted life in all its vivacity, ugliness and beauty, squalor and heroism; it was realism still; but it was realism carried to some higher pitch, in which facts were transformed by the more vivid light in which they were seen. He seemed to see things more profoundly through the grave eyes of those dead noblemen of Castile; and the gestures of the saints, which at first had seemed wild and distorted, appeared to have some mysterious significance. But he could not tell what that significance was. It was like a message which it was very important for him to receive, but it was given him in an unknown tongue, and he could not understand. He was always seeking for a meaning in life, and here it seemed to him that a meaning was offered; but it was obscure and vague. He was profoundly troubled. He saw what looked like the truth as by flashes of lightning on a dark, stormy night you might see a mountain range. He seemed to see that a man need not leave his life to chance, but that his will was powerful; he seemed to see that self-control might be as passionate and as active as the surrender to passion; he seemed to see that the inward life might be as manifold, as varied, as rich with experience, as the life of one who conquered realms and explored unknown lands.

CHAPTER 3
OF HUMAN CONDUCT

> Oh, wearisome condition of humanity!
> Born under one law, to another bound;
> Vainly begot and yet forbidden vanity,
> Created sick, commanded to be sound.
> What meaneth Nature by these diverse laws?
> Passion and reason self-division cause.
>
> —Fulke Greville, *Mustapha*.

". . . But pray tell me what is the meaning of life?"

Maugham's question is insistent: what indeed *is* the meaning of life? If it is true, as Bradley says, that "our lives are wasted in the pursuit of the impalpable, the search for the impossible and the unmeaning," the problem of this chapter is perhaps the key one for all philosophy. For it is concerned with the effort of man to define that for which he strives, to discover the goal worthy of his seeking.

The problem receives formulation through posing the antithesis of objectivity and relativity in value theory. Wordsworth, in the "Ode to Duty," expresses the absolutism of that "Stern Daughter of the Voice of God." Victor and his friends, abandoned on a solitary ridge in the Spanish Civil War, demonstrate the power of this absolutistic conviction even in the face of apparently useless self-sacrifice. Relativistic attacks upon this position are introduced by MacLeish's ironic "Lines for an Interment." ("We are all acting again like civilized beings . . . The Facts of Life we have learned are Economic.") Sophocles has Odysseus urge, "Be bold today and honest afterwards. . . . If thou wouldst profit thou must have no qualms." G. L. Dickinson, Dostoevsky, Russell, and others continue the debate.

Indecision and moral skepticisms are often answered by a pleasure ethic; the chapter turns to the "eat, drink, and be merry" philosophy as a reply to the problem of life. Butler asks us as mortals if it is not our business to make the most of the world we have, to seek those means that promote a comfortable long life. He defends the position with eloquence and reason. Less rational, more emotional are the short pieces following that sing the praises of the Aristippian ideal, "Eat thou and drink; tomorrow thou shalt die." Logan Pearsall Smith's bright flippancies and the more sober reflections of Lucretius are followed by the discerning inquiry into the grounds of enjoyment by Dostoevsky.

Is happiness a sufficient basis for right living? Carlyle inveighs against it: not happiness but work is our reason for being. Mill replies with the classic formulation of utilitarianism. Subsequently the reader is introduced to stoicism by Matthew Arnold. The plea is for nothing more nor less than "a chainless soul, with courage to endure." Housman and Unamuno repeat and amplify the austere theme, the coda receiving familiar expression in Henley's "Invictus."

Santayana's profound and quiet protest against his generation, "that talks of freedom and is slave to riches . . . ," prepares the way for the concluding selection from *Marius the Epicurean,* in which Pater quotes the magnificent testament of Marcus Aurelius, "Sayest thou, 'I have not played five acts'? True. But in human life, three acts only make sometimes a whole play. That is the composer's business, not thine. Withdraw thyself with a good will; for that too hath, perchance, a good will which dismisses thee from thy part."

FROM OF HUMAN BONDAGE, Chapter 45 *

W. SOMERSET MAUGHAM

". . . But pray tell me what is the meaning of life?"

"I say, that's rather a difficult question. Won't you give the answer yourself?"

"No, because it's worthless unless you yourself discover it. But what do you suppose you are in the world for?"

Philip had never asked himself, and he thought for a moment before replying.

"Oh, I don't know; I suppose to do one's duty, and make the best possible use of one's faculties, and avoid hurting other people."

"In short, to do unto others as you would they should do unto you?"

"I suppose so."

"Christianity."

"No, it isn't," said Philip indignantly. "It has nothing to do with Christianity. It's just abstract morality."

"But there's no such thing as abstract morality."

"In that case, supposing under the influence of liquor you left your purse behind when you leave here and I picked it up, why do you imagine that I should return it to you? It's not the fear of the police."

"It's the dread of hell if you sin and the hope of Heaven if you are virtuous."

"But I believe in neither."

"That may be. Neither did Kant when he devised the Categorical Imperative. You have thrown aside a creed, but you have preserved the ethic which was based upon it. To all intents you are a Christian still, and if there is a God in Heaven you will undoubtedly receive your reward. The Almighty can hardly be such a fool as the churches make out. If you keep His laws I don't think He can care a packet of pins whether you believe in Him or not."

"But if I left my purse behind you would certainly return it to me," said Philip.

"Not from motives of abstract morality, but only from fear of the police."

"It's a thousand to one that the police would never find out."

"My ancestors have lived in a civilized state so long that the fear of the police has eaten into my bones. The daughter of my *concierge* would not hesitate for a moment. You answer that she belongs to the criminal classes; not at all, she is merely devoid of vulgar prejudice."

"But then that does away with honor and virtue and goodness and decency and everything," said Philip.

"Have you ever committed a sin?"

"I don't know, I suppose so," answered Philip.

"You speak with the lips of a dissenting minister. I have never committed a sin."

Cronshaw in his shabby great-coat, with the collar turned up, and his hat well down on his head, with his red fat face and his little gleaming eyes, looked extraordinarily comic; but Philip was too much in earnest to laugh.

"Have you never done anything you regret?"

"How can I regret when what I did was inevitable?" asked Cronshaw in return.

"But that's fatalism."

"The illusion which man has that his will is free is so deeply rooted that I am ready to accept it. I act as though I were a free agent. But when an action is performed it is clear that all the forces of the universe from all eternity conspired to cause it, and nothing I could do could have prevented it. It was inevitable. If it was good I can claim no merit; if it was bad I accept no censure."

"My brain reels," said Philip.

"Have some whiskey," returned Cronshaw, passing over the bottle. "There's nothing like it for clearing the head. You must expect to be thick-witted if you insist upon drinking beer."

Philip shook his head, and Cronshaw proceeded:

"You're not a bad fellow, but you won't drink. Sobriety disturbs conversation. But when I speak of good and bad . . ." Philip saw he was taking up the thread of his discourse. "I speak conventionally. I attach no meaning to those words. I refuse to make a hierarchy of human actions and ascribe worthiness to some and ill-repute to others. The terms vice and virtue have no signification for me. I do not confer praise or blame: I accept. I am the measure of all things. I am the center of the world."

"But there are one or two other people in the world," objected Philip.

"I speak only for myself. I know them only as they limit my activities. Round each of them too the world turns, and each one for himself is the center of the universe. My right over them extends only as far as my power. What I can do is the only limit of what I may do. Because we are gregarious we live in society, and society holds together by means of force, force of arms (that is the policeman) and force of public opinion (that is Mrs. Grundy). You have society on one hand and the individual on the other: each is an organism striving for self-preservation. It is might against might. I stand alone, bound to accept society and not unwilling, since in return for the taxes I pay it protects me, a weakling, against the tyranny of another stronger than I am; but I submit to its laws because I must; I do not acknowledge their justice: I do not know justice, I only know power. And when I have paid for the policeman who protects me and, if I live in a country where conscription is in force, served in the army which guards my house and land from the invader, I am quits with society: for the rest I counter its might with my wiliness. It makes laws for its self-preservation, and if I break them it imprisons or kills me: it has the might to do so and therefore the right. If I break the laws I will accept the vengeance of the state, but I will not regard it as punishment nor shall I feel myself convicted of wrong-doing. Society tempts me to its service by honors and riches and the good opinion of my fellows; but I am indifferent to their good opinion, I despise honors and I can do very well without riches."

"But if everyone thought like you things would go to pieces at once."

"I have nothing to do with others, I am only concerned with myself. I take advantage of the fact that the majority of mankind are led by certain rewards to do things which directly or indirectly tend to my convenience."

"It seems to me an awfully selfish way of looking at things," said Philip.

"But are you under the impression that men ever do anything except for selfish reasons?"

"Yes."

"It is impossible that they should. You will find as you grow older that the first thing needful to make the world a tolerable place to live in is to recognize the inevitable selfishness of humanity. You demand unselfishness from others, which is a preposterous claim that they should sacrifice their desires to yours. Why should they? When you are reconciled to the fact that each is for himself in the world you will ask less from your fellows. They will not disappoint you, and you will look upon them more charitably. Men seek but one thing in life—their pleasure."

"No, no, no!" cried Philip.

Cronshaw chuckled.

"You rear like a frightened colt, because I use a word to which your Christianity ascribes a deprecatory meaning. You have a hierarchy of values; pleasure is at the bottom of the ladder, and you speak with a little thrill of self-satisfaction, of duty, charity, and truthfulness. You think pleasure is only of the senses; the wretched slaves who manufactured your morality despised a satisfaction which they had small means of enjoying. You would not be so frightened if I had spoken of happiness instead of pleasure: it sounds less shocking, and your mind wanders from the sty of Epicurus to his garden. But I will speak of pleasure, for I see that men aim at that, and I do not know that they aim at happiness. It is pleasure that lurks in the practice of every one of your virtues. Man performs actions because they are good for him, and when they are good for other people as well they are thought virtuous: if he finds pleasure in giving alms he is charitable; if he finds pleasure in helping others he is benevolent; if he finds pleasure in working for society he is public-spirited; but it is for your private pleasure that you give twopence to a beggar as much as it is for my private pleasure that I drink another whiskey and soda. I, less of a humbug than you, neither applaud myself for my pleasure nor demand your admiration."

"But have you never known people do things they didn't want to instead of things they did?"

"No. You put your question foolishly. What you mean is that people accept an immediate pain rather than an immediate pleasure. The objection is as foolish as your manner of putting it. It is clear that men accept an immediate pain rather than an immediate pleasure, but only because they expect a greater pleasure in the future. Often the pleasure is illusory, but their error in calculation is no refutation of the rule. You are puzzled because you cannot get over the idea that pleasures are only of the senses; but, child, a man who dies for his country dies because he likes it as surely as a man eats pickled cabbage because he likes it. It is a law of creation. If it were possible for men to prefer pain to pleasure the human race would have long since become extinct."

"But if all that is true," cried Philip, "what is the use of anything? If you take away duty and goodness and beauty why are we brought into the world?"

.   .   .   .

It looked as though you did not act in a certain way because you thought in a certain way, but rather that you thought in a certain way because you were made in a certain way. Truth had nothing to do with it. There was no such thing as truth. Each man was his own philosopher, and the elaborate systems which the great men of the past had composed were only valid for the writers.

The thing then was to discover what one was and one's system of philosophy would devise itself. It seemed to Philip that there were three things to find out: man's relation to the world he lives in, man's relation with the men among whom he lives, and finally man's relation to himself. He made an elaborate plan of study.

The advantage of living abroad is that, coming in contact with the manners and customs of the people among whom you live, you observe them from the outside and see that they have not the necessity which those who practice them believe. You cannot fail to discover that the beliefs which to you are self-evident to the foreigner are absurd. The year in Germany, the long stay in Paris, had prepared Philip to receive the skeptical teaching which came to him now with such a feeling of relief. He saw that nothing was good and nothing was evil; things were merely adapted to an end. He read *The Origin of Species*. It seemed to offer an explanation of much that troubled him. He was like an explorer now who has reasoned that certain natural features must present themselves, and, beating up a broad river, finds here the tributary that he expected, there the fertile, populated plains, and farther on the mountains. When some great discovery is made the world is surprised afterwards that it was not accepted at once, and even on those who acknowledge its truth the effect is unimportant. The first readers of *The Origin of Species* accepted it with their reason; but their emotions, which are the ground of conduct, were untouched. Philip was born a generation after this great book was published, and much that horrified its contemporaries had passed into the feeling of the time, so that he was able to accept it with a joyful heart. He was intensely moved by the grandeur of the struggle for life, and the ethical rule which it suggested seemed to fit in with his predispositions. He said to himself that might was right. Society stood on one side, an organism with its own laws of growth and self-preservation, while the individual stood on the other. The actions which were to the advantage of society it termed virtuous and those which were not it called vicious. Good and evil meant nothing more than that. Sin was a prejudice from which the free man should rid himself. Society had three arms in its contest with the individual, laws, public opinion, and conscience: the first two could be met by guile, guile is the only weapon of the weak against the strong: common opinion put the matter well when it stated that sin consisted in being found out; but conscience was the traitor within the gates; it fought in each heart the battle of society, and caused the individual to throw himself, a wanton sacrifice, to the prosperity of his enemy. For it was clear that the two were irreconcilable, the state and the individual conscious of himself. *That* uses the individual for its own ends, trampling upon him if he thwarts it, rewarding him with medals, pensions, honors, when he served it faithfully; *this,* strong only in his independence, threads his way through the state, for convenience's sake, paying in money or service for certain benefits, but with no sense of obligation; and, indifferent to the rewards, asks only to be left alone. He is the independent traveler, who uses Cook's tickets because they save trouble, but looks with good-humored contempt on the personally conducted parties. The free man can do no wrong. He does everything he likes —if he can. His power is the only measure of his morality. He recognizes the laws of the state and he can break them without sense of sin, but if he is punished he accepts the punishment without rancour. Society has the power.

But if for the individual there was no right and no wrong, then it seemed to Philip that conscience lost its power. It was with a cry of triumph that he seized the knave and flung him from his breast. But he was no nearer to the meaning of life than he had been before. Why the world was there and what men had come into existence for at all was as inexplicable as ever.

ODE TO DUTY

WILLIAM WORDSWORTH

Stern Daughter of the Voice of God!
O Duty! if that name thou love,
Who art a light to guide, a rod
To check the erring, and reprove;
Thou, who art victory and law
When empty terrors overawe;
From vain temptations dost set free;
And calm'st the weary strife of frail humanity!

There are who ask not if thine eye
Be on them; who, in love and truth,
Where no misgiving is, rely
Upon the genial sense of youth:
Glad Hearts! without reproach or blot;
Who do thy work, and know it not:
O! if through confidence misplaced
They fail, thy saving arms, dread Power, around them cast.

Serene will be our days and bright,
And happy will our nature be,
When love is an unerring light,
And joy its own security.
And they a blissful course may hold
Even now, who, not unwisely bold,
Live in the spirit of this creed;
Yet seek thy firm support, according to their need.

I, loving freedom, and untried;
No sport of every random gust,
Yet being to myself a guide,
Too blindly have reposed my trust:
And oft, when in my heart was heard
Thy timely mandate, I deferred
The task, in smoother walks to stray;
But thee I now would serve more strictly, if I may.

Through no disturbance of my soul,
Or strong compunction in me wrought,
I supplicate for thy control;
But in the quietness of thought:
Me this unchartered freedom tires;
I feel the weight of chance-desires:

My hopes no more must change their name,
I long for a repose that ever is the same.

Stern Lawgiver! yet thou dost wear
The Godhead's most benignant grace;
Nor know we anything so fair
As is the smile upon thy face:
Flowers laugh before thee on their beds
And fragrance in thy footing treads;
Thou dost preserve the stars from wrong;
And the most ancient heavens through Thee, are fresh and strong.

To humbler functions, awful Power!
I call thee: I myself commend
Unto thy guidance from this hour;
Oh, let my weakness have an end!
Give unto me, made lowly wise,
The spirit of self-sacrifice;
The confidence of reason give;
And in the light of truth thy Bondman let me live!

MORALITY

MATTHEW ARNOLD

We cannot kindle when we will
The fire which in the heart resides;
The spirit bloweth and is still,
In mystery our soul abides.
    But tasks in hours of insight will'd
    Can be through hours of gloom fulfill'd.

With aching hands and bleeding feet
We dig and heap, lay stone on stone;
We bear the burden and the heat
Of the long day, and wish 'twere done.
    Not till the hours of light return,
    All we have built do we discern.

Then, when the clouds are off the soul,
When thou dost bask in Nature's eye,
Ask, how *she* view'd thy self-control,
Thy struggling, task'd morality—
    Nature, whose free, light, cheerful air,
    Oft made thee, in thy gloom, despair.

And she, whose censure thou dost dread,
Whose eye thou wast afraid to seek,
See, on her face a glow is spread,
A strong emotion on her cheek!
    "Ah, child!" she cries, "that strife divine,
    Whence was it, for it is not mine?

"There is no effort on *my* brow—
I do not strive, I do not weep;
I rush with the swift spheres and glow
In joy, and when I will, I sleep.
    Yet that severe, that earnest air,
    I saw, I felt it once—but where?

"I knew not yet the gauge of time,
Nor wore the manacles of space;
I felt it in some other clime,
I saw it in some other place.
    'Twas when the heavenly house I trod,
    And lay upon the breast of God."

FROM KEY LARGO: PROLOGUE

MAXWELL ANDERSON

VICTOR: Isn't this a graver matter
    than you pretend, King?
KING: It's running for your life.
    That's grave enough.
VICTOR: If we go it's more than an end
    to our crusade.   It's an end to everything
    we were, everything we talked of in your room
    under the skylight, an end to all the meaning
    you found in the world.   We haven't talked much lately.
    I thought it was only because there wasn't time,
    but maybe you've changed and haven't told us.
KING: I have.
    I was trying to hold on.   When you've believed
    that right wins in the end it's a little hard
    to turn round suddenly on a battle-front
    and say the hell with it.
VICTOR: But you've turned round now,
    and said it?
KING: Yes.
VICTOR: But right does win in the end.
KING: Only if you believe whoever wins
    is right in the end.   Because we're losing here—
    and dying here!
VICTOR: You have been our leader, King.
    Certainly you've been mine.   We haven't been cowards,
    any of us, but we've let you show the way
    most of the time.   Are we suddenly afraid
    to die, when suddenly it's necessary?
    Are you afraid?   If you are then it's come about
    between tonight and this morning.
KING: Nobody's afraid
    to die when he sees good reason for it.   Hell,
    we're not here for fun!   We came believing

there was some use in it!   Maybe some of us think
there still is use.   I've been trying to hold on
this last half-year—I've been trying to believe
the whole world would rise up and step on this evil
that crawls over Spain—and it has risen up,
and stepped on us.   And now I'm beginning to wonder
if a cause is sacred when it's lost.   Did we volunteer
to die in a lost cause?

VICTOR: What's gone?   What's changed
since yesterday?

KING: Our cause is lost, that's all.
Maybe because there isn't any God
and nobody cares who wins.   Anyway if you win
you never get what you fight for, never get
the least approximation of the thing
you were sold on when you enlisted.   No, you find
instead that you were fighting to impose
some monstrous, bloody injustice, some revenge
that would end in another war.

MONTE: Why do you say
our cause is lost, and Franco will win in Spain?
Is there news of Franco?   Is the war lost for us?
We've told ourselves we couldn't lose.

KING: Well, we can.
This was between the lines of what they said—
the officers—the war's at an end in Spain—
this withdrawal, it's part of a larger movement—
falling back on Madrid, getting ready to ask for terms;
I don't know what else—but the end.

MONTE: Then I understand you.

KING: I should think you would.

JERRY: And the war's over.

KING: That I can't swear to.   It was never said,
only by hints, indirectly, but I got it,
enough to convince me.

NIMMO: I never thought of the end.
I never thought of that part.

MONTE: So it's not only
we cover a retreat—but the war's lost
and we die for a lost cause.

KING: So get your duffle,
and we'll move out.   Look, we were children,
suckled in one of these nutmeg Alma Maters,
and Spain was a bugle call.   Up and to Spain
and save the world!   Byron went out to Greece
about a hundred years ago and died
in a swamp of the fever.   Don Quixote
went out against the windmills.   It was a Spaniard
who knew his Spain well enough to write Quixote—
and we should have read it.—I know I'm a turncoat;

it was my romantic notion to save Spain,
and I was eloquent about it. Yes,
maybe I thought I talked like Rupert Brooke—
for all I know maybe I thought I looked
like that poor Galahad of Gallipoli,
saving heaven for the angels.—The best I can do now
is be fairly honest about it, and get you out
and get myself out. They say there's just one test
for whether a man's a fool—it's how long he lives
and how well.

JERRY: There's not much to carry. It won't take long.
Shall we pack up?

NIMMO: I think so.

MONTE: And those three hundred
on the ridge to the south—if we're not here they're caught;
they'll be wide open crossing the valley. Look,
couldn't we get word to them?

NIMMO: Not before morning.

JERRY: Well, let it go.

VICTOR: Is it decided?

NIMMO: Yes. What can we do?

VICTOR: Then I'll play anarchist
tonight. I'll stay here.

MONTE: Alone?

VICTOR: I like company—
but if I'm alone, I'm alone. Don't think I blame you.
You went into it for any number of reasons,
mostly perishable, as King says. You could leave
and go on living, but I couldn't. I'm a Spaniard,
or my father is, and all my blood and belief
are in this fight here. I was brought up to think
of Spain and freedom first in the morning, and first
at night. It took the place of prayers with us;
but that's because my father's a little crazy,
according to the neighbors, and I'm infected—
not that I mind.

KING: Wait a minute, Victor!
You can't stay here alone.

VICTOR: Oh, yes, I can.
That's the anarchist angle of this army—
every man his own captain. I can stay
if I wish, and those who wish to go, can go.
So I'll sit here.

KING: You can't hold them alone, you know.
You'll die for nothing. They'll walk right over you.
Won't even pause.

VICTOR: Well—

KING: Then why do it? Why sit here
and get yourself murdered?

VICTOR: Because there is no God.

KING: What do you mean?

VICTOR: Because the sky's quite empty,
  just as you said.   The scientists have been over it
  with a fine-tooth comb and a telescope, and the verdict
  is, No God, nothing there.   Empty and sterilized,
  like a boiled test-tube.   But if there's no God there
  and nothing inside me I have any respect for
  then I'm done.   Then I don't live, and I couldn't.
  So I stay here to keep whatever it is
  alive that's alive inside me.
KING: It's not only the sky
  that's empty, remember.   They've looked us through pretty
  well,
  and men and horses are pure chemistry
  so far as anybody knows.   The soul—
  or psyche—has the same composition
  as eggs and butter.
VICTOR: It's too late
  to change.   I know what I live by, and I'll die by it.
  It's more important than living.
KING: What you live by?
VICTOR: Yes.
KING: Then what is it?   Tell us.
VICTOR: I'd rather not.
KING: If it's like all the other faiths I've ever known
  it's nothing you can put your finger on,
  or say in words, or put any trust in, and so
  it's nothing.   A pocket of air under the vest.
  That's why it can't be stated.
VICTOR: I have to believe
  there's something in the world that isn't evil—
  I have to believe there's something in the world
  that would rather die than accept injustice—something
  positive for good—that can't be killed —
  or I'll die inside.   And now that the sky's found empty
  a man has to be his own god for himself—
  has to prove to himself that a man can die
  for what he believes—if ever the time comes to him
  when he's asked to choose, and it just so happens
  it's up to me tonight.—And I stay here.
  I don't say it's up to you—I couldn't tell
  about another man—or any of you—
  but I know it's up to me.
KING: Is it up to us still,
  after all the betrayals, after the game's changed
  and we're cheated on both sides?   After the Russian
  secret police taking over our own brigade?   And Munich,
  and Czechoslovakia, and this last betrayal
  of Spain by France and England?   We should know
  by this time—we've looked at Europe long enough
  to know there's nothing to fight for here—that nothing
  you win means freedom or equality
  or justice—that all the formulas are false—

and known to be false—democracy, communism,
socialism, naziism—dead religions
nobody believes in—or if he does believe
he's quietly made use of by the boys
who long ago learned better, and believe
in nothing but themselves. Let it end—let them end it—
these idiot ideologies that snarl
across borders at each other. Stalin walking
his swamps in blood, Hitler's swastikas
in blood above the lintels, the English and French
desperate because everything has failed,
because life itself has failed, and capitalism,
and they may even lose their colonies,
unless God can be revived. And here in Spain,
Franco will win in Spain, they'll see to that—
but if he didn't, Stalin would win in Spain,
and it's one blood-purge or the other, but never justice,
only the rat-men ratting on each other
in a kind of rat despair.—I tell you it was a dream,
all a dream we had, in a dream world,
of brothers who put out a helping hand
to brothers, and might save them.—Long ago
men found out the sky was empty; it follows
that men are a silly accident, meaningless,
here in the empty sky, like a flag on the moon,
as meaningless as an expedition led
to take possession of it—in the name of Marx—
or maybe democracy—or social justice!
Why should we die here for a dead cause, for a symbol,
on these empty ramparts, where there's nothing to win,
even if you could win it?
VICTOR: Yes, but if I die
then I know men will never give in;
then I'll know there's something in the race
of men, because even I had it, that hates injustice
more than it wants to live.—Because even I had it—
and I'm no hero.—And that means the Hitlers
and the Mussolinis always lose in the end—
force loses in the long run, and the spirit wins,
whatever spirit is. Anyway it's the thing
that says it's better to sit here with the moon
and hold them off while I can. If I went with you
I'd never know whether the race was turning
down again, to the dinosaurs—this way
I keep my faith. In myself and what men are.
And in what we may be.
KING: Well—
VICTOR: Oh, I know all this
sounds priggish—it's the manly thing to joke
in extremis—but just for the record let it stand,
and now we'll forget it,

KING: If you won't argue
  there's no arguing. I only wish
  we could all stick together. Are we ready?
JERRY: One minute.
       (NIMMO *and* JERRY *pick up to go.*)
MONTE: I guess I'll stick with Victor.
JERRY:
       (*stopping suddenly*)
  Yes. I'll stay.
  I'll stay, too.
KING: It's Nimmo and me then.
NIMMO: I can't go.
  With the four of us we might hold them. Long enough—
  while the shock troops got away.
JERRY: By God, we might—
  with the four of us.
KING: It seems I was wrong
  and nobody needs advice. I could have saved
  the walk up here and down. Why, you God damn fools,
  what do you care what the Sunday-school teachers say
  if you can live?
JERRY:
       (*tremulously*)
  That's all right.
       (KING *picks up his gun and pack and steps to the embankment by*
        which he entered. As he stands silhouetted he turns to them.)
KING: It's not cowardice, you know.
  It's plain, common, everyday horse-sense;
  it's not me that's crazy.
       (*They are silent, looking up at him.*)
  Don't you see I can't save you,
  but you can save yourselves, and if you don't
  I'll run from you all like a pack of ghosts?
VICTOR: But you shouldn't.
  You shouldn't, King. Why can't you think of us
  as among the fortunate few whose lives have had
  a meaning right up to the end? And not as heroes—
  just ordinary fellows who ate breakfast
  on a certain morning—and then ate lunch and dinner
  and slept exceptionally long that night—
  as why shouldn't they?
KING: Well, anything I can do?
  You were writing a letter.
VICTOR: It isn't finished,
  and it wasn't important. Give me your hand, though.
KING: Good-bye.
VICTOR: You're doing what you believe, and that's all that
  matters.
       (KING *comes down and takes* VICTOR'S *hand, then turns and goes*
        down the hill.)

MONTE: Has it occurred to you—here in the moonlight—
there's a resemblance between these Spanish mountains
and the mountains of the moon?
(*Again the flash, and the detonation.*)

LINES FOR AN INTERMENT

ARCHIBALD MacLEISH

Now it is fifteen years you have lain in the meadow:
The boards at your face have gone through: the earth is
Packed down and the sound of the rain is fainter:
The roots of the first grass are dead:

It's a long time to lie in the earth with your honor:
The world, Soldier, the world has been moving on:

The girls wouldn't look at you twice in the cloth cap:
Six years old they were when it happened:

It bores them even in books: "Soissons besieged!"
As for the gents they have joined the American Legion:

Belts and a brass band and the ladies' auxiliaries:
The Californians march in the OD silk:

We are all acting again like civilized beings:
People mention it at tea . . .

The Facts of Life we have learned are Economic:
You were deceived by the detonations of bombs:

You thought of courage and death when you thought of warfare:
Hadn't they taught you the fine words were unfortunate?

Now that we understand we judge without bias:
We feel of course for those who had to die:

Women have written us novels of great passions
Proving the useless death of the dead was a tragedy:

Nevertheless it is foolish to chew gall:
The foremost writers on both sides have apologized:

The Germans are back in the Midi with cropped hair:
The English are drinking the better beer in Bavaria:

You can rest now in the rain in the Belgian meadow—
Now that it's all explained away and forgotten:
Now that the earth is hard and the wood rots:

Now you are dead . . .

PHILOCTETES, lines 79-122

SOPHOCLES

ODYSSEUS

I know, my son, thy honest nature shrinks
From glozing words and practice of deceit;
But (for 'tis sweet to snatch a victory)
Be bold to-day and honest afterwards.
For one brief hour of lying follow me;
All time to come shall prove thy probity.

NEOPTOLEMUS

Son of Laertes, what upon my ear
Grates in the telling, I should hate to do.
Such is my nature; any taint of guile
I loathe, and such, they tell me, was my sire.
But I am ready, not by fraud, but force,
To bring the man; for, crippled in one foot,
Against our numbers he can prove no match.
Natheless, since I was sent to aid thee, prince,
I fear to seem a laggard; yet prefer
To fail with honor than succeed by fraud.

ODYSSEUS

Son of a gallant sire, I too in youth
Was slow of tongue and forward with my hand;
But I have learnt by trial of mankind
Mightier than deeds of puissance is the tongue.

NEOPTOLEMUS

It comes to this that thou would'st have me lie.

ODYSSEUS

Entangle Philoctetes by deceit.

NEOPTOLEMUS

Why not persuade him rather than deceive?

ODYSSEUS

Persuasion's vain, and force of no avail.

NEOPTOLEMUS

What arms hath he of such miraculous might?

ODYSSEUS

Unerring arrows, tipp'd with instant death.

NEOPTOLEMUS

Might not a bold man come to grips with him?

ODYSSEUS

No, as I told thee, guile alone avails.

NEOPTOLEMUS

Thou deem'st it, then, no shame to tell a lie?

ODYSSEUS

Not if success depends upon a lie.

NEOPTOLEMUS

With what face shall one dare to speak such words?

ODYSSEUS

If thou would'st profit thou must have no qualms.

NEOPTOLEMUS

What gain to *me,* should he be brought to Troy?

ODYSSEUS

Without these arms Troy-town cannot be sacked.

NEOPTOLEMUS

Ye told me *I* should take it.   Was that false?

ODYSSEUS

Not thou apart from these nor these from thee.

NEOPTOLEMUS

The quarry's worth the chase, if this be so.

ODYSSEUS

Know that success a double meed shall win.

NEOPTOLEMUS

Make plain this twofold prize and I'll essay.

ODYSSEUS

Thou wilt be hailed as wise no less than brave.

NEOPTOLEMUS

I'll do it—here's my hand—and risk the shame.

ODYSSEUS

Good.   My instructions—thou rememberest them?

NEOPTOLEMUS

I have consented; trust me for the rest.

(F. Storr, tr.)

THE LATEST DECALOGUE

ARTHUR HUGH CLOUGH

Thou shalt have one God only; who
Would be at the expense of two?
No graven images may be
Worshiped, except the currency:
Swear not at all; for, for thy curse
Thine enemy is none the worse:
At church on Sunday to attend
Will serve to keep the world thy friend:
Honor thy parents; that is, all
From whom advancement may befall;
Thou shalt not kill; but need'st not strive
Officiously to keep alive:
Do not adultery commit;
Advantage rarely comes of it:
Thou shalt not steal; an empty feat,
When it's so lucrative to cheat:
Bear not false witness; let the lie
Have time on its own wings to fly:
Thou shalt not covet, but tradition
Approves all forms of competition.

FROM THE MEANING OF GOOD, I

G. LOWES DICKINSON

"What do you do, then, if you do not read books?"

"I talk to as many people as I can, and especially to those who have had no special education in philosophy; and try to find out to what conclusions they have been led by their own direct experience."

"Conclusions about what?"

"About many things. But in particular about the point we used to be fondest of discussing in the days before you had, as you say, given up the subject—I mean the whole question of the values we attach, or ought to attach, to things."

"Oh!" he said, "well, as to all that, my opinion is the same as of old. 'There's nothing good or bad but thinking makes it so.' So I used to say at college and so I say now."

"I remember," I replied, "that that is what you always used to say; but I thought I had refuted you over and over again."

"So you may have done, as far as logic can refute; but every bit of experience which I have had since last we met has confirmed me in my original view."

"That," I said, "is very interesting, and is just what I want to hear about. What is it that experience has done for you? For, as you know, I have so little of my own, I try to get all I can get out of other people's."

"Well," he said, "the effect of mine has been to bring home to me, in a way I could never realize before, the extraordinary diversity of men's ideals."

"That, you find, is the effect of travel?"

"I think so. Traveling really does open the eyes. For instance, until I went to the East I never really felt the antagonism between the Oriental view of life and our own. Now, it seems to me clear that either they are mad or we are; and upon my word, I don't know which. Of course, when one is here, one supposes it is they. But when one gets among them and really talks to them, when one realizes how profound and intelligent is their contempt for our civilization, how worthless they hold our aims and activities, how illusory our progress, how futile our intelligence, one begins to wonder whether, after all, it is not merely by an effect of habit that one judges them to be wrong and ourselves right, and whether there is anything at all except blind prejudice in any opinions and ideas about Right and Wrong."

"In fact," interposed Audubon, "you agree, like me, with Sir Richard Burton:

'There is no good, there is no bad, these be the whims of mortal will;
What works me weal that call I good, what harms and hurts I hold as ill.
They change with space, they shift with race, and in the veriest span
    of time,
Each vice has worn a virtue's crown, all good been banned as sin or
    crime.' "

"Yes," he assented, "and that is what is brought home to one by travel. Though really, if one had penetration enough, it would not be necessary to travel to make the discovery. A single country, a single city, almost a single village, would illustrate, to one who can look below the surface, the same truth. Under the professed uniformity of beliefs, even here in England, what discrepancies and incongruities are concealed! Every type, every individual almost, is distinguished from every other in precisely this point of the judgments he makes about Good. What does the soldier and adventurer think of the life of a studious recluse? or the city man of that of the artist? and vice versa? Behind the mask of good manners we all of us go about judging and condemning one another root and branch. We are in no real agreement as to the worth either of men or things. It is an illusion of the 'canting moralist' (to use Stevenson's phrase) that there is any fixed and final standard of Good. Good is just what any one thinks it to be; and one man has as much right to his opinion as another."

"But," I objected, "it surely does not follow that because there are different opinions about Good, they are all equally valuable."

"No. I should infer rather that they are all equally worthless."

"That does not seem to me legitimate either; and I venture to doubt whether you really believe it yourself."

"Well, at any rate I am inclined to think I do."

"In a sense perhaps you do; but not in the sense which seems to me most important. I mean that when it comes to the point, you act, and are practically bound to act, upon your opinion about what is good, as though you did believe it to be true."

"How do you mean 'practically bound'?"

"I mean that it is only by so acting that you are able to introduce any order or system into your life, or in fact to give it to yourself any meaning at all. Without the belief that what you hold to be good really somehow is so, your life, I think, would resolve itself into mere chaos."

"I don't see that."

"Well, I may be wrong, but my notion is that what systematizes a life is choice; and choice, I believe. means choice of what we hold to be good."

"Surely not!　Surely we may choose what we hold to be bad."

"I doubt it."

"But how then do you account for what you call bad men?"

"I should say they are men who choose what I think bad but they think good."

"But are there not men who deliberately choose what they think bad, like Milton's Satan—'Evil be thou my Good'?"

"Yes, but by the very terms of the expression he was choosing what he thought good; only he thought that evil was good."

"But that is a contradiction."

"Yes, it is the contradiction in which he was involved, and in which I believe everyone is involved who chooses, as you say, the Bad.　To them it is not only bad, it is somehow also good."

"Does that apply to Nero, for example?"

"Yes, I think it very well might; the things which he chose, power and wealth and the pleasures of the senses, he chose because he thought them good; if his choice also involved what he thought bad, such as murder and rapine and the like (if he did think these bad, which I doubt), then there was a contradiction not so much in his choice as in its consequences.　But even if I were to admit that he and others have chosen and do choose what they believe to be bad, it would not affect the point I want to make.　For to choose Bad must be, in your view, as absurd as to choose Good; since, I suppose, you do not believe, that our opinions about the one have any more validity than our opinions about the other.　So that if we are to abandon Good as a principle of choice, it is idle to say we may fall back upon Bad."

"No, I don't say that we may; nor do I see that we must.　We do not need either the one or the other.　You must have noticed—I am sure I have—that men do not in practice choose with any direct reference to Good or Bad; they choose what they think will bring them pleasure, or fame, or power, or, it may be, barely a livelihood."

"But believing, surely, that these things are good?"

"Not necessarily; not thinking at all about it, perhaps."

"Perhaps not thinking about it as we are now; but still, so far believing that what they have chosen is good, that if you were to go to them and suggest that, after all, it is bad they would be seriously angry and distressed."

"But, probably," interposed Audubon, "like me, they could not help themselves. We are none of us free, in the way you seem to imagine.　We have to choose the best we can, and often it is bad enough."

"No doubt," I replied, "but still, as you say yourself, what we choose is the best we can, that is, the most good we can.　The criterion is Good, only it is very little of it that we are able to realize."

"No," objected Ellis, "I am not prepared to admit that the criterion is Good. You will find that men will frankly confess that other pursuits or occupations are, in their opinion, better than those they have chosen, and that these better things were and are open to themselves, and yet they continue to devote themselves to the worse, knowing it all the time to be the worse."

"But in most cases," I replied, "these better things, surely, are not really 'open' to them, except so far as external circumstances are concerned.　They are hampered in their choice by passions and desires, by that part of them which does not choose, but is passively carried away by alien attractions; and the course they actually adopt is the best they can choose, though they see a better which they would choose if they could.　The choice is always of Good, but it may be diverted by passion to less Good."

"I don't know," he said, "that that is a fair account of the matter."

"Nor do I. It is so hard to analyze what goes on in one's own consciousness, much more what goes on in other people's. Still, that is the kind of way I should describe my own experience, and I should expect that most people who reflect would agree with me. They would say, I think, that they always choose the best they can, though regretting that they cannot choose better than they do; and it would seem to them, I think, absurd to suggest that they choose Bad, or choose without any reference either to Good or Bad."

"Well," he said, "granting, for the moment, that you are right—what follows?"

"Why, then," I said, "it follows that we are, as I said, 'practically bound' to accept as valid, for the moment at least, our opinions about what is good; for otherwise we should have no principle to choose by, if it be true that the principle of choice is Good."

"Very well," he said, "then we should have to do without choosing!"

"But could we?"

"I don't see why not; many people do."

"But what sort of people? I mean what sort of life would it be?" . . .

"Why, . . . without choice one would be a mere slave of passion, a creature of every random mood and impulse, a beast, a thing, not a man at all!"

Ellis looked round rather amused.

"Well," he said, "you fire-eater, and why not? I don't know that impulse is such a bad thing. A good impulse is better than a bad calculation any day!"

"Yes, but you deny the validity of the distinction between Good and Bad, so it's absurd for you to talk about a good impulse." . . .

"Considering, as I was saying, that there are so many different opinions about what things are good, and that no criterion has been discovered for testing them, I hold that we have no reason to attach any validity to these opinions, or to suppose that it is possible to have any true opinions on the subject at all."

"And what do you say to that?" asked Parry, turning to me.

"I said, or rather I suggested, for the whole matter is very difficult to me, that in spite of the divergency of opinions on the point, and the difficulty of bringing them into harmony, we are nevertheless practically bound, whether we can justify it to our reason or not, to believe that our own opinions about what is good have somehow some validity."

"But how 'practically bound'?" asked Leslie.

"Why, as I was trying to get Ellis to admit when you interrupted—and your interruption really completed my argument—I imagine it to be impossible for us not to make choices; and in making choices, as I think, we use our ideas about Good as a principle of choice."

"But you must remember," said Ellis, "that I have never admitted the truth of that last statement."

"But," I said, "if you do not admit it generally—and generally, I confess, I do not see how it could be proved or disproved, except by an appeal to every individual's experience—do you not admit it in your own case? Do you not find that, in choosing, you follow your idea of what is good, so far as you can under the limitations of your own passions and of external circumstances?"

"Well," he replied, "I wish to be candid, and I am ready to admit that I do."

"And that you cannot conceive yourself as choosing otherwise? I mean that if you had to abandon as a principle of choice your opinion about Good, you would have nothing else to fall back upon?"

"No; I think in that case I should simply cease to choose."

"And can you conceive yourself doing that? Can you conceive yourself living, as perhaps many men do, at random and haphazard, from moment to moment, following blindly any impulse that may happen to turn up, without any principle by which you might subordinate one to the other?"

"No," he said, "I don't think I can."

"That, then," I said, "is what I meant, when I suggested that you, at any rate, and I, and other people like us, are practically bound to believe that our opinions about what is good have some validity, even though we cannot say what or how much."

"You say, then, that we have to accept in practice what we deny in theory?"

"Yes, if you like. I say, at least, that the consequence of the attempt to bring our theoretical denial to bear upon our practice would be to reduce our life to a moral chaos, by denying the only principle of choice which we find ourselves actually able to accept. In your case and mine, as it seems, it is our opinion about Good that engenders order among our passions and desires; and without it we should sink back to be mere creatures of blind impulse, such as perhaps in fact, many men really are."

"What!" cried Audubon, interrupting in a tone of half indignant protest, "do you mean to say that it is some idea about Good that brings order into a man's life? All I can say is that, for my part, I never once think, from one year's end to another, of anything so abstract and remote. I simply go on, day after day, plodding the appointed round, without reflection, without reason, simply because I have to. There's order in my life, heaven knows! but it has nothing to do with ideas about Good. And altogether," he ejaculated, in a kind of passion, "it's a preposterous thing to tell me that I believe in Good, merely because I lead a life like a mill-horse! That would be an admirable reason for believing in Bad—but Good!"

He lapsed again into silence; and I was half unwilling to press him further, knowing that he felt our dialectics to be a kind of insult to his concrete woes. However, it seemed to be necessary for the sake of the argument to give some answer, so I began:—

"But if you don't like the life of a mill-horse, why do you lead it?"

"Why? because I have to!" he replied; "you don't suppose I would do it if I could help it?"

"No," I said, "but why can't you help it?"

"Because," he said, "I have to earn my living."

"Then is it a good thing to earn your living?"

"No, but it's a necessary thing."

"Necessary, why?"

"Because one must live."

"Then it is a good thing to live?"

"No, it's a very bad one."

"Why do you live, then?"

"Because I can't help it."

"But it is always possible to stop living."

"No, it isn't."

"But why not?"

"Because there are other people dependent on me, and I don't choose to be such a mean skunk as to run away myself and leave other people here to suffer. Besides, it's a sort of point of honor. As I'm here, I'm going to play the game. All I say is that the game is not worth the playing; and you will never persuade me into the belief that it is."

"But, my dear Philip," I said, "there is no need for me to persuade you, for it is clear that you are persuaded already. You believe, as you have really admitted in principle, that it is good to live rather than to die; and to live, moreover, a monotonous, laborious life, which you say you detest. Take away that belief, and your whole being is transformed. Either you change your manner of life, abandon the routine which you hate, break up the order imposed (as I said at first) by your idea about Good, and give yourself up to the chaos of chance desires; or you depart from life altogether, on the hypothesis that that is the good thing to do. But in any case the truth appears to remain that somehow or other you do believe in Good; and that it is this belief which determines the whole course of your life."

"Well," he said, "it's no use arguing the point, but I am unconvinced." And he sank back to his customary silence.

from NOTES FROM UNDERGROUND, I, ix, x

FYODOR DOSTOEVSKY

With the ant-heap the respectable race of ants began and with the ant-heap they will probably end, which does the greatest credit to their perseverance and good sense. But man is a frivolous and incongruous creature, and perhaps, like a chess player, loves the process of the game, not the end of it. And who knows (there is no saying with certainty), perhaps the only goal on earth to which mankind is striving lies in this incessant process of attaining, in other words, in life itself, and not in the thing to be attained, which must always be expressed as a formula, as positive as twice two makes four, and such positiveness is not life, gentlemen, but is the beginning of death. Anyway, man has always been afraid of this mathematical certainty, and I am afraid of it now. Granted that man does nothing but seek that mathematical certainty, he traverses oceans, sacrifices his life in the quest, but to succeed, really to find it, he dreads, I assure you. He feels that when he has found it there will be nothing for him to look for. When workmen have finished their work they do at least receive their pay, they go to the tavern, then they are taken to the police-station—and there is occupation for a week. But where can man go? Anyway, one can observe a certain awkwardness about him when he has attained such objects. He loves the process of attaining, but does not quite like to have attained, and that, of course, is very absurd. In fact, man is a comical creature; there seems to be a kind of jest in it all. But yet mathematical certainty is, after all, something insufferable. Twice two makes four seems to me simply a piece of insolence. Twice two makes four is a pert coxcomb who stands with arms akimbo barring your path and spitting. I admit that twice two makes four is an excellent thing, but if we are to give everything its due, twice two makes five is sometimes a very charming thing too.

And why are you so firmly, so triumphantly, convinced that only the normal and the positive—in other words, only what is conducive to welfare—is for the advantage of man? Is not reason in error as regards advantage? Does not man, perhaps, love something besides well-being? Perhaps he is just as fond of suffering? Perhaps suffering is just as great a benefit to him as well-being? Man is sometimes extraordinarily, passionately, in love with suffering, and that is a fact. There is no need to appeal to universal history to prove that; only ask yourself, if you are a man and have lived at all. As far as my personal opinion is concerned, to care only for well-being seems to me positively ill-bred. Whether it's good or bad, it is sometimes very pleasant, too, to smash things. I hold no brief for suffering nor for well-being either. I am standing for . . . my caprice, and for its being guaranteed to me when necessary. Suffering would be out of place in vaudevilles, for instance; I know that. In the "Palace of Crystal" it is unthinkable; suffering means doubt, negation, and what would be the good of a "palace of crystal" if there could be any doubt about it? And yet I think man will never renounce real suffering, that is, destruction and chaos. Why, suffering is the sole origin of consciousness. Though I did lay it down at the beginning that consciousness is the greatest misfortune for man, yet I know man prizes it and would not give it up for any satisfaction. Consciousness, for instance, is infinitely superior to twice two makes four. Once you have mathematical certainty there is nothing left to do or to understand. There will be nothing left but to bottle up your five senses and plunge into contemplation. While if you stick to consciousness, even though the same result is attained, you can at least flog yourself at times, and that will, at any rate, liven you up. Reactionary as it is, corporal punishment is better than nothing.

X

You believe in a palace of crystal that can never be destroyed—a palace at which one will not be able to put out one's tongue or make a long nose on the sly. And perhaps that is just why I am afraid of this edifice, that it is of crystal and can never be destroyed and that one cannot put one's tongue out at it even on the sly.

You see, if it were not a palace, but a henhouse, I might creep into it to avoid getting wet, and yet I would not call the henhouse a palace out of gratitude to it for keeping me dry. You laugh and say that in such circumstances a henhouse is as good as a mansion. Yes, I answer, if one had to live simply to keep out of the rain.

But what is to be done if I have taken it into my head that that is not the only object in life, and that if one must live one had better live in a mansion. That is my choice, my desire. You will only eradicate it when you have changed my preference. Well, do change it, allure me with something else, give me another ideal. But meanwhile I will not take a henhouse for a mansion. The palace of crystal may be an idle dream, it may be that it is inconsistent with the laws of nature and that I have invented it only through my own stupidity, through the old-fashioned irrational habits of my generation. But what does it matter to me that it is inconsistent? That makes no difference since it exists in my desires, or rather exists as long as my desires exist. Perhaps you are laughing again? Laugh away; I will put up with any mockery rather than pretend that I am satisfied when I am hungry. I know, anyway, that I will not be put off with a compromise, with a recurring zero, simply because it is consistent with the laws of nature and actually exists. I will not accept as the crown of my desires a block of buildings with tenements for the poor on a lease of a thousand years, and perhaps with a sign-board of a dentist hanging out. Destroy my desires, eradicate my ideals, show me something better, and I will follow you. You will say, perhaps, that it is not worth your trouble; but in that case I can give you the same answer. We are discussing things seriously; but if you won't deign to give me your attention, I will drop your acquaintance. I can retreat into my underground hole.

But while I am alive and have desires I would rather my hand were withered off than bring one brick to such a building! Don't remind me that I have just rejected the palace of crystal for the sole reason that one cannot put out one's tongue at it. I did not say because I am so fond of putting my tongue out. Perhaps the thing I resented was, that of all your edifices there has not been one at which one could not put out one's tongue. On the contrary, I would let my tongue be cut off out of gratitude if things could be so arranged that I should lose all desire to put it out. It is not my fault that things cannot be so arranged, and that one must be satisfied with model flats. Then why am I made with such desires? Can I have been constructed simply in order to come to the conclusion that all my construction is a cheat? Can this be my whole purpose? I do not believe it.

(Constance Garnett, tr.)

FROM THE HARM THAT GOOD MEN DO *

BERTRAND RUSSELL

I

A hundred years ago there lived a philosopher named Jeremy Bentham, who was universally recognized to be a very wicked man. I remember to this day the first time that I came across his name when I was a boy. It was in a statement by the Rev. Sydney Smith to the effect that Bentham thought people ought to make soup of their dead grandmothers. This practice appeared to me as undesirable from a culinary as from a moral point of view, and I therefore conceived a bad opinion of Bentham. Long afterwards, I discovered that the statement was one of those reckless lies in which respectable people are wont to indulge in the interests of virtue. I also discovered what was the really serious charge against him. It was no less than this: that he defined a "good" man as a man who does good. This definition, as the reader will perceive at once if he is right-minded, is subversive of all true morality. How much more exalted is the attitude of Kant, who lays it down that a kind action is not virtuous if it springs from affection for the beneficiary, but only if it is inspired by the moral law, which is, of course, just as likely to inspire unkind actions. We know that the exercise of virtue should be its own reward, and it seems to follow that the enduring of it on the part of the patient should be its own punishment. Kant, therefore, is a more sublime moralist than Bentham, and has the suffrages of all those who tell us that they love virtue for its own sake.

It is true that Bentham fulfilled his own definition of a good man: he did much good. The forty middle years of the nineteenth century in England were years of incredibly rapid progress, materially, intellectually, and morally. At the beginning of the period comes the Reform Act, which made Parliament representative of the middle class, not, as before, of the aristocracy. This Act was the most difficult of the steps towards democracy in England, and was quickly followed by other important reforms, such as the abolition of slavery in Jamaica. At the beginning of the period the penalty for petty theft was death by hanging; very soon the death penalty was confined to those who were guilty of murder or high treason. The Corn Laws, which made food so dear as to cause atrocious poverty, were abolished in 1846. Compulsory education was introduced in 1870. It is the fashion to decry the Victorians, but I wish our age had half as good a record as theirs. This, however, is beside the point. My point is that a very large proportion of the progress during those years must be attributed to the influence of Bentham. There can be no doubt that nine-tenths of the people living in England in the latter part of last century were happier than they would have been if he had never lived. So shallow was his philosophy that he would have regarded this as a vindication of his activities. We, in our more enlightened age, can see that such a view is preposterous; but it may fortify us to review the grounds for rejecting a groveling utilitarianism such as that of Bentham.

* Reprinted from *Sceptical Essays* by Bertrand Russell by permission of W. W. Norton & Company, Inc. Copyright, 1928, by Bertrand Russell.

II

We all know what we mean by a "good" man. The ideally good man does not drink or smoke, avoids bad language, converses in the presence of men only exactly as he would if there were ladies present, attends church regularly, and holds the correct opinions on all subjects. He has a wholesome horror of wrongdoing, and realizes that it is our painful duty to castigate Sin. He has a still greater horror of wrong thinking, and considers it the business of the authorities to safeguard the young against those who question the wisdom of the views generally accepted by middle-aged successful citizens. Apart from his professional duties, at which he is assiduous, he spends much time in good works: he may encourage patriotism and military training; he may promote industry, sobriety, and virtue among wage-earners and their children by seeing to it that failures in these respects receive due punishment; he may be a trustee of a university and prevent an ill-judged respect for learning from allowing the employment of professors with subversive ideas. Above all, of course, his "morals," in the narrow sense, must be irreproachable.

It may be doubted whether a "good" man, in the above sense, does, on the average, any more good than a "bad" man. I mean by a "bad" man the contrary of what we have been describing. A "bad" man is one who is known to smoke and to drink occasionally, and even to say a bad word when some one treads on his toe. His conversation is not always such as could be printed, and he sometimes spends fine Sundays out-of-doors instead of at church. Some of his opinions are subversive; for instance, he may think that if you desire peace you should prepare for peace, not for war. Towards wrongdoing he takes a scientific attitude, such as he would take towards his motor-car if it misbehaved; he argues that sermons and prison will no more cure vice than mend a broken tire. In the matter of wrong thinking he is even more perverse. He maintains that what is called "wrong thinking" is simply thinking, and what is called "right thinking" is repeating words like a parrot; this gives him a sympathy with all sorts of undesirable cranks. His activities outside his working hours may consist merely in enjoyment, or, worse still, in stirring up discontent with preventable evils which do not interfere with the comfort of the men in power. And it is even possible that in the matter of "morals" he may not conceal his lapses as carefully as a truly virtuous man would do, defending himself by the perverse contention that it is better to be honest than to pretend to set a good example. A man who fails in any or several of these respects will be thought ill of by the average respectable citizen, and will not be allowed to hold any position conferring authority, such as that of a judge, a magistrate, or a schoolmaster. Such positions are open only to "good" men. . . .

To speak seriously: the standards of "goodness" which are generally recognized by public opinion are not those which are calculated to make the world a happier place. This is due to a variety of causes, of which the chief is tradition, and the next most powerful is the unjust power of dominant classes. Primitive morality seems to have developed out of the notion of taboo; that is to say, it was originally purely superstitious, and forbade certain perfectly harmless acts (such as eating out of the chief's dish) on the supposed ground that they produced disaster by magical means. In this way there came to be prohibitions, which continued to have authority over people's feelings when the supposed reasons for them were forgotten. A considerable part of current morals is still of this sort: certain kinds of conduct produce emotions of horror, quite regardless of the question whether they have bad effects or not. In many cases the conduct which inspires horror is in fact harmful; if this were not the case, the need for a revision of our moral standards would be more generally recognized. Murder, for example, can obviously not be tolerated in a civilized society; yet the origin of the prohibition of murder is purely superstitious. It was thought that the murdered man's blood (or, later, his ghost) demanded vengeance, and might punish not only the guilty man, but any one who showed him kindness. The superstitious character of the prohibition of murder is shown by the fact that it was possible to be purified from blood-guiltiness by certain ritual ceremonies, which were apparently designed, originally, to disguise the murderer so that the ghost would not recognize him. This, at least, is the theory of Sir J. G. Frazer. When we speak of repentance as "washing out" guilt we are using a metaphor derived from the fact that long ago actual washing was used to remove blood-stains. Such notions as "guilt" and "sin" have an emotional background connected with this source in remote antiquity. Even in the case of murder a rational ethic will view the matter differently: it will be concerned with prevention and cure, as in the case of illness, rather than with guilt, punishment, and expiation.

Our current ethic is a curious mixture of superstition and rationalism. Murder is an ancient crime, and we view it through a mist of age-long horror. Forgery is a modern crime, and we view it rationally. We punish forgers, but we do not feel them strange beings set apart, as we do murderers. And we still think in social practice, whatever we may hold in theory, that virtue consists in not doing rather than in doing. The man who abstains from certain acts labeled "sin" is a good man, even though he never does anything to further the welfare of others. This, of course, is not the attitude inculcated in the Gospels: "Love thy neighbor as thyself" is a positive precept. But in all Christian communities the man who obeys this precept is persecuted, suffering at least poverty, usually imprisonment, and sometimes death. The world is full of injustice, and those who profit by injustice are in a position to administer rewards and punishments. The rewards go to those who invent ingenious justifications for inequality, the punishments to those who try to remedy it. I do not know of any country where a man who has a genuine love for his neighbor can long avoid obloquy. In Paris, just before the outbreak of the war, Jean Jaurès, the best citizen of France, was murdered; the murderer was acquitted, on the ground that he had performed a public service. This case was peculiarly dramatic, but the same sort of thing happens everywhere.

Those who defend traditional morality will sometimes admit that it is not perfect, but contend that any criticism will make all morality crumble. This will not be the case if the criticism is based upon something positive and constructive, but only if it is conducted with a view to nothing more than momentary pleasure. To return to Bentham: he advocated, as the basis of morals, "the greatest happiness of the greatest number." A man who acts upon this principle will have a much more arduous life than a man who merely obeys conventional precepts. He will necessarily make himself the champion of the oppressed, and so incur the enmity of the great. He will proclaim facts which the powers that be wish to conceal; he will deny falsehoods designed to alienate sympathy from those who need it. Such a mode of life does not lead to a collapse of genuine morality. Official morality has always been oppressive and negative: it has said "thou shalt not," and has not troubled to investigate the effect of activities not forbidden by the code. Against this kind of morality all the great mystics and religious teachers have protested in vain: their followers ignored their most explicit pronouncements. It seems unlikely, therefore, that any large-scale improvements will come through their methods.

More is to be hoped, I think, from the progress of reason and science. Gradually men will come to realize that a world whose institutions are based upon hatred and injustice is not the one most likely to produce happiness. The late war taught this lesson to a few, and would have taught it to many more if it had ended in a draw. We need a morality based upon love of life, upon pleasure in growth and positive achievement, not upon repression and prohibition. A man should be regarded as "good" if he is happy, expansive, generous, and glad when others are happy; if so, a few peccadillos should be regarded as of little importance. But a man who acquires a fortune by cruelty and exploitation should be regarded as at present we regard what is called an "immoral" man; and he should be so regarded even if he goes to church regularly and gives a portion of his ill-gotten gains to public objects. To bring this about, it is only necessary to instill a rational attitude towards ethical questions, instead of the mixture of superstition and oppression which still passes muster as "virtue" among important personages. The power of reason is thought small in these days, but I remain an unrepentant rationalist. Reason may be a small force, but it is constant, and works always in one direction, while the forces of unreason destroy one another in futile strife. Therefore every orgy of unreason in the end strengthens the friends of reason, and shows afresh that they are the only true friends of humanity.

FROM THE WAY OF ALL FLESH, Chapter 19 *

SAMUEL BUTLER

Mr. Pontifex's life not only continued a long time, but was prosperous right up to the end. Is not this enough? Being in this world is it not our most obvious business to make the most of it—to observe what things do *bona fide* tend to long life and comfort, and to act accordingly? All animals, except man, know that the principal business of life is to enjoy it—and they do enjoy it as much as man and other circumstances will allow. He has spent his life best who has enjoyed it most; God will take care that we do not enjoy it any more than is good for us. If Mr. Pontifex is to be blamed it is for not having eaten and drunk less and thus suffered less from his liver, and lived perhaps a year or two longer.

Goodness is naught unless it tends towards old age and sufficiency of means. I speak broadly and *exceptis excipiendis*. So the psalmist says, "The righteous shall not lack any thing that is good." Either this is mere poetical license, or it follows that he who lacks anything that is good is not righteous; there is a presumption also that he who has passed a long life without lacking anything that is good has himself also been good enough for practical purposes.

Mr. Pontifex never lacked anything that he much cared about. True, he might have been happier than he was if he had cared about things which he did not care for, but the gist of this lies in the "if he had cared." We have all sinned and come short of the glory of making ourselves as comfortable as we easily might have done, but in this particular case Mr. Pontifex did not care, and would not have gained much by getting what he did not want.

There is no casting of swine's meat before men worse than that which would flatter virtue as though her true origin were not good enough for her, but she must have a lineage, deduced as it were by spiritual heralds, from some stock with which she has nothing to do. Virtue's true lineage is older and more respectable than any that can be invented for her. She springs from man's experience concerning his own well-being—and this, though not infallible, is still the least fallible thing we have. A system which cannot stand without a better foundation than this must have something so unstable within itself that it will topple over on whatever pedestal we place it.

The world has long ago settled that morality and virtue are what bring men peace at the last. "Be virtuous," says the copy-book, "and you will be happy." Surely if a reputed virtue fails often in this respect it is only an insidious form of vice, and if a reputed vice brings no very serious mischief on a man's later years it is not so bad a vice as it is said to be. Unfortunately, though we are all of a mind about the main opinion that virtue is what tends to happiness, and vice what ends in sorrow, we are not so unanimous about details—that is to say as to whether any given course, such, we will say, as smoking, has a tendency to happiness or the reverse.

I submit it as the result of my own poor observation, that a good deal of unkindness and selfishness on the part of parents towards children is not generally followed by ill consequences to the parents themselves. They may cast a gloom over their children's lives for many years without having to suffer anything that will hurt them. I should say, then, that it shows no great moral obliquity on the part of parents if within certain limits they make their children's lives a burden to them.

Granted that Mr. Pontifex's was not a very exalted character, ordinary men are not required to have very exalted characters. It is enough if we are of the same moral and mental stature as the "main" or "mean" part of men—that is to say as the average.

It is involved in the very essence of things that rich men who die old shall have been mean. The greatest and wisest of mankind will be almost always found to be the meanest—the ones who have kept the "mean" best between excess either of virtue or vice. They hardly ever have been prosperous if they have not done this, and, considering how many miscarry altogether, it is no small feather in a man's cap if he has been no worse than his neighbors. Homer tells us about some one who made it his business . . . always to excel and to stand higher than other people. What an uncompanionable, disagreeable person he must have been! Homer's heroes generally come to a bad end, and I doubt not that this gentleman, whoever he was, did so sooner or later.

A very high standard, again, involves the possession of rare virtues, and rare virtues are like rare plants or animals, things that have not been able to hold their own in the world. A virtue to be serviceable must, like gold, be alloyed with some commoner but more durable metal.

People divide off vice and virtue as though they were two things, neither of which had with it anything of the other. This is not so. There is no useful virtue which has not some alloy of vice, and hardly any vice, if any, which carries not with it a little dash of virtue; virtue and vice are like life and death, or mind and matter—things which cannot exist without being qualified by their opposite. The most absolute life contains death, and the corpse is still in many respects living; so also it has been said, "If thou, Lord, wilt be extreme to mark what is done amiss," which shows that even the highest ideal we can conceive will yet admit so much compromise with vice as shall countenance the poor abuses of the time, if they are not too outrageous. That vice pays homage to virtue is notorious; we call this hypocrisy; there should be a word found for the homage which virtue not infrequently pays, or at any rate would be wise in paying, to vice.

I grant that some men will find happiness in having what we all feel to be a higher moral standard than others. If they go in for this, however, they must be content with virtue as her own reward, and not grumble if they find lofty Quixotism an expensive luxury, whose rewards belong to a kingdom that is not of this world. They must not wonder if they cut a poor figure in trying to make the most of both worlds. Disbelieve as we may the details of the accounts which record the growth of the Christian religion, yet a great part of Christian teaching will remain as true as though we accepted the details.

We cannot serve God and Mammon; strait is the way and narrow is the gate which leads to what those who live by faith hold to be best worth having, and there is no way of saying this better than the Bible has done. It is well there should be some who think thus, as it is well there should be speculators in commerce, who will often burn their fingers—but it is not well that the majority should leave the "mean" and beaten path.

For most men, and most circumstances, pleasure—tangible material prosperity in this world—is the safest test of virtue. Progress has ever been through the pleasures rather than through the extreme sharp virtues, and the most virtuous have leaned to excess rather than to asceticism. To use a commercial metaphor, competition is so keen, and the margin of profits has been cut down so closely that virtue cannot afford to throw away any *bona fide* chance, and must base her action rather on the actual moneying out of conduct than on a flattering prospectus. She will not therefore neglect—as some do who are prudent and economical enough in other matters—the important factor of our chance of escaping detection, or at any rate of our dying first. A reasonable virtue will give this chance its due value, neither more nor less.

Pleasure, after all, is a safer guide than either right or duty. For hard as it is to know what gives us pleasure, right and duty are often still harder to distinguish and, if we go wrong with them, will lead us into just as sorry a plight as a mistaken opinion concerning pleasure. When men burn their fingers through following after pleasure they find out their mistake and get to see where they have gone wrong more easily than when they have burnt them through following after a fancied duty, or a fancied idea concerning right virtue. The devil, in fact, when he dresses himself in angel's clothes, can only be detected by experts of exceptional skill, and so often does he adopt this disguise that it is hardly safe to be seen talking to an angel at all, and prudent people will follow after pleasure as a more homely but more respectable and on the whole much more trustworthy guide.

TO HIS COY MISTRESS

ANDREW MARVELL

Had we but world enough, and time,
This coyness, Lady, were no crime
We would sit down and think which way
To walk and pass our long love's day.
Thou by the Indian Ganges' side
Shouldst rubies find: I by the tide
Of Humber would complain. I would
Love you ten years before the Flood,
And you should, if you please, refuse
Till the conversion of the Jews.
My vegetable love should grow
Vaster than empires, and more slow;
An hundred years should go to praise
Thine eyes and on thy forehead gaze;
Two hundred to adore each breast,
But thirty thousand to the rest;

An age at least to every part,
And the last age should show your heart.
For, Lady, you deserve this state,
Nor would I love at lower rate.
    But at my back I always hear
Time's wingèd chariot hurrying near;
And yonder all before us lie
Deserts of vast eternity.
Thy beauty shall no more be found,
Nor, in thy marble vault, shall sound
My echoing song: then worms shall try
That long preserved virginity,
And your quaint honor turn to dust,
And into ashes all my lust:
The grave's a fine and private place,
But none, I think, do there embrace.
Now therefore, while the youthful hue
Sits on thy skin like morning dew,
And while thy willing soul transpires
At every pore with instant fires,
Now let us sport us while we may,
And now, like amorous birds of prey,
Rather at once our time devour
Than languish in his slow-chapt power.
Let us roll all our strength and all
Our sweetness up into one ball,
And tear our pleasures with rough strife
Thorough the iron gates of life:
Thus, though we cannot make our sun
Stand still, yet we will make him run.

GAUDEAMUS IGITUR

(ANON.)

Let us live then and be glad
    While young life's before us!
        After youthful pastime had,
        After old age hard and sad,
    Earth will slumber o'er us.

Where are they who in this world,
    Ere we kept, were keeping?
        Go ye to the gods above:
        Go to hell; inquire thereof:
    They are not; they're sleeping.

Brief is life, and brevity
    Briefly shall be ended:
        Death comes like a whirlwind strong,
        Bears us with his blast along;
    None shall be defended.

Live this university,
    Men that learning nourish;
        Live each member of the same,
        Long live all that bear its name;
    Let them ever flourish!

Live the commonwealth also,
    And the men that guide it!
        Live our town in strength and health,
        Founders, patrons, by whose wealth
    We are here provided!

Live all girls!   A health to you,
    Melting maids and beauteous!
        Live the wives and women too,
        Gentle, loving, tender, true,
    Good, industrious, duteous!

Perish cares that pule and pine!
    Perish envious blamers!
        Die the Devil, thine and mine!
        Die the starch-necked Philistine!
    Scoffers and defamers!
                    (John Addington Symonds, tr.)

CAVIARE *

LOGAN PEARSALL SMITH

"Aren't you ashamed of yourself?" asked my hostess, when she found me alone in the supper-room, after all the other guests had gone.

"Ashamed? Why should I be ashamed?" I asked, as I went on eating. "I am simply following the precepts of Aristippus of Cyrene, who maintains that we should live wholly in the present moment, which alone exists, and in which alone the absolute Good of life is before us. It is only by regarding each Moment as an eternity, with no before or after, and by calmly and resolutely culling, without fear, or passion, or prejudice, the Good it offers—it is only thus, he says, that Wisdom is made manifest; only thus," I explained, as I took another caviare-sandwich, "that mortals may participate in the felicity of the Gods—the bright Gods, who feed on happiness for ever."

THE BUSY BEES †

LOGAN PEARSALL SMITH

Sitting for hours idle in the shade of an apple tree, near the garden-hives, and under the aerial thoroughfares of those honey-merchants,—sometimes when the noonday heat is loud with their minute industry, or when they fall in crowds out of the late sun to their night-long labors,—I have sought instructions from the Bees, and tried to appropriate to myself the old industrious lesson.

* From All Trivia by Logan Pearsall Smith, copyright, 1945, by Harcourt, Brace and Company, Inc.
    † From: Trivia by Logan Pearsall Smith. Copyright 1917 by Doubleday & Company, Inc.

And yet, hang it all, who by rights should be the teacher and who the learners? For those peevish, over-toiled, utilitarian insects, was there no lesson to be derived from the spectacle of Me? Gazing out at me with myriad eyes from their joyless factories, might they not learn at last—could I not finally teach them—a wiser and more generous-hearted way to improve the shining hours?

DE RERUM NATURA, II, lines 1-61

LUCRETIUS

'Tis pleasant, safely to behold from shore
The rolling ship, and hear the tempest roar:
Not that another's pain is our delight;
But pains unfelt produce the pleasing sight.
'Tis pleasant also to behold from afar
The moving legions mingled in the war:
But much more sweet thy laboring steps to guide
To virtue's heights, with wisdom well supplied,
And all the magazines of learning fortified:
From thence to look below on human kind,
Bewildered in the maze of life, and blind:
To see vain fools ambitiously contend
For wit and power; their last endeavors bend
T' outshine each other, waste their time and health
In search of honor, and pursuit of wealth.
O wretched man! in what a mist of life,
Inclosed with dangers and with noisy strife,
He spends his little span; and overfeeds
His crammed desires with more than nature needs!
For Nature wisely stints our appetite,
And craves no more than undisturbed delight:
Which minds unmixed with cares, and fears, obtain;
A soul serene, a body void of pain.
So little this corporeal frame requires;
So bounded are our natural desires,
That wanting all, and setting pain aside,
With bare privation sense is satisfied.
If golden sconces hang not on the walls,
To light the costly suppers and the balls;
If the proud palace shines not with the state
Of burnished bowls, and of reflected plate;
If well tuned harps, nor the more pleasing sound
Of voices, from the vaulted roofs rebound;
Yet on the grass, beneath a poplar shade,
By the cool stream our careless limbs are laid;
With cheaper pleasures innocently blessed,
When the warm spring with gaudy flowers is dressed.
Nor will the raging fever's fire abate,
With golden canopies and beds of State:
But the poor patient will as soon be sound

On the hard mattress, or the Mother ground.
Then since our bodies are not eased the more
By birth, or power, or Fortune's wealthy store,
'Tis plain, these useless toys of every kind
As little can relieve the laboring mind;
Unless we could suppose the dreadful sight
Of marshalled legions moving to the fight,
Could, with their sound and terrible array,
Expel our fears, and drive the thoughts of death away;
But, since the supposition vain appears,
Since clinging cares, and trains of inbred fears,
Are not with sounds to be affrighted thence,
But in the midst of pomp pursue the prince,
Not awed by arms, but in the presence bold,
Without respect to purple, or to gold;
Why should not we these pageantries despise,
Whose worth but in our want of reason lies?
For life is all in wandering errors led;
And just as children are surprised with dread,
And tremble in the dark, so riper years
Even in broad daylight are possessed with fears,
And shake at shadows fanciful and vain,
As those which in the breasts of children reign.
These bugbears of the mind, this inward Hell,
No rays of outward sunshine can dispel;
But nature and right reason must display
Their beams abroad, and bring the darksome soul to day.

(John Dryden, tr.)

NOTES FROM UNDERGROUND, I, iv

FYODOR DOSTOEVSKY

"Ha, ha, ha! You will be finding enjoyment in toothache next," you cry, with a laugh.

"Well? Even in toothache there is enjoyment," I answer. I had toothache for a whole month and I know there is. In that case, of course, people are not spiteful in silence, but moan; but they are not candid moans, they are malignant moans, and the malignancy is the whole point. The enjoyment of the sufferer finds expression in those moans; if he did not feel enjoyment he would not moan. It is a good example, gentlemen, and I will develop it. Those moans express in the first place all the aimlessness of your pain, which is so humiliating to your consciousness; the whole legal system of nature on which you spit disdainfully, of course, but from which you suffer all the same while she does not. They express the consciousness that you have no enemy to punish, but that you have pain; the consciousness that in spite of all possible Vagenheims you are in complete slavery to your teeth; that if some one wishes it, your teeth will leave off aching, and if he does not, they will go on aching another three months; and that finally if you are still contumacious and still protest, all that is left you for your own gratification is to thrash yourself or beat your wall with your fist as hard as you can, and absolutely nothing more.

Well, these mortal insults, these jeers on the part of some one unknown, end at last in an enjoyment which sometimes reaches the highest degree of voluptuousness. I ask you, gentlemen, listen sometimes to the moans of an educated man of the nineteenth century suffering from toothache, on the second or third day of the attack, when he is beginning to moan, not as he moaned on the first day, that is, not simply because he has toothache, not just as any coarse peasant, but as a man affected by progress and European civilization, a man who is "divorced from the soil and the national elements," as they express it now-a-days. His moans become nasty, disgustingly malignant, and go on for whole days and nights. And of course he knows himself that he is doing himself no sort of good with his moans; he knows better than any one that he is only lacerating and harassing himself and others for nothing; he knows that even the audience before whom he is making his efforts, and his whole family, listen to him with loathing, do not put a ha'porth of faith in him, and inwardly understand that he might moan differently, more simply, without trills and flourishes, and that he is only amusing himself like that from ill-humor, from malignancy. Well, in all these recognitions and disgraces it is that there lies a voluptuous pleasure. As though he would say: "I am worrying you, I am lacerating your hearts, I am keeping every one in the house awake. Well, stay awake then, you, too, feel every minute that I have toothache. I am not a hero to you now, as I tried to seem before, but simply a nasty person, an impostor. Well, so be it, then! I am very glad that you see through me. It is nasty for you to hear my despicable moans: well, let it be nasty; here I will let you have a nastier flourish in a minute. . . ." You do not understand even now, gentlemen? No, it seems our development and our consciousness must go further to understand all the intricacies of this pleasure. You laugh? Delighted. My jests, gentlemen, are of course in bad taste, jerky, involved, lacking self-confidence. But of course that is because I do not respect myself. Can a man of perception respect himself at all?

(Constance Garnett, tr.)

THE MODERN WORKER

In *Past and Present* (Chapter 4)

THOMAS CARLYLE

All work, even cotton-spinning, is noble; work is alone noble; be that here said and asserted once more. And in like manner, too, all dignity is painful; a life of ease is not for any man, nor for any god. The life of all gods figures itself to us as a Sublime Sadness,—earnestness of Infinite Battle against Infinite Labor. Our highest religion is named the "Worship of Sorrow." For the son of man there is no noble crown, well worn, or even ill worn, but is a crown of thorns!—These things, in spoken words, or still better, in felt instincts alive in every heart, were once well known.

Does not the whole wretchedness, the whole *Atheism* as I call it, of man's ways, in these generations, shadow itself for us in that unspeakable Life-philosophy of his: The pretension to be what he calls "happy"? Every pitifulest whipster that walks within a skin has his head filled with the notion that he is, shall be, or by all human and divine laws ought to be, "happy." His wishes, the pitifulest whipster's, are to be fulfilled for him; his days, the pitifulest whipster's, are to flow on in ever-gentle current of enjoyment, impossible even for the gods. The prophets preach to us, Thou shalt be happy; thou shalt love pleasant things, and find them. The people clamor, Why have we not found pleasant things?

We construct our theory of Human Duties, not on any Greatest-Nobleness Principle, never so mistaken; no, but on a Greatest-Happiness Principle. "The word *Soul* with us, as in some Slavonic dialects, seems to be synonymous with *Stomach*." We plead and speak, in our Parliaments and elsewhere, not as from the Soul, but from the Stomach;—wherefore, indeed, our pleadings are so slow to profit. We plead not for God's Justice; we are not ashamed to stand clamoring and pleading for our own "interests," our own rents and trade-profits; we say, They are the "interests" of so many; there is such an intense desire in us for them! We demand Free-Trade, with much just vociferation and benevolence, That the poorer classes, who are terribly ill-off at present, may have cheaper New-Orleans bacon. Men ask on Free-trade platforms, How can the indomitable spirit of Englishmen be kept up without plenty of bacon? We shall become a ruined Nation!—Surely, my friends, plenty of bacon is good and indispensable: but I doubt, you will never get even bacon by aiming only at that. You are men, not animals of prey, well-used or ill-used! Your Greatest-Happiness Principle seems to me fast becoming a rather unhappy one.—What if we should cease babbling about "happiness," and leave *it* resting on its own basis, as it used to do!

A gifted Byron rises in his wrath; and feeling too surely that he for his part is not "happy," declares the same in very violent language, as a piece of news that may be interesting. It evidently has surprised him much. One dislikes to see a man and poet reduced to proclaim on the streets such tidings; but on the whole, as matters go, that is not the most dislikable. Byron speaks the *truth* in this matter. Byron's large audience indicates how true it is felt to be.

"Happy," my brother? First of all, what difference is it whether thou art happy or not! Today becomes Yesterday so fast, all Tomorrows become Yesterdays; and then there is no question whatever of the "happiness," but quite another question. Nay, thou hast such a sacred pity left at least for thyself, thy very pains, once gone over into Yesterday, become joys to thee. Besides, thou knowest not what heavenly blessedness and indispensable sanative virtue was in them; thou shalt only know it after many days, when thou art wiser!—A benevolent old Surgeon sat once in our company, with a Patient fallen sick by gourmandising, whom he had just, too briefly in the Patient's judgment, been examining. The foolish Patient still at intervals continued to break in on our discourse, which rather promised to take a philosophic turn: "But I have lost my appetite," said he, objurgatively, with a tone of irritated pathos; "I have no appetite; I can't eat!"—"My dear fellow," answered the Doctor in mildest tone, "it isn't of the slightest consequence;"—and continued his philosophical discoursings with us!

Or does the reader not know the history of that Scottish iron Misanthrope? The inmates of some town-mansions, in those Northern parts, were thrown into the fearfulest alarm by indubitable symptoms of a ghost inhabiting the next house, or perhaps even the partition-wall! Ever at a certain hour, with preternatural gnarring, growling, and screeching, which attended as running bass, there began, in a horrid, semi-articulate, unearthly voice, this song: "Once I was hap-hap-happy, but now I'm *mees*-erable! Clack-clack-clack, gnarr-r-r, whuz-z: Once I was hap-hap-happy, but now I'm mees-erable!"—Rest, rest, perturbed spirit;—or indeed, as the good old Doctor said: My dear fellow, it isn't of the slightest consequence! But no; the perturbed spirit could not rest; and to the neighbors, fretted, affrighted, or at least insufferably bored by him, it *was* of such consequence that they had to go and examine in his haunted chamber. In his haunted chamber, they find that the perturbed spirit is an unfortunate—imitator of Byron?   No, is an unfortunate rusty Meat-jack, gnarring and creaking with rust and work; and this, in Scottish dialect, is *its* Byronian musical Life-philosophy, sung according to ability!

Truly, I think the man who goes about pothering and uproaring for his "happiness,"—pothering, and were it ballot-boxing, poem-making, or in what way soever fussing and exerting himself,—he is not the man that will help us to "get our knaves and dastards arrested!"   No; he rather is on the way to increase the number,—by at least one unit and his tail!   Observe, too, that this is all a modern affair; belongs not to the old heroic times, but to these dastard new times.   "Happiness our being's end and aim," all that very paltry speculation, is at bottom, if we will count well, not yet two centuries old in the world.

The only happiness a brave man ever troubled himself with asking much about was, happiness enough to get his work done.   Not "I can't eat!" but "I can't work!" that was the burden of all wise complaining among men.   It is, after all, the one unhappiness of a man.   That he cannot work; that he cannot get his destiny as a man fulfilled.

Behold, the day is passing swiftly over, our life is passing swiftly over; and the night cometh when no man can work.   The night once come, our happiness, our unhappiness,—it is all abolished; vanished, clean gone; a thing that has been: "not of the slightest consequence" whether we were happy as eupeptic Curtis, as the fattest pig of Epicurus, or unhappy as Job with potsherds, as musical Byron with Giaours and sensibilities of the heart; as the unmusical Meat-jack with hard labor and rust!   But our work,—behold that is not abolished, that has not vanished: our work, behold, it remains, or the want of it remains;—for endless Times and Eternities, remains; and that is now the sole question with us forevermore!   Brief brawling Day, with its noisy phantasms, its poor paper-crowns tinsel-gilt, is gone; and divine everlasting Night with her star-diadems, with her silences and her veracities, is come!   What hast thou done, and how?   Happiness, unhappiness: all that was but the *wages* thou hadst; thou hast spent all that, in sustaining thyself hitherward; not a coin of it remains with thee, it is all spent, eaten: and now thy work, where is thy work?   Swift, out with it, let us see thy work!

Of a truth, if man were not a poor hungry dastard, and even much of a blockhead withal, he would cease criticizing his victuals to such extent; and criticize himself rather, what he does with his victuals!

from UTILITARIANISM

JOHN STUART MILL

The creed which accepts as the foundation of morals *utility*, or the *greatest happiness principle*, holds that actions are right in proportion as they tend to promote happiness, wrong as they tend to produce the reverse of happiness.   By "happiness" is intended pleasure, and the absence of pain; by "unhappiness," pain, and the privation of pleasure.   To give a clear view of the moral standard set up by the theory, much more requires to be said; in particular, what things it includes in the ideas of pain and pleasure; and to what extent this is left an open question.   But these supplementary explanations do not affect the theory of life on which this theory of morality is grounded—namely, that pleasure, and freedom from pain, are the only things desirable as ends; and that all desirable things (which are as numerous in the utilitarian as in any other scheme) are desirable either for the pleasure inherent in themselves, or as means to the promotion of pleasure and the prevention of pain.

Now such a theory of life excites in many minds, and among them in some of the most estimable in feeling and purpose, inveterate dislike. To suppose that life has (as they express it) no higher end than pleasure—no better and nobler object of desire and pursuit—they designate as utterly mean and groveling; as a doctrine worthy only of swine, to whom the followers of Epicurus were, at a very early period, contemptuously likened; and modern holders of the doctrine are occasionally made the subject of equally polite comparisons by its German, French, and English assailants.

When thus attacked, the Epicureans have always answered that it is not they but their accusers who represent human nature in a degrading light; since the accusation supposes human beings to be capable of no pleasures except those of which swine are capable. If this supposition were true, the charge could not be gainsaid, but would then be no longer an imputation; for if the sources of pleasure were precisely the same to human beings and to swine, the rule of life which is good enough for the one would be good enough for the other. The comparison of the Epicurean life to that of beasts is felt as degrading, precisely because a beast's pleasures do not satisfy a human being's conceptions of happiness. Human beings have faculties more elevated than the animal appetites, and when once made conscious of them, do not regard anything as happiness which does not include their gratification. I do not, indeed, consider the Epicureans to have been by any means faultless in drawing out their scheme of consequences from the utilitarian principle. To do this in any sufficient manner, many Stoic, as well as Christian elements require to be included. But there is no known Epicurean theory of life which does not assign to the pleasures of the intellect, of the feelings and imagination, and of the moral sentiments, a much higher value as pleasures than to those of mere sensation. It must be admitted, however, that utilitarian writers in general have placed the superiority of mental over bodily pleasures chiefly in the greater permanency, safety, uncostliness, etc., of the former—that is, in their circumstantial advantages rather than in their intrinsic nature. And on all these points utilitarians have fully proved their case; but they might have taken the other, and, as it may be called, higher ground, with entire consistency. It is quite compatible with the principle of utility to recognize the fact, that some *kinds* of pleasure are more desirable and more valuable than others. It would be absurd that while, in estimating all other things, quality is considered as well as quantity, the estimation of pleasures should be supposed to depend on quantity alone.

If I am asked what I mean by difference of quality in pleasures, or what makes one pleasure more valuable than another merely as a pleasure, except its being greater in amount, there is but one possible answer. Of two pleasures, if there be one to which all or almost all who have experience of both give a decided preference, irrespective of any feeling of moral obligation to prefer it, that is the more desirable pleasure. If one of the two is, by those who are competently acquainted with both, placed so far above the other that they prefer it, even though knowing it to be attended with a greater amount of discontent, and would not resign it for any quantity of the other pleasure which their nature is capable of, we are justified in ascribing to the preferred enjoyment a superiority in quality, so far outweighing quantity as to render it, in comparison, of small account.

Now it is an unquestionable fact that those who are equally acquainted with, and equally capable of appreciating and enjoying both, do give a most marked preference to the manner of existence which employs their higher faculties. Few human creatures would consent to be changed into any of the lower animals, for a promise of the fullest allowance of a beast's pleasures; no intelligent human being would consent to be a fool, no instructed person would be an ignoramus, no person of feeling and conscience would be selfish and base, even though they should be persuaded that the fool, the dunce, or the rascal is better satisfied with his lot than they are with theirs. They would not resign what they possess more than he for the most complete satisfaction of all the desires which they have in common with him. If they ever fancy they would, it is only in cases of unhappiness so extreme, that to escape from it they would exchange their lot for almost any other, however undesirable in their own eyes. A being of higher faculties requires more to make him happy, is capable probably of more acute suffering, and certainly accessible to it at more points, than one of an inferior type; but in spite of these liabilities, he can never really wish to sink into what he feels to be a lower grade of existence. We may give what explanation we please of this unwillingness: we may attribute it to pride, a name which is given indiscriminately to some of the most and to some of the least estimable feelings of which mankind are capable; we may refer it to the love of liberty and personal independence, an appeal to which was with the Stoics one of the most effective means for the inculcation of it; to the love of power, or to the love of excitement, both of which do really enter into and contribute to it: but its most appropriate appellation is a sense of dignity, which all human beings possess in one form or other; and in some, though by no means in exact, proportion to their higher faculties, and which is so essential a part of the happiness of those in whom it is strong, that nothing which conflicts with it could be, otherwise than momentarily, an object of desire to them. Whoever supposes that this preference takes place at a sacrifice of happiness—that the superior being, in anything like equal circumstances, is not happier than the inferior—confounds the two very different ideas, of *happiness* and *content*. It is indisputable that the being whose capacities of enjoyment are low, has the greatest chance of having them fully satisfied; and a highly endowed being will always feel that any happiness which he can look for, as the world is constituted, is imperfect. But he can learn to bear its imperfections, if they are at all bearable; and they will not make him envy the being who is indeed unconscious of the imperfections, but only because he feels not at all the good which those imperfections qualify. It is better to be a human being dissatisfied than a pig satisfied; better to be Socrates dissatisfied than a fool satisfied. And if the fool, or the pig, are of a different opinion, it is because they only know their own side of the question. The other party to the comparison knows both sides.

It may be objected that many who are capable of the higher pleasures, occasionally, under the influence of temptation, postpone them to the lower. But this is quite compatible with a full appreciation of the intrinsic superiority of the higher. Men often, from infirmity of character, make their election for the nearer good, though they know it to be the less valuable; and this no less when the choice is between two bodily pleasures, than when it is between bodily and mental. They pursue sensual indulgences to the injury of health, though perfectly aware that health is the greater good. It may be further objected that many who begin with youthful enthusiasm for everything noble, as they advance in years sink into indolence and selfishness. But I do not believe that those who undergo this very common change, voluntarily choose the lower description of pleasures in preference to the higher. I believe that before they devote themselves exclusively to the one, they have already become incapable of the other. Capacity for the nobler feelings is in most natures a very tender plant, easily killed, not only by hostile influences, but by mere want of sustenance; and in the majority of young persons it speedily dies away if the occupations to which their position in life has devoted them, and the society into which it has thrown them, are not favorable to keeping that higher capacity in exercise. Men lose their high aspirations as they lose their intellectual tastes, because they have not time or opportunity for indulging them; and they addict themselves to inferior pleasures not because they deliberately prefer them, but because they are either the only ones to which they have access or the only ones which they are any longer capable of enjoying. It may be questioned whether anyone who has remained equally susceptible to both classes of pleasures, ever knowingly and calmly preferred the lower; though many, in all ages, have broken down in an ineffectual attempt to combine both.

From this verdict of the only competent judges I apprehend there can be no appeal. On a question which is the best worth having of two pleasures, or which of two modes of existence is the most grateful to the feelings, apart from its moral attributes and from its consequences, the judgment of those who are qualified by knowledge of both, or, if they differ, that of the majority among them, must be admitted as final. And there need be the less hesitation to accept this judgment respecting the quality of pleasures, since there is no other tribunal to be referred to even on the question of quantity. What means are there of determining which is the acutest of two pains, or the intensest of two pleasurable sensations, except the general suffrage of those who are familiar with both? Neither pains nor pleasures are homogeneous, and pain is always heterogeneous with pleasure. What is there to decide whether a particular pleasure is worth purchasing at the cost of a particular pain, except the feelings and judgment of the experienced? When, therefore, those feelings and judgment declare the pleasures derived from the higher faculties to be preferable *in kind,* apart from the question of intensity, to those of which the animal nature, disjoined from the higher faculties, is susceptible, they are entitled on this subject to the same regard.

I have dwelt on this point, as being a necessary part of a perfectly just conception of utility, or happiness, considered as the directive rule of human conduct. But it is by no means an indispensable condition to the acceptance of the utilitarian standard; for that standard is not the agent's own greatest happiness, but the greatest amount of happiness altogether; and if it may possibly be doubted whether a noble character is always the happier for its nobleness, there can be no doubt that it makes other people happier, and that the world in general is immensely a gainer by it. Utilitarianism, therefore, could only attain its end by the general cultivation of nobleness of character, even if each individual were only benefited by the nobleness of others, and his own, so far as happiness is concerned, were a sheer deduction from the benefit. But the bare enunciation of such an absurdity as this last renders refutation superfluous.

According to the "greatest happiness principle," as above explained, the ultimate end, with reference to and for the sake of which all other things are desirable (whether we are considering our own good or that of other people), is an existence exempt as far as possible from pain, and as rich as possible in enjoyments, both in point of quantity and quality; the test of quality, and the rule for measuring it against quantity, being the preference felt by those who in their opportunities of experience, to which must be added their habits of self-consciousness and self-observation, are best furnished with the means of comparison. This, being, according to the utilitarian opinion, the end of human action, is necessarily also the standard of morality; which may accordingly be defined, the rules and precepts for human conduct, by the observance of which an existence such as has been described might be, to the greatest extent possible, secured to all mankind; and not to them only, but, so far as the nature of things admits, to the whole sentient creation.

SELF-DEPENDENCE

MATTHEW ARNOLD

Weary of myself, and sick of asking
What I am, and what I ought to be,
At this vessel's prow I stand, which bears me
Forwards, forwards, o'er the starlit sea.

And a look of passionate desire
O'er the sea and to the stars I send:
"Ye who from my childhood up have calmed me,
Calm me, ah, compose me to the end!

"Ah, once more," I cried, "ye stars, ye waters,
On my heart your mighty charm renew;
Still, still let me, as I gaze upon you,
Feel my soul becoming vast like you!"

From the intense, clear, star-sown vault of heaven,
Over the lit sea's unquiet way,
In the restling night-air came the answer:
"Wouldst thou *be* as these are? *Live* as they.

"Unaffrighted by the silence round them,
Undistracted by the sights they see,
These demand not that the things without them
Yield them love, amusement, sympathy.

"And with joy the stars perform their shining,
And the sea its long moon-silvered roll;
For self-poised they live, nor pine with noting
All the fever of some differing soul.

"Bounded by themselves, and unregardful
In what state God's other works may be,
In their own tasks all their powers pouring,
These attain the mighty life you see."

O air-born voice! long since, severely clear,
A cry like thine in mine own heart I hear:
"Resolve to be thyself; and know that he,
Who finds himself, loses his misery!"

THE LAST WORD

MATTHEW ARNOLD

Creep into thy narrow bed,
Creep, and let no more be said!
Vain thy onset! all stands fast.
Thou thyself must break at last.

Let the long contention cease!
Geese are swans, and swans are geese.
Let them have it how they will!
Thou art tired; best be still.

They out-talked thee, hissed thee, tore thee?
Better men fared thus before thee;
Fired their ringing shot and passed,
Hotly charged—and sank at last.

Charge once more, then, and be dumb!
Let the victors, when they come,
When the forts of folly fall,
Find thy body by the wall!

FROM A SHROPSHIRE LAD (LXII, XLV)

A. E. HOUSMAN

LXII

"Terence, this is stupid stuff:
You eat your victuals fast enough;
There can't be much amiss, 'tis clear,
To see the rate you drink your beer.
But oh, good Lord, the verse you make,
It gives a chap the belly-ache.
The cow, the old cow, she is dead;
It sleeps well, the horned head:
We poor lads, 'tis our turn now
To hear such tunes as killed the cow.
Pretty friendship 'tis to rhyme
Your friends to death before their time
Moping melancholy mad:
Come, pipe a tune to dance to, lad."

Why, if 'tis dancing you would be,
There's brisker pipes than poetry.
Say, for what were hop-yards meant,
Or why was Burton built on Trent?
Oh many a peer of England brews
Livelier liquor than the Muse,

And malt does more than Milton can
To justify God's ways to man.
Ale, man, ale's the stuff to drink
For fellows whom it hurts to think:
Look into the pewter pot
To see the world as the world's not.
And faith, 'tis pleasant till 'tis past:
The mischief is that 'twill not last.
Oh I have been to Ludlow fair
And left my necktie God knows where,
And carried half way home, or near,
Pints and quarts of Ludlow beer:
Then the world seemed none so bad,
And I myself a sterling lad;
And down in lovely muck I've lain,
Happy till I woke again.
Then I saw the morning sky;
Heigho, the tale was all a lie;
The world, it was the old world yet,
I was I, my things were wet,
And nothing now remained to do
But begin the game anew.

Therefore, since the world has still
Much good, but much less good than ill,
And while the sun and moon endure
Luck's a chance, but trouble's sure,
I'd face it as a wise man would,
And train for ill and not for good.
'Tis true, the stuff I bring for sale
Is not so brisk a brew as ale:
Out of a stem that scored the hand
I wrung it in a weary land.
But take it: if the smack is sour,
The better for the embittered hour;
It should do good to heart and head
When your soul is in my soul's stead;
And I will friend you, if I may
In the dark and cloudy day.

There was a king reigned in the East:
There, when kings will sit to feast,
They get their fill before they think
With poisoned meat and poisoned drink.
He gathered all that springs to birth
From the many-venomed earth;
First a little, thence to more,
He sampled all her killing store;
And easy, smiling, seasoned sound,
Sate the king when healths went round.
They put arsenic in his meat
And stared aghast to watch him eat;

They poured strychnine in his cup
And shook to see him drink it up:
They shook, they stared as white's their shirt:
Them it was their poison hurt.
—I tell the tale that I heard told.
Mithridates, he died old.

XLV

If it chance your eye offend you,
  Pluck it out, lad, and be sound:
'Twill hurt, but here are salves to friend you,
  And many a balsam grows on ground.

And if your hand or foot offend you,
  Cut it off, lad, and be whole;
But play the man, stand up and end you,
  When your sickness is your soul.

FROM THE PRACTICAL PROBLEM

In *The Tragic Sense of Life*

MIGUEL DE UNAMUNO

My conduct must be the best proof, the moral proof, of my supreme desire; and if I do not end by convincing myself, within the bounds of the ultimate and irremediable uncertainty, of the truth of what I hope for, it is because my conduct is not sufficiently pure. Virtue, therefore, is not based upon dogma, but dogma upon virtue, and it is not faith that creates martyrs but martyrs who create faith. There is no security or repose—so far as security and repose are obtainable in this life, so essentially insecure and unreposeful—save in conduct that is passionately good.

Conduct, practice, is the proof of doctrine, theory. "If any man will do His will—the will of Him that sent me," said Jesus, "he shall know of the doctrine, whether it be of God or whether I speak of myself" (John vii. 17); and there is a well-known saying of Pascal: "Begin by taking holy water and you will end by becoming a believer." And pursuing a similar train of thought, Johann Jakob Moser, the pietist, was of the opinion that no atheist or naturalist had the right to regard the Christian religion as void of truth so long as he had not put it to the proof by keeping its precepts and commandments (Ritschl, *Geschichte des Pietismus*, Book vii., 43).

What is our heart's truth, anti-rational though it be? The immortality of the human soul, the truth of the persistence of our consciousness without any termination whatsoever, the truth of the human finality of the Universe. And what is its moral proof? We may formulate it thus: Act so that in your own judgment and in the judgment of others you may merit eternity, act so that you may become irreplaceable, act so that you may not merit death. Or perhaps thus: Act as if you were to die tomorrow, but to die in order to survive and be eternalized. The end of morality is to give personal, human finality to the Universe; to discover the finality that belongs to it—if indeed it has any finality—and to discover it by acting.

More than a century ago, in 1804, in Letter XC of that series that constitutes the

immense monody of his *Obermann*, Sénancour wrote the words which I have put
at the head of this chapter ["L'homme est périssable. Il se peut; mais périssons en
résistant, et, si le néant nous est reservé, ne faisons pas que ce soit une justice."]—
and of all the spiritual descendants of the patriarchal Rousseau, Sénancour was the
most profound and the most intense; of all the men of heart and feeling that France
has produced, not excluding Pascal, he was the most tragic. "Man is perishable.
That may be; but let us perish resisting, and if it is nothingness that awaits us, do
not let us so act that it shall be a just fate." Change this sentence from its negative
to the positive form—"And if it is nothingness that awaits us, let us so act that it
shall be an unjust fate" and you get the firmest basis of action for the man who
cannot or will not be a dogmatist.

That which is irreligious and demoniacal, that which incapacitates us for action
and leaves us without any ideal defense against our evil tendencies, is the pessimism
that Goethe puts into the mouth of Mephistopheles when he makes him say, "All
that has achieved existence deserves to be destroyed" (*denn alles was ensteht ist
wert dass es zugrunde geht*). This is the pessimism which we men call evil, and not
that other pessimism that consists in lamenting what it fears to be true and struggling against this fear—namely, that everything is doomed to annihilation in the
end. Mephistopheles asserts that everything that exists deserves to be destroyed,
annihilated, but not that everything will be destroyed or annihilated; and we assert
that everything that exists deserves to be exalted and eternalized, even though no
such fate is in store for it. The moral attitude is the reverse of this.

Yes, everything deserves to be eternalized, absolutely everything, even evil itself,
for that which we call evil would lose its evilness in being eternalized, because it
would lose its temporal nature. For the essence of evil consists in its temporal nature, in its not applying itself to any ultimate and permanent end.

And it might not be superfluous here to say something about that distinction,
more overlaid with confusion than any other, between what we are accustomed to
call optimism and pessimism, a confusion not less than that which exists with regard to the distinction between individualism and socialism. Indeed, it is scarcely
possible to form a clear idea as to what pessimism really is.

I have just this very day read in the *Nation* (July 6, 1912) an article, entitled "A
Dramatic Inferno," that deals with an English translation of the works of Strind-
berg, and it opens with the following judicious observations: "If there were in the
world a sincere and total pessimism, it would of necessity be silent. The despair
which finds a voice is a social mood, it is the cry of misery which brother utters to
brother when both are stumbling through a valley of shadows which is peopled with
—comrades. In its anguish it bears witness to something that is good in life, for it
presupposes sympathy. . . . The real gloom, the sincere despair, is dumb and
blind; it writes no books, and feels no impulse to burden an intolerable universe
with a monument more lasting than brass." Doubtless there is something of
sophistry in this criticism, for the man who is really in pain weeps and even cries
aloud, even if he is alone and there is nobody to hear him, simply as a means of al-
leviating his pain, although this perhaps may be a result of social habits. But does
not the lion, alone in the desert, roar if he has an aching tooth? But apart from
this, it cannot be denied that there is a substance of truth underlying these remarks.
The pessimism that protests and defends itself cannot be truly said to be pessimism.
And, in truth, still less is it pessimism to hold that nothing ought to perish although all things may be doomed to annihilation, while on the other hand it is
pessimism to affirm that all things ought to be annihilated even though nothing may
perish.

Pessimism, moreover, may possess different values. There is a eudemonistic or economic pessimism, that which denies happiness; there is an ethical pessimism, that which denies the triumph of moral good; and there is a religious pessimism, that which despairs of the human finality of the Universe, of the eternal salvation of the individual soul.

All men deserve to be saved, but, as I have said in the previous chapter, he above all deserves immortality who desires it passionately and even in the face of reason. An English writer, H. G. Wells, who has taken upon himself the rôle of the prophet (a thing not uncommon in his country), tells us in *Anticipations* that "active and capable men of all forms of religious profession tend in practice to disregard the question of immortality altogether." And this is because the religious professions of these active and capable men to whom Wells refers are usually simply a lie, and their lives are a lie, too, if they seek to base them upon religion. But it may be that at bottom there is not so much truth in what Wells asserts as he and others imagine. These active and capable men live in the midst of society imbued with Christian principles, surrounded by institutions and social feelings that are the product of Christianity, and faith in the immortality of the soul exists deep down in their own souls like a subterranean river, neither seen nor heard, but watering the roots of their deeds and their motives.

But to turn back, I repeat that if the attainment of eternal happiness could be bound up with any particular belief, it would be with the belief in the possibility of its realization. And yet, strictly speaking, not even with this. The reasonable man says in his head, "There is no other life after this," but only the wicked says it in his heart. But since the wicked man is possibly only a man who has been driven to despair, will a human God condemn him because of his despair? His despair alone is misfortune enough.

If it is nothingness that awaits us, let us make an injustice of it; let us fight against destiny, even though without hope of victory; let us fight against it quixotically.

(J. E. Crawford Flitch, tr.)

INVICTUS

WILLIAM ERNEST HENLEY

Out of the night that covers me,
 Black as the Pit from pole to pole,
I thank whatever gods may be
 For my unconquerable soul.

In the fell clutch of circumstance
 I have not winced nor cried aloud.
Under the bludgeonings of chance
 My head is bloody, but unbowed.

Beyond this place of wrath and tears
 Looms but the Horror of the shade,
And yet the menace of the years
 Finds, and shall find me, unafraid.

It matters not how strait the gate,
How charged with punishments the scroll,
I am the master of my fate:
I am the captain of my soul.

"MY HEART REBELS AGAINST MY GENERATION" *
(Ode II)

GEORGE SANTAYANA

My heart rebels against my generation
That talks of freedom and is slave to riches,
And, toiling 'neath each day's ignoble burden,
Boasts of the morrow.

No space for noonday rest or midnight watches,
No purest joy of breathing under heaven!
Wretched themselves, they heap, to make them happy,
Many possessions.

But thou, O silent Mother, wise, immortal,
To whom our toil is laughter,—take, divine one,
This vanity away, and to thy lover
Give what is needful:—

A staunch heart, nobly calm, averse to evil,
The windy sky for breath, the sea, the mountain,
A well-born, gentle friend, his spirit's brother,
Ever beside him.

What would you gain, ye seekers, with your striving,
Or what vast Babel raise you on your shoulders?
You multiply distresses, and your children
Surely will curse you.

O leave them rather friendlier gods, and fairer
Orchards and temples, and a freer bosom!
What better comfort have we, or what other
Profit in living,

Than to feed, sobered by the truth of Nature,
Awhile upon her bounty and her beauty,
And hand her torch of gladness to the ages
Following after?

She hath not made us, like her other children,
Merely for peopling of her spacious kingdoms,
Beasts of the wild, or insects of the summer,
Breeding and dying,

* Reprinted from *Poems* by George Santayana; copyright 1923 by Charles Scribner's Sons; used by permission of the publishers.

But also that we might, half knowing, worship
The deathless beauty of her guiding vision,
And learn to love, in all things mortal, only
What is eternal.

FROM THE DIVINITY THAT DOTH HEDGE A KING

In *Marius the Epicurean*

WALTER PATER

The rays of the early November sunset slanted full upon the audience, and made it necessary for the officers of the Court to draw the purple curtains over the windows, adding to the solemnity of the scene.   In the depth of those warm shadows, surrounded by her ladies, the empress Faustina was seated to listen.   The beautiful Greek statue of Victory, which since the days of Augustus had presided over the assemblies of the Senate, had been brought into the hall, and placed near the chair of the emperor; who, after rising to perform a brief sacrificial service in its honor, bowing reverently to the assembled fathers left and right, took his seat and began to speak.

There was a certain melancholy grandeur in the very simplicity or triteness of the theme: as it were the very quintessence of all the old Roman epitaphs, of all that was monumental in that city of tombs, layer upon layer of dead things and people. As if in the very fervor of disillusion, he seemed to be composing,—ὥσπερ ἐπιγραφὰς χρόνων καὶ ὅλων ἐθνῶν—the sepulchral titles of ages and whole peoples; nay! the very epitaph of the living Rome itself.   The grandeur of the ruins of Rome,— heroism in ruin: it was under the influence of an imaginative anticipation of this, that he appeared to be speaking.   And though the impression of the actual greatness of Rome on that day was but enhanced by the strain of contempt, falling with an accent of pathetic conviction from the emperor himself, and gaining from his pontifical pretensions the authority of a religious intimation, yet the curious interest of the discourse lay in this, that Marius, for one, as he listened, seemed to foresee a grass-grown Forum, the broken ways of the Capitol, and the Palatine hill itself in humble occupation.   That impression connected itself with what he had already noted of an actual change even then coming over Italian scenery.   Throughout, he could trace something of a humor into which Stoicism at all times tends to fall, the tendency to cry, *Abase yourselves!*   There was here the almost inhuman impassibility of one who had thought too closely on the paradoxical aspect of the love of posthumous fame.   With the ascetic pride which lurks under all Platonism, resultant from its opposition of the seen to the unseen, as falsehood to truth—the imperial Stoic, like his true descendant, the hermit of the middle age, was ready, in no friendly humor, to mock, there in its narrow bed, the corpse which had made so much of itself in life.   Marius could but contrast all that with his own Cyrenaic eagerness, just then, to taste and see and touch; reflecting on the opposite issues deducible from the same text.   "The world, within me and without, flows away like a river," he had said; "therefore let me make the most of what is here and now."— "The world and the thinker upon it, are consumed like a flame," said Aurelius, "therefore will I turn away my eyes from vanity: renounce: withdraw myself alike from all affections."   He seemed tacitly to claim as a sort of personal dignity, that he was very familiarly versed in this view of things, and could discern a death's-head everywhere.   Now and again Marius was reminded of the saying that "with the

Stoics all people are the vulgar save themselves;" and at times the orator seemed to have forgotten his audience, and to be speaking only to himself.

"Art thou in love with men's praises, get thee into the very soul of them, and see!—see what judges they be, even in those matters which concern themselves. Wouldst thou have their praise after death, bethink thee, that they who shall come hereafter, and with whom thou wouldst survive by thy great name, will be but as these, whom here thou hast found so hard to live with. For of a truth, the soul of him who is aflutter upon renown after death, presents not this aright to itself, that of all whose memory he would have each one will likewise very quickly depart, until memory herself be put out, as she journeys on by means of such as are themselves on the wing but for a while, and are extinguished in their turn.—Making so much of those thou wilt never see! It is as if thou wouldst have had those who were before thee discourse fair things concerning thee.

"To him, indeed, whose wit hath been whetted by true doctrine, that well-worn sentence of Homer sufficeth, to guard him against regret and fear.—

'Like the race of leaves

The race of man is:—

The wind in autumn strows
The earth with old leaves: then the spring the woods with new endows.'

Leaves! little leaves!—thy children, thy flatterers, thine enemies! Leaves in the wind, those who would devote thee to darkness, who scorn or miscall thee here, even as they also whose great fame shall outlast them. For all these, and the like of them, are born indeed in the spring season— ἔαρος ἐπιγίγνεται ὥρη: and soon a wind hath scattered them, and thereafter the wood peopleth itself again with another generation of leaves. And what is common to all of them is but the littleness of their lives: and yet wouldst thou love and hate, as if these things should continue for ever. In a little while thine eyes also will be closed, and he on whom thou perchance hast leaned thyself be himself a burden upon another.

"Bethink thee often of the swiftness with which the things that are, or are even now coming to be, are swept past thee: that the very substance of them is but the perpetual motion of water: that there is almost nothing which continueth: of that bottomless depth of time, so close at thy side. Folly! to be lifted up, or sorrowful, or anxious, by reason of things like these! Think of infinite matter, and thy portion—how tiny a particle, of it! of infinite time, and thine own brief point there; of destiny, and the joy thou art in it; and yield thyself readily to the wheel of Clotho, to spin of thee what web she will.

"As one casting a ball from his hand, the nature of things hath had its aim with every man, not as to the ending only, but the first beginning of his course, and passage thither. And hath the ball any profit of its rising, or loss as it descendeth again, or in its fall? or the bubble, as it groweth or breaketh on the air? or the flame of the lamp, from the beginning to the end of its brief story?

"All but at this present that future is, in which nature, who disposeth all things in order, will transform whatsoever thou now seest, fashioning from its substance somewhat else, and therefrom somewhat else in its turn, lest the world grow old. We are such stuff as dreams are made of—disturbing dreams. Awake, then! and see thy dream as it is, in comparison with that erewhile it seemed to thee.

"And for me, especially, it were well to mind those many mutations of empire in time past; therein peeping also upon the future, which must needs be of like species with what hath been, continuing ever within the rhythm and number of things which really are; so that in forty years one may note of man and of his ways little less than in a thousand. Ah! from this higher place, look we down upon the shipwrecks and the calm! Consider, for example, how the world went, under the emperor Vespasian. They are married and given in marriage, they breed children; love hath its way with them; they heap up riches for others or for themselves; they are murmuring at things as then they are; they are seeking for great place; crafty, flattering, suspicious, waiting upon the death of others:—festivals, business, war, sickness, dissolution: and now their whole life is no longer anywhere at all. Pass on to the reign of Trajan: all things continue the same: and that life also is no longer anywhere at all. Ah! but look again, and consider, one after another, as it were the sepulchral inscriptions of all peoples and times, according to one pattern.— What multitudes, after their utmost striving—a little afterwards! were dissolved again into their dust.

"Think again of life as it was far off in the ancient world; as it must be when we shall be gone; as it is now among the wild heathen. How many have never heard your names and mine, or will soon forget them! How soon may those who shout my name today begin to revile it, because glory, and the memory of men, and all things beside, are but vanity—a sandheap under the senseless wind, the barking of dogs, the quarrelling of children, weeping incontinently upon their laughter.

"This hasteth to be; that other to have been: of that which now cometh to be, even now somewhat hath been extinguished. And wilt thou make thy treasure of any one of these things? It were as if one set his love upon the swallow, as it passeth out of sight through the air!

"Bethink thee often, in all contentions public and private, of those whom men have remembered by reason of their anger and vehement spirit—those famous rages, and the occasions of them—the great fortunes, and misfortunes, of men's strife of old. What are they all now, and the dust of their battles? Dust and ashes indeed; a fable, a mythus, or not so much as that. Yes! keep those before thine eyes who took this or that, the like of which happeneth to thee, so hardly; were so querulous, so agitated. And where again are they? Wouldst thou have it not otherwise with thee?

"Consider how quickly all things vanish away—their bodily structure into the general substance; the very memory of them into that great gulf and abysm of past thoughts. Ah! 'tis on a tiny space of earth thou art creeping through life—a pigmy soul carrying a dead body to its grave.

"Let death put thee upon the consideration both of thy body and thy soul: what an atom of all matter hath been distributed to thee; what a little particle of the universal mind. Turn thy body about, and consider what thing it is, and that which old age, and lust, and the languor of disease can make of it. Or come to its substantial and causal qualities, its very type: contemplate that in itself, apart from the accidents of matter, and then measure also the span of time for which the nature of things, at the longest, will maintain that special type. Nay! in the very principles and first constituents of things corruption hath its part—so much dust, humor, stench, and scraps of bone! Consider that thy marbles are but the earth's callosities, thy gold and silver its *faeces;* this silken robe but a worm's bedding, and thy purple an unclean fish. Ah! and thy life's breath is not otherwise, as it passeth out of matters like these, into the like of them again.

"For the one soul in things, taking matter like wax in the hands, molds and re-molds—how hastily!—beast, and plant, and the babe, in turn: and that which dieth hath not slipped out of the order of nature, but, remaining therein, hath also its changes there, disparting into those elements of which nature herself, and thou too, art compacted. She changes without murmuring. The oaken chest falls to pieces with no more complaining than when the carpenter fitted it together. If one told thee certainly that on the morrow thou shouldst die, or at the furthest on the day after, it would be no great matter to thee to die on the day after tomorrow rather than tomorrow. Strive to think it a thing no greater that thou wilt die—not tomorrow, but a year, or two years, or ten years from today.

"I find that all things are now as they were in the days of our buried ancestors—all things sordid in their elements, trite by long usage, and yet ephemeral. How ridiculous, then, how like a countryman in town, is he, who wonders at aught. Doth the sameness, the repetition of the public shows, weary thee? Even so doth that likeness of events in the spectacle of the world. And so must it be with thee to the end. For the wheel of the world hath ever the same motion, upward and downward, from generation to generation. When, when, shall time give place to eternity?

"If there be things which trouble thee thou canst put them away, inasmuch as they have their being but in thine own notion concerning them. Consider what death is, and how, if one does but detach from it the appearances, the notions, that hang about it, resting the eye upon it as in itself it really is, it must be thought of but as an effect of nature, and that man but a child whom an effect of nature shall affright. Nay! not function and effect of nature, only; but a thing profitable also to herself.

"To cease from action—the ending of thine effort to think and do: there is no evil in that. Turn thy thought to the ages of man's life, boyhood, youth, maturity, old age: the change in every one of these also is a dying, but evil nowhere. Thou climbedst into the ship, thou hast made thy voyage and touched the shore: go forth now! Be it into some other life: the divine breath is everywhere, even there. Be it into forgetfulness for ever; at least thou wilt rest from the beating of sensible images upon thee, from the passions which pluck thee this way and that like an unfeeling toy, from those long marches of the intellect, from thy toilsome ministry to the flesh.

"Art thou yet more than dust and ashes and bare bone—a name only, or not so much as that, which, also, is but whispering and a resonance, kept alive from mouth to mouth of dying objects who have hardly known themselves; how much less thee, dead so long ago!

"When thou lookest upon a wise man, a lawyer, a captain of war, think upon another gone. When thou seest thine own face in the glass, call up there before thee one of thine ancestors—one of those old Caesars. Lo! everywhere, thy double before thee! Thereon, let the thought occur to thee: And where are they? anywhere at all, for ever? And thou, thyself—how long? Art thou blind to that thou art—thy matter, how temporal; and thy function, the nature of thy business? Yet tarry, at least, till thou hast assimilated even these things to thine own proper essence, as a quick fire turneth into heat and light whatsoever be cast upon it.

"As words once in use are antiquated to us, so is it with the names that were once on all men's lips: Camillus, Volesus, Leonnatus: then, in a little while, Scipio and Cato, and then Augustus, and then Hadrian, and then Antoninus Pius. How many great physicians who lifted wise brows at other men's sickbeds have sickened and died! Those wise Chaldeans, who foretold, as a great matter, another man's last hour, have themselves been taken by surprise. Ay! and all those others, in their pleasant places: those who doted on a Capreae like Tiberius, on their gardens, on the baths: Pythagoras and Socrates, who reasoned so closely upon immortality: Alexander, who used the lives of others as though his own should last for ever—he and his mule-driver alike now!—one upon another. Well-nigh the whole court of Antoninus is extinct. Panthea and Pergamus sit no longer beside the sepulchre of their lord. The watchers over Hadrian's dust have slipped from his sepulchre.—It were jesting to stay longer. Did they sit there still, would the dead feel it? or feeling it, be glad? or glad, hold those watchers for ever? The time must come when they too shall be aged men and aged women, and decease, and fail from their places; and what shift were there then for imperial service? This too is but the breath of the tomb, and a skinful of dead men's blood.

"Think again of those inscriptions, which belong not to one soul only, but to whole families: Ἔσχατος τοῦ ἰδίου γένους: *He was the last of his race.* Nay! of the burial of whole cities: Helice, Pompeii: of others, whose very burial place is unknown.

"Thou hast been a citizen in this wide city. Count not for how long, nor re-pine; since that which sends thee hence is no unrighteous judge, no tyrant, but Nature, who brought thee hither; as when a player leaves the stage at the bidding of the conductor who hired him. Sayest thou, 'I have not played five acts'? True! but in human life, three acts only make sometimes an entire play. That is the composer's business, not thine. Withdraw thyself with a good will; for that too hath, perchance, a good will which dismisseth thee from thy part."

The discourse ended almost in darkness, the evening having set in somewhat suddenly, with a heavy fall of snow. The torches, made ready to do him a useless honor, were of real service now, as the emperor was solemnly conducted home; one man rapidly catching light from another—a long stream of moving lights across the white Forum, up the great stairs, to the palace.

CHAPTER 4

IN SEARCH OF GOD

Who lifteth in the eastern sky the dark, gold moon?
Who painteth green and purple on the blackbird's throat?
—William Alexander Percy, "A Canticle."

"Mine eyes have seen the glory of the coming of the Lord." The god of the vintage and the fateful lightnings is a great god and greatly to be feared. He is also said to be a god that man has created in his own image, purely anthropomorphic. But in considering deity man deals with two things, one perhaps problematic, the other intensely real: The first is God; the second the idea of God. To the believer in God the terrible swift sword of justice and righteousness may be the very source of all human justice and equity. He will have implemented his social concern (as well as his hope for immortality) with a conviction of the reality of a Being that Is and Knows. But if there is only the idea of God, that idea is still acknowledged to be a primary force in shaping human affairs. Whatever its form, its importance to humanity is so manifest as almost to cancel need for comment. Religion, however founded, more effectively unites and divides mankind than politics. The sects of religion draw sharper lines than the boundaries of state and language. International differences themselves take on the color of religion, and the medieval cry, "God for Harry! England and St. George!" has a modern counterpart in the perorations of our leaders.

The yearning of man for the infinite is perhaps the deepest instinct in his nature, as Mary Coleridge suggests in the poem beginning the selections in this chapter. Though philosophy cannot explore the unknown, it can and must examine this inner prompting, this urgency in man's nature towards something higher than himself—which is for him a god.

Nowhere in all literature is the grandeur of the idea of God more richly imaged than in the Psalms, which, with a vision almost foreseeing our modern discoveries about the extent of the universe, chant a God exalted above the heavens. Yet this God is anthropomorphic, not just an immanent spirit—or should we say that the great poet spoke as a poet in human symbols that he does not mean us to take literally? That he appears to have been literally interpreted, or that poets and prophets find it necessary to use human symbolism in interpreting their feeling, a great part of our best religious literature, represented essentially by the selections from

133

Addison and Tennyson, attests.   The God of David marks the gradual emergence of religion from the worship of many gods.

These opening selections illustrate the orthodox concept of an omnipotent, omniscient, good, and just God; but even the Psalms make allowance for a God whose dark ways are such as to raise the question about evil in the universe, and thus we have a conflict in values.   This conflict is realized by Boethius, who accepts God as the efficient cause and architect of the universe but asks in deep puzzlement why God, with his manifest care for order in the world of Nature, has no discernible care for order in mankind.   The traditional answer, of course, is that evil may be only appearance, as Francis Thompson believes, "Shade of His hand, outstretched caressingly."   What this means in human experience is graphically imagined by James Stephens. Is it possible that God has "no choice in this sad maze" or worse—no care?

Thus we are introduced to deism, the watch-maker concept of God and the universe, a view representing God as creating the machine of the universe, setting it going, and then letting it take care of itself.   It is but natural that bitterness and resentment should be roused by this idea of an absentee God, and this resentment breaks out in eloquent hate in the selection from Swinburne.

It is also natural that man, feeling thus deserted, little, and lonely in a world he never made, should draw the tragic inference that there is no God. Lucian even takes up the weapon of laughter against belief.   His dialogue, besides mocking at faith (the faith of his time hardly deserved reverence), also illustrates the workings of Greek theology, a system at once polytheistic and anthropomorphic.   Faith and anthropomorphism both are reduced to an absurdity by Rupert Brooke in "Heaven."   A good example of modern (Victorian) youth assailed by doubt leading to atheism is furnished us by Somerset Maugham in his portrait of Philip Carey.

The doubter, waiting for a special sign from God, finds it hard to believe in him.   But, William Alexander Percy asks, "Who lifteth in the eastern sky the dark, gold moon?"   The gods are dead, but beauty will continue forever to fashion in Nature the forms it loves.   Man, it appears, cannot live godless. In a mysterious beauty, as Percy conceives it, atheists and naturalists commonly tend to rebuild God intellectually.

Contrasting with naturalism and yet akin is pantheism, which sees God as creator and thing itself, manifested in everything, and often idealized: "not in vain I had been taught to reverence a Power That is the visible quality and shape And image of right reason" (Wordsworth, "Imagination and Taste").   But pantheism also provides for a God-universe of good and evil, as in Emerson's "Brahma."

William Pepperell Montague finds that we *are* confronted with God, or something very like him, in the universe.   What is the nature of this God? Is he finite or infinite, and what is the answer to the problem of evil pre-

sented earlier in this chapter? Vaughan returns us to the personal God of
Christianity and suggests once more the idealized attributes; but he, like
Hopkins, is baffled about God's nature, of which he sees everywhere the
broken hieroglyphics.

It is one thing to believe in a personal God. It is another to attempt to
justify that belief by reason. But may not God be a blind energy? No,
says Robinson Jeffers, for we ourselves are conscious. "Nobody that I
know of ever poured grain from an empty sack." God is conscious and
personal. So sure is Pascal of his faith in this personal God that he pro-
poses his famed wager on the thesis "God is or He is not." Reason, and all
authorities agree on this point, cannot serve us in deciding this question;
but, says Pascal, what have we to lose in siding with faith? William James
cites with approval the difficult but noble argument of Clifford, that, "It
is wrong always, everywhere, and for everyone to believe anything upon
insufficient evidence"; but he goes on to reveal strong sympathies with Pascal's position.

What, then, is God? Can creeds or reasons explain him? The mystery
of his nature, like the mystery of immortality, must ever remain unexplained.
We cannot analyze God or measure his being. But, C. Day Lewis asserts, the
nightingale knows. Instinct is knowledge.

SELF-QUESTION

MARY E. COLERIDGE

Is this wide world not large enough to fill thee,
     Nor nature, nor that deep man's Nature, Art?
Are they too thin, too weak and poor to still thee,
     Thou little heart?

Dust art thou, and to dust again returnest,
     A spark of fire within a beating clod.
Should that be infinite for which thou burnest,
     Must it be God?

SELF-KNOWLEDGE

—E coelo descendit γνῶθι σεαυτόν [From the sky comes down the counsel,
"Know thyself"].—Juvenal, xi. 27.

SAMUEL TAYLOR COLERIDGE

Γνῶθι σεαυτόν!—and is this the prime
And heaven-sprung adage of the olden time!—
Say, canst thou make thyself?—Learn first that trade;—
Haply thou mayst know what thyself had made.
What hast thou, Man, that thou dar'st call thine own?—
What is there in thee, Man, that can be known?—

Dark fluxion, all unfixable by thought,
A phantom dim of past and future wrought,
Vain sister of the worm,—life, death, soul, clod—
Ignore thyself, and strive to know thy God!

THE BOOK OF PSALMS, VIII, XIX, XXIII, XCI

PSALM VIII

O Lord our Lord, how excellent is thy name in all the earth! who hast set thy glory above the heavens.

Out of the mouth of babes and sucklings hast thou ordained strength because of thine enemies; that thou mightest still the enemy and the avenger.

When I consider thy heavens, the work of thy fingers; the moon and the stars, which thou hast ordained;

What is man, that thou art mindful of him? and the son of man, that thou visitest him?

For thou hast made him a little lower than the angels, and hast crowned him with glory and honor.

Thou madest him to have dominion over the works of thy hands; thou hast put all things under his feet:

All sheep and oxen, yea, and the beasts of the field;

The fowl of the air, and the fish of the sea, and whatsoever passeth through the paths of the seas.

O Lord our Lord, how excellent is thy name in all the earth!

PSALM XIX

The heavens declare the glory of God; and the firmament sheweth his handi-work.

Day unto day uttereth speech, and night unto night sheweth knowledge.

There is no speech nor language, where their voice is not heard.

Their line is gone out through all the earth, and their words to the end of the world. In them hath he set a tabernacle for the sun,

Which is as a bridegroom coming out of his chamber, and rejoiceth as a strong man to run a race.

His going forth is from the end of the heaven, and his circuit unto the ends of it: and there is nothing hid from the heat thereof.

The law of the Lord is perfect, converting the soul: the testimony of the Lord is sure, making wise the simple.

The statutes of the Lord are right, rejoicing the heart: the commandment of the Lord is pure, enlightening the eyes.

The fear of the Lord is clean, enduring for ever: the judgments of the Lord are true and righteous altogether.

More to be desired are they than gold, yea, than much fine gold: sweeter also than honey and the honeycomb.

Moreover, by them is thy servant warned; and in keeping of them there is great reward.

Who can understand his errors? cleanse thou me from secret faults.

Keep back thy servant also from presumptuous sins; let them not have dominion over me: then shall I be upright, and I shall be innocent from the great transgression.

Let the words of my mouth, and the meditation of my heart, be acceptable in thy sight, O Lord, my strength, and my redeemer.

PSALM XXIII

The Lord is my shepherd; I shall not want.

He maketh me to lie down in green pastures: he leadeth me beside the still waters.

He restoreth my soul: he leadeth me in the paths of righteousness for his name's sake.

Yea, though I walk through the valley of the shadow of death, I will fear no evil: for thou art with me; thy rod and thy staff they comfort me.

Thou preparest a table before me in the presence of mine enemies: thou anointest my head with oil; my cup runneth over.

Surely goodness and mercy shall follow me all the days of my life; and I will dwell in the house of the Lord for ever.

PSALM XCI

He that dwelleth in the secret place of the Most High shall abide under the shadow of the Almighty.

I will say of the Lord, He is my refuge and my fortress: my God; in him will I trust.

Surely he shall deliver thee from the snare of the fowler, and from the noisome pestilence.

He shall cover thee with his feathers, and under his wings shalt thou trust: his truth shall be thy shield and buckler.

Thou shalt not be afraid for the terror by night; nor for the arrow that flieth by day;

Nor for the pestilence that walketh in darkness; nor for the destruction that wasteth at noon-day.

A thousand shall fall at thy side, and ten thousand at thy right hand; but it shall not come nigh thee.

Only with thine eyes shalt thou behold and see the reward of the wicked.

Because thou hast made the Lord, which is my refuge, even the Most High, thy habitation;

There shall no evil befall thee, neither shall any plague come nigh thy dwelling.

For he shall give his angels charge over thee, to keep thee in all thy ways.

They shall bear thee up in their hands, lest thou dash thy foot against a stone.

Thou shalt tread upon the lion and adder: the young lion and the dragon shalt thou trample under feet.

Because he hath set his love upon me, therefore will I deliver him: I will set him on high, because he hath known my name.

He shall call upon me, and I will answer him: I will be with him in troubles; I will deliver him, and honor him.

With long life will I satisfy him, and shew him my salvation.

THE BOOK OF THE PROPHET ISAIAH, Chapters 40, 55

CHAPTER 40

Comfort ye, comfort ye my people, saith your God. Speak ye comfortably to Jerusalem, and cry unto her, that her warfare is accomplished, that her iniquity is pardoned: for she hath received of the Lord's hand double for all her sins.

The voice of him that crieth in the wilderness, Prepare ye the way of the Lord, make straight in the desert a highway for our God. Every valley shall be exalted, and every mountain and hill shall be made low: and the crooked shall be made straight, and the rough places plain. And the glory of the Lord shall be revealed, and all flesh shall see it together: for the mouth of the Lord hath spoken it.

The voice said, Cry. And he said, What shall I cry? All flesh is grass, and all the goodliness thereof is as the flower of the field. The grass withereth, the flower fadeth: Because the spirit of the Lord bloweth upon it: surely the people is grass. The grass withereth, the flower fadeth: but the word of our God shall stand for ever.

O Zion, that bringest good tidings, get thee up into the high mountain. O Jerusalem, that bringest good tidings, lift up thy voice with strength; lift it up, be not afraid; say unto the cities of Judah, Behold your God! Behold the Lord God will come with strong hand, and his arm shall rule for him: behold, his reward is with him, and his work before him. He shall feed his flock like a shepherd: he shall gather the lambs with his arm, and carry them in his bosom, and shall gently lead those that are with young.

Who hath measured the waters in the hollow of his hand, and meted out heaven with the span, and comprehended the dust of the earth in a measure, and weighed the mountains in scales, and the hills in a balance? Who hath directed the Spirit of the Lord, or being his counsellor hath taught him? With whom took he counsel, and who instructed him, and taught him in the path of judgment, and taught him knowledge, and shewed to him the way of understanding?

Behold, the nations are as a drop of a bucket, and are counted as the small dust of the balance: behold, he taketh up the isles as a very little thing. And Lebanon is not sufficient to burn, nor the beasts thereof sufficient for a burnt-offering. All nations before him are as nothing; and they are counted to him less than nothing, and vanity.

To whom then will ye liken God? or what likeness will ye compare unto him?

The workman melteth a graven image, and the goldsmith spreadeth it over with gold, and casteth silver chains. He that is so impoverished that he hath no oblation chooseth a tree that will not rot; he seeketh unto him a cunning workman to prepare a graven image that shall not be moved.

Have ye not known? have ye not heard? hath it not been told you from the beginning? have ye not understood from the foundations of the earth?

It is he that sitteth upon the circle of the earth, and the inhabitants thereof are as grasshoppers; that stretcheth out the heavens as a curtain, and spreadeth them out as a tent to dwell in; that bringeth the princes to nothing; he maketh the judges of the earth as vanity.

Yea, they shall not be planted: yea, they shall not be sown: yea, their stock shall not take root in the earth: and he shall also blow upon them, and they shall wither, and the whirlwind shall take them away as stubble.

To whom then will ye liken me, or shall I be equal? saith the Holy One.

Lift up your eyes on high, and behold who hath created these things, that bringeth out their host by number: he calleth them all by names, by the greatness of his might, for that he is strong in power; not one faileth.

Why sayest thou, O Jacob, and speakest, O Israel, My way is hid from the Lord, and my judgment is passed over from my God?

Hast thou not known, hast thou not heard, that the everlasting God, the Lord, the Creator of the ends of the earth, fainteth not, neither is weary? There is no searching of his understanding. He giveth power to the faint; and to them that have no might he increaseth strength. Even the youths shall faint and be weary, and the young men shall utterly fall. But they that wait upon the Lord shall renew their strength; they shall mount up with wings as eagles; they shall run, and not be weary; and they shall walk, and not faint.

CHAPTER 55

Ho, every one that thirsteth, come ye to the waters, and he that hath no money; come ye, buy, and eat; yea, come, buy wine and milk without money and without price.

Wherefore do ye spend money for that which is not bread? and your labour for that which satisfieth not? hearken diligently unto me, and eat ye that which is good, and let your soul delight itself in fatness.

Incline your ear, and come unto me; hear, and your soul shall live; and I will make an everlasting covenant with you, even the sure mercies of David. Behold, I have given him for a witness to the people, a leader and commander to the people. Behold, thou shalt call a nation that thou knowest not, and nations that knew not thee shall run unto thee, because of the Lord thy God, and for the Holy One of Israel; for he hath glorified thee.

Seek ye the Lord while he may be found, call ye upon him while he is near. Let the wicked forsake his way, and the unrighteous man his thoughts: and let him return unto the Lord, and he will have mercy upon him; and to our God, for he will abundantly pardon.

For my thoughts are not your thoughts, neither are your ways my ways, saith the Lord. For as the heavens are higher than the earth, so are my ways higher than your ways, and my thoughts than your thoughts.

For as the rain cometh down, and the snow from heaven, and returneth not thither, but watereth the earth, and maketh it bring forth and bud, that it may give seed to the sower, and bread to the eater: so shall my word be that goeth forth out of my mouth: it shall not return unto me void, but it shall accomplish that which I please, and it shall prosper in the thing whereto I sent it.

For ye shall go out with joy, and be led forth with peace: the mountains and the hills shall break forth before you into singing, and all the trees of the field shall clap their hands. Instead of the thorn shall come up the fir-tree, and instead of the brier shall come up the myrtle tree: and it shall be to the Lord for a name, for an everlasting sign that shall not be cut off.

HYMN

JOSEPH ADDISON

The spacious firmament on high,
With all the blue ethereal sky,
And spangled heavens, a shining frame,
Their great Original proclaim.

The unwearied Sun from day to day
Does his Creator's power display;
And publishes to every land
The work of an Almighty hand.

Soon as the evening shades prevail,
The Moon takes up the wondrous tale;
And nightly to the listening Earth
Repeats the story of her birth:
Whilst all the stars that round her burn,
And all the planets in their turn,
Confirm the tidings as they roll,
And spread the truth from pole to pole.

What though in solemn silence all
Move round the dark terrestrial ball;
What though nor real voice nor sound
Amidst their radiant orbs be found?
In Reason's ear they all rejoice,
And utter forth a glorious voice;
For ever singing as they shine,
"The Hand that made us is divine."

FROM IN MEMORIAM

ALFRED LORD TENNYSON

Strong Son of God, immortal Love,
    Whom we, that have not seen thy face,
    By faith, and faith alone, embrace,
Believing where we cannot prove.

Thine are these orbs of light and shade;
    Thou madest Life in man and brute;
    Thou madest Death; and lo, thy foot
Is on the skull which thou hast made.

Thou wilt not leave us in the dust:
    Thou madest man, he knows not why;
    He thinks he was not made to die;
And thou hast made him: thou art just.

Thou seemest human and divine,
    The highest, holiest manhood, thou:
    Our wills are ours, we know not how;
Our wills are ours, to make them thine.

Our little systems have their day;
    They have their day and cease to be:
    They are but broken lights of thee,
And thou, O Lord, art more than they.

We have but faith: we cannot know:
For knowledge is of things we see;
And yet we trust it comes from thee,
A beam in darkness: let it grow.

Let knowledge grow from more to more,
But more of reverence in us dwell;
That mind and soul, according well,
May make one music as before,

But vaster. We are fools and slight;
We mock thee when we do not fear:
But help thy foolish ones to bear;
Help thy vain worlds to bear thy light.

"O THOU GREAT BUILDER OF THIS STARRY FRAME"

In *Consolation of Philosophy, I, v*

ANICIUS MANLIUS SEVERINUS BOETHIUS

O thou great builder of this starry frame
Who fixt in thy eternal throne dost tame
The rapid Spheres, and lest they jar
Hast given a law to every star!
Thou art the Cause that now the Moon
With full orb dulls the stars, and soon
Again grows dark, her light being done,
The nearer still she's to the Sun.
Thou in the early hours of night
Mak'st the cool Evening-star shine bright,
And at Sun-rising ('cause the least)
Look pale and sleepy in the East.
Thou, when the leaves in Winter stray,
Appoint'st the Sun a shorter way,
And in the pleasant Summer-light
With nimble hours dost wing the night.
Thy hand the various year quite through
Discreetly tempers, that what now
The North-wind tears from every tree
In Spring again restored we see.
Then what the winter-stars between
The furrows in mere seed have seen
The Dog-star since (grown up and born)
Hath burnt in stately, full-eared Corn.
  Thus by Creation's law controlled
All things their proper stations hold
Observing (as thou didst intend)
Why they were made, and for what end.
Only human actions thou
Hast no Care of, but to the flow

And Ebb of Fortune leav'st them all.
Hence the Innocent endures that thrall
Due to the wicked, whilst alone
They sit possessors of his throne,
The Just are killed, and Virtue lies
Buried in obscurities,
And (which of all things is most sad)
The good man suffers by the bad.
No perjuries, nor damned pretense
Colored with holy, lying sense
Can them annoy, but when they mind
To try their force, which most men find,
They from the highest sway of things
Can pull down great, and pious Kings.
 O then at length, thus loosely hurled
Look on this miserable world
Who e'er thou art, that from above
Dost in such order all things move!
And let not man (of divine art
Not the least, nor vilest part)
By Casual evils thus bandied, be
The sport of fate's obliquity.
But with that faith thou guid'st the heaven,
Settle this Earth, and make them even.

(Henry Vaughan, tr.)

THE HOUND OF HEAVEN

FRANCIS THOMPSON

I fled Him, down the nights and down the days;
 I fled Him, down the arches of the years;
I fled Him, down the labyrinthine ways
 Of my own mind; and in the mist of tears
I hid from Him, and under running laughter.
  Up vistaed hopes I sped;
  And shot, precipitated,
Adown Titanic glooms of chasmèd fears,
 From those strong Feet that followed, followed after.
  But with unhurrying chase,
  And unperturbèd pace,
 Deliberate speed, majestic instancy,
  They beat—and a Voice beat
  More instant than the Feet—
"All things betray thee, who betrayest Me!"

 I pleaded, outlaw-wise,
By many a hearted casement, curtained red,
 Trellised with intertwining charities;
(For, though I knew His love Who followèd,
  Yet was I sore adread,

Lest, having Him, I must have naught beside.)
But, if one little casement parted wide,
     The gust of His approach would clash it to:
Fear wist not to evade, as Love wist to pursue.
Across the margent of the world I fled,
     And troubled the gold gateways of the stars,
     Smiting for shelter on their clangèd bars;
          Fretted to dulcet jars
And silvern chatter the pale ports o' the moon.
I said to Dawn: Be sudden—to Eve: Be soon;
     With thy young skiey blossoms heap me over
          From this tremendous Lover—
Float thy vague veil about me, lest He see!
     I tempted all His servitors, but to find
My own betrayal in their constancy,
In faith to Him their fickleness to me,
     Their traitorous trueness, and their loyal deceit.
To all swift things for swiftness did I sue;
     Clung to the whistling mane of every wind.
     But whether they swept, smoothly fleet,
     The long savannahs of the blue;
          Or whether, Thunder-driven,
          They clanged his chariot 'thwart a heaven,
Plashy with flying lightnings round the spurn o' their feet:—
     Fear wist not to evade as Love wist to pursue.
          Still with unhurrying chase,
          And unperturbèd pace,
     Deliberate speed, majestic instancy,
          Came on the following Feet,
          And a Voice above their beat—
"Naught shelters thee, who wilt not shelter Me."

I sought no more that after which I strayed
     In face of man or maid;
But still within the little children's eyes
     Seems something, something that replies,
They at least are for me, surely for me!
I turned me to them very wistfully;
But just as their young eyes grew sudden fair
     With dawning answers there,
Their angel plucked them from me by the hair.
"Come then, ye other children, Nature's—share
With me" (said I) "your delicate fellowship;
     Let me greet you lip to lip,
     Let me twine with you caresses,
          Wantoning
     With our Lady-Mother's vagrant tresses,
          Banqueting
     With her in her wind-walled palace,
     Underneath her azured daïs,
     Quaffing, as your taintless way is,

From a chalice
Lucent-weeping out of the dayspring."
　　So it was done:
I in their delicate fellowship was one—
Drew the bolt of Nature's secrecies.
I knew all the swift importings
　　On the wilful face of skies;
　　I knew how the clouds arise
　　Spumèd of the wild sea-snortings;
　　　　All that's born or dies
　　Rose and drooped with; made them shapers
Of mine own moods, or wailful or divine;
　　With them joyed and was bereaven.
　　I was heavy with the even,
　　When she lit her glimmering tapers
　　Round the day's dead sanctities.
　　I laughed in the morning's eyes.
I triumphed and I saddened with all weather,
　　Heaven and I wept together,
And its sweet tears were salt with mortal mine;
Against the red throb of its sunset-heart
　　I laid my own to beat,
　　And share commingling heat;
But not by that, by that, was eased my human smart.
In vain my tears were wet on Heaven's grey cheek.
For ah! we know not what each other says,
　　These things and I; in sound *I* speak—
Their sound is but their stir, they speak by silences.
Nature, poor stepdame, cannot slake my drouth;
　　Let her, if she would owe me,
Drop yon blue bosom-veil of sky, and show me
　　The breasts o' her tenderness:
Never did any milk of hers once bless
　　My thirsting mouth.
　　Nigh and nigh draws the chase,
　　With unperturbèd pace,
　Deliberate speed, majestic instancy;
　　And past those noisèd Feet
　　A voice comes yet more fleet—
"Lo! naught contents thee, who content'st not Me."

Naked I wait Thy love's uplifted stroke!
My harness piece by piece Thou hast hewn from me,
　　And smitten me to my knee;
　　I am defenseless utterly.
　　I slept, methinks, and woke,
And, slowly gazing, find me stripped in sleep.
In the rash lustihead of my young powers,
　　I shook the pillaring hours
And pulled my life upon me; grimed with smears,

I stand amid the dust o' the mounded years—
My mangled youth lies dead beneath the heap.
My days have crackled and gone up in smoke,
Have puffed and burst as sun-starts on a stream.
    Yea, faileth now even dream
The dreamer, and the lute the lutanist;
Even the linkèd fantasies, in whose blossomy twist
I swung the earth a trinket at my wrist,
Are yielding; cords of all too weak account
For earth with heavy griefs so overplussed.
    Ah! is Thy love indeed
A weed, albeit an amaranthine weed,
Suffering no flowers except its own to mount?
        Ah! must—
        Designer infinite!—
Ah! must Thou char the wood ere Thou canst limn with it?
My freshness spent its wavering shower i' the dust;
And now my heart is as a broken fount,
Wherein tear-drippings stagnate, spilt down ever
    From the dank thoughts that shiver
Upon the sighful branches of my mind.
    Such is; what is to be?
The pulp so bitter, how shall taste the rind?
I dimly guess what Time in mists confounds;
Yet ever and anon a trumpet sounds
From the hid battlements of Eternity;
Those shaken mists a space unsettle, then
Round the half-glimpsèd turrets slowly wash again.
    But not ere him who summoneth
    I first have seen, enwound
With glooming robes purpureal, cypress-crowned;
His name I know, and what his trumpet saith.
Whether man's heart or life it be which yields
    Thee harvest, must Thy harvest-fields
    Be dunged with rotten death?

    Now of that long pursuit
    Comes on at hand the bruit;
That Voice is round me like a bursting sea:
    "And is thy earth so marred,
    Shattered in shard on shard?
    Lo, all things fly thee, for thou fliest Me!
    Strange, piteous, futile thing!
Wherefore should any set thee love apart?
Seeing none but I makes much of naught" (He said),
"And human love needs human meriting:
    How hast thou merited—
Of all man's clotted clay the dingiest clot?
    Alack, thou knowest not
How little worthy of any love thou art!

Whom wilt thou find to love ignoble thee,
  Save Me, save only Me?
All which I took from thee I did but take,
  Not for thy harms,
But just that thou might'st seek it in My arms.
  All which thy child's mistake
Fancies as lost, I have stored for thee at home:
  Rise, clasp My hand, and come!"

  Halts by me that footfall:
    Is my gloom, after all,
Shade of His hand, outstretched caressingly?
  "Ah, fondest, blindest, weakest,
  I am He Whom thou seekest!
Thou dravest love from thee, who dravest Me."

THE WHISPERER

JAMES STEPHENS

The moon was round!
And, as I walked along,
There was no sound,
Save where the wind with long,
Low hushes, whispered to the ground
A snatch of song.

No thought had I
Save that the moon was fair,
And fair the sky,
And God was everywhere:
I chanted, as the wind went by,
A poet's prayer.

Then came a voice
—Why is it that you praise
And why rejoice,
O stranger to the ways
Of Providence?　God has no choice
In this sad maze!

—His law He laid
Down at the dread beginnings,
When He made
The world and set it spinning;
And His casual hand betrayed
Us into sinning.

—I fashion you;
And then, for weal or woe,
My business through
I care not how ye go,
Or struggle, win or lose, nor do
I want to know.

—Is no appeal,
For I am far from sight;
And cannot feel
The rigor of your plight;
And if ye faint just when ye kneel,
That, too, is right!

—Then do not sing,
O poet in the night!
That everything
Is beautiful and right:
What if a wind come now and fling
At thee its spite!

All in amaze
I listened to the tone
Mocking my praise:
And then I heard the moan
That all tormented nature did upraise:
From tree and stone!

And, as I went,
I heard it once again,
That harsh lament!
And fire came to my brain!
Deep anger unto me was lent
To write this strain!

FROM ATALANTA IN CALYDON

ALGERNON CHARLES SWINBURNE

    . . . one saith
The gods are gracious, praising God; and one,
When hast thou seen? or hast thou felt his breath
    Touch, nor consume thine eyelids as the sun,
Nor fill thee to the lips with fiery death?
    None hath beheld him, none
Seen above other gods and shapes of things,
Swift without feet and flying without wings,
Intolerable, not clad with death or life,
    Insatiable, not known of night or day,
The lord of love and loathing and of strife
    Who gives a star and takes a sun away;
Who shapes the soul, and makes her a barren wife
    To the earthly body and grievous growth of clay;
Who turns the large limbs to a little flame
    And binds the great sea with a little sand;
Who makes desire, and slays desire with shame;
    Who shakes the heaven as ashes in his hand;
Who, seeing the light and shadow for the same,
    Bids day waste night as fire devours a brand,

Smites without sword, and scourges without rod;
　　The supreme evil, God.
Yea, with thine hate, O God, thou hast covered us,
　　One saith, and hidden our eyes away from sight,
And made us transitory and hazardous,
　　Light things and slight;
Yet have men praised thee, saying, He hath made man thus,
　　And he doeth right.
Thou hast kissed us, and hast smitten; thou hast laid
Upon us with thy left hand life, and said,
Live: and again thou hast said, Yield up your breath,
And with thy right hand laid upon us death.
Thou hast sent us sleep, and stricken sleep with dreams,
　　Saying, Joy is not, but love of joy shall be;
Thou hast made sweet springs for all the pleasant streams,
　　In the end thou hast made them bitter with the sea.
Thou hast fed one rose with dust of many men;
　　Thou hast marred one face with fire of many tears;
Thou hast taken love, and given us sorrow again;
　　With pain thou hast filled us full to the eyes and ears.
Therefore because thou art strong, our father, and we
　　Feeble; and thou art against us, and thine hand
Constrains us in the shallows of the sea
　　And breaks us at the limits of the land;
Because thou hast bent thy lightnings as a bow,
　　And loosed the hours like arrows; and let fall
Sins and wild words and many a wingèd woe
　　And wars among us, and one end of all;
Because thou hast made the thunder, and thy feet
　　Are as a rushing water when the skies
Break, but thy face as an exceeding heat
　　And flames of fire the eyelids of thine eyes;
Because thou art over all who are over us;
　　Because thy name is life and our name death;
Because thou art cruel and men are piteous,
　　And our hands labor and thine hand scattereth;
Lo, with hearts rent and knees made tremulous,
　　Lo, with ephemeral lips and casual breath,
　　　At least we witness of thee ere we die
That these things are not otherwise, but thus;
　　That each man in his heart sigheth, and saith,
　　　That all men even as I,
All we are against thee, against thee, O God most high.

FROM ZEUS RAVES

LUCIAN

Scene . . . the Theater at Athens. The benches crowded with citizens. TIMO-
CLES *and* DAMIS *on the stage, and the Gods invisible to the audience, looking on.*

.   .   .   .

TIMOCLES: What! you blasphemous villain, you! you don't believe in the Gods and in Providence?

DAMIS: I see no proof of their existence. I wait your reasons why I should have a positive opinion about it.

TIMOCLES: I will give you no reasons, you wretch. Give me yours for your atheism.

ZEUS: Our man is doing well. He has the rudest manner and the loudest voice. Well done, Timocles! give him hard words. That is your strong point. Begin to reason and you will be as dumb as a fish.

TIMOCLES: By Athene, you shall have no reasons from me.

DAMIS: Very well, then; ask me questions and I will answer them. Don't use foul language if you can help it.

TIMOCLES: Speak, then, you accursed monster. Do you or do you not believe in Divine Providence?

DAMIS: I do not.

TIMOCLES: What? Do you mean that the Gods do not foresee future events?

DAMIS: I do not know that they do.

TIMOCLES: And there is no divine order in the universe?

DAMIS: None that I am aware of.

TIMOCLES: And the world is not governed by reason and intelligence?

DAMIS: I do not perceive that it is.

TIMOCLES: Will you bear this, good people? Will you not stone the blasphemer?

DAMIS: Why inflame the people against me, Timocles? The Gods show no displeasure. They have heard me (if hear they do) without interposing. Why should you be so fierce in their behalf?

TIMOCLES: They hear you. They hear you? They will give it to you by-and-bye.

DAMIS: They will not have much leisure to bestow on me if they are so busy as you say, Timocles, managing the universe. They have not punished you for certain perjuries that I have heard of. I will not go into particulars, but they could scarcely have a better opportunity of vindicating their existence than by bringing you to question. They are away across the ocean, perhaps, among the Ethiopians. They dine there frequently on their own invitation, do they not?

TIMOCLES: What reply can I make to such horrible irreverence?

DAMIS: You can give me the reply for which I have been so long waiting. You can tell me why you yourself believe in Providence.

TIMOCLES: I believe in it first on account of the order which is visible throughout the universal scheme of things. The sun and moon move in their alloted path; the seasons revolve; the plants spring; the animals come to the birth, and are organized with exquisite skill. Man, yet more wonderful than they, thinks and acts and makes shoes and builds houses—all evident proofs of design and purpose.

DAMIS: You beg the question, Timocles. You have not proved that things are as they are by design. What is, is. That it has been so ordered by Providence is no sure conclusion. Once there may have been disorder where there is now order. You look at the universe as it exists, you examine the movements of it, you admire them, you assume that those movements were intended, and you fly into a passion with those who cannot agree with you; but passion is not argument, as they say in the play. What is the second reason for your belief?

TIMOCLES: There is no need of a second; but you shall have no excuse for your impiety. You allow that Homer is the first of poets?

DAMIS: I do.

TIMOCLES: Well, then, Homer says that there is a Providence, and I believe Homer.

DAMIS: My excellent friend, Homer may be a first-rate poet, but neither he nor any of his kind are authorities on matters of fact. The object of poetry is to amuse, not to instruct. Poets arrange their words in metre, they invent legends out of their imagination, they desire to give their hearers pleasure, and that is all. But to what passages in Homer do you refer? He tells us, if I remember, that the wife and brothers and daughter of Jupiter conspired to dethrone and imprison him, and that if Thetis had not called in the help of Briareus they would have succeeded. He tells us that Jupiter, to reward Thetis, cheated Agamemnon with a false dream, and that tens of thousands of Achaeans perished in consequence. Or you believe, perhaps, because Athene set on Diomed to wound Aphrodite and Ares, because the whole celestial company fell afterwards into fighting one with another; then Ares, who I suppose had not recovered from his hurt, was thrashed by Athene, and

"Up against Leto arose the doughty champion Hermes."

Or you have been convinced by the story about Artemis. Artemis was angry because Oeneus had not asked her to dinner, and sent a monstrous boar to ravage the country. These, I presume, are the illustrations of divine power mentioned by Homer which you have found so satisfactory.

(Applause from all parts of the Theatre.)

ZEUS: Bless me, how they cheer; and our fellow is looking over his shoulder. . . . He trembles. He will drop his shield in a moment, and run.

TIMOCLES: Euripides brings the Gods upon the very stage. He shows them in the act of rewarding the good heroes, and punishing wretches like you. Is Euripides mistaken too?

DAMIS: Most wise philosopher, if you argue from the stage, why then the actors Polus, Aristodemus, Satyrus must be Gods; or perhaps it is their masks, and boots, and shawls, and gloves and false stomachs? When Euripides speaks his own opinion, he says:

"Thou seest the ether, stretching infinite,
Enveloping the earth in moist embrace,
This—this is Zeus—this is the Deity."

And again:

"Zeus be Zeus whate'er he may,
I know but what the legends say,"

and more to the same purpose.

TIMOCLES: Then the multitudes of men and nations who have believed in the existence of the Gods, and have worshiped them, have all been deceived?

DAMIS: Thank you for reminding me of national religious customs. Nothing exhibits more plainly the foundations on which theology is built. There is one religion on one side of a border, and another on the other. The Scythian worships Acinaces, the Thracian a slave, Zalmoxis, who escaped from Samos. The Phrygian adores the moon or the month; the Ethiopian the day. The Cyllenian prays to Phanes; the Assyrian to a dove; the Persians to fire; the Egyptians to water. At Memphis a bull is a God; at Pelusium an onion. Elsewhere in Egypt they worship an ibis, a crocodile, a cat, a monkey, a dog-headed ape. In some villages the right shoulder is sacred, in others the left; in others a skull cut in half; in others a bowl or plate. Do you really mean, Timocles, that such things are a serious proof that the Gods exist?

MOMUS (*to the Gods*): I warned you, my friends, that there would be an inquiry into these matters, and that the truth would come out.

ZEUS: You did so, and you were right, Momus. If we survive our present trouble I will try to mend them.

TIMOCLES: Oh, thou enemy of God! What dost thou say to oracles and prophecies? Whence come they, save from divine foreknowledge?

DAMIS: To what oracles do you refer? You mean, I presume, the answer that Croesus got from the Pythoness, for which he paid so dearly, that ruined him and his city. An oracle with a double face, like the statues of Hermes.

MOMUS: Exactly what most I feared. Where is our soothsayer? Go in, Apollo, and answer for yourself.

ZEUS: S'death, Momus, this is no time for irony.

TIMOCLES: See'st thou not, thou sinner thou, that thy arguments will make an end of Church and Altar?

DAMIS: Not all Churches and not all Altars, Timocles. We will let the Altars stand where they burn only incense. Of the Shrine of our Lady in Tauris I would not leave a stone.

ZEUS: Frightful. The fellow spares none of us. He speaks as if from the back of a wagon, and curses you all in a heap, alike the guilty and guiltless.

MOMUS: Not many of us can plead not guilty, Zeus. Wait; he will strike higher presently. (*A thunderstorm*).

TIMOCLES: Dost thou hear, thou impious Damis? Dost thou hear the voice of Zeus himself?

DAMIS: I hear the thunder; but whether it be the voice of Zeus you know better than I. You have been in Heaven, I presume, and have seen him. Travelers from Crete tell me they show his grave in that island. If he has been long dead, I do not perceive how he can be thundering.

MOMUS: I knew he would say that; I was sure of it. You change color, Zeus. Your teeth chatter. Pluck up your spirits. Never mind what these monkeys say.

ZEUS: Never mind! It is very well to say never mind. Don't you see that Damis has the whole Hall with him?

MOMUS: Let down that gold chain of yours, and drag them all up in the air with earth and ocean together.

TIMOCLES: Have you ever been at sea, miserable man?

DAMIS: Many times, Timocles.

TIMOCLES: And did not the winds in the sails help you more than the rowers? And was there not a pilot at the helm to keep the vessel true upon its course?

DAMIS: Assuredly.

TIMOCLES: The ship could not reach its port without a pilot; and the ship of the Universe, you think, requires neither captain nor helmsman?

ZEUS: Well put, Timocles. A good illustration that.

DAMIS: Most inspired Timocles, the captain you speak of arranges his plans beforehand. He settles his course and adheres to it. His men are all in order and obey his word of command. Spars, ropes, chains, oars are on board in their places, and ready to his hand. But the great captain of the Universe shows none of this forethought. The forestay is made fast to the stern, and the sheets to the bow. The anchors are sometimes of gold, and the bulwarks of lead. The bottom is painted and carved; the upper works are plain and unsightly. The crew are disposed at random; the craven fool is a commissioned officer; the swimmer is sent aloft to man the yards; the skilled navigator to work at the pumps. As to the passengers—knaves sit at the captain's table; honest men are huddled into corners. Socrates and Aristides and Phocion lie on the bare boards, without room to stretch their feet, and without food enough to eat. Callias and Midas and Sardanapalus revel in luxury, and look down on the rest of mankind. This is the state of your ship, Timocles, and it explains the number of shipwrecks. Had there been a captain in command, he would have distinguished the good from the bad, have promoted worth and capacity, and have set vice and folly in the place belonging to it. The able seaman would be master or lieutenant; the skulker and poltroon would be tied to the triangles. In short, my friend, if your ship has had a commander, he has not been fit for his place, and there is need of a revolution.

MOMUS: Damis is sailing with wind and stream direct into victory.

ZEUS: It is so indeed. Timocles produces nothing but commonplaces, and one after another they are overturned.

TIMOCLES: As the example of the ship does not convince you, I will give you one more argument, the last, the best, the sheet-anchor of theology.

ZEUS: What is he going to say?

TIMOCLES: Attend to the positions as they follow one from the other, and discover a flaw if you can. If there are altars, then there must be Gods. But there are altars, therefore there are Gods. There, what say you now? Laughing? What is there to amuse you?

DAMIS: My dear friend, I doubt if this sheet-anchor of yours will hold. You hang the existence of the Gods on the existence of altars, and you fancy the link will hold; but if this is your last position, we may as well close the discussion.

TIMOCLES: You admit that you are vanquished.

DAMIS: Of course; you have taken refuge at the altar as men do in extremities. On that altar and in the name of your sheet-anchor we will swear a truce, and contend no more.

TIMOCLES: Oh! oh! you are sarcastic, are you! you grave-digger! you wretch! you abomination! you gaol bird! you cess-pool! we know where you came from; your mother was a whore; and you killed your brother and seduced your friend's wife; you are an adulterer, a sodomite, a glutton, and a beast. Stay till I can thrash you. Stay, I say, villain, abhorred villain!

ZEUS: One has gone off laughing, and the other follows railing and throwing tiles at him. Well, what are we to do?

HERMES: The old play says, you are not hurt, if you don't acknowledge it. Suppose a few people have gone away believing in Damis, what then? A great many more believe the reverse; the whole mass of uneducated Greeks and the barbarians everywhere.

ZEUS: True, Hermes, but that was a good thing which Darius said about Zopyrus. "I had rather have one Zopyrus than a thousand Babylons."

(James Anthony Froude, tr.)

HEAVEN

RUPERT BROOKE

Fish (fly-replete, in depth of June,
Dawdling away their wat'ry noon)
Ponder deep wisdom, dark or clear,
Each secret fishy hope or fear.

Fish say, they have their Stream and Pond;
But is there anything Beyond?
This life cannot be All, they swear,
For how unpleasant, if it were!
One may not doubt that, somehow, Good
Shall come of Water and of Mud;
And, sure, the reverent eye must see
A Purpose in Liquidity.
We darkly know, by Faith we cry,
The future is not Wholly Dry.
Mud unto mud!—Death eddies near—
Not here the appointed End, not here!
But somewhere, beyond Space and Time,
Is wetter water, slimier slime!
And there (they trust) there swimmeth One
Who swam ere rivers were begun,
Immense, of fishy form and mind,
Squamous, omnipotent, and kind;
And under that Almighty Fin,
The littlest fish may enter in.
Oh! never fly conceals a hook,
Fish say, in the Eternal Brook,
But more than mundane weeds are there,
And mud, celestially fair;
Fat caterpillars drift around,
And Paradisal grubs are found;
Unfading moths, immortal flies,
And the worm that never dies.
And in that Heaven of all their wish,
There shall be no more land, say fish.

FROM OF HUMAN BONDAGE, Chapter 28 *

W. SOMERSET MAUGHAM

It looked as though knowing that you were right meant nothing; they all knew
they were right. Weeks had no intention of undermining the boy's faith, but he
was deeply interested in religion, and found it an absorbing topic of conversation.
He had described his own views accurately when he said that he very earnestly
disbelieved in almost everything that others believed. Once Philip asked him a
question, which he had heard his uncle put when the conversation at the vicarage
had fallen upon some mildly rationalistic work which was then exciting discussion
in the newspapers.

"But why should you be right and all those fellows like St. Anselm and St. Augustine be wrong?"

"You mean that they were very clever and learned men, while you have grave
doubts whether I am either?" asked Weeks.

"Yes," answered Philip uncertainly, for put in that way his question seemed
impertinent.

"St. Augustine believed that the earth was flat and that the sun turned round it."

"I don't know what that proves."

"Why, it proves that you believe with your generation. Your saints lived in an age of faith, when it was practically impossible to disbelieve what to us is positively incredible."

"Then how d'you know that we have the truth now?"

"I don't."

Philip thought this over for a moment, then he said:

"I don't see why the things we believe absolutely now shouldn't be just as wrong as what they believed in the past."

"Neither do I."

"Then how can you believe anything at all?"

"I don't know."

Philip asked Weeks what he thought of Hayward's religion.

"Men have always formed gods in their own image," said Weeks. "He believes in the picturesque."

Philip paused for a little while, then he said:

"I don't see why one should believe in God at all."

The words were no sooner out of his mouth than he realized that he had ceased to do so. It took his breath away like a plunge into cold water. He looked at Weeks with startled eyes. Suddenly he felt afraid. He left Weeks as quickly as he could. He wanted to be alone. It was the most startling experience that he had ever had. He tried to think it all out; it was very exciting, since his whole life seemed concerned (he thought his decision on this matter must profoundly affect its course) and a mistake might lead to eternal damnation; but the more he reflected the more convinced he was; and though during the next few weeks he read books, aids to skepticism, with eager interest it was only to confirm him in what he felt instinctively. The fact was that he had ceased to believe not for this reason or the other, but because he had not the religious temperament. Faith had been forced upon him from the outside. It was a matter of environment and example. A new environment and a new example gave him the opportunity to find himself. He put off the faith of his childhood quite simply, like a cloak that he no longer needed. At first life seemed strange and lonely without the belief which, though he never realized it, had been an unfailing support. He felt like a man who has leaned on a stick and finds himself forced suddenly to walk without assistance. It really seemed as though the days were colder and the nights more solitary. But he was upheld by the excitement; it seemed to make life a more thrilling adventure; and in a little while the stick which he had thrown aside, the cloak which had fallen from his shoulders, seemed an intolerable burden of which he had been eased. The religious exercises which for so many years had been forced upon him were part and parcel of religion to him. He thought of the collects and epistles which he had been made to learn by heart, and the long services at the Cathedral through which he had sat when every limb itched with the desire for movement; and he remembered those walks at night through muddy roads to the parish church at Blackstable, and the coldness of that bleak building; he sat with his feet like ice, his fingers numb and heavy, and all around was the sickly odor of pomatum. Oh, he had been so bored! His heart leaped when he saw he was free from all that.

He was surprised at himself because he ceased to believe so easily, and, not knowing that he felt as he did on account of the subtle workings of his inmost nature, he ascribed the certainty he had reached to his own cleverness. He was unduly pleased with himself. With youth's lack of sympathy for an attitude other than its own he despised not a little Weeks and Hayward because they were content with the vague emotion which they called God and would not take the further step which to himself seemed so obvious. One day he went alone up a certain hill so that he might see a view which, he knew not why, filled him always with wild exhilaration. It was autumn now, but often the days were cloudless still, and then the sky seemed to glow with a more splendid light: it was as though nature consciously sought to put a fuller vehemence into the remaining days of fair weather. He looked down upon the plain, a-quiver with the sun, stretching vastly before him: in the distance were the roofs of Mannheim and ever so far away the dimness of Worms. Here and there a more piercing glitter was the Rhine. The tremendous spaciousness of it was glowing with rich gold. Philip, as he stood there, his heart beating with sheer joy, thought how the tempter had stood with Jesus on a high mountain and shown him the kingdoms of the earth. To Philip, intoxicated with the beauty of the scene, it seemed that it was the whole world which was spread before him, and he was eager to step down and enjoy it. He was free from degrading fears and free from prejudice. He could go his way without the intolerable dread of hell-fire. Suddenly he realized that he had lost also that burden of responsibility which made every action of his life a matter of urgent consequence. He could breathe more freely in a lighter air. He was responsible only to himself for the things he did. Freedom! He was his own master at last. From old habit, unconsciously he thanked God that he no longer believed in Him.

Drunk with pride in his intelligence and in his fearlessness, Philip entered deliberately upon a new life. But his loss of faith made less difference in his behavior than he expected. Though he had thrown on one side the Christian dogmas it never occurred to him to criticize the Christian ethics; he accepted the Christian virtues, and indeed thought it fine to practice them for their own sake, without a thought of reward or punishment. There was small occasion for heroism in the Frau Professor's house, but he was a little more exactly truthful than he had been, and he forced himself to be more than commonly attentive to the dull, elderly ladies who sometimes engaged him in conversation. The gentle oath, the violent adjective, which are typical of our language and which he had cultivated before as a sign of manliness, he now elaborately eschewed.

Having settled the whole matter to his satisfaction he sought to put it out of his mind, but that was more easily said than done; and he could not prevent the regrets nor stifle the misgivings which sometimes tormented him. He was so young and had so few friends that immortality had had no particular attractions for him, and he was able without trouble to give up belief in it; but there was one thing which made him wretched; he told himself that he was unreasonable, he tried to laugh himself out of such pathos; but the tears really came to his eyes when he thought that he would never see again the beautiful mother whose love for him had grown more precious as the years since her death passed on. And sometimes, as though the influence of innumerable ancestors, God-fearing and devout, were working in him unconsciously, there seized him a panic fear that perhaps after all it was all true, and there was, up there behind the blue sky, a jealous God who would punish in everlasting flames the atheist. At these times his reason could offer him no help, he imagined the anguish of physical torment which would last endlessly, he felt quite sick with fear and burst into a violent sweat. At last he would say to himself desperately:

"After all, it's not my fault. I can't force myself to believe. If there is a God after all and he punishes me because I honestly don't believe in Him I can't help it."

A CANTICLE *

WILLIAM ALEXANDER PERCY

Lovely is daytime when the joyful sun goes singing,
Lovely is night with stars and round or sickled moon,
Lovely are trees, forever lovely, whether in winter
Or musical midsummer or when they bud and tassel
Or crown themselves with stormy splendors in the fall.
But lovelier than day or night or trees in blossom
Is there no secret infinite loveliness behind?

Beautiful is water, running on rocks in mountains,
Or bosoming sunsets where the valley rivers ponder;
Beautiful is ocean with its myriad colors,
Its southern blues and purples, its arctic gray and silver,
Blown into green frost-fretted or wine-dark in the evening.
But still more beautiful than waters calm or cloven,
Than ocean thunder-maned or floored for delicate springtime,
Is there no beauty visible save to our eyes?

Marvelous is the grass, friendly and very clean,
Though intimate with all the dead, the ceaseless dead,
It has great heart and makes the ancient earth forgetful;
It is not troubled by the wind and from the storm
It learns a radiance; all night it wears the dew
And in the morning it is glad with a pure gladness.
More marvelous than dew-strown morning grasses, is there
No brave immortal joyousness that wrought the grass?

Who lifteth in the eastern sky the dark, gold moon?
Who painteth green and purple on the blackbird's throat?
What hand of rapture scattereth sunshine through the rain
And flingeth round the barren boughs of spring returned
Dim fire?   Who stenciled with caught breath the moth's wide wing
And lit the ruby in his eyes?   Whose ecstasy
Set silver ripples on the racing thunder-cloud
And flared the walls of storm with terrible dead green?
What dreamer fretted dew upon the flat-leafed corn
And twined in innocence of useless perfect art
The morning-glory with its bubble blue, soon gone?
Was there no hand that braided autumn branches in
Their solemn brede and stained them with a somber rust?
Was there no love conceived the one-starred, rivered evening,
And dipped in crocus fire the gray horns of the moon?

They say there never was a god men loved but died—
Dead is Astarte, Astoreth is dead, and Baal;

Zeus and Jehovah share a single grave and deep;
Olympus hears no laughter, Sinai no voice;
Spring comes, but Freia comes not nor Persephone:
On temple plinth and porch the random grasses run;
Of all their priests alone the white-stoled stars are faithful.
Dead are the gods, forever dead!   And yet—and yet—
Who lifteth in the eastern sky the dark, gold moon? . . .
There is a loveliness outlasts the temporal gods,
A beauty that, when all we know as beautiful
Is gone, will fashion in delight the forms it loves,
In that wide room where all our stars are but a drift
Of glimmering petals down an air from far away.

"MY HEART LEAPS UP WHEN I BEHOLD"

WILLIAM WORDSWORTH

My heart leaps up when I behold
   A rainbow in the sky:
So was it when my life began;
So is it now I am a man;
So be it when I shall grow old,
   Or let me die!
The Child is father of the Man;
And I could wish my days to be
Bound each to each by natural piety.

FROM IMAGINATION AND TASTE

In *The Prelude (XIII)*

WILLIAM WORDSWORTH

From Nature doth emotion come, and moods
Of calmness equally are Nature's gift:
This is her glory; these two attributes
Are sister horns that constitute her strength.
Hence Genius, born to thrive by interchange
Of peace and excitation, finds in her
His best and purest friend; from her receives
That energy by which he seeks the truth,
From her that happy stillness of the mind
Which fits him to receive it when unsought.

   Such benefit the humblest intellects
Partake of, each in their degree; 'tis mine
To speak, what I myself have known and felt;
Smooth task! for words find easy way, inspired
By gratitude, and confidence in truth.
Long time in search of knowledge did I range
The field of human life, in heart and mind

Benighted; but, the dawn beginning now
To re-appear, 'twas proved that not in vain
I had been taught to reverence a Power
That is the visible quality and shape
And image of right reason; that matures
Her processes by steadfast laws; gives birth
To no impatient or fallacious hopes,
No heat of passion or excessive zeal.
No vain conceits; provokes to no quick turns
Of self-applauding intellect; but trains
To meekness, and exalts by humble faith;
Holds up before the mind intoxicate
With present objects, and the busy dance
Of things that pass away, a temperate show
Of objects that endure; and by this course
Disposes her, when over-fondly set
On throwing off encumbrances, to seek
In man, and in the frame of social life,
What e'er there is desirable and good
Of kindred permanence, unchanged in form
And function, or, through strict vicissitude
Of life and death, revolving.   Above all
Were re-established now those watchful thoughts
Which, seeing little worthy or sublime
In what the Historian's pen so much delights
To blazon—power and energy detached
From moral purpose—early tutored me
To look with feelings of fraternal love
Upon the unassuming things that hold
A silent station in this beauteous world.

from LINES COMPOSED A FEW MILES ABOVE TINTERN ABBEY

On Revisiting the Banks of the Wye During a Tour

WILLIAM WORDSWORTH

And now, with gleams of half-extinguished thought,
With many recognitions dim and faint,
And somewhat of a sad perplexity,
The picture of the mind revives again:
While here I stand, not only with the sense
Of present pleasure, but with pleasing thoughts
That in this moment there is life and food
For future years.   And so I dare to hope,
Though changed, no doubt, from what I was when first
I came among these hills; when like a roe
I bounded o'er the mountains, by the sides
Of the deep rivers, and the lonely streams,
Wherever nature led: more like a man

Flying from something that he dreads than one
Who sought the thing he loved. For nature then
(The coarser pleasure of my boyish days,
And their glad animal movements all gone by)
To me was all in all.—I cannot paint
What then I was. The sounding cataract
Haunted me like a passion: the tall rock,
The mountain, and the deep and gloomy wood,
Their colors and their forms, were then to me
An appetite; a feeling and a love,
That had no need of a remoter charm,
By thought supplied, nor any interest
Unborrowed from the eye.—That time is past,
And all its aching joys are now no more,
And all its dizzy raptures. Not for this
Faint I, nor mourn nor murmur; other gifts
Have followed; for such loss, I would believe,
Abundant recompense. For I have learned
To look on nature, not as in the hour
Of thoughtless youth; but hearing often-times
The still, sad music of humanity,
Nor harsh nor grating, though of ample power
To chasten and subdue. And I have felt
A presence that disturbs me with the joy
Of elevated thoughts; a sense sublime
Of something far more deeply interfused,
Whose dwelling is the light of setting suns,
And the round ocean and the living air,
And the blue sky, and in the mind of man:
A motion and a spirit, that impels
All thinking things, all objects of all thought,
And rolls through all things. Therefore am I still
A lover of the meadows and the woods,
And mountains; and of all that we behold
From this green earth; of all the mighty world
Of eye, and ear,—both what they half create,
And what perceive; well pleased to recognize
In nature and the language of the sense
The anchor of my purest thoughts, the nurse,
The guide, the guardian of my heart, and soul
Of all my moral being.

BRAHMA

RALPH WALDO EMERSON

If the red slayer think he slays,
    Or if the slain think he is slain,
They know not well the subtle ways
    I keep, and pass, and turn again.

Far or forgot to me is near;
   Shadow and sunlight are the same;
The vanished gods to me appear;
   And one to me are shame and fame.

They reckon ill who leave me out;
   When me they fly, I am the wings;
I am the doubter and the doubt
   And I the hymn the Brahmin sings.

The strong gods pine for my abode,
   And pine in vain the sacred Seven;
But thou, meek lover of the good!
   Find me, and turn thy back on heaven.

FROM GOD FINITE AND GOD INFINITE

In *Belief Unbound*

WILLIAM PEPPERELL MONTAGUE

In our opening discussion we defined religion as the belief in a power greater than ourselves that makes for good. We defended this definition on the ground that it left religion free from the proven falsities, ethical and physical, embodied in traditional creeds, while at the same time it avoided the emptiness and platitude of those schools of ultra-modernism which cling to the word "religion," but use it to mean only the recognition of some sort of unity and mystery in the universe, plus a praiseworthy devotion to whatever is praiseworthy, as, for example, the perfecting of humanity. Taking religion as we took it, we see at once that it is neither certainly and obviously true nor certainly and obviously false, but possibly true, and, if true, tremendously exciting. The question of its truth or falsity is exciting and momentous because it is a question, not of the validity of this or that theory as to the nature of the physical world or as to the origin and destiny of the human race, but because it is the question whether the things we care for most are at the mercy of the things we care for least. If God is not, then the existence of all that is beautiful and in any sense good, is but the accidental and ineffective by-product of blindly swirling atoms, or of the equally unpurposeful, though more conceptually complicated, mechanisms of present-day physics. A man may well believe that this dreadful thing is true. But only the fool will say in his heart that he is glad that it is true. For to wish there should be no God is to wish that the things which we love and strive to realize and make permanent, should be only temporary and doomed to frustration and destruction. If life and its fulfilments are good, why should one rejoice at the news that God is dead and that there is nothing in the whole world except our frail and perishable selves that is concerned with anything that matters? Not that such a prospect would diminish the duty to make the best of what we have while we have it. Goodness is not made less good by a lack of cosmic support for it. Morality is sanctionless, and an ideal can never derive its validity from what is external to itself and to the life whose fulfilment it is. Atheism leads not to badness but only to an incurable sadness and loneliness. For it is the nature of life everywhere to outgrow its present and its past, and, in the life of man, the spirit has outgrown the body on which it depends and seeks an expansion which no finite fulfilment can satisfy. It is this yearning for the infinite and the sense of desolation attending the prospect of its frustration that constitutes the motive to seek religion and to make wistful and diligent inquiry as to the possibility of its truth.

There are two great problems which, taken together, comprise the prolegomena to every possible theology or atheology. They are the Problem of Evil and the Problem of Good.

How can the amount of evil and purposelessness in the world be compatible with the existence of a God? And how can the amount of goodness and purposefulness in the world be compatible with the nonexistence of a God?

1. *The Problem of Evil.* The first of these problems has already been touched upon, but its importance justifies us in considering it again. Of one thing we can be certain, since the existing world contains evil, God's alleged attributes of infinite power and perfect goodness can be reconciled only by altering the one or the other of those attributes. For surely it would seem that since God does not abolish evil it must be either because he can't or because he won't, which means that he is limited either in his power or in his goodness. The line more commonly adopted by theological apologetics is to preserve the infinite power of God at any cost and do what one can with the goodness. Since evil occurs, God must be willing that it should occur. Why? Well, perhaps evil is a mere negation or illusion; perhaps it is good in disguise, a necessary ingredient of divine satisfaction; or a desirable and natural punishment of human sin; or a lesson and opportunity for human good. Or God's ideal of goodness may be quite different from ours, etc. To each and all of these suggestions there are two answers, one theoretical, the other practical. In the theoretical retort we ask, if evil is only a negation or illusion or disguise, then why should we and all other creatures suffer the failure to realize this? The experience of what is alleged to be unreal evil becomes itself the real evil. As for the portion of the world's evil that serves as a wholesome punishment or wholesome lesson for anybody, it is but an infinitesimal fraction of the total of the world's misery. Finally, if God's purposes are other than what we call good, then his nature is other than what we mean by good, while to go further and assume, as some absolute idealists have assumed, that our sin and agony actually contribute to God's enjoyment, would be to make him not merely lacking in good, but a demon of evil. In short, the explanations do not explain. But if they did (and this is the practical retort that follows and clinches the theoretical), the case of the theologians would be still worse; for if evil is really nothing, it is nothing to avoid; while if it is some disguised or indirect form of good, it is a duty to abet it, not oppose it. If the Vessels of Wrath, like the Vessels of Grace, contribute to the divine happiness, why should we care which sort of vessels our brothers and ourselves become? We should not only be *"willing* to be damned for the glory of God," we should strive for it. Surely no such vicious nonsense as that perpetrated by these defenders of God's unlimited power would ever have blackened the history of religious apologetics had it not been for man's ignoble and masochistic craving to have at any price a monarch or master, no matter how evil in the light of his own conscience such a master might be.

If our analysis of the Problem of Evil is valid, there can exist no omnipotent God. Possibly an omnipotent It, conceivably an omnipotent Demon, but not an omnipotent Goodness.

2. *The Problem of Good.* The world that we know contains a quantity of good which, though limited, is still far in excess of what could be expected in a purely mechanistic system.

If the Universe were composed entirely of a vast number of elementary entities, particles of matter or electricity, or pulses of radiant energy, which preserved themselves and pushed and pulled one another about according to merely physical laws, we should expect that they would occasionally agglutinate into unified structures, which in turn, though far less frequently, might combine to form structures still more complex, and so on.   But that any considerable number of these higher aggregates would come about by mere chance would itself be a chance almost infinitely small.   Moreover, there would be a steady tendency for such aggregates, as soon as they were formed, to break down and dissipate the matter and energy that had been concentrated in them.   This increase of leveling, scattering, and disorganization to which all differentiated, concentrated, and organized aggregates are subject in our world, and in any world in which there is random motion alone, or random motion supplemented by such reciprocal *ab extra* determinations as are formulated in the laws of physics, is named the Increase of Entropy.   This principle is exemplified in many familiar ways.   The intense and concentrated waves caused by the stone dropped in the pool spread out and become less intense as their extensity increases.   The hot stove in the cool room dissipates its differentiated and concentrated heat until a uniform level of temperature is reached.   Stars radiate their energy and their mass into space, heavy and complex atoms break down into their simpler and lighter atomic constituents.   Even the electrons and protons themselves are supposed to amalgamate and by so doing dissipate into space as short pulses of energy the very stuff of which they were made.   And living organisms, with their minds, their societies, and their cultures, grow old, degenerate, and die, which is not merely the way of all flesh, but the way of all things.

And yet within this world that is forever dying, there have been born or somehow come to be, protons and electrons, atoms of hydrogen and helium, and the whole series of increasingly complex chemical elements culminating in radium and uranium.   And these atoms not only gather loosely into nebulae, but in the course of time combine tightly into molecules, which in turn combine into the various complicated crystals and colloids that our senses can perceive.   And on the only planet we really know, certain of the compounds of carbon gain the power of building themselves up by assimilation, and so growing and reproducing.   Life thus started "evolves," as we say, into higher and higher forms, such as fishes, reptiles, and birds, mammals, primates, men, and, among men, sages and heroes.

Now the serious atheist must take his world seriously and seriously ask: What is the chance that all this ascent is, in a universe of descent, the result of chance? And of course by chance, as here used, we mean not absence of any causality, but absence of any causality except that recognized in physics.   Thus it would be "chance" if a bunch of little cards, each with a letter printed on it, when thrown up into the breeze, should fall so as to make a meaningful sentence like "See the cat."   Each movement of each letter would be mechanically caused, but it would be a chance and a real chance, though a small one, that they would so fall.   And if a sufficiently large bundle of letters were thrown into the air there would also be a chance that they would fall back so as to spell out the entire play of Hamlet.   The chance of this happening would be real enough, but it would be so small that, if properly expressed as a fraction, $\frac{1}{n}$, the string of digits contained in the denominator would, I suspect, reach from here to one of the fixed stars.   And as for the probability that the atoms composing the brain of the author of *Hamlet,* if left to the mercy of merely mechanistic breezes, would fall into the combinations which that brain embodied—well, that is a chance that is smaller still.   Surely we need not pursue the game further. Let the atheist lay the wager and name the odds that he will demand of us. Given the number of corpuscles, waves, or what not, that compose the universe, he is to bet that with only the types of mechanistic causality (or, if you are modern and fussy about the word "cause" you can call them "functional correlations") that are recognized in physics, there would result, I will not say the cosmos that we actually have, but any cosmos with an equal quantity of significant structures and processes. He certainly will not bet with us on even terms, and I am afraid that the odds that he will feel bound to ask of us will be so heavy that they will make him sheepish, because it is, after all, the truth of his own theory on which he is betting.

But what is the alternative to all this? Nothing so very terrible; merely the hypothesis that the kind of causality that we know best, the kind that we find in the only part of matter that we can experience directly and from within, the causality, in short, that operates in our lives and minds, is not an alien accident but an essential ingredient of the world that spawns us. The alternative to mere mechanistic determination is not some unknown thing concocted *ad hoc* to help us out of a difficulty. Surely, mind is a *vera causa* if ever there was one, and we merely suggest that the kind of anabolic and anti-entropic factor of whose existence we are certain in ourselves, is present and operative in varying degree in all nature. If we are right, we escape the universe of perpetual miracle, on which the atheist sets his heart. The organized structures and currents of ascent and evolution, from the atoms themselves to the lives of men, cease to be outrageously improbable runs of luck and become the normal expression of something akin to us. Material nature makes altogether too many winning throws for us not to suspect that she is playing with dice that are loaded, loaded with life and mind and purpose. This is the solution that seems to me almost inevitable of the problem which, for want of a better name, I have called the Problem of Good.

And so we are confronted with a God, or something very like a God, that exists, not as an omnipotent monarch, a giver of laws and punishments, but as an ascending force, a nisus, a thrust toward concentration, organization, and life. This power appears to labor slowly and under difficulties. We can liken it to a yeast that, through the aeons, pervades the chaos of matter and slowly leavens it with spirit.

The great difficulty of any theory of a finite God turns on his relation to the cosmic whole within which he functions. Legitimately or not, the mind rejects the kind of dualism involved. Moreover, a divine mind or personality can scarcely be conceived as other than a cosmic mind. It is, of course, possible that the earth, the solar system, or the galaxy to which we belong, has a unified consciousness associated with it, but no such limited system could be the body of God. Our interest in the problem of deity would not be satisfied by discovering a mind that was merely larger than our own. Nor would any such limited mind throw light upon the anti-entropic factor which we have accepted as a finite God, and which, despite its finitude, appears to pervade the entire cosmos and hence to indicate a relationship to the totality different from and more intimate than that of a part to its whole. Are we then forced to conclude that the finite God, which solved for us the Problem of Good, requires as correlate the infinite God of religious tradition who seemed to be precluded by the Problem of Evil?

VANITY OF SPIRIT

HENRY VAUGHAN

Quite spent with thoughts I left my cell, and lay
Where a shrill spring tuned to the early day.
    I begged here long, and groaned to know
    Who gave the clouds so brave a bow,
    Who bent the spheres, and circled in
    Corruption with this glorious Ring,
    What is his name, and how I might
    Descry some part of his great light.
I summoned nature: pierced through all her store,
Broke up some seals, which none had touched before,
    Her womb, her bosom, and her head
    Where all her secrets lay abed
    I rifled quite, and having past
    Through all the creatures, came at last
    To search my self, where I did find
    Traces, and sounds of a strange kind.
Here of this mighty spring, I found some drills,
With echoes beaten from the eternal hills;
    Weak beams, and fires flashed to my sight,
    Like a young East, or moon-shine night,
    Which showed me in a nook cast by
    A piece of much antiquity,
    With hieroglyphics quite dismembered,
    And broken letters scarce remembered.
I took them up, and (much joyed,) went about
To unite those pieces, hoping to find out
    The mystery; but this near done,
    That little light I had was gone:
    It grieved me much.   At last, said I,
    Since in these veils my eclipsed eye
    May not approach thee, (for at night
    Who can have commerce with the light?)
    I'll disapparel, and to buy
    But one half glance, most gladly die.

NONDUM

"Verily Thou art a God that hidest Thyself."—Isa. 45: 15

GERARD MANLEY HOPKINS

God, though to Thee our psalm we raise
No answering voice comes from the skies;
To Thee the trembling sinner prays
But no forgiving voice replies;
Our prayer seems lost in desert ways,
Our hymn in the vast silence dies.

We see the glories of the earth
But not the hand that wrought them all:
Night to a myriad worlds gives birth,
Yet like a lighted empty hall
Where stands no host at door or hearth
Vacant creation's lamps appal.

We guess; we clothe Thee, unseen King,
With attributes we deem are meet;
Each in his own imagining
Sets up a shadow in Thy seat;
Yet know not how our gifts to bring,
Where seek thee with unsandalled feet.

And still th'unbroken silence broods
While ages and while aeons run,
As erst upon chaotic floods
The Spirit hovered ere the sun
Had called the seasons' changeful moods
And life's first germs from death had won.

And still th'abysses infinite
Surround the peak from which we gaze.
Deep calls to deep and blackest night
Giddies the soul with blinding daze
That dares to cast its searching sight
On being's dread and vacant maze.

And Thou art silent, whilst Thy world
Contends about its many creeds
And hosts confront with flags unfurled
And zeal is flushed and pity bleeds
And truth is heard, with tears impearled,
A moaning voice among the reeds.

My hand upon my lips I lay;
The breast's desponding sob I quell;
I move along life's tomb-decked way
And listen to the passing bell
Summoning men from speechless day
To death's more silent, darker spell.

Oh! till Thou givest that sense beyond,
To show Thee that Thou art, and near,
Let patience with her chastening wand
Dispel the doubt and dry the tear;
And lead me child-like by the hand;
If still in darkness not in fear.

Speak! whisper to my watching heart
One word—as when a mother speaks
Soft, when she sees her infant start,
Till dimpled joy steals o'er its cheeks.
Then, to behold Thee as Thou art,
I'll wait till morn eternal breaks.

FROM THE INHUMANIST

ROBINSON JEFFERS

An old man with a double-bit axe
Is caretaker at the Gore place. The cattle, except a few wild
    horns, died in that fire; the horses
Graze high up the dark hill; nobody ever comes to the infamous
    house; the pain, the hate and the love
Have left no ghost. Old men and gray hawks need solitude,
Here it is deep and wide.

     "Winter and summer," the old man says, "rain and the
    drought;
Peace creeps out of war, war out of peace; the stars rise and they
    set; the clouds go north
And again they go south.—Why does God hunt in circles?
  Has he lost something? Is it possible—himself?
In the darkness between the stars did he lose himself and become
    godless, and seeks—himself?"

"Does God exist?—No doubt of that," the old man says.
  "The cells of my old camel of a body,
Because they feel each other and are fitted together—through
    nerves and blood feel each other—all the little animals
Are the one man: there is not an atom in all the universes
But feels every other atom; gravitation, electromagnetism, light,
    heat, and the other
Flamings, the nerves in the night's black flesh, flow them together;
    the stars, the winds and the people: one energy,
One existence, one music, one organism, one life, one God: star-fire
    and rock-strength, the sea's cold flow
And man's dark soul."

     "Not a tribal nor an anthropoid God.
Not a ridiculous projection of human fears, needs, dreams, justice
    and love-lust."

"A conscious God?—The question has no importance. But
  I am conscious: where else
Did this consciousness come from? Nobody that I know of ever
    poured grain from an empty sack.
And who, I would say, but God, and a conscious one,
Ended the chief war-makers with their war, so humorously, such
    accurate timing, and such
Appropriate ends? . . ."

OF THE NECESSITY OF THE WAGER

In *Pensées* (233)

BLAISE PASCAL

Infinite—nothing.—Our soul is cast into a body, where it finds number, time, dimension. Thereupon it reasons, and calls this nature, necessity, and can believe nothing else.

Unity joined to infinity adds nothing to it, no more than one foot to an infinite measure. The finite is annihilated in the presence of the infinite, and becomes a pure nothing. So our spirit before God, so our justice before divine justice. There is not so great a disproportion between our justice and that of God, as between unity and infinity.

The justice of God must be vast like His compassion. Now justice to the outcast is less vast, and ought less to offend our feelings than mercy towards the elect.

We know that there is an infinite, and are ignorant of its nature. As we know it to be false that numbers are finite, it is therefore true that there is an infinity in number. But we do not know what it is. It is false that it is even, it is false that it is odd; for the addition of a unit can make no change in its nature. Yet it is a number, and every number is odd or even (this is certainly true of every finite number). So we may well know that there is a God without knowing what He is. Is there not one substantial truth, seeing there are so many things which are not truth itself?

We know then the existence and nature of the finite, because we also are finite and have extension. We know the existence of the infinite, and are ignorant of its nature, because it has extension like us, but not limits like us. But we know neither the existence nor the nature of God, because He has neither extension nor limits.

But by faith we know His existence; in glory we shall know His nature. Now, I have already shown that we may well know the existence of a thing, without knowing its nature.

Let us now speak according to natural lights.

If there is a God, He is infinitely incomprehensible, since, having neither parts nor limits, He has no affinity to us. We are then incapable of knowing either what He is or if He is. This being so, who will dare to undertake the decision of the question? Not we, who have no affinity to Him.

Who then will blame Christians for not being able to give a reason for their belief, since they profess a religion for which they cannot give a reason? They declare, in expounding it to the world, that it is a foolishness, *stultitiam;* and then you complain that they do not prove it! If they proved it, they would not keep their word; it is in lacking proofs, that they are not lacking in sense. "Yes, but although this excuses those who offer it as such, and takes away from them the blame of putting it forward without reason, it does not excuse those who receive it." Let us then examine this point, and say, "God is, or He is not." But to which side shall we incline? Reason can decide nothing here. There is an infinite chaos which separates us. A game is being played at the extremity of this infinite distance where heads or tails will turn up. What will you wager? According to reason, you can do neither the one thing nor the other; according to reason, you can defend neither of the propositions.

Do not then reprove for error those who have made a choice; for you know nothing about it. "No, but I blame them for having made, not this choice, but a choice; for again both he who chooses heads and he who chooses tails are equally at fault, they are both in the wrong. The true course is not to wager at all."

—Yes; but you must wager. It is not optional. You are embarked. Which will you choose then? Let us see. Since you must choose, let us see which interests you least. You have two things to lose, the true and the good; and two things to stake, your reason and your will, your knowledge and your happiness; and your nature has two things to shun, error and misery. Your reason is no more shocked in choosing one rather than the other, since you must of necessity choose. This is one point settled. But your happiness? Let us weigh the gain and the loss in wagering that God is. Let us estimate these two chances. If you gain, you gain all; if you lose, you lose nothing. Wager then without hesitation that He is.—"That is very fine. Yes, I must wager; but I may perhaps wager too much."—Let us see. Since there is an equal risk of gain and of loss, if you had only to gain two lives, instead of one, you might still wager. But if there were three lives to gain, you would have to play (since you are under the necessity of playing), and you would be imprudent, when you are forced to play, not to chance your life to gain three at a game where there is an equal risk of loss and gain. But there is an eternity of life and happiness. And this being so, if there were an infinity of chances, of which one only would be for you, you would still be right in wagering one to win two, and you would act stupidly, being obliged to play, by refusing to stake one life against three at a game in which out of an infinity of chances there is one for you, if there were an infinity of an infinitely happy life to gain. But there is here an infinity of an infinitely happy life to gain, a chance of gain against a finite number of chances of loss, and what you stake is finite. It is all divided; wherever the infinite is and there is not an infinity of chances of loss against that of gain, there is no time to hesitate, you must give all. And thus, when one is forced to play, he must renounce reason to preserve his life, rather than risk it for infinite gain, as likely to happen as the loss of nothingness.

For it is no use to say it is uncertain if we will gain, and it is certain that we risk, and that the infinite distance between the *certainty* of what is staked and the *uncertainty* of what will be gained, equals the finite good which is certainly staked against the uncertain infinite. It is not so, as every player stakes a certainty to gain an uncertainty, and yet he stakes a finite certainty to gain a finite uncertainty, without transgressing against reason. There is not an infinite distance between the certainty staked and the uncertainty of the gain; that is untrue. In truth, there is an infinity between the certainty of gain and the certainty of loss. But the uncertainty of the gain is proportioned to the certainty of the stake according to the proportion of the chances of gain and loss. Hence it comes that, if there are as many risks on one side as on the other, the course is to play even; and then the certainty of the stake is equal to the uncertainty of the gain, so far is it from fact that there is an infinite distance between them. And so our proposition is of infinite force, when there is the finite to stake in a game where there are equal risks of gain and of loss, and the infinite to gain. This is demonstrable; and if men are capable of any truths, this is one.

"I confess it, I admit it. But still is there no means of seeing the faces of the cards?"—Yes, Scripture and the rest, &c.—"Yes, but I have my hands tied and my mouth closed; I am forced to wager, and am not free. I am not released, and am so made that I cannot believe. What then would you have me do?"

True. But at least learn your inability to believe, since reason brings you to this, and yet you cannot believe. Endeavor then to convince yourself, not by increase of proofs of God, but by the abatement of your passions. You would like to attain faith, and do not know the way; you would like to cure yourself of unbelief, and ask the remedy for it. Learn of those who have been bound like you, and who now stake all their possessions. These are people who know the way which you would follow, and who are cured of an ill of which you would be cured. Follow the way by which they began; by acting as if they believe, taking the holy water, having masses said, &c. Even this will naturally make you believe, and deaden your acuteness.—"But this is what I am afraid of."—And why? What have you to lose?

But to show you that this leads you there, it is this which will lessen the passions, which are your stumbling-blocks.

The end of this discourse.—Now what harm will befall you in taking this side? You will be faithful, honest, humble, grateful, generous, a sincere friend, truthful. Certainly you will not have those poisonous pleasures, glory and luxury; but will you not have others? I will tell you that you will thereby gain in this life, and that, at each step you take on this road, you will see so great certainty of gain, so much nothingness in what you risk, that you will at last recognize that you have wagered for something certain and infinite, for which you have given nothing.

"Ah! This discourse transports me, charms me," &c.

If this discourse pleases you and seems impressive, know that it is made by a man who has knelt, both before and after it, in prayer to that Being, infinite and without parts, before whom he lays all he has, for you also to lay before Him all you have for your own good and for His glory, that so strength may be given to lowliness.

234

If we must not act save on a certainty, we ought not to act on religion, for it is not certain. But how many things we do on an uncertainty, sea voyages, battles! I say then we must do nothing at all, for nothing is certain, and that there is more certainty in religion than there is as to whether we may see tomorrow; for it is not certain that we may see tomorrow, and it is certainly possible that we may not see it. We cannot say as much about religion. It is not certain that it is; but who will venture to say that it is certainly possible that it is not? Now when we work for tomorrow, and so on an uncertainty, we act reasonably; for we ought to work for an uncertainty according to the doctrine of chance which was demonstrated above. . . .

236

According to the doctrine of chance, you ought to put yourself to the trouble of searching for the truth; for if you die without worshiping the True Cause, you are lost.—"But," say you, "if He had wished me to worship Him, He would have left me signs of His will."—He has done so; but you neglect them. Seek them, therefore; it is well worth it.

277

The heart has its reasons, which reason does not know. We feel it in a thousand things. I say that the heart naturally loves the Universal Being, and also itself naturally, according as it gives itself to them; and it hardens itself against one or the other at its will. You have rejected the one, and kept the other. Is it by reason that you love yourself?

(W. F. Trotter, tr.)

FROM THE WILL TO BELIEVE
WILLIAM JAMES

In Pascal's *Thoughts* there is a celebrated passage known in literature as Pascal's wager. In it he tries to force us into Christianity by reasoning as if our concern with truth resembled our concern with the stakes in a game of chance. Translated freely his words are these: You must either believe or not believe that God is—which will you do? Your human reason cannot say. A game is going on between you and the nature of things which at the day of judgment will bring out either heads or tails. Weigh what your gains and your losses would be if you should stake all you have on heads, or God's existence: if you win in such case, you gain eternal beatitude; if you lose, you lose nothing at all. If there were an infinity of chances, and only one for God in this wager, still you ought to stake your all on God; for though you surely risk a finite loss by this procedure, any finite loss is reasonable, even a certain one is reasonable, if there is but the possibility of infinite gain. Go, then, and take holy water, and have masses said; belief will come and stupefy your scruples,—*Cela vous fera croire et vous abêtira.* Why should you not? At bottom, what have you to lose?

You probably feel that when religious faith expresses itself thus, in the language of the gaming-table, it is put to its last trumps. Surely Pascal's own personal belief in masses and holy water had far other springs; and this celebrated page of his is but an argument for others, a last desperate snatch at a weapon against the hardness of the unbelieving heart. We feel that a faith in masses and holy water adopted wilfully after such a mechanical calculation would lack the inner soul of faith's reality; and if we were ourselves in the place of the Deity, we should probably take particular pleasure in cutting off believers of this pattern from their infinite reward. It is evident that unless there be some pre-existing tendency to believe in masses and holy water, the option offered to the will by Pascal is not a living option. Certainly no Turk ever took to masses and holy water on its account; and even to us Protestants these means of salvation seem such foregone impossibilities that Pascal's logic, invoked for them specifically, leaves us unmoved. As well might the Mahdi write to us, saying, "I am the Expected One whom God has created in his effulgence. You shall be infinitely happy if you confess me; otherwise you shall be cut off from the light of the sun. Weigh, then, your infinite gain if I am genuine against your finite sacrifice if I am not!" His logic would be that of Pascal; but he would vainly use it on us, for the hypothesis he offers us is dead. No tendency to act on it exists in us to any degree.

The talk of believing by our volition seems, then, from one point of view, simply silly. From another point of view it is worse than silly, it is vile. When one turns to the magnificent edifice of the physical sciences, and sees how it was reared; what thousands of disinterested moral lives of men lie buried in its mere foundations; what patience and postponement, what choking down of preference, what submission to the icy laws of outer fact are wrought into its very stones and mortar; how absolutely impersonal it stands in its vast augustness,—then how besotted and contemptible seems every little sentimentalist who comes blowing his voluntary smoke-wreaths, and pretending to decide things from out of his private dream! Can we wonder if those bred in the rugged and manly school of science should feel like spewing such subjectivism out of their mouths? The whole system of loyalties which grow up in the schools of science go dead against its toleration; so that it is only natural that those who have caught the scientific fever should pass over to the opposite extreme, and write sometimes as if the incorruptibly truthful intellect ought positively to prefer bitterness and unacceptableness to the heart in its cup.

> "It fortifies my soul to know
> That, though I perish, Truth is so—"

sings Clough, while Huxley exclaims: "My only consolation lies in the reflection that, however bad our posterity may become, so far as they hold by the plain rule of not pretending to believe what they have no reason to believe, because it may be to their advantage so to pretend [the word "pretend" is surely here redundant], they will not have reached the lowest depth of immorality." And that delicious *enfant terrible* Clifford writes: "Belief is desecrated when given to unproved and unquestioned statements for the solace and private pleasure of the believer. . . . Whoso would deserve well of his fellows in this matter will guard the purity of his belief with a very fanaticism of jealous care, lest at any time it should rest on an unworthy object, and catch a stain which can never be wiped away. . . . If [a] belief has been accepted on insufficient evidence [even though the belief be true, as Clifford on the same page explains] the pleasure is a stolen one. . . . It is sinful because it is stolen in defiance of our duty to mankind. That duty is to guard ourselves from such beliefs as from a pestilence which may shortly master our own body and then spread to the rest of the town. . . . It is wrong always, everywhere, and for every one, to believe anything upon insufficient evidence."

III

All this strikes one as healthy, even when expressed, as by Clifford, with somewhat too much of robustious pathos in the voice. Free-will and simple wishing do seem, in the matter of our credences, to be only fifth wheels to the coach. Yet if any one should thereupon assume that intellectual insight is what remains after wish and will and sentimental preference have taken wing, or that pure reason is what then settles our opinions, he would fly quite as directly in the teeth of the facts.

It is only our already dead hypotheses that our willing nature is unable to bring to life again. But what has made them dead for us is for the most part a previous action of our willing nature of an antagonistic kind. When I say "willing nature," I do not mean only such deliberate volitions as may have set up habits of belief that we cannot now escape from,—I mean all such factors of belief as fear and hope, prejudice and passion, imitation and partisanship, the circumpressure of our caste and set. As a matter of fact we find ourselves believing, we hardly know how or why. Mr. Balfour gives the name of "authority" to all those influences, born of the intellectual climate, that make hypotheses possible or impossible for us, alive or dead. Here in this room, we all of us believe in molecules and the conservation of energy, in democracy and necessary progress, in Protestant Christianity and the duty of fighting for "the doctrine of the immortal Monroe," all for no reasons worthy of the name. We see into these matters with no more inner clearness, and probably with much less, than any disbeliever in them might possess. His unconventionality would probably have some grounds to show for its conclusions; but for us, not insight, but the *prestige* of the opinions, is what makes the spark shoot from them and light up our sleeping magazines of faith. Our reason is quite satisfied, in nine hundred and ninety-nine cases out of every thousand of us, if it can find a few arguments that will do to recite in case our credulity is criticized by some one else. Our faith is faith in some one else's faith, and in the greatest matters this is most the case. Our belief in truth itself, for instance, that there is a truth, and that our minds and it are made for each other,—what is it but a passionate affirmation of desire, in which our social system backs us up? We want to have a truth; we want to believe that our experiments and studies and discussions must put us in a continually better and better position towards it; and on this line we agree to fight out our thinking lives. But if a pyrrhonistic skeptic asks us *how we know* all this, can our logic find a reply? No! certainly it cannot. It is just one volition against another,—we willing to go in for life upon a trust or assumption which he, for his part, does not care to make.

As a rule we disbelieve all facts and theories for which we have no use. Clifford's cosmic emotions find no use for Christian feelings. Huxley belabors the bishops because there is no use for sacerdotalism in his scheme of life. Newman, on the contrary, goes over to Romanism, and finds all sorts of reasons good for staying there, because a priestly system is for him an organic need and delight. Why do so few "scientists" even look at the evidence for telepathy, so called? Because they think, as a leading biologist, now dead, once said to me, that even if such a thing were true, scientists ought to band together to keep it suppressed and concealed. It would undo the uniformity of Nature and all sorts of other things without which scientists cannot carry on their pursuits. But if this very man had been shown something which as a scientist he might *do* with telepathy, he might not only have examined the evidence, but even have found it good enough. This very law which the logicians would impose upon us—if I may give the name of logicians to those who would rule out our willing nature here—is based on nothing but their own natural wish to exclude all elements for which they, in their professional quality of logicians, can find no use.

Evidently, then, our non-intellectual nature does influence our convictions. There are passional tendencies and volitions which run before and others which come after belief, and it is only the latter that are too late for the fair; and they are not too late when the previous passional work has been already in their own direction. Pascal's argument, instead of being powerless, then seems a regular clincher, and is the last stroke needed to make our faith in masses and holy water complete. The state of things is evidently far from simple; and pure insight and logic, whatever they might do ideally, are not the only things that really do produce our creeds.

IV

Our next duty, having recognized this mixed-up state of affairs, is to ask whether it be simply reprehensible and pathological, or whether, on the contrary, we must treat it as a normal element in making up our minds. The thesis I defend is, briefly stated, this: *Our passional nature not only lawfully may, but must, decide an option between propositions, whenever it is a genuine option that cannot by its nature be decided on intellectual grounds; for to say, under such circumstances, "Do not decide, but leave the question open," is itself a passional decision,—just like deciding yes or no,—and is attended with the same risk of losing the truth.*

FROM FEUILLES DÉTACHÉES
ERNEST RENAN

"There are many chances that the world may be nothing but a fairy pantomime of which no God has care. We must therefore arrange ourselves so that on neither hypothesis we shall be completely wrong. We must listen to the superior voices, but in such a way that if the second hypothesis were true we should not have been too completely duped. If in effect the world be not a serious thing, it is the dogmatic people who will be the shallow ones, and the worldly minded whom the theologians now call frivolous will be those who are really wise.

"*In utrumque paratus*, then. Be ready for anything—that perhaps is wisdom. Give ourselves up, according to the hour, to confidence, to skepticism, to optimism, to irony, and we may be sure that at certain moments at least we shall be with the truth. . . . Good-humor is a philosophic state of mind; it seems to say to Nature that we take her no more seriously than she takes us. I maintain that one should always talk of philosophy with a smile. We owe it to the Eternal to be virtuous; but we have the right to add to this tribute our irony as a sort of personal reprisal. In this way we return to the right quarter jest for jest; we play the trick that has been played on us. Saint Augustine's phrase: *Lord, if we are deceived, it is by thee!* remains a fine one, well suited to our modern feeling. Only we wish the Eternal to know that if we accept the fraud, we accept it knowingly and willingly. We are resigned in advance to losing the interest on our investments of virtue, but we wish not to appear ridiculous by having counted on them too securely."

(William James, tr.)

FROM THE LITTLE DUCK *

DONALD C. BABCOCK

Now we are ready to look at something pretty special.
It is a duck riding the ocean a hundred feet beyond the surf.
No, it isn't a gull.
A gull always has a raucous touch about him.
This is some sort of duck, and he cuddles in the swells.
He isn't cold, and he is thinking things over.
There is a big heaving in the Atlantic,
And he is part of it.
He looks a bit like a mandarin, or the Lord Buddha meditating under the Bo tree,
But he has hardly enough above the eyes to be a philosopher.
He has poise, however, which is what philosophers must have.
He can rest while the Atlantic heaves, because he rests in the Atlantic.
Probably he doesn't *know* how large the ocean is.
And neither do you.
But he realizes it.
And what does he do, I ask you. He sits down in it.
He reposes in the immediate as if it were infinity—which it is.
That is religion, and the duck has it.
He has made himself part of the boundless, by easing himself into it just where
    it touches him.

The people of the Middle Ages were more like this duck than we are.
They took life as it presented itself, and ran it up in spires of Gothic.
They crossed few oceans, but they floated on the sea of time.
And a cat is more like this duck than we are.
We can radio to the moon and get back a pip for an answer,
But a cat can make a hearthrug a haven in the infinite,
Or launch four kittens into life in a cracker box by the furnace,
Purring with pride because she has tuned in on cosmic waves.

I like the little duck.
He doesn't know much,
But he has religion.

FROM THE MAGNETIC MOUNTAIN

C. DAY-LEWIS

21

Third Enemy speaks
God is a proposition,
And we that prove him are his priests, his chosen.
From bare hypothesis
Of strata and wind, of stars and tides, watch me
Construct his universe,
A working model of my majestic notions,
A sum done in the head,
Last week I measured the light, his little finger;
The rest is a matter of time.

God is an electrician,
And they that worship him must worship him
In ampere and volt.
Scrap sun and moon, your twilight of false gods:
X. is not here or there;
Whose lightning scrawls brief cryptograms on sky,
Easy for us to solve;
Whose motions fit our formulae, whose temple
Is a pure apparatus.

God is a statistician:
Offer him all the data; tell him your dreams.
What is your lucky number?
How do you react to bombs?   Have you a rival?
Do you really love your wife?
Get yourself taped.   Put soul upon the table:
Switch on the arc-lights; watch
Heart's beat, the secret agents of the blood,
Let every cell be observed.

God is a Good Physician,
Gives fruit for hygiene, crops for calories.
Don't touch that dirty man,
Don't drink from the same cup, sleep in one bed:
You know He will not like it.
Young men, cut out those visions, they're bad for the eyes:
I'll show you face to face
Eugenics, Eupeptics and Euthanasia,
The clinic Trinity.

22

Where is he, where?   How the man stares!
Do you think he is there, buttoned up in your stars?
Put by that telescope;
You can't bring him nearer, you can't, sir, you haven't a hope.
Is he the answer to your glib equations,
The lord of light, the destroyer of nations?
To be seen on a slide, to be caught on a filter?   The Cause
Limed in his own laws?
Analyst, you've missed him, Or worse and worst
You've got him inside?   You must feel fit to burst.
Here, there, everywhere
Or nowhere.   At least you know where.   And how much do you care?

Where then, Oh where?   In earth or in air?
The master of mirth, the corrector of care?
Nightingale knows, if any,
And poplar flowing with wind; and high on the sunny
Hill you may find him, and low on the lawn
When every dew-drop is a separate dawn.
In the moment before the bombardment, poised at peace
He hides.   And whoever sees
The cloud on the sky-line, the end of grief.
Dust in the distance that spells a relief,
Has found.   Shall have his share
Who naked emerges on the far side of despair.

This one shall hear, though from afar,
The clear first call of new life, through fear
Piercing and padded walls:
Shall arise, shall scatter his heirlooms, shall run till he falls.
That one is slower, shall know by growing,
Not aware of his hour, but suddenly blowing
With leaves and roses, living from springs of the blood.
These ones have found their good:
Facing the rifles in a blind alley
Or stepping through ruins to sound reveille
They feel the father here,
They have him at heart, they shake hands, they know he is near.

CHAPTER 5

IF A MAN DIE

Ay, but to die, and go we know not where;
To lie in cold obstruction and to rot;
This sensible warm motion to become
A kneaded clod, and the delighted spirit
To bathe in fiery floods or to reside
In thrilling region of thick-ribbed ice—
                                        —Shakespeare

Why is death so feared?   Why do people living lives of disaster and pain prefer their wretchedness of breathing to death?   Why is a natural process that is the inevitable result of birth regarded with so much sorrow?   A first death or a few hundred deaths might be considered uncanny and distressing; but a million, no, untold millions of deaths!   Is it not strange that after thousands of centuries man still stands unreconciled with helpless awe before the fact of death?

Part of our attitude towards death, it is true, is conditioned in us.   Just as lovers learn to kiss by the book and much of their emotion is social, inherited from their customs and literature, each person investing the loved one with fictional qualities hardly his own, so with our customs and ceremonies and inherited fears we have magnified death.   In every drive through the countryside we can read the "heavy page of death Printed by gravestones in the cemetery."   Our expensive memorials, our tombs, our mausoleums, our wreaths, the costly mummeries of our undertakers—all the ghoulish machinery of death—what do all these things mean if death is merely a natural process—or what do they mean if death involves the supernatural?

All these things, even those manifestations that reason and taste may deplore, testify to man's craving for, if not belief in, immortality.   "If a man die, shall he live again?"   This agonized cry of Job is the large theme of human grief.   To live again! to live if only in name!

But Death is not just a matter of ceremony and desire for permanence. It is bleak separation of friend and friend, of lover and beloved.   In its bleakest final sense it is felt in the poignant human lament of Catullus for his brother *("Ave atque vale")*, a desolate lament unlighted with any hope. This attitude towards death represents in essence the response of the naturalists and those whose religion does not embrace the concept of immortality. Such is the mood of the chorus in Sophocles' *Antigone,* which chants, "Many wonders there be, but naught more wondrous than man . . . Yet for death he hath found no cure."

What should man's attitude be toward this universal incurable disease, this "Bugbear Death" as Lucretius calls it? He argues that we need not fear death for the simple reason (as he sees it) that death means the end of existence for us. When our possessions are taken from us, our desire for them is taken too. Bacon goes yet further in reproving our fear by reminding us that there is "no passion in the mind so weak but it mates and masters" this fear. One should "count the end of life among the blessings of nature." Antoine de Saint-Exupéry also dismisses such fear as unimportant: "I have never known a man to think of himself when dying. Never." And William Cullen Bryant counsels us to accept our approaching dissolution as we accept a pleasant sleep. Humbert Wolfe and Leopardi both agree that we should face death unafraid, but the habitual bitterness of Leopardi illustrates the fear. The distress exists and cannot be denied. Edna St. Vincent Millay is openly impatient with the attitude of noble resignation. Particularly eloquent on this theme is Don Marquis, who says that we must "Give up the dream that Love may trick the fates." The flame of our love could not be a flame if there were no dark (a metaphor that could be interpreted otherwise, if one thinks of the present light of now dark stars). All humanity is doomed to drown in space and time like its forgotten gods.

These conclusions, however, are not necessarily true. Robert Frost, though agnostic in "The Strong Are Saying Nothing," presents us with a reasonable hope. The farmer, he says, plants his seed in cold spring weather. Will it grow and bloom? There may be little or nothing beyond the grave (we have the white promise of the plum tree), but the strong hold their peace. In this poem, Frost has introduced a new theme, the theme of biological immortality. Probably the first reason why men conceived of immortality lies in their observation of the immortality of the seed, the natural immortality that man shares with plants and animals, a theme touched upon by Shakespeare in his twelfth sonnet.

Allied with the concept of biological immortality is that of social immortality, a concept of large importance in our life and thought. Robinson Jeffers rejects this secular immortality (together with the religious one) as a bargain in glass beads. This hunger for perpetuity in a name has reared many a costly monument, as Sir Thomas Browne points out in *Hydriotaphia*: "But the iniquity of Oblivion blindly scattereth her poppy." No memorial can save any of us from the "uncomfortable night of nothing." There is nothing strictly immortal but immortality itself.

One of the most common arguments for religious immortality is based on the thesis that our world is a reasonable world, a world of order and law (incidentally the same argument advanced by the naturalist for his position). Coleridge proceeds on this assumption. If life ceases with death, man is an accident without meaning. Life itself has no meaning. With this view Tennyson is in full accord; unless life is eternal, it is "best at once to sink to peace." Both poets intimate that immortality is required by the logic of existence. Whitman (cited by G. Lowes Dickinson) also argues for the reasonableness of immortality. All the facts of Nature, he says, are miraculous; all are as wonderful as immortality and no more incredible.

Emily Brontë in avowed faith resorts to teleology. God is Being and Breath and he cannot be destroyed. The mind as part of God is anchored on immortality. Shakespeare seems to share this spiritual belief in his Sonnet CXLVI, but his concern is largely directed at the thralldom of the soul to sin. Richer in spiritual value is the Platonism of Sir Philip Sidney's "Leave me, O Love, that reachest but to dust," a sonnet which directs our thought away from life and death to eternal love. Wordsworth and Shelley also are visited by this mystical vision, this "master-light of all our seeing," this "beauty in which all things work and move."

To Santayana a celestial "reduplication of earthly society," however idealized, is a wearisome prospect. In short, he meets the charge that there must be immortality since this is a reasonable universe by insisting that the concept of immortality itself is unreasonable. No humanly conceivable immortality can satisfy our reason. Is it true that no poet or prophet has ever been able to suggest to us a paradise meeting our intellectual requirements?

It is left for Dean Inge to attempt an answer to Santayana. Inge sums up the quarrel between naturalism and idealism. He finds many facts hard to explain unless, like Emily Brontë, he assumes the teleological Final Cause. Basing his stand on the absolute in terms of values, he concludes that so far as we can identify ourselves in thought and mind with the absolute values, we are sure of our immortality. Inge believes that personality, like other facts, is teleological—"here in the making, elsewhere in fact and power." Death only will bring the achievement of personality.

How shall we know the answer to these mysteries? Death will tell us. So we come back to the individual person, face to face with death, and we are reminded of the defenseless nobility of Socrates, standing before the Athenian jury twenty-four hundred years ago. "The hour of departure has arrived, and we go our ways. . . ."

AVE ATQUE VALE

CATULLUS

Through many lands and over many waters
To these sad rites, my brother, I am come
To pay you this last tribute of devotion,
Vainly to greet your ashes cold and dumb,—
Vainly since fortune snatched your self from me,
Alas, my brother, reft so cruelly!

Yet take these offerings which from ancient years
Are tribute due the dead, our customs tell;
Take them, my brother, wet with many tears:
Forever hail!   Forever fare you well.

(James A. S. McPeek, tr.)

FROM LAVENGRO, Chapter 25

GEORGE BORROW

. . . I now wandered along the heath, till I came to a place where, beside a thick furze, sat a man, his eyes fixed intently on the red ball of the setting sun.

"That's not you, Jasper?"

"Indeed, brother!"

"I've not seen you for years."

"How should you, brother?"

"What brings you here?"

"The fight, brother."

"Where are the tents?"

"On the old spot, brother."

"Any news since we parted?"

"Two deaths, brother."

"Who are dead, Jasper?"

"Father and mother, brother."

"Where did they die?"

"Where they were sent, brother."

"And Mrs. Herne?"

"She's alive, brother."

"Where is she now?"

"In Yorkshire, brother."

"What is your opinion of death, Mr. Petulengro?" said I, as I sat down beside him.

"My opinion of death, brother, is much the same as that in the old song of Pharaoh, which I have heard my grandam sing:—

"Cana marel o manus chivios andé puv,
    Ta rovel pa leste o chavo ta romi."

When a man dies, he is cast into the earth, and his wife and child sorrow over him. If he has neither wife nor child, then his father and mother, I suppose; and if he is quite alone in the world, why, then, he is cast into the earth, and there is an end of the matter."

"And do you think that is the end of a man?"

"There's an end of him, brother, more's the pity."

"Why do you say so?"

"Life is sweet, brother."

"Do you think so?"

"Think so!   There's night and day, brother, both sweet things; sun, moon, and stars, brother, all sweet things: there's likewise the wind on the heath. Life is very sweet, brother: who would wish to die?"

"I would wish to die—"

"You talk like a gorgio—which is the same as talking like a fool—were you a Romany chal you would talk wiser. Wish to die, indeed!   A Romany chal would wish to live for ever!"

"In sickness, Jasper?"

"There's the sun and stars, brother."

"In blindness, Jasper?"

"There's the wind on the heath, brother; if I could only feel that, I would gladly live for ever. Dosta, we'll now go to the tents and put on the gloves; and I'll try to make you feel what a sweet thing it is to be alive, brother!"

"MANY WONDERS THERE BE, BUT NAUGHT MORE WONDROUS THAN MAN"

In *Antigone* (lines 332-347)

SOPHOCLES

Many wonders there be, but naught more wondrous than man:
Over the surging sea, with a whitening south wind wan,
Through the foam of the firth, man makes his perilous way;
And the eldest of deities Earth that knows not toil nor decay
Ever he furrows and scores, as his team, year in year out,
With breed of the yokèd horse, the ploughshare turneth about.

The light-witted birds of the air, the beasts of the weald and the wood
He traps with his woven snare, and the brood of the briny flood.
Master of cunning he: The savage bull, and the hart
Who roams the mountain free, are tamed by his infinite art;
And the shaggy rough-maned steed is broken to bear the bit.

Speech and the wind-swift speed of counsel and civic wit,
He hath learnt for himself all these; and the arrowy rain to fly
And the nipping airs that freeze, 'neath the open winter sky.
He hath provision for all: Fell plague he hath learnt to endure;
Safe whate'er may befall: yet for death he hath found no cure.

(F. Storr, tr.)

from AGAINST THE FEAR OF DEATH
In *De Rerum Natura* (*III, 830-1094*)
LUCRETIUS

What has this Bugbear Death to frighten Man,
If Souls can die, as well as Bodies can?
For, as before our birth we felt no pain,
When Punic arms infested land and main,
When Heaven and Earth were in confusion hurled,
For the debated Empire of the World,
Which awed with dreadful expectation lay,
Sure to be slaves, uncertain who should sway:
So, when our mortal frame shall be disjoined,
The lifeless lump uncoupled from the mind,
From sense of grief and pain we shall be free;
We shall not feel, because we shall not *Be.*
Though Earth in Seas, and Seas in Heav'n were lost,
We should not move, we only should be tost.
Nay, even suppose when we have suffered Fate,
The Soul could feel, in her divided state,
What's that to us? for we are only we
While Souls and Bodies in one frame agree.
Nay, tho' our atoms should revolve by chance,
And matter leap into the former dance,
Tho' time our life and motion could restore,
And make our bodies what they were before,
What gain to us would all this bustle bring?
The new-made Man would be another thing;
When once an interrupting pause is made,
That individual Being is decayed.
We, who are dead and gone, shall bear no part
In all the pleasures, nor shall feel the smart,
Which to that other Mortal shall accrue,
Whom, of our matter Time shall mold anew.
For backward if you look, on that long space
Of Ages past, and view the changing face
Of Matter, tost and variously combined
In sundry shapes, 'tis easy for the mind
From thence t'infer, that Seeds of things have been
In the same order as they now are seen:
Which yet our dark remembrance cannot trace,
Because a pause of Life, a gaping space,
Has come betwixt, where memory lies dead,
And all the wandering motions from the sense are fled.
For who so e'er shall in misfortunes live,
Must *Be,* when those misfortunes shall arrive;
And since the Man who *Is* not, feels not woe,
(For death exempts him and wards off the blow,
Which we, the living, only feel and bear)
What is there left for us in Death to fear?

When once that pause of life has come between,
'Tis just the same as we had never been.
And therefore if a Man bemoan his lot,
That after death his moldering limbs shall rot,
Or flames, or jaws of beast devour his mass,
Know, he's an unsincere, unthinking Ass.

  .   .   .   .   .   .

And last, suppose great Nature's voice should call
To Thee, or me, or any of us all,
What dost thou mean, ungrateful wretch, thou vain,
Thou mortal thing, thus idly to complain,
And sigh and sob, that thou shalt be no more?
For if thy Life were pleasant heretofore,
If all the bounteous blessings, I could give,
Thou hast enjoyed, if thou hast known to live,
And pleasure not leaked through thee like a sieve,
Why dost thou not give thanks as at a plenteous feast,
Crammed to the throat with life, and rise and take thy rest?
But if my blessings thou hast thrown away,
If undigested joys passed thro', and would not stay,
Why dost thou wish for more to squander still?
If Life be grown a load, a real ill,
And I would all thy cares and labors end,
Lay down thy burden, fool, and know thy friend.

  .   .   .   .   .   .

Is nature to be blamed if thus she chide?
No, sure; for 'tis her business to provide
Against this ever-changing frame's decay,
New things to come, and old to pass away.
One Being, worn, another Being makes;
Changed, but not lost; for Nature gives and takes:
New Matter must be found for things to come,
And these must waste like those, and follow Nature's doom.
All things, like thee, have time to rise and rot;
And from each other's ruin are begot:
For Life is not confin'd to him or thee:
'Tis giv'n to all for use, to none for Property.

  .   .   .   .   .   .

Mean time when thoughts of death disturb thy head;
Consider, Ancus great and good is dead;
Ancus thy better far, was born to die;
And thou, dost thou bewail mortality?
So many monarchs with their mighty State,
Who ruled the World, were over-ruled by fate.
That haughty king, who lorded o'er the Main,
And whose stupendous bridge did the wild waves restrain,
(In vain they foamed, in vain they threatened wreck,
While his proud legions marched upon their back:)
Him Death, a greater monarch, overcame;
Nor spared his guards the more, for their immortal name.

The Roman chief, the Carthaginian dread,
Scipio, the Thunder Bolt of War, is dead,
And like a common slave, by fate in triumph led.
The founders of invented arts are lost;
And wits who made eternity their boast.
Where now is Homer, who possessed the Throne?
The immortal work remains, the mortal author's gone.
Democritus, perceiving age invade,
His body weakened, and his mind decayed,
Obeyed the summons with a cheerful face;
Made haste to welcome death, and met him half the race.
That stroke even Epicurus could not bar,
Though he in wit surpassed mankind as far
As does the midday sun the midnight star.
And thou, dost thou disdain to yield thy breath,
Whose very Life is little more than Death?
More than one half by lazy sleep possessed;
And when awake thy soul but nods at best,
Day-dreams and sickly thoughts revolving in thy breast.
Eternal troubles haunt thy anxious mind,
Whose cause and cure thou never hop'st to find;
But still uncertain, with thyself at strife,
Thou wander'st in the labyrinth of life.

(John Dryden, tr.)

OF DEATH

FRANCIS BACON

Men fear Death, as children fear to go in the dark; and as that natural fear in children is increased with tales, so is the other. Certainly, the contemplation of death, as the wages of sin and passage to another world, is holy and religious; but the fear of it, as a tribute due unto nature, is weak. Yet in religious meditations there is sometimes mixture of vanity and of superstition. You shall read in some of the friars' books of mortification, that a man should think with himself what the pain is if he have but his finger's end pressed or tortured, and thereby imagine what the pains of death are, when the whole body is corrupted and dissolved; when many times death passeth with less pain than the torture of a limb; for the most vital parts are not the quickest of sense. And by him that spake only as a philosopher and natural man, it was well said, *Pompa mortis magis terret, quàm, mors ipsa*: [it is the accompaniments of death that are frightful rather than death itself.] Groans and convulsions, and a discolored face, and friends weeping, and blacks, and obsequies, and the like, show death terrible. It is worthy the observing, that there is no passion in the mind of man so weak, but it mates and masters the fear of death; and therefore death is no such terrible enemy when a man hath so many attendants about him that can win the combat of him. Revenge triumphs over death; Love slights it; Honor aspireth to it; Grief flieth to it; Fear preoccupateth it; nay we read, after Otho the emperor had slain himself, Pity (which is the tenderest of affections) provoked many to die, out of mere compassion to their sovereign, and as the truest sort of followers. Nay Seneca adds niceness and satiety: *Cogita quamdiu eadem feceris; mori velle, non tantum fortis, aut miser, sed etiam fastidiosus potest.* A man would die, though he were neither valiant nor miserable, only upon a weariness to do the same thing so oft over and over. It is no less worthy to observe, how little alteration in good spirits the approaches of death make; for they appear to be the same men till the last instant. Augustus Caesar died in a compliment; *Livia, conjugii nostri memor, vive et vale:* [farewell, Livia; and forget not the days of our marriage.] Tiberius in dissimulation; as Tacitus saith of him, *Jam Tiberium vires et corpus, non dissimulatio, deserebant:* [his powers of body were gone, but his power of dissimulation still remained.] Vespasian in a jest; sitting upon the stool, *Ut puto Deus fio:* [I think I am becoming a god.] Galba with a sentence; *Feri, si ex re sit populi Romani:* [strike, if it be for the good of Rome;] holding forth his neck. Septimius Severus in despatch; *Adeste si quid mihi restat agendum:* [make haste, if there is anything more for me to do.] And the like. Certainly the Stoics bestowed too much cost upon death, and by their great preparations made it appear more fearful. Better saith he, *qui finem vitae extremum inter munera ponat naturae:* [who accounts the close of life as one of the benefits of nature.] It is as natural to die as to be born; and to a little infant, perhaps, the one is as painful as the other. He that dies in an earnest pursuit, is like one that is wounded in hot blood; who, for the time, scarce feels the hurt; and therefore a mind fixed and bent upon somewhat that is good doth avert the dolors of death. But above all, believe it, the sweetest canticle is, *Nunc dimittis;* when a man hath obtained worthy ends and expectations. Death hath this also; that it openeth the gate to good fame, and extinguisheth envy. *Extinctus amabitur idem:* [the same man that was envied while he lived, shall be loved when he is gone].

FROM MEDITATIONS (IX, III; XI, XXVII)

MARCUS AURELIUS

Thou must not in matter of death carry thyself scornfully, but as one that is well pleased with it, as being one of those things that nature hath appointed. For what thou dost conceive of these, of a boy to become a young man, to wax old, to grow, to ripen, to get teeth, or a beard, or gray hairs; to beget, to bear, or to be delivered; or what other action soever it be, that is natural unto man according to the several seasons of his life; such a thing is it also to be dissolved. It is therefore the part of a wise man, in matter of death, not in any wise to carry himself either violently, or proudly; but patiently to wait for it, as one of nature's operations: that with the same mind as now thou dost expect when that which yet is but an embryo in thy wife's belly shall come forth, thou mayst expect also when thy soul shall fall off from that outward coat or skin: wherein as a child in the belly it lieth involved and shut up. But if thou desirest a more popular, and though not so direct and philosophical, yet a very powerful and penetrative recipe against the fear of death, nothing can make thee more willing to part with thy life, than if thou shalt consider, both what the subjects themselves are that thou shalt part with, and what manner of dispositions thou shalt no more have to do with. True it is, that offended with them thou must not be by no means, but take care of them, and meekly bear with them. However, this thou mayst remember, that whensoever it happens that thou depart, it shall not be from men that held the same opinions that thou dost. For that indeed, (if it were so) is the only thing that might make thee averse from death, and willing to continue here, if it were thy hap to live with men that had obtained the same belief that thou hast. But now, what

a toil it is for thee to live with men of different opinions, thou seest: so that thou
hast rather occasion to say, Hasten, I thee pray, O Death; lest I also in time forget
myself. . . .

To stir up a man to the contempt of death this among other things, is of good
power and efficacy, that even they who esteemed pleasure to be happiness, and pain
misery, did nevertheless many of them contemn death as much as any. And can
death be terrible to him, to whom that only seems good, which in the ordinary
course of nature is seasonable? to him, to whom, whether his actions be many or
few, so they be all good, is all one; and who whether he behold the things of the
world being always the same either for many years, or for few years only, is altogether indifferent? O man! as a citizen thou hast lived, and conversed in this
great city the world. Whether just for so many years, or no, what is it unto thee?
Thou hast lived (thou mayest be sure) as long as the laws and orders of the city
required; which may be the common comfort of all. Why then should it be
grievous unto thee, if (not a tyrant, nor an unjust judge, but) the same nature that
brought thee in, doth now send thee out of the world? As if the praetor should
fairly dismiss him from the stage, whom he had taken in to act a while. Oh, but
the play is not yet at an end, there are but three acts yet acted of it? Thou hast
well said: for in matter of life, three acts is the whole play. Now to set a certain
time to every man's acting, belongs unto him only, who as first he was of thy composition, so is now the cause of thy dissolution. As for thyself, thou hast to do
with neither. Go thy ways then well pleased and contented: for so is He that
dismisseth thee.

(Meric Casaubon, tr.)

from FLIGHT TO ARRAS, Chapter 19 *

ANTOINE DE SAINT EXUPÉRY

. . . I used to wonder as I was dressing for a sortie what a man's last moments
were like. And each time, life would give the lie to the ghosts I evoked. Here I
was, now, naked and running the gauntlet, unable so much as to guard my head by
arm or shoulder from the crazy blows raining down upon me. I had always assumed that the ordeal, when it came, would be an ordeal that concerned my flesh.
My flesh alone, I assumed, would be subjected to the ordeal. It was unavoidable
that in thinking of these things I should adopt the point of view of my body.
Like all men, I had given it a good deal of time. I had dressed it, bathed it, fed
it, quenched its thirst. I had identified myself with this domesticated animal. I
had taken it to the tailor, the surgeon, the barber. I had been unhappy with it,
cried out in pain with it, loved with it. I had said of it, "This is me." And now
of a sudden my illusion vanished. What was my body to me? A kind of flunkey
in my service. Let but my anger wax hot, my love grow exalted, my hatred collect
in me, and that boasted solidarity between me and my body was gone.

Your son is in a burning house. Nobody can hold you back. You may burn up;
but do you think of that? You are ready to bequeath the rags of your body to any
man who will take them. You discover that what you set so much store by is
trash. You would sell your hand, if need be, to give a hand to a friend. It is in
your act that you exist, not in your body. Your act is yourself, and there is no
other you. Your body belongs to you: it is not you. Are you about to strike an

enemy? No threat of bodily harm can hold you back. You? It is the death of your enemy that is you. You? It is the rescue of your child that is you. In that moment you exchange yourself against something else; and you have no feeling that you lost by the exchange. Your members? Tools. A tool snaps in your hand: how important is that tool? You exchange yourself against the death of your enemy, the rescue of your child, the recovery of your patient, the perfection of your theorem. Here is a pilot of my Group wounded and dying. A true citation in general orders would read: "Called out to his observer, 'They've got me! Beat it! And for God's sake don't lose those notes!'" What matters is the notes, the child, the patient, the theorem. Your true significance becomes dazzlingly evident. Your true name is duty, hatred, love, child, theorem. There is no other you than this.

The flames of the house, of the diving plane, strip away the flesh; but they strip away the worship of the flesh too. Man ceases to be concerned with himself: he recognizes of a sudden what he forms part of. If he should die, he would not be cutting himself off from his kind, but making himself one with them. He would not be losing himself, but finding himself. This that I affirm is not the wishful thinking of a moralist. It is an everyday fact. It is a commonplace truth. But a fact and a truth hidden under the veneer of our everyday illusion. Dressing and fretting over the fate that might befall my body, it was impossible for me to see that I was fretting over something absurd. But in the instant when you are giving up your body, you learn to your amazement—all men always learn to their amazement—how little store you set by your body. It would be foolish to deny that during all those years of my life when nothing insistent was prompting me, when the meaning of my existence was not at stake, it was impossible for me to conceive that anything might be half so important as my body. But here in this plane I say to my body (in effect), "I don't care a button what becomes of you. I have been expelled out of you. There is no hope of your surviving this, and yet I lack for nothing. I reject all that I have been up to this very instant. For in the past it was not I who thought, not I who felt: it was you, my body. One way and another, I have dragged you through life to this point; and here I discover that you are of no importance."

Already at the age of fifteen I might have learnt this lesson. I had a younger brother who lay dying. One morning towards four o'clock his nurse woke me and said that he was asking for me.

"Is he in pain?" I asked.

The nurse said nothing, and I dressed as fast as I could.

When I came into his room he said to me in a matter-of-fact voice, "I wanted to see you before I died. I am going to die." And with that he stiffened and winced and could not go on. Lying in pain, he waved his hand as if saying "No!" I did not understand. I thought it was death he was rejecting. The pain passed, and he spoke again. "Don't worry," he said. "I'm all right. I can't help it. It's my body." His body was already foreign territory, something not himself.

He was very serious, this younger brother who was to die in twenty minutes. He had called me in because he felt a pressing need to hand on part of himself to me. "I want to make my will," he said; and he blushed with pride and embarrassment to be talking like a grown man. Had he been a builder of towers he would have bequeathed to me the finishing of his tower. Had he been a father, I should have inherited the education of his children. A reconnaissance pilot, he would have passed on to me the intelligence he had gleaned. But he was a child, and what he confided to my care was a toy steam engine, a bicycle, and a rifle.

Man does not die. Man imagines that it is death he fears; but what he fears is the unforeseen, the explosion. What man fears is himself, not death. There is no death when you meet death. When the body sinks into death, the essence of man is revealed. Man is a knot, a web, a mesh into which relationships are tied. Only those relationships matter. The body is an old crock that nobody will miss. I have never known a man to think of himself when dying. Never.

(Lewis Galantière, tr.)

THANATOPSIS

WILLIAM CULLEN BRYANT

To him who in the love of Nature holds
Communion with her visible forms, she speaks
A various language; for his gayer hours
She has a voice of gladness, and a smile
And eloquence of beauty, and she glides
Into his darker musings, with a mild
And healing sympathy, that steals away
Their sharpness, ere he is aware. When thoughts
Of the last bitter hour come like a blight
Over thy spirit, and sad images
Of the stern agony, and shroud, and pall,
And breathless darkness, and the narrow house,
Make thee to shudder, and grow sick at heart;—
Go forth, under the open sky, and list
To Nature's teachings, while from all around—
Earth and her waters, and the depths of air—
Comes a still voice—Yet a few days, and thee
The all-beholding sun shall see no more
In all his course; nor yet in the cold ground,
Where thy pale form was laid, with many tears,
Nor in the embrace of Ocean, shall exist
Thy image. Earth, that nourished thee, shall claim
Thy growth, to be resolved to earth again,
And, lost each human trace, surrendering up
Thine individual being, shalt thou go
To mix for ever with the elements,
To be a brother to the insensible rock
And to the sluggish clod, which the rude swain
Turns with his share, and treads upon. The oak
Shall send his roots abroad, and pierce thy mold.

Yet not to thine eternal resting-place
Shalt thou retire alone, nor couldst thou wish
Couch more magnificent. Thou shalt lie down
With patriarchs of the infant world—with kings,
The powerful of the earth—the wise, the good,
Fair forms, and hoary seers of ages past,
All in one mighty sepulchre. The hills
Rock-ribbed and ancient as the sun,—the vales
Stretching in pensive quietness between;

The venerable woods—rivers that move
In majesty and the complaining brooks
That make the meadows green; and, poured round all,
Old Ocean's gray and melancholy waste,—
Are but the solemn decorations all
Of the great tomb of man. The golden sun,
The planets, all the infinite host of heaven.
Are shining on the sad abodes of death,
Through the still lapse of ages. All that tread
The globe are but a handful to the tribes
That slumber in its bosom.—Take the wings
Of morning, pierce the Barcan wilderness,
Or lose thyself in the continuous woods
Where rolls the Oregon, and hears no sound,
Save his own dashings—yet the dead are there:
And millions in those solitudes, since first
The flight of years began, have laid them down
In their last sleep—the dead reign there alone.
So shalt thou rest, and what if thou withdraw
In silence from the living, and no friend
Take note of thy departure? All that breathe
Will share thy destiny. The gay will laugh
When thou art gone, the solemn brood of care
Plod on, and each one as before will chase
His favorite phantom; yet all these shall leave
Their mirth and their employments, and shall come
And make their bed with thee. As the long train
Of ages glides away, the sons of men,
The youth in life's green spring, and he who goes
In the full strength of years, matron and maid,
The speechless babe, and the gray-headed man—
Shall one by one be gathered to thy side,
By those, who in their turn shall follow them.

So live, that when thy summons comes to join
The innumerable caravan, which moves
To that mysterious realm, where each shall take
His chamber in the silent halls of death,
Thou go not, like the quarry-slave at night,
Scourged to his dungeon, but, sustained and soothed
By an unfaltering trust, approach thy grave,
Like one who wraps the drapery of his couch
About him, and lies down to pleasant dreams.

THE UNCOURAGEOUS VIOLET

HUMBERT WOLFE

If God had given man the power
to warn the blade, and warn the flower,
"Death is the guerdon of all that live!"
and they refrained—would they forgive?

Would daffodil the spring desert
because her golden ballet-skirt,
poised on a slim green-stockinged toe,
with the first pirouette, must go?

Would primrose lay aside her yellow
competition with her fellow?
Would violet refuse to be
blue in spring's lapis lazuli?

Would crocus timidly disclaim
her silver heart of candle flame?
Would ragged-robin fail to make
her universal red mistake?

And if the smallest flower or weed
demands her bright specific need,
and tosses death behind her stem,
are we too proud to learn from them?

Are we afraid to tell the sage
(who warns us) that the heritage
of certain death, which does not fret
the uncourageous violet,

we shall accept, and, being heirs
to his disorderly affairs,
will teach him that a gentleman
will spend his credit while he can.

FROM THE BROOM, OR THE DESERT FLOWER

And men loved darkness rather than light.
—John 3:19

GIACOMO LEOPARDI

Here on the arid spine
Of formidable mount
Vesevus, the destroyer,
Ungladdened by any tree or flower save thine,
Thou scatterest thy solitary tufts,
O fragrant-scented broom,
Amid the wastes at home.   So I have seen
Thy lovely stems on the lone plains take pity
Encompassing the city,
Once of all mortal men acknowledged queen,
And seeming, as they lie
Solemn and silent, of her lost empire
Pledge and reminder to the passer-by.
Now in this soil again I see thee, lover
Of melancholy, man-forsaken places,

Faithful companion of adversity.
These fields, which cinders cover
Unfertile, and which lava now encases,
Adamantine and barren,
Ringing metallic 'neath the traveler's feet,
Where the adder makes his nest and coils himself
In the sun, where conies fleet
Scurry to refuge in their cavernous warren—
These fields once smiled with hamlets
And fruitful tilth and harvest's golden glory
And rang with cattle lowing;
Here, for the noble's leisure,
Stood palaces with glowing
Gardens; here flourished cities famed in story,
Which, with all those therein, the haughty mountain's
Fierce breath, poured flashing forth in fiery fountains,
Blasted forever. Now all things around
One common ruin o'erwhelms,
Among which thou art rooted, gentle flower,
And, as if pitying others' overthrow,
Waftest abroad thy sweetest scents that so
The desert may be comforted. These slopes
Let him come visit who is wont to exalt
With praise our mortal state; here let him judge
With what a loving mind
Nature tends humankind. Here shall he too
All that is needful find
Justly to gauge the sovereign power of Man,
Whom his hard nurse, when least he fears it, can
By a slight movement instantly blot out
In part, and could with movements
Only less slight, swiftly, without a trace,
Wholly annihilate.
Stamped on these shores one sees
How the great human race
Pursues its grand, progressive destinies.

Here gaze, here see thyself,
Thou proud and foolish age,
That hast the pathway spurned
Which re-born thought pushed forward till thy feet
Abandoned it, and now, straight backward turned,
Thou boastest thy retreat
By calling it advance.
Thine idle, childish prattle do all minds
Whose evil destiny made thee their sire,
Flatter, tho' they are bold
Oft privately to hold
Thee up to scorn.

. . . . . .

Nature recks not, and cares
No more for what befalls

Mankind than for the ant: and slays she less
Of that stock than of this,
No cause thereof we find
Save Man is less prolific of his kind.

.   .   .   .   .   .

So, knowing not Man, nor what the ages are
That Man calls old, careless how mortals trace
From sire to son their race,
Stands Nature ever green; nay, she proceeds,
But on a path so long,
That she appears to stand.   Meanwhile realms fall,
Nations and tongues collapse: she nothing heeds:
And Mankind dares itself eternal call.

And thou, O limber broom,
Whose fragrant shaws adorn
These fields despoiled of life and wastes forlorn,
Thou too shalt soon succumb, like unto them,
Beneath the fiery torrent's cruel power,
Which, creeping in its hour
Back to familiar channels, a greedy hem
Shall fling o'er thy soft thickets.   And thou beneath
The deadly weight shalt unresisting bow
Thine innocent head full low:
But not bowed up till then in fruitless prayer
Or mien that cowards show to supplicate
The future tyrant: neither held erect,
With frantic pride aspiring to the stars,
Scorning the desert, where
Thou hadst both birth and home,
Not of thy choice but such as chance allowed:
But wiser, but so far
Less weak in this than Man, that thou didst never
Deem thy frail stock endowed
By fate or thee with power to live forever.

(G. L. Bickersteth, tr.)

TO DAFFODILS

ROBERT HERRICK

Fair Daffodils, we weep to see
    You haste away so soon;
As yet the early-rising sun
    Has not attained his noon.
        Stay, stay
    Until the hasting day
        Has run
    But to the evensong:
And, having prayed together, we
    Will go with you along.

We have short time to stay, as you;
　　We have as short a spring;
As quick a growth to meet decay,
　　As you or any thing.
　　　We die,
　As your hours do, and dry
　　　Away,
　Like to the summer's rain;
Or as the pearls of morning's dew,
　Ne'er to be found again.

DIRGE WITHOUT MUSIC *

EDNA ST. VINCENT MILLAY

I am not resigned to the shutting away of loving hearts in the hard ground.
So it is, and so it will be, for so it has been, time out of mind:
Into the darkness they go, the wise and the lovely.　Crowned
With lilies and with laurel they go; but I am not resigned.

Lovers and thinkers, into the earth with you.
Be one with the dull, the indiscriminate dust.
A fragment of what you felt, of what you knew,
A formula, a phrase remains,—but the best is lost.

The answers quick and keen, the honest look, the laughter, the love,—
They are gone.　They are gone to feed the roses.　Elegant and curled
Is the blossom.　Fragrant is the blossom.　I know.　But I do not approve.
More precious was the light in your eyes than all the roses of the world.

Down, down, down into the darkness of the grave
Gently they go, the beautiful, the tender, the kind;
Quietly they go, the intelligent, the witty, the brave.
I know.　But I do not approve.　And I am not resigned.

TRANSIENT

DON MARQUIS

Give up the dream that Love may trick the fates
To live again somewhere beyond the gleam
Of dying stars, or shatter the strong gates
Some god has builded high: give up the dream.
Flame were not flame unless it met the dark—
The beauty of our doomed, bewildered loves
Dwells in the transience of the moving spark
Which pricks oblivion's blackness as it moves;
A few more heartbeats and our hearts shall lie
Dusty and done with raptures and with rhyme:
Let us not babble of eternity
Who stand upon this little ledge of time!
Even old godheads sink in space and drown,
Their arks like foundered galleons sucked down.

* From *The Buck in the Snow and Other Poems*, published by Harper & Bros., copyright,
1928, by Edna St. Vincent Millay.

THE STRONG ARE SAYING NOTHING

ROBERT FROST

The soil now gets a rumpling soft and damp,
And small regard to the future of any weed.
The final flat of the hoe's approval stamp
Is reserved for the bed of a few selected seed.

There is seldom more than a man to a harrowed piece.
Men work alone, their lots plowed far apart,
One stringing a chain of seed in an open crease,
And another stumbling after a halting cart.

To the fresh and black of the squares of early mould
The leafless bloom of a plum is fresh and white;
Though there's more than a doubt if the weather is not
        too cold
For the bees to come and serve its beauty aright.

Wind goes from farm to farm in wave on wave,
But carries no cry of what is hoped to be.
There may be little or much beyond the grave,
But the strong are saying nothing until they see.

"WHEN I DO COUNT THE CLOCK THAT TELLS THE TIME"

(Sonnet XII)

WILLIAM SHAKESPEARE

When I do count the clock that tells the time,
And see the brave day sunk in hideous night;
When I behold the violet past prime,
And sable curls, all silvered o'er with white;
When lofty trees I see barren of leaves,
Which erst from heat did canopy the herd,
And summer's green all girded up in sheaves,
Borne on the bier with white and bristly beard,
Then of thy beauty do I question make,
That thou among the wastes of time must go,
Since sweets and beauties do themselves forsake
And die as fast as they see others grow;
And nothing 'gainst Time's scythe can make defense
Save breed, to brave him when he takes thee hence.

THE GIANT'S RING: BALLYLESSON, NEAR BELFAST

ROBINSON JEFFERS

Whoever is able will pursue the plainly
False immortality of not having lived in vain but leaving
    some mark in the world.

Secretly mocking at his own insanity
He labors the same, he knows that no dead man's lip was ever curled
    in self-scorn,
And immortality is for the dead.
Jesus and Caesar out of the bricks of man's weakness,
    Washington out of the brittle
Bones of man's strength built their memorials,
This nameless chief of a knot of forgotten tribes in the
    Irish darkness used faithfuller
Simpler materials: to diadem a hill-top
That sees the long loughs and the Mourne Mountains, with
    a ring of enormous embankment, and to build
In the center that great toad of a dolmen
Piled up of ponderous basalt that sheds the centuries like
    raindrops. He drove the labor,
And has ear-marked already some four millenniums.
His very presence is here, thick-bodied and brutish, a brutal
    and senseless will-power.
Immortality? While Homer and Shakespeare are names,
Not of men but verses, and the elder has not lived nor the
    younger will, such treadings of time.
—Conclude that secular like Christian immortality's
Too cheap a bargain: the name, the work or the soul: glass
    beads are the trade for savages.

"I THINK CONTINUALLY OF THOSE WHO WERE TRULY GREAT"

STEPHEN SPENDER

I think continually of those who were truly great.
Who, from the womb, remembered the soul's history
Through corridors of light where the hours are suns
Endless and singing, whose lovely ambition
Was that their lips, still touched with fire,
Should tell of the Spirit clothed from head to foot in song.
And who hoarded from the Spring branches
The desires falling across their bodies like blossoms.

What is precious is never to forget
The essential delight of the blood drawn from ageless springs
Breaking through rocks in worlds before our earth.
Never to deny its pleasure in the morning simple light
Nor its grave evening demand for love.
Never to allow gradually the traffic to smother
With noise and fog the flowering of the spirit.

Near the sun, near the snow, in the highest fields,
See how these names are fêted by the waving grass
And by the streamers of white cloud
And whispers of wind in the listening sky.

The names of those who in their lives fought for life.
Who wore at their hearts the fire's center.
Born of the sun they traveled a short while towards the sun,
And left the vivid air signed with their honor.

FROM HYDRIOTAPHIA: URN-BURIAL, Chapter 5

SIR THOMAS BROWNE

What song the Syrens sang, or what name Achilles assumed when he hid himself among women, though puzzling questions, are not beyond all conjecture. What time the persons of these ossuaries entered the famous nations of the dead, and slept with princes and counsellors, might admit a wide solution. But who were the proprietaries of these bones, or what bodies these ashes made up, were a question above antiquarism, not to be resolved by man, nor easily perhaps by spirits, except we consult the provincial guardians, or tutelary observators. Had they made as good provision for their names as they have done for their relics, they had not so grossly erred in the art of perpetuation. But to subsist in bones, and be but pyramidally extant, is a fallacy in duration. Vain ashes, which, in the oblivion of names, persons, times and sexes, have found unto themselves a fruitless continuation, and only arise unto late posterity as emblems of mortal vanities, antidotes against pride, vain-glory, and madding vices! Pagan vain-glories, which thought the world might last forever, had encouragement for ambition, and finding no Atropos unto the immortality of their names, were never damped with the necessity of oblivion. Even old ambitions had the advantage of ours in the attempts of their vain-glories, who acting early, and before the probable meridian of time, have by this time found great accomplishment of their designs, whereby the ancient heroes have already out-lasted their monuments and mechanical preservations. But in this latter scene of time we cannot expect such mummies unto our memories, when ambition may fear the prophecy of Elias; and Charles the Fifth can never hope to live within two Methuselahs of Hector.

And therefore restless inquietude for the diuturnity of our memories unto present considerations seems a vanity almost out of date, and a superannuated piece of folly. We cannot hope to live so long in our names as some have done in their persons: one face of Janus holds no proportion to the other. 'Tis too late to be ambitious. The great mutations of the world are acted, or time may be too short for our designs. To extend our memories by monuments, whose death we daily pray for, and whose duration we cannot hope without injury to our expectations in the advent of the last day, were a contradiction to our beliefs. We, whose generations are ordained in this setting part of time, are providentially taken off from such imaginations; and, being necessitated to eye the remaining particle of futurity, are naturally constituted unto thoughts of the next world, and cannot excusably decline the consideration of that duration which maketh pyramids pillars of snow, and all that's past a moment.

Circles and right lines limit and close all bodies, and the mortal right-lined circle must conclude and shut up all. There is no antidote against the opium of time, which temporally considereth all things. Our fathers find their graves in our short memories, and sadly tell us how we may be buried in our survivors. Gravestones tell truth scarce forty years. Generations pass while some trees stand, and old families last not three oaks. To be read by bare inscriptions, like many in Gruter, to hope for eternity by enigmatical epithets or first letters of our names, to be studied by antiquaries who we were, and have new names given us like many of the mummies, are cold consolations unto the students of perpetuity, even by everlasting languages.

To be content that times to come should only know there was such a man, not caring whether they knew more of him was a frigid ambition in Cardan, disparaging his horoscopal inclination and judgment of himself. Who cares to subsist like Hippocrates' patients, or Achilles' horses in Homer, under naked nominations, without deserts and noble acts, which are the balsam of our memories, the entelechia and soul of our subsistences? To be nameless in worthy deed exceeds an infamous history. The Canaanitish woman lives more happily without a name, than Herodias with one. And who had not rather have been the good thief, than Pilate?

But the iniquity of oblivion blindly scattereth her poppy, and deals with the memory of men without distinction to merit of perpetuity. Who can but pity the founder of the pyramids? Herostratus lives that burnt the temple of Diana; he is almost lost that built it. Time hath spared the epitaph of Adrian's horse, confounded that of himself. In vain we compute our felicities by the advantage of our good names, since bad have equal durations; and Thersites is like to live as long as Agamemnon. Who knows whether the best of men be known? or whether there be not more remarkable persons forgot, than any that stand remembered in the known account of time? Without the favor of the everlasting register the first man had been as unknown as the last, and Methuselah's long life had been his only chronicle.

Oblivion is not to be hired: the greater part must be content to be as though they had not been, to be found in the register of God, not in the record of man. Twenty-seven names make up the first story, and the recorded names ever since contain not one living century. The number of the dead long exceedeth all that shall live. The night of time far surpasseth the day, and who knows when was the equinox? Every hour adds unto that current arithmetic, which scarce stands one moment. And since death must be the Lucina of life, and even pagans could doubt whether thus to live were to die; since our longest sun sets at right descensions, and makes but winter arches, and therefore it cannot be long before we lie down in darkness, and have our light in ashes; since the brother of death daily haunts us with dying mementoes, and time, that grows old itself, bids us hope no long duration: diuturnity is a dream and folly of expectation.

Darkness and light divide the course of time, and oblivion shares with memory a great part even of our living beings; we slightly remember our felicities, and the smartest strokes of affliction leave but short smart upon us. Sense endureth no extremities, and sorrows destroy us or themselves. To weep into stones are fables. Afflictions induce callosities, miseries are slippery, or fall like snow upon us, which notwithstanding is no stupidity. To be ignorant of evils to come, and forgetful of evils past, is a merciful provision in nature, whereby we digest the mixture of our few and evil days, and our delivered senses not relapsing into cutting remembrances, our sorrows are not kept raw by the edge of repetitions. A great part of antiquity contented their hopes of subsistency with a transmigration of their souls. A good way to continue their memories, while having the advantage of plural successions, they could not but act something remarkable in such variety of beings, and enjoying the fame of their passed selves, make accumulation of glory unto their last durations. Others, rather than be lost in the uncomfortable night of nothing, were content to recede into the common being, and make one particle of the public soul of all things, which was no more than to return into their unknown and divine original again. Egyptian ingenuity was more unsatisfied, contriving their bodies in sweet consistencies to attend the return of their souls. But all was vanity, feeding the wind, and folly. The Egyptian mummies, which Cambyses or time hath spared, avarice now consumeth. Mummy is become merchandise, Mizraim cures wounds, and Pharaoh is sold for balsams.

In vain do individuals hope for immortality, or any patent from oblivion, in preservations below the moon; men have been deceived even in their flatteries above the sun, and studied conceits to perpetuate their names in heaven. The various cosmography of that part hath already varied the names of contrived constellations; Nimrod is lost in Orion, and Osiris in the dog-star. While we look for incorruption in the heavens, we find they are but like the earth; durable in their main bodies, alterable in their parts: whereof, beside comets and new stars, perspectives begin to tell tales; and the spots that wander about the sun, with Phaethon's favor, would make clear conviction.

There is nothing strictly immortal but immortality; whatever hath no beginning may be confident of no end: (all others have a dependent being, and within the reach of destruction) which is the peculiar of that necessary essence that cannot destroy itself; and the highest strain of omnipotency, to be so powerfully constituted, as not to suffer even from the power of itself. But the sufficiency of Christian immortality frustrates all earthly glory, and the quality of either state after death makes a folly of posthumous memory. God, who can only destroy our souls, and hath assured our resurrection, either of our bodies or names hath directly promised no duration; wherein there is so much of chance, that the boldest expectants have found unhappy frustration; and to hold long subsistence, seems but a scape in oblivion. But man is a noble animal, splendid in ashes, and pompous in the grave, solemnizing nativities and deaths with equal luster nor omitting ceremonies of bravery in the infamy of his nature.

Life is a pure flame, and we live by an invisible sun within us. . . .

HUMAN LIFE: ON THE DENIAL OF IMMORTALITY
SAMUEL TAYLOR COLERIDGE

If dead, we cease to be; if total gloom
  Swallow up life's brief flash for aye, we fare
As summer-gusts, of sudden birth and doom,
  Whose sound and motion not alone declare,
But are their whole of being! If the breath
  Be life itself, and not its task and tent,
If even a soul like Milton's can know death;
  O Man! thou vessel purposeless, unmeant,
Yet drone-hive strange of phantom purposes!
  Surplus of nature's dread activity,
Which, as she gazed on some nigh-finished vase
Retreating slow, with meditative pause,
  She formed with restless hands unconsciously!
  Blank accident! nothing's anomaly!
  If rootless thus, thus substanceless thy state,
Go, weigh thy dreams, and be thy hopes, thy fears,
The counter-weights!—Thy laughter and thy tears
  Mean but themselves, each fittest to create,
  And to repay the other! Why rejoices

Thy heart with hollow joy for hollow good?
Why cowl thy face beneath the mourner's hood,
Why waste thy sighs, and thy lamenting voices,
Image of image, ghost of ghostly elf,
That such a thing as thou feel'st warm or cold?
Yet what and whence thy gain, if thou withhold
These costly shadows of thy shadowy self?
Be sad! be glad! be neither! seek, or shun!
Thou hast no reason why!   Thou can'st have none;
Thy being's being is contradiction.

IN MEMORIAM, XXXIV

ALFRED LORD TENNYSON

My own dim life should teach me this,
That life shall live for evermore,
Else earth is darkness at the core,
And dust and ashes all that is;

This round of green, this orb of flame,
Fantastic beauty; such as lurks
In some wild poet, when he works
Without a conscience or an aim.

What then were God to such as I?
'Twere hardly worth my while to choose
Of things all mortal, or to use
A little patience ere I die;

'Twere best at once to sink to peace,
Like birds the charming serpent draws,
To drop head-foremost in the jaws
Of vacant darkness and to cease.

PERSONAL IMMORTALITY

In *The Meaning of Good, II, iii*

G. LOWES DICKINSON

"To me, for example, the immortality of the soul does not seem any harder to imagine than birth and life, and death and consciousness. It's all such a mystery together, if once one begins trying to realize it."

"No one," interposed Ellis, "has put that point better than Walt Whitman."

"True," I replied, "and that reminds me that I think you hardly did justice to his view when you were quoting him a little while ago. It is true that he does, as you said, accept all facts, good and bad, and even appears at times to obliterate the distinction between them. But also, whether consistently or no, he regards them all as phases of a process, good only because of what they promise to be. So that his view really requires a belief in immortality to justify it; and to him such belief is as natural and simple as to Wilson it is absurd. There is a passage somewhere, I remember—perhaps you can quote it—it begins, 'Is it wonderful that I should be immortal?'

"Yes," he said, "I remember:

'Is it wonderful that I should be immortal? as every one is immortal;

'I know it is wonderful—but my eyesight is equally wonderful, and how I was conceived in my mother's womb is equally wonderful,

'And passed from a babe, in the creeping trance of a couple of summers and winters to articulate and walk. All this is equally wonderful.

'And that my soul embraces you this hour, and we affect each other without ever seeing each other, and never perhaps to see each other, is every bit as wonderful.

'And that I can think such thoughts as these is just as wonderful,

'And that I can remind you, and you think them and know them to be true, is just as wonderful.

'And that the moon spins round the earth, and on with the earth, is equally wonderful,

'And that they balance themselves with the sun and stars is equally wonderful.' "

"That," I said, "is the passage I meant, and it shows that Whitman, at any rate, did not share Wilson's feeling that the immortality of the soul is unimaginable."

"Well," said Wilson, "imaginable or no, we have no reason to believe it to be true."

"No reason, indeed," I agreed, "so far as demonstration is concerned, though equally, as I think, no reason to deny it. But the point I raised was, whether, if we are to take a positive view of life and hold that it somehow has a good significance, we are not bound to adopt this hypothesis of immortality—to believe, that is, that, somehow or other, there awaits us a state of being in which all souls shall be bound together in that harmonious and perfect relation of which we have a type and foretaste in what we call love. For, if it be true that perfect Good does involve some such relation, and yet that it is one unattainable under the conditions of our present life, then we must say either that such Good is unattainable—and in that case why should we idly pursue it?—or that we believe we shall attain it under some other conditions of existence. And according as we adopt one or the other position —so it seems to me—our attitude towards life will be one of affirmation or of negation."

"But," he objected, "even if you were right in your conception of Good, and even if it be true that Good in its perfection is unattainable, yet we might still choose to get at least what Good we can—and some Good you admit we can get— and might find in that pursuit a sufficient justification for life."

"We might, indeed," I admitted, "but also we might very well find that the Good we can attain is so small, and the Evil so immensely preponderant, that we ought to labor rather to bring to an end an existence so pitiful than to perpetuate it indefinitely in the persons of our luckless descendants."

"That, thank heaven," said Parry, "is not the view which is taken by the Western world."

"The West," I replied, "has not yet learned to reflect. Its activity is the slave of instinct, blind and irresponsible."

"Yes," he assented eagerly, "and that is its saving grace! This instinct, which you call blind, is health and sanity and vigor."

"I know," I said, "that you think so, and so does Mr. Kipling, and all the train of violent and bloody bards who follow the camp of the modern army of progress. I have no quarrel with you or with them; you may very well be right in your somewhat savage worship of activity. I am only trying to ascertain the conditions of your being right, and I seem to find it in personal immortality."

"No," he persisted. "We are right without condition, right absolutely and beyond all argument. Pursue Good is the one ultimate law; whether or no it can be attained is a minor matter; and if to inquire into the conditions of its attainment is only to weaken us in the pursuit, then I say the inquiry is wrong, and ought to be discouraged."

PROSPICE

ROBERT BROWNING

Fear death? to feel the fog in my throat,
    The mist in my face,
When the snows begin, and the blasts denote
    I am nearing the place,
The power of the night, the press of the storm,
    The post of the foe;
Where he stands, the Arch Fear in a visible form,
    Yet the strong man must go:
For the journey is done and the summit attained,
    And the barriers fall,
Though a battle's to fight ere the guerdon be gained,
    The reward of it all.
I was ever a fighter, so—one fight more,
    The best and the last!
I would hate that death bandaged my eyes, and forbore,
    And bade me creep past.
No! let me taste the whole of it, fare like my peers
    The heroes of old,
Bear the brunt, in a minute pay glad life's arrears
    Of pain, darkness and cold.
For sudden the worst turns the best to the brave,
    The black minute's at end,
And the elements' rage, the fiend-voices that rave,
    Shall dwindle, shall blend,
Shall change, shall become first a peace out of pain,
    Then a light, then thy breast,
O thou soul of my soul! I shall clasp thee again,
    And with God be the rest!

LAST LINES

EMILY BRONTË

No coward soul is mine,
No trembler in the world's storm-troubled sphere:
    I see Heaven's glories shine,
And faith shines equal, arming me from fear.

O God within my breast,
Almighty, ever-present Deity!
    Life—that in me has rest,
As I—undying Life—have power in Thee!

    Vain are the thousand creeds
That move men's hearts: unutterably vain;
    Worthless as withered weeds,
Or idlest froth amid the boundless main,

    To waken doubt in one
Holding so fast by Thine infinity;
    So surely anchored on
The steadfast rock of immortality.

    With wide-embracing love
Thy Spirit animates eternal years,
    Pervades and broods above,
Changes, sustains, dissolves, creates, and rears.

    Though earth and man were gone,
And suns and universes cease to be,
    And Thou were left alone,
Every existence would exist in Thee.

    There is not room for Death,
Nor atom that his might could render void:
    Thou—Thou art Being and Breath,
And what Thou art may never be destroyed.

"POOR SOUL, THE CENTER OF MY SINFUL EARTH"
(Sonnet CXLVI)

WILLIAM SHAKESPEARE

Poor soul, the center of my sinful earth,
Thrall to these rebel powers that thee array,
Why dost thou pine within and suffer dearth,
Painting thy outward walls so costly gay?
Why so large cost, having so short a lease,
Dost thou upon thy fading mansion spend?
Shall worms, inheritors of this excess,
Eat up thy charge?   Is this thy body's end?
Then soul, live thou upon thy servant's loss,
And let that pine to aggravate thy store;
Buy terms divine in selling hours of dross;
Within be fed, without be rich no more:
So shalt thou feed on Death, that feeds on men,
And Death once dead. there's no more dying then.

"LEAVE ME, O LOVE WHICH REACHEST BUT TO DUST"

SIR PHILIP SIDNEY

Leave me, O love which reachest but to dust;
And thou, my mind, aspire to higher things!
Grow rich in that which never taketh rust:
Whatever fades but fading pleasure brings.
Draw in thy beams, and humble all thy might
To that sweet yoke where lasting freedoms be;
Which breaks the clouds and opens forth the light,
That doth both shine and gave us sight to see.
O take fast hold! let that light be thy guide
In this small course which birth draws out to death,
And think how evil becometh him to slide,
Who seeketh Heaven, and comes of heavenly breath.
Then farewell, world; thy uttermost I see;
Eternal Love, maintain thy life in me.

ODE

INTIMATIONS OF IMMORTALITY FROM RECOLLECTIONS OF EARLY CHILDHOOD

WILLIAM WORDSWORTH

I

There was a time when meadow, grove, and stream,
The earth, and every common sight, to me did seem
    Apparelled in celestial light,
The glory and the freshness of a dream.
It is not now as it hath been of yore;—
        Turn whereso'er I may,
        By night or day,
The things which I have seen I now can see no more.

II

        The rainbow comes and goes,
        And lovely is the rose,
        The moon doth with delight
Look round her when the heavens are bare,
        Waters on a starry night
        Are beautiful and fair;
        The sunshine is a glorious birth;
        But yet I know, where'er I go,
That there hath past away a glory from the earth.

III

Now, while the birds thus sing a joyous song,
        And while the young lambs bound
        As to the tabor's sound,

To me alone there came a thought of grief;
A timely utterance gave that thought relief,
 And I again am strong:
The cataracts blow their trumpets from the steep;
No more shall grief of mine the season wrong;
I hear the echoes through the mountains throng,
The winds come to me from the fields of sleep,
 And all the earth is gay;
 Land and sea
Give themselves up to jollity,
 And with the heart of May
Doth every beast keep holiday;—
 Thou child of joy,
Shout round me, let me hear thy shouts, thou happy shepherd-
boy!

IV

Ye blessed creatures, I have heard the call
 Ye to each other make; I see
The heavens laugh with you in your jubilee;
 My heart is at your festival,
 My head hath its coronal,
The fulness of your bliss, I feel—I feel it all.
 Oh evil day! if I were sullen
 While Earth herself is adorning
 This sweet May-morning,
 And the children are culling,
 On every side,
 In a thousand valleys far and wide,
 Fresh flowers; while the sun shines warm,
And the babe leaps up on his mother's arm:—
 I hear, I hear, with joy I hear!
 —But there's a tree, of many, one,
A single field which I have looked upon,
Both of them speak of something that is gone:
 The pansy at my feet
 Doth the same tale repeat:
Whither is fled the visionary gleam?
Where is it now, the glory and the dream?

V

Our birth is but a sleep and a forgetting:
The soul that rises with us, our life's star,
 Hath had elsewhere its setting,
 And cometh from afar:
 Not in entire forgetfulness,
 And not in utter nakedness,
But trailing clouds of glory do we come
 From God, who is our home:
Heaven lies about us in our infancy!
Shades of the prison-house begin to close
 Upon the growing boy,

But he beholds the light, and whence it flows,
    He sees it in his joy;
The youth, who daily farther from the east
    Must travel, still is Nature's priest,
    And by the vision splendid
    Is on his way attended;
At length the man perceives it die away,
And fade into the light of common day.

VI

Earth fills her lap with pleasures of her own;
Yearnings she hath in her own natural kind,
And, even with something of a mother's mind,
    And no unworthy aim,
    The homely nurse doth all she can
To make her foster-child, her inmate man,
    Forget the glories he hath known,
And that imperial palace whence he came.

VII

Behold the child among his new-born blisses,
A six years' darling of a pigmy size!
See, where 'mid work of his own hand he lies,
Fretted by sallies of his mother's kisses,
With light upon him from his father's eyes!
See, at his feet, some little plan or chart,
Some fragment from his dream of human life,
Shaped by himself with newly-learned art;
    A wedding or a festival,
    A mourning or a funeral;
      And this hath now his heart,
    And unto this he frames his song:
      Then will he fit his tongue
To dialogues of business, love, or strife;
    But it will not be long
    Ere this be thrown aside,
    And with new joy and pride
The little actor cons another part:
Filling from time to time his "humorous stage"
With all the persons, down to palsied age,
That Life brings with her in her equipage;
    As if his whole vocation
    Were endless imitation.

VIII

Thou, whose exterior semblance doth belie thy soul's **immensity**;
Thou best philosopher, who yet dost keep
Thy heritage, thou eye among the blind,
That, deaf and silent, read'st the eternal deep,
Haunted forever by the eternal mind,—
    Mighty prophet! Seer blest!
    On whom those truths do rest,

Which we are toiling all our lives to find,
In darkness lost, the darkness of the grave;
Thou, over whom thy immortality
Broods like the day, a master o'er a slave,
A presence which is not to be put by;
Thou little child, yet glorious in the might
Of heaven-born freedom on thy being's height,
Why with such earnest pains dost thou provoke
The years to bring the inevitable yoke,
Thus blindly with thy blessedness at strife?
Full soon thy soul shall have her earthly freight,
And custom lie upon thee with a weight,
Heavy as frost, and deep almost as life!

IX

Oh joy! that in our embers
Is something that doth live,
That nature yet remembers
What was so fugitive!
The thought of our past years in me doth breed
Perpetual benediction: not indeed
For that which is most worthy to be blest—
Delight and liberty, the simple creed
Of childhood, whether busy or at rest,
With new-fledged hope still fluttering in his breast:—
Not for these I raise
The song of thanks and praise;
But for those obstinate questionings
Of sense and outward things,
Fallings from us, vanishings;
Blank misgivings of a creature
Moving about in worlds not realized,
High instincts before which our mortal nature
Did tremble like a guilty thing surprised:
But for those first affections,
Those shadowy recollections,
Which, be they what they may,
Are yet the fountain light of all our day,
Are yet a master light of all our seeing;
Uphold us, cherish, and have power to make
Our noisy years seem moments in the being
Of the eternal silence: truths that wake,
To perish never;
Which neither listlessness, nor mad endeavor,
Nor man nor boy,
Nor all that is at enmity with joy,
Can utterly abolish or destroy!
Hence in a season of calm weather
Though inland far we be,
Our souls have sight of that immortal sea
Which brought us hither,
Can in a moment travel thither,

And see the children sport upon the shore,
And hear the mighty waters rolling evermore.

X

Then sing, ye birds, sing, sing a joyous song!
  And let the young lambs bound
  As to the tabor's sound!
We in thought will join your throng,
  Ye that pipe and ye that play,
  Ye that through your hearts today
  Feel the gladness of the May!
What though the radiance which was once so bright
Be now for ever taken from my sight,
  Though nothing can bring back the hour
Of splendor in the grass, of glory in the flower;
  We will grieve not, rather find
  Strength in what remains behind;
  In the primal sympathy
  Which having been must ever be;
  In the soothing thoughts that spring
  Out of human suffering;
  In the faith that looks through death,
In years that bring the philosophic mind.

XI

And O, ye fountains, meadows, hills, and groves,
Forebode not any severing of our loves!
Yet in my heart of hearts I feel your might;
I only have relinquished one delight
To live beneath your more habitual sway.
I love the brooks which down their channels fret,
Even more than when I tripped lightly as they;
The innocent brightness of a new-born day is lovely yet;
The clouds that gather round the setting sun
Do take a sober coloring from an eye
That hath kept watch o'er man's mortality;
Another race hath been, and other palms are won.
Thanks to the human heart by which we live,
Thanks to its tenderness, its joys, and fears,
To me the meanest flower that blows can give
Thoughts that do often lie too deep for tears.

FROM ADONAIS

PERCY BYSSHE SHELLEY

Peace, peace! he is not dead, he doth not sleep—
He hath awakened from the dream of life—
'Tis we, who lost in stormy visions, keep
With phantoms an unprofitable strife,
And in mad trance, strike with our spirit's knife

Invulnerable nothings.—*We* decay
Like corpses in a charnel; fear and grief
Convulse us and consume us day by day,
And cold hopes swarm like worms within our living clay.

He has outsoared the shadow of our night;
Envy and calumny and hate and pain,
And that unrest which men miscall delight,
Can touch him not and torture not again;
From the contagion of the world's slow stain
He is secure, and now can never mourn
A heart grown cold, a head grown gray in vain;
Nor, when the spirit's self has ceased to burn,
With sparkless ashes load an unlamented urn.

He lives, he wakes—'tis Death is dead, not he;
Mourn not for Adonais.—Thou young Dawn,
Turn all thy dew to splendor, for from thee
The spirit thou lamentest is not gone;
Ye caverns and ye forests, cease to moan!
Cease, ye faint flowers and fountains, and thou Air,
Which like a mourning veil thy scarf hadst thrown
O'er the abandoned Earth, now leave it bare
Even to the joyous stars which smile on its despair!

He is made one with Nature: there is heard
His voice in all her music, from the moan
Of thunder, to the song of night's sweet bird;
He is a presence to be felt and known
In darkness and in light, from herb and stone,
Spreading itself where'er that Power may move
Which has withdrawn his being to its own;
Which wields the world with never-wearied love,
Sustains it from beneath, and kindles it above.

He is a portion of the loveliness
Which once he made more lovely: he doth bear
His part, while the one Spirit's plastic stress
Sweeps through the dull dense world, compelling there,
All new successions to the forms they wear;
Torturing th' unwilling dross that checks its flight
To its own likeness, as each mass may bear;
And bursting in its beauty and its might
From trees and beasts and men into the Heaven's light.

The splendors of the firmament of time
May be eclipsed, but are extinguished not;
Like stars to their appointed height they climb,
And death is a low mist which cannot blot
The brightness it may veil.   When lofty thought

Lifts a young heart above its mortal lair,
And love and life contend in it, for what
Shall be its earthly doom, the dead live there
And move like winds of light on dark and stormy air.

. . . .

The One remains, the many change and pass;
Heaven's light forever shines, Earth's shadows fly;
Life, like a dome of many-colored glass,
Stains the white radiance of Eternity,
Until Death tramples it to fragments.—Die,
If thou wouldst be with that which thou dost seek!
Follow where all is fled!—Rome's azure sky,
Flowers, ruins, statues, music, words, are weak
The glory they transfuse with fitting truth to speak.

Why linger, why turn back, why shrink, my Heart?
Thy hopes are gone before: from all things here
They have departed; thou shouldst now depart!
A light is passed from the revolving year,
And man, and woman; and what still is dear
Attracts to crush, repels to make thee wither.
The soft sky smiles,—the low wind whispers near:
'Tis Adonais calls! oh, hasten thither,
No more let Life divide what Death can join together.

That Light whose smile kindles the Universe,
That Beauty in which all things work and move,
That Benediction which the eclipsing Curse
Of birth can quench not, that sustaining Love
Which through the web of being blindly wove
By man and beast and earth and air and sea,
Burns bright or dim, as each are mirrors of
The fire for which all thirst; now beams on me,
Consuming the last clouds of cold mortality.

The breath whose might I have invoked in song
Descends on me; my spirit's bark is driven,
Far from the shore, far from the trembling throng
Whose sails were never to the tempest given;
The massy earth and spherèd skies are riven!
I am borne darkly, fearfully, afar;
Whilst, burning through the inmost veil of Heaven,
The soul of Adonais, like a star,
Beacons from the abode where the Eternal are.

FROM THE BELIEF IN A FUTURE LIFE *

In *Reason in Religion (Chapter 13)*

GEORGE SANTAYANA

Many a man dies too soon and some are born in the wrong age or station. Could these persons drink at the fountain of youth at least once more they might do themselves fuller justice and cut a better figure at last in the universe. Most people think they have stuff in them for greater things than time suffers them to perform. To imagine a second career is a pleasing antidote for ill-fortune; the poor soul wants another chance. But how should a future life be constituted if it is to satisfy this demand, and how long need it last? It would evidently have to go on in an environment closely analogous to earth; I could not, for instance, write in another world the epics which the necessity of earning my living may have stifled here, did that other world contain no time, no heroic struggles, or no metrical language. Nor is it clear that my epics, to be perfect, would need to be quite endless. If what is foiled in me is really poetic genius and not simply a tendency toward perpetual motion, it would not help me if in heaven, in lieu of my dreamt-of epics, I were allowed to beget several robust children. In a word, if hereafter I am to be the same man improved I must find myself in the same world corrected. Were I transformed into a cherub or transported into a timeless ecstasy, it is hard to see in what sense I should continue to exist. Those results might be interesting in themselves and might enrich the universe; they would not prolong my life nor retrieve my disasters.

For this reason a future life is after all best represented by those frankly material ideals which most Christians—being Platonists—are wont to despise. It would be genuine happiness for a Jew to rise again in the flesh and live for ever in Ezekiel's New Jerusalem, with its ceremonial glories and civic order. It would be truly agreeable for any man to sit in well-watered gardens with Mohammed, clad in green silks, drinking delicious sherbets, and transfixed by the gazelle-like glance of some young girl, all innocence and fire. Amid such scenes a man might remain himself and might fulfil hopes that he had actually cherished on earth. He might also find his friends again, which in somewhat generous minds is perhaps the thought that chiefly sustains interest in a posthumous existence. But to recognize his friends a man must find them in their bodies, with their familiar habits, voices, and interests; for it is surely an insult to affection to say that he could find them in an eternal formula expressing their idiosyncrasy. When, however, it is clearly seen that another life, to supplement this one, must closely resemble it, does not the magic of immortality altogether vanish? Is such a reduplication of earthly society at all credible? And the prospect of awakening again among houses and trees, among children and dotards, among wars and rumors of wars, still fettered to one personality and one accidental past, still uncertain of the future, is not this prospect wearisome and deeply repulsive? Having passed through these things once and bequeathed them to posterity, is it not time for each soul to rest? The universe doubtless contains all sorts of experiences, better and worse than the human; but it is idle to attribute to a particular man a life divorced from his circumstances and his body.

Dogmas about such a posthumous experience find some shadowy support in various illusions and superstitions that surround death, but they are developed into articulate prophecies chiefly by certain moral demands.   One of these requires rewards and punishments more emphatic and sure than those which conduct meets with in this world.   Another requires merely a more favorable and complete opportunity for the soul's development.   Considerations like these are pertinent to moral philosophy.   It touches the notion of duty whether an exact hedonistic retribution is to be demanded for what is termed merit and guilt: so that without such supernatural remuneration virtue, perhaps, would be discredited and deprived of a motive.   It likewise touches the ideality and nobleness of life whether human aims can be realized satisfactorily only in the agent's singular person, so that the fruits of effort would be forthwith missed if the laborer himself should disappear.

To establish justice in the world and furnish an adequate incentive to virtue was once thought the chief business of a future life.   The Hebraic religions somewhat overreached themselves on these points: for the grotesque alternative between hell and heaven in the end only aggravated the injustice it was meant to remedy. Life is unjust in that it subordinates individuals to a general mechanical law, and the deeper and longer hold fate has on the soul, the greater that injustice.   A perpetual life would be a perpetual subjection to arbitrary power, while a last judgment would be but a last fatality.   That hell may have frightened a few villains into omitting a crime is perhaps credible; but the embarrassed silence which the churches, in a more sensitive age, prefer to maintain on that wholesome doctrine— once, as they taught, the only rational basis for virtue—shows how their teaching has to follow the independent progress of morals.   Nevertheless, persons are not wanting, apparently free from ecclesiastical constraint, who still maintain that the value of life depends on its indefinite prolongation.   By an artifice of reflection they substitute vanity for reason, and selfish for ingenuous instincts in man.   Being apparently interested in nothing but their own careers, they forget that a man may remember how little he counts in the world and suffer that rational knowledge to inspire his purposes.   Intense morality has always envisaged earthly goods and evils, and even when a future life has been accepted vaguely, it has never given direction to human will or aims, which at best it could only proclaim more emphatically.   It may indeed be said that no man of any depth of soul has made his prolonged existence the touchstone of his enthusiasms.   Such an instinct is carnal, and if immortality is to add a higher inspiration to life it must not be an immortality of selfishness.   What a despicable creature must a man be, and how sunk below the level of the most barbaric virtue, if he cannot bear to live and to die for his children, for his art, or for his country!

FROM SURVIVAL AND IMMORTALITY

WILLIAM RALPH INGE

Faith in human immortality stands or falls with the belief in *absolute values*. The interest of consciousness, as Professor Pringle-Pattison has said in his admirable Gifford Lectures, lies in the ideal values of which it is the bearer, not in its mere existence as a more refined kind of fact.   Idealism is most satisfactorily defined as the interpretation of the world according to a scale of value, or, in Plato's phrase, by the Idea of the Good.   The highest values in this scale are absolute, eternal, and super-individual, and lower values are assigned their place in virtue of their correspondence to or participation in these absolute values.   I agree with Münsterberg that the conditional and subjective values of the pragmatist have no meaning unless we have acknowledged beforehand the independent value of truth.   If the proof of the merely individual significance of truth has itself only individual importance, it cannot claim any general meaning. If, on the other hand, it demands to be taken as generally valid, the possibility of a general truth is acknowledged from the start. If this one exception is granted, the whole illusory universe of relativism is overthrown. To deny any thought which is more than relative is to deprive even skepticism itself of the presuppositions on which it rests. The logical skeptic has no *ego* to doubt with. "Every doubt of absolute values destroys itself. As thought it contradicts itself; as doubt it denies itself; as belief it despairs of itself." It is not necessary or desirable to follow Münsterberg in identifying valuation with will. He talks of the will judging; but the will cannot judge. In contemplating existence we use our will to fix our attention, and then try conscientiously to prevent it from influencing the verdict. But this illegitimate use of the word "will" does not impair the force of the argument for absolute values.

Now, valuation arranges experience in a different manner from natural science. The attributes of reality, in our world of values, are Goodness, Truth, and Beauty. And we assert that we have as good reason to claim objective reality for these Ideas as for anything in the world revealed to our senses. "All claims on man's behalf," says Professor Pringle-Pattison, "must be based on the objectivity of the values revealed in his experience, and brokenly realized there. Man does not make values any more than he makes reality." Our contention is that the world of values, which forms the content of idealistic thought and aspiration, is the real world; and in this world we find our own immortality.

But there could be no greater error than to leave the two worlds, or the two "judgments," that of existence and that of value, contrasted with each other, or treated as unrelated in our experience. A value-judgment which is not also a judgment of existence is in the air; it is the baseless fabric of a vision. Existence is itself a value, and an ingredient in every valuation; that which has no existence has no value. And, on the other side, it is a delusion to suppose that any science can dispense with valuation. Even mathematics admits that there is a right and a wrong way of solving a problem, though by confining itself to quantitative measurements it can assert no more than a hypothetical reality for its world. It is quite certain that we can think of no existing world without valuation.

"The ultimate identity of existence and value is the venture of faith to which mysticism and speculative idealism are committed." [1] It is indeed the presupposition of all philosophy and all religion; without this faith there can, properly speaking, be no belief in God. But the difference between naturalism and idealism may, I think, be better stated otherwise than by emphasizing the contrast between existence and value, which it is impossible for either side to maintain. Naturalism seeks to interpret the world by investigation of origins; idealism by investigation of ends. The one finds the explanation of evolution in that from which it started, the other in that to which it tends. The one explains the higher by the lower; the other the lower by the higher. This is a plain issue; either the world shows a teleology or it does not. If it does, the philosophy based on the inorganic sciences is wrong. And the attempt to explain the higher by the lower becomes mischievous or impossible when we pass from one *order* to another. In speaking of different "orders," we do not commit ourselves to any sudden breaks or leaps in evolution. The organic may be linked to the inorganic, soul to the lower forms of life, spirit to soul. But whether the "scale of perfection" is a ladder or an inclined plane, new categories are necessary as we ascend it. And unless we

[1] Quoted by Professor Pringle-Pattison from an article by me in the *Times* Literary Supplement.

admit an inner teleology as a determining factor in growth, many facts even in physiology are hard to explain.

If the basis of our faith in the world-order is the conviction that the Ideas of the Good, the True, and the Beautiful are fully real and fully operative, we must try to form some clear notion of what these Ideas mean, and how they are related to each other. The goal of Truth, as an absolute value, is unity, which in the outer world means harmony, in the intercourse of spirit with spirit, love; and in the inner world, peace or happiness. The goal of Goodness as an absolute value is the realization of the ought-to-be in victorious moral effort. Beauty is the self-recognition of creative Spirit in its own works; it is the expression of Nature's own deepest character. Beauty gives neither information nor advice; but it satisfies a part of our nature which is not less Divine than that which pays homage to Truth and Goodness.

Now, these absolute values are supra-temporal. If the soul were in time, no value could arise; for time is always hurling its own products into nothingness, and the present is an unextended point, dividing an unreal past from an unreal future. The soul is not in time; time is rather in the soul. Values are eternal and indestructible. When Plotinus says that "nothing that really *is* can ever perish" (ἀπολεῖται οὐδὲν τῶν ὄντων), and when Höffding says that "no value perishes out of the world," they are saying the same thing. In so far as we can identify ourselves in thought and mind with the absolute values, we are sure of our immortality.

But it will be said that in the first place this promise of immortality carries with it no guarantee of survival in time, and in the second place that it offers us, at last, only an impersonal immortality. Let us take these two objections in turn, though they are in reality closely connected.

We must not regard time as an external, inhuman, unconscious process. Time is the frame of soul-life; outside this it has no existence. The entire cosmic process is the life-frame of the universal Soul, the Divine Logos. With this life we are vitally connected, however brief and unimportant the span and the task of an individual career may seem to us. If my particular life-meaning passes out of activity, it will be because the larger life, to which I belong, no longer needs that form of expression. My death, like my birth, will have a teleological justification, to which my supra-temporal self will consent. When a good man's work in this world is done, when he is able to say, without forgetting his many failures, "I have finished the work that Thou gavest me to do," surely his last word will be, "Lord, now lettest Thou Thy servant depart in peace"; not, "Grant that I may flit for a while over my former home, and hear what is happening to my country and my family." We may leave it to our misguided necromancers to describe the adventures of the disembodied ghost—

"Quo cursu deserta petiverit, et quibus ante
Infelix sua tecta supervolitaverit alis."

The most respectable motive which leads men to desire a continuance of active participation in the affairs of time is that which Tennyson expresses in the often-quoted line, "Give her the wages of going on, and not to die." We may feel that we have it in us to do more for God and our fellow-men than we shall be able to accomplish in this life, even if it be prolonged to old age. Is not this a desire which we may prefer as a claim? And in any case, it is admitted that time is the form of the will. Are we to have no more will after death? Further, is our probation over when we die? What is to be the fate of that large majority who, so far as we can see, are equally undeserving of heaven and of hell? To these questions no answer is possible, because we are confronted with a blank wall of ignorance. We do not know whether there will be any future probation. We do not know whether Robert Browning's expectation of "other tasks in other lives, God willing," will be fulfiled.

> "And I shall thereupon
> Take rest, ere I be gone
> Once more on my adventure brave and new. . . ."

The second objection, which, as I have said, is closely connected with the first, is that idealism offers us a merely impersonal immortality. But what is personality? The notion of a world of spiritual atoms, *"solida pollentia simplicitate,"* as Lucretius says, seems to be attractive to some minds. There are thinkers of repute who even picture the Deity as the constitutional President of a *collegium* of souls. This kind of pluralism is of course fundamentally incompatible with the presuppositions of my paper. The idea of the "self" seems to me to be an arbitrary fixation of our average state of mind, a half-way house which belongs to no order of real existence. The conception of an abstract ego seems to involve three assumptions, none of which is true. The first is that there is a sharp line separating subject from object and from other subjects. The second is that the subject, thus sundered from the object, remains identical through time. The third is that this indiscerptible entity is in some mysterious way both myself and my property. In opposition to the first, I maintain that the foci of consciousness flow freely into each other even on the psychical plane, while in the eternal world there are probably no barriers at all. In opposition to the second, it is certain that the empirical self is by no means identical throughout, and that the spiritual life, in which we may be said to attain real personality for the first time, is only "ours" potentially. In opposition to the third, I repeat that the question whether it is "my" soul that will live in the eternal world seems to have no meaning at all. In philosophy as in religion, we had better follow the advice of the Theologia Germanica and banish, as far as possible, the words "me and mine" from our vocabulary. For personality is not something given to start with. It does not belong to the world of claims and counter-claims in which we chiefly live. We must be willing to lose our soul on this level of experience, before we can find it unto life eternal. Personality is a teleological fact; it is here in the making, elsewhere in fact and power. So in the case of our friends. The man whom we love is not the changing psychophysical organism; it is the Christ in him that we love, the perfect man who is struggling into existence in his life and growth. If we ask what a man is, the answer may be either, "He is what he loves," or "He is what he is worth." The two are not very different. Thus I cannot agree with Keyserling, who in criticizing this type of thought (with which, none the less, he has great sympathy) says that "mysticism, whether it likes it or not, ends in an impersonal immortality." For impersonality is a purely negative conception, like timelessness. What is negated in "timelessness" is not the reality of the present, but the unreality of the past and future. So the "impersonality" which is here (not without warrant from the mystics themselves) said to belong to eternal life is really the liberation of the idea of personality. Personality is allowed to expand as far as it can, and only so can it come into its own. When Keyserling adds, "The instinct of immortality really affirms that the individual is not ultimate," I entirely agree with him. . . .

We are sometimes inclined to think, with a natural regret, that the conditions of life in the eternal world are so utterly unlike those of the world which we know, that we must either leave our mental picture of that life in the barest outline, or fill it in with the colors which we know on earth, but which, as we are well aware, cannot portray truly the life of blessed spirits. To some extent this is true; and whereas a bare and colorless sketch of the richest of all facts is as far from the truth as possible, we may allow ourselves to fill in the picture as best we can, if we remember the risks which we run in doing so. There are, it seems to me, two chief risks in allowing our imagination to create images of the bliss of heaven. One is that the eternal world, thus drawn and painted with the forms and colors of earth, takes substance in our minds as a second physical world, either supposed to exist somewhere in space, or expected to come into existence somewhen in time. This is the heaven of popular religion; and being a geographical or historical expression, it is open to attacks which cannot be met. Hence in the minds of many persons the whole fact of human immortality seems to belong to dreamland. The other danger is that, since a geographical and historical heaven is found to have no actuality, the hope of eternal life, with all that the spiritual world contains, should be relegated to the sphere of the "ideal." This seems to be the position of Höffding, and is quite clearly the view of thinkers like Santayana. They accept the dualism of value and existence, and place the highest hopes of humanity in a world which has value only and no existence. This seems to me to be offering mankind a stone for bread. Martineau's protest against this philosophy is surely justified:

"Amid all the sickly talk about 'ideals,' it is well to remember that as long as they are a mere self-painting of the yearning spirit, they have no more solidity than floating air-bubbles, gay in the sunshine and broken by the passing wind. You do not so much as touch the threshold of religion, so long as you are detained by the phantoms of your thought; the very gate of entrance to religion, the moment of its new birth, is the discovery that your gleaming ideal is the everlasting real." [2]

But though our knowledge of the eternal world is much less than we could desire, it is much greater than many thinkers allow. We are by no means shut off from realization and possession of the eternal values while we live here. We are not confined to local and temporal experience. We know what Truth and Beauty mean, not only for ourselves but for all souls throughout the universe, and for God Himself. Above all, we know what Love means. Now Love, which is the realization in experience of spiritual existence, has an unique value as a hierophant of the highest mysteries. And Love guarantees personality, for it needs what has been called *otherness*. In all love there must be a subject and an object, and a bond between them which transcends without annulling their separateness. What this means for personal immortality has been seen by many great minds. As an example I will quote from Plotinus' picture of life in the spiritual world. This writer is certainly not inclined to overestimate the claims of separate individuality, and he is under no obligation to make his doctrine conform to the dogmas of any creed.

"Spirits yonder see themselves in others. For there all things are transparent, and there is nothing dark or resisting, but everyone is manifest to everyone internally, and all things are manifest; for light is manifest to light. For everyone has all things in himself and sees all things in another, so that all things are everywhere and all is all and each is all, and infinite the glory." [3]

2 *Study of Religion*, vol. i. 12.
3 *Ennead*, v. 8, 4.

This eternal world is about us and within us while we live here. "Heaven is nearer to our souls than the earth is to our bodies." The world which we ordinarily think of as real is an arbitrary selection from experience, corresponding roughly to the average reaction of life upon the average man. Some values, such as existence, persistence, and rationality, are assumed to be "real"; others are relegated to the "ideal." Under the influence of natural science, special emphasis is laid on those values with which that science is engaged. But our world changes with us. It rises as we rise, and falls as we fall. It puts on immortality as we do. "Such as men themselves are, such will God appear to them to be." [4] Spinoza rightly says that all true knowledge takes place *sub specie aeternitatis*. For the πνευματικὸς the whole of life is spiritual, and, as Eucken says, he recognizes the whole of the spiritual life as his own life-being. He learns, as Plotinus declares in a profound sentence, that "all things that are Yonder are also Here below."

APOLOGY (CONCLUSION)

PLATO

Friends, who would have acquitted me, I would like also to talk with you about the thing which has come to pass, while the magistrates are busy, and before I go to the place at which I must die. Stay then a little, for we may as well talk with one another while there is time. You are my friends, and I should like to show you the meaning of this event which has happened to me. O my judges—for you I may truly call judges—I should like to tell you of a wonderful circumstance. Hitherto the divine faculty of which the internal oracle is the source has constantly been in the habit of opposing me even about trifles, if I was going to make a slip or error in any matter; and now as you see there has come upon me that which may be thought, and is generally believed to be, the last and worst evil. But the oracle made no sign of opposition, either when I was leaving my house in the morning, or when I was on my way to the court, or while I was speaking, at anything which I was going to say; and yet I have often been stopped in the middle of a speech, but now in nothing I either said or did touching the matter in hand has the oracle opposed me. What do I take to be the explanation of this silence? I will tell you. It is an intimation that what has happened to me is a good, and that those of us who think that death is an evil are in error. For the customary sign would surely have opposed me had I been going to evil and not to good.

Let us reflect in another way, and we shall see that there is great reason to hope that death is a good; for one of two things—either death is a state of nothingness and utter unconsciousness, or, as men say, there is a change and migration of the soul from this world to another. Now if you suppose that there is no consciousness, but a sleep like the sleep of him who is undisturbed even by dreams, death will be an unspeakable gain. For if a person were to select the night in which his sleep was undisturbed even by dreams, and were to compare with this the other days and nights of his life, and then were to tell us how many days and nights he had passed in the course of his life better and more pleasantly than this one, I think that any man, I will not say a private man, but even the great king will not find many such days or nights, when compared with the others. Now if death be of such a nature, I say that to die is a gain; for eternity is then only a single night. But if death is the journey to another place, and there, as men say, all

---

[4] From John Smith, the Cambridge Platonist.

the dead abide, what good, O my friends and judges, can be greater than this? If indeed when the pilgrim arrives in the world below, he is delivered from the professors of justice in this world, and finds the true judges who are said to give judgment there, Minos and Rhadamanthus and Aeacus and Triptolemus, and other sons of God who were righteous in their own life, that pilgrimage will be worth making. What would not a man give if he might converse with Orpheus and Musaeus and Hesiod and Homer? Nay, if this be true, let me die again and again. I myself, too, shall have a wonderful interest in there meeting and conversing with Palamedes, and Ajax the son of Telamon, and any other ancient hero who has suffered death through an unjust judgment; and there will be no small pleasure, as I think, in comparing my own sufferings with theirs. Above all, I shall then be able to continue my search into true and false knowledge; as in this world, so also in the next; and I shall find out who is wise, and who pretends to be wise, and is not. What would not a man give, O judges, to be able to examine the leader of the great Trojan expedition; or Odysseus or Sisyphus, or numberless others, men and women too! What infinite delight would there be in conversing with them and asking them questions! In another world they do not put a man to death for asking questions; assuredly not. For besides being happier than we are, they will be immortal, if what is said is true.

Wherefore, O judges, be of good cheer about death, and know of a certainty, that no evil can happen to a good man, either in life or after death. He and his are not neglected by the gods; nor has my own approaching end happened by mere chance. But I see clearly that the time had arrived when it was better for me to die and be released from trouble; wherefore the oracle gave no sign. For which reason, also, I am not angry with my condemners, or with my accusers; they have done me no harm, although they did not mean to do me any good; and for this I may gently blame them.

Still I have a favor to ask of them. When my sons are grown up, I would ask you, O my friends, to punish them; and I would have you trouble them, as I have troubled you, if they seem to care about riches, or anything, more than about virtue; or if they pretend to be something when they are really nothing,—then reprove them, as I have reproved you, for not caring about that for which they ought to care, and thinking that they are something when they are really nothing. And if you do this, both I and my sons will have received justice at your hands.

The hour of departure has arrived, and we go our ways—I to die, and you to live. Which is better God only knows.

(Benjamin Jowett, tr.)

CHAPTER 6

THE PROBLEM OF EVIL

Evil, do I say?
But speak not evil of the evil:
Evil and good they braided play
Into one cord.
—Herman Melville, *Clarel,* IV, iv.

What is man to make of this paradoxical world, a world in which every virtue is opposed by an opposite vice, a world in which Good can be explained only in terms that imply the existence of Evil, a world in which our very existence commonly depends on intolerable cruelty? If the shoes on our feet were to come to life, if our food could know again its recent mangled death-throes, what a chorus of agony would appal us! And when we consider man's long history, dark with his propensity for repeating old crimes with new refinements, what a revulsion we experience! Moreover, if sickened with the evil in humanity, we seek comfort in the seemingly innocent world of Nature, we meet once more with the signs of unimagined cruelty. On every hand creatures live on flesh and blood torn quivering and warm from frightened things; and over half the species of animate life are parasites, sapping the lives of others.

What are we to think of a world filled with infinite evil? One assumption is made at the outset in this problem: God *is.* A mechanistic view of the universe largely eliminates the problem of evil as a problem by rejecting the doctrine of a Final Cause. In a universe so conceived, ills are regarded as the outgrowth of purely natural causes, and there is no possible relationship between them and any external spiritual force. Only in a God-constituted world can these phenomena be regarded in an absolute sense as evil.

What, then, is the relation of these ugly facts to our concepts of God? Did God frame the evil of the universe as well as the good? Blake, rapt in the contemplation of this mystery, symbolized in his Tiger, asks, "Did he smile his work to see? Did he who made the Lamb make thee?"

One of the most common answers is that the ways of God are inscrutable, an answer that suggests law, but makes room for caprice. The early Hebrew psalmist appears to have accepted this explanation imperturbably. All the facts of the earth attest God's glory, and death is no evil. There was one famous early rebel against this attitude, the righteous Job, but his protests

win the answer out of the whirlwind.   Robert Frost examines the implications of this great dramatic epic in a philosophical play of his own.   What
was God's hidden purpose in afflicting Job?   It is characteristic of Frost's
gentle humor and wisdom that he keeps to the text of the Bible in his answer.

But it is not in man's nature to be content with this answer.   Byron's Cain,
not resigned to man's lot, asks the questions that epitomize the problem:
Because God is all-powerful, must he be all-good?   And if he is all-good, why
then is evil?   The assumption is clear: A perfect God would not create an
imperfect world.   The *Rubaiyat* seizes on the idea of God's presumed omniscience and perfection to absolve man from sin: "Thou wilt not with Predestined Evil round Enmesh, and then impute my fall to sin."

But others will not release man from blame thus easily.   Landor's Mole,
after justifying his own animal existence, thrusts home so pointed a truth
about man himself that the Gardener will not listen further.   Robinson
Jeffers is savage and direct on the same theme: The torturer deserves the
death cup.

Such a repudiation of man is private, alien to man's self-love.   Tennyson,
who sees Man as Nature's last work with "splendid purpose in his eyes," feels
that evil will ultimately be transformed: "O yet we trust that somehow
good Will be the final goal of ill."   Since faith is not knowledge, Tennyson
admits his helplessness in the face of this problem; he is "an infant crying
in the night, And with no language but a cry."

The thesis that evil is only illusion, as suggested by Meredith, is examined
in full by G. Lowes Dickinson.   At the end of his dialogue he arrives at the
important crux: What is the place of right and wrong in a system in which
evil is only appearance?   And what, Dostoevsky asks, of innocent children
tortured to death?   Can one accept an ultimate happiness that requires as
part of its fabric the death-throes of a child?   Reason and sympathy must
answer no.

All these conjectures assume the omnipotence of God.   But Alfred Noyes
argues that it is conceivable that some things are impossible even to Omnipotence, and that it may be impossible even for a perfect God to develop
a race to its full heights without suffering.   The necessity of suffering in
the scheme of man's spiritual evolution is the timeless answer of mysticism,
given since thought began.   T. E. Brown insists that through griefs we attain
to unity with God.   Our pains are as ripples from the gold-beaked stem of
God's onward surging galley.   Suffering, of course, has long been exalted
as the Way and the Life by Jesus of Nazareth.   The goodness of suffering
becomes a spiritual revelation in the writings of Miguel Unamuno.   Man
must choose, he says, between happiness and love; and love, which alone is
good, is suffering.

Rightly weighed, these several considerations explain much.   If they do
not explain all, the believer may content himself with Browning's view that

the broken arcs we see on earth will become, in heaven, a perfect sphere. One truth is sure: Though man's own baseness produces untold agony, his nature is at its grandest in response to suffering. "Our sweetest songs are those that tell of saddest thought," and our greatest works of art present man's conquest of fear and pain and death.

THE TIGER

WILLIAM BLAKE

Tiger! Tiger! burning bright
In the forests of the night,
What immortal hand or eye
Could frame thy fearful symmetry?

In what distant deeps or skies
Burnt the fire of thine eyes?
On what wings dare he aspire?
What the hand dare seize the fire?

And what shoulder, and what art,
Could twist the sinews of thy heart?
And when thy heart began to beat,
What dread hand? and what dread feet?

What the hammer? what the chain?
In what furnace was thy brain?
What the anvil? what dread grasp
Dare its deadly terrors clasp?

When the stars threw down their spears,
And watered heaven with their tears,
Did he smile his work to see?
Did he who made the Lamb make thee?

Tiger! Tiger! burning bright
In the forests of the night,
What immortal hand or eye
Dare frame thy fearful symmetry?

THE BOOK OF PSALMS, CIV

Bless the Lord, O my soul. O Lord my God, thou art very great; thou art clothed with honor and majesty.

Who coverest thyself with light as with a garment: who stretchest out the heavens like a curtain:

Who layeth the beams of his chambers in the waters: who maketh the clouds his chariot: who walketh upon the wings of the wind:

Who maketh his angels spirits; his ministers a flaming fire:

Who laid the foundations of the earth, that it should not be removed for ever.

Thou coveredst it with the deep as with a garment: the waters stood above the mountains.

At thy rebuke they fled; at the voice of thy thunder they hasted away.

They go up by the mountains; they go down by the valleys unto the place which thou hast founded for them.

Thou hast set a bound that they may not pass over; that they turn not again to cover the earth.

He sendeth the springs into the valleys, which run among the hills.

They give drink to every beast of the field: the wild asses quench their thirst.

By them shall the fowls of the heaven have their habitation, which sing among the branches.

He watereth the hills from his chambers: the earth is satisfied with the fruit of thy works.

He causeth the grass to grow for the cattle, and herb for the service of man: that he may bring forth food out of the earth;

And wine that maketh glad the heart of man, and oil to make his face to shine, and bread which strengtheneth man's heart.

The trees of the Lord are full of sap; the cedars of Lebanon, which he hath planted;

Where the birds make their nests: as for the stork, the fir trees are her house.

The high hills are a refuge for the wild goats; and the rocks for the conies.

He appointed the moon for seasons: the sun knoweth his going down.

Thou makest darkness, and it is night: wherein all the beasts of the forest do creep forth.

The young lions roar after their prey, and seek their meat from God.

The sun ariseth, they gather themselves together, and lay them down in their dens.

Man goeth forth unto his work and to his labor until the evening.

O Lord, how manifold are thy works! in wisdom hast thou made them all: the earth is full of thy riches.

So is this great and wide sea, wherein are things creeping innumerable, both small and great beasts.

There go the ships: there is that leviathan, whom thou hast made to play therein.

These wait all upon thee; that thou mayest give them their meat in due season.

That thou givest them they gather: thou openest thine hand, they are filled with good.

Thou hidest thy face, they are troubled: thou takest away their breath, they die, and return to their dust.

Thou sendest forth thy spirit, they are created: and thou renewest the face of the earth.

The glory of the Lord shall endure for ever: the Lord shall rejoice in his works.

He looketh on the earth, and it trembleth: he toucheth the hills, and they smoke.

I will sing unto the Lord as long as I live: I will sing praise to my God while I have my being.

My meditation of him shall be sweet: I will be glad in the Lord.

Let the sinners be consumed out of the earth, and let the wicked be no more. Bless thou the Lord, O my soul. Praise ye the Lord.

FROM THE BOOK OF JOB

CHAPTER 1

There was a man in the land of Uz, whose name was Job; and that man was perfect and upright, and one that feared God, and eschewed evil.

And there were born unto him seven sons and three daughters.

His substance also was seven thousand sheep, and three thousand camels, and five hundred yoke of oxen, and five hundred she-asses, and a very great household; so that this man was the greatest of all the men of the east.

And his sons went and feasted in their houses, every one his day; and sent and called for their three sisters to eat and to drink with them.

And it was so, when the days of their feasting were gone about, that Job sent and sanctified them, and rose up early in the morning, and offered burnt offerings according to the number of them all: for Job said, It may be that my sons have sinned, and cursed God in their hearts. Thus did Job continually.

Now there was a day when the sons of God came to present themselves before the Lord, and Satan came also among them.

And the Lord said unto Satan, Whence comest thou? Then Satan answered the Lord, and said, From going to and fro in the earth, and from walking up and down in it.

And the Lord said unto Satan, Hast thou considered my servant Job, that there is none like him in the earth, a perfect and an upright man, one that feareth God, and escheweth evil?

Then Satan answered the Lord, and said, Doth Job fear God for nought?

Hast not thou made an hedge about him, and about his house, and about all that he hath on every side? thou hast blessed the work of his hands, and his substance is increased in the land.

But put forth thine hand now, and touch all that he hath, and he will curse thee to thy face.

And the Lord said unto Satan, Behold, all that he hath is in thy power; only upon himself put not forth thine hand. So Satan went forth from the presence of the Lord.

And there was a day when his sons and his daughters were eating and drinking wine in their eldest brother's house:

And there came a messenger unto Job, and said, The oxen were plowing, and the asses feeding beside them:

And the Sabeans fell upon them, and took them away; yea, they have slain the servants with the edge of the sword; and I only am escaped alone to tell thee.

While he was yet speaking, there came also another, and said, The fire of God is fallen from heaven, and hath burned up the sheep, and the servants, and consumed them; and I only am escaped alone to tell thee.

While he was yet speaking, there came also another, and said, The Chaldeans made out three bands, and fell upon the camels, and have carried them away, yea, and slain the servants with the edge of the sword; and I only am escaped alone to tell thee.

While he was yet speaking, there came also another, and said, Thy sons and thy daughters were eating and drinking wine in their eldest brother's house:

And, behold, there came a great wind from the wilderness, and smote the four corners of the house, and it fell upon the young men, and they are dead; and I only am escaped alone to tell thee,

Then Job arose, and rent his mantle, and shaved his head, and fell down upon the ground, and worshiped,

And said, Naked came I out of my mother's womb, and naked shall I return thither: the Lord gave, and the Lord hath taken away; blessed be the name of the Lord.

In all this Job sinned not, nor charged God foolishly.

CHAPTER 2

Again there was a day when the sons of God came to present themselves before the Lord, and Satan came also among them to present himself before the Lord.

And the Lord said unto Satan, From whence comest thou?   And Satan answered the Lord, and said, From going to and fro in the earth, and from walking up and down in it.

And the Lord said unto Satan, Hast thou considered my servant Job, that there is none like him in the earth, a perfect and an upright man, one that feareth God, and escheweth evil? and still he holdeth fast his integrity, although thou movedst me against him, to destroy him without cause.

And Satan answered the Lord, and said, Skin for skin, yea, all that a man hath will he give for his life.

But put forth thine hand now, and touch his bone and his flesh, and he will curse thee to thy face.

And the Lord said unto Satan, Behold, he is in thine hand; but save his life.

So went Satan forth from the presence of the Lord, and smote Job with sore boils from the sole of his foot unto his crown.

And he took him a potsherd to scrape himself withal; and he sat down among the ashes.

Then said his wife unto him, Dost thou still retain thine integrity? curse God, and die.

But he said unto her, Thou speakest as one of the foolish women speaketh. What? shall we receive good at the hand of God, and shall we not receive evil?   In all this did not Job sin with his lips.

Now when Job's three friends heard of all this evil that was come upon him, they came every one from his own place; Eliphaz the Temanite, and Bildad the Shuhite, and Zophar the Naamathite: for they had made an appointment together to come to mourn with him and to comfort him.

And when they lifted up their eyes afar off, and knew him not, they lifted up their voice, and wept; and they rent every one his mantle, and sprinkled dust upon their heads toward heaven.

So they sat down with him upon the ground seven days and seven nights, and none spake a word unto him: for they saw that his grief was very great. . . .

CHAPTER 3

After this opened Job his mouth, and cursed his day.

And Job spake, and said,

Let the day perish wherein I was born, and the night in which it was said, There is a man child conceived.

Let that day be darkness; let not God regard it from above, neither let the light shine upon it.

Let darkness and the shadow of death stain it; let a cloud dwell upon it; let the blackness of the day terrify it.

As for that night, let darkness seize upon it; let it not be joined unto the days of the year, let it not come into the number of the months.

Lo, let that night be solitary, let no joyful voice come therein.

Let them curse it that curse the day, who are ready to raise up their mourning.

Let the stars of the twilight thereof be dark; let it look for light, but have none; neither let it see the dawning of the day:

Because it shut not up the doors of my mother's womb, nor hid sorrow from mine eyes.

Why died I not from the womb? why did I not give up the ghost when I came out of the belly?

Why did the knees prevent me? or why the breasts that I should suck?

For now should I have lain still and been quiet, I should have slept: then had I been at rest. . . .

CHAPTER 21

. . . .

Hear diligently my speech, and let this be your consolations.

Suffer me that I may speak; and after that I have spoken, mock on.

As for me, is my complaint to man? and if it were so, why should not my spirit be troubled?

Mark me, and be astonished, and lay your hand upon your mouth.

Even when I remember I am afraid, and trembling taketh hold on my flesh.

Wherefore do the wicked live, become old, yea, are mighty in power?

Their seed is established in their sight with them, and their offspring before their eyes.

Their houses are safe from fear, neither is the rod of God upon them.

Their bull gendereth, and faileth not; their cow calveth, and casteth not her calf.

They send forth their little ones like a flock, and their children dance.

They take the timbrel and harp, and rejoice at the sound of the organ.

They spend their days in wealth, and in a moment go down to the grave.

Therefore they say unto God, Depart from us; for we desire not the knowledge of thy ways.

What is the Almighty, that we should serve him? and what profit should we have, if we pray unto him?

Lo, their good is not in their hand: the counsel of the wicked is far from me.

How oft is the candle of the wicked put out! and how oft cometh their destruction upon them! God distributeth sorrows in his anger.

They are as stubble before the wind, and as chaff that the storm carrieth away.

God layeth up his iniquity for his children: he rewardeth him, and he shall know it.

His eyes shall see his destruction, and he shall drink of the wrath of the Almighty.

For what pleasure hath he in his house after him, when the number of his months is cut off in the midst?

Shall any teach God knowledge? seeing he judgeth those that are high.

One dieth in his full strength, being wholly at ease and quiet.

His breasts are full of milk, and his bones are moistened with marrow.

And another dieth in the bitterness of his soul, and never eateth with pleasure.

They shall lie down alike in the dust, and the worms shall cover them. . . .

CHAPTER 31

I made a covenant with mine eyes; why then should I think upon a maid?

For what portion of God is there from above? and what inheritance of the Almighty from on high?

Is not destruction to the wicked? and a strange punishment to the workers of iniquity?

Doth not he see my ways, and count all my steps?

If I have walked with vanity, or if my foot hath hasted to deceit;

Let me be weighed in an even balance, that God may know mine integrity.

If my step hath turned out of the way, and mine heart walked after mine eyes, and if any blot hath cleaved to mine hands;

Then let me sow, and let another eat; yea, let my offspring be rooted out.

If mine heart have been deceived by a woman, or if I have laid wait at my neighbor's door;

Then let my wife grind unto another, and let others bow down upon her.

For this is an heinous crime; yea, it is an iniquity to be punished by the judges.

For it is a fire that consumeth to destruction, and would root out all mine increase.

If I did despise the cause of my manservant or of my maidservant, when they contended with me;

What then shall I do when God riseth up? and when he visiteth, what shall I answer him?

Did not he that made me in the womb make him? and did not one fashion us in the womb?

If I have withheld the poor from their desire, or have caused the eyes of the widow to fail;

Or have eaten my morsel myself alone, and the fatherless hath not eaten thereof;

(For from my youth he was brought up with me, as with a father, and I have guided her from my mother's womb;)

If I have seen any perish for want of clothing, or any poor without covering;

If his loins have not blessed me, and if he were not warmed with the fleece of my sheep;

If I have lifted up my hand against the fatherless, when I saw my help in the gate:

Then let mine arm fall from my shoulder-blade, and mine arm be broken from the bone.

For destruction from God was a terror to me, and by reason of his highness I could not endure.

If I have made gold my hope, or have said to the fine gold, Thou art my confidence;

If I rejoiced because my wealth was great, and because mine hand had gotten much;

If I beheld the sun when it shined, or the moon walking in brightness;

And my heart hath been secretly enticed, or my mouth hath kissed my hand:

This also were an iniquity to be punished by the judge: for I should have denied the God that is above.

If I rejoiced at the destruction of him that hated me, or lifted up myself when evil found him:

Neither have I suffered my mouth to sin by wishing a curse to his soul.

If the men of my tabernacle said not, Oh that we had of his flesh! we cannot be satisfied.

The stranger did not lodge in the street: but I opened my doors to the traveler.

If I covered my transgressions as Adam, by hiding mine iniquity in my bosom:

Did I fear a great multitude, or did the contempt of families terrify me, that I kept silence, and went not out of the door?

Oh that one would hear me! behold, my desire is, that the Almighty would answer me, and that mine adversary had written a book.

Surely I would take it upon my shoulder, and bind it as a crown to me.

I would declare unto him the number of my steps; as a prince would I go near unto him.

If my land cry against me, or that the furrows likewise thereof complain;

If I have eaten the fruits thereof without money, or have caused the owners thereof to lose their life:

Let thistles grow instead of wheat, and cockle instead of barley. The words of Job are ended.

.   .   .   .

CHAPTER 38

Then the Lord answered Job out of the whirlwind, and said,

Who is this that darkeneth counsel by words without knowledge?

Gird up now thy loins like a man; for I will demand of thee, and answer thou me.

Where wast thou when I laid the foundations of the earth? declare, if thou hast understanding.

Who hath laid the measures thereof, if thou knowest? or who hath stretched the line upon it?

Whereupon are the foundations thereof fastened? or who laid the corner stone thereof;

When the morning stars sang together, and all the sons of God shouted for joy?

Or who shut up the sea with doors, when it brake forth, as if it had issued out of the womb?

When I made the cloud the garment thereof, and thick darkness a swaddling-band for it.

And brake up for it my decreed place, and set bars and doors,

And said, Hitherto shalt thou come, but no further: and here shall thy proud waves be stayed?

Hast thou commanded the morning since thy days; and caused the dayspring to know his place;

That it might take hold of the ends of the earth, that the wicked might be shaken out of it?

It is turned as clay to the seal; and they stand as a garment.

And from the wicked their light is withholden, and the high arm shall be broken.

Hast thou entered into the springs of the sea? or hast thou walked in the search of the depth?

Have the gates of death been opened unto thee? or hast thou seen the doors of the shadow of death?

Hast thou perceived the breadth of the earth? declare if thou knowest it all.

Where is the way where light dwelleth? and as for darkness, where is the place thereof,

That thou shouldest take it to the bound thereof, and that thou shouldest know the paths to the house thereof?

Knowest thou it, because thou wast then born? or because the number of thy days is great?

Hast thou entered into the treasures of the snow? or hast thou seen the treasures of the hail,

Which I have reserved against the time of trouble, against the day of battle and war?

By what way is the light parted, which scattereth the east wind upon the earth?

Who hath divided a watercourse for the overflowing of waters, or a way for the lightning of thunder;

To cause it to rain on the earth, where no man is; on the wilderness, wherein there is no man;

To satisfy the desolate and waste ground; and to cause the bud of the tender herb to spring forth?

Hath the rain a father? or who hath begotten the drops of dew?

Out of whose womb came the ice? and the hoary frost of heaven, who hath gendered it?

The waters are hid as with a stone, and the face of the deep is frozen.

Canst thou bind the sweet influences of Pleiades, or loose the bands of Orion?

Canst thou bring forth Mazzaroth in his season? or canst thou guide Arcturus with his sons?

Knowest thou the ordinances of heaven? canst thou set the dominion thereof in the earth?

Canst thou lift up thy voice to the clouds, that abundance of waters may cover thee?

Canst thou send lightnings, that they may go, and say unto thee, Here we are?

Who hath put wisdom in the inward parts? or who hath given understanding to the heart?

Who can number the clouds in wisdom? or who can stay the bottles of heaven,

When the dust groweth into hardness, and the clods cleave fast together?

Wilt thou hunt the prey for the lion? or fill the appetite of the young lions,

When they couch in their dens, and abide in the covert to lie in wait?

Who provideth for the raven his food? when his young ones cry unto God, they wander for lack of meat.

.   .   .   .

CHAPTER 42

Then Job answered the Lord, and said,

I know that thou canst do every thing, and that no thought can be withholden from thee.

Who is he that hideth counsel without knowledge? therefore have I uttered that I understood not; things too wonderful for me, which I knew not.

Hear, I beseech thee, and I will speak: I will demand of thee, and declare thou unto me.

I have heard of thee by the hearing of the ear: but now mine eye seeth thee.

Wherefore I abhor myself, and repent in dust and ashes.

.   .   .   .

And the Lord turned the captivity of Job, when he prayed for his friends: also the Lord gave Job twice as much as he had before.

Then came there unto him all his brethren, and all his sisters, and all they that had been of his acquaintance before, and did eat bread with him in his house: and they bemoaned him, and comforted him over all the evil that the Lord had brought upon him: every man also gave him a piece of money, and every one an earring of gold.

So the Lord blessed the latter end of Job more than his beginning: for he had fourteen thousand sheep, and six thousand camels, and a thousand yoke of oxen, and a thousand she-asses.

He had also seven sons and three daughters.

And he called the name of the first, Jemima; and the name of the second, Kezia; and the name of the third, Keren-happuch.

And in all the land were no women found so fair as the daughters of Job: and their father gave them inheritance among their brethren.

After this lived Job an hundred and forty years, and saw his sons, and his sons' sons, even four generations.

So Job died, being old and full of days.

from A MASQUE OF REASON
ROBERT FROST

GOD: Oh, I remember well: you're Job, my Patient.
How are you now? I trust you're quite recovered,
And feel no ill effects from what I gave you.
JOB: Gave me in truth: I like the frank admission.
I am a name for being put upon.
But, yes, I'm fine, except for now and then
A reminiscent twinge of rheumatism.
The let-up's heavenly. You perhaps will tell us
If that is all there is to be of Heaven,
Escape from so great pains of life on earth
It gives a sense of let-up calculated
To last a fellow to Eternity.
GOD: Yes, by and by. But first a larger matter.
I've had you on my mind a thousand years
To thank you someday for the way you helped me
Establish once for all the principle
There's no connection man can reason out
Between his just deserts and what he gets.
Virtue may fail and wickedness succeed.
'Twas a great demonstration we put on.
I should have spoken sooner had I found
The word I wanted. You would have supposed
One who in the beginning *was* the Word
Would be in a position to command it.
I have to wait for words like anyone.
Too long I've owed you this apology
For the apparently unmeaning sorrow
You were afflicted with in those old days.
But it was of the essence of the trial
You shouldn't understand it at the time.

It had to seem unmeaning to have meaning.
And it came out all right. I have no doubt
You realize by now the part you played
To stultify the Deuteronomist
And change the tenor of religious thought.
My thanks are to you for releasing me
From moral bondage to the human race.
The only free will there at first was man's,
Who could do good or evil as he chose.
I had no choice but I must follow him
With forfeits and rewards he understood—
Unless I liked to suffer loss of worship.
I had to prosper good and punish evil.
You changed all that. You set me free to reign.
You are the Emancipator of your God,
And as such I promote you to a saint.

JOB: You hear him, Thyatira: we're a saint.
Salvation in our case is retroactive.
We're saved, we're saved, whatever else it means.

JOB's WIFE: Well, after all these years!

JOB: This is my wife.

JOB's WIFE: If you're the deity I assume You are—
(I'd know You by Blake's picture anywhere) —

GOD: The best, I'm told, I ever have had taken.

JOB's WIFE:—I have a protest I would lodge with You.
I want to ask You if it stands to reason
That women prophets should be burned as witches
Whereas men prophets are received with honor.

JOB: Except in their own country, Thyatira.

GOD: You're not a witch?

JOB's WIFE: No.

GOD: Have you ever been one?

JOB: Sometimes she thinks she has and gets herself
Worked up about it.   But she really hasn't—
Not in the sense of having to my knowledge
Predicted anything that came to pass.

JOB's WIFE: The witch of Endor was a friend of mine.

GOD: You wouldn't say she fared so very badly.
I noticed when she called up Samuel
His spirit had to come.   Apparently
A witch was stronger than a prophet there.

JOB's WIFE: But she was burned for witchcraft.

GOD: That is not
Of record in my Note Book.

JOB's WIFE: Well, she was
And I should like to know the reason why.

GOD: There you go asking for the very thing
We've just agreed I didn't have to give.
(*The throne collapses. But He picks it up*
And this time locks it up and leaves it.)
Where has she been the last half hour or so?

She wants to know why there is still injustice.
I answer flatly: That's the way it is,
And bid my will avouch it like Macbeth.
We may as well go back to the beginning
And look for justice in the case of Segub.
JOB: Oh, Lord, let's not go *back* to anything.
GOD: Because your wife's past won't bear looking into?
In our great moment what did you do, Madam?
What did you try to make your husband say?
JOB'S WIFE: No, let's not live things over.   I don't care.
I stood by Job.   I may have turned on You.
Job scratched his boils and tried to think what he
Had done or not done to or for the poor.
The test is always how we treat the poor.
It's time the poor were treated by the state
In some way not so penal as the poorhouse.
That's one thing more to put on Your agenda.
Job hadn't done a thing, poor innocent.
I told him not to scratch: it made it worse.
If I said it once I said a thousand times,
Don't scratch!   And when, as rotten as his skin,
His tents blew all to pieces, I picked up
Enough to build him every night a pup tent
Around him so it wouldn't touch and hurt him.
I did my wifely duty.   I should tremble!
All You can seem to do is lose Your temper
When reason-hungry mortals ask for reasons.
Of course, in the abstract high singular
There isn't any universal reason;
And no one but a man would think there was.
You don't catch women trying to be Plato.
Still there must be lots of unsystematic
Stray scraps of palliative reason
It wouldn't hurt You to vouchsafe the faithful.

.   .   .   .

GOD: It would be too bad if Columbus-like
You failed to see the worth of your achievement.
JOB: You call it mine.
GOD: We groped it out together.
Any originality it showed
I give you credit for.   My forte is truth,
Or metaphysics, long the world's reproach
For standing still in one place true forever;
While science goes self-superseding on.
Look at how far we've left the current science
Of Genesis behind.   The wisdom there though,
Is just as good as when I uttered it.
Still, novelty has doubtless an attraction.
JOB: So it's important who first thinks of things?
GOD: I'm a great stickler for the author's name.

By proper names I find I do my thinking.

JOB'S WIFE: God, who invented earth?

JOB: What, still awake?

GOD: Any originality it showed
    Was of the Devil. He invented Hell,
    False premises that are the original
    Of all originality, the sin
    That felled the angels, Wolsey should have said.
    As for the earth, we groped that out together,
    Much as your husband Job and I together
    Found out the discipline man needed most
    Was to learn his submission to unreason;
    And that for man's own sake as well as mine,
    So he won't find it hard to take his orders
    From his inferiors in intelligence
    In peace and war—especially in war.

JOB: So he won't find it hard to take his war.

GOD: You have the idea. There's not much I can tell you.

JOB: All very splendid. I am flattered proud
    To have been in on anything with You.
    'Twas a great demonstration if You say so.
    Though incidentally I sometimes wonder
    Why it had had to be at my expense.

GOD: It had to be at somebody's expense.
    Society can never think things out:
    It has to see them acted out by actors,
    Devoted actors at a sacrifice—
    The ablest actors I can lay my hands on.
    Is that your answer?

JOB: No, for I have yet
    To ask my question. We disparage reason.
    But all the time it's what we're most concerned with.
    There's will as motor and there's will as brakes.
    Reason is, I suppose, the steering gear.
    The will as brakes can't stop the will as motor
    For very long. We're plainly made to go.
    We're going anyway and may as well
    Have some say as to where we're headed for;
    Just as we will be talking anyway
    And may as well throw in a little sense.
    Let's do so now. Because I let You off
    From telling me your reason, don't assume
    I thought You had none. Somewhere back
    I knew You had one. But this isn't it
    You're giving me. You say we groped this out.
    But if You will forgive me the irreverence,
    It sounds to me as if You thought it out,
    And took Your time to it. It seems to me
    An afterthought, a long long afterthought.
    I'd give more for one least beforehand reason
    Than all the justifying ex-post-facto

Excuses trumped up by You for theologists.
The front of being answerable to no one
I'm with You in maintaining to the public.
But Lord, we showed them what. The audience
Has all gone home to bed. The play's played out.
Come, after all these years—to satisfy me.
I'm curious. And I'm a grown-up man:
I'm not a child for You to put me off
And tantalize me with another "Oh, because,"
You'd be the last to want me to believe
All Your effects were merely lucky blunders.
That would be unbelief and atheism.
The artist in me cries out for design.
Such devilish ingenuity of torture
Did seem unlike You, and I tried to think
The reason might have been some other person's.
But there is nothing You are not behind.
I did not ask then, but it seems as if
Now after all these years You might indulge me.
Why did You hurt me so? I am reduced
To asking flatly for a reason—outright.
GOD: I'd tell you, Job—
JOB: All right, don't tell me then
If you don't want to. I don't want to know.
But what is all this secrecy about?
I fail to see what fun, what satisfaction
A God can find in laughing at how badly
Men fumble at the possibilities
When left to guess forever for themselves.
The chances are when there's so much pretense
Of metaphysical profundity
The obscurity's a fraud to cover nothing.
I've come to think no so-called hidden value's
Worth going after. Get down into things
It will be found there's no more given there
Than on the surface. If there ever was,
The crypt was long since rifled by the Greeks.
We don't know where we are, or who we are.
We don't know one another; don't know You;
Don't know what time it is. We don't know, don't we?
Who says we don't? Who got up these misgivings?
Oh, we know well enough to go ahead with.
I mean we seem to know enough to act on.
It comes down to a doubt about the wisdom
Of having children—after having had them,
So there is nothing we can do about it
But warn the children they perhaps should have none.
You could end this by simply coming out
And saying plainly and unequivocally
Whether there's any part of man immortal.
Yet You don't speak. Let fools bemuse themselves

By being baffled for the sake of being.
I'm sick of the whole artificial puzzle.
JOB'S WIFE: You won't get any answers out of God.
GOD: My kingdom, what an outbreak!
JOB'S WIFE: Job is right,
Your kingdom, yes, Your kingdom come on earth.
Pray tell me what does that mean.   Anything?
Perhaps that earth is going to crack someday
Like a big egg and hatch a heaven out
Of all the dead and buried from their graves.
One simple little statement from the throne
Would put an end to such fantastic nonsense;
And, too, take care of twenty of the four
And twenty freedoms on the party docket.
Or is it only four?   My extra twenty
Are freedoms from the need of asking questions.
   (I hope You know the game called twenty questions.)
For instance, is there such a thing as Progress?
Job says there's no such thing as Earth's becoming
An easier place for man to save his soul in.
Except as a hard place to save his soul in,
A trial ground where he can try himself
And find out whether he is any good,
It would be meaningless.   It might as well
Be Heaven at once and have it over with.
GOD: Two pitching on like this tend to confuse me.
One at a time, please.   I will answer Job first.
I'm going to tell Job why I tortured him
And trust it won't be adding to the torture.
I was just showing off to the devil, Job,
As is set forth in Chapters One and Two.
   (Job takes a few steps pacing.)   Do you mind?
   (God eyes him anxiously.)
JOB: No.   No, I mustn't.
'Twas human of You.   I expected more
Than I could understand and what I get
Is almost less than I can understand.
But I don't mind.   Let's leave it as it stood.
The point was it was none of my concern.
I stick to that.   But talk about confusion!
How is that for a mix-up, Thyatira?
Yet I suppose what seems to us confusion
Is not confusion, but the form of forms,
The serpent's tail stuck down the serpent's throat,
Which is the symbol of eternity
And also of the way all things come round,
Or of how rays return upon themselves,
To quote the greatest Western poem yet.

FROM CAIN

A MYSTERY

LORD BYRON

ACT I

SCENE I

The Land without Paradise.—Time, Sunrise.

ADAM, EVE, CAIN, ABEL, ADAH, ZILLAH, *offering a Sacrifice.*
ADAM: God, the Eternal! Infinite! All-wise!—
Who out of darkness on the deep didst make
Light on the waters with a word—all hail!
Jehovah, with returning light, all hail!
EVE: God! who didst name the day, and separate
Morning from night, till then divided never—
Who didst divide the wave from wave, and call
Part of thy work the firmament—all hail!
ABEL: God! who didst call the elements into
Earth—ocean—air—and fire, and with the day
And night, and worlds which these illuminate,
Or shadow, madest beings to enjoy them,
And love both them and thee—all hail! all hail!
ADAH: God, the Eternal! Parent of all things!
Who didst create these best and beauteous beings,
To be beloved, more than all, save thee—
Let me love thee and them:—All hail! all hail!
ZILLAH: Oh, God! who loving, making, blessing all,
Yet didst permit the Serpent to creep in,
And drive my father forth from Paradise,
Keep us from further evil:—Hail! all hail!
ADAM: Son Cain, my first-born, wherefore art thou silent?
CAIN: Why should I speak?
ADAM: To pray.
CAIN: Have ye not prayed?
ADAM: We have, most fervently.
CAIN: And loudly: I
Have heard you.
ADAM: So will God, I trust.
ABEL: Amen!
ADAM: But thou, my eldest born, art silent still.
CAIN: 'Tis better I should be so.
ADAM: Wherefore so?
CAIN: I have nought to ask.
ADAM: Nor aught to thank for?
CAIN: No.
ADAM: Dost thou not live?
CAIN: Must I not die?
EVE: Alas.
The fruit of our forbidden tree begins
To fall.

ADAM: And we must gather it again.
Oh, God! why didst thou plant the tree of knowledge?
CAIN: And wherefore plucked ye not the tree of life?
Ye might have then defied him.
ADAM: Oh! my son,
Blaspheme not: these are serpent's words.
CAIN: Why not?
The snake spoke *truth*: it *was* the tree of knowledge;
It *was* the tree of life: knowledge is good,
And life is good; and how can both be evil?
EVE: My boy! thou speakest as I spoke, in sin,
Before thy birth: let me not see renewed
My misery in thine.   I have repented.
Let me not see my offspring fall into
The snares beyond the walls of Paradise,
Which e'en in Paradise destroyed his parents.
Content thee with what *is*.   Had we been so,
Thou now hadst been contented.—Oh, my son!
ADAM: Our orisons completed, let us hence,
Each to his task of toil—not heavy, though
Needful: the earth is young, and yields us kindly
Her fruits with little labor.
EVE: Cain, my son,
Behold thy father cheerful and resigned,
And do as he doth.
                                  [*Exeunt* ADAM *and* EVE.

ZILLAH: Wilt thou not, my brother?
ABEL: Why wilt thou wear this gloom upon thy brow,
Which can avail thee nothing, save to rouse
The Eternal anger?
ADAH: My beloved Cain,
Wilt thou frown even on me?
CAIN: No, Adah! no;
I fain would be alone a little while.
Abel, I'm sick at heart; but it will pass.
Precede me, brother—I will follow shortly.
And you, too, sisters, tarry not behind;
Your gentleness must not be harshly met:
I'll follow you anon.
ADAH: If not, I will
Return to seek you here.
ABEL: The peace of God
Be on your spirit, brother!
                                  [*Exeunt* ABEL, ZILLAH, *and* ADAH.

CAIN: (*solus*)   And this is
Life!—Toil! and wherefore should I toil?—because
My father could not keep his place in Eden.
What had *I* done in this—I was unborn:
I sought not to be born; nor love the state
To which that birth has brought me.   Why did he
Yield to the serpent and the woman? or,

Yielding, why suffer? What was there in this?
The tree was planted, and why not for him?
If not, why place him near it, where it grew,
The fairest in the center? They have but
One answer to all questions, " 'T was *his* will,
And *he* is good." How know I that? Because
He is all-powerful, must all-good, too, follow?
I judge but by the fruits—and they are bitter—
Which I must feed on for a fault not mine. . . .

ACT II

SCENE II

CAIN: . . . Why do I exist?
Why art *thou* wretched? why are all things so?
Ev'n he who made us must be, as the maker
Of things unhappy! To produce destruction
Can surely never be the task of joy,
And yet my sire says he's omnipotent:
Then why is evil—he being good? I asked
This question of my father; and he said,
Because this evil only was the path
To good. Strange good, that must arise from out
Its deadly opposite. I lately saw
A lamb stung by a reptile: the poor suckling
Lay foaming on the earth, beneath the vain
And piteous bleating of its restless dam;
My father plucked some herbs, and laid them to
The wound; and by degrees the helpless wretch
Resumed its careless life, and rose to drain
The mother's milk, who o'er it tremulous
Stood licking its reviving limbs with joy.
Behold, my son! said Adam, how from evil
Springs good!
LUCIFER: What didst thou answer?
CAIN: Nothing; for
He is my father: but I thought, that 'twere
A better portion for the animal
Never to have been *stung at all,* than to
Purchase renewal of its little life
With agonies unutterable, though
Dispelled by antidotes.
LUCIFER: But as thou saidst
Of all beloved things thou lovest her
Who shared thy mother's milk, and giveth hers
Unto thy children—
CAIN: Most assuredly:
What should I be without her?
LUCIFER: What am I?
CAIN: Dost thou love nothing?
LUCIFER: What does thy God love?

CAIN: All things, my father says; but I confess
    I see it not in their allotment here.
LUCIFER: And, therefore, thou canst not see if *I* love
    Or no, except some vast and general purpose,
    To which particular things must melt like snows.
CAIN: Snows! what are they?
LUCIFER: Be happier in not knowing
    What thy remoter offspring must encounter;
    But bask beneath the clime which knows no winter. . . .

RUBAIYAT, LXXVIII-LXXXI

OMAR KHAYYAM

LXXVIII

What! out of senseless Nothing to provoke
A conscious Something to resent the yoke
    Of unpermitted Pleasure, under pain
Of Everlasting Penalties, if broke!

LXXIX

What! from his helpless Creature be repaid
Pure Gold for what he lent him dross-allayed—
    Sue for a Debt he never did contract,
And cannot answer—Oh the sorry trade!

LXXX

Oh Thou, who didst with pitfall and with gin
Beset the Road I was to wander in,
    Thou wilt not with Predestined Evil round
Enmesh, and then impute my Fall to Sin!

LXXXI

Oh Thou, who Man of baser Earth didst make,
And ev'n with Paradise devise the Snake:
    For all the Sin wherewith the Face of Man
Is blackened—Man's forgiveness give—and take!

THE GARDENER AND THE MOLE

WALTER SAVAGE LANDOR

A gardener had watched a mole
And caught it coming from its hole.
"Mischievous beast!" he cried, "to harm
The garden as thou dost the farm.

Here thou hast had thy wicked will
Upon my tulip and jonquil.
Behold them drooping and half dead
Upon this torn and tumbled bed."
   The mole said meekly in reply,
"My star is more to blame than I.
To undermine is mole's commission,
Our house still holds it from tradition.
What lies the nearest us is ours.
Decreed so by the higher Powers.
We hear of conies and of hares.
But when commit we deeds like theirs?
We never touch the flowers that blow,
And only bulbs that lurk below.
'Tis true, where we have run, the ground
Is raised a trifle, nor quite sound,
Yet, after a few days of rain,
Level and firm it lies again;
Wise men, like you, will rather wait
For these than argue against fate,
Or quarrel with us moles because
We simply follow Nature's laws.
We raise the turf to keep us warm,
Surely in this there is no harm.
Ye break it up to set thereon
A fortress or perhaps a throne,
And pray that God cast down his eyes
Benignly on burnt sacrifice,
The sacrifice of flesh and bone
Fashioned, they tell us, like His own.
Ye in the cold lie all the night
Under thin tents, at morn to fight.
Neither for horned nor fleecy cattle
Start we to mingle in the battle,
Or in the pasture shed their blood
To pamper idleness with food.
Indeed we do eat worms; what then?
Do not those very worms eat men,
And have the impudence to say
Ye shall ere long be such as they?
We never kill or wound a brother,
Men kill by thousands one another,
And, though ye swear ye wish but peace,
Your feuds and warfares never cease."
   Such homebrought truths the gardener,
Though mild by nature, could not bear,
And lest the mole might more have said
He chopt its head off with the spade.

THE KING OF BEASTS

ROBINSON JEFFERS

Cattle in the slaughter-pens, laboratory dogs
Slowly tortured to death, flogged horses, trapped fur-bearers,
Agonies in the snow, splintering your needle teeth on chill steel—look:
Mankind, your Satans, are not very happy either. I wish you had seen the battle-
    squalor, the bombings,
The screaming fire-deaths. I wish you could watch the endless hunger, the cold,
    the moaning, the hopelessness.
I wish you could smell the Russian and German torture-camps. It is quite natural
    the two-footed beast
That inflicts terror, the cage, enslavement, torment and death on all other animals
Should eat the dough that he mixes and drink the death cup. It is just and decent.
    And it will increase, I think.

IN MEMORIAM, LIV-LVI

ALFRED LORD TENNYSON

LIV

O, yet we trust that somehow good
    Will be the final goal of ill,
    To pangs of nature, sins of will,
Defects of doubt, and taints of blood;

That nothing walks with aimless feet;
    That not one life shall be destroyed,
    Or cast as rubbish to the void,
When God hath made the pile complete;

That not a worm is cloven in vain;
    That not a moth with vain desire
    Is shrivelled in a fruitless fire,
Or but subserves another's gain.

Behold, we know not anything;
    I can but trust that good shall fall
    At last—far-off—at last, to all,
And every winter change to spring.

So runs my dream; but what am I?
    An infant crying in the night;
    An infant crying for the light,
And with no language but a cry.

LV

The wish, that of the living whole
    No life may fail beyond the grave,
    Derives it not from what we have
The likest God within the soul?

Are God and Nature then at strife,
    That Nature lends such evil dreams?
    So careful of the type she seems,
So careless of the single life,

That I, considering everywhere
    Her secret meaning in her deeds,
    And finding that of fifty seeds
She often brings but one to bear,

I falter where I firmly trod,
    And falling with my weight of cares
    Upon the great world's altar-stairs
That slope thro' darkness up to God,

I stretch lame hands of faith, and grope,
    And gather dust and chaff, and call
    To what I feel is Lord of all,
And faintly trust the larger hope.

LVI

"So careful of the type?" but no.
    From scarped cliff and quarried stone
    She cries, "A thousand types are gone;
I care for nothing, all shall go.

"Thou makest thine appeal to me.
    I bring to life, I bring to death;
    The spirit does but mean the breath:
I know no more." And he, shall he,

Man, her last work, who seem'd so fair,
    Such splendid purpose in his eyes,
    Who rolled the psalm to wintry skies,
Who built him fanes of fruitless prayer,

Who trusted God was love indeed
    And love Creation's final law—
    Tho' Nature, red in tooth and claw
With ravine, shrieked against his creed—

Who loved, who suffered countless ills,
    Who battled for the True, the Just,
    Be blown about the desert dust,
Or sealed within the iron hills?

No more? A monster then, a dream,
    A discord. Dragons of the prime,
    That tare each other in their slime,
Were mellow music matched with him.

O life as futile, then, as frail!
O for thy voice to soothe and bless!
What hope of answer, or redress?
Behind the veil, behind the veil.

THE END

In *White-Jacket*

HERMAN MELVILLE

As a man-of-war that sails through the sea, so this earth that sails through the air. We mortals are all on board a fast-sailing, never-sinking world-frigate, of which God was the shipwright; and she is but one craft in a Milky-Way fleet, of which God is the Lord High Admiral. The port we sail from is forever astern. And though far out of sight of land, for ages and ages we continue to sail with sealed orders, and our last destination remains a secret to ourselves and our officers; yet our final haven was predestinated ere we slipped from the stocks at creation.

Thus sailing with sealed orders, we ourselves are the repositories of the secret packet, whose mysterious contents we long to learn. There are no mysteries out of ourselves. But let us not give ear to the superstitious, gun-deck gossip about whither we may be gliding, for, as yet, not a soul on board of us knows—not even the commodore himself; assuredly not the chaplain; even our professor's scientific surmisings are vain. On that point, the smallest cabin-boy is as wise as the captain. And believe not the hypochondriac dwellers below hatches, who will tell you, with a sneer, that our world-frigate is bound to no final harbor whatever; that our voyage will prove an endless circumnavigation of space. Not so. For how can this world frigate prove our eventual abiding place, when, upon our first embarkation, as infants in arms, her violent rolling—in after life unperceived—makes every soul of us sea-sick? Does not this show, too, that the very air we here inhale is uncongenial, and only becomes endurable at last through gradual habituation, and that some blessed, placid haven, however remote at present, must be in store for us all?

Glance fore and aft our flush decks. What a swarming crew! All told, they muster hard upon eight hundred millions of souls. Over these we have authoritative Lieutenants, a sword-belted Officer of Marines, a Chaplain, a Professor, a Purser, a Doctor, a Cook, a Master-at-arms.

Oppressed by illiberal laws, and partly oppressed by themselves, many of our people are wicked, unhappy, inefficient. We have skulkers and idlers all round, and brow-beaten waisters, who, for a pittance, do our craft's shabby work. Nevertheless, among our people we have gallant fore, main, and mizzen-top men aloft, who, well treated or ill, still trim our craft to the blast.

We have a *brig* for trespassers; a bar by our main-mast, at which they are arraigned; a cat-o'-nine-tails and a gangway, to degrade them in their own eyes and in ours. These are not always employed to convert Sin to Virtue, but to divide them, and protect Virtue and legalized Sin from unlegalized Vice.

We have a Sick-bay for the smitten and helpless, whither we hurry them out of sight, and, however they may groan beneath hatches, we hear little of their tribulations on deck; we still sport our gay streamer aloft. Outwardly regarded, our craft is a lie; for all that is outwardly seen of it is the clean-swept deck, and oft-painted planks comprised above the water-line; whereas, the vast mass of our fabric, with all its store-rooms of secrets, forever slides along far under the surface.

When a shipmate dies, straightway we sew him up, and overboard he goes; our world-frigate rushes by, and never more do we behold him again; though, sooner or later, the everlasting under-tow sweeps him toward our own destination.

We have both a quarter-deck to our craft and a gun-deck; subterranean shot-lockers and gunpowder magazines; and the Articles of War form our domineering code.

Oh, shipmates and world-mates, all round! we the people suffer many abuses. Our gun-deck is full of complaints. In vain from Lieutenants do we appeal to the Captain; in vain—while on board our world-frigate—to the indefinite Navy Commissioners, so far out of sight aloft. Yet the worst of our evils we blindly inflict upon ourselves; our officers cannot remove them, even if they would. From the last ills no being can save another; therein each man must be his own saviour. For the rest, whatever befall us, let us never train our murderous guns inboard; let us not mutiny with bloody pikes in our hands. Our Lord High Admiral will yet interpose; and though long ages should elapse, and leave our wrongs unredressed, yet, shipmates and world-mates! let us never forget, that,

> "Whoever afflict us, whatever surround,
> Life is a voyage that's homeward bound!"

MARTIN'S PUZZLE

GEORGE MEREDITH

There she goes up the street with her book in her hand,
  And her Good morning, Martin! Ay, lass, how d' ye do?
Very well, thank you, Martin!—I can't understand!
  I might just as well never have cobbled a shoe!
I can't understand it. She talks like a song;
  Her voice takes your ear like the ring of a glass;
She seems to give gladness while limping along,
  Yet sinner ne'er suffered like that little lass.

First, a fool of a boy ran her down with a cart.
  Then, her fool of a father—a blacksmith by trade—
Why the deuce does he tell us it half broke his heart?
  His heart!—where's the leg of the poor little maid!
Well, that's not enough; they must push her downstairs,
  To make her go crooked: but why count the list?
If it's right to suppose that our human affairs
  Are all ordered by heaven—there, bang goes my fist!

For if angels can look on such sights—never mind!
  When you're next to blaspheming, it's best to be mum.
The parson declares that her woes weren't designed;
  But, then, with the parson it's all kingdom-come.
Lose a leg, save a soul—a convenient text;
  I call it Tea doctrine, not savoring of God
When poor little Molly wants "chastening," why, next
  The Archangel Michael might taste of the rod.

But to see the poor darling go limping for miles
  To read books to sick people!—and just of an age
When girls learn the meaning of ribands and smiles!
  Makes me feel like a squirrel that turns in a cage.

The more I push thinking the more I revolve:
    I never get farther:—and as to her face,
It starts up when near on my puzzle I solve.
    And says, "This crushed body seems such a sad case."

Not that she's for complaining: she reads to earn pence;
    And from those who can't pay, simple thanks are enough.
Does she leave lamentation for chaps without sense?
    Howsoever, she's made up of wonderful stuff.
Ay, the soul in her body must be a stout cord;
    She sings little hymns at the close of the day.
Though she has but three fingers to lift to the Lord,
    And only one leg to kneel down with to pray.

What I ask is, Why persecute such a poor dear,
    If there's Law above all?   Answer that if you can!
Irreligious I'm not; but I look on this sphere
    As a place where a man should just think like a man.
It isn't fair dealing!   But, contrariwise,
    Do bullets in battle the wicked select?
Why, then it's all chance-work!   And yet, in her eyes,
    She holds a fixed something by which I am checked.

Yonder riband of sunshine aslope on the wall,
    If you eye it a minute'll have the same look:
So kind! and so merciful!   God of us all!
    It's the very same lesson we get from the Book.
Then, is Life but a trial?   Is that what is meant?
    Some must toil, and some perish, for others below:
The injustice to each spreads a common content;
    Ay!   I've lost it again, for it can't be quite so.

She's the victim of fools: that seems nearer the mark.
    On earth there are engines and numerous fools.
Why the Lord can permit them, we're still in the dark;
    He does, and in some sort of way they're His tools.
It's a roundabout way, with respect let me add,
    If Molly goes crippled that we may be taught:
But, perhaps, it's the only way, though it's so bad;
    In that case we'll bow down our heads,—as we ought.

But the worst of *me* is, that when I bow my head,
    I perceive a thought wriggling away in the dust,
And I follow its tracks, quite forgetful, instead
    Of humble acceptance: for, question I must!
Here's a creature made carefully—carefully made!
    Put together with craft, and then stamped on, and why?
The answer seems nowhere: it's discord that's played.
    The sky's a blue dish!—an implacable sky!

Stop a moment: I seize an idea from the pit.
They tell us that discord, though discord alone,
Can be harmony when the notes properly fit:
    Am I judging all things from a single false tone?
Is the Universe one immense Organ, that rolls
    From devils to angels? I'm blind with the sight.
It pours such a splendor on heaps of poor souls!
I might try at kneeling with Molly to-night.

FROM IS EVIL ONLY APPEARANCE?

In *The Meaning of Good*

G. LOWES DICKINSON

"What we call Evil, you mean, is nothing but appearance."

"Yes."

"You think, in fact, with the poet, that 'all that is, is good'?"

"Yes," he replied, "all that really is."

"Ah!" I said, "but in that 'really' lies the crux of the matter. Take, for instance, a simple fact of our own experience—pain. Would you say, perhaps, that pain is good?"

"No," he replied, "not as it appears to us; but as it really is."

"As it really is to whom, or in whom?"

"To the Absolute, we will say; to God, if you like."

"Well, but what is the relation of the pain as it is in God to the pain that appears to us?"

"I don't pretend to know," he said, "but that is hardly the point. The point is, that it is only in connection with what is in God that the word Good has any real meaning. Appearance is neither good nor bad; it is simply not real."

"But," cried Audubon, interrupting in a kind of passion, "it is in appearance that we live and move and have our being. What is the use of saying that appearance is neither good nor bad, when we are feeling it as the one or the other every moment of our lives? And as to the Good that is in God, who knows or cares about it? What consolation is it to me when I am suffering from the toothache, to be told that God is enjoying the pain that tortures me? It is simply absurd to call God's Good good at all, unless it has some kind of relation to our Good."

"Well," said Dennis, "as to that, I can only say that, in my opinion, it is nothing but our weakness that leads us to take such a view. When I am really at my best, when my intellect and imagination are working freely, and the humors and passions of the flesh are laid to rest, I seem to see, with a kind of direct intuition, that the world, just as it is, is good, and that it is only the confusion and obscurity due to imperfect vision that makes us call it defective and wish to alter it for the better. When I perceive Truth at all, I perceive that it is also Good; and I cannot then distinguish between what is, and what ought to be."

"Really," cried Audubon, "really? Well, that I cannot understand."

"I hardly know how to make it clear," he replied, "unless it were by a concrete example. I find that when I think out any particular aspect of things, so far, that is to say, as I can think it out at all, all the parts and details fall into such perfect order and arrangement that it becomes impossible for me any longer to desire that anything should be other than it is. And that, even in the regions where at other times I am most prone to discover error and defect. You know, for instance, that I am something of an economist?"

"What are you not?" I said. "If you sin, it is not from lack of light!"

"Well," he continued, "there is, I suppose, no department of affairs which one is more inclined to criticize than this. And yet the more one investigates the more one discovers, even here, the harmony and necessity that pervade the whole universe. The ebb and flow of business from this trade or country to that, the rise and fall of wages, or of the rate of interest, the pouring of capital into or out of one industry or another, the varying relations of imports to exports, the periods of depression and recovery, and in close connection with all this the ever-changing conditions of the lives of countless workmen throughout the world, their well-being or ill-being, it may be their very life and death, together with the whole fate of future generations in health, capacity, opportunity, and the like,—all this complexus of things, so chaotic and unintelligible at the first view, so full, as we say, of iniquity, injustice, and the like, falls, as we penetrate further, into one vast and harmonious system, so inspiring to the imagination, so inevitable to the understanding, that our objections and cavillings, ethical, aesthetic, or what you will, simply vanish away at the clearer vision, or, if they persist, persist as mere irrelevant illusions; while we abandon ourselves to the contemplation of the whole, as of some world-symphony, whose dissonances, no less than its concords, are taken up and resolved in the irresistible march and progress, the ocean-flooding of the Whole. You will think," he continued, "that I am absurdly rhapsodical over what, after all, is matter prosaic enough; but what I wanted to suggest was that it is Reality so conceived that appeals to me at once as Truth and as Good. This partial vision of mine in the economic sphere is a kind of type of the way in which I conceive the Absolute. I conceive Him to be a Being necessary and therefore perfect; a Being in face of whom our own incoherent and tentative criticisms, our complaints that this or that should, if only it could, be otherwise, our regrets, desires, aspirations, and the like, show but as so many testimonies to our own essential imperfection, weaknesses to be surmounted, rather than signs of worth to stamp us, as we vainly boast, the elect of creation."

He finished; and I half expected that Leslie would intervene, since I saw, as I thought, many weak points in the position. But he kept silence, impressed, perhaps, by that idea of the Perfect and Eternal which has a natural home in the minds of the generous and young. So I began myself rather tentatively:

"I think," I said, "I understand the position you wish to indicate; and so stated, in general terms, no doubt it is attractive. It is when we endeavor to work it out in detail that the difficulties appear. The position, as I understand it, is, that, from the point of view of the Absolute, what we call Evil and what we call Good simply have no existence. Good and Evil, in our sense, are mere appearances; and Good, in the absolute sense, is identical with the Absolute or with God?"

"Yes," he said, "that is my notion."

"And so, for example, to apply the idea in detail, in the region which you yourself selected, all that we regret, or hate, or fear in our social system—poverty, disease, starvation and the rest—is not really evil at all, does not in fact exist, but is merely what appears to us? There is, in fact, no social evil?"

"No," he replied, "in the sense I have explained there is none."

"Well then," I continued, "how is it with all our social and other ideals? Our desire to make our own lives and other people's lives happier? Our efforts to subdue nature, to conquer disease, to introduce order and harmony where there appears to be discord and confusion? How is it with those finer and less directly practical impulses by which you yourself are mainly preoccupied—the quest of knowledge or of beauty for their own sake, the mere putting of ourselves into right relations with the universe, apart from any attempt to modify it? Are all these desires and activities mere illusions of ours, or worse than illusions, errors and even vices, impious misapprehensions of the absolutely Good, frivolous attempts to adapt the Perfect to our own imperfections?"

"No," he replied, "I would not put it so. Some meaning, I apprehend, there must be in time and change, and some meaning also in our efforts, though not, I believe, the meaning which we imagine. The divine life, as I conceive it, is a process; only a process that is somehow eternal, circular, so to speak, not rectilinear, much as Milton appears to imagine it when he describes the blessed spirits 'progressing the dateless and irrevoluble circle of eternity'; and of this eternal process our activity, which we suppose to be moving towards an end, is somehow or other an essential element. So that, in this way, it is necessary and right that we should strive after ideals; only, when we are thinking philosophically, we ought to make clear to ourselves that in truth the Ideal is eternally fulfilled, its fulfilment consisting precisely in that process which we are apt to regard as a mere means to its realization. This, as Hegel has it, is the 'cunning' of the Absolute Reason, which deludes us into the belief that there is a purpose to be attained, and by the help of that delusion preserves that energy of action which all the time is really itself the End."

I looked up at him as he finished, to see whether he was quite serious; and as he appeared to be so, and as Leslie still kept silence, I took up the argument as follows.

"I understand," I said, "in a sort of way what you mean; but still the same difficulty recurs which Audubon has already put forward. On your hypothesis there seems to be an impassable gulf between God's conception of Good and ours. To God, as it seems, the world is eternally good; and in its goodness is included that illusion by which it appears to us so bad, that we are continually employed in trying to make it better. The maintenance of this illusion is essential to the nature of the world; to us, evil always must appear. But, as we know by experience, the evil that *appears* is just as terrible and just as hateful as it would be if it really *were*. A toothache, as Audubon put it, is no less a pain to us because it is a pleasure to God. We cannot, if we would, adopt His point of view; and clearly it would be impious to try, since we should be endeavoring to defeat His ingenious plan to keep the world going by hoodwinking us. We therefore are chained and bound to the whirling wheel of appearance; to us what seems good is good, and what seems bad, bad; and your contention that all existence is somehow eternally good is for us simply irrelevant; it belongs to the point of view of God to which we have no access."

"Yes," cried Audubon, "and what a God to call God at all! Why not just as much the devil? What are we to think of the Being who is responsible for a world of whose economy our evil is not merely an accident, a mistake, but positively an essential, inseparable condition!"

"What, indeed!" exclaimed Leslie. "Call Him God, by all means, if you like, but such a God as Zeus was to Prometheus, omnipotent, indeed, and able to exact with infallible precision His daily and hourly toll of blood and tears, but powerless at least to chain the mind He has created free, or to exact allegiance and homage from spirits greater, though weaker, than Himself."

This was the sort of talk, I knew, that rather annoyed Dennis. I did not therefore, for the moment, leave him time to reply, but proceeded to a somewhat different point:

"Even putting aside," I said, "the moral character of God, as it appears in your scheme of the universe, must we not perhaps accuse Him of a slight lapse of intelligence? For, as I understand the matter, it was essential to the success of the Absolute's plan that we should never discover the deception that is being played upon us. But, it seems, we do discover it. Hegel, for example, by your own confession, has not only detected but exposed it. Well then, what is to be done? Do you suppose that we could, even if we would, continue to lend ourselves to the imposition? Must not our aims and purposes cease to have any interest for us, once we are clear that they are not true ends? And that which, according to the hypothesis, *is* the true end, the 'dateless and irrevoluble circle' of activity, that, surely, we at least cannot sanction or approve, seeing that it involves and perpetuates the very misery and pain whose destruction was our only motive for acting at all. For, whatever may be the case with God, we, you will surely admit, are forbidden by all that in us is highest and best, to approve or even to acquiesce in the deliberate perpetuation of a world of whose existence all that we call evil is an essential and eternal constituent. So that, as I said at first, it looks as if the Absolute Reason had not been, after all, quite as cunning as it thought, since it has allowed us to discover and expose the very imposition it had invented to cheat us into concurrence with its plans. . . ."

"Our aim should be not to abolish what we call evil, by successive modifications of physical and social conditions, but rather, all these remaining essentially the same, to come to see that what appears to be evil is not really so."

"Yes," he said, "that is the view I would suggest."

"So that, for example, though we might still experience a toothache, we should no longer regard it as an evil; and so with all the host of things we are in the habit of calling bad: they would continue unchanged 'in themselves,' as you Hegelians say, only to us they would appear no longer bad, but good?"

"Yes; as I said at first, all reality is good, and all Evil, so-called, is merely illusion."

I was about to reply when I was forestalled by Bartlett. For some time past the discussion had been left pretty much to Dennis and myself, with an occasional incursion from Audubon and Leslie. Ellis had gone indoors; Parry and Wilson were talking together about something else; and Bartlett appeared to be still absorbed in the *Chronicle*. I noticed, however, that for the last few moments he had been getting restless, and I suspected that he was listening, behind his newspaper, to what we were saying. I was not therefore altogether surprised when, upon Dennis' last remark, he suddenly broke into our debate with the exclamation:

"Would it be 'in order' to introduce a concrete example? There is a curiously apt one here in the *Chronicle*."

And upon our assenting, he read us a long extract about phosphorus-poisoning, the details of which I now forget, but at any rate it brought before us, very vividly, a tale of cruel suffering and oppression.

"Now," he said, as he finished, "is that, may I ask, the kind of thing that it amuses you to call mere illusion?"

"Yes," replied Dennis stoutly, "that will do very well for an example."

"Well," he rejoined, "I do not propose to dispute about words; but for my own part I should have thought that, if anything is real, that is; and so, I think, you would find it, if you yourself were the sufferer."

"But," objected Dennis, "do you think that it is in the moment of suffering that one is most competent to judge about the reality of pain?"

"Certainly, for it is only in the moment of suffering that one really knows what it is that one is judging about."

"I am not sure about that. I doubt whether it is true that experience involves knowledge and *vice versa*. It is, indeed, to my mind, part of the irony of life, that we know so much which we can never experience, and experience so much which we can never know."

"I don't follow that," said Bartlett, "but of one thing I am sure, that you will never get rid of evil by calling it illusion."

"No," Dennis conceded, "you will never of course get rid of it, in the sense you mean, by that, or indeed, in my opinion, by any other means. But we were discussing not what we are to do with evil, but how we are to conceive it."

"But," he objected, "if you begin by conceiving it as illusion, you will never do anything with it at all."

"Perhaps not, but I am not sure that that is my business."

"At any rate, Dennis," I interposed, "you will, I expect, admit, that for us, while we live in the region of what you call 'Appearance,' Evil is at least as pressing and as obvious as Good."

"Yes," he said, "I am ready to admit that."

"And," I continued, "for my part I agree with Bartlett and with Leslie, that it is Appearance with which we are concerned. What I have been contending for throughout, is that in the world in which we live (whether we are to call it Reality or Appearance), Evil and Good are the really dominating facts; and that we cannot dismiss them from our consideration either on the ground that we know nothing of them (as Ellis was inclined to maintain) or on the ground that we know all about them (as Parry and Wilson seemed to think). On the contrary, it is, I believe, our main business to find out about them; and that we can find out about them is with me an article of faith, and so, I believe, it is with most people, whether or no they are aware of it or are ready to admit it."

Dennis was preparing to reply, when Ellis reappeared to summon us to lunch. We followed him in gladly enough, for it was past our usual hour and we were hungry; and the conversation naturally taking a lighter turn, I have nothing further to record until we reassembled in the afternoon. . . .

"Why, the Bad is all part of the Good; one takes the rough with the smooth. Or rather the Good stands above what you call good and bad; it consists in the activity itself which feeds upon both alike. If I were Dennis I should say it is the synthesis of both."

"Well," said Leslie, "I never heard before of a synthesis produced by one side of the antithesis simply swallowing the other."

"Didn't you?" said Ellis. "Then you have a great deal yet to learn. This is known as the synthesis of the lion and the lamb."

"Oh, synthesis!" cried Parry. "Heaven save us from synthesis! What is it you are trying to say?"

"That's what I want to know," I said. "We seem to be coming perilously near to Dennis's position, that what we call Evil is mere appearance."

"Well," said Ellis, "extremes meet! Dennis arrived at his view by a denial of the world; I arrive at mine by an affirmation of it."

"But do you really think," I urged, "that everything in the world is good?"

"I think," he replied, "that everything may be made to minister to Good if you approach it in the proper way."

"That reads," said Audubon, "like an extract from a sermon."

"As I remarked before," replied Ellis, "extremes meet."

"But, Ellis," I protested, "do explain! How are you going to answer Leslie?"

"Leslie is really too young," he replied, "to be answerable at all. But if you insist on my being serious, what I meant to suggest is, that when our activity is freshest and keenest we find delight in what is called Evil no less than in what is called Good. The complexity of the world charms us, its 'downs' as well as its 'ups,' its abysses and glooms no less than its sunny levels. We would not alter it if we could; it is better than we could make it; and we accept it not merely with acquiescence but with triumph."

"Oh, do we!" said Audubon.

"We," answered Ellis, "not you! You, of course, do not accept anything."

"But who are 'we'?" asked Leslie.

"All of us," he replied, "who try to make an art of living. Yes, art, that is the word! To me life appears like a great tragicomedy. It has its shadows as well as its lights, but we would not lose one of them, for fear of destroying the harmony of the whole. Call it good, or call it bad, no matter, so it is. The villain no less than the hero claims our applause; it would be dull without him. We can't afford to miss anything or anyone."

"In fact," cried Audubon, " 'Konx Ompax! Totality!' You and Dennis are strangely agreed for once!"

"Yes," he replied, "but for very different reasons, as the judge said on the one occasion when he concurred with his colleagues. Dennis accepts the Whole because he finds it a perfect logical system; I, because I find it a perfect work of art. His prophet is Hegel; mine is Walt Whitman."

"Walt Whitman! And you profess to be an artist!"

"So was he, not in words but in life. One thing to him was no better nor worse than another; small and great, high and low, good and bad, he accepts them all, with the instinctive delight of an actual physical contact. Listen to him!" And he began to quote:

> " 'I do not call one greater and one smaller,
> 'That which fills its period and place is equal to any.
> 'I believe a leaf of grass is no less than the journey-work of
>   the stars.
> 'And the pismire is equally perfect, and a grain of sand, and the
>   egg of the wren,
> 'And the tree-toad is a "chef-d'oeuvre" for the highest;
> 'And the running blackberry would adorn the parlors of heaven,
> 'And the narrowest hinge in my hand puts to scorn all machinery,
> 'And the cow crunching with depressed head surpasses any statue,
> 'And a mouse is a miracle enough to stagger sextillions of infidels.' "

"That's all very well," objected Leslie, "though, of course, it's rather absurd; but it does not touch the question of evil at all."

"Wait a bit," cried Ellis, "he's ready for you there."

> " 'I am not the poet of goodness only, I do not decline to be
>   the poet of wickedness also.
>
>   .   .   .   .
>
> 'What blurt is this about virtue and about vice?
> 'Evil propels me and reform of evil propels me, I stand
>   indifferent;

'My gait is no fault-finder's or rejector's gait,
'I moisten the roots of all that grows.' "

.   .   .   .

" 'This is the meal equally set, this is the meat for natural
     hunger,
'It is for the wicked just the same as the righteous, I make
     appointment with all,
'I will not have a single person slighted or kept away,
'The kept-woman, sponger, thief are hereby invited,
'The heavy-lipped slave is invited, the venerealee is invited;
'There shall be no difference between them and the rest.' "

"That's rather strong," remarked Parry.

"Don't you like it?" Ellis inquired.

"I think I might like it if I were drunk."

"Ah, but a poet, you see, is always drunk!"

"Well, I unfortunately, am often sober; and then I find the sponger and the venerealee anything but agreeable objects."

"Besides," said Audubon, "though it's very good of Walt Whitman to invite us all, the mere fact of dining with him, however miscellaneous the company, doesn't alter the character of the dinner."

"No," cried Leslie, "and that's just the point Ellis has missed all through. Even if it be true that the world appears to him as a work of art, it doesn't appear so to the personages of the drama. What's play to him is grim earnest to them; and, what's more, he himself is an actor, not a mere spectator, and may have that fact brought home to him, any moment, in his flesh and blood."

"Of course!" replied Ellis, "and I wouldn't have it otherwise. The point of the position is that one should play one's part oneself, but play it as an artist with one's eye upon the total effect, never complaining of Evil merely because one happens to suffer, but taking the suffering itself as an element in the aesthetic perfection of the Whole."

"I should like to see you doing that," said Bartlett, rather brutally, "when you were down with a fit of yellow fever."

"Or shut up in a mad-house," said Leslie.

"Or working eight hours a day at business," said Audubon, "with the thermometer 100° in the shade."

"Oh well," answered Ellis, "those are the confounded accidents of our unhealthy habits of life."

"I am afraid," I said, "they are accidents very essential to the substance of the world."

"Besides," cried Parry, "there's the whole moral question, which you seem to ignore altogether. If there be any activity that is good, it must be, I suppose, the one that is right; and the activity you describe seems to have nothing to do with right and wrong."

from PRO AND CONTRA

In *The Brothers Karamazov*

FYODOR DOSTOEVSKY

"Well, tell me where to begin, give your orders. The existence of God, eh?"

"Begin where you like. You declared yesterday at father's that there was no God." Alyosha looked searchingly at his brother.

"I said that yesterday at dinner on purpose to tease you and I saw your eyes glow. But now I've no objection to discussing with you, and I say so very seriously. I want to be friends with you, Alyosha, for I have no friends and want to try it. Well, only fancy, perhaps I too accept God," laughed Ivan, "that's a surprise for you, isn't it?"

"Yes of course, if you are not joking now."

"Joking? I was told at the elder's yesterday that I was joking. You know, dear boy, there was an old sinner in the eighteenth century who declared that, if there were no God, he would have to be invented. *S'il n'existait pas Dieu, il faudrait l'inventer.* And man has actually invented God. And what's strange, what would be marvelous, is not that God should really exist; the marvel is that such an idea, the idea of the necessity of God, could enter the head of such a savage, vicious beast as man. So holy it is, so touching, so wise and so great a credit it does to man. As for me, I've long resolved not to think whether man created God or God man. And I won't go through all the axioms laid down by Russian boys on that subject, all derived from European hypotheses; for what's a hypothesis there, is an axiom with the Russian boy, and not only with the boys but with their teachers too, for our Russian professors are often just the same boys themselves. And so I omit all the hypotheses. For what are we aiming at now? I am trying to explain as quickly as possible my essential nature, that is what manner of man I am, what I believe in, and for what I hope, that's it, isn't it? And therefore I tell you that I accept God simply. But you must note this: if God exists and if He really did create the world, then, as we all know, He created it according to the geometry of Euclid and the human mind with the conception of only three dimensions in space. Yet there have been and still are geometricians and philosophers, and even some of the most distinguished, who doubt whether the whole universe, or to speak more widely the whole of being, was only created in Euclid's geometry; they even dare to dream that two parallel lines, which according to Euclid can never meet on earth, may meet somewhere in infinity. I have come to the conclusion that, since I can't understand even that, I can't expect to understand about God. I acknowledge humbly that I have no faculty for settling such questions, I have a Euclidian earthly mind, and how could I solve problems that are not of this world? And I advise you never to think about it either, my dear Alyosha, especially about God, whether He exists or not. All such questions are utterly inappropriate for a mind created with an idea of only three dimensions. And so I accept God and am glad to, and what's more I accept His wisdom, His purpose—which are utterly beyond our ken; I believe in the underlying order and the meaning of life; I believe in the eternal harmony in which they say we shall one day be blended. I believe in the Word to Which the universe is striving, and Which Itself was 'with God,' and Which Itself is God and so on, and so on, to infinity. There are all sorts of phrases for it. I seem to be on the right path, don't I? Yet would you believe it, in the final result I don't accept this world of God's, and, although I know it exists, I don't accept it at all. It's not that I don't accept God, you must understand, it's the world created by Him I don't and cannot accept. Let me make it plain. I believe like a child that suffering will be healed and made up for, that all the humiliating absurdity of human contradictions will vanish like a pitiful mirage, like the despicable fabrication of the impotent and infinitely small Euclidian mind of man, that in the world's finale, at the moment of eternal harmony, something so precious will come to pass that it will suffice for all hearts, for the comforting of all resentments, for the atonement of all the crimes of humanity, of all the blood they've shed; that it will make it not only possible to forgive but to justify all that has happened with men—but though all that may come to pass, I don't accept it. I won't accept it. Even if parallel lines do meet and I see it myself, I shall see it and say that they've met, but still I won't accept it. That's what's at the root of me, Alyosha; that's my creed.

". . . Do you understand why this infamy must be and is permitted? Without it, I am told, man could not have known good and evil. Why should he know that diabolical good and evil when it costs so much? Why, the whole world of knowledge is not worth that child's prayer to 'dear, Kind God'! I say nothing of the sufferings of grown-up people, they have eaten the apple, damn them, and the devil take them all! But these little ones! I am making you suffer, Alyosha, you are not yourself. I'll leave off if you like."

"Never mind. I want to suffer too," muttered Alyosha.

"One picture, only one more, because it's so curious, so characteristic, and I have only just read it in some collection of Russian antiquities. I've forgotten the name. I must look it up. It was in the darkest days of serfdom at the beginning of the century, and long live the Liberator of the People! There was in those days a general of aristocratic connections, the owner of great estates, one of these men—somewhat exceptional, I believe, even then—who, retiring from the service into a life of leisure, are convinced that they've earned absolute power over the lives of their subjects. There were such men then. So our general, settled on his property of two thousand souls, lives in pomp and domineers over his poor neighbors as though they were dependents and buffoons. He has kennels of hundreds of hounds and nearly a hundred dog-boys—all mounted, and in uniform. One day a serf boy, a little child of eight, threw a stone in play and hurt the paw of the general's favorite hound. 'Why is my favorite dog lame?' He is told that the boy threw a stone that hurt the dog's paw. 'So you did it.' The general looked the child up and down. 'Take him.' He was taken—taken from his mother and kept shut up all night. Early that morning the general comes out on horseback, with the hounds, his dependents, dog-boys, and huntsmen, all mounted around him in full hunting parade. The servants are summoned for their edification, and in front of them all stands the mother of the child. The child is brought from the lock-up. It's a gloomy, cold, foggy autumn day, a capital day for hunting. The general orders the child to be undressed; the child is stripped naked. He shivers, numb with terror not daring to cry. . . . 'Make him run,' commands the general. 'Run! run!' shout the dog-boys. The boy runs. . . . 'At him!' yells the general, and he sets the whole pack of hounds on the child. The hounds catch him, and tear him to pieces before his mother's eyes! . . . I believe the general was afterwards declared incapable of administering his estates. Well—what did he deserve? To be shot? to be shot for the satisfaction of our moral feelings? Speak, Alyosha!"

"To be shot," murmured Alyosha, lifting his eyes to Ivan with a pale twisted smile.

"Bravo!" cried Ivan delighted. "If even you say so . . . You're a pretty monk! So there is a little devil sitting in your heart, Alyosha Karamazov!"

"What I said was absurd, but—"

"That's just the point that 'but'!" cried Ivan. "Let me tell you, novice, that the absurd is only too necessary on earth. The world stands on absurdities, and perhaps nothing would have come to pass in it without them. We know what we know!"

"What do you know?"

"I understand nothing," Ivan went on, as though in delirium. "I don't want to understand anything now. I want to stick to the fact. I made up my mind long ago not to understand. If I try to understand anything, I shall be false to the fact and I have determined to stick to the fact."

"Why are you trying me?" Alyosha cried, with sudden distress. "Will you say what you mean at last?"

"Of course, I will; that's what I've been leading up to. You are dear to me, I don't want to let you go, and I won't give you up to your Zossima."

Ivan for a minute was silent, his face became all at once very sad.

"Listen! I took the case of the children only to make my case clearer. Of the other tears of humanity with which the earth is soaked from its crust to its center, I will say nothing. I have narrowed my subject on purpose. I am a bug, and I recognize in all humility that I cannot understand why the world is arranged as it is. Men are themselves to blame, I suppose; they were given paradise, they wanted freedom, and stole fire from heaven, though they knew they would become unhappy, so there is no need to pity them. With my pitiful, earthly, Euclidian understanding, all I know is that there is suffering and that there are none guilty; that cause follows effect, simply and directly; that everything flows and finds its level—but that's only Euclidian nonsense, I know that, and I can't consent to live by it! What comfort is it to me that there are none guilty and that cause follows effect simply and directly, and that I know it—I must have justice, or I will destroy myself. And not justice in some remote infinite time and space, but here on earth, and that I could see myself. I have believed in it. I want to see it, and if I am dead by then, let me rise again, for if it all happens without me, it will be too unfair. Surely I haven't suffered, simply that I, my crimes and my sufferings, may manure the soil of the future harmony for somebody else. I want to see with my own eyes the hind lie down with the lion and the victim rise up and embrace his murderer. I want to be there when every one suddenly understands what it has all been for. All the religions of the world are built on this longing, and I am a believer. But then there are the children, and what am I to do about them? That's a question I can't answer. For the hundredth time I repeat, there are numbers of questions, but I've only taken the children, because in their case what I mean is so unanswerably clear. Listen! If all must suffer to pay for the eternal harmony, what have children to do with it, tell me, please? It's beyond all comprehension why they should suffer, and why they should pay for the harmony. Why should they, too, furnish material to enrich the soil for the harmony of the future? I understand solidarity in sin among men. I understand solidarity in retribution, too; but there can be no such solidarity with children. And if it is really true that they must share responsibility for all their fathers' crimes, such a truth is not of this world and is beyond my comprehension. Some jester will say, perhaps, that the child would have grown up and have sinned, but you see he didn't grow up, he was torn to pieces by the dogs, at eight years old. Oh, Alyosha, I am not blaspheming! I understand, of course, what an upheaval of the universe it will be, when everything in heaven and earth blends in one hymn of praise and everything that lives and has lived cries aloud: 'Thou art just, O Lord, for Thy ways are revealed,' when the mother embraces the fiend who threw her child to the dogs, and all three cry aloud with tears, 'Thou are just, O Lord!' then, of course, the crown of knowledge will be reached and all will be made clear. But what pulls me up here is that I can't accept that harmony. And while I am on earth, I make haste to take my own measures. You see, Alyosha, perhaps it really may happen that if I live to that moment, or rise again to see it, I, too, perhaps, may cry aloud with the rest, looking at the mother embracing the child's torturer, 'Thou art just, O Lord!' but I don't want to cry aloud then. While there is still time, I hasten to protect myself and so I renounce the higher harmony altogether. It's not worth the tears of that one tortured child who beat itself on the breast with its little fist and prayed in its stinking outhouse, with its unexpiated tears to 'dear, kind God'! It's not worth it, because those tears are unatoned for. They must be atoned for, or there can be no harmony. But how? How are you going to atone for them? Is it possible? By their being avenged? But what do I care for avenging them? What do I care for a hell for oppressors? What good can hell do, since those children have already been tortured? And what becomes of harmony, if there is hell? I want to forgive. I want to embrace. I don't want more suffering. And if the sufferings of children go to swell the sum of sufferings which was necessary to pay for truth, then I protest that the truth is not worth such a price. I don't want the mother to embrace the oppressor who threw her son to the dogs! She dare not forgive him! Let her forgive him for herself, if she will, let her forgive the torturer for the immeasurable suffering of her mother's heart. But the sufferings of her tortured child she has no right to forgive; she dare not forgive the torturer, even if the child were to forgive him! And if that is so, if they dare not forgive what becomes of harmony? Is there in the whole world a being who would have the right to forgive and could forgive? I don't want harmony. From love for humanity I don't want it. I would rather be left with the unavenged suffering. I would rather remain with my unavenged suffering and unsatisfied indignation, *even if I were wrong*. Besides, too high a price is asked for harmony; it's beyond our means to pay so much to enter on it. And so I hasten to give back my entrance ticket, and if I am an honest man I am bound to give it back as soon as possible. And that I am doing. It's not God that I don't accept, Alyosha, only I most respectfully return Him the ticket."

"That's rebellion," murmured Alyosha, looking down.

"Rebellion? I am sorry you call it that," said Ivan earnestly. "One can hardly live in rebellion, and I want to live. Tell me yourself, I challenge you—answer. Imagine that you are creating a fabric of human destiny with the object of making men happy in the end, giving them peace and rest at last, but that it was essential and inevitable to torture to death only one tiny creature—that baby beating its breast with its fist, for instance—and to found that edifice on its unavenged tears, would you consent to be the architect on those conditions? Tell me, and tell the truth."

"No, I wouldn't consent," said Alyosha softly.

"And can you admit the idea that men for whom you are building it would agree to accept their happiness on the foundation of the unexpiated blood of a little victim? And accepting it would remain happy for ever?"

"No, I can't admit it. . . ."

FROM THE UNKNOWN GOD

ALFRED NOYES

. . . The sufferings inflicted by animals on one another are certainly less than the sufferings that man, of his own free-will, has often inflicted upon them. We cannot account for them, as a French wit has remarked, on the ground that their ancestors "had eaten forbidden hay." Neither, as an English writer remarked, can we criticize the lion for obtaining his meat in a probably far more merciful method than that whereby man obtains his chop. But animals do not seem to lack joy in their lives; and, while the greater part of the human race does enjoy its chop, and even bishops ask blessings on the meal, it seems to be mere cant to pretend that the human race has a right to criticize its Creator for the pain involved in the process. Mr. Thomas Hardy indulged in a great deal of this criticism; but he once informed me that he was not a vegetarian and that the animals' paradise he was planning would be chiefly for the uneatable.

A great deal of the questioning is made from very comfortable armchairs after a hearty meal on some portion of one of the animals chiefly concerned, and I could never understand either the skeptic or the curate who, after quoting Blake's "Little lamb, who made thee," could go home to his roast shoulder and mint-sauce, and question the Creator's kindness for allowing him to do so. We are living in a weird universe, where—if we could see ourselves—stranger things happen than ever Dante dreamed of. We sustain ourselves, as a famous statement has it, by thrusting pieces of other animals into holes in our heads; and if this were even whispered to denizens of some other planets, they would probably ridicule the teller as hopelessly insane. Yet this weird system of transubstantiation whereby

"Whatever Miss T. eats
Turns into Miss T,"

is the most vivid fact of our lives; and, if it fails to startle us, it is only because custom lies heavy upon us, and we live and move and have our being in a somnambulistic routine.

But the problem of physical suffering (which I propose to take first) cannot be dismissed lightly; and I must confess, at the outset, that I have never been satisfied with the bland argument of philosophers, or the ardent proclamations of Browning, that

"The evil is null, is nought, is silence implying sound."

Long before Browning, the scholastics had affirmed with greater depth that *malum est privatio ordinis ad finem debitum.* But to the woman dying of cancer the words ring hollow and remit no pang. To say that evil is relative, while good is absolute, is all very well for the philosopher in his library. But most men would shrink from offering that wise remark as an anodyne to anyone who was actually being stretched on one of the many racks of this tough world. Certainly the maker of such a remark—unless he were very insensitive—would find it difficult to meet the patient gaze of any real victim.

It is more honest to face the facts without minimizing them; and there is a more possible answer in which my own mind rested, an answer which the philosophers have strangely neglected, perhaps because it was too simple for them. It is surely possible that these pangs of Nature may be the price that has to be paid for something else, something that could be achieved in no other way, without that self-contradiction which, as the philosophers themselves affirm, is impossible even to Omnipotence,

Omnipotence in the Creator does not imply, for instance, the power to make a thing entirely black and entirely white simultaneously.   It is therefore surely possible that some profound contradiction may be involved in the idea that finely sensitive creatures might have been produced incapable of any but pleasurable sensations.   If we can imagine such a creature, and compare it with the highest types of humanity, there is little doubt as to which will be the more admirable, and no doubt at all as to which will be the more lovable.   It may be impossible, even for Omnipotence, without some fundamental self-contradiction, to evolve a race which, ignorant of suffering and unacquainted with grief, should also achieve the heights and sound the depths of intellectual and spiritual life.   It may be that those heights and depths are actually made up of the very experience which we would forego, and that there may be a deeper meaning than is always realized in the saying of the supreme victim and victor of suffering on earth: *I am the Way.*

We may conceive of a Virgil without the sense of tears; a Shakespeare, wandering through Arden, without a hint of tragedy; a Beethoven, untouched by compassion, in a world that had no need of it; but the thinkers and artists would be the very first to affirm that such a world had somehow lost all its greatness.   What does this mean, this hesitation as to whether we could accept our own improved and extremely comfortable universe?   Does it not again suggest that—dimly as we may apprehend it—we are here groping around some profound necessity which cannot be overcome, even by the Omnipotent, without self-contradiction?

PAIN

T. E. BROWN

The man that hath great griefs I pity not;
   'Tis something to be great
   In any wise, and hint the larger state,
Though but in shadow of a shade, God wot!

Moreover, while we wait the possible,
   This man has touched the fact,
   And probed till he has felt the core, where, packed
In pulpy folds, resides the ironic ill.

And while we others sip the obvious sweet—
   Lip-licking after-taste
   Of glutinous rind, lo! this man hath made haste,
And pressed the sting that holds the central seat.

For thus it is God stings us into life,
   Provoking actual souls
   From bodily systems, giving us the poles
That are His own, not merely balanced strife.

Nay, the great passions are His veriest thought,
   Which whoso can absorb,
   Nor, querulous halting, violate their orb,
In him the mind of God is fullest wrought.

Thrice happy such an one!   Far other he
   Who dallies on the edge
   Of the great vortex, clinging to a sedge
Of patent good, a timorous Manichee;

Who takes the impact of a long-breathed force,
   And fritters it away
   In eddies of disgust, that else might stay
His nerveless heart, and fix it to the course.

For there is threefold oneness with the One;
   And he is one, who keeps
   The homely laws of life; who, if he sleeps,
Or wakes, in his true flesh God's will is done.

And he is one, who takes the deathless forms,
   Who schools himself to think
   With the All-thinking, holding fast the link,
God-riveted, that bridges casual storms.

But tenfold one is he, who feels all pains
   Not partial, knowing them
   As ripples parted from the gold-beaked stem,
Wherewith God's galley onward ever strains.

To him the sorrows are the tension-thrills
   Of that serene endeavor,
   Which yields to God for ever and for ever
The joy that is more ancient than the hills.

FROM FAITH, HOPE, AND CHARITY

In *The Tragic Sense of Life*

MIGUEL DE UNAMUNO

Suffering is the substance of life and the root of personality, for it is only suffering that makes us persons.   And suffering is universal, suffering is that which unites all us living beings together; it is the universal or divine blood that flows through us all.   That which we call will, what is it but suffering?

And suffering has its degrees, according to the depth of its penetration, from the suffering that floats upon the sea of appearances to the eternal anguish, the source of the tragic sense of life, which seeks a habitation in the depths of the eternal and there awakens consolation; from the physical suffering that contorts our bodies to the religious anguish that flings us upon the bosom of God, there to be watered by the divine tears.

Anguish is something far deeper, more intimate, and more spiritual than suffering.   We are wont to feel the touch of anguish even in the midst of that which we call happiness, and even because of this happiness itself, to which we cannot resign ourselves and before which we tremble.   The happy who resign themselves to their apparent happiness, to a transitory happiness, seem to be as men without substance, or, at any rate, men who have not discovered this substance in themselves, who have not touched it. Such men are usually incapable of loving or of being loved, and they go through life without really knowing either pain or bliss.

There is no true love save in suffering, and in this world we have to choose either love, which is suffering, or happiness. And love leads us to no other happiness than that of love itself and its tragic consolation of uncertain hope. The moment love becomes happy and satisfied, it no longer desires and it is no longer love. The satisfied, the happy, do not love; they fall asleep in habit, near neighbor to annihilation. To fall into a habit is to begin to cease to be. Man is the more man—that is, the more divine—the greater his capacity for suffering, or, rather, for anguish.

At our coming into the world it is given to us to choose between love and happiness, and we wish—poor fools!—for both: the happiness of loving and the love of happiness. But we ought to ask for the gift of love and not of happiness, and to be preserved from dozing away into habit, lest we should fall into a fast sleep, a sleep without waking, and so lose our consciousness beyond power of recovery. We ought to ask God to make us conscious of ourselves in ourselves, in our suffering.

What is Fate, what is Fatality, but the brotherhood of love and suffering? What is it but that terrible mystery in virtue of which love dies as soon as it touches the happiness towards which it reaches out, and true happiness dies with it? Love and suffering mutually engender one another, and love is charity and compassion, and the love that is not charitable and compassionate is not love. Love, in a word, is resigned despair.

That which the mathematicians call the problem of maxima and minima, which is also called the law of economy, is the formula for all existential—that is, passional —activity. In material mechanics and in social mechanics, in industry and in political economy, every problem resolves itself into an attempt to obtain the greatest possible resulting utility with the least possible effort, the greatest income with the least expenditure, the most pleasure with the least pain. And the terrible and tragic formula of the inner, spiritual life is either to obtain the most happiness with the least love, or the most love with the least happiness. And it is necessary to choose between the one and the other, and to know that he who approaches the infinite of love, the love that is infinite, approaches the zero of happiness, the supreme anguish. And in reaching this zero he is beyond the reach of the misery that kills. "Be not, and thou shalt be mightier than aught that is," said Brother Juan de los Angeles in one of his *Diálogos de la conquista del reino de Dios* (Dial. iii. 8).

And there is something still more anguishing than suffering. A man about to receive a much-dreaded blow expects to have to suffer so severely that he may even succumb to the suffering, and when the blow falls he feels scarcely any pain; but afterwards, when he has come to himself and is conscious of his insensibility, he is seized with terror, a tragic terror, the most terrible of all, and choking with anguish he cries out: "Can it be that I no longer exist?" Which would you find most appalling—to feel such pain as would deprive you of your senses on being pierced through with a white-hot iron, or to see yourself thus pierced through without feeling any pain? Have you never felt the horrible terror of feeling yourself incapable of suffering and of tears? Suffering tells us that we exist; suffering tells us that those whom we love exist; suffering tells us that the world in which we live exists; and suffering tells us that God exists and suffers; but it is the suffering of anguish, the anguish of surviving and being eternal. Anguish discovers God to us and makes us love Him.

To believe in God is to love Him, and to love Him is to feel Him suffering, to pity Him.

It may perhaps appear blasphemous to say that God suffers, for suffering implies limitation. Nevertheless, God, the Consciousness of the Universe, is limited by the brute matter in which He lives, by the unconscious, from which He seeks to liberate Himself and to liberate us. And we, in our turn, must seek to liberate Him. God suffers in each and all of us, in each and all of the consciousnesses imprisoned in transitory matter, and we all suffer in Him. Religious anguish is but the divine suffering, the feeling that God suffers in me and that I suffer in Him.

The universal suffering is the anguish of all in seeking to be all else but without power to achieve it, the anguish of each in being he that he is, being at the same time all that he is not, and being so for ever. The essence of a being is not only its endeavor to persist for ever, as Spinoza taught us, but also its endeavor to universalize itself; it is the hunger and thirst for eternity and infinity. Every created being tends not only to preserve itself in itself, but to perpetuate itself, and, moreover, to invade all other beings, to be others without ceasing to be itself, to extend its limits to the infinite, but without breaking them. It does not wish to throw down its walls and leave everything laid flat, common and undefended, confounding and losing its own individuality, but it wishes to carry its walls to the extreme limits of creation and to embrace everything within them. It seeks the maximum of individuality with the maximum also of personality; it aspires to the identification of the Universe with itself; it aspires to God.

And this vast I, within which each individual I seeks to put the Universe—what is it but God? And because I aspire to God, I love Him; and this aspiration of mine towards God is my love for Him, and just as I suffer in being He, He also suffers in being I, and in being each one of us.

I am well aware that in spite of my warning that I am attempting here to give a logical form to a system of alogical feelings, I shall be scandalizing not a few of my readers in speaking of a God who suffers, and in applying to God Himself, as God, the passion of Christ. The God of so-called rational theology excludes in effect all suffering. And the reader will no doubt think that this idea of suffering can have only a metaphorical value when applied to God, similar to that which is supposed to attach to those passages in the Old Testament which describe the human passions of the God of Israel. For anger, wrath, and vengeance are impossible without suffering. And as for saying that God suffers through being bound by matter, I shall be told that, in the words of Plotinus (*Second Ennead,* ix., 7), the Universal Soul cannot be bound by the very thing—namely, bodies or matter—which is bound by It.

Herein is involved the whole problem of the origin of evil, the evil of sin no less than the evil of pain, for if God does not suffer, He causes suffering; and if His life, since God lives, is not a process of realizing in Himself a total consciousness which is continually becoming fuller—that is to say, which is continually becoming more and more God—it is a process of drawing all things towards Himself, of imparting Himself to all, of constraining the consciousness of each part to enter into the consciousness of the All, which is He Himself, until at last He comes to be all in all— πάντα ἐν πᾶσι , according to the expression of St. Paul, the first Christian mystic. We will discuss this more fully, however, in the next chapter on the apocatastasis or beatific union.

For the present let it suffice to say that there is a vast current of suffering urging living beings towards one another, constraining them to love one another and to seek one another, and to endeavor to complete one another, and to be each himself and others at the same time. In God everything lives, and in His suffering everything suffers, and in loving God we love His creatures in Him, just as in loving and pitying His creatures we love and pity God in them. No single soul can be free so long as there is anything enslaved in God's world, neither can God Himself, who lives in the soul of each one of us, be free so long as our soul is not free.

My most immediate sensation is the sense and love of my own misery, my anguish, the compassion I feel for myself, the love I bear for myself. And when this compassion is vital and superabundant, it overflows from me upon others, and frc_ the excess of my own compassion I come to have compassion for my neighbors. My own misery is so great that the compassion for myself which it awakens within me soon overflows and reveals to me the universal misery.

And what is charity but the overflow of pity? What is it but reflected pity that overflows and pours itself out in a flood of pity for the woes of others and in the exercise of charity?

When the overplus of our pity leads us to the consciousness of God within us, it fills us with so great anguish for the misery shed abroad in all things, that we have to pour our pity abroad, and this we do in the form of charity. And in this pouring abroad of our pity we experience relief and the painful sweetness of goodness. This is what Teresa de Jesús, the mystical doctor, called "sweet-tasting suffering" (dolor sabroso), and she knew also the lore of suffering loves. It is as when one looks upon some thing of beauty and feels the necessity of making others sharers in it. For the creative impulse, in which charity consists, is the work of suffering love.

We feel, in effect, a satisfaction in doing good when good superabounds within us, when we are swollen with pity; and we are swollen with pity when God, filling our soul, gives us the suffering sensation of universal life, of the universal longing for eternal divinization. For we are not merely placed side by side with others in the world, having no common root with them, neither is their lot indifferent to us, but their pain hurts us, their anguish fills us with anguish, and we feel our community of origin and of suffering even without knowing it. Suffering, and pity which is born of suffering, are what reveal to us the brotherhood of every existing thing that possesses life and more or less of consciousness. "Brother Wolf" St. Francis of Assisi called the poor wolf that feels a painful hunger for the sheep, and feels, too, perhaps, the pain of having to devour them; and this brotherhood reveals to us the Fatherhood of God, reveals to us that God is a Father and that He exists. And as a Father He shelters our common misery.

(J. E. Crawford Flitch, tr.)

FROM ABT VOGLER

ROBERT BROWNING

IX

Therefore to whom turn I but to thee, the ineffable Name?
    Builder and maker, thou, of houses not made with hands!
What, have fear of change from thee who art ever the same?
    Doubt that thy power can fill the heart that thy power expands?
There shall never be one lost good! What was, shall live as before;
    The evil is null, is naught, is silence implying sound;
What was good shall be good, with, for evil, so much good more;
    On the earth the broken arcs; in the heaven, a perfect round.

X

All we have willed or hoped or dreamed of good shall exist;
  Nor its semblance, but itself; no beauty, nor good, nor power
Whose voice has gone forth, but each survives for the melodist
  When eternity affirms the conception of an hour.
The high that proved too high, the heroic for each too hard,
  The passion that left the ground to lose itself in the sky,
Are music sent up to God by the lover and the bard;
  Enough that he heard it once: we shall hear it by-and-by.

XI

And what is our failure here but a triumph's evidence
  For the fulness of the days?   Have we withered or agonized?
Why else was the pause prolonged but that singing might issue thence?
  Why rushed the discords in but that harmony should be prized?
Sorrow is hard to bear, and doubt is slow to clear,
  Each sufferer says his say, his scheme of the weal and woe:
But God has a few of us whom he whispers in the ear;
  The rest may reason and welcome: 'tis we musicians know.

XII

Well, it is earth with me; silence resumes her reign:
  I will be patient and proud, and soberly acquiesce.
Give me the keys.   I feel for the common chord again,
  Sliding by semitones, till I sink to the minor,—yes,
And I blunt it into a ninth, and I stand on alien ground,
  Surveying awhile the heights I rolled from into the deep;
Which, hark, I have dared and done, for my resting-place is found,
  The C Major of this life: so, now I will try to sleep.

CHAPTER 7

THE VALUE OF LIFE: AS THE PESSIMIST SEES IT

The times are nightfall, look, their light grows less;
The times are winter, watch, a world undone:
They waste, they wither worse; they as they run
Or bring more or more blazon man's distress.
And I not help. Nor word now of success:
All is from wreck, here, there, to rescue one—
Work which to see scarce so much as begun
Makes welcome death, does dear forgetfulness.

Or what is else? There is your world within.
There rid the dragons, root out there the sin.
Your will is law in that small commonweal. . . .
—Gerard Manley Hopkins.

Seen down the perspective of the centuries, the history of man's moral evaluation of the world and life appears as a panorama of light and dark. Thus it is generally agreed that the Age of Pericles, its ugly features dimmed by time, was a dynamic period of idealism and order, a glorious age of the affirmation of reason and beauty; that the Middle Ages were a time whose apparent negation of this life is perhaps too easily symbolized by Dürer's engraving of Melancholy or the popular theme of the Dance of Death; that the Renaissance, beginning in fourteenth-century Italy and extending through the spacious times of great Elizabeth, was an era of abundant vitality; and that this age was followed by others in which man's thinking seems to have been dominantly pessimistic or optimistic in tone down to our own age of bewildering revelation and disillusionment. The very terms, "Dark Ages," "Renaissance," and "Age of Doubt" signify in themselves that men and civilizations were dominated (as it seems to us) by the conviction that life in itself was "stale, flat, and unprofitable," or knew a resurgence of belief in the value of life, or the darkness of uncertainty.

Though these larger aspects, the fluctuations in mood from period to period, interest the philosopher as well as the social historian, in this text we must be content with the presentation of the typical attitudes of pessimism and optimism as expressed in the literature of poets and philosophers. In taking this approach to the problem, we shall not, after all, be entirely neglecting the almost cyclical changes, since great men—indeed all men to some extent—both reflect and shape their ages. It is to this varying response to life that men commonly refer when they speak of their philosophy.   To some degree everyone exemplifies one or the other of these attitudes: he is primarily an optimist or a pessimist.

Though the reader will find it desirable to study the selections illustrating these two evaluations of life together, for convenience in developing the theme of each we have divided the material into two chapters.   This chapter presents variations of the pessimistic view.

Our first selection, from *Candide,* shows the conflict between these two diverse evaluations of life.   *Candide* as a whole was written to repudiate Leibnitz's doctrine of pre-established harmony, the theory that all the universe is a result of wise design, that this is the best of all possible worlds. Voltaire insists that this view (which is developed in detail by Pope in the next chapter) will not meet the test of practical experience: evil is a fact, not an illusion; worst of all, men are conditioned to evil by nature.

Pessimism may manifest itself in a variety of ways, but it is basically always a disillusionment with life or religion.   Sometimes this disillusionment may be an individual uneasiness, a lack of personal adjustment to one's time and circumstances.   Yet the main reason why we approve of Wordsworth's sonnet, "The World Is Too Much with Us," is that it expresses the oppression that we all feel in our too complex world.   This uneasiness, this depression that comes from the loss of inward light, this suspension in us of the "shaping spirit of imagination" as Coleridge calls it ("Ode to Dejection"), is not just the private cry of individual distress.   However much the lost child of the poem may symbolize the poet himself, it suggests also the atmosphere of doubt in which the thought arose.   This inner unhappiness becomes a discontent with life itself in Santayana's "I Would I Might Forget That I Am I."

What in these preceding poems is felt as representing the individual affected with gloomy misgivings about the value of life becomes intensified and widened in Leopardi, most pessimistic of all poets, to apply to mankind in general.   In his "Dialogue Between Nature and the Soul," humanity is seen doomed to unhappiness.   Man may attain to greatness, never to any real satisfaction.   It would be better, he concludes, to be nothing than to live in the mockery of the unattainable.   This almost unrelieved gloom, which is made blacker to us by our own modern misgivings about our civilization, has its ancient parallel in the words of the Preacher, whose admonition has long sobered the thoughtful: "I have seen all the works that are done under the sun; and behold all is vanity and vexation of spirit."

One encounters this theme of the vanity and painful futility of human affairs in poetry and philosophy everywhere.   In the defeat of the pretensions of a tyrant ("Ozymandias"), one may take a gloomy pleasure, but the larger application of the idea to all our systems that Santayana makes leaves no comfort.   To be told that our discoveries have resulted in a smaller earth and smaller hope of heaven, and that our race is reverting to the darkness from which it rose is not reassuring.

More piteous than the general pattern of futility and misery is the evidence of the incidental cruelty of the world, the pathos of the individual creature and his capacity for grief. Everyone's experience will supply incidents to match the brutality of the vignettes of Pater in *Marius the Epicurean*. Leopardi, Francis Thompson, and Arnold in particular inveigh against the injustice of ills self-incurred when one was a child, the inequalities of our world, a world in which one's future depends on the shape of one's nose, a world in which beauty dies and old age grows foul even to itself. Ours is a life, Leopardi asserts, in which "Mere relief from pain is counted joy."

Worse still than the wanton cruelty of chance and man's own malice to man is the desolation that comes from the loss of one's ideals. To most people, as to Philip Carey in *Of Human Bondage,* dark moments come when all that they have been taught to revere seems false. But the darkness of the man who has deserted his ideals is yet more hideous: with him, Life is "a tale Told by an idiot, full of sound and fury, Signifying nothing." Trapped by such bitterness, men naturally think of escape, of a refuge in death, a theme illustrated here in the reflections from Leopardi, Swinburne, and Hopkins. This mood has its nadir in Swinburne's ironic thankfulness that "no life lives forever, That dead men rise up never, That even the weariest river Winds somewhere safe to sea." Can men really invert their thinking so far as to acclaim death a boon?

If death is a refuge, and the only refuge from our certain ills, if life is meaningless, why live? ask Leopardi and Robinson ("From the Greek of Simonides," "The Man Against the Sky"). Man should scorn a life, says Robinson, in which "All comes to Nought." Why not commit suicide? This escape of despair is rejected by Hamlet on supernatural grounds—the "dread of something after death." What this "something after death" may be is visualized by Claudio in *Measure for Measure.* Thus Shakespeare, though he might have devised other nobler answers, leads away from the worst pessimism, worst since it ends the possibility of a right solution, and we are back in our normal unhappy world in which men fear death.

Is there no escape from death? asks Whitman. We think of the escape offered by faith. But the thoroughgoing pessimist rejects this. The faiths that contented our fathers no longer satisfy him. He sees humanity as the puppets of the gods, who enjoy the spectacle of the Tragedy of Man with its hero, Conqueror Worm (Poe). God is a mockery, man-invented, whose fear blights our lives (Shelley). James Thomson, after dallying hopelessly on the hopes of religion, returns to bleak nihilism again.

There is, the pessimist maintains, no escape from the terrible lot of mortality. What, then, is the place of the individual in a purposeless, lost world? Leopardi suggests that we should prize the sweet illusions of youth and turn with the "iron days" of age to the great questions of philosophy. And Carlyle's hero in *Sartor Resartus,* confronted with a universe "void of Life, of Purpose, of Volition," emerges from utter pessimism through the strength of his spirit: "The Everlasting No had said: 'Behold thou art fatherless, outcast, and the Universe is mine' (the Devil's); to which my whole Me now made answer: 'I am not thine, but Free, and forever hate thee!'" But though this picture of the deserted spirit defying a hostile universe is not petty, it is still a dark view; and dark, too, is the noble mind of Arnold, who can find solace only in human love.

Finally it should be evident that the pessimistic view in its best aspects is not ignoble. Examination of the chapters dealing with naturalism and humanism, basically pessimistic so far as orthodox religious views are concerned, will convince one of the essential nobility of the nature of man. This is the untarnished glory of the dark view of life.

FROM WHAT HAPPENED TO CANDIDE AND MARTIN IN FRANCE

In *Candide (Chapter 22)*

VOLTAIRE

Then, turning to him, Candide said:

"Sir, no doubt you think that all is for the best in the physical world and in the moral, and that nothing could be otherwise than as it is?"

"Sir," replied the man of letters, "I do not think anything of the sort. I think everything goes awry with us, that nobody knows his rank or his office, nor what he is doing, nor what he ought to do, and that except at supper, which is quite gay and where there appears to be a certain amount of sociability, all the rest of their time is passed in senseless quarrels: Jansenists with Molinists, lawyers with churchmen, men of letters with men of letters, courtiers with courtiers, financiers with the people, wives with husbands, relatives with relatives—'tis an eternal war."

Candide replied:

"I have seen worse things; but a wise man, who has since had the misfortune to be hanged, taught me that it is all for the best; these are only the shadows in a fair picture."

"Your wise man who was hanged, was poking fun at the world," said Martin; "and your shadows are horrible stains."

"The stains are made by men," said Candide, "and they cannot avoid them."

"Then it is not their fault," said Martin.

"THE WORLD IS TOO MUCH WITH US"

WILLIAM WORDSWORTH

The world is too much with us; late and soon,
Getting and spending, we lay waste our powers:
Little we see in Nature that is ours;
We have given our hearts away, a sordid boon!
This Sea that bares her bosom to the moon;

The winds that will be howling at all hours,
And are up-gathered now like sleeping flowers;
For this, for everything, we are out of tune;
It moves us not.—Great God! I'd rather be
A Pagan suckled in a creed outworn;
So might I, standing on this pleasant lea,
Have glimpses that would make me less forlorn;
Have sight of Proteus rising from the sea;
Or hear old Triton blow his wreathèd horn.

DEJECTION: AN ODE

SAMUEL TAYLOR COLERIDGE

Late, late yestreen I saw the new Moon,
With the old Moon in her arms;
And I fear, I fear, my Master dear!
We shall have a deadly storm.

—Ballad of Sir Patrick Spence.

I

Well! If the Bard was weather-wise, who made
   The grand old ballad of Sir Patrick Spence,
   This night, so tranquil now, will not go hence
Unroused by winds, that ply a busier trade
Than those which mould yon cloud in lazy flakes,
Or the dull sobbing draft, that moans and rakes
      Upon the strings of this Aeolian lute,
      Which better far were mute.
   For lo! the New-moon winter-bright!
   And overspread with phantom light,
      (With swimming phantom light o'erspread
   But rimmed and circled by a silver thread)
I see the old Moon in her lap, foretelling
   The coming on of rain and squally blast.
And oh! that even now the gust were swelling,
   And the slant night-shower driving loud and fast!
Those sounds which oft have raised me, whilst they awed,
      And sent my soul abroad,
Might now, perhaps, their wonted impulse give,
Might startle this dull pain, and make it move and live!

II

A grief without a pang, void, dark, and drear,
   A stifled, drowsy, unimpassioned grief,
   Which finds no natural outlet, no relief,
      In word, or sigh, or tear—
O Lady! in this wan and heartless mood,
To other thoughts by yonder throstle woo'd,
   All this long eve, so balmy and serene,
Have I been gazing on the western sky,

And its peculiar tint of yellow green:
And still I gaze—and with how blank an eye!
And those thin clouds above, in flakes and bars,
That give away their motion to the stars;
Those stars, that glide behind them or between,
Now sparkling, now bedimmed, but always seen
Yon crescent Moon as fixed as if it grew
In its own cloudless, starless lake of blue;
I see them all so excellently fair,
I see, not feel how beautiful they are!

III

My genial spirits fail;
And what can these avail
To lift the smothering weight from off my breast?
It were a vain endeavor,
Though I should gaze forever
On that green light that lingers in the west:
I may not hope from outward forms to win
The passion and the life, whose fountains are within.

IV

O Lady! we receive but what we give,
And in our life alone does nature live:
Ours is her wedding-garment, ours her shroud!
And would we aught behold, of higher worth
Than that inanimate cold world allowed
To the poor loveless ever-anxious crowd,
Ah! from the soul itself must issue forth,
A light, a glory, a fair luminous cloud
Enveloping the Earth—
And from the soul itself must there be sent
A sweet and potent voice, of its own birth,
Of all sweet sounds the life and element!

V

O pure of heart; thou need'st not ask of me
What this strong music in the soul may be!
What, and wherein it doth exist,
This light, this glory, this fair luminous mist,
This beautiful and beauty-making power.
Joy, virtuous lady! Joy that ne'er was given,
Save to the pure, and in their purest hour,
Life, and Life's effluence, cloud at once and shower
Joy, Lady! is the spirit and the power
Which wedding Nature to us gives in dower,
A new Earth and new Heaven,
Undreamt of by the sensual and the proud—
Joy is the sweet voice, Joy the luminous cloud—

We in ourselves rejoice!
And thence flows all that charms or ear or sight,
    All melodies the echoes of that voice,
All colors a suffusion from that light.

VI

There was a time when, though my path was rough,
This joy within me dallied with distress,
And all misfortunes were but as the stuff
    Whence Fancy made me dreams of happiness:
For hope grew round me, like the twining vine,
And fruits, and foliage, not my own, seemed mine.
But now afflictions bow me down to earth:
Nor care I that they rob me of my mirth,
        But oh! each visitation
Suspends what nature gave me at my birth,
    My shaping spirit of Imagination.
For not to think of what I needs must feel,
    But to be still and patient, all I can;
And haply by abstruse research to steal
    From my own nature all the natural man—
    This was my sole resource, my only plan:
Till that which suits a part infects the whole,
And now is almost grown the habit of my soul.

VII

Hence viper thoughts, that coil around my mind,
        Reality's dark dream!
I turn from you, and listen to the wind,
    Which long has raved unnoticed.   What a scream
Of agony by torture lengthened out
That lute sent forth!   Thou Wind, that ravest without,
    Bare craig, or mountain-tarn, or blasted tree,
Or pine-grove whither woodman never clomb,
Or lonely house, long held the witches' home,
    Methinks were fitter instruments for thee,
Mad Lutanist! who in this month of showers,
Of dark-brown gardens, and of peeping flowers,
Mak'st Devils' yule, with worse than wintry song,
The blossoms, buds, and timorous leaves among.
    Thou Actor, perfect in all tragic sounds!
Thou mighty Poet, e'en to frenzy bold!
        What tell'st thou now about?
        'Tis of the rushing of a host in rout,
    With groans of trampled men, with smarting wounds—
At once they groan with pain, and shudder with the cold!
But hush! there is a pause of deepest silence!
    And all that noise, as of a rushing crowd,
With groans and tremulous shudderings—all is over—
    It tells another tale, with sounds less deep and loud!
        A tale of less affright,
        And tempered with delight,

As Otway's self had framed the tender lay,
'Tis of a little child,
Upon a lonesome wild,
Not far from home, but she hath lost her way:
And now moans low in bitter grief and fear,
And now screams loud, and hopes to make her mother hear.

VIII

'Tis midnight, but small thoughts have I of sleep;
Full seldom may my friends such vigils keep!
Visit her, gentle Sleep! with wings of healing,
　And may this storm be but a mountain-birth,
May all the stars hang bright above her dwelling,
　Silent as though they watched the sleeping Earth!
　　With light heart may she rise,
　　Gay fancy, cheerful eyes,
　Joy lift her spirit, joy attune her voice;
To her may all things live, from pole to pole,
Their life the eddying of her living soul!
O simple spirit, guided from above,
Dear Lady! friend devoutest of my choice,
Thus mayest thou ever, evermore rejoice.

WISDOM

SARA TEASDALE

When I have ceased to break my wings
Against the faultiness of things,
And learned that compromises wait
Behind each hardly opened gate,
When I can look Life in the eyes,
Grown calm and very coldly wise,
Life will have given me the Truth,
And taken in exchange—my youth.

"I WOULD I MIGHT FORGET THAT I AM I" *

GEORGE SANTAYANA

I would I might forget that I am I,
And break the heavy chain that binds me fast,
Whose links about myself my deeds have cast.
What in the body's tomb doth buried lie
Is boundless; 'tis the spirit of the sky,
Lord of the future, guardian of the past,
And soon must forth, to know his own at last.
In his large life to live, I fain would die.

* Reprinted from *Poems* by George Santayana; copyright 1923 by Charles Scribner's Sons; used by permission of the publishers.

Happy the dumb beast, hungering for food,
But calling not his suffering his own;
Blessèd the angel, gazing on all good,
But knowing not he sits upon a throne;
Wretched the mortal, pondering his mood,
And doomed to know his aching heart alone.

DIALOGUE BETWEEN NATURE AND A SOUL

GIACOMO LEOPARDI

NATURE: Go now, my favorite daughter, for such thou shalt be called for a long series of ages—go, live, and be great and miserable.

SOUL: What sin have I committed prior to my birth that you doom me to such a punishment?

NATURE: What punishment, my child?

SOUL: Have you not doomed me to be unhappy?

NATURE: Ay; for I have destined thee to be great, and thou can'st not be that without being unhappy. Moreover, thou art appointed to animate a human form, and all men of necessity are from their birth unhappy.

SOUL: Instead of this being so, it were but reasonable that you should provide that they should of necessity be happy; and if this be beyond your power, surely you ought at least to refrain from placing them in the world.

NATURE: Neither of these courses is within my power, for I myself am subject to Destiny, who hath ordained it otherwise, whatever the reason for this may be, and neither you nor I can penetrate it. Now, seeing that you have been created and destined to occupy a human body, no power existing either in me or in any other being can possibly deliver you from the unhappiness appointed to men. Nay, in addition to that unhappiness, it will be necessary for you to endure a special and still greater measure of misery, peculiar to yourself by reason of the very nobility and excellence with which I have endowed you.

SOUL: Having just come into existence, of course I have all things to learn, and this probably is the reason why I fail to understand you. But tell me, are nobility of disposition and extraordinary unhappiness substantially the same thing; and if not, could you not contrive to separate them?

NATURE: In the case of mankind, and indeed to a certain extent in that of all animals, it may be said that these two things are practically one and the same, since the more elevated the faculties are, the more clear becomes the perception of the conditions of life, and of the unhappiness inseparable from existence; and thus that unhappiness itself becomes intensified. At the same time increased vividness of perception tends to enlarge the scope of self-love, and to increase the craving for happiness, resulting only in increased regret for the impossibility of attaining it, and greater intolerance of the inevitable woes of life. All this was from the beginning involved in the primeval and eternal constitution of created things, which it is beyond my power to change.

But furthermore, the very keenness of your intellect, coupled with the vividness of your imagination, will tend to diminish to a great degree your command over your emotions. The lower animals readily apply their faculties and powers to the accomplishment of the ends which they have in view; but men seldom put forth their full and unrestricted capacities on any occasion, since their powers of action are usually more or less impeded by the influence of their reason and their imagination, which introduce a thousand doubts into their deliberations, and raise up a thousand obstacles to the execution of their designs. Indeed, those of them who are the least capable of weighing their thoughts and analyzing their intentions, or who are the least addicted to this habit, are generally found to be the most prompt in their decisions, and the most direct in their operations; whereas beings like you, perpetually involved in introspection, and hampered by the very magnitude of their powers, are comparatively impotent for practical purposes, and are too often a prey to irresolution in thought and deed, that most baneful of all the mischiefs which can affect the transactions of life.

Add to this, that while by the superiority of your faculties you will easily and swiftly surpass your fellow-creatures in profound knowledge and difficult attainments, nevertheless you will frequently find it almost impossible to put into practice numerous things, trifling in appearance, but most necessary to the business of life; and at the same time you will see these things accomplished without difficulty and practiced with ease by persons far inferior to yourself, if not actually contemptible in their character. These and other infinite difficulties and mortifications await on and environ great souls. Yet they are abundantly compensated for these trials by fame, by the praises and honors which are won for these noble spirits by their greatness, and by the enduring memory which they leave behind to posterity.

SOUL: But who will accord to me the praises and honors of which you speak? Will they be rendered to me by Heaven, or by you, or by whom?

NATURE: They will be rendered to you by men, since they alone can confer them.

SOUL: But I pray you to consider. It occurs to me that since I shall be unable to perform actions so necessary to the conduct of human affairs, and which yet are capable, as you say, of accomplishment by the poorest intelligences, the result must be that instead of being praised and honored, I shall inevitably be vituperated and shunned by men, or at least shall have to pass through life almost unknown to them, as one ill fitted for human society.

NATURE: To me it is not given to read the future with absolute exactness, or to predict infallibly all that men may think or do in relation to you during your sojourn on earth. But from the experience of the past, I should judge it to be most probable that they will pursue you with envy, the usual fate of noble souls, or vex you with contumely or neglect. Besides which, Fortune herself, and even ordinary chance, are wont to be hostile to such as you.

Nevertheless, immediately after your death, as happened to one called Camoëns, or at most a few years later, as occurred in the case of another named Milton, you will be praised and exalted to the skies, I will not say by all men, but at least by that small portion of them who are possessed of judgment and discrimination; and possibly the mortal remains of the person in whom you dwelt when on earth will repose in a sumptuous tomb, and his features, imitated in various costly materials, be preserved among men; while all the incidents of his life will be described by many writers, and their memory be diligently preserved, till at last the whole civilized world shall ring with his renown. All this will probably happen, unless by the malignity of fortune, or by reason of the very excess of your gifts, you should be hindered from exhibiting to mankind any due proof of your worth, as indeed has happened in many cases, known only to me and to Fate.

SOUL: Oh! mother, although I am as yet destitute of all other knowledge, nevertheless I know and feel that the strongest desire you have implanted in me, indeed the only one of which I am conscious, is the desire of happiness. And even granting that I may be capable of desiring glory, and whether that be a good or an evil, assuredly I could never desire it if it does not insure happiness, or is not at least conducive to its attainment. Now, according to what you have said, the qualities with which you have endowed me may possibly be necessary or serviceable for the attainment of glory, but it is evident that they do not lead to happiness, but on the contrary to misery. Furthermore, it appears that these qualities will not lead me even to glory until I shall be dead; and when I am dead, what benefit or what pleasure can possibly accrue to me even from the greatest advantages earth can bestow? Finally, you yourself admit that this phantom glory, which can only be purchased at the price of so much misery, may never be attained by me at all, not even after death. These things being so, and judging from your own words, I am forced to the conclusion that instead of loving me tenderly, as you professed in your opening address, you in reality hate me even more malignantly than mankind and Fortune herself are likely to be capable of doing during my sojourn on earth, since you have not scrupled to present to me a gift so fatal as this nobility of character for which you take so much credit to yourself, but which is itself calculated to prove so effectual an obstacle to my attainment of my sole desire—happiness.

NATURE: My child, every soul of man, as I have already told you, is doomed to infelicity, in spite of me; but in the universal unhappiness which is the inevitable lot of men, and in the infinite vanity of all their pleasures and hopes, glory has ever been regarded by them as the greatest good which is conceded to mortals, and the most worthy object of their efforts; and therefore, not from hatred of you, but from a sincere and special good will and benevolence, I resolved to endow you with all the qualities in my power to bestow, for the attainment of that end.

SOUL: Tell me—of all the inferior creatures which you mentioned is there any one furnished with less perfection of vitality, and less capacity for feeling than man?

NATURE: Surely. From the plants upwards all creatures are in this respect more or less inferior to man, who is gifted with a greater exuberance of life and feeling than any other created thing, inasmuch as he is the most perfect of all earthly creatures.

SOUL: Well then, if you truly love me, lodge me in the most imperfect of them all; or if you cannot do this, at least strip me of those fatal gifts which you fancy ennoble me, and adapt me to occupy the most stupid and insensate human creature you have ever fashioned.

NATURE: This it is in my power to grant; and I am willing to do so, since you reject the immortality for which I had destined you.

SOUL: And instead of immortality, I beseech you to send me death as soon as possible.

NATURE: On that point I will consult Destiny.

(Patrick Maxwell, tr.)

from ECCLESIASTES; or THE PREACHER
CHAPTER I

The words of the Preacher, the son of David, king in Jerusalem.

Vanity of vanities, saith the Preacher, vanity of vanities; all is vanity.

What profit hath a man of all his labor which he taketh under the sun?

One generation passeth away, and another generation cometh: but the earth abideth for ever.

The sun also ariseth, and the sun goeth down, and hasteth to his place where he arose.

The wind goeth toward the south, and turneth about unto the north; it whirleth about continually, and the wind returneth again according to his circuits.

All the rivers run into the sea; yet the sea is not full; unto the place from whence the rivers come, thither they return again.

All things are full of labor; man cannot utter it: the eye is not satisfied with seeing, nor the ear filled with hearing.

The thing that hath been, it is that which shall be; and that which is done is that which shall be done: and there is no new thing under the sun.

Is there any thing whereof it may be said, See, this is new? it hath been already of old time, which was before us.

There is no remembrance of former things; neither shall there be any remembrance of things that are to come with those that shall come after.

I the Preacher was king over Israel in Jerusalem.

And I gave my heart to seek and search out by wisdom concerning all things that are done under heaven: this sore travail hath God given to the sons of man to be exercised therewith.

I have seen all the works that are done under the sun; and, behold, all is vanity and vexation of spirit.

.   .   .   .

CHAPTER II

I said in mine heart, Go to now, I will prove thee with mirth, therefore enjoy pleasure: and, behold, this also is vanity.

I said of laughter, It is mad: and of mirth: What doeth it?

I sought in mine heart to give myself unto wine, yet acquainting mine heart with wisdom; and to lay hold on folly, till I might see what was that good for the sons of men, which they should do under the heaven all the days of their life.

I made me great works; I builded me houses; I planted me vineyards:

I made me gardens and orchards, and I planted trees in them of all kind of fruits:

I made me pools of water, to water therewith the wood that bringeth forth trees:

I got me servants and maidens, and had servants born in my house; also I had great possessions of great and small cattle above all that were in Jerusalem before me:

I gathered me also silver and gold, and the peculiar treasure of kings and of the provinces: I gat me men singers and women singers, and the delights of the sons of men, as musical instruments, and that of all sorts.

So I was great, and increased more than all that were before me in Jerusalem: also my wisdom remained with me.

And whatsoever mine eyes desired I kept not from them, I withheld not my heart from any joy; for my heart rejoiced in all my labor: and this was my portion of all my labor.

Then I looked on all the works that my hands had wrought, and on the labor that I had labored to do: and, behold, all was vanity and vexation of spirit, and there was no profit under the sun.

And I turned myself to behold wisdom, and madness, and folly: for what can the man do that cometh after the king? even that which hath been already done.

Then I saw that wisdom excelleth folly, as far as light excelleth darkness.

The wise man's eyes are in his head; but the fool walketh in darkness: and I myself perceived also that one event happeneth to them all.

Then said I in my heart, As it happeneth to the fool, so it happeneth even to me; and why was I then more wise? Then I said in my heart, that this also is vanity.

For there is no remembrance of the wise more than of the fool for ever; seeing that which now is in the days to come shall all be forgotten. And how dieth the wise man? as the fool.

Therefore I hated life; because the work that is wrought under the sun is grievous unto me: for all is vanity and vexation of spirit.

Yea, I hated all my labor which I had taken under the sun: because I should leave it unto the man that shall be after me.

And who knoweth whether he shall be a wise man or a fool? yet shall he have rule over all my labor wherein I have labored, and wherein I have shewed myself wise under the sun. This is also vanity.

Therefore I went about to cause my heart to despair of all the labor which I took under the sun.

For there is a man whose labor is in wisdom, and in knowledge, and in equity; yet to a man that hath not labored therein shall he leave it for his portion. This also is vanity and a great evil.

For what hath man of all his labor, and of the vexation of his heart, wherein he hath labored under the sun?

For all his days are sorrows, and his travail grief; yea, his heart taketh not rest in the night. This is also vanity.

There is nothing better for a man, than that he should eat and drink, and that he should make his soul enjoy good in his labor. This also I saw, that it was from the hand of God.

For who can eat, or who else can hasten hereunto, more than I?

For God giveth to a man that is good in his sight wisdom, and knowledge, and joy: but to the sinner he giveth travail, to gather and to heap up, that he may give to him that is good before God. This also is vanity and vexation of spirit.

CHAPTER IX

For all this I considered in my heart even to declare all this, that the righteous, and the wise, and their works, are in the hand of God: no man knoweth either love or hatred by all that is before them.

All things come alike to all: there is one event to the righteous, and to the wicked; to the good and to the clean, and to the unclean; to him that sacrificeth, and to him that sacrificeth not: as is the good, so is the sinner; and he that sweareth, as he that feareth an oath.

This is an evil among all things that are done under the sun, that there is one event unto all: yea, also the heart of the sons of men is full of evil, and madness is in their heart while they live, and after that they go to the dead.

For to him that is joined to all the living there is hope: for a living dog is better than a dead lion.

For the living know that they shall die: but the dead know not any thing, neither have they any more a reward; for the memory of them is forgotten.

Also their love, and their hatred, and their envy, is now perished; neither have they any more a portion for ever in any thing that is done under the sun.

Go thy way, eat thy bread with joy, and drink thy wine with a merry heart; for God now accepteth thy works.

Let thy garments be always white and let thy head lack no ointment.

Live joyfully with the wife whom thou lovest all the days of the life of thy vanity, which he hath given thee under the sun, all the days of thy vanity: for that is thy portion in this life, and in thy labor which thou takest under the sun.

Whatsoever thy hand findeth to do, do it with thy might; for there is no work, nor device, nor knowledge, nor wisdom, in the grave, whither thou goest.

I returned, and saw under the sun, that the race is not to the swift, nor the battle to the strong, neither yet bread to the wise, nor yet riches to men of understanding, nor yet favor to men of skill; but time and chance happeneth to them all.

For man also knoweth not his time: as the fishes that are taken in an evil net, and as the birds that are caught in the snare; so are the sons of men snared in an evil time, when it falleth suddenly upon them.

This wisdom have I seen also under the sun, and it seemed great unto me:

There was a little city, and few men within it; and there came a great king against it, and besieged it, and built great bulwarks against it:

Now there was found in it a poor wise man, and he by his wisdom delivered the city; yet no man remembered that same poor man.

Then said I, Wisdom is better than strength: nevertheless the poor man's wisdom is despised, and his words are not heard.

The words of wise men are heard in quiet more than the cry of him that ruleth among fools.

Wisdom is better than weapons of war: but one sinner destroyeth much good.

CHAPTER XII

Remember now thy Creator in the days of thy youth, while the evil days come not, nor the years draw nigh, when thou shalt say, I have no pleasure in them;

While the sun, or the light, or the moon, or the stars, be not darkened, nor the clouds return after the rain:

In the day when the keepers of the house shall tremble, and the strong men shall bow themselves, and the grinders cease because they are few, and those that look out of the windows be darkened,

And the doors shall be shut in the streets, when the sound of the grinding is low, and he shall rise up at the voice of the bird, and all the daughters of music shall be brought low;

Also when they shall be afraid of that which is high, and fears shall be in the way, and the almond tree shall flourish, and the grasshopper shall be a burden, and desire shall fail: because man goeth to his long home, and the mourners go about the streets:

Or ever the silver cord be loosed, or the golden bowl be broken, or the pitcher be broken at the fountain, or the wheel broken at the cistern.

Then shall the dust return to the earth as it was: and the spirit shall return unto God who gave it.

Vanity of vanities, saith the preacher; all is vanity.

OZYMANDIAS

PERCY BYSSHE SHELLEY

I met a traveler from an antique land
Who said: Two vast and trunkless legs of stone
Stand in the desert. Near them, on the sand,
Half sunk, a shattered visage lies, whose frown,
And wrinkled lip, and sneer of cold command,
Tell that the sculptor well those passions read
Which yet survive, stamped on these lifeless things,
The hand that mocked them and the heart that fed;
And on the pedestal these words appear:
"My name is Ozymandias, king of kings:
Look on my works, ye Mighty, and despair!"
Nothing beside remains. Round the decay
Of that colossal wreck, boundless and bare
The lone and level sands stretch far away.

"GATHERING THE ECHOES OF FORGOTTEN WISDOM" *
(Ode III)

GEORGE SANTAYANA

Gathering the echoes of forgotten wisdom,
And mastered by a proud, adventurous purpose,
Columbus sought the golden shores of India
    Opposite Europe.

He gave the world another world, and ruin
Brought upon blameless, river-loving nations,
Cursed Spain with barren gold, and made the Andes
    Fiefs of Saint Peter;

While in the cheerless North the thrifty Saxon
Planted his corn, and narrowing his bosom,
Made covenant with God, and by keen virtue
    Trebled his riches.

What venture hast thou left us, bold Columbus?
What honor left thy brothers, brave Magellan?
Daily the children of the rich for pastime
    Circle the planet.

And what good comes to us of all your dangers?
A smaller earth and smaller hope of heaven.
Ye have but cheapened gold, and, measuring ocean,
    Counted the islands.

* Reprinted from *Poems* by George Santayana; copyright 1923 by Charles Scribner's Sons; used by permission of the publishers.

No Ponce de Leon shall drink in fountains,
On any flowering Easter, youth eternal;
No Cortes look upon another ocean;
    No Alexander

Found in the Orient dim a boundless kingdom,
And, clothing his Greek strength in barbarous splendor,
Build by the sea his throne, while sacred Egypt
    Honors his godhead.

The earth, the mother once of godlike Theseus
And mighty Heracles, at length is weary,
And now brings forth a spawn of antlike creatures.
    Blackening her valleys,

Inglorious in their birth and in their living,
Curious and querulous, afraid of battle,
Rummaging earth for coals, in camps of hovels
    Crouching from winter,

As if grim fate, amid our boastful prating,
Made us the image of our brutish fathers,
When from their caves they issued, crazed with terror,
    Howling and hungry.

For all things come about in sacred cycles,
And life brings death, and light eternal darkness,
And now the world grows old apace; its glory
    Passes for ever.

Perchance the earth will yet for many ages
Bear her dead child, her moon, around her orbit;
Strange craft may tempt the ocean streams, new forests
    Cover the mountains.

If in those latter days men still remember
Our wisdom and our travail and our sorrow,
They never can be happy, with that burden
    Heavy upon them,

Knowing the hideous past, the blood, the famine,
The ancestral hate, the eager faith's disaster,
All ending in their little lives, and vulgar
    Circle of troubles.

But if they have forgot us, and the shifting
Of sands has buried deep our thousand cities,
Fell superstition then will seize upon them;
    Protean error

Will fill their panting heart with sickly phantoms
Of sudden blinding good and monstrous evil;
There will be miracles again, and torment,
    Dungeon, and fagot,—

Until the patient earth, made dry and barren,
Sheds all her herbage in a final winter,
And the gods turn their eyes to some far distant
Bright constellation.

FROM SUNT LACRIMAE RERUM

In *Marius the Epicurean*

WALTER PATER

. . . "Then, how if appetite, be it for real or ideal, should itself fail one after awhile? Ah, yes! is it of cold always that men die; and on some of us it creeps very gradually. In truth, I can remember just such a lack-luster condition of feeling once or twice before. But I note, that it was accompanied then by an odd indifference, as the thought of them occurred to me, in regard to the sufferings of others—a kind of callousness, so unusual with me, as at once to mark the humor it accompanied as a palpably morbid one that could not last. Were those sufferings, great or little, I asked myself then, of more real consequence to them than mine to me, as I remind myself that 'nothing that will end is really long'—long enough to be thought of importance? But today, my own sense of fatigue, the pity I conceive for myself, disposed me strongly to a tenderness for others. For a moment the whole world seemed to present itself as a hospital of sick persons; many of them sick in mind; all of whom it would be a brutality not to humor, not to indulge.

"Why, when I went out to walk off my wayward fancies, did I confront the very sort of incident (my unfortunate *genius* had surely beckoned it from afar to vex me) likely to irritate them further? A party of men were coming down the street. They were leading a fine race-horse; a handsome beast, but badly hurt somewhere, in the circus, and useless. They were taking him to slaughter; and I think the animal knew it: he cast such looks, as if of mad appeal, to those who passed him, as he went among the strangers to whom his former owner had committed him, to die, in his beauty and pride, for just that one mischance or fault; although the morning air was still so animating, and pleasant to snuff. I could have fancied a human soul in the creature, swelling against its luck. And I had come across the incident just when it would figure to me as the very symbol of our poor humanity, in its capacities for pain, its wretched accidents, and those imperfect sympathies, which can never quite identify us with one another; the very power of utterance and appeal to others seeming to fail us, in proportion as our sorrows come home to ourselves, are really our own. We are constructed for suffering! What proofs of it does but one day afford, if we care to note them, as we go—a whole long chaplet of sorrowful mysteries! *Sunt lacrimae rerum et mentem mortalia tangunt.*

"Men's fortunes touch us! The little children of one of those institutions for the support of orphans, now become fashionable among us by way of memorial of eminent persons deceased, are going, in long file, along the street, on their way to a holiday in the country. They halt, and count themselves with an air of triumph, to show that they are all there. Their gay chatter has disturbed a little group of peasants; a young woman and her husband, who have brought the old mother, now past work and witless, to place her in a house provided for such afflicted people. They are fairly affectionate, but anxious how the thing they have to do may go— hope only she may permit them to leave her there behind quietly. And the poor old soul is excited by the noise made by the children, and partly aware of what is going to happen with her. She too begins to count—one, two, three, five—on her trembling fingers, misshapen by a life of toil. 'Yes! yes! and twice five make ten'—they say, to pacify her. It is her last appeal to be taken home again; her proof that all is not yet up with her; that she is, at all events, still as capable as those joyous children.

"At the baths, a party of laborers are at work upon one of the great brick furnaces, in a cloud of black dust. A frail young child has brought food for one of them, and sits apart, waiting till his father comes—watching the labor, but with a sorrowful distaste for the din and dirt. He is regarding wistfully his own place in the world, there before him. His mind, as he watches, is grown up for a moment; and he foresees, as it were, in that moment, all the long tale of days, of early awakings, of his own coming life of drudgery at work like this.

"A man comes along carrying a boy whose rough work has already begun—the only child—whose presence beside him sweetened the father's toil a little. The boy has been badly injured by a fall of brick-work, yet, with an effort, he rides boldly on his father's shoulders. It will be the way of natural affection to keep him alive as long as possible, though with that miserably shattered body—'Ah! with us still, and feeling our care beside him!'—and yet surely not without a heartbreaking sigh of relief, alike from him and them, when the end comes.

"On the alert for incidents like these, yet of necessity passing them by on the other side, I find it hard to get rid of a sense that I, for one, have failed in love. I could yield to the humor till I seemed to have had my share in those great public cruelties, the shocking legal crimes which are on record, like that cold-blooded slaughter, according to law, of the four hundred slaves in the reign of Nero, because one of their number was thought to have murdered his master. The reproach of that, together with the kind of facile apologies those who had no share in the deed may have made for it, as they went about quietly on their own affairs that day, seems to come very close to me, as I think upon it. And to how many of those now actually around me, whose life is a sore one, must I be indifferent, if I ever become aware of their soreness at all? To some, perhaps, the necessary conditions of my own life may cause me to be opposed, in a kind of natural conflict, regarding those interests which actually determine the happiness of theirs. I would that a stronger love might arise in my heart!

"Yet there is plenty of charity in the world. My patron, the Stoic emperor, has made it even fashionable. To celebrate one of his brief returns to Rome lately from the war, over and above a largess of gold pieces to all who would, the public debts were forgiven. He made a nice show of it: for once, the Romans entertained themselves with a good-natured spectacle, and the whole town came to see the great bonfire in the Forum, into which all bonds and evidence of debt were thrown on delivery, by the emperor himself; many private creditors following his example. That was done well enough! But still the feeling returns to me, that no charity of ours can get at a certain natural unkindness which I find in things themselves.

. . . .

"For there is a certain grief in things as they are, in man as he has come to be, as he certainly is, over and above those griefs of circumstance which are in a measure removable—some inexplicable shortcoming, or misadventure, on the part of nature itself—death, and old age as it must needs be, and that watching for their approach, which makes every stage of life like a dying over and over again. Almost all death is painful, and in every thing that comes to an end a touch of death, and therefore of wretched coldness struck home to one, of remorse, of loss and parting, of outraged attachments. Given faultless men and women, given a perfect state of society which should have no need to practice on men's susceptibilities for its own selfish ends, adding one turn more to the wheel of the great rack for its own inter-est or amusement, there would still be this evil in the world, of a certain necessary sorrow and desolation, felt, just in proportion to the moral, or nervous perfection men have attained to. And what we need in the world, over against that, is a cer-tain permanent and general power of compassion—humanity's standing force of self-pity—as an elementary ingredient of our social atmosphere, if we are to live in it at all. I wonder, sometimes, in what way man has cajoled himself into the bearing of his burden thus far, seeing how every step in the capacity of apprehension his labor has won for him, from age to age, must needs increase his dejection. It is as if the increase of knowledge were but an increasing revelation of the radical hope-lessness of his position: and I would that there were one even as I, behind this vain show of things!

"At all events, the actual conditions of our life being as they are, and the ca-pacity for suffering so large a principle in things—since the only principle, perhaps, to which we may always safely trust is a ready sympathy with the pain one actually sees—it follows that the practical and effective difference between men will lie in their power of insight into those conditions, their power of sympathy. The future will be with those who have most of it; while for the present, as I persuade myself, those who have much of it, have something to hold by, even in the dissolution of a world, or in that dissolution of self, which is, for every one, no less than the dis-solution of the world it represents for him. Nearly all of us, I suppose, have had our moments, in which any effective sympathy for us on the part of others has seemed impossible; in which our pain has seemed a stupid outrage upon us, like some overwhelming physical violence, from which we could take refuge, at best, only in some mere general sense of good will—somewhere in the world perhaps. And then, to one's surprise, the discovery of that good will, if it were only in a not unfriendly animal, may seem to have explained, to have actually justified to us, the fact of our pain. There have been occasions, certainly, when I have felt that if others cared for me as I cared for them, it would be, not so much a consolation, as an equivalent, for what one has lost or suffered: a realized profit on the summing up of one's accounts: a touching of that absolute ground amid all the changes of phenomena, which our philosophers have of late confessed themselves quite un-able to discover. In the mere clinging of human creatures to each other, nay! in one's own solitary self-pity, amid the effects even of what might appear irredeem-able loss, I seem to touch the eternal. Something in that pitiful contact, some-thing new and true, fact or apprehension of fact, is educed, which, on a review of all the perplexities of life, satisfies our moral sense, and removes that appearance of unkindness in the soul of things themselves, and assures us that not everything has been in vain.

"And I know not how, but in the thought thus suggested, I seem to take up, and reknit myself to, a well-remembered hour, when by some gracious accident—it was on a journey—all things about me fell into a more perfect harmony than is their wont. Everything seemed to be, for a moment, after all, almost for the best. Through the train of my thoughts, one against another, it was as if I became aware of the dominant power of another person in controversy, wrestling with me. I seem to be come round to the point at which I left off then. The antagonist has closed with me again. A protest comes, out of the very depths of man's radically hopeless condition in the world, with the energy of one of those suffering yet prevailing deities, of which old poetry tells. Dared one hope that there is a heart, even as ours, in that divine 'Assistant' of one's thoughts—a heart even as mine, behind this vain show of things!"

FROM SAPPHO'S LAST SONG

GIACOMO LEOPARDI

What fault, what monstrous crime did I commit
Ere birth, that Heav'n on my polluted soul
Should frown, and Fortune turn from me her face?
What sin was mine in babyhood, the age
Unconscious of misdoing, that afterwards
The spindle of unconquerable Fate
Should wind for me the rusty thread of life
Without youth and youth's bloom?   A rash word there
Thy lips have uttered: that which must be, is,
By an inscrutable will.   Inscrutable
Is all, save pain.   Neglected children, born
To weep are we, whereof the reason lies
Upon the lap of the gods.   Oh anxious hope
Of budding girlhood!   To the fair of face,
The fair of face alone, All-Father gave
Eternal empire over Man.   If cloaked
In ugliness, the worth
Of noble deed or song shines never forth.

Death be our choice.   Casting to earth the veil
It scorns, the naked soul shall fly to Dis
And mend the brutal blunder of the blind
Distributor of luck.   And thou, for whom
I have been long tormented with vain love,
Vain faith and ever unappeased desire,
Live on, be happy, if ever mortal man
Lived happy here on earth.   Myself the God
With the sweet liquor from his niggard jar
Ne'er sprinkled after childhood's dear deceits
And dreams had perished.   All our loveliest days
Of life are first to flit away: instead,
Disease creeps on, and old age, and the shades
Of chilly death.   The palms I hoped to win,
My pleasant dreams, where are they?   Nought remains
But Hades; and my valiant soul belongs
To the goddess of Taenarum
And to the silent shore and Stygian gloom.

(G. L. Bickersteth, tr.)

SPRING AND FALL

To a Young Child

GERARD MANLEY HOPKINS

Márgarét, are you gríeving
Over Goldengrove unleaving?
Leáves, líke the things of man, you
With your fresh thoughts care for, can you?

Áh! ás the heart grows older
It will come to such sights colder
By and by, nor spare a sigh
Though worlds of wanwood leafmeal lie;
And yet you wíll weep and know why.
Now no matter, child, the name:
Sórrow's springs are the same.
Nor mouth had, no nor mind, expressed
What heart heard of, ghost guessed:
It ís the blight man was born for,
It is Margaret you mourn for.

TIME

BHARTRIHARI

Time is the root of all this earth;
These creatures, who from Time had birth,
Within his bosom at the end
Shall sleep; Time hath nor enemy nor friend.

All we in one long caravan
Are journeying since the world began;
We know not whither, but we know
Time guideth at the front, and all must go.

Like as the wind upon the field
Bows every herb, and all must yield,
So we beneath Time's passing breath
Bow each in turn,—why tears for birth or death?
(Paul Elmer More, tr.)

GROWING OLD

MATTHEW ARNOLD

What is it to grow old?
Is it to lose the glory of the form,
The luster of the eye?
Is it for beauty to forego her wreath?
—Yes, but not this alone.

Is it to feel our strength—
Not our bloom only, but our strength—decay?
Is it to feel each limb
Grow stiffer, every function less exact,
Each nerve more loosely strung?

Yes, this, and more; but not
Ah, 'tis not what in youth we dreamed 'twould be!
'Tis not to have our life
Mellowed and softened as with sunset-glow,
A golden day's decline.

'Tis not to see the world
As from a height, with rapt prophetic eyes,
And heart profoundly stirred;
And weep, and feel the fulness of the past,
The years that are no more.

It is to spend long days
And not once feel that we were ever young;
It is to add, immured
In the hot prison of the present, month
To month with weary pain.

It is to suffer this,
And feel but half, and feebly, what we feel.
Deep in our hidden heart
Festers the dull remembrance of a change,
But no emotion—none.

It is—last stage of all—
When we are frozen up within, and quite
The phantom of ourselves,
To hear the world applaud the hollow ghost
Which blamed the living man.

THE CALM AFTER THE STORM
GIACOMO LEOPARDI

The storm has passed away:
Birds sing a roundelay, I hear the hen,
Back on the road once more,
Chanting her old refrain.   Above yon hills
To westward, look, the blue breaks forth serene.
The clouds lift, fields are seen,
And in the valley runs the river clear.
All hearts rejoice, now on all sides is heard
The hum of life, again
To wonted labor stirred.
The workman, at the rainy sky to gaze,
Singing, with work in hand,
Comes to his door: out run
In rivalry the wenches to draw water
From the late downpour won:
The fruiterer has begun
Again the daily cry
He shouts as he goes by.

See, there's the Sun returning, see him smile
On hill and hamlet. Servants open fling
Windows and balconies and shuttered rooms:
And, from the high street, far away one hears
The jingle of bells, the traveler's coach the while
Rumbling along as he his road resumes.

 Now joy doth all men move.
When is existence e'er
So sweet as now, so fair?
When with such ardent love
Doth Man his work pursue,
Resume old tasks, or bend his strength to new?
When doth he less recall his misery?
Ah, pleasure born of woe;
Vain joy, which, terror past,
Is but the fruit thereof, whenas the wretch,
Who loathed his life till then,
Trembled and dreaded death;
Whenas cold, speechless, pale,
In their long torture men
Broke into sweat and shuddered to behold
Upon us swooping down
Lightning and cloud and gale.

 O courteous Nature, these
Thy gifts are, and 'tis thus
That thou dispensest joy
To mortal beings.   Mere relief from pain
Is counted joy by us.
Pains dost thou strew with lavish hand; unbidden
Sorrow arises: and of pleasure, only
So much as springs by some rare miracle
From tribulation, is great profit. Oh,
Mankind beloved of Heaven! Fortunate
Indeed if slight rebate
Of any woe be thine;
Blest only if death heals thee of all woe.
      (G. L. Bickersteth, tr.)

FROM OF HUMAN BONDAGE, Chapter 29 *
SOMERSET MAUGHAM

. . . He did not know how wide a country, arid and precipitous, must be crossed before the traveler through life comes to an acceptance of reality. It is an illusion that youth is happy, an illusion of those who have lost it; but the young know they are wretched, for they are full of the truthless ideals which have been instilled into them, and each time they come in contact with the real they are bruised and wounded. It looks as if they were victims of a conspiracy; for the books they read, ideal by the necessity of selection, and the conversation of their elders who look back upon the past through a rosy haze of forgetfulness, prepare them for an unreal life. They must discover for themselves that all they have read and all they have been told are lies, lies, lies; and each discovery is another nail driven into the body on the cross of life. The strange thing is that each one who has gone through that bitter disillusionment adds to it in his turn, unconsciously by the power within him which is stronger than himself. The companionship of Hayward was the worst possible thing for Philip. He was a man who was nothing for himself, but only through a literary atmosphere, and he was dangerous because he had deceived himself into sincerity. He honestly mistook his sensuality for romantic emotion, his vacillation for the artistic temperament, and his idleness for philosophic calm. His mind, vulgar in its effort at refinement, saw everything a little larger than life size, with the outlines blurred, in a golden mist of senti-mentality. He lied and never knew that he lied, and when it was pointed out to him said that lies were beautiful. He was an idealist.

MACBETH, V, v, 16-28

WILLIAM SHAKESPEARE

SEYTON: The queen, my lord, is dead.
MACBETH: She should have died hereafter;
 There would have been a time for such a word.
 Tomorrow, and tomorrow, and tomorrow,
 Creeps in this petty pace from day to day,
 To the last syllable of recorded time;
 And all our yesterdays have lighted fools
 The way to dusty death. Out, out, brief candle!
 Life's but a walking shadow, a poor player
 That struts and frets his hour upon the stage,
 And then is heard no more; it is a tale
 Told by an idiot, full of sound and fury,
 Signifying nothing.

TO HIMSELF

GIACOMO LEOPARDI

 Now shalt thou rest forever,
My weary heart. Dead is the last illusion
That I believed eternal: dead; and perished
Not hope alone, but even
Desire, for the illusions which we cherished.
Rest then for aye. Sufficient
Hath been thine agitaticn. Nought is worthy
Thine agonies, earth merits not thy sighing.
Mere bitterness and tedium
Is life, nought else; the world is dust and ashes.
Now rest thee. For the last time
Abandon hope. Fate to our kind hath given

No boon but death.   Now scorn thyself, scorn Nature,
Scorn the brute Power whose reign
We know but by our woes, which are its pastime;
Scorn all that is, for all is vain, vain, vain.

(G. L. Bickersteth, tr.)

THE GARDEN OF PROSERPINE

ALGERNON CHARLES SWINBURNE

Here, where the world is quiet;
   Here, where all trouble seems
Dead winds' and spent waves' riot
   In doubtful dreams of dreams;
I watch the green field growing
For reaping folk and sowing,
For harvest-time and mowing,
   A sleepy world of streams.

I am tired of tears and laughter,
   And men that laugh and weep;
Of what may come hereafter
   For men that sow to reap:
I am weary of days and hours,
Blown buds of barren flowers,
Desires and dreams and powers
   And everything but sleep.

Here life has death for neighbor,
   And far from eye or ear
Wan waves and wet winds labor,
   Weak ships and spirits steer;
They drive adrift, and whither
They wot not who make thither;
But no such winds blow hither,
   And no such things grow here.

No growth of moor or coppice,
   No heather-flower or vine,
But bloomless buds of poppies,
   Green grapes of Proserpine,
Pale beds of blowing rushes
Where no leaf blooms or blushes
Save this whereout she crushes
   For dead men deadly wine.

Pale, without name or number,
   In fruitless fields of corn,
They bow themselves and slumber
   All night till light is born;
And like a soul belated,
In hell and heaven unmated,
By cloud and mist abated
   Comes out of darkness morn.

Though one were strong as seven,
    He too with death shall dwell,
Nor wake with wings in heaven,
    Nor weep for pains in hell;
Though one were fair as roses,
His beauty clouds and closes;
And well though love reposes,
    In the end it is not well.

Pale, beyond porch and portal,
    Crowned with calm leaves, she stands
Who gathers all things mortal
    With cold immortal hands;
Her languid lips are sweeter
Than love's who fears to greet her
To men that mix and meet her
    From many times and lands.

She waits for each and other,
    She waits for all men born;
Forgets the earth her mother,
    The life of fruits and corn;
And spring and seed and swallow
Take wing for her and follow
Where summer song rings hollow
    And flowers are put to scorn.

There go the loves that wither,
    The old loves with wearier wings;
And all dead years draw thither,
    And all disastrous things;
Dead dreams of days forsaken,
Blind buds that snows have shaken,
Wild leaves that winds have taken,
    Red strays of ruined springs.

We are not sure of sorrow,
    And joy was never sure;
Today will die tomorrow;
    Time stoops to no man's lure;
And love grown faint and fretful,
With lips but half regretful
Sighs, and with eyes forgetful
    Weeps that no loves endure.

From too much love of living,
    From hope and fear set free,
We thank with brief thanksgiving
    Whatever gods may be
That no life lives for ever;
That dead men rise up never;
That even the weariest river
    Winds somewhere safe to sea.

Then star nor sun shall waken,
  Nor any change of light:
Nor sound of waters shaken,
  Nor any sound or sight:
Nor wintry leaves nor vernal,
Nor days nor things diurnal;
  Only the sleep eternal
  In an eternal night.

"NO WORST, THERE IS NONE"

GERARD MANLEY HOPKINS

No worst, there is none. Pitched past pitch of grief,
More pangs will, schooled at forepangs, wilder wring.
Comforter, where, where is your comforting?
Mary, mother of us, where is your relief?
My cries heave, herds-long; huddle in a main, a chief
Woe, world-sorrow; on an age-old anvil wince and sing—
Then lull, then leave off. Fury had shrieked "No ling-
    ering! Let me be fell: force I must be brief."

  O the mind, mind has mountains; cliff of fall
Frightful, sheer, no-man-fathomed. Hold them cheap
May who ne'er hung there. Nor does long our small
Durance deal with that steep or deep. Here! creep,
Wretch, under a comfort serves in a whirlwind: all
Life death does end and each day dies with sleep.

FROM THE MAN AGAINST THE SKY

EDWIN ARLINGTON ROBINSON

Whatever the dark road he may have taken,
This man who stood on high
And faced alone the sky,
Whatever drove or lured or guided him,—
A vision answering a faith unshaken,
An easy trust assumed of easy trials,
A sick negation born of weak denials,
A crazed abhorrence of an old condition,
A blind attendance on a brief ambition,—
Whatever stayed him or derided him,
His way was even as ours;
And we, with all our wounds and all our powers,
Must each await alone at his own height
Another darkness or another light;
And there, of our poor self dominion reft,
If inference and reason shun
Hell, Heaven, and Oblivion,
May thwarted will (perforce precarious,
But for our conservation better thus)

Have no misgiving left
Of doing yet what here we leave undone?
Or if unto the last of these we cleave,
Believing or protesting we believe
In such an idle and ephemeral
Florescence of the diabolical,—
If, robbed of two fond old enormities,
Our being had no onward auguries,
What then were this great love of ours to say
For launching other lives to voyage again
A little farther into time and pain,
A little faster in a futile chase
For a kingdom and a power and a Race
That would have still in sight
A manifest end of ashes and eternal night?
Is this the music of the toys we shake
So loud,—as if there might be no mistake
Somewhere in our indomitable will?
Are we no greater than the noise we make
Along one blind atomic pilgrimage
Whereon by crass chance billeted we go
Because our brains and bones and cartilage
Will have it so?
If this we say, then let us all be still
About our share in it, and live and die
More quietly thereby.
Where was he going, this man against the sky?
You know not, nor do I.
But this we know, if we know anything:
That we may laugh and fight and sing
And of our transience here make offering
To an orient Word that will not be erased,
Or, save in incommunicable gleams
Too permanent for dreams,
Be found or known.
No tonic and ambitious irritant
Of increase or of want
Has made an otherwise insensate waste
Of ages overthrown
A ruthless, veiled, implacable foretaste
Of other ages that are still to be
Depleted and rewarded variously
Because a few, by fate's economy,
Shall seem to move the world the way it goes;
No soft evangel of equality,
Safe-cradled in a communal repose
That huddles into death and may at last
Be covered well with equatorial snows—
And all for what, the devil only knows—
Will aggregate an inkling to confirm
The credit of a sage or of a worm,
Or tell us why one man in five

Should have a care to stay alive
While in his heart he feels no violence
Laid on his humor and intelligence
When infant Science makes a pleasant face
And waves again that hollow toy, the Race;
No planetary trap where souls are wrought
For nothing but the sake of being caught
And sent again to nothing will attune
Itself to any key of any reason
Why man should hunger through another season
To find out why 'twere better late than soon
To go away and let the sun and moon
And all the silly stars illuminate
A place for creeping things,
And those that root and trumpet and have wings,
And herd and ruminate,
Or dive and flash and poise in rivers and seas,
Or by their loyal tails in lofty trees
Hang screeching lewd victorious derision
Of man's immortal vision.
Shall we, because Eternity records
Too vast an answer for the time-born words
We spell, whereof so many are dead that once
In our capricious lexicons
Were so alive and final, hear no more
The Word itself, the living word
That none alive has ever heard
Or ever spelt,
And few have ever felt
Without the fears and old surrenderings
And terrors that began
When Death let fall a feather from his wings
And humbled the first man?
Because the weight of our humility,
Wherefrom we gain
A little wisdom and much pain,
Falls here too sore and there too tedious,
Are we in anguish or complacency,
Not looking far enough ahead
To see by what mad couriers we are led
Along the roads of the ridiculous,
To pity ourselves and laugh at faith
And while we curse life bear it?
And if we see the soul's dead end in death,
Are we to fear it?
What folly is here that has not yet a name
Unless we say outright that we are liars?
What have we seen beyond our sunset fires
That lights again the way by which we came?
Why pay we such a price, and one we give
So clamoringly, for each racked empty day
That leads one more last human hope away,

As quiet fiends would lead past our crazed eyes
Our children to an unseen sacrifice?
If after all that we have lived and thought,
All comes to Nought,—
If there be nothing after Now,
And we be nothing anyhow,
And we know that,—why live?
'Twere sure but weaklings' vain distress
To suffer dungeons where so many doors
Will open on the cold eternal shores
That look sheer down
To the dark tideless floods of Nothingness
Where all who know may drown.

HAMLET, III, i, 56-88

WILLIAM SHAKESPEARE

HAMLET: To be, or not to be: that is the question:
Whether 'tis nobler in the mind to suffer
The slings and arrows of outrageous fortune,
Or to take arms against a sea of troubles,
And by opposing end them. To die: to sleep;
No more: and, by a sleep to say we end
The heart-ache and the thousand natural shocks
That flesh is heir to, 'tis a consummation
Devoutly to be wished. To die, to sleep;
To sleep; perchance to dream: ay, there's the rub;
For in that sleep of death what dreams may come
When we have shuffled off this mortal coil,
Must give us pause. There's the respect
That makes calamity of so long life;
For who would bear the whips and scorns of time,
The oppressor's wrong, the proud man's contumely,
The pangs of despised love, the law's delay,
The insolence of office and the spurns
That patient merit of the unworthy takes,
When he himself might his quietus make
With a bare bodkin? who would these fardels bear,
To grunt and sweat under a weary life,
But that the dread of something after death,
The undiscovered country from whose bourn
No traveler returns, puzzles the will,
And makes us rather bear those ills we have
Than fly to others that we know not of?
Thus conscience does make cowards of us all;
And thus the native hue of resolution
Is sicklied o'er with the pale cast of thought,
And enterprises of great pith and moment
With this regard their currents turn awry,
And lose the name of action.

MEASURE FOR MEASURE, III, i, 74-89, 116-132

WILLIAM SHAKESPEARE

ISABELLA: O, I do fear thee, Claudio; and I quake,
Lest thou a feverous life shouldst entertain,
And six or seven winters more respect
Than a perpetual honor. Dar'st thou die?
The sense of death is most in apprehension,
And the poor beetle, that we tread upon,
In corporal sufferance finds a pang as great
As when a giant dies.
CLAUDIO: Why give you me this shame?
Think you I can a resolution fetch
From flowery tenderness?   If I must die,
I will encounter darkness as a bride,
And hug it in mine arms.
ISABELLA: There spake my brother: there my father's
    grave
Did utter forth a voice. Yes, thou must die:
Thou art too noble to conserve a life
In base appliances . . .
CLAUDIO: Death is a fearful thing.
ISABELLA: And shamed life a hateful.
CLAUDIO: Ay, but to die, and go we know not where;
To lie in cold obstruction and to rot;
This sensible warm motion to become
A kneaded clod; and the delighted spirit
To bathe in fiery floods, or to reside
In thrilling region of thick-ribbed ice;
To be imprisoned in the viewless winds,
And blown with restless violence round about
The pendant world; or to be worse than worst
Of those that lawless and incertain thought
Imagines howling! 'Tis too horrible!
The weariest and most loathed worldly life
That age, ache, penury and imprisonment
Can lay on nature is a paradise
To what we fear of death.

PARADISE LOST, II, lines 142-51

JOHN MILTON

Thus repulsed, our final hope
Is flat despair: we must exasperate
The Almighty Victor to spend all his rage;
And that must end us; that must be our cure—
To be no more. Sad cure! For who would lose,
Though full of pain, this intellectual being,
Those thoughts that wander through eternity,
To perish rather, swallowed up and lost
In the wide womb of uncreated Night,
Devoid of sense and motion?

YET, YET, YE DOWNCAST HOURS
WALT WHITMAN

Yet, yet, ye downcast hours, I know ye also,
Weights of lead, how ye clog and cling at my ankles,
Earth to a chamber of mourning turns—I hear the o'erweening,
  mocking voice,
Matter is conqueror—matter, triumphant only, continues onward.

Despairing cries float ceaselessly toward me,
The call of my nearest lover, putting forth, alarmed, uncertain,
The sea I am quickly to sail, come tell me,
Come tell me where I am speeding, tell me my destination.

I understand your anguish, but I cannot help you,
I approach, hear, behold, the sad mouth, the look out of the
  eyes, your mute inquiry,
Whither I go from the bed I recline on, come tell me;
Old age, alarmed, uncertain—a young woman's voice, appealing
  to me for comfort;
A young man's voice, *Shall I not escape?*

THE CONQUEROR WORM
EDGAR ALLAN POE

Lo! 'tis a gala night
  Within the lonesome latter years!
An angel throng, bewinged, bedight
  In veils, and drowned in tears,
Sit in a theater, to see
  A play of hopes and fears,
While the orchestra breathes fitfully
  The music of the spheres.

Mimes, in the form of God on high,
  Mutter and mumble low,
And hither and thither fly;
  Mere puppets they, who come and go
At bidding of vast formless things,
  That shift the scenery to and fro,
Flapping from out their condor wings
  Invisible woe!

That motley drama—oh, be sure
  It shall not be forgot;
With its phantom chased for evermore
  By a crowd that seize it not,
Through a circle that ever returneth in
  To the self-same spot;
And much of madness, and more of sin,
  And horror the soul of the plot.

But, see, amid the mimic rout
  A crawling shape intrude—
A blood-red thing that writhes from out
  The scenic solitude!
It writhes!—it writhes!—with mortal pangs
  The mimes become its food,
And the angels sob at vermin fangs
  In human gore imbued.

Out, out are the lights—out all!
  And over each quivering form
The curtain, a funeral pall,
  Comes down with the rush of a storm;
And the angels, all pallid and wan,
  Uprising, unveiling, affirm
That the play is the tragedy, "Man,"
  And its hero the Conqueror Worm.

THE REVOLT OF ISLAM, CANTO VIII, iv-viii
PERCY BYSSHE SHELLEY

" 'What dream ye?   Your own hands have built an home,
  Even for yourselves on a beloved shore:
For some, fond eyes are pining till they come,
  How they will greet him when his toils are o'er,
  And laughing babes rush from the well-known door!
Is this your care?   ye toil for your own good—
  Ye feel and think—has some immortal power
Such purposes?   or in a human mood,
Dream ye some Power thus builds for man in solitude?

" 'What is that Power?   Ye mock yourselves, and give
  A human heart to what ye cannot know:
As if the cause of life could think and live!
  'Twere as if man's own works should feel, and show
  The hopes, and fears, and thoughts from which they flow,
And he be like to them!   Lo!   Plague is free
  To waste, Blight, Poison, Earthquake, Hail, and Snow,
Disease, and Want, and worse Necessity
Of hate and ill, and Pride, and Fear, and Tyranny!

" 'What is that Power?   Some moon-struck sophist stood
  Watching the shade from his own soul upthrown
Fill Heaven and darken Earth, and in such mood
  The Form he saw and worshiped was his own,
  His likeness in the world's vast mirror shown;
And 'twere an innocent dream, but that a faith
  Nursed by fear's dew of poison, grows thereon,
And that men say, that Power has chosen Death
On all who scorn its laws, to wreak immortal wrath.

" 'Men say that they themselves have heard and seen,
Or known from others who have known such things,
A Shade, a Form, which Earth and Heaven between
Wields an invisible rod—that Priests and Kings,
Custom, domestic sway, ay, all that brings
Man's freeborn soul beneath the oppressor's heel,
Are his strong ministers, and that the stings
Of death will make the wise his vengeance feel,
Though truth and virtue arm their hearts with tenfold steel.

" 'And it is said, this Power will punish wrong;
Yes, add despair to crime, and pain to pain!
And deepest hell, and deathless snakes among,
Will bind the wretch on whom is fixed a stain,
Which, like a plague, a burden, and a bane,
Clung to him while he lived;—for love and hate,
Virtue and vice, they say are difference vain—
The will of strength is right—this human state
Tyrants, that they may rule, with lies thus desolate.' "

FROM PROEM

JAMES THOMSON

O antique fables! beautiful and bright
And joyous with the joyous youth of yore;
O antique fables! for a little light
Of that which shineth in you evermore,
To cleanse the dimness from our weary eyes,
And bathe our old world with a new surprise
Of golden dawn entrancing sea and shore.

We stagger under the enormous weight
Of all the heavy ages piled on us,
With all their grievous wrongs inveterate,
And all their disenchantments dolorous,
And all the monstrous tasks they have bequeathed;
And we are stifled with the airs they breathed;
And read in theirs our dooms calamitous.

Our world is all stript naked of their dreams;
No deities in sky or sun or moon,
No nymphs in woods and hills and seas and streams;
Mere earth and water, air and fire, their boon;
No God in all our universe we trace,
No heaven in the infinitude of space,
No life beyond death—coming not too soon.

Our souls are stript of their illusions sweet,
Our hopes at best in some far future years
For others, not ourselves; whose bleeding feet

Wander this rocky waste where broken spears
And bleaching bones lie scattered on the sand;
Who know *we* shall not reach the Promised Land;
Perhaps a mirage glistening through our tears.

And if there be this Promised Land indeed,
Our children's children's children's heritage,
Oh, what a prodigal waste of precious seed,
Of myriad myriad lives from age to age,
Of woes and agonies and blank despairs,
Through countless cycles, that some fortunate heirs
May enter, and conclude the pilgrimage!

But if it prove a mirage after all!
Our last illusion leaves us wholly bare,
To bruise against Fate's adamantine wall,
Consumed or frozen in the pitiless air;
In all our world, beneath, around, above,
One only refuge, solace, triumph,—Love,
Sole star of light in infinite black despair.

FROM THE CITY OF DREADFUL NIGHT

JAMES THOMSON

II

.   .   .   .

When he had spoken thus, before he stirred,
    I spoke, perplexed by something in the signs
Of desolation I had seen and heard
    In this drear pilgrimage to ruined shrines:
"When Faith and Love and Hope are dead indeed,
Can Life still live?   By what doth it proceed?"

As whom his one intense thought overpowers,
    He answered coldly, "Take a watch, erase
The signs and figures of the circling hours,
    Detach the hands, remove the dial-face;
The works proceed until run down; although
Bereft of purpose, void of use, still go."

Then turning to the right paced on again,
    And traversed squares and traveled streets whose glooms
Seemed more and more familiar to my ken;
    And reached that sullen temple of the tombs;
And paused to murmur with the old despair,
"Here Faith died, poisoned by this charnel air."

I ceased to follow, for the knot of doubt
    Was severed sharply with a cruel knife:
He circled thus for ever tracing out
    The series of the fraction left of Life;
Perpetual recurrence in the scope
Of but three terms, dead Faith, dead Love, dead Hope.

VIII

.   .   .   .

"Who is most wretched in this dolorous place?
  I think myself; yet I would rather be
  My miserable self than He, than He
Who formed such creatures to His own disgrace.

"The vilest thing must be less vile than Thou
  From whom it had its being, God and Lord!
  Creator of all woe and sin! abhorred,
Malignant and implacable! I vow

"That not for all Thy power furled and unfurled,
  For all the temples to Thy glory built,
  Would I assume the ignominious guilt
Of having made such men in such a world.

"As if a Being, God or Fiend, could reign,
At once so wicked, foolish, and insane,
As to produce men when He might refrain!

"The world rolls round for ever like a mill;
It grinds out death and life and good and ill;
It has no purpose, heart or mind or will.

"While air of Space, and Time's full river flow
The mill must blindly whirl unresting so:
It may be wearing out, but who can know?

"Man might know one thing were his sight less dim;
That it whirls not to suit his petty whim,
That it is quite indifferent to him.

"Nay, does it treat him harshly as he saith?
It grinds him some slow years of bitter breath,
Then grinds him back into eternal death."

.   .   .   .

XIV

Large glooms were gathered in the mighty fane,
  With tinted moongleams slanting here and there;
And all was hush: no swelling organ-strain,
  No chant, no voice or murmuring of prayer;
No priests came forth, no tinkling censers fumed,
And the high altar space was unillumed.

Around the pillars and against the walls
  Leaned men and shadows; others seemed to brood
Bent or recumbent in secluded stalls.
  Perchance they were not a great multitude
Save in that city of so lonely streets
Where one may count up every face he meets.

All patiently awaited the event
  Without a stir or sound, as if no less
Self-occupied, doomstricken, while attent.
  And then we heard a voice of solemn stress
From the dark pulpit, and our gaze there met
Two eyes which burned as never eyes burned yet:

Two steadfast and intolerable eyes
  Burning beneath a broad and rugged brow;
The head behind it of enormous size,
  And as black fir-groves in a large wind bow,
Our rooted congregation, gloom-arrayed,
By that great sad voice deep and full were swayed:—

"O melancholy Brothers, dark, dark, dark!
O battling in black floods without an ark!
  O spectral wanderers of unholy Night!
My soul hath bled for you these sunless years,
With bitter blood-drops running down like tears:
  Oh, dark, dark, dark, withdrawn from joy and light!

My heart is sick with anguish for your bale!
Your woe hath been my anguish; yea, I quail
  And perish in your perishing unblest.
And I have searched the heights and depths, the scope
Of all our universe, with desperate hope
  To find some solace for your wild unrest.

And now at last authentic word I bring,
Witnessed by every dead and living thing;
  Good tidings of great joy for you, for all:
There is no God; no Fiend with names divine
Made us and tortures us; if we must pine,
  It is to satiate no Being's gall.

It was the dark delusion of a dream,
That living Person conscious and supreme,
  Whom we must curse for cursing us with life;
Whom we must curse because the life He gave
Could not be buried in the quiet grave,
  Could not be killed by poison or by knife.

This little life is all we must endure,
The grave's most holy peace is ever sure,
  We fall asleep and never wake again;
Nothing is of us but the moldering flesh,
Whose elements dissolve and merge afresh
  In earth, air, water, plants, and other men.

We finish thus; and all our wretched race
Shall finish with its cycle, and give place
        To other beings, with their own time-doom
Infinite aeons ere our kind began;
Infinite aeons after the last man
        Has joined the mammoth in earth's tomb and womb.

We bow down to the universal laws,
Which never had for man a special clause
        Of cruelty or kindness, love or hate:
If toads and vultures are obscene to sight,
If tigers burn with beauty and with might,
        Is it by favor or by wrath of fate?

All substance lives and struggles evermore
Through countless shapes continually at war,
        By countless interactions interknit:
If one is born a certain day on earth,
All times and forces tended to that birth,
        Not all the world could change or hinder it.

I find no hint throughout the Universe
Of good or ill, of blessing or of curse;
        I find alone Necessity Supreme;
With infinite Mystery, abysmal, dark,
Unlighted ever by the faintest spark
        For us the flitting shadows of a dream.

O Brothers of sad lives! they are so brief;
A few short years must bring us all relief:
        Can we not bear these years of laboring breath?
But if you would not this poor life fulfil,
Lo, you are free to end it when you will,
        Without the fear of waking after death."—

The organ-like vibrations of his voice
        Thrilled through the vaulted aisles and died away;
The yearning of the tones which bade rejoice
        Was sad and tender, as a requiem lay:
Our shadowy congregation rested still
As brooding on that "End it when you will."

.   .   .   .

XVI

Our shadowy congregation rested still,
        As musing on that message we had heard
And brooding on that "End it when you will;"
        Perchance awaiting yet some other word;
When keen as lightning through a muffled sky
Sprang forth a shrill and lamentable cry:—

"The man speaks sooth, alas! the man speaks sooth:
  We have no personal life beyond the grave;
There is no God; Fate knows nor wrath nor ruth:
  Can I find here the comfort which I crave?

In all eternity I had one chance,
  One few years' term of gracious human life:
The splendors of the intellect's advance,
  The sweetness of the home with babes and wife;

The social pleasures with their genial wit;
  The fascination of the worlds of art,
The glories of the worlds of natures, lit
  By large imagination's glowing heart;

The rapture of mere being, full of health;
  The careless childhood and the ardent youth,
The strenuous manhood winning various wealth,
  The reverend age serene with life's long truth:

All the sublime prerogatives of Man;
  The storied memories of the times of old,
The patient tracking of the world's great plan
  Through sequences and changes myriadfold.

This chance was never offered me before;
  For me the infinite Past is blank and dumb:
This chance recurreth never, nevermore;
  Blank, blank for me the infinite To-come.

And this sole chance was frustrate from my birth,
  A mockery, a delusion; and my breath
Of noble human life upon this earth
  So racks me that I sigh for senseless death.

My wine of life is poison mixed with gall,
  My noonday passes in a nightmare dream,
I worse than lose the years which are my all:
  What can console me for the loss supreme?

Speak not of comfort where no comfort is,
  Speak not at all: can words make foul things fair?
Our life's a cheat, our death a black abyss:
  Hush and be mute envisaging despair."—

This vehement voice came from the northern aisle
  Rapid and shrill to its abrupt harsh close;
And none gave answer for a certain while,
  For words must shrink from these most wordless woes;
At last the pulpit speaker simply said,
With humid eyes and thoughtful drooping head:—

"My Brother, my poor Brothers, it is thus;
This life itself holds nothing good for us,
   But it ends soon and nevermore can be;
And we knew nothing of it ere our birth,
And shall know nothing when consigned to earth:
   I ponder these thoughts and they comfort me."

TO COUNT CARLO PEPOLI

GIACOMO LEOPARDI

How comes it, Pepoli, that you endure
This travail-vexéd and benightmared sleep
That we call life? What hopes buoy up your heart
That you support it? in what thoughts and how,
In irksome toil or pleasant, do you spend
Your idleness, that tiresome legacy
Bequeathed you by your fathers? Life is all,
For rich and poor alike, mere idleness,
If rightly we call idleness such work,
Such strenuous filling-up of time as tends
Unto no end worth while, nor can achieve
The end it aims at. Those industrious folk,
Whom tranquil morning sees, as evening sees,
Ploughing the soil and tending plants and herds,
Were you to call them idle, since their life
Is to sustain life, whereas life when spent
For life's sake, has no value in men's eyes,
You would be right. The mariner drags out
His nights and days in idleness; to sweat
In factories is idle; idle too
Are soldiers' vigils and their perilous frays;
The grasping merchant lives in idleness:
For by no industry, no sweat of brow,
No peril, no night-vigils can a man
Gain for himself or others what alone
Our nature craves and strives for—happiness.
Yet for that chafing, irritable desire,
Which ever since creation-day has made
Mortals sigh vainly for a state of bliss,
Nature by way of medicine had prepared
In this unhappy life necessities
Of divers kinds, whereby no day should pass
But that the human family should find
Full work for hand and brain and, though deprived
Of joy, be always busy: thus perplexed
And frenzied, the desire should have less chance
Of torturing the heart. So too brute beasts,
Endless in kind, within whose hearts, like ours,
One sole desire, to wit, for happiness,
As fruitless as our own, resides; intent

On that, their single aim in life, are found
To lead less evil, less laborious days
Than we, nor blame the slowness of the hours.
But we, who unto others' hands commit
Provision of the means whereby we live,
Must yet ourselves with weariness and pain
Fulfil a far more stern necessity,
Which we to others cannot delegate,
That absolute, imperious constraint
Laid on us of mere living, of which no hoard
Of gold, no wealth of herds, or rich estates,
No palace or kingly raiment can relieve
Us wretched mortals.   Now if one, in scorn
Of his unfruitful years and loathing heaven's
Fair light, is prompted to anticipate
Reluctant death, yet will not on himself
Lay homicidal hand; he, gnawed at heart
By that undying worm, the vain desire
For happiness, forever casts about
On all sides, seeking cures and tries in vain
A thousand nostrums, which ill compensate
The remedy by Nature's self supplied.

Behold him make a cult of hair and dress,
And gait and carriage, vainly spend his zeal
On coach and horses, join the envied rout
In fashionable salons, noisy squares
And public parks, all day and night absorbed
In gaming, supping, dancing; on his lips
Perpetual laughter; ah, but in his heart,
Deep down within his heart, a dull, dead weight,
Like adamantine pillar unremoved,
Sits deathless Ennui throned, to shake whom youth
For all its strength is powerless, and nought
Avail the dulcet tones of rosy lips,
And nought the tender glance of twin black eyes,
Tremulously gleaming, that belovéd glance,
Of all things mortal worthiest named divine.

Another, as if bent on fleeing man's
Sad lot, spends all his days in voyaging
From clime to clime, a wanderer over hills,
And oceans, traversing the whole wide world,
A pilgrim through all confines of all space
That Nature opes to Man in the infinite
Fields of the Universe.   Alas, black Care
Sits on the lofty prow; in every land,
Beneath all skies, is Happiness invoked
Vainly, for Sorrow rules us everywhere.

And some there are who choose to spend the hours
In savage warfare, from sheer idleness
Shedding their brethren's blood; and some who salve
Their own with others' losses and would make
Themselves less sorrowful by others' woe,
Hence strive to spend their lives in doing harm.
Some by pursuit of high philosophy
And of the arts, and some by trampling down
Their own and foreign folk, or ruining
The ancient peace of remote virgin shores
By trade, by arms and by dishonesty,
Consume the destined portion of their days.

You more humane ambition, milder thought
Rules in the heyday of your youth, the fair
April of life, to all men else Heaven's first
And joyous boon, but harmful, bitter, grave
To one who has no country. You are moved
To study numbers and portray in words
The Beautiful, to few, not oft, nor long
Revealed on earth, and shapes which, kinder far
Than Heaven or Nature, Fancy and inborn
Illusion in abundance body forth
For our delight. A thousand, thousand times
Blest is the man, who as his years increase
Retains—what is so lightly lost—the power
Of dear imagination; whom the Fates
Endowed with an eternal youth of heart;
Who in his prime and in old age alike
As was his wont in budding manhood's bloom,
Deep in his thought makes Nature beautiful,
Death and the desert live. May Heaven grant
To you this great good fortune; may the fire,
Which warms your bosom now, preserve your love
For poetry, when you are gray-haired. I
Already feel the sweet illusions fade
Of life's spring-season; to my eyes grow dim
The entrancing images which were to me
So dear, that always to my latest hour
I shall look back and yearn for them with tears.
Now in that day when all congealed and cold
Shall be this bosom, when no more the calm
And solitary smile of sunny fields,
No more the spring-song of the birds at dawn,
No more above the hills and lone sea-marge
Beneath a limpid heaven the silent moon
Shall move my soul; when all the loveliness
Of Nature or of Art shall be to me
Lifeless and dumb; and every noble feeling,
All soft emotion be unknown and strange;
Then, beggared of my one solace, will I turn

To other studies less beloved, whereby
The hateful remnant of my iron days
May be consumed. I will investigate
The bitter truth and the blind destinies
Of mortal and immortal things, why born,
Why burdened with intolerable woe
Is human kind; unto what final end
Nature and Fate be urging us; who finds
Support or pleasure in our monstrous pain;
What laws, what purpose regulate the round
Of this mysterious universe, so praised
By sages, a mere puzzle unto me.

In such inquiries I shall while away
My idleness: for Truth, when known, tho' sad,
Has its delights. And if at times when I
Reason of truth, good folk shall find my words
Unpalatable or hard to comprehend,
I shall not grieve; for long before that day
I shall have ceased to feel desire for Fame;
Vain goddess, ay and goddess blinder far
Than Fortune is, or Destiny, or Love.

(G. L. Bickersteth, tr.)

FROM THE EVERLASTING NO

In *Sartor Resartus*

THOMAS CARLYLE

. . . Alas! the fearful Unbelief is unbelief in yourself; and how could I believe? Had not my first, last Faith in myself, when even to me the Heavens seemed laid open, and I dared to love, been all too cruelly belied? The speculative Mystery of Life grew ever more mysterious to me: neither in the practical Mystery had I made the slightest progress, but been everywhere buffeted, foiled, and contemptuously cast out. A feeble unit in the middle of a threatening Infinitude, I seemed to have nothing given me but eyes, whereby to discern my own wretchedness. Invisible yet impenetrable walls, as of Enchantment, divided me from all living: was there, in the wide world, any true bosom I could press trustfully to mine? O Heaven, No, there was none! I kept a lock upon my lips: why should I speak much with that shifting variety of so-called Friends, in whose withered, vain and too-hungry souls Friendship was but an incredible tradition? In such cases, your resource is to talk little, and that little mostly from the Newspapers. Now when I look back, it was a strange isolation I then lived in. The men and women around me, even speaking with me, were but Figures; I had, practically, forgotten that they were alive, that they were not merely automatic. In midst of their crowded streets and assemblages, I walked solitary; and (except as it was my own heart, not another's, that I kept devouring) savage also, as the tiger in his jungle. Some comfort it would have been, could I, like a Faust, have fancied myself tempted and tormented of the Devil; for a Hell, as I imagine, without Life, though only diabolic Life, were more frightful: but in our age of Down-pulling and Disbelief, the very Devil has been pulled down, you cannot so much as believe in a Devil. To me the Universe was all void of Life, of Purpose, of Volition, even of Hostility: it was one huge, dead, immeasurable Steam-engine, rolling on, in its dead indifference, to grind me limb from limb. O, the vast, gloomy, solitary Golgotha, and Mill of Death! Why was the Living banished thither companionless, conscious? Why, if there is no Devil; nay, unless the Devil is your God?

A prey incessantly to such corrosions, might not, moreover, as the worst aggravation to them, the iron constitution even of a Teufelsdröckh threaten to fail? We conjecture that he has known sickness; and, in spite of his locomotive habits, perhaps sickness of the chronic sort. Hear this, for example: "How beautiful to die of broken heart, on Paper! Quite another thing in practice; every window of your Feeling, even of your Intellect, as it were, begrimed and mud-bespattered, so that no pure ray can enter; a whole Drugshop in your inwards; the fordone soul drowning slowly in quagmires of Disgust!"

Putting all which external and internal miseries together, may we not find in the following sentences, quite in our Professor's still vein, significance enough? "From Suicide a certain aftershine (Nachschein) of Christianity withheld me: perhaps also a certain indolence of character; for, was not that a remedy I had at any time within reach? Often, however, was there a question present to me: Should some one now, at the turning of that corner, blow thee suddenly out of Space, into the other World, or other No-World, by pistol-shot,—how were it? On which ground, too, I have often, in sea-storms and sieged cities and other death-scenes, exhibited an imperturbability, which passed, falsely enough, for courage.

"So had it lasted," concludes the Wanderer, "so had it lasted, as in bitter protracted Death-agony, through long years. The heart within me, unvisited by any heavenly dewdrop, was smouldering in sulphurous slow-consuming fire. Almost since earliest memory I had shed no tear; or once only when I, murmuring half-audibly, recited Faust's Deathsong, that wild *Selig der den er im Siegesglanze findet* (Happy whom *he* finds in Battle's splendor), and thought that of this last Friend even I was not forsaken, that Destiny itself could not doom me not to die. Having no hope, neither had I any definite fear, were it of Man or of Devil: nay, I often felt as if it might be solacing, could the Arch-Devil himself, though in Tartarean terrors, but rise to me, that I might tell him a little of my mind. And yet, strangely enough, I lived in a continual, indefinite, pining fear; tremulous, pusillanimous, apprehensive of I knew not what: it seemed as if all things in the Heavens above and the Earth beneath would hurt me; as if the Heavens and the Earth were but boundless jaws of a devouring monster, wherein I, palpitating, waited to be devoured.

"Full of such humor, and perhaps the miserablest man in the whole French Capital, or Suburbs, was I, one sultry Dog-day, after much perambulation, toiling along the dirty little *Rue Saint-Thomas de l'Enfer*, among civic rubbish enough, in a close atmosphere, and over pavements hot as Nebuchadnezzar's Furnace; whereby doubtless my spirits were little cheered; when, all at once, there rose a Thought in me, and I asked myself: 'What *art* thou afraid of? Wherefore, like a coward, dost thou forever pip and whimper, and go cowering and trembling? Despicable biped! what is the sum-total of the worst that lies before thee? Death? Well, Death; and say the pangs of Tophet too, and all that the Devil and Man may, will or can do against thee! Hast thou not a heart: canst thou not suffer whatsoever it be; and, as a Child of Freedom, thou outcast, trample Tophet itself under thy feet, while it consumes thee? Let it come, then: I will meet it and defy it!' And as I so thought, there rushed like a stream of fire over my whole soul; and I shook base Fear away from me forever. I was strong, of unknown strength, a spirit, almost a god. Ever from that time, the temper of my misery was changed: not Fear or whining Sorrow was it, but Indignation and grim fire-eyed Defiance.

"Thus had the EVERLASTING NO (*das ewige Nein*) pealed authoritatively through all the recesses of my Being, of my ME; and then was it that my whole ME stood up in native God-created majesty, and with emphasis recorded its Protest. Such a Protest, the most important transaction in Life, may that same Indignation and Defiance, in a psychological point of view, be fitly called. The Everlasting No had said: 'Behold, thou are fatherless, outcast, and the Universe is mine (the Devil's)'; to which my whole Me now made answer: '*I* am not thine, but Free, and forever hate thee!'

"It is from this hour that I incline to date my Spiritual New-birth, or Baphometic Fire-baptism; perhaps I directly thereupon began to be a Man."

DOVER BEACH

MATTHEW ARNOLD

The sea is calm tonight.
The tide is full, the moon lies fair
Upon the straits:—on the French coast, the light
Gleams, and is gone; the cliffs of England stand,
Glimmering and vast, out in the tranquil bay.
Come to the window, sweet is the night-air!
Only, from the long line of spray
Where the sea meets the moon-blanched land,
Listen! you hear the grating roar
Of pebbles which the waves draw back, and fling,
At their return, up the high strand,
Begin, and cease, and then again begin,
With tremulous cadence slow, and bring
The eternal note of sadness in.

Sophocles long ago
Heard it on the Aegean, and it brought
Into his mind the turbid ebb and flow
Of human misery; we
Find also in the sound a thought,
Hearing it by this distant northern sea.

The Sea of Faith
Was once, too, at the full, and round earth's shore
Lay like the folds of a bright girdle furled;
But now I only hear
Its melancholy, long, withdrawing roar,
Retreating, to the breath
Of the night-wind, down the vast edges drear
And naked shingles of the world.

Ah, love, let us be true
To one another! for the world, which seems
To lie before us like a land of dreams,
So various, so beautiful, so new,
Hath really neither joy, nor love, nor light,
Nor certitude, nor peace, nor help for pain;
And we are here as on a darkling plain
Swept with confused alarms of struggle and flight,
Where ignorant armies clash by night.

RUBAIYAT, XCIX

OMAR KHAYYAM

Ah Love! could you and I with Him conspire
To grasp this sorry Scheme of Things entire,
    Would not we shatter it to bits—and then
Remold it nearer to the Heart's Desire!

(Edward Fitzgerald, tr.)

CHAPTER 8

THE VALUE OF LIFE: AS THE OPTIMIST SEES IT

If Luther's day expands to Darwin's year,
Shall that exclude the hope—foreclose the fear?
—Herman Melville, *Clarel*, XXXV.

In an age exceeding all others in individual and mass atrocities, an age in which the repulsive doctrine that the end—usually a selfish one—justifies the means is accepted by whole national groups, it is not easy to maintain an optimistic view of life. Our ingenious creations, so beneficial if properly used, have become destroying monsters. Men have won political freedoms only to renounce them in hoarse acclaim of mass-murdering leaders. And from one generation rejecting the idea of God has sprung a new generation of lost illusions that seriously questions all our values. Even the most sanguine humanist is now being shaken in his hope that man through his own efforts alone can build a better society.

What can the optimist offer to fortify us against these dark facts and darker apprehensions? Let us examine the answers that various poets and thinkers have given us, the answers that they found heartening when confronted with evil.

In a somewhat gentler age than ours (smallpox and slavery would appear less evil than atomic and bacteriological warfare and genocide), Robert Browning wrote the most famous of all statements of religious optimism, "God's in his heaven, All's right with the world," lines often quoted with sardonic wryness, and sometimes a sneer at the shallow and unthinking philosophy of the author. If, however, these lines are read in their context, it is apparent that Browning's meaning is deeper. He is well aware of evil.

But what of the many creatures of violence not intercepted in their crimes by a singing girl—that is, by some recollection of a better self? This difficult question is considered in substance in the chapter on the problem of evil. Does Emerson's "Music" present a solution? Is there a "cheerful song" to be found in the evils shadowed forth thus far in these comments? Though, as Wilfred Owen says, in speaking of war, "The poetry is in the pity," the nobility of men in response to horror may be a music of sad beauty, but hardly a cheerful song.

These answers leave too much in the murkiness of doubt, doubt that has existed to some degree since thinking began. But Pope (*Essay on Man*) tries, as one should, to reason his way out of the perplexity, "to vindicate the ways of God to man." Living in an age that believed in the efficacy of reason—an age fundamentally optimistic—he defends at length the thesis that the world is ideally conceived, the best of all possible worlds: "And spite of pride, in erring reason's spite, One truth is clear, Whatever is, is right."

This position, though faith may incline to sustain it, as Pope does in shrewdly reasoned argument, is not altogether convincing to "erring" reason; and Voltaire's ridicule of it (observed also in the preceding chapter) is the natural response of the incredulous. His emendation of the doctrine, "all is well," to read, "if all is not well, all is tolerable," comes perhaps closer to the position of most thoughtful optimists. Yet so late as 1860 we find a poet maintaining the idea that our world is perfect ("Song at Sunset"): "I do not see one imperfection in the universe; And I do not see one cause or result lamentable at last in the universe." The whole scheme of things, says Whitman, is illimitably, ineffably grand. And Browning, in yet another celebrated statement of optimism ("Rabbi ben Ezra") maintains in effect the same position, though he gives more space to doubt. Central in his argument is the idea that life is a crucible that tests men's souls. The evils that we face are necessary for our own perfection. We should welcome doubt, welcome difficulties, all that "turns earth's smoothness rough." Of less importance but still worthy of note is his answer to the pessimists who have lamented the unhappiness of growing old.

The assurance of faith with its serene vision has its most appealing intellectual justification in *Paracelsus*. In this poem, which anticipates the publication of Darwin's *Origin of Species* by twenty-four years, Browning sketches the outlines of a theory of evolution, an evolution that has no end. Throughout the poem runs the teleological argument: "God renews his ancient rapture" in the process of life, "From Life's minute beginnings up at last To Man—the consummation of this scheme Of being." But progress, he continues, is the law of all life: man is not man as yet; man's ideal shaping has not even begun.

Just when did doubt enter in to shake this robust acceptance of faith, a faith that had, despite the skepticism of various poets and philosophers, remained down the centuries the secure stay of a great part of the people of the Western world? The publication by Darwin of scientific argument for the theory of evolution—the same theory in essence that to Browning (and many a poet and philosopher since his time) was a new vision of the glory of God, seems to mark the beginning of uncertainty for many, a turning away from religious assurance to agnosticism. Hints of this spiritual struggle are apparent in some of Browning's poems already cited; and Herman Melville openly acknowledges the conflict between traditional religion and the findings of science: "If Luther's day expand to Darwin's year, Shall that exclude the hope—foreclose the fear?" From this time on down to the present, much of the best literature reflects increasing doubt and insecurity. It is a time of readjustment of values, a time not unlike our own in which the human spirit is ill at ease in its suddenly enlarged home.

The general tendency towards pessimism is observable in Tennyson's "Two Voices." In this state of perplexity, if one sees the "distant gates of Eden" gleaming, one fears it is a dream. After a desperate struggle with doubt, Tennyson is reassured by the Second Voice: " 'What is it thou knowest, sweet voice?' I cried. 'A hidden hope,' the voice replied." This is still optimism, as is Hopkins' rejection of despair in "Carrion Comfort," but how far removed both expressions are from the vigorous certainty of *Rabbi ben Ezra!* No defense is left for religion except faith—but, Tennyson reminds us in *The Ancient Sage,* faith is a mighty force: "Cleave ever to the sunnier side of doubt, And cling to Faith beyond the forms of Faith!" To Alfred North Whitehead in *Science and the Modern World* this vision of the "hidden hope" redeems us from despair: "The fact of the religious vision and its history of persistent expansion, is our one ground for optimism. Apart from it, human life is a flash of occasional enjoyments lighting up a mass of pain and misery, a bagatelle of transient experience."

The conflict between faith and doubt is reviewed dramatically by Thomas Hardy in the final choruses of *The Dynasts* (quoted in Chapter 12, "Of Time and Change"). His amazing conclusion, though based on naturalism, arrives at a hope that most naturalists cannot quite envision. And this hope glows through the blackness of "God's Funeral" and "The Darkling Thrush." Still others, refusing even this naturalistic dream, cling to the hope of the perfectibility of man and counsel us to work to achieve a paradise in Nature ("The Optimist"). On this plane, the optimist who believes in humanity despite his loss of faith in the supernatural and the pessimist who likewise affirms human values in the absence of religious faith tend to meet and merge in conviction. But the humanistic optimist goes further: instead of visualizing man as nobly facing ultimate extinction of life and hope, he sees mankind going indomitably on, despite recessions of error, towards an ever-receding goal of increasing perfection (see Chapter 14, "The Humanist Way of Life"). And after all, life itself may be adequate foundation for a resurgent optimism, as Aldous Huxley and Thomas Wolfe testify.

Though a shallow optimism is to be deplored, a philosophy that is essentially hopeful, one that does not think that we can cure our ills by ignoring them, needs no defense. It is the essential character of our race:

> Where said the Race of Man, "Here let me drown"?
> "Here let me die of hunger"?—"let me freeze"?
> By nightfall he has built another town:
> This boiling pot, this clearing in the trees.

PIPPA PASSES, I, lines 214-269

ROBERT BROWNING

SEBALD: I kiss you now, dear Ottima, now and now!
This way? Will you forgive me—be once more
My great queen?

OTTIMA: Bind it thrice about my brow;
Crown me your queen, your spirit's arbitress,
Magnificent in sin. Say that!

SEBALD: I crown you
My great white queen, my spirit's arbitress,
Magnificent . . .

        (*From without is heard the voice of* PIPPA, *singing—*

            The year's at the spring
            And day's at the morn;
            Morning's at seven;
            The hill-side's dew-pearled;
            The lark's on the wing;
            The snail's on the thorn:
            God's in his heaven—
            All's right with the world! [PIPPA *passes.*)

SEBALD: God's in his heaven!   Do you hear that?
Who spoke?
You, you spoke!

OTTIMA: Oh—that little ragged girl!
She must have rested on the step: we give them
But this one holiday the whole year round.
Did you ever see our silk-mills—their inside?
There are ten silk-mills now belong to you.
She stoops to pick my double heartsease . . . Sh!
She does not hear: call you out louder!

SEBALD: Leave me!
Go, get your clothes on—dress those shoulders!

OTTIMA: Sebald?

SEBALD: Wipe off that paint!   I hate you.

OTTIMA: Miserable!

SEBALD: My God, and she is emptied of it now!
Outright now!—how miraculously gone
All of the grace—had she not strange grace once?
Why, the blank cheek hangs listless as it likes,
No purpose holds the features up together,
Only the cloven brow and puckered chin
Stay in their places: and the very hair,
That seemed to have a sort of life in it,
Drops, a dead web!

OTTIMA: Speak to me—not of me!

SEBALD: That round great full-orbed face, where
    not an angle
Broke the delicious indolence—all broken!

OTTIMA: To me—not of me! Ungrateful, perjured cheat!
  A coward too: but ingrate's worse than all.
  Beggar—my slave—a fawning, cringing lie!
  Leave me! Betray me! I can see your drift!
  A lie that walks and eats and drinks!
SEBALD: My God!
  Those morbid olive faultless shoulder-blades—
  I should have known there was no blood beneath!
OTTIMA: You hate me then? You hate me then?
SEBALD: To think
  She would succeed in her absurd attempt,
  And fascinate by sinning, show herself
  Superior—guilt from its excess superior
  To innocence! That little peasant's voice
  Has righted all again. Though I be lost,
  I know which is the better, never fear,
  Of vice or virtue, purity or lust,
  Nature or trick! I see what I have done,
  Entirely now! Oh I am proud to feel
  Such torments—let the world take credit thence—
  I, having done my deed, pay too its price!
  I hate, hate—curse you! God's in his heaven!

MUSIC

RALPH WALDO EMERSON

  Let me go where'er I will
  I hear a sky-born music still:
  It sounds from all things old,
  It sounds from all things young,
  From all that's fair, from all that's foul,
  Peals out a cheerful song.
  It is not only in the rose,
  It is not only in the bird,
  Not only where the rainbow glows,
  Nor in the song of woman heard,
  But in the darkest, meanest things
  There alway, alway something sings.
  'T is not in the high stars alone,
  Nor in the cups of budding flowers,
  Nor in the redbreast's mellow tone,
  Nor in the bow that smiles in showers,
  But in the mud and scum of things
  There alway, alway something sings.

FROM AN ESSAY ON MAN

ALEXANDER POPE

EPISTLE I

Awake, my St. John! leave all meaner things
To low ambition, and the pride of kings.
Let us, since life can little more supply
Than just to look about us and to die,
Expatiate free o'er all this scene of man;
A mighty maze but not without a plan;
A wild, where weeds and flowers promiscuous shoot;
Or garden tempting with forbidden fruit.
Together let us beat this ample field,
Try what the open, what the covert yield;
The latent tracts, the giddy heights, explore,
Of all who blindly creep, or sightless soar;
Eye Nature's walks, shoot folly as it flies,
And catch the manners living as they rise;
Laugh where we must, be candid where we can;
But vindicate the ways of God to man.
   I. Say first, of God above or Man below,
What can we reason but from what we know?
Of man, what see we but his station here,
From which to reason, or to which refer?
Through worlds unnumbered though the God be known,
'Tis ours to trace him only in our own.
He, who through vast immensity can pierce,
See worlds on worlds compose one universe,
Observe how system into system runs,
What other planets circle other suns,
What varied being peoples every star,
May tell why heaven has made us as we are.
But of this frame, the bearings and the ties,
The strong connections, nice dependencies,
Gradations just, has thy pervading soul
Looked through; or can a part contain a whole?
   Is the great chain that draws all to agree,
And drawn supports, upheld by God or thee?
   II. Presumptuous man! the reason wouldst thou find,
Why formed so weak, so little, and so blind?
First, if thou canst, the harder reason guess,
Why formed no weaker, blinder, and no less?
Ask of thy mother earth, why oaks are made
Taller or stronger than the weeds they shade!
Or ask of yonder argent fields above
Why Jove's satellites are less than Jove!
   Of systems possible, if 'tis confessed
That wisdom infinite must form the best,
Where all must fall or not coherent be,
And all that rises rise in due degree,

Then, in the scale of reasoning life, 'tis plain,
There must be, somewhere, such a rank as Man:
And all the question (wrangle e'er so long)
Is only this, if God has placed him wrong.
  Respecting Man, whatever wrong we call,
May, must be right, as relative to all.
In human works, though labored on with pain,
A thousand movements scarce one purpose gain;
In God's, one single can its end produce;
Yet serves to second too some other use.
So man, who here seems principal alone,
Perhaps acts second to some sphere unknown,
Touches some wheel, or verges to some goal;
'Tis but a part we see, and not a whole.
  When the proud steed shall know why man restrains
His fiery course, or drives him o'er the plains;
When the dull ox, why now he breaks the clod,
Is now a victim, and now Egypt's god;
Then shall man's pride and dulness comprehend
His actions', passions', being's, use and end;
Why doing, suffering, checked, impelled; and why
This hour a slave, the next a deity.
  Then say not man's imperfect, heaven in fault;
Say rather man's as perfect as he ought:
His knowledge measured to his state and place,
His time a moment, and a point his space.

   .   .   .   .

  IV. Go, wiser thou! and in thy scale of sense,
Weigh thy opinion against Providence;
Call imperfection what thou fanciest such,
Say, Here he gives too little, there too much!
Destroy all creatures for thy sport or gust,
Yet cry, If man's unhappy, God's unjust;
If man alone ingross not heaven's high care,
Alone made perfect here, immortal there:
Snatch from his hand the balance and the rod,
Rejudge his justice, be the god of God.
In pride, in reasoning pride, our error lies;
All quit their sphere and rush into the skies!
Pride still is aiming at the blessed abodes,
Men would be Angels, Angels would be gods.
Aspiring to be gods if Angels fell,
Aspiring to be Angels men rebel:
And who but wishes to invert the laws
Of order, sins against the Eternal Cause.
  V. Ask for what end the heavenly bodies shine,
Earth for whose use, Pride answers, " 'Tis for mine!
For me kind Nature wakes her genial power,
Suckles each herb, and spreads out every flower;
Annual for me, the grape, the rose renew
The juice nectareous, and the balmy dew;

For me the mine a thousand treasures brings;
For me health gushes from a thousand springs;
Seas roll to waft me, suns to light me rise;
My footstool earth, my canopy the skies!"
  But errs not nature from this gracious end,
From burning suns when livid deaths descend,
When earthquakes swallow, or when tempests sweep
Towns to one grave, whole nations to the deep?
"No," 'tis replied, "the first Almighty Cause
Acts not by partial but by general laws:
The exceptions few; some change since all began;
And what created perfect?"—Why then man?
If the great end be human happiness,
Then Nature deviates; and can man do less?
As much that end a constant course requires
Of showers and sunshine, as of man's desires:
As much eternal springs and cloudless skies,
As men for ever temperate, calm, and wise.
If plagues or earthquakes break not heaven's design,
Why then a Borgia or a Cataline?
Who knows but He, whose hand the lightning forms,
Who heaves old ocean, and who wings the storms;
Pours fierce ambition in a Caesar's mind,
Or turns young Ammon loose to scourge mankind?
From pride, from pride our very reasoning springs;
Account for moral, as for natural things:
Why charge we heaven in those, in these acquit?
In both to reason right is to submit.
  Better for us, perhaps, it might appear,
Were there all harmony, all virtue here;
That never air or ocean felt the wind;
That never passion discomposed the mind.
But all subsists by elemental strife;
And passions are the elements of life.
The general order, since the whole began,
Is kept in Nature, and is kept in Man.

.   .   .   .

  VIII. See, through this air, this ocean, and this earth,
All matter quick, and bursting into birth.
Above, how high progressive life may go!
Around, how wide! how deep extend below!
Vast chain of being! which from God began,
Natures ethereal, human, angel, man,
Beast, bird, fish, insect, what no eye can see,
No glass can reach; from infinite to thee,
From thee to nothing. On superior powers
Were we to press, inferior might on ours:
Or in full creation leave a void,
Where, one step broken, the great scale's destroyed:
From Nature's chain whatever link you strike,
Tenth or ten thousandth, breaks the chain alike.

And if each system in gradation roll
Alike essential to the amazing Whole,
The least confusion but in one, not all
That system only, but the Whole must fall.
Let earth unbalanced from her orbit fly,
Planets and stars run lawless through the sky;
Let ruling angels from their spheres be hurled,
Being on being wrecked, and world on world;
Heaven's whole foundations to their center nod,
And Nature tremble to the throne of God!
All this dread order break—for whom? for thee?
Vile worm!—O madness! pride! impiety!

IX. What if the foot, ordained the dust to tread,
Or hand, to toil, aspired to be the head?
What if the head, the eye, or ear repined
To serve mere engines to the ruling mind?
Just as absurd for any part to claim
To be another, in this general frame:
Just as absurd, to mourn the tasks or pains
The great directing Mind of all ordains.

All are but parts of one stupendous whole,
Whose body Nature is, and God the soul;
That, changed through all, and yet in all the same,
Great in the earth, as in the ethereal frame,
Warms in the sun, refreshes in the breeze,
Glows in the stars, and blossoms in the trees,
Lives through all life, extends through all extent,
Spreads undivided, operates unspent;
Breathes in our soul, informs our mortal part,
As full, as perfect in a hair as heart;
As full, as perfect in vile man that mourns,
As the rapt Seraph that adores and burns:
To him no high, no low, no great, no small;
He fills, he bounds, connects, and equals all.

X. Cease then, nor Order imperfection name:
Our proper bliss depends on what we blame.
Know thy own point: this kind, this due degree
Of blindness, of weakness, heaven bestows on thee.
Submit: in this, or any other sphere,
Secure to be as blessed as thou canst bear;
Safe in the hand of one disposing Power,
Or in the natal, or the mortal hour.
All Nature is but Art unknown to thee,
All chance, direction which thou canst not see;
All discord, harmony not understood;
All partial evil, universal good;
And, spite of Pride, in erring Reason's spite,
One truth is clear, *Whatever is, is right.*

EPISTLE II

I. Know then thyself, presume not God to scan,
The proper study of mankind is Man.
Placed on this isthmus of a middle state,
A being darkly wise, and rudely great:
With too much knowledge for the Skeptic side,
With too much weakness for the Stoic's pride,
He hangs between; in doubt to act, or rest;
In doubt to deem himself a God or Beast;
In doubt his mind or body to prefer;
Born but to die, and reasoning but to err;
Alike in ignorance, his reason such,
Whether he thinks too little or too much;
Chaos of thought and passion, all confused;
Still by himself abused, or disabused;
Created half to rise, and half to fall;
Great lord of all things, yet a prey to all;
Sole judge of truth, in endless error hurled;
The glory, jest, and riddle of the world!

Go, wondrous creature! mount where Science guides,
Go, measure earth, weigh air, and state the tides;
Instruct the planets in what orbs to run,
Correct old Time, and regulate the sun;
Go, soar with Plato to the empyreal sphere,
To the first good, first perfect, and first fair;
Or tread the mazy round his followers trod;
And quitting sense call imitating God;
As eastern priests in giddy circles run,
And turn their heads to imitate the sun.
Go, teach Eternal Wisdom how to rule—
Then drop into thyself, and be a fool!

Superior beings, when of late they saw
A mortal man unfold all Nature's law,
Admired such wisdom in an earthly shape,
And showed a NEWTON, as we show an ape.
Could he, whose rules the rapid comet bind,
Describe or fix one movement of his mind?
Who saw its fires here rise, and there descend,
Explain his own beginning or his end?
Alas! what wonder! Man's superior part
Unchecked may rise, and climb from art to art;
But when his own great work is but begun,
What Reason weaves, by Passion is undone,

Trace Science then, with modesty thy guide;
First strip off all her equipage of pride;
Deduct what is but vanity or dress,
Or learning's luxury, or idleness;
Or tricks to show the stretch of human brain,
Mere curious pleasure, or ingenious pain;

Expunge the whole, or lop the excrescent parts
Of all our vices have created arts;
Then see how little the remaining sum,
Which served the past, and must the times to come!

  .   .   .   .

    The Eternal Art, educing good from ill,
Grafts on this passion our best principle:
'Tis thus the mercury of man is fixed,
Strong grows the virtue with his nature mixed;
The dross cements what else were too refined,
And in one interest body acts with mind.
    As fruits, ungrateful to the planter's care,
On savage stocks inserted learn to bear,
The surest Virtues thus from Passions shoot,
Wild Nature's vigor working at the root.
What crops of wit and honesty appear
From spleen, from obstinacy, hate or fear!
See anger, zeal and fortitude supply;
Even avarice, prudence; sloth, philosophy;
Lust, through some certain strainers well refined,
Is gentle love, and charms all womankind;
Envy, to which the ignoble mind's a slave,
Is emulation in the learned or brave;
Nor virtue, male or female can we name,
But what will grow on pride, or grow on shame.
    Thus Nature gives us (let it check our pride)
The Virtue nearest to our vice allied;
Reason the bias turns to good from ill,
And Nero reigns a Titus if he will.
The fiery soul abhorred in Catiline,
In Decius charms, in Curtius is divine:
The same ambition can destroy or save,
And makes a patriot as it makes a knave.
    IV. This light and darkness in our chaos joined,
What shall divide?   The god within the mind.

  .   .   .   .

EPISTLE III

    I. Here then we rest: "The Universal Cause
Acts to one end, but acts by various laws."
In all the madness of superfluous Health,
The trim of Pride, the impudence of Wealth,
Let this great truth be present night and day:
But most be present if we preach or pray.
    Look round our world, behold the chain of love
Combining all below and all above.
See plastic Nature working to this end,
The single atoms each to other tend,
Attract, attracted to, the next in place
Formed and impelled its neighbor to embrace.

See matter next with various life endued,
Press to one center still, the general good.
See dying vegetables life sustain,
See life dissolving vegetate again:
All forms that perish other forms supply,
(By turns we catch the vital breath and die)
Like bubbles on the sea of Matter born,
They rise, they break, and to that sea return.
Nothing is foreign; parts relate to whole;
One all-extending, all-preserving soul
Connects each being, greatest with the least;
Made beast in aid of man, and man of beast;
All served, all serving: nothing stands alone;
The chain holds on, and where it ends unknown.
    Has God, thou fool! worked solely for thy good,
Thy joy, thy pastime, thy attire, thy food?
Who for thy table feeds the wanton fawn,
For him as kindly spreads the flowery lawn:
Is it for thee the lark ascends and sings?
Joy tunes his voice, joy elevates his wings.
Is it for thee the linnet pours his throat?
Loves of his own and raptures swell the note.
The bounding steed you pompously bestride,
Shares with his lord the pleasure and the pride.
Is thine alone the seed that strews the plain?
The birds of heaven shall vindicate their grain.
Thine the full harvest of the golden year?
Part pays, and justly, the deserving steer;
The hog, that ploughs not, nor obeys thy call,
Lives on the labors of this lord of all.
Know, Nature's children all divide her care;
The fur that warms a monarch warmed a bear.
While Man exclaims, "See all things for my use!"
"See man for mine!" replies a pampered goose:
And just as short of Reason he must fall,
Who thinks all made for one, not one for all.
Grant that the powerful still the weak control;
Be Man the wit, and tyrant of the whole:
Nature that tyrant checks; he only knows,
And helps, another creature's wants and woes.
Say, will the falcon, stooping from above,
Smit with her varying plumage, spare the dove?
Admires the jay the insect's gilded wings?
Or hears the hawk when Philomela sings?
Man cares for all: to birds he gives his woods,
To beasts his pastures, and to fish his floods.
For some his interest prompts him to provide,
For more his Pleasure, yet for more his Pride:
All feed on one vain patron, and enjoy
The extensive blessing of his luxury.
That very life his learned hunger craves,
He saves from famine, from the savage saves;

Nay, feasts the animal he dooms his feast,
And, till he ends the being, makes it blessed,
Which sees no more the stroke, or feels the pain,
Than favored man by touch ethereal slain.
The creature had his feast of life before;
Thou too must perish, when thy feast is o'er!
   To each unthinking being, heaven, a friend,
Gives not the useless knowledge of its end:
To man imparts it; but with such a view
As, while he dreads it, makes him hope it too;
The hour concealed, and so remote the fear,
Death still draws nearer, never seeming near.
Great standing miracle! that heaven assigned
Its only thinking thing this turn of mind.

.   .   .   .

EPISTLE IV

   O HAPPINESS! our being's end and aim,
Good, Pleasure, Ease, Content! whate'er thy name:
That something still which prompts the eternal sigh,
For which we bear to live, or dare to die;
Which still so near us, yet beyond us lies,
O'erlooked, seen double by the fool and wise:
Plant of celestial seed! if dropped below,
Say, in what mortal soil thou deign'st to grow?
Fair opening to some court's propitious shine,
Or deep with diamonds in the flaming mine?
Twined with wreaths Parnassian laurels yield,
Or reaped in iron harvests of the field?
Where grows?—where grows it not? If vain our toil,
We ought to blame the culture, not the soil:
Fixed to no spot is Happiness sincere,
'Tis no where to be found, or everywhere:
'Tis never to be bought, but always free;
And, fled from monarchs, St. John! dwells with thee.
   Ask of the Learned the way! The Learned are blind;
This bids to serve, and that to shun mankind;
Some place the bliss in Action, some in Ease,
Those call it Pleasure, and Contentment these;
Some sunk to beasts find pleasure end in Pain;
Some swelled to Gods confess e'en Virtue vain;
Or indolent, to each extreme they fall,
To trust in every thing, or doubt of all.
   Who thus define it, say they more or less
Than this, that happiness is happiness?
   II. Take Nature's path, and mad Opinion's leave;
All states can reach it, and all heads conceive;
Obvious her goods, in no extreme they dwell;
There needs but thinking right, and meaning well;
And mourn our various portions as we please,
Equal is common sense, and common ease.
   Remember, Man, "the Universal Cause

Acts not by partial, but by general laws";
And makes what happiness we justly call,
Subsist, not in the good of one, but all.
There's not a blessing individuals find,
But some way leans and hearkens to the kind;
No bandit fierce, no tyrant mad with pride,
No caverned hermit rests self-satisfied:
Who most to shun or hate mankind pretend,
Seek an admirer, or would fix a friend.
Abstract what others feel, what others think,
All pleasures sicken, and all glories sink:
Each has his share; and who would more obtain,
Shall find the pleasure pays not half the pain.

Order is Heaven's first law; and, this confest,
Some are, and must be, greater than the rest,
More rich, more wise; but who infers from hence
That such are happier, shocks all common sense.
Heaven to mankind impartial we confess,
If all are equal in their happiness:
But mutual wants this happiness increase;
All Nature's difference keeps all Nature's peace.
Condition, circumstance is not the thing;
Bliss is the same in subject or in king,
In who obtain defense, or who defend,
In him who is, or who finds a friend:
Heaven breathes through every member of the whole
One common blessing, as one common soul.
But Fortune's gifts if each alike possessed,
And each were equal, must not all contest?
If then to all men happiness was meant,
God in externals could not place content.

Fortune her gifts may variously dispose,
And these be happy called, unhappy those;
But heaven's just balance equal will appear,
While those are placed in hope, and these in fear:
Not present good or ill, the joy or curse,
But future views of better, or of worse.

O sons of earth! attempt ye still to rise,
By mountains piled on mountains, to the skies?
Heaven still with laughter the vain toil surveys,
And buries madmen in the heaps they raise.
Know, all good that individuals find,
Or God and Nature meant to mere mankind,
Reason's whole pleasure, all the joys of sense,
Lie in three words, Health, Peace, and Competence.

· · · · · · · · · ·

O blind to truth, and God's whole scheme below,
Who fancy bliss to vice, to virtue woe!
Who sees and follows that great scheme the best,
Best knows the blessing, and will most be blessed.

But fools the good alone unhappy call,
For ills or accidents that chance to all.
See Falkland dies, the virtuous and the just!
See God-like Turenne prostrate on the dust!
See Sidney bleeds amid the martial strife!
Was this their virtue, or contempt of life?
Say, was it virtue, more though heaven ne'er gave?
Lamented Digby! sunk thee to the grave?
Tell me, if virtue made the son expire,
Why, full of days and honor, lives the sire?
Why drew Marseilles' good bishop purer breath,
When Nature sickened, and each gale was death?
Or why so long (in life if long can be)
Lent heaven a parent to the poor and me?
    What makes all physical or moral ill?
There deviates Nature, and here wanders Will.
God sends not ill, if rightly understood,
Or partial ill is universal good,
Or change admits, or Nature lets it fall
Short, and but rare, till man improved it all.
We just as wisely might of Heaven complain,
That Righteous Abel was destroyed by Cain,
As that the virtuous son is ill at ease
When his lewd father gave the dire disease.
Think we like some weak prince, the Eternal Cause,
Prone for his favorites to reverse his laws?
    Shall burning Aetna, if a sage requires,
Forget to thunder, and recall her fires?
On air or sea new motions be impressed,
O blameless Bethel! to relieve thy breast?
When the loose mountain trembles from on high,
Shall gravitation cease if you go by?
Or some old temple nodding to its fall,
For Chartres' head reserve the hanging wall?
    But still this world, so fitted for the knave,
Contents us not. A better shall we have?
A kingdom of the just then let it be:
But first consider how those just agree.
The good must merit God's peculiar care;
But who, but God, can tell us who they are?
One thinks on Calvin heaven's own Spirit fell;
Another deems him instrument of hell;
If Calvin feel heaven's blessing, or its rod,
This cries there is, and that, there is no God.
What shocks one part will edify the rest,
Nor with one system can they all be blessed.
The very best will variously incline,
And what rewards your virtue, punish mine.
Whatever is, is right.—This world, 'tis true,
Was made for Caesar—but for Titus too:
And which more blessed? who chained his country, say,
Or he whose virtue sighed to lose a day?

"But sometimes virtue starves, while vice is fed."
What then?   Is the reward of virtue bread?
That vice may merit, 'tis the price of toil;
The knave deserves it when he tills the soil,
The knave deserves it when he tempts the main,
Where folly fights for kings, or dives for gain.
The good man may be weak, be indolent;
Nor is his claim to plenty, but content.
But grant him riches, your demand is o'er?
"No—shall the good want health, the good want power?"
Add health, and power, and every earthly thing:
"Why bounded power? why private? why no king?
Nay, why external for internal given?
Why is not man a God, and earth a Heaven?"
Who ask and reason thus, will scarce conceive
God gives enough while he has more to give:
Immense the power, immense were the demand;
Say, at what part of Nature will they stand?
    What nothing earthly gives or can destroy,
The soul's calm sunshine, and the heartfelt joy,
Is Virtue's prize. A better would you fix?
Then give humility a coach and six,
Justice a conqueror's sword, or truth a gown,
Or public spirit its great cure, a crown.
Weak, foolish man! will heaven reward us there,
With the same trash mad mortals wish for here?
The boy and man an individual makes,
Yet sighest thou now for apples and for cakes?
Go, like the Indian, in another life
Expect thy dog, thy bottle, and thy wife;
As well as dream such trifles are assigned,
As toys and empires, for a god-like mind:
Rewards, that either would to Virtue bring
No joy, or be destructive of the thing:
How oft by these at sixty are undone
The virtues of a saint at twenty-one!

    .   .   .   .

    VII. Know then this truth (enough for man to know),
"Virtue alone is happiness below."
The only point where human bliss stands still,
And tastes the good without the fall to ill;
Where only merit constant pay receives,
Is blessed in what it takes, and what it gives;
The joy unequaled, if its end it gain,
And if it lose, attended with no pain:
Without satiety, though e'er so blessed,
And but more relished as the more distressed:
The broadest mirth unfeeling Folly wears,
Less pleasing far than Virtue's very tears:
Good, from each object, from each place acquired,
For ever exercised, yet never tired;

Never elated while one man's oppressed;
Never dejected, while another's blessed;
And where no wants, no wishes can remain,
Since but to wish more virtue is to gain.
See the sole bliss Heaven could on all bestow!
Which who but feels can taste, but thinks can know;
Yet poor with fortune, and with learning blind,
The bad must miss; the good, untaught, will find;
Slave to no sect, who takes no private road,
But looks through Nature up to Nature's God;
Pursues that chain which links the immense design,
Joins Heaven and earth, and mortal and divine;
Sees, that no being any bliss can know,
But touches some above and some below;
Learns from this union of the rising whole,
The first, last purpose of the human soul;
And knows where faith, law, morals, all began.
All end, in love of God, and love of Man.

FROM CANDIDE, Chapter 28
VOLTAIRE

"Well! my dear Pangloss," said Candide, "when you were hanged, dissected, stunned with blows and made to row in the galleys, did you always think that everything was for the best in this world?"

"I am still of my first opinion," replied Pangloss, "for after all, I am a philosopher; and it would be unbecoming for me to recant, since Leibnitz could not be in the wrong and Pre-established harmony is the finest thing imaginable like the plenum and subtle matter."

FROM BABOUC'S VISION, Chapter 17
VOLTAIRE

He rendered his account in the following way. He caused the best metal founder of the town to make a statuette composed of every metal and of the most precious and most worthless stones and earths. And he took it to Ituriel.

"Will you break this pretty statuette," he said, "because it is not all gold and diamonds?"

Ituriel guessed his meaning; he resolved not even to think of correcting Persepolis and to let the world go on as it is; for, said he, if all is not well, all is tolerable. Persepolis, then, was allowed to remain and Babouc was very far from complaining like Jonah, who was angry because Nineveh was not destroyed. But when a man has been three days in the belly of a whale, he is not so good-tempered as when he has been at the opera, to the theater and has supped in good company.

SONG AT SUNSET

WALT WHITMAN

Splendor of ended day, floating and filling me!
Hour prophetic—hour resuming the past!
Inflating my throat—you, divine average!
You, Earth and Life, till the last ray gleams, I sing.

Open mouth of my Soul, uttering gladness,
Eyes of my Soul, seeing perfection,
Natural life of me, faithfully praising things;
Corroborating forever the triumph of things.

Illustrious every one!
Illustrious what we name space—sphere of unnumbered spirits;
Illustrious the mystery of motion, in all beings, even the
    tiniest insect;
Illustrious the attribute of speech—the senses—the body;
Illustrious the passing light! Illustrious the pale reflection
    on the new moon in the western sky!
Illustrious whatever I see, or hear, or touch, to the last.

Good in all,
In the satisfaction and aplomb of animals,
In the annual return of the seasons,
In the hilarity of youth,
In the strength and flush of manhood,
In the grandeur and exquisiteness of old age,
In the superb vistas of Death.

Wonderful to depart;
Wonderful to be here!
The heart, to jet the all-alike and innocent blood!
To breathe the air, how delicious!
To speak! to walk! to seize something by the hand!
To prepare for sleep, for bed—to look on my rose-colored
    flesh;
To be conscious of my body, so satisfied, so large;
To be this incredible God I am;
To have gone forth among other Gods—these men and
    women I love.

Wonderful how I celebrate you and myself!
How my thoughts play subtly at the spectacles around!
How the clouds pass silently overhead!
How the earth darts on and on! and how the sun, moon,
    stars, dart on and on!
How the water sports and sings! (Surely it is alive!)
How the trees rise and stand up—with strong trunks—with
    branches and leaves!
(Surely there is something more in each of the trees—some
    living Soul.)

O amazement of things! even the least particle!
O spirituality of things!
O strain musical, flowing through ages and continents—now
    reaching me and America!
I take your strong chords—I intersperse them, and cheerfully
    pass them forward.
I too carol the sun, ushered, or at noon, or, as now, setting,
I too throb to the brain and beauty of the earth, and of all
    the growths of the earth,
I too have felt the resistless call of myself.

As I sailed down the Mississippi,
As I wandered over the prairies,
As I have lived—as I have looked through my windows, my
    eyes,
As I went forth in the morning—as I beheld the light breaking
    in the east;
As I bathed on the beach of the Eastern Sea, and again on the
    beach of the Western Sea;
As I roamed the streets of inland Chicago—whatever streets
    I have roamed;
Or cities, or silent woods, or even amid the sights of war;
Wherever I have been, I have charged myself with contentment
    and triumph.

I sing to the last the Equalities, modern or old,
I sing the endless finalés of things;
I say Nature continues—Glory continues;
I praise with electric voice;
For I do not see one imperfection in the universe;
And I do not see one cause or result lamentable at last in the
    universe.

O setting sun! though the time has come,
I still warble under you, if none else does, unmitigated
    adoration.

RABBI BEN EZRA

ROBERT BROWNING

Grow old along with me!
The best is yet to be,
The last of life for which the first was made:
Our times are in His hand
Who saith "A whole I planned,
Youth shows but half; trust God: see all, nor be afraid!"

Not that amassing flowers
Youth sighed "Which rose make ours,
Which lily leave and then as best recall?"

Not that, admiring stars,
　　It yearned "Nor Jove, nor Mars;
Mine be some figured flame which blends, transcends
　　them all!"

　　Not for such hopes and fears
　　Annulling youth's brief years,
Do I remonstrate: folly wide the mark!
　　Rather I prize the doubt
　　Low kinds exist without,
Finished and finite clods, untroubled by a spark.

　　Poor vaunt of life indeed,
　　Were man but formed to feed
On joy, to solely seek and find and feast:
　　Such feasting ended, then
　　As sure an end to men;
Irks care the crop-full bird? Frets doubt the maw-crammed
　　beast?

　　Rejoice we are allied
　　To That which doth provide
And not partake, effect and not receive!
　　A spark disturbs our clod;
　　Nearer we hold of God
Who gives, than of His tribes that take, I must believe.

　　Then, welcome each rebuff
　　That turns earth's smoothness rough,
Each sting that bids nor sit nor stand but go!
　　Be our joys three-parts pain!
　　Strive, and hold cheap the strain;
Learn, nor account the pang; dare, never grudge the throe!

　　For thence,—a paradox
　　Which comforts while it mocks,—
Shall life succeed in that it seems to fail:
　　What I aspired to be,
　　And was not, comforts me:
A brute I might have been, but would not sink i' the scale.

　　What is he but a brute
　　Whose flesh hath soul to suit,
Whose spirit works lest arms and legs want play?
　　To man, propose this test—
　　Thy body at its best,
How far can that project thy soul on its lone way?

　　Yet gifts should prove their use:
　　I own the Past profuse
Of power each side, perfection every turn:

AS THE OPTIMIST SEES IT

Eyes, ears took in their dole,
Brain treasured up the whole;
Should not the heart beat once "How good to live
and learn"?

Not once beat "Praise be Thine!
I see the whole design,
I, who saw Power, see now Love perfect too:
Perfect I call Thy plan:
Thanks that I was a man!
Maker, remake, complete,—I trust what Thou shalt do!"

For pleasant is this flesh;
Our soul in its rose-mesh
Pulled ever to the earth, still yearns for rest:
Would we some prize might hold
To match those manifold
Possessions of the brute,—gain most, as we did best!

Let us not always say
"Spite of this flesh to-day
I strove, made head, gained ground upon the whole!"
As the bird wings and sings,
Let us cry "All good things
Are ours, nor soul helps flesh more, now, than flesh
helps soul!"

Therefore I summon age
To grant youth's heritage,
Life's struggle having so far reached its term:
Thence shall I pass, approved
A man, for aye removed
From the developed brute; a God though in the germ.

And I shall thereupon
Take rest, ere I be gone
Once more on my adventure, brave and new:
Fearless and unperplexed,
When I wage battle next,
What weapons to select, what armor to indue.

Youth ended, I shall try
My gain or loss thereby;
Leave the fire ashes, what survives is gold:
And I shall weigh the same,
Give life its praise or blame:
Young, all lay in dispute; I shall know, being old.

For note, when evening shuts,
A certain moment cuts
The deed off, calls the glory from the gray:

A whisper from the west
Shoots—"Add this to the rest,
Take it and try its worth: here dies another day."

So, still within this life,
Though lifted o'er its strife,
Let me discern, compare, pronounce at last,
"This rage was right i' the main,
That acquiescence vain:
The Future I may face now I have proved the Past."

For more is not reserved
To man, with soul just nerved
To act tomorrow what he learns today;
Here, work enough to watch
The Master work, and catch
Hints of the proper craft, tricks of the tools' true play.

As it was better, youth
Should strive, through acts uncouth,
Toward making, than repose on aught found made;
So, better, age, exempt
From strife, should know, than tempt
Further.   Thou waitedest age; wait death nor be afraid!

Enough now, if the Right
And Good and Infinite
Be named here, as thou callest thy hand thine own,
With knowledge absolute,
Subject to no dispute
From fools that crowded youth, nor let thee feel alone.

Be there, for once and all,
Severed great minds from small,
Announced to each his station in the Past!
Was I, the world arraigned,
Were they, my soul disdained,
Right?   Let age speak the truth and give us peace at last!

Now, who shall arbitrate?
Ten men love what I hate,
Shun what I follow, slight what I receive;
Ten, who in ears and eyes
Match me: we all surmise
They, this thing, and I, that; whom shall my soul believe?

Not on the vulgar mass
Called "work," must sentence pass,
Things done, that took the eye and had the price;
O'er which, from level stand,
The low world laid its hand,
Found straightway to its mind, could value in a trice:

But all, the world's coarse thumb
And finger failed to plumb,
So passed in making up the main account:
All instincts immature,
All purposes unsure,
That weighed not as his work, yet swelled the man's amount:

Thoughts hardly to be packed
Into a narrow act,
Fancies that broke through language and escaped:
All I could never be,
All, men ignored in me,
This, I was worth to God, whose wheel the pitcher shaped.

Aye, note that Potter's wheel,
That metaphor! and feel
Why time spins fast, why passive lies our clay,—
Thou, to whom fools propound,
When the wine makes its round,
"Since life fleets, all is change: the Past gone, seize
today!"

Fool! All that is, at all,
Lasts ever, past recall;
Earth changes, but thy soul and God stand sure:
What entered into thee
That was, is, and shall be:
Time's wheel runs back or stops; Potter and clay endure.

He fixed thee mid this dance
Of plastic circumstance,
This Present, thou, forsooth, wouldst fain arrest:
Machinery just meant
To give thy soul its bent,
Try thee and turn thee forth, sufficiently impressed.

What though the earlier grooves
Which ran the laughing loves
Around thy base, no longer pause and press?
What though, about thy rim,
Skull-things in order grim
Grow out, in graver mood, obey the sterner stress?

Look not thou down but up!
To uses of a cup,
The festal board, lamp's flash and trumpet's peal,
The new wine's foaming flow,
The Master's lips aglow!
Thou, heaven's consummate cup, what needest thou with
earth's wheel?

from PARACELSUS

ROBERT BROWNING

I knew, I felt (perception unexpressed,
Uncomprehended by our narrow thought,
But somehow felt and known in every shift
And change in the spirit,—nay, in every pore
Of the body, even)—what God is, what we are,
What life is—how God tastes an infinite joy
In infinite ways—one everlasting bliss,
From whom all being emanates, all power
Proceeds; in whom is life for evermore,
Yet whom existence in its lowest form
Includes; where dwells enjoyment there is he:
With still a flying point of bliss remote,
A happiness in store afar, a sphere
Of distant glory in full view; thus climbs
Pleasure its heights forever and forever.
The center-fire heaves underneath the earth,
And the earth changes like a human face;
The molten ore bursts up among the rocks,
Winds into the stone's heart, outbranches bright
In hidden mines, spots barren river-beds,
Crumbles into fine sand where sunbeams bask—
God joys therein. The wroth sea's waves are edged
With foam, white as the bitten lip of hate,
When, in the solitary waste, strange groups
Of young volcanoes come up, cyclops-like,
Staring together with their eyes on flame—
God tastes a pleasure in their uncouth pride.
Then all is still; earth is a wintry clod:
But spring-wind, like a dancing psaltress passes
Over its breast to waken it, rare verdure
Buds tenderly upon rough banks, between
The withered tree-roots and the cracks of frost,
Like a smile striving with a wrinkled face;
The grass grows bright, the boughs are swoln with blooms
Like chrysalids impatient for the air,
The shining dorrs are busy, beetles run
Along the furrow, ants make their ado;
Above, birds fly in merry flocks, the lark
Soars up and up, shivering for very joy;
Afar the ocean sleeps; white fishing-gulls
Flit where the strand is purple with its tribe
Of nested limpets; savage creatures seek
Their loves in wood and plain—and God renews
His ancient rapture. Thus he dwells in all,
From life's minute beginnings, up at last
To man—the consummation of this scheme
Of being, the completion of this sphere
Of life: whose attributes had here and there

Been scattered o'er the visible world before,
Asking to be combined, dim fragments meant
To be united in some wondrous whole,
Imperfect qualities throughout creation,
Suggesting some one creature yet to make,
Some point where all those scattered rays should meet
Convergent in the faculties of man.
Power—neither put forth blindly, nor controlled
Calmly by perfect knowledge; to be used
At risk, inspired or checked by hope and fear:
Knowledge—not intuition, but the slow
Uncertain fruit of an enhancing toil,
Strengthened by love: love—not serenely pure,
But strong from weakness, like a chance-sown plant
Which, cast on stubborn soil, puts forth changed buds
And softer stains, unknown in happier climes;
Love which endures and doubts and is oppressed
And cherished, suffering much and much sustained,
And blind, oft-failing, yet believing love,
A half-enlightened, often-chequered trust:—
Hints and previsions of which faculties,
Are strewn confusedly everywhere about
The inferior natures, and all lead up higher,
All shape out dimly the superior race,
The heir of hopes too fair to turn out false,
And man appears at last.   So far the seal
Is put on life; one stage of being complete,
One scheme wound up: and from the grand result
A supplementary reflux of light,
Illustrates all the inferior grades, explains
Each back stop in the circle . . .

    .   .   .   .

With apprehension of his passing worth,
Desire to work his proper nature out,
And ascertain his rank and final place,
For these things tend still upward, progress is
The law of life, man is not Man as yet.
Nor shall I deem his object served, his end
Attained, his genuine strength put fairly forth,
While only here and there a star dispels
The darkness, here and there a towering mind
O'erlooks its prostrate fellows: when the host
Is out at once to the despair of night,
When all mankind alike is perfected,
Equal in full-blown powers—then, not till then,
I say, begins man's general infancy.
For wherefore make account of feverish starts
Of restless members of a dormant whole,
Impatient nerves which quiver while the body
Slumbers as in a grave?   Oh long ago
The brow was twitched, the tremulous lids astir,

The peaceful mouth disturbed; half-uttered speech
Ruffled the lip, and then the teeth were set,
The breath drawn sharp, the strong right-hand clenched stronger,
As it would pluck a lion by the jaw;
The glorious creature laughed out even in sleep!
But when full roused, each giant-limb awake,
Each sinew strung, the great heart pulsing fast,
He shall start up and stand on his own earth,
Then shall his long triumphant march begin,
Thence shall his being date,—thus wholly roused,
What he achieves shall be set down to him.
When all the race is perfected alike
As man, that is; all tended to mankind,
And, man produced, all has its end thus far:
But in completed man begins anew
A tendency to God.   Prognostics told
Man's near approach; so in man's self arise
August anticipations, symbols, types
Of a dim splendor ever on before
In that eternal circle life pursues.
For men begin to pass their nature's bound,
And find new hopes and cares which fast supplant
Their proper joys and griefs; they grow too great
For narrow creeds of right and wrong, which fade
Before the unmeasured thirst for good: while peace
Rises within them ever more and more.
Such men are even now upon the earth,
Serene amid the half-formed creatures round
Who should be saved by them and joined with them.

EPILOGUE TO ASOLANDO

ROBERT BROWNING

At the midnight in the silence of the sleep-time,
   When you set your fancies free,
Will they pass to where—by death, fools think, imprisoned—
Low he lies who once so loved you, whom you loved so,
      —Pity me?

Oh to love so, be so loved, yet so mistaken!
   What had I on earth to do
With the slothful, with the mawkish, the unmanly?
Like the aimless, helpless, hopeless, did I drivel
      —Being—who?

One who never turned his back but marched breast forward,
   Never doubted clouds would break,
Never dreamed, though right were worsted, wrong would triumph,
Held we fall to rise, are baffled to fight better,
      Sleep to wake.

No, at noonday in the bustle of man's work-time
  Greet the unseen with a cheer!
Bid him forward, breast and back as either should be,
"Strive and thrive!" cry "Speed,—fight on, fare ever
    There as here!"

FROM CLAREL, XXXV

HERMAN MELVILLE

If Luther's day expand to Darwin's year,
Shall that exclude the hope—foreclose the fear?

  Unmoved by all the claims our times avow,
The ancient Sphinx still keeps the porch of shade
And comes Despair, whom not her calm may cow,
And coldly on that adamantine brow
Scrawls undeterred his bitter pasquinade.
But Faith (who warm from the scrawl indignant turns),
With blood warm oozing from her wounded trust,
Inscribes even on her shards of broken urns
The sign o' the cross—*the spirit above the dust!*

  Yea, ape and angel, strife and old debate—
The harps of heaven and dreary gongs of hell;
Science the feud can only aggravate—
No umpire she betwixt the chimes and knell:
The running battle of the star and clod
Shall run for ever—if there be no God.

  Degrees we know, unknown in days before;
The light is greater, hence the shadow more;
And tantalized and apprehensive Man
Appealing—Wherefore ripen us to pain?
Seems there the spokesman of dumb Nature's train.

  But through such strange illusions have they passed
Who in life's pilgrimage have baffled striven—
Even death may prove unreal at the last,
And stoics be astounded into heaven.

FROM THE TWO VOICES

ALFRED LORD TENNYSON

A still small voice spake unto me,
"Thou art so full of misery,
Were it not better not to be?"

Then to the still small voice I said:
"Let me not cast in endless shade
What is so wonderfully made."

To which the voice did urge reply:
"Today I saw the dragonfly
Come from the wells where he did lie.

"An inner impulse rent the veil
Of his old husk; from head to tail
Came out clear plates of sapphire mail.

"He dried his wings; like gauze they grew;
Through crofts and pastures wet with dew
A living flash of light he flew."

I said: "When first the world began,
Young Nature through five cycles ran,
And in the sixth she molded man.

"She gave him mind, the lordliest
Proportion, and, above the rest
Dominion in the head and breast."

Thereto the silent voice replied:
"Self-blinded are you by your pride;
Look up through night; the world is wide.

"This truth within thy mind rehearse,
That in a boundless universe
Is boundless better, boundless worse.

"Think you this mold of hopes and fears
Could find no statelier than his peers
In yonder hundred million spheres?"

It spake, moreover, in my mind:
"Though thou wert scattered to the wind,
Yet is there plenty of the kind."

Then did my response clearer fall:
"No compound of this earthly ball
Is like another, all in all."

To which he answer'd scoffingly:
"Good soul! suppose I grant it thee,
Who'll weep for thy deficiency?

"Or will one beam be less intense,
When thy peculiar difference
Is canceled in the world of sense?"

I would have said, "Thou canst not know";
But my full heart, that worked below,
Rained through my sight its overflow.

Again the voice spake unto me:
"Thou art so steeped in misery,
Surely 't were better not to be.

"Thine anguish will not let thee sleep,
Nor any train of reason keep;
Thou canst not think, but thou wilt weep."

I said: "The years with change advance;
If I make dark my countenance,
I shut my life from happier chance.

"Some turn this sickness yet might take,
Even yet." But he: "What drug can make
A withered palsy cease to shake?"

I wept: "Tho' I should die, I know
That all about the thorn will blow
In tufts of rosy-tinted snow;

"And men, through novel spheres of thought
Still moving after truth long sought,
Will learn new things when I am not."

"Yet," said the secret voice, "some time,
Sooner or later, will gray prime
Make thy grass hoar with early rime.

"Not less swift souls that yearn for light,
Rapt after heaven's starry flight,
Would sweep the tracts of day and night.

"Not less the bee would range her cells,
The furzy prickle fire the dells,
The foxglove cluster dappled bells."

I said that "all the years invent;
Each month is various to present
The world with some development.

"Were this not well, to bide mine hour,
Though watching from a ruined tower
How grows the day of human power?"

"The highest-mounted mind," he said,
"Still sees the sacred morning spread
The silent summit overhead.

"Will thirty seasons render plain
Those lonely lights that still remain,
Just breaking over land and main?

"Or make that morn, from his cold crown
And crystal silence creeping down,
Flood with full daylight glebe and town?

"Forerun thy peers, thy time, and let
Thy feet, millenniums hence, be set
In midst of knowledge, dreamed not yet.

"Thou hast not gained a real height,
Nor art thou nearer to the light,
Because the scale is infinite.

" 'T were better not to breathe or speak,
Than cry for strength, remaining weak,
And seem to find, but still to seek.

"Moreover, but to seem to find
Asks what thou lackest, thought resigned,
A healthy frame, a quiet mind."

.   .   .   .

"If straight thy track, or if oblique,
Thou knowest not. Shadows thou dost strike,
Embracing cloud, Ixion-like;

"And owning but a little more
Than beasts, abidest lame and poor,
Calling thyself a little lower

"Than angels. Cease to wail and brawl!
Why inch by inch to darkness crawl?
There is one remedy for all."

"O dull, one-sided voice," said I,
"Wilt thou make everything a lie,
To flatter me that I may die?

"I know that age to age succeeds,
Blowing a noise of tongues and deeds,
A dust of systems and of creeds.

"I cannot hide that some have striven,
Achieving calm, to whom was given
The joy that mixes man with Heaven;

"Who, rowing hard against the stream,
Saw distant gates of Eden gleam,
And did not dream it was a dream;

"But heard, by secret transport led,
Even in the charnels of the dead,
The murmur of the fountain-head—

"Which did accomplish their desire,
Bore and forebore, and did not tire,
Like Stephen, an unquenched fire.

"He heeded not reviling tones,
Nor sold his heart to idle moans,
Though cursed and scorned, and bruised with stones;

"But looking upward, full of grace,
He prayed, and from a happy place
God's glory smote him on the face."

.   .   .   .

"Moreover, something is or seems,
That touches me with mystic gleams,
Like glimpses of forgotten dreams—

"Of something felt, like something here;
Of something done, I know not where;
Such as no language may declare."

The still voice laughed.   "I talk," said he,
"Not with thy dreams.   Suffice it thee
Thy pain is a reality."

"But thou," said I, "hast missed thy mark,
Who sought'st to wreck my mortal ark,
By making all the horizon dark.

"Why not set forth, if I should do
This rashness, that which might ensue
With this old soul in organs new?

"Whatever crazy sorrow saith,
No life that breathes with human breath
Has ever truly long'd for death.

" 'Tis life, whereof our nerves are scant,
O, life, not death, for which we pant;
More life, and fuller, that I want."

I ceased, and sat as one forlorn.
Then said the voice, in quiet scorn,
"Behold, it is the Sabbath morn."

And I arose, and I released
The casement, and the light increased
With freshness in the dawning east.

Like softened airs that blowing steal,
When meres begin to uncongeal,
The sweet church bells began to peal.

On to God's house the people prest;
Passing the place where each must rest,
Each entered like a welcome guest.

One walked between his wife and child,
With measured footfall firm and mild,
And now and then he gravely smiled.

The prudent partner of his blood
Leaned on him, faithful, gentle, good,
Wearing the rose of womanhood.

And in their double love secure,
The little maiden walked demure,
Pacing with downward eyelids pure.

These three made unity so sweet,
My frozen heart began to beat,
Remembering its ancient heat.

I blest them, and they wandered on;
I spoke, but answer came there none;
The dull and bitter voice was gone.

A second voice was at mine ear,
A little whisper silver-clear,
A murmur, "Be of better cheer."

As from some blissful neighborhood,
A notice faintly understood,
"I see the end, and know the good."

A little hint to solace woe,
A hint, a whisper breathing low,
"I may not speak of what I know."

Like an Aeolian harp that wakes
No certain air, but overtakes
Far thought with music that it makes;

Such seemed the whisper at my side:
"What is it thou knowest, sweet voice?" I cried.
"A hidden hope," the voice replied;

So heavenly-toned, that in that hour
From out my sullen heart a power
Broke, like the rainbow from the shower,

To feel, although no tongue can prove,
That every cloud, that spreads above
And veileth love, itself is love.

And forth into the fields I went,
And Nature's living motion lent
The pulse of hope to discontent.

I wondered at the bounteous hours,
The slow result of winter showers;
You scarce could see the grass for flowers.

I wondered, while I paced along;
The woods were filled so full with song,
There seemed no room for sense of wrong;

And all so variously wrought,
I marveled how the mind was brought
To anchor by one gloomy thought;

And wherefore rather I made choice
To commune with that barren voice,
Than him that said, "Rejoice! Rejoice!"

CARRION COMFORT

GERARD MANLEY HOPKINS

Not, I'll not carrion comfort, Despair, not feast on thee;
Not untwist—slack they may be—these last strands of man
In me ór, most weary, cry *I can no more.* I can;
Can something, hope, wish day come, not choose not to be.
But ah, but O thou terrible, why wouldst thou rude on me
Thy wring-world right foot rock? lay a lionlimb against me? scan
With darksome devouring eyes my bruisèd bones? and fan,
O in turns of tempest, me heaped there; me frantic to avoid
        thee and flee?
    Why?   That my chaff might fly; my grain lie, sheer and clear.
Nay in all that toil, that coil, since (seems) I kissed the rod,
Hand rather, my heart lo! lapped strength, stole joy, would
        laugh, cheer.
Cheer whom though? the hero whose heaven-handling flung me,
        fóot tród
Me? or me that fought him?   O which one? is it each one?
        That night, that year
Of now done darkness I wretch lay wrestling with (my God!)
        my God.

FROM THE ANCIENT SAGE

ALFRED LORD TENNYSON

Thou canst not prove the Nameless, O my son,
Nor canst thou prove the world thou movest in,
Thou canst not prove that thou art body alone,
Nor canst thou prove that thou art spirit alone,

Nor canst thou prove that thou art both in one.
Thou canst not prove thou art immortal, no,
Nor yet that thou art mortal—nay, my son,
Thou canst not prove that I, who speak with thee,
Am not thyself in converse with thyself,
For nothing worthy proving can be proven,
Nor yet disproven.   Wherefore thou be wise,
Cleave ever to the sunnier side of doubt,
And cling to Faith beyond the forms of Faith!
She reels not in the storm of warring words,
She brightens at the clash of "Yes" and "No,"
She sees the best that glimmers through the worst,
She feels the sun is hid but for a night,
She spies the summer through the winter bud,
She tastes the fruit before the blossom falls,
She hears the lark within the songless egg.
She finds the fountain where they wailed "Mirage!"

GOD'S FUNERAL

THOMAS HARDY

I

I saw a slowly-stepping train—
Lined on the brows, scoop-eyed and bent and hoar—
Following in files across a twilit plain
A strange and mystic form the foremost bore.

II

And by contagious throbs of thought
Or latent knowledge that within me lay
And had already stirred me, I was wrought
To consciousness of sorrow even as they.

III

The fore-borne shape, to my blurred eyes,
At first seemed man-like, and anon to change
To an amorphous cloud of marvelous size,
Sometimes endowed with wings of glorious range.

IV

And this phantasmal variousness
Ever possessed it as they drew along:
Yet throughout all it symboled none the less
Potency vast and loving-kindness strong.

V

Almost before I knew I bent
Toward the moving columns without a word;
They, growing in bulk and numbers as they went,
Struck out sick thought that could be overheard:—

VI

"O man-projected Figure, of late
Imaged as we, thy knell who shall survive?
Whence came it we were tempted to create
One whom we can no longer keep alive?

VII

"Framing him jealous, fierce, at first
We gave him justice as the ages rolled,
Will to bless those by circumstance accurst,
And longsuffering, and mercies manifold.

VIII

"And, tricked by our own early dream
And need of solace, we grew self-deceived,
Our making soon our maker did we deem,
And what we had imagined we believed.

IX

"Till, in Time's stayless stealthy swing,
Uncompromising rude reality
Mangled the Monarch of our fashioning,
Who quavered, sank; and now has ceased to be.

X

"So, toward our myth's oblivion,
Darkling, and languid-lipped, we creep and grope
Sadlier than those who wept in Babylon,
Whose Zion was a still abiding hope.

XI

"How sweet it was in years far hied
To start the wheels of day with trustful prayer,
To lie down liegely at the eventide
And feel a blest assurance he was there!

XII

"And who or what shall fill his place?
Whither will wanderers turn distracted eyes
For some fixed star to stimulate their pace
Towards the goal of their enterprise?" . . .

XIII

Some in the background then I saw,
Sweet women, youths, men, all incredulous,
Who chimed: "This is a counterfeit of straw,
This requiem mockery! Still he lives to us!"

XIV

I could not buoy their faith; and yet
Many I had known: with all I sympathized;
And though struck speechless, I did not forget
That what was mourned for, I, too, long had prized.

XV

Still, how to bear such loss I deemed
The insistent question for each animate mind,
And gazing, to my growing sight there seemed
A pale yet positive gleam low down behind,

XVI

Whereof, to lift the general night,
A certain few who stood aloof had said
"See you upon the horizon that small light—
Swelling somewhat?"   Each mourner shook his head.

XVII

And they composed a crowd of whom
Some were right good, and many nigh the best . . .
Thus dazed and puzzled 'twixt the gleam and gloom
Mechanically I followed with the rest.

THE DARKLING THRUSH

THOMAS HARDY

I leant upon a coppice gate
    When Frost was specter-gray,
And Winter's dregs made desolate
    The weakening eye of day.
The tangled bine-stems scored the sky
    Like strings of broken lyres,
And all mankind that haunted nigh
    Had sought their household fires.

The land's sharp features seemed to be
    The Century's corpse outleant,
His crypt the cloudy canopy,
    The wind his death-lament.
The ancient pulse of germ and birth
    Was shrunken hard and dry,
And every spirit upon earth
    Seemed fervorless as I.

At once a voice arose among
    The bleak twigs overhead
In a full-hearted evensong
    Of joy illimited;

An aged thrush, frail, gaunt, and small,
  In blast-beruffled plume,
Had chosen thus to fling his soul
  Upon the growing gloom.

So little cause for carolings
  Of such ecstatic sound
Was written on terrestrial things
  Afar or nigh around,
That I could think there trembled through
  His happy good-night air
Some blessed Hope, whereof he knew
  And I was unaware.

OPTIMIST

JAMES STEPHENS

(1)

All ye that labor!   Every broken man
Bending beneath his load!   Each tired heart
That cannot quit its burden!   All the clan
Black-browed and fierce, who feel the smart

Of fortune's lances, wayward, uncontrolled:
All ye who writhe in silence 'neath the sin
That no man knows about!   And ye that sold
The freedom of your souls if ye might win

A little ease from strife, and hate the thing
That bought it!   Ye that droop, trembling with pain,
And hunger-haunted, lacking everything
That dignifies existence, and are fain

To lay ye down and die!   Hear the behest
—All ye that labor, come to Me, and rest—

(2)

Let ye be still, ye tortured ones!   Nor strive
Where striving's futile!   Ye can ne'er attain
To lay your burdens down!   All things alive
Must bear the woes of life, and if the pain

Be more than ye can bear, then ye can die!
That is the law!   And bootless 'tis to seek
In the deeps of space; beyond the high
Pearl-tincted clouds; out where the moon doth peak

Her silver horns; for all that vastness bows
To Tyrant Toil, and weeps to find
Somewhere an aid.   Be ye patient!   Rouse
Your shoulders to the load to ye assigned,

And dree your weird! Be sure ye shall not moan
Stretched in the narrow bed, beneath the stone!

(3)

Lo, we are mocked with fancies! And we stretch
Our unavailing arms to anywhere
Where help is none. The north wind will not fetch
An answer to our cries! Nor on the air,

Fanned by the south wind's fan, is friend or aid!
What then is left, but this—that we be brave,
And steadfast in our places! Not afraid
However fell our lot! And we will lave

Us deep in human waters, till the mind
Grows wise and kindly, and we haply steal
A paradise from Nature! Naught can bind
Man closer unto man than that he feel

The trouble of his comrade! So we grope
Through courage, truth, and kindness, back to Hope.

THE CICADAS *

ALDOUS HUXLEY

Sightless, I breathe and touch; this night of pines
Is needly, resinous and rough with bark.
Through every crevice in the tangible dark
The moonlessness above it all but shines.

Limp hangs the leafy sky; never a breeze
Stirs, nor a foot in all this sleeping ground;
And there is silence underneath the trees—
The living silence of continuous sound.

For like inveterate remorse, like shrill
Delirium throbbing in the fevered brain,
An unseen people of cicadas fill
Night with their one harsh note, again, again.

Again, again, with what insensate zest!
What fury of persistence, hour by hour!
Filled with what devil that denies them rest,
Drunk with what source of pleasure and of power!

Life is their madness, life that all night long
Bids them to sing and sing, they know not why;
Mad cause and senseless burden of their song;
For life commands, and Life! is all their cry.

I hear them sing, who in the double night
Of clouds and branches fancied that I went
Through my own spirit's dark discouragement,
Deprived of inward as of outward sight:

Who, seeking, even as here in the wild wood,
A lamp to beckon through my tangled fate,
Found only darkness and, disconsolate,
Mourned the lost purpose and the vanished good.

Now in my empty heart the crickets' shout
Re-echoing denies and still denies
With stubborn folly all my learned doubt,
In madness more than I in reason wise.

Life, life! The word is magical. They sing,
And in my darkened soul the great sun shines;
My fancy blossoms with remembered spring,
And all my autumns ripen on the vines.

Life! and each knuckle of the fig-tree's pale
Dead skeleton breaks out with emerald fire.
Life! and the tulips blow, the nightingale
Calls back the rose, calls back the old desire:

And old desire that is for ever new,
Desire, life's earliest and latest birth,
Life's instrument to suffer and to do,
Springs with the roses from the teeming earth;

Desire that from the world's bright body strips
Deforming time and makes each kiss the first;
That gives to hearts, to satiated lips
The endless bounty of tomorrow's thirst.

Time passes, and the watery moonrise peers
Between the tree-trunks. But no outer light
Tempers the chances of our groping years,
No moon beyond our labyrinthine night.

Clueless we go; but I have heard thy voice,
Divine Unreason! harping in the leaves,
And grieve no more; for wisdom never grieves,
And thou hast taught me wisdom; I rejoice.

FROM THIS IS MAN *

In *A Stone, A Leaf, A Door*

THOMAS WOLFE

This is man,
Who, if he can remember ten golden moments of joy
    and happiness
Out of all his years,
Ten moments unmarked by care,
Unseamed by aches or itches,
Has power to lift himself with his expiring breath,
And say: "I have lived upon this earth
And known glory!"

This is man,
And one wonders why he wants to live at all.
A third of his life is lost and deadened under sleep;
Another third is given to a sterile labor;
A sixth is spent in all his goings and his comings,
In the moil and shuffle of the streets,
In thrusting, shoving, pawing.
How much of him is left, then,
For a vision of the tragic stars?
How much of him is left
To look upon the everlasting earth?
How much of him is left for glory
And the making of great songs?
A few snatched moments only
From the barren glut and suck of living.
Here, then, is man,
This moth of time,
This dupe of brevity and numbered hours,
This travesty of waste and sterile breath.

Yet if the gods could come here
To a desolate, deserted earth
Where only the ruin of man's cities remained,
Where only a few marks and carvings of his hand
Were legible upon his broken tablets,
Where only a wheel lay rusting in the desert sand,
A cry would burst out of their hearts
And they would say:
"He lived, and he was here!"

Behold his works:

He needed speech to ask for bread—and he had Christ!
He needed songs to sing in battle—and he had Homer!
He needed words to curse his enemies—

And he had Dante, he had Voltaire, he had Swift!
He needed cloth to cover up his hairless, puny flesh
      against the seasons—
And he wove the robes of Solomon,
He made the garments of great kings,
He made the samite for the young knights!
He needed walls and a roof to shelter him—
And he made Blois!
He needed a temple to propitiate his God—
And he made Chartres and Fountains Abbey!
He was born to creep upon the earth—
And he made great wheels,
He sent great engines thundering down the rails,
He launched great wings into the air,
He put great ships upon the angry sea!

Plagues wasted him,
And cruel wars destroyed his strongest sons,
But fire, flood, and famine could not quench him.
No, nor the inexorable grave—
His sons leaped shouting from his dying loins.
The shaggy bison with his thews of thunder
Died upon the plains;
The fabled mammoths of the unrecorded ages
Are vast scaffoldings of dry insensate loam;
The panthers have learned caution
And move carefully among tall grasses to the water-
      hole;
And man lives on
Amid the senseless nihilism of the universe.

For there is one belief, one faith,
That is man's glory, his triumph, his immortality—
And that is his belief in life.
Man loves life,
And loving life, hates death,
And because of this he is great, he is glorious,
He is beautiful, and his beauty is everlasting.
He lives below the senseless stars
And writes his meanings in them.
He lives in fear, in toil,
In agony, and in unending tumult,
But if the blood foamed bubbling from his wounded
      lungs
At every breath he drew,
He would still love life more dearly
Than an end of breathing.
Dying, his eyes burn beautifully,
And the old hunger shines more fiercely in them—
He has endured all the hard and purposeless suffering,
And still he wants to live.

Thus it is impossible to scorn this creature.
For out of his strong belief in life,
This puny man made love.
At his best,
He *is* love.
Without him
There can be no love,
No hunger, no desire.
So this is man—the worst and best of him—
This frail and petty thing
Who lives his day
And dies like all the other animals,
And is forgotten.
And yet, he is immortal, too.
For both the good and evil that he does
Live after him.
Why, then, should any living man
Ally himself with death,
And, in his greed and blindness,
Batten on his brother's blood?

(Arranged in verse by John S. Barnes.)

"SAY NOT, THE STRUGGLE NAUGHT AVAILETH"

ARTHUR HUGH CLOUGH

Say not, the struggle naught availeth,
    The labor and the wounds are vain,
The enemy faints not, nor faileth,
    And as things have been they remain.

If hopes were dupes, fears may be liars;
    It may be, in yon smoke concealed,
Your comrades chase e'en now the fliers,
    And, but for you, possess the field.

For while the tired waves, vainly breaking,
    Seem here no painful inch to gain,
Far back, through creeks and inlets making,
    Comes silent, flooding in, the main.

And not by eastern windows only,
    When daylight comes, comes in the light;
In front, the sun climbs slow, how slowly!
    But westward, look, the land is bright.

"HE WOKE IN TERROR TO A SKY MORE BRIGHT" *

In *Epitaph for the Race of Man* (*IX*)

EDNA ST. VINCENT MILLAY

He woke in terror to a sky more bright
Than middle day; he heard the sick earth groan,
And ran to see the lazy-smoking cone
Of the fire-mountain, friendly to his sight
As his wife's hand, gone strange and full of fright;
Over his fleeing shoulder it was shown
Rolling its pitchy lake of scalding stone
Upon his house that had no feet for flight.
Where did he weep?   Where did he sit him down
And sorrow, with his head between his knees?
Where said the Race of Man, "Here let me drown"?
"Here let me die of hunger"?—"let me freeze"?
By nightfall he has built another town:
This boiling pot, this clearing in the trees.

*From *Wine from These Grapes*, published by Harper & Bros., copyright, 1928, by Edna St. Vincent Millay.

CHAPTER 9

OF HUMAN FREEDOM

Of old sat Freedom on the heights,
    The thunders breaking at her feet;
Above her shook the starry lights;
    She heard the torrents meet.

There in her place she did rejoice,
    Self-gathered in her prophet-mind,
But fragments of her mighty voice
    Came rolling on the wind.

Then stepped she down through town and field
    To mingle with the human race,
And part by part to men revealed
    The fulness of her face—

—Alfred Lord Tennyson.

"Man is born free, and everywhere he is in chains."

This splendid half-truth of Rousseau sums half the history and nine-tenths the sorrow of mankind. Seeming to be a matter-of-fact description of both man and history, it has motivated progressive social action—sometimes of the supremely violent type. Men have died for freedom—for others, and for themselves. Dostoevsky will tell us, in the present chapter, that a man may even choose suicide to prove the ultimate freedom of his own assertive will. Strange contradiction, yet having its own sad logic! The idea of freedom, in whatever guise, grips the spirit, testifying to its own ultimacy in establishing a pattern for living; assaulting even the conscience of God as He seeks to justify, through his spokesmen, His ways to men. It is a craving instinctive in all creatures, from Ariel to Caliban.

If men will die for freedom, they will also say that there is no significant life without it. That which ought to be cannot be impossible. What man ought to do he must be free to do. This must be true at two levels: that of political liberty and all the manifold "freedoms" defined by sorts of relationships between man and man (such as freedom of speech) and Nature and man (freedom from want): also it must be true at the fundamental level of metaphysics—the so-called freedom of the will. This chapter is almost entirely about the latter, that is, about philosophical freedom. This is basic, for unless man is free in this sense it is absurd to talk of or wish for liberty of action: the tyrant would no more be master than would be the slave. He would only be what he must be. But *can* he be different?

The terrible voice of Melville's Ahab takes up the question (as the readings open): "Is Ahab, Ahab? Is it I, God, or who, that lifts this arm? . . . By heaven, man, we are turned round and round in this world, like yonder windlass, and Fate is the handspike . . . Who's to doom, when the judge himself is dragged to the bar?" The *Rubaiyat* yields the same appalling refrain: "The Moving Finger writes; and having writ, Moves on. . . . Lift not your hands to It for help—for It As impotently moves as you or I." In *Death the Leveler* Shirley says of all men that "Early or late They stoop to fate," and to Hardy even sickness and death are but subalterns. "I, too," says Death, "am a slave." The real master is the Spinner of the Years who prepared the planet-shaking "Convergence of the Twain."

Ahab returns to testify that "Ahab is forever Ahab." Some things *must* be, according to Melville: the Fates require a specific sort of destiny for a man, and it is idle to think that anything else can be. "This whole act's immutably decreed." Here we have displayed one of the forms the conviction of determinism can take. "I act under orders."

When this doctrine is wedded to a theology, one invites the devastating irony of Voltaire: ". . . the Lisbon roads had been expressly created for the Anabaptist to be drowned in them." Furthermore, "all this is for the best" and "it was necessary that we should be free." By contrast Pope's magnificent hymn displays the reverent attitude and expresses the dualism that finds all determined except the will of man.

The passages from *Antigone* and *Oedipus the King* by Sophocles give regrettably only a suggestion of the great idea of Fate that pervades so much of Greek tragedy. "O pray not," the Chorus responds to Creon when he asks for a speedy end, "prayers are idle; from the doom Of fate for mortals refuge is there none." Oedipus, too, feels the "heavy hand" of fate. A modern echo is heard in the pathetic lament of Maugham's Philip to whom it seems that life lives itself. The illusion of free will cannot be escaped—but it is only an illusion. And so the futility of regret. (But isn't the regretting itself fore-doomed? Maugham here illustrates an inconsistency as old certainly as ancient stoicism: since all is determined, man might as well not cry over spilt milk: "all the forces of the universe were bent on spilling it." *And* on making me cry over it.)

Palmer probes deeply the natural resentment to the suggestion of complete human predictability. He displays the types of conditions under which we feel that prediction is something derogatory. This should be so, he reasons, only on the assumption that some value can attach to irrational caprice. The *more* I know of chess (and the more committed I am to winning), the more certainly an expert can tell what my next move will be.

In "The Dilemma of Determinism" James works out a pragmatic argument for freedom based upon the irrationality of judgments of regret, which, presumably, we all do make, since we really do not believe in thorough-going subjectivism. On deterministic grounds the only escape from pessimism is the abandonment of the judgment of regret. Otherwise we are left with the kind of universe, defined in James's words, "as a place in which what ought to be is impossible." Chance, and so open possibility, is real: the disconnectedness of things is harmless. This *is* a pluralistic, restless universe!

Dostoevsky in *Notes from Underground* passionately denies that there can be any formula for all our caprices. The one certain thing we cannot say about the universe is that it is rational. As for human life it is ". . . often worthless, yet it is life and not simply extracting square roots." For reason is simply reason, but will is *all* of life. And a man will preserve his most fantastic dreams just to prove he is still a man. He adds (in *The Possessed*) that man may also be a deliberate suicide to assert his will—to be a free man. It may well be, as James has said elsewhere, that my first act of freedom shall be to assert my freedom. Logan Pearsall Smith, who never loses his sense of "the whimsical and perilous charms of daily life," in his own personal fashion recalls the theme of the narrow-margined chance that invests our lives with the unexpected—the might-have-been.

To Melville also, now with high seriousness, Chance works at the Loom of Time. Chance, he says, works "within the right lines of necessity" yet has "the last featuring blow at events." But before this we have "chance, free will, and necessity—no wise incompatible—all interweavingly working together." The theme is left thus: not, either freedom or necessity, but freedom *and* necessity—and chance. "I, with my own hand I ply my own shuttle and weave my own destiny into these unalterable threads."

FROM THE SYMPHONY

In *Moby Dick*, Chapter CXXXII

HERMAN MELVILLE

But Ahab's glance was averted; like a blighted fruit tree he shook, and cast his last, cindered apple to the soil.

"What is it, what nameless, inscrutable, unearthly thing is it; what cozening, hidden lord and master, and cruel, remorseless emperor commands me; that against all natural lovings and longings, I so keep pushing, and crowding, and jamming myself on all the time; recklessly making me ready to do what in my own proper, natural heart, I durst not so much as dare? Is Ahab, Ahab? Is it I, God, or who, that lifts this arm? But if the great sun move not of himself; but is as an errand-boy in heaven; nor one single star can revolve, but by some invisible power; how then can this one small heart beat; this one small brain think thoughts; unless God does that beating, does that thinking, does that living, and not I. By heaven, man, we are turned round and round in this world, like yonder windlass, and Fate is the handspike. And all the time, lo! that smiling sky, and this unsounded sea! Look! see yon Albicore! who put it into him to chase and fang that flying-fish? Where do murderers go, man! Who's to doom, when the judge himself is dragged to the bar? But it is a mild, mild wind, and a mild looking sky; and the air smells now, as if it blew from a far-away meadow; they have been making hay somewhere under the slopes of the Andes, Starbuck, and the mowers are sleeping among the new mown hay. Sleeping? Aye, toil we how we may, we all sleep at last on the field.

RUBAIYAT, LXII-LXXIII

OMAR KHAYYAM

I must abjure the Balm of Life, I must,
Scared by some After-reckoning ta'en on trust,
   Or lured with Hope of some Diviner Drink,
To fill the Cup—when crumbled into Dust!

Oh threats of Hell and Hopes of Paradise!
One thing at least is certain—*This* Life flies;
   One thing is certain and the rest is Lies;
The Flower that once has blown for ever dies.

Strange, is it not? that of the myriads who
Before us passed the door of Darkness through,
   Not one returns to tell us of the Road,
Which to discover we must travel too.

The Revelations of Devout and Learned
Who rose before us, and as Prophets burned,
   Are all but Stories, which, awoke from Sleep
They told their comrades, and to Sleep returned.

I sent my Soul through the Invisible,
Some Letter of that After-life to spell:
   And by and by my Soul returned to me,
And answered "I myself am Heaven and Hell:"

Heaven but the Vision of fulfilled Desire,
And Hell the Shadow from a Soul on fire,
   Cast on the Darkness into which Ourselves,
So late emerged from, shall so soon expire.

We are no other than a moving row
Of Magic Shadow-shapes that come and go
   Round with the Sun-illumined Lantern held
In Midnight by the Master of the Show;

But helpless Pieces of the Game He plays
Upon this Chequer-board of Nights and Days;
   Hither and thither moves, and checks, and slays,
And one by one back in the Closet lays.

The Ball no question makes of Ayes and Noes,
But Here or There as strikes the Player goes;
   And He that tossed you down into the Field,
He knows about it all—He knows—HE knows!

The Moving Finger writes; and, having writ,
Moves on: nor all your Piety nor Wit
   Shall lure it back to cancel half a Line,
Nor all your Tears wash out a Word of it.

And that inverted Bowl they call the Sky,
Whereunder crawling cooped we live and die,
   Lift not your hands to *It* for help—for It
As impotently moves as you or I.

With Earth's first Clay They did the Last Man knead,
And there of the Last Harvest sowed the Seed:
   And the first Morning of Creation wrote
What the Last Dawn of Reckoning shall read.

                    (Edward Fitzgerald, tr.)

DEATH THE LEVELER

JAMES SHIRLEY

The glories of our blood and state
   Are shadows, not substantial things;
There is no armor against Fate;
   Death lays his icy hand on kings:
     Scepter and Crown
     Must tumble down,
And in the dust be equal made
With the poor crookèd scythe and spade.

Some men with swords may reap the field,
   And plant fresh laurels where they kill:
But their strong nerves at last must yield;
   They tame but one another still:
     Early or late
     They stoop to fate,
And must give up their murmuring breath
When they, pale captives, creep to death.

The garlands wither on your brow;
   Then boast no more your mighty deeds!
Upon Death's purple altar now
   See where the victor-victim bleeds.
     Your heads must come
     To the cold tomb:
Only the actions of the just
Smell sweet and blossom in their dust.

THE SUBALTERNS

THOMAS HARDY

I

"Poor wanderer," said the leaden sky,
  "I fain would lighten thee,
But there are laws in force on high
  Which say it must not be."

II

"I would not freeze thee, shorn one," cried
  The North, "knew I but how
To warm my breath, to slack my stride;
  But I am ruled as thou."

III

"Tomorrow I attack thee, wight,"
  Said Sickness. "Yet I swear
I bear thy little ark no spite,
  But am bid enter there."

IV

"Come hither, Son," I heard Death say;
  "I did not will a grave
Should end thy pilgrimage today,
  But I, too, am a slave!"

V

We smiled upon each other then,
  And life to me had less
Of that fell look it wore ere when
  They owned their passiveness.

THE CONVERGENCE OF THE TWAIN

Lines on the loss of the Titanic

THOMAS HARDY

I

In a solitude of the sea
Deep from human vanity,
And the Pride of Life that planned her, stilly couches she.

II

Steel chambers, late the pyres
Of her salamandrine fires,
Cold currents thrid, and turn to rhythmic tidal lyres.

III

Over the mirrors meant
To glass the opulent
The sea-worm crawls—grotesque, slimed, dumb, indifferent.

IV

Jewels in joy designed
To ravish the sensuous mind
Lie lightless, all their sparkles bleared and black and blind.

V

Dim moon-eyed fishes near
Gaze at the gilded gear
And query: "What does this vaingloriousness down here?" . . .

VI

Well: while was fashioning
This creature of cleaving wing,
The Immanent Will that stirs and urges everything

VII

Prepared a sinister mate
For her—so gaily great—
A Shape of Ice, for the time far and dissociate.

VIII

And as the smart ship grew
In stature, grace, and hue,
In shadowy silent distance grew the Iceberg too.

IX

Alien they seemed to be:
No mortal eye could see
The intimate welding of their later history,

X

Or sign that they were bent
By paths coincident
On being anon twin halves of one august event,

XI

Till the Spinner of the Years
Said "Now!"   And each one hears,
And consummation comes, and jars two hemispheres.

FROM "THE WHALE WATCH" AND "THE CHASE"

In *Moby Dick*

HERMAN MELVILLE

CHAPTER CXVII

The four whales slain that evening had died wide apart; one, far to windward; one, less distant, to leeward; one ahead; one astern. These last three were brought alongside ere nightfall; but the windward one could not be reached till morning; and the boat that had killed it lay by its side all night; and that boat was Ahab's.

The waif-pole was thrust upright into the dead whale's spout-hole and the lantern hanging from its top, cast a troubled flickering glare upon the black, glossy back, and far out upon the midnight waves, which gently chafed the whale's broad flank, like soft surf upon a beach.

Ahab and all his boat's crew seemed asleep but the Parsee; who crouching in the bow, sat watching the sharks, that spectrally played round the whale, and tapped the light cedar planks with their tails. A sound like the moaning in squadrons over Asphaltites of unforgiven ghosts of Gomorrah, ran shuddering through the air.

Started from his slumbers, Ahab, face to face, saw the Parsee; and hooped round by the gloom of the night they seemed the last men in a flooded world. "I have dreamed it again," said he.

"Of the hearses? Have I not said, old man, that neither hearse nor coffin can be thine?"

"And who are hearsed that die on the sea?"

"But I said, old man, that ere thou couldst die on this voyage, two hearses must verily be seen by thee on the sea; the first not made by mortal hands; and the visible wood of the last one must be grown in America."

"Aye, aye! a strange sight that, Parsee:—a hearse and its plumes floating over the ocean with the waves for the pall-bearers. Ha! Such a sight we shall not soon see."

"Believe it or not, thou canst not die till it be seen, old man."

"And what was that saying about thyself?"

"Though it come to the last, I shall still go before thee thy pilot."

"And when thou art so gone before—if that ever befall—then ere I can follow, thou must still appear to me, to pilot me still?— Was it not so? Well, then, did I believe all ye say, oh my pilot! I have here two pledges that I shall yet slay Moby-Dick and survive it."

"Take another pledge, old man," said the Parsee, as his eyes lighted up like fire-flies in the gloom—"Hemp only can kill thee."

"The gallows, ye mean.—I am immortal then, on land and on sea," cried Ahab, with a laugh of derision:—"Immortal on land and on sea!"

Both were silent again, as one man. The gray dawn came on, and the slumbering crew arose from the boat's bottom, and ere noon the dead whale was brought to the ship.

CHAPTER CXXXIV

. . . "Great God! but for one single instant show thyself," cried Starbuck; "never, never wilt thou capture him, old man—In Jesus' name no more of this, that's worse than devil's madness. Two days chased; twice stove to splinters; thy very leg once more snatched from under thee; thy evil shadow gone—all good angels mobbing thee with warnings:—what more wouldst thou have?—Shall we keep chasing this murderous fish till he swamps the last man? Shall we be dragged by him to the bottom of the sea? Shall we be towed by him to the infernal world? Oh, oh,—Impiety and blasphemy to hunt him more!"

"Starbuck, of late I've felt strangely moved to thee; ever since that hour we both saw—thou know'st what, in one another's eyes. But in this matter of the whale, be the front of thy face to me as the palm of this hand—a lipless, unfeatured blank. Ahab is for ever Ahab, man. This whole act's immutably decreed. 'Twas re-hearsed by thee and me a billion years before this ocean rolled. Fool! I am the Fates' lieutenant; I act under orders. Look thou, underling! that thou obeyest mine.—Stand round me, men. Ye see an old man cut down to the stump; lean-ing on a shivered lance; propped up on a lonely foot. 'Tis Ahab—his body's part; but Ahab's soul's a centipede, that moves upon a hundred legs. I feel strained, half-stranded, as ropes that tow dismasted frigates in a gale; and I may look so. But ere I break, ye'll hear me crack; and till ye hear *that*, know that Ahab's hawser tows his purpose yet. Believe ye, men, in the things called omens? Then laugh aloud, and cry encore! For ere they drown, drowning things will twice rise to the surface; then rise again, to sink for evermore. So with Moby-Dick—two days he's floated—to-morrow will be the third. Aye, men, he'll rise once more,—but only to spout his last! D'ye feel brave, men, brave?"

"As fearless fire," cried Stubb.

"And as mechanical," muttered Ahab. Then as the men went forward, he mut-tered on: "The things called omens! And yesterday I talked the same to Starbuck there, concerning my broken boat. Oh! how valiantly I seek to drive out of others' hearts what's clinched so fast in mine!—The Parsee—the Parsee!—gone, gone? and he was to go before:—but still was to be seen again ere I could perish—How's that?— There's a riddle now might baffle all the lawyers backed by the ghosts of the whole line of judges:—like a hawk's beak it pecks my brain. *I'll, I'll* solve it, though!"

When dusk descended, the whale was still in sight to leeward.

So once more the sail was shortened, and everything passed nearly as on the previous night; only, the sound of hammers, and the hum of the grindstone was heard till nearly daylight, as the men toiled by lanterns in the complete and careful rigging of the spare boats and sharpening their fresh weapons for the morrow. Meantime, of the broken keel of Ahab's wrecked craft the carpenter made him another leg; while still as on the night before, slouched Ahab stood fixed within his scuttle; his hid, heliotrope glance anticipatingly gone backward on its dial; sat due eastward for the earliest sun. . . .

CHAPTER CXXXV

. . . The boats had not gone very far, when by a signal from the mastheads— a downward pointed arm, Ahab knew that the whale had sounded; but intending to be near him at the next rising, he held on his way a little sideways from the vessel; the becharmed crew maintaining the profoundest silence, as the head-beat waves hammered and hammered against the opposing bow.

"Drive, drive in your nails, oh ye waves! to their uttermost heads drive them in! ye but strike a thing without a lid; and no coffin and no hearse can be mine:—and hemp only can kill me! Ha! ha!"

Suddenly the waters around them slowly swelled in broad circles; then quickly upheaved, as if sideways sliding from a submerged berg of ice, swiftly rising to the surface. A low rumbling sound was heard; a subterraneous hum; and then all held their breaths; as bedraggled with trailing ropes, and harpoons, and lances, a vast form shot lengthwise, but obliquely from the sea. Shrouded in a thin drooping veil of mist, it hovered for a moment in the rainbowed air; and then fell swamping back into the deep. Crushed thirty feet upwards, the waters flashed for an instant like heaps of fountains, then brokenly sank in a shower of flakes, leaving the circling surface creamed like new milk round the marble trunk of the whale.

"Give way!" cried Ahab to the oarsmen, and the boats darted forward to the attack; but maddened by yesterday's fresh irons that corroded in him, Moby-Dick seemed combinedly possessed by all the angels that fell from heaven. The wide tiers of welded tendons overspreading his broad white forehead, beneath the transparent skin, looked knitted together; as head on, he came churning his tail among the boats; and once more flailed them apart; spilling out the irons and lances from the two mates' boats, and dashing in one side of the upper part of their bows, but leaving Ahab's almost without a scar.

While Daggoo and Queequeg were stopping the strained planks; and as the whale swimming out from them, turned, and showed one entire flank as he shot by them again; at that moment a quick cry went up. Lashed round and round to the fish's back; pinioned in the turns upon turns in which, during the past night, the whale had reeled the involutions of the lines around him, the half torn body of the Parsee was seen; his sable raiment frayed to shreds; his distended eyes turned full upon old Ahab.

The harpoon dropped from his hand.

"Befooled, befooled!"—drawing in a long lean breath—"Aye, Parsee! I see thee again.—Aye, and thou goest before; and this, *this* then is the hearse that thou didst promise. But I hold thee to the last letter of thy word. Where is the second hearse? Away, mates, to the ship! those boats are useless now; repair them if ye can in time, and return to me; if not, Ahab is enough to die—Down, men! the first thing that but offers to jump from this boat I stand in, that thing I harpoon. Ye are not other men, but my arms and my legs; and so obey me.—Where's the whale? gone down again?"

But he looked too nigh the boat; for as if bent upon escaping with the corpse he bore, and as if the particular place of the last encounter had been a stage in his leeward voyage, Moby-Dick was now again steadily swimming forward; and had almost passed the ship,—which thus far had been sailing in the contrary direction to him, though for the present her headway had been stopped. He seemed swimming with his utmost velocity, and now only intent upon pursuing his own straight path in the sea.

"Oh! Ahab," cried Starbuck, "not too late is it, even now, the third day, to desist. See! Moby-Dick seeks thee not. It is thou, thou, that madly seekest him!" . . .

From the ship's bows, nearly all the seamen now hung inactive; hammers, bits of plank, lances, and harpoons, mechanically retained in their hands, just as they had darted from their various employments; all their enchanted eyes intent upon the whale, which from side to side strangely vibrating his predestinating head, sent a broad band of overspreading semicircular foam before him as he rushed. Retribution, swift vengeance, eternal malice were in his whole aspect, and spite of all that mortal man could do, the solid white buttress of his forehead smote the ship's starboard bow, till men and timbers reeled. Some fell flat upon their faces. Like dislodged trucks, the heads of the harpooneers aloft shook on their bull-like necks. Through the breach, they heard the waters pour, as mountain torrents down a flume.

"The ship! The hearse!—the second hearse!" cried Ahab from the boat; "its wood could only be American!"

Diving beneath the settling ship, the whale ran quivering along its keel; but turning under water, swiftly shot to the surface again, far off the other bow, but within a few yards of Ahab's boat, where, for a time, he lay quiescent.

"I turn my body from the sun. What ho, Tashtego! let me hear thy hammer. Oh! ye three unsurrendered spires of mine; thou uncracked keel; the only god-bullied hull; thou firm deck, and haughty helm, and Pole-pointed prow,—death-glorious ship! must ye then perish, and without me? Am I cut off from the last fond pride of meanest shipwrecked captains? Oh, lonely death on lonely life! Oh, now I feel my topmost greatness lies in my topmost grief! Ho, ho! from all your furthest bounds, pour ye now in, ye bold billows of my whole foregone life, and top this one piled comber of my death! Towards thee I roll, thou all-destroying but unconquering whale; to the last I grapple with thee; from hell's heart I stab at thee; for hate's sake I spit my last breath at thee. Sink all coffins and hearses to one common pool! and since neither can be mine, let me then tow to pieces, while still chasing thee, though tied to thee, thou damned whale! *Thus I give up the spear!*"

The harpoon was darted; the stricken whale flew forward; with igniting velocity the line ran through the groove;—ran foul. Ahab stooped to clear it; he did clear it; but the flying turn caught him round the neck, and voicelessly as Turkish mutes bowstring their victim, he was shot out of the boat, ere the crew knew he was gone. Next instant, the heavy eye-splice in the rope's final end flew out of the stark-empty tub, knocked down an oarsman, and smiting the sea, disappeared in its depths.

For an instant, the tranced boat's crew stood still; then turned. "The ship? Great God, where is the ship?" Soon they through dim, bewildering mediums saw her sidelong fading phantom, as in the gaseous Fata Morgana; only the uppermost masts out of water; while fixed by infatuation, or fidelity, or fate, to their once lofty perches, the pagan harpooneers still maintained their sinking lookouts on the sea. And now, concentric circles seized the lone boat itself, and all its crew, and each floating oar, and every lance-pole, and spinning, animate and inanimate, all round and round in one vortex, carried the smallest chip of the Pequod out of sight.

But as the last whelmings intermixingly poured themselves over the sunken head of the Indian at the mainmast, leaving a few inches of the erect spar yet visible, together with long streaming yards of the flag, which calmly undulated, with ironical coincidings, over the destroying billows they almost touched;—at that instant, a red arm and a hammer hovered backwardly uplifted in the open air, in the act of nailing the flag faster and yet faster to the subsiding spar. A sky-hawk that tauntingly had followed the main-truck downwards from its natural home among the stars, pecking at the flag, and incommoding Tashtego there; this bird now chanced to intercept its broad fluttering wings between the hammer and the wood; and simultaneously feeling that ethereal thrill, the submerged savage beneath, in his death-gasp, kept his hammer frozen there; and so the bird of heaven, with archangelic shrieks, and his imperial beak thrust upwards, and his whole captive form folded in the flag of Ahab, went down with his ship, which, like Satan, would not sink to hell till she had dragged a living part of heaven along with her, and helmeted herself with it.

Now small fowls flew screaming over the yet yawning gulf; a sullen white surf beat against its steep sides; then all collapsed, and the great shroud of the sea rolled on as it rolled five thousand years ago.

CANDIDE, Chapter 5

VOLTAIRE

Storm, Shipwreck, earthquake, and what happened
to Dr. Pangloss, to Candide and the Anabaptist Jacques

Half the enfeebled passengers, suffering from that inconceivable anguish which the rolling of a ship causes in the nerves and in all the humors of bodies shaken in contrary directions, did not retain strength enough even to trouble about the danger.   The other half screamed and prayed; the sails were torn, the masts broken, the vessel leaking.   Those worked who could, no one cooperated, no one commanded.   The Anabaptist tried to help the crew a little; he was on the main-deck; a furious sailor struck him violently and stretched him on the deck: but the blow he delivered gave him so violent a shock that he fell head-first out of the ship. He remained hanging and clinging to part of the broken mast.   The good Jacques ran to his aid, helped him to climb back, and from the effort he made was flung into the sea in full view of the sailor, who allowed him to drown without condescending even to look at him.   Candide came up, saw his benefactor reappear for a moment and then be engulfed for ever.   He tried to throw himself after him into the sea; he was prevented by the philosopher Pangloss, who proved to him that the Lisbon roads had been expressly created for the Anabaptist to be drowned in them.   While he was proving this *a priori,* the vessel sank, and every one perished except Pangloss, Candide and the brutal sailor who had drowned the virtuous Anabaptist; the blackguard swam successfully to the shore and Pangloss and Candide were carried there on a plank.

When they had recovered a little, they walked towards Lisbon; they had a little money by the help of which they hoped to be saved from hunger after having escaped the storm.

Weeping the death of their benefactor, they had scarcely set foot in the town when they felt the earth tremble under their feet; the sea rose in foaming masses in the port and smashed the ships which rode at anchor.   Whirlwinds of flame and ashes covered the streets and squares; the houses collapsed, the roofs were thrown upon the foundations, and the foundations were scattered; thirty thousand inhabitants of every age and both sexes were crushed under the ruins.   Whistling and swearing, the sailor said:

"There'll be something to pick up here."

"What can be the sufficient reason for this phenomenon?" said Pangloss.

"It is the last day!" cried Candide.

The sailor immediately ran among the debris, dared death to find money, found it, seized it, got drunk, and having slept off his wine, purchased the favors of the first woman of good will he met on the ruins of the houses and among the dead and dying.   Pangloss, however, pulled him by the sleeve.

"My friend," said he, "this is not well, you are disregarding universal reason, you choose the wrong time."

"Blood and 'ounds!" he retorted, "I am a sailor and I was born in Batavia; four times have I stamped on the crucifix during four voyages to Japan; you have found the right man for your universal reason!"

Candide had been hurt by some falling stones; he lay in the street covered with debris.   He said to Pangloss:

"Alas!   Get me a little wine and oil; I am dying."

"This earthquake is not a new thing," replied Pangloss.   "The town of Lima felt the same shocks in America last year; similar causes produce similar effects; there must certainly be a train of sulphur underground from Lima to Lisbon."

"Nothing is more probable," replied Candide; "but for God's sake, a little oil and wine."

"What do you mean, probable?" replied the philosopher; "I maintain that it is proved."

Candide lost consciousness, and Pangloss brought him a little water from a neighboring fountain.

Next day, they found a little food as they wandered among the ruins and regained a little strength. Afterwards they worked like others to help the inhabitants who had escaped death. Some citizens they had assisted gave them as good a dinner as could be expected in such a disaster; true, it was a dreary meal; the hosts watered their bread with their tears, but Pangloss consoled them by assuring them that things could not be otherwise.

"For," said he, "all this is for the best; for, if there is a volcano at Lisbon, it cannot be anywhere else; for it is impossible that things should not be where they are; for all is well."

A little dark man, a familiar of the Inquisition, who sat beside him, politely took up the conversation, and said:

"Apparently you do not believe in original sin; for, if everything is for the best, there was neither fall nor punishment."

"I most humbly beg your excellency's pardon," replied Pangloss, still more politely, "for the fall of man and the curse necessarily entered into the best of all possible worlds."

"Then you do not believe in freewill?" said the familiar.

"Your excellency will pardon me," said Pangloss; "freewill can exist with absolute necessity; for it was necessary that we should be free; for in short, limited will . . ."

Pangloss was in the middle of his phrase when the familiar nodded to his armed attendant who was pouring out port or Oporto wine for him.

(Richard Aldington, tr.)

THE UNIVERSAL PRAYER

ALEXANDER POPE

Father of all! in ev'ry age,
    In every clime adored,
By saint, by savage, and by sage,
    Jehovah, Jove, or Lord!

Thou Great First Cause, least understood!
    Who all my sense confined
To know but this, that thou art good,
    And that myself am blind;

Yet gave me in this dark estate,
    To see the good from ill:
And binding nature fast in fate,
    Left free the human will.

What conscience dictates to be done,
　Or warns me not to do,
This teach me more than hell to shun,
　That, more than heaven pursue.

What blessings thy free bounty gives
　Let me not cast away;
For God is paid when man receives:
　T' enjoy is to obey.

Yet not to earth's contracted span
　Thy goodness let me bound,
Or think thee Lord alone of man,
　When thousand worlds are round:

Let not this weak, unknowing hand
　Presume thy bolts to throw,
And deal damnation round the land
　On each I judge thy foe.

If I am right, thy grace impart
　Still in the right to stay:
If I am wrong, oh teach my heart
　To find that better way.

Save me alike from foolish pride,
　Or impious discontent,
At aught thy wisdom has denied,
　Or aught thy goodness lent.

Teach me to feel another's woe,
　To hide the fault I see;
That mercy I to others show,
　That mercy show to me.

Mean though I am, not wholly so,
　Since quickened by thy breath:
Oh lead me wheresoe'er I go,
　Through this day's life or death.

This day be bread and peace my lot:
　All else beneath the sun,
Thou know'st if best bestowed or not,
　And let thy will be done.

To Thee, whose temple is all space,
　Whose altar, earth, sea, skies,
One chorus let all being raise;
　All nature's incense rise!

ANTIGONE, lines 607-624, 872-928
SOPHOCLES

CHORUS

Thy might, O Zeus, what mortal power can quell?
Not sleep that lays all else beneath its spell,
Nor moons that never tire: untouched by Time,
    Throned in the dazzling light
    That crowns Olympus' height,
Thou reignest King, omnipotent, sublime.

    Past, present, and to be,
    All bow to thy decree,
    All that exceeds the mean by Fate
    Is punished, Love or Hate.

Hope flits about on never-wearying wings;
Profit to some, to some light loves she brings,
But no man knoweth how her gifts may turn,
Till 'neath his feet the treacherous ashes burn.
Sure 'twas a sage inspired that spake this word;
    If evil good appear
    To any, Fate is near;
And brief the respite from her flaming sword.

.   .   .   .

CHORUS

Religion has her claims, 'tis true,
Let rites be paid when rites are due.
Yet is it ill to disobey
The powers who hold by might the sway.
Thou hast withstood authority,
A self-willed rebel, thou must die.

ANTIGONE

Unwept, unwed, unfriended, hence I go,
    No longer may I see the day's bright eye;
Not one friend left to share my bitter woe,
    And o'er my ashes heave one passing sigh.

CREON

If wail and lamentation aught availed
To stave off death, I trow they'd never end.
Away with her, and having walled her up
In a rock-vaulted tomb, as I ordained,
Leave her alone at liberty to die,
Or, if she choose, to live in solitude,
The tomb her dwelling. We in either case
Are guiltless as concerns this maiden's blood.
Only on earth no lodging shall she find.

ANTIGONE

O grave, O bridal bower, O prison house
Hewn from the rock, my everlasting home,
Whither I go to join the mighty host
Of kinsfolk, Persephassa's guests long dead,
The last of all, of all most miserable,
I pass, my destined span of years cut short.
And yet good hope is mine that I shall find
A welcome from my sire, a welcome too,
From thee, my mother, and my brother dear;
For with these hands, I laved and decked your limbs
In death, and poured libations on your grave.
And last, my Polyneices, unto thee
I paid due rites, and this my recompense!
Yet am I justified in wisdom's eyes.
For even had it been some child of mine,
Or husband moldering in death's decay,
I had not wrought this deed despite the State.
What is the law I call in aid? 'Tis thus
I argue. Had it been a husband dead
I might have wed another, and have borne
Another child, to take the dead child's place.
But, now my sire and mother both are dead,
No second brother can be born for me.
Thus by the law of conscience I was led
To honor thee, dear brother, and was judged
By Creon guilty of a heinous crime.
And now he drags me like a criminal,
A bride unwed, amerced of marriage-song
And marriage-bed and joys of motherhood,
By friends deserted to a living grave.
What ordinance of heaven have I transgressed?
Hereafter can I look to any god
For succour, call on any man for help?
Alas, my piety is impious deemed.
Well, if such justice is approved of heaven,
I shall be taught by suffering my sin;
But if the sin is theirs, O may they suffer
No worse ills than the wrongs they do to me!
                                   (F. Storr, tr.)

OEDIPUS THE KING, lines 771-833, 1176-1231

SOPHOCLES

OEDIPUS

And thou shalt not be frustrate of thy wish,
Now my imaginings have gone so far.
Who has a higher claim than thou to hear
My tale of dire adventures? Listen then.

My sire was Polybus of Corinth, and
My mother Meropè, a Dorian;
And I was held the foremost citizen,
Till a strange thing befell me, strange indeed,
Yet scarce deserving all the heat it stirred.
A roisterer at some banquet, flown with wine,
Shouted "Thou art no true son of thy sire."
It irked me, but I stomached for the nonce
The insult; on the morrow I sought out
My mother and my sire and questioned them.
They were indignant at the random slur
Cast on my parentage and did their best
To comfort me, but still the venomed barb
Rankled, for still the scandal spread and grew.
So privily without their leave I went
To Delphi, and Apollo sent me back
Balked of the knowledge that I came to seek.
But other grievous things he prophesied,
Woes, lamentations, mourning, portents dire;
To wit I should defile my mother's bed
And raise up seed too loathsome to behold,
And slay the father from whose loins I sprang.
Warned by the oracle I turned and fled,—
And Corinth henceforth was to me unknown
Save as I knew its region by the stars;—
Whither, I cared not, so I never might
Behold my doom of infamy fulfilled.
And in my wanderings I reached the place
Where, as thy story runs, the king was slain.
Then, lady,—thou shalt hear the very truth—
As I drew near the triple-branching roads,
A herald met me and a man who sat
In a car drawn by colts—as in thy tale—
The man in front and the old man himself
Threatened to thrust me rudely from the path,
Then jostled by the charioteer in wrath
I struck him, and the old man, seeing this,
Watched till I passed and from his car brought down
Full on my head the double-pointed goad.
   Yet was I quits with him and more; one stroke
Of my good staff sufficed to fling him clean
Out of the chariot seat and laid him prone.
And so I slew them every one.   But if
Betwixt this stranger there was aught in common
With Laïus, who more miserable than I,
What mortal could you find more god-abhorred?
Wretch whom no sojourner, no citizen
May harbor or address, whom all are bound
To harry from their homes.   And this same curse
Was laid on me, and laid by none but me.
Yea with these hands all gory I pollute
The bed of him I slew.   Say, am I vile?

Am I not utterly unclean, a wretch
Doomed to be banished, and in banishment
Forgo the sight of all my dearest ones,
And never tread again my native earth;
Or else to wed my mother and slay my sire,
Polybus, who begat me and upreared?
If one should say, this is the handiwork
Of some inhuman power, who could blame
His judgment?   But, ye pure and awful gods,
Forbid, forbid that I should see that day!
May I be blotted out from living men
Ere such a plague spot set on me its brand!

.   .   .   .

HERDSMAN

'Twas told that he should slay his sire.

OEDIPUS

Why didst thou give it then to this old man?

HERDSMAN

Through pity, master, for the babe.   I thought
He'd take it to the country whence he came;
But he preserved it for the worst of woes.
For if thou art in sooth what this man saith,
God pity thee! thou wast to misery born.

OEDIPUS

Ah me! ah me! all brought to pass, all true!
O light, may I behold thee nevermore!
I stand a wretch, in birth, in wedlock cursed,
A parricide, incestuous, triply cursed.

[*Exit* OEDIPUS

CHORUS

        Races of mortal man
        Whose life is but a span,
I count ye but the shadow of a shade!
        For he who most doth know
        Of bliss, hath but the show;
A moment, and the visions pale and fade.
Thy fall, O Oedipus, thy piteous fall
Warns me none born of woman blest to call.

        For he of marksmen best,
        O Zeus, outshot the rest,
And won the prize supreme of wealth and power.
        By him the vulture maid
        Was quelled, her witchery laid;
He rose our savior and the land's strong tower.

We hailed thee king and from that day adored
Of mighty Thebes the universal lord.

O heavy hand of fate!
Who now more desolate,
Whose tale more sad than thine, whose lot more dire?
O Oedipus, discrownèd head,
Thy cradle was thy marriage bed;
One harborage sufficed for son and sire.
How could the soil thy father eared so long
Endure to bear in silence such a wrong?

All-seeing Time hath caught
Guilt, and to justice brought
The son and sire commingled in one bed.
O child of Laïus' ill-starred race
Would I had ne'er beheld thy face!
I raise for thee a dirge as o'er the dead.
Yet, sooth to say, through thee I drew new breath,
And now through thee I feel a second death.

Enter SECOND MESSENGER.

SECOND MESSENGER

Most grave and reverend senators of Thebes,
What deeds ye soon must hear, what sights behold
How will ye mourn, if, true-born patriots,
Ye reverence still the race of Labdacus!
Not Ister nor all Phasis' flood, I ween,
Could wash away the blood-stains from this house,
The ills it shrouds or soon will bring to light,
Ills wrought of malice, not unwittingly,
The worst to bear are self-inflicted wounds.

FROM OF HUMAN BONDAGE, Chapter 67 *

W. SOMERSET MAUGHAM

Macalister was a big-boned fellow, much too short for his width, with a large, fleshy face and a soft voice. He was a student of Kant and judged everything from the standpoint of pure reason. He was fond of expounding his doctrines. Philip listened with excited interest. He had long come to the conclusion that nothing amused him more than metaphysics, but he was not so sure of their efficacy in the affairs of life. The neat little system which he had formed as the result of his meditations at Blackstable had not been of conspicuous use during his infatuation for Mildred. He could not be positive that reason was much help in the conduct of life. It seemed to him that life lived itself. He remembered very vividly the violence of the emotion which had possessed him and his inability, as if he were tied down to the ground with ropes, to react against it. He read many wise things in books, but he could only judge from his own experience (he did not know

* From: *Of Human Bondage* by W. Somerset Maugham. Copyright 1917 by Doubleday & Company, Inc.

whether he was different from other people); he did not calculate the pros and cons of an action, the benefits which must befall him if he did it, the harm which might result from the omission; but his whole being was urged on irresistibly. He did not act with a part of himself but altogether. The power that possessed him seemed to have nothing to do with reason: all that reason did was to point out the methods of obtaining what his whole soul was striving for.

Macalister reminded him of the Categorical Imperative.

"Act so that every action of yours should be capable of becoming a universal rule of action for all men."

"That seems to me perfect nonsense," said Philip.

"You're a bold man to say that of anything stated by Emanuel Kant," retorted Macalister.

"Why? Reverence for what somebody said is a stultifying quality: there's a damned sight too much reverence in the world. Kant thought things not because they were true, but because he was Kant."

"Well, what is your objection to the Categorical Imperative?"

(They talked as though the fate of empires were in the balance.)

"It suggests that one can choose one's course by an effort of will. And it suggests that reason is the surest guide. Why should its dictates be any better than those of passion? They're different. That's all."

"You seem to be a contented slave of your passions."

"A slave because I can't help myself, but not a contented one," laughed Philip.

While he spoke he thought of that hot madness which had driven him in pursuit of Mildred. He remembered how he had chafed against it and how he had felt the degradation of it.

"Thank God, I'm free from all that now," he thought.

And yet even as he said it he was not quite sure whether he spoke sincerely. When he was under the influence of passion he had felt a singular vigor, and his mind had worked with unwonted force. He was more alive, there was an excitement in sheer being, an eager vehemence of soul, which made life now a trifle dull. For all the misery he had endured there was a compensation in that sense of rushing, overwhelming existence.

But Philip's unlucky words engaged him in a discussion on the freedom of the will, and Macalister, with his well-stored memory, brought out argument after argument. He had a mind that delighted in dialectics, and he forced Philip to contradict himself; he pushed him into corners from which he could only escape by damaging concessions; he tripped him up with logic and battered him with authorities.

At last Philip said:

"Well, I can't say anything about other people. I can only speak for myself. The illusion of free will is so strong in my mind that I can't get away from it, but I believe it is only an illusion. But it is an illusion which is one of the strongest motives of my actions. Before I do anything I feel that I have choice, and that influences what I do; but afterwards, when the thing is done, I believe that it was inevitable from all eternity."

"What do you deduce from that?" asked Hayward.

"Why, merely the futility of regret. It's no good crying over spilt milk, because all the forces of the universe were bent on spilling it."

FROM THE IMPROBABILITY OF FREEDOM

In *The Problem of Freedom*

GEORGE HERBERT PALMER

V

But beside the disproof of libertarianism furnished by scientific observation and the nature of the human mind, there remains a third class of evidence which has carried even wider popular conviction. Belief in determinism is embedded in the structure of society. The predictability of conduct is a condition of man's associating with man. We have already seen how difficult life would be in a physical world where calculation was subject to dual possibilities. Figure the situation. I do not know whether the sun will rise tomorrow. It did rise today. I noticed it yesterday, and people tell me it has risen for many years. But after all, if the causal sequence is not tight, why expect that coming times will resemble past? It is grounded expediency which makes our world a fit place to dwell in. Equally true is this of the world of men. I at least do not see how we could live together had we no power to forecast each other's conduct. My act has reference to yours. In proportion as yours is uncertain, mine must be thrown out of gear. I am a teacher; would my class assemble at nine o'clock if they could not reckon on my presence? Should I myself appear if I had no reasonable expectation of finding them? How could commerce proceed, or travel, churches, theaters, courts, or governments, if the act of one man could not be coordinated with fair certainty to that of another?

It may be said that this certainty is only fair, that members of my class surprise me by their absence every day. But I should not be surprised if I regarded them as beings endowed with ambiguous futures, as likely therefore to act in one way as another, beings whose conduct not even divine wisdom could foresee. No, the uncertainty here is not unlike that felt in watching an approaching storm-cloud. Will it rain? Undoubtedly, if such and such conditions are present. And are they? Of this we have only partial knowledge. In both cases, connections may be recognized as unalterably fixed and yet about the result our judgment may waver. All the determinist asserts is that given antecedents are followed by invariable consequents even in the very complex circumstances of human intercourse; that the more fully these antecedents are understood, the more confidently we can predict results; and that regularly among friends and acquaintances they are in fact so fully understood that here we have something like a working certitude. All this predictability of conduct he finds incompatible with the libertarian fancy of multiple possibilities. Hume has so powerful a passage comparing our assurance of personal and physical events that I transcribe it entire:—

"When we consider how aptly natural and moral evidence unite together and form only one chain of argument, we shall make no scruple to allow that they are of the same nature and derived from the same principles. A prisoner who has neither money nor interest discovers the impossibility of his escape as well when he considers the obstinacy of the gaoler as the walls and bars with which he is surrounded; and in all attempts for his freedom chooses rather to work upon the stone and iron of the one than upon the inflexible nature of the other. The same person, when conducted to the scaffold, foresees his death as certainly from the constancy and fidelity of his guards as from the operation of the axe or wheel. His mind runs along a certain train of ideals: the refusal of the soldiers to consent to his escape; the action of the executioner; the separation of the head and body; bleeding, convulsive motions, and death. Here is a connected chain of natural causes and voluntary actions; but the mind feels no difference between them in passing from one link to another, nor is less certain of the future event than if it were connected with the objects present to the memory or senses by a train of causes, cemented together by what we are pleased to call a physical necessity. The same experienced union has the same effect on the mind, whether the united objects be motives, volition, and actions, or figure and motion. We may change the names of things, but their nature and their operation on the understanding never change.

"Were a man whom I know to be honest and opulent and with whom I lived in intimate friendship, to come to my house, where I am surrounded with my servants, I rest assured that he is not to stab me before he leaves it in order to rob me of my silver standish; and I no more suspect this event than the falling of the house itself, which is new and solidly built and founded. *But he may have been seized with a sudden and unknown frenzy.* So may a sudden earthquake arise, and shake and tumble my house about my ears. I shall therefore change the suppositions. I shall say that I know with certainty that he is not to put his hand into the fire and hold it there till it be consumed; and this event I think I can foretell with the same assurance as if he throw himself out of the window, and meet with no obstruction, he will not remain a moment suspended in the air. No suspicion of an unknown frenzy can give the least possibility to the former event, which is so contrary to all the known principles of human nature. A man who at noon leaves his purse full of gold on the pavement of Charing Cross may as well expect that it will fly away like a feather as that he will find it untouched an hour after. About one half of human reasonings contain inferences of a similar nature attended with more or less of certainty, proportioned to our experience of the usual conduct of mankind in each particular situation." (Essay XXXIX, sec. VIII.)

VI

Possibly we may find such prediction offensive, and feel that if it applies to us our character is impaired. Were I completely a person, I may imagine, prediction of my acts would be impossible. So long as I am but a creature of habit, not widely different from the objects about me, of course I can be predicted. In all of us there are large tracts which have not come under personal control. Within this region, it may be thought, prediction works. But in whatever degree we conceive a human being as a person we remove him from the sphere of prediction. Prediction is something derogatory. As we honor the dignity of mankind we must hold hard to a belief in freedom.

I remember how surprised I was years ago on suddenly discovering that this sort of talk expresses exactly the opposite of the truth. Like everybody else, I grew up a libertarian. When a young man, I was fond of playing chess. One day as I was deliberating over a move in the middle of a game I suddenly asked myself whether an expert standing beside me could predict what that move would be. Not, I saw, unless I had a past history as a chess player with which he was familiar. If I were a beginner, he could not tell whether I would advance a pawn three squares, or move a castle aslant, or expose my queen to capture. All these, and a multitude of other possibilities would be open to me and therefore to his prediction. But if I had a knowledge of the game, these possibilities would be closed. And if I were an accomplished player, the expert at my elbow might whisper to his neighbor, "There is only one move he can make. He must attack his opponent's king with his black bishop." As I then, without hearing the remark, proceed to make that move, should I feel belittled to have the expert announce that it was foreknown? Should I feel that having supposed my act to be one of freedom, I had now been deprived of something precious and myself degraded into a mere thing? On the contrary, I should probably feel much flattered and congratulate myself on being, and being known to be, a player guided by law. Evidently, then, as personality enlarges, conduct becomes more predictable. That was the impressive lesson taught me by this striking case. An endowment of freedom, where all things are equally likely, is no blessing but a sign of incapacity. We should desire to be rid of it and should count ourselves well off when we come under such necessity as is here described.

But how widely does this principle obtain? Apparently throughout human intercourse. Suppose, for example, that John and I were summoned to report on an affair in which we two were engaged last week, and I should say, "Since John is a free person, there is no telling what account he will give. It may be the truth, or an utterly false tale. We cannot predict." He certainly would not think me complimentary; nor, on the other hand, would he resent my saying that there was only one statement open to him, that nothing but the truth could issue from his lips. That is in reality what we all desire, to be such truthful persons that we simply cannot tell a lie, such courteous persons that no word of querulousness ever escapes us. The more thoroughly we are narrowed down to such single issues, the prouder we justly are.

It may be suspected, however, that what we like here is not the escape from freedom but the attribution to us of some praiseworthy act. Let us examine then an indifferent case, into which no praise or blame enters. Suppose John and I have been living together intimately for a long time, and one morning as I am dressing, another acquaintance enters the room. To him John whispers, "Observe him! When he comes to his coat, he will put in his left arm first." If John should tell me of this after I was dressed, I should not be annoyed. I should smile and say, "How pleasant, my dear fellow, to have you know me rather better than I know myself."

Yet I do not profess that it is always agreeable to be predicted. In the last case prediction would be offensively intimate if offered by a stranger. And for a still more questionable case take the following: When I am beginning my lecture some morning I notice that Mr. Smith is absent. I tell the class that he will appear at four minutes past nine, on entering will pass in front of my desk, waving his hand as he goes, will advance a dozen steps beyond, and then turn back to take a seat beside the door. When he has gone through this performance, I address him thus: "Mr. Smith, you evidently think yourself a free man and bear yourself with a good deal of confidence. But let me say that you are completely determined. In each of your late movements there was only a single issue open to you, and I foretold it. To all this company I explained precisely what you were going to do." Would he not feel uncomfortable, as if wound up with a spring to which somebody else held the key?

Probably what strikes us here as uncanny in contrast with the preceding cases, is that Mr. Smith's actions do not seem his own, but to have been so shaped by outside influence as to be comprehensible without regard to himself. Remove suspicion of this sort, and the annoyance ceases. Seeing Mr. Smith's perplexity, I hasten to add, "Do not imagine that you have been calculated like an eclipse. It is yourself that has interested me. I knew your wish to be present today and that you would come as promptly as possible. But the train does not arrive, I noticed, till a few minutes past nine. Your dislike, too, of bad air in lecture-rooms is well known. Before you took your seat I expected you to make sure that the window was open, which, with your poor sight, you cannot ascertain without pressing forward to examine; and I recalled the deprecatory gesture with which you usually pass my desk. Your seat is by the door, and to that you would naturally return when secure of proper ventilation." In all likelihood remarks of this kind would put an end to his annoyance; for what troubles us is not prediction, but the possibility that prediction is based on something external to ourselves. Let it be once seen that forecast comes from observation of established character, and we are not perturbed.

from THE DILEMMA OF DETERMINISM

WILLIAM JAMES

What does determinism profess?

It professes that those parts of the universe already laid down absolutely appoint and decree what the other parts shall be. The future has no ambiguous possibilities hidden in its womb: the part we call the present is compatible with only one totality. Any other future complement than the one fixed from eternity is impossible. The whole is in each and every part, and welds it with the rest into an absolute unity, an iron block, in which there can be no equivocation or shadow of turning.

> "With earth's first clay they did the last man knead,
> And there of the last harvest sowed the seed.
> And the first morning of creation wrote
> What the last dawn of reckoning shall read."

Indeterminism, on the contrary, says that the parts have a certain amount of loose play on one another, so that the laying down of one of them does not necessarily determine what the others shall be. It admits that possibilities may be in excess of actualities, and that things not yet revealed to our knowledge may really in themselves be ambiguous. Of two alternative futures which we conceive, both may now be really possible; and the one become impossible only at the very moment when the other excludes it by becoming real itself. Indeterminism thus denies the world to be one unbending unit of fact. It says there is a certain ultimate pluralism in it; and, so saying, it corroborates our ordinary unsophisticated view of things. To that view, actualities seem to float in a wider sea of possibilities from out of which they are chosen; and *somewhere,* indeterminism says, such possibilities exist, and form a part of truth.

Determinism, on the contrary, says they exist *nowhere,* and that necessity on the one hand and impossibility on the other are the sole categories of the real. Possibilities that fail to get realized are, for determinism, pure illusion: they never were possibilities at all. There is nothing inchoate, it says, about this universe of ours, all that was or is or shall be actual in it having been from eternity virtually there. The cloud of alternatives our minds escort this mass of actuality withal is a cloud of sheer deceptions, to which "impossibilities" is the only name that rightfully belongs.

The issue, it will be seen, is a perfectly sharp one, which no eulogistic terminology can smear over or wipe out. The truth *must* lie with one side or the other, and its lying with one side makes the other false.

The question relates solely to the existence of possibilities, in the strict sense of the term, as things that may, but need not, be. Both sides admit that a volition, for instance, has occurred. The indeterminists say another volition might have occurred in its place: the determinists swear that nothing could possibly have occurred in its place. Now, can science be called in to tell us which of these two point-blank contradicters of each other is right? Science professes to draw no conclusions but such as are based on matters of fact, things that have actually happened; but how can any amount of assurance that something actually happened give us the least grain of information as to whether another thing might or might not have happened in its place? Only facts can be proved by other facts. With things that are possibilities and not facts, facts have no concern. If we have no other evidence than the evidence of existing facts, the possibility-question must remain a mystery never to be cleared up.

And the truth is that facts practically have hardly anything to do with making us either determinists or indeterminists. Sure enough, we make a flourish of quoting facts this way or that; and if we are determinists, we talk about the infallibility with which we can predict one another's conduct; while if we are indeterminists, we lay great stress on the fact that it is just because we cannot foretell one another's conduct, either in war or statecraft or in any of the great and small intrigues and businesses of men, that life is so intensely anxious and hazardous a game. But who does not see the wretched insufficiency of this so-called objective testimony on both sides? What fills up the gaps in our minds is something not objective, not external. What divides us into possibility men and anti-possibility men is different faiths or postulates,—postulates of rationality. To this man the world seems more rational with possibilities in it,—to that man more rational with possibilities excluded; and talk as we will about having to yield to evidence, what makes us monists or pluralists, determinists or indeterminists, is at bottom always some sentiment like this.

The stronghold of the deterministic sentiment is the antipathy to the idea of chance. As soon as we begin to talk indeterminism to our friends, we find a number of them shaking their heads. This notion of alternative possibility, they say, this admission that any one of several things may come to pass, is, after all, only a roundabout name for chance; and chance is something the notion of which no sane mind can for an instant tolerate in the world. What is it, they ask, but barefaced crazy unreason, the negation of intelligibility and law? And if the slightest particle of it exist anywhere, what is to prevent the whole fabric from falling together, the stars from going out, and chaos from recommencing her topsy-turvy reign?

Remarks of this sort about chance will put an end to discussion as quickly as anything one can find. I have already told you that "chance" was a word I wished to keep and use. Let us then examine exactly what it means, and see whether it ought to be such a terrible bugbear to us. I fancy that squeezing the thistle boldly will rob it of its sting.

The sting of the word "chance" seems to lie in the assumption that it means something positive, and that if anything happens by chance, it must needs be something of an intrinsically irrational and preposterous sort. Now, chance means nothing of the kind. It is a purely negative and relative term, giving us no information about that of which it is predicated, except that it happens to be disconnected with something else,—not controlled, secured, or necessitated by other things in advance of its own actual presence. As this point is the most subtile one of the whole lecture, and at the same time the point on which all the rest hinges, I beg you to pay particular attention to it. What I say is that it tells us nothing about what a thing may be in itself to call it "chance." It may be a bad thing, it may be a good thing. It may be lucidity, transparency, fitness incarnate, matching the whole system of other things, when it has once befallen, in an unimaginably perfect way. All you mean by calling it "chance" is that this is not guaranteed, that it may also fall out otherwise. For the system of other things has no positive hold on the chance-thing. Its origin is in a certain fashion negative: it escapes, and says Hands off! coming, when it comes, as a free gift, or not at all.

This negativeness, however, and this opacity of the chance-thing when thus considered *ab extra,* or from the point of view of previous things or distant things, do not preclude its having any amount of positiveness and luminosity from within, and at its own place and moment. All that its chance-character asserts about it is that there is something in it really of its own, something that is not the unconditional property of the whole. If the whole wants this property, the whole must wait till it can get it, if it be a matter of chance. That the universe may actually be a sort of joint-stock society of this sort, in which the sharers have both limited liabilities and limited powers, is of course a simple and conceivable notion.

Nevertheless, many persons talk as if the minutest dose of disconnectedness of one part with another, the smallest modicum of independence, the faintest tremor of ambiguity about the future, for example, would ruin everything, and turn this goodly universe into a sort of insane sand-heap or nulliverse, no universe at all. Since future human volitions are as a matter of fact the only ambiguous things we are tempted to believe in, let us stop for a moment to make ourselves sure whether their independent and accidental character need be fraught with such direful consequences to the universe as these.

What is meant by saying that my choice of which way to walk home after the lecture is ambiguous and matter of chance as far as the present moment is concerned? It means that both Divinity Avenue and Oxford Street are called; but that only one, and that one *either* one, shall be chosen. Now, I ask you seriously to suppose that this ambiguity of my choice is real; and then to make the impossible hypothesis that the choice is made twice over, and each time falls on a different street. In other words, imagine that I first walk through Divinity Avenue, and then imagine that the powers governing the universe annihilate ten minutes of time with all that it contained, and set me back at the door of this hall just as I was before the choice was made. Imagine then that, everything else being the same, I now make a different choice and traverse Oxford Street. You, as passive spectators, look on and see the two alternative universes,—one of them with me walking through Divinity Avenue in it, the other with the same me walking through Oxford Street. Now, if you are determinists you believe one of these universes to have been from eternity impossible: you believe it to have been impossible because of the intrinsic irrationality of accidentality somewhere involved in it. But looking outwardly at these universes, can you say which is the impossible and accidental one, and which the rational and necessary one? I doubt if the most ironclad determinist among you could have the slightest glimmer of light on this point. In other words, either universe *after the fact* and once there would, to our means of observation and understanding, appear just as rational as the other. There would be absolutely no criterion by which we might judge one necessary and the other matter of chance. Suppose now we relieve the gods of their hypothetical task and assume my choice, once made, to be made forever. I go through Divinity Avenue for good and all. If, as good determinists, you now begin to affirm, what all good determinists punctually do affirm, that in the nature of things I *couldn't* have gone through Oxford Street,—had I done so it would have been chance, irrationality, insanity, a horrid gap in nature,—I simply call your attention to this, that your affirmation is what the Germans call a *Machtspruch,* a mere conception fulminated as a dogma and based on no insight into details. Before my choice, either street seemed as natural to you as to me.   Had I happened to take Oxford Street, Divinity Avenue would have figured in your philosophy as the gap in nature; and you would have so proclaimed it with the best deterministic conscience in the world.

But what a hollow outcry, then, is this against a chance which, if it were present to us, we could by no character whatever distinguish from a rational necessity!   I have taken the most trivial of examples, but no possible example could lead to any different result.   For what are the alternatives which, in point of fact, offer themselves to human volition?   What are those futures that now seem matters of chance? Are they not one and all like the Divinity Avenue and Oxford Street of our example?   Are they not all of them *kinds* of things already here and based in the existing frame of nature?   Is any one ever tempted to produce an *absolute* accident, something utterly irrelevant to the rest of the world?   Do not all the motives that assail us, all the futures that offer themselves to our choice, spring equally from the soil of the past; and would not either one of them, whether realized through chance or through necessity, the moment it was realized, seem to us to fit that past, and in the completest and most continuous manner to interdigitate with the phenomena already there?

The more one thinks of the matter, the more one wonders that so empty and gratuitous a hubbub as this outcry against chance should have found so great an echo in the hearts of men.   It is a word which tells us absolutely nothing about what chances, or about the *modus operandi* of the chancing; and the use of it as a war-cry shows only a temper of intellectual absolutism, a demand that the world shall be a solid block, subject to one control,—which temper, which demand, the world may not be bound to gratify at all.   In every outwardly verifiable and practical respect, a world in which the alternatives that now actually distract *your* choice were decided by pure chance would be by *me* absolutely undistinguished from the world in which I now live.   I am, therefore, entirely willing to call it, so far as your choices go, a world of chance for me.   To *yourselves,* it is true, those very acts of choice, which to me are so blind, opaque, and external, are the opposites of this, for you are within them and effect them.   To you they appear as decisions; and decisions, for him who makes them, are altogether peculiar psychic facts.   Self-luminous and self-justifying at the living moment at which they occur, they appeal to no outside moment to put its stamp upon them or make them continuous with the rest of nature.   Themselves it is rather who seem to make nature continuous; and in their strange and intense function of granting consent to one possibility and withholding it from another, to transform an equivocal and double future into an inalterable and simple past.

But with the psychology of the matter we have no concern this evening.   The quarrel which determinism has with chance fortunately has nothing to do with this or that psychological detail.   It is a quarrel altogether metaphysical.   Determinism denies the ambiguity of future volitions, because it affirms that nothing future can be ambiguous.   But we have said enough to meet the issue.   Indeterminate future volitions *do* mean chance.   Let us not fear to shout it from the house-tops if need be; for we now know that the idea of chance is, at bottom, exactly the same thing as the idea of gift,—the one simply being a disparaging, and the other a eulogistic, name for anything on which we have no effective *claim*.   And whether the world be the better or the worse for having either chances or gifts in it will depend altogether on *what* these uncertain and unclaimable things turn out to be.

And this at last brings us within sight of our subject.   We have seen what determinism means: we have seen that indeterminism is rightly described as meaning chance; and we have seen that chance, the very name of which we are urged to shrink from as from a metaphysical pestilence, means only the negative fact that no part of the world, however big, can claim to control absolutely the destinies of the whole. But although, in discussing the word "chance," I may at moments have seemed to be arguing for its real existence, I have not meant to do so yet. We have not yet ascertained whether this be a world of chance or no; at most, we have agreed that it seems so. And I now repeat what I said at the outset, that, from any strict theoretical point of view, the question is insoluble. To deepen our theoretic sense of the *difference* between a world with chances in it and a deterministic world is the most I can hope to do; and this I may now at last begin upon, after all our tedious clearing of the way.

I wish first of all to show you just what the notion that this is a deterministic world implies. The implications I call your attention to are all bound up with the fact that it is a world in which we constantly have to make what I shall, with your permission, call judgments of regret. Hardly an hour passes in which we do not wish that something might be otherwise; and happy indeed are those of us whose hearts have never echoed the wish of Omar Khayyam—

> "That we might clasp, ere closed, the book of fate,
>   And make the writer on a fairer leaf
> Inscribe our names, or quite obliterate.

> "Ah! Love, could you and I with fate conspire
> To mend this sorry scheme of things entire,
>   Would we not shatter it to bits, and then
> Remold it nearer to the heart's desire?"

Now, it is undeniable that most of these regrets are foolish, and quite on a par in point of philosophic value with the criticisms on the universe of that friend of our infancy, the hero of the fable The Atheist and the Acorn,—

> "Fool! had that bough a pumpkin bore,
>   Thy whimsies whould have worked no more," etc.

Even from the point of view of our own ends, we should probably make a botch of remodeling the universe. How much more then from the point of view of ends we cannot see! Wise men therefore regret as little as they can. But still some regrets are pretty obstinate and hard to stifle,—regrets for acts of wanton cruelty or treachery, for example, whether performed by others or by ourselves. Hardly any one can remain *entirely* optimistic after reading the confession of the murderer at Brockton the other day: how, to get rid of the wife whose continued existence bored him, he inveigled her into a desert spot, shot her four times, and then, as she lay on the ground and said to him, "You didn't do it on purpose, did you, dear?" replied, "No, I didn't do it on purpose," as he raised a rock and smashed her skull. Such an occurrence, with the mild sentence and self-satisfaction of the prisoner, is a field for a crop of regrets, which one need not take up in detail. We feel that, although a perfect mechanical fit to the rest of the universe, it is a bad moral fit, and that something else would really have been better in its place.

But for the deterministic philosophy the murder, the sentence, and the prisoner's optimism were all necessary from eternity; and nothing else for a moment had a ghost of a chance of being put into their place. To admit such a chance, the determinists tell us, would be to make a suicide of reason; so we must steel our hearts against the thought. And here our plot thickens, for we see the first of those difficult implications of determinism and monism which it is my purpose to make you feel. If this Brockton murder was called for by the rest of the universe, if it had to come at its preappointed hour, and if nothing else would have been consistent with the sense of the whole, what are we to think of the universe? Are we stubbornly to stick to our judgment of regret, and say, though it *couldn't* be, yet it *would* have been in a better universe with something different from this Brockton murder in it? That, of course, seems the natural and spontaneous thing for us to do; and yet it is nothing short of deliberately espousing a kind of pessimism. The judgment of regret calls the murder bad. Calling a thing bad means, if it mean anything at all, that the thing ought not to be, that something else ought to be in its stead. Determinism, in denying that anything else can be in its stead, virtually defines the universe as a place in which what ought to be is impossible,—in other words, as an organism whose constitution is afflicted with an incurable taint, an irremediable flaw. The pessimism of a Schopenhauer says no more than this,—that the murder is a symptom; and that it is a vicious symptom because it belongs to a vicious whole, which can express its nature no otherwise than by bringing forth just such a symptom as that at this particular spot. Regret for the murder must transform itself, if we are determinists and wise, into a larger regret. It is absurd to regret the murder alone. Other things being what they are, *it* could not be different. What we should regret is that whole frame of things of which the murder is one member. I see no escape whatever from this pessimistic conclusion, if, being determinists, our judgment of regret is to be allowed to stand at all.

The only deterministic escape from pessimism is everywhere to abandon the judgment of regret. That this can be done, history shows to be not impossible. The devil, *quoad existentiam,* may be good. That is, although he be a *principle* of evil, yet the universe, with such a principle in it, may practically be a better universe than it could have been without. On every hand, in a small way, we find that a certain amount of evil is a condition by which a higher form of good is brought. There is nothing to prevent anybody from generalizing this view, and trusting that if we could but see things in the largest of all ways, even such matters as this Brockton murder would appear to be paid for by the uses that follow in their train. An optimism *quand même,* a systematic and infatuated optimism like that ridiculed by Voltaire in his Candide, is one of the possible ideal ways in which a man may train himself to look on life. Bereft of dogmatic hardness and lit up with the expression of a tender and pathetic hope, such an optimism has been the grace of some of the most religious characters that ever lived.

> "Throb thine with Nature's throbbing breast,
> And all is clear from east to west."

Even cruelty and treachery may be among the absolutely blessed fruits of time, and to quarrel with any of their details may be blasphemy. The only real blasphemy, in short, may be that pessimistic temper of the soul which lets it give way to such things as regrets, remorse, and grief.

Thus, our deterministic pessimism may become a deterministic optimism at the price of extinguishing our judgments of regret.

But does not this immediately bring us into a curious logical predicament? Our determinism leads us to call our judgments of regret wrong, because they are pessimistic in implying that what is impossible yet ought to be. But how then about the judgments of regret themselves? If they are wrong, other judgments, judgments of approval presumably, ought to be in their place. But as they are necessitated, nothing else *can* be in their place; and the universe is just what it was before,—namely, a place in which what ought to be appears impossible. We have got one foot out of the pessimistic bog, but the other one sinks all the deeper. We have rescued our actions from the bonds of evil, but our judgments are now held fast. When murders and treacheries cease to be sins, regrets are theoretic absurdities and errors. The theoretic and the active life thus play a kind of seesaw with each other on the ground of evil. The rise of either sends the other down. Murder and treachery cannot be good without regret being bad: regret cannot be good without treachery and murder being bad. Both, however, are supposed to have been foredoomed; so something must be fatally unreasonable, absurd, and wrong in the world. It must be a place of which either sin or error forms a necessary part. From this dilemma there seems at first sight no escape. Are we then so soon to fall back into the pessimism from which we thought we had emerged? And is there no possible way by which we may, with good intellectual consciences, call the cruelties and the treacheries, the reluctances and the regrets, *all* good together?

Certainly there is such a way, and you are probably most of you ready to formulate it yourselves. But, before doing so, remark how inevitably the question of determinism and indeterminism slides us into the question of optimism and pessimism, or, as our fathers called it, "the question of evil." The theological form of all these disputes is the simplest and the deepest, the form from which there is the least escape,—not because, as some have sarcastically said, remorse and regret are clung to with a morbid fondness by the theologians as spiritual luxuries, but because they are existing facts of the world, and as such must be taken into account in the deterministic interpretation of all that is fated to be. If they are fated to be error, does not the bat's wing of irrationality still cast its shadow over the world?

.   .   .   .

But this brings us right back, after such a long détour, to the question of indeterminism and to the conclusion of all I came here to say to-night. For the only consistent way of representing a pluralism and a world whose parts may affect one another through their conduct being either good or bad is the indeterministic way. What interest, zest, or excitement can there be in achieving the right way, unless we are enabled to feel that the wrong way is also a possible and a natural way,—nay, more, a menacing and an imminent way? And what sense can there be in condemning ourselves for taking the wrong way, unless we need have done nothing of the sort, unless the right way was open to us as well? I cannot understand the willingness to act, no matter how we feel, without the belief that acts are really good and bad. I cannot understand the belief that an act is bad, without regret at its happening. I cannot understand regret without the admission of real, genuine possibilities in the world. Only *then* is it other than a mockery to feel, after we have failed to do our best, that an irreparable opportunity is gone from the universe, the loss of which it must forever after mourn.

If you insist that this is all superstition, that possibility is in the eye of science and reason impossibility, and that if I act badly 'tis that the universe was foredoomed to suffer this defect, you fall right back into the dilemma, the labyrinth, of pessimism and subjectivism, from out of whose toils we have just wound our way.

Now, we are of course free to fall back, if we please. For my own part, though, whatever difficulties may beset the philosophy of objective right and wrong, and the indeterminism it seems to imply, determinism, with its alternatives of pessimism or romanticism, contains difficulties that are greater still. But you will remember that I expressly repudiated awhile ago the pretension to offer any arguments which could be coercive in a so-called scientific fashion in this matter. And I consequently find myself, at the end of this long talk, obliged to state my conclusions in an altogether personal way. This personal method of appeal seems to be among the very conditions of the problem; and the most any one can do is to confess as candidly as he can the grounds for the faith that is in him, and leave his example to work on others as it may.

Let me, then, without circumlocution say just this. The world is enigmatical enough in all conscience, whatever theory we may take up toward it. The indeterminism I defend, the free-will theory of popular sense based on the judgment of regret, represents that world as vulnerable, and liable to be injured by certain of its parts if they act wrong. And it represents their acting wrong as a matter of possibility or accident, neither inevitable nor yet to be infallibly warded off. In all this, it is a theory devoid either of transparency or of stability. It gives us a pluralistic, restless universe, in which no single point of view can ever take in the whole scene; and to a mind possessed of the love of unity at any cost, it will, no doubt, remain forever inacceptable. A friend with such a mind once told me that the thought of my universe made him sick, like the sight of the horrible motion of a mass of maggots in their carrion bed.

But while I freely admit that the pluralism and the restlessness are repugnant and irrational in a certain way, I find that every alternative to them is irrational in a deeper way. The indeterminism with its maggots, if you please to speak so about it, offends only the native absolutism of my intellect,—an absolutism which, after all, perhaps, deserves to be snubbed and kept in check. But the determinism with its necessary carrion, to continue the figure of speech, and with no possible maggots to eat the latter up, violates my sense of moral reality through and through. When, for example, I imagine such carrion as the Brockton murder, I cannot conceive it as an act by which the universe, as a whole, logically and necessarily expresses its nature without shrinking from complicity with such a whole. And I deliberately refuse to keep on terms of loyalty with the universe by saying blankly that the murder, since it does flow from the nature of the whole, is not carrion. There are *some* instinctive reactions which I, for one, will not tamper with. The only remaining alternative, the attitude of gnostical romanticism, wrenches my personal instincts in quite as violent a way. It falsifies the simple objectivity of their deliverance. It makes the goose-flesh the murder excites in me a sufficient reason for the perpetration of the crime. It transforms life from a tragic reality into an insincere melodramatic exhibition, as foul or as tawdry as any one's diseased curiosity pleases to carry it out. And with its consecration of the "roman naturaliste" state of mind, and its enthronement of the baser crew of Parisian *littérateurs* among the eternally indispensable organs by which the infinite spirit of things attains to that subjective illumination which is the task of its life, it leaves me in presence of a sort of subjective carrion considerably more noisome than the objective carrion I called it in to take away.

No! better a thousand times, than such systematic corruption of our moral sanity, the plainest pessimism, so that it be straightforward; but better far than that the world of chance. Make as great an uproar about chance as you please, I know that chance means pluralism and nothing more. If some of the members of the pluralism are bad, the philosophy of pluralism, whatever broad views it may deny me, permits me, at least, to turn to the other members with a clean breast of affection and an unsophisticated moral sense. And if I still wish to think of the world as a totality, it lets me feel that a world with a *chance* in it of being altogether good, even if the chance never come to pass, is better than a world with no such chance at all. That "chance" whose very notion I am exhorted and conjured to banish from my view of the future as the suicide of reason concerning it, that "chance" is—what? Just this,—the chance that in moral respects the future may be other and better than the past has been. This is the only chance we have any motive for supposing to exist. Shame, rather, on its repudiation and its denial! For its presence is the vital air which lets the world live, the salt which keeps it sweet.

. . . .

But now you will bring up your final doubt. Does not the admission of such an unguaranteed chance or freedom preclude utterly the notion of a Providence governing the world? Does it not leave the fate of the universe at the mercy of the chance-possibilities, and so far insecure? Does it not, in short, deny the craving of our nature for an ultimate peace behind all tempests, for a blue zenith above all clouds?

To this my answer must be very brief. The belief in free-will is not in the least incompatible with the belief in Providence, provided you do not restrict the Providence to fulminating nothing but *fatal* decrees. If you allow him to provide possibilities as well as actualities to the universe, and to carry on his own thinking in those two categories, just as we do ours, chances may be there, uncontrolled even by him, and the course of the universe be really ambiguous; and yet the end of all things may be just what he intended it to be from all eternity.

An analogy will make the meaning of this clear. Suppose two men before a chessboard,—the one a novice, the other an expert player of the game. The expert intends to beat. But he cannot foresee exactly what any one actual move of his adversary may be. He knows, however, all the *possible* moves of the latter; and he knows in advance how to meet each of them by a move of his own which leads in the direction of victory. And the victory infallibly arrives, after no matter how devious a course, in the one predestined form of check-mate to the novice's king.

Let now the novice stand for us finite free agents, and the expert for the infinite mind in which the universe lies. Suppose the latter to be thinking out his universe before he actually creates it. Suppose him to say, I will lead things to a certain end, but I will not *now* decide on all the steps thereto. At various points, ambiguous possibilities shall be left open, *either* of which, at a given instant, become actual. But whichever branch of these bifurcations become real, I know what I shall do at the *next* bifurcation to keep things from drifting away from the final result I intend.

The creator's plan of the universe would thus be left blank as to many of its actual details, but all possibilities would be marked down. The realization of some of these would be left absolutely to chance; that is, would only be determined when the moment of realization came. Other possibilities would be *contingently* determined; that is, their decision would have to wait till it was seen how the matters of absolute chance fell out. But the rest of the plan, including its final upshot, would be rigorously determined once for all. So the creator himself would not need to know *all* the details of actuality until they came; and at any time his own view of the world would be a view partly of facts and partly of possibilities, exactly as ours is now. Of one thing, however, he might be certain; and that is that his world was safe, and that no matter how much it might zigzag he could surely bring it home at last.

Now, it is entirely immaterial, in this scheme, whether the creator leave the absolute chance-possibilities to be decided by himself, each when its proper moment arrives, or whether, on the contrary, he alienate this power from himself, and leave the decision out and out to finite creatures such as we men are. The great point is that the possibilities are really *here*. Whether it be we who solve them, or he working through us, at those soul-trying moments when fate's scales seem to quiver, and good snatches the victory from evil or shrinks nerveless from the fight, is of small account, so long as we admit that the issue is decided nowhere else than *here* and *now*. *That* is what gives the palpitating reality to our moral life and makes it tingle, as Mr. Mallock says, with so strange and elaborate an excitement.   This reality, this excitement, are what the determinisms, hard and soft alike, suppress by their denial that *anything* is decided here and now, and their dogma that all things were foredoomed and settled long ago.   If it be so, may you and I then have been foredoomed to the error of continuing to believe in liberty.   It is fortunate for the winding up of controversy that in every discussion with determinism this *argumentum ad hominem* can be its adversary's last word.

NOTES FROM UNDERGROUND, I, viii

FYODOR DOSTOEVSKY

"Ha! ha! ha!   But you know there is no such thing as choice in reality, say what you like," you will interpose with a chuckle.   "Science has succeeded in so far analyzing man that we know already that choice and what is called freedom of will is nothing else than—"

Stay, gentlemen, I meant to begin with that myself.   I confess, I was rather frightened.   I was just going to say that the devil only knows what choice depends on, and that perhaps that was a very good thing, but I remembered the teaching of science . . . and pulled myself up.   And here you have begun upon it.   Indeed, if there really is some day discovered a formula for all our desires and caprices— that is, an explanation of what they depend upon, by what laws they arise, how they develop, what they are aiming at in one case and in another and so on, that is a real mathematical formula—then, most likely, man will at once cease to feel desire, indeed, he will be certain to.   For who would want to choose by rule? Besides, he will at once be transformed from a human being into an organ-stop or something of the sort; for what is a man without desires, without free will and without choice, if not a stop in an organ?   What do you think?   Let us reckon the chances—can such a thing happen or not?

"H'm!" you decide.   "Our choice is usually mistaken from a false view of our advantage.   We sometimes choose absolute nonsense because in our foolishness we see in that nonsense the easiest means for attaining a supposed advantage.   But when all that is explained and worked out on paper (which is perfectly possible, for it is contemptible and senseless to suppose that some laws of nature man will never understand), then certainly so-called desires will no longer exist.   For if a desire should come into conflict with reason we shall then reason and not desire, because it will be impossible retaining our reason to be *senseless* in our desires, and in that way knowingly act against reason and desire to injure ourselves.   And as all choice and reasoning can be really calculated—because there will some day be discovered the laws of our so-called free will—so, joking apart, there may one day be something like a table constructed of them, so that we really shall choose in accordance with it.   If, for instance, some day they calculate and prove to me that I made a long nose at some one because I could not help making a long nose at him and that I had to do it in that particular way, what *freedom* is left me, especially if I am a learned man and have taken my degree somewhere?   Then I should be able to calculate my whole life for thirty years beforehand.   In short, if this could be arranged there would be nothing left for us to do; anyway, we should have to understand that.   And, in fact, we ought unwearyingly to repeat to our-selves that at such and such a time and in such and such circumstances nature does not ask our leave; that we have got to take her as she is and not fashion her to suit

our fancy, and if we really aspire to formulas and tables of rules, and well, even
. . . to the chemical retort, there's no help for it, we must accept the retort too,
or else it will be accepted without our consent. . . ."

Yes, but here I come to a stop! Gentlemen, you must excuse me for being over-
philosophical; it's the result of forty years underground! Allow me to indulge my
fancy. You see, gentlemen, reason is an excellent thing, there's no disputing that,
but reason is nothing but reason and satisfies only the rational side of man's
nature, while will is a manifestation of the whole life, that is, of the whole human
life including reason and all the impulses. And although our life, in this manifestation of it, is often worthless, yet it is life and not simply extracting square
roots. Here I, for instance, quite naturally want to live, in order to satisfy all my
capacities for life, and not simply my capacity for reasoning, that is, not simply
one twentieth of my capacity for life. What does reason know? Reason only
knows what it has succeeded in learning (some things, perhaps, it will never learn;
this is a poor comfort, but why not say so frankly?) and human nature acts as a
whole, with everything that is in it, consciously or unconsciously, and, even if it
goes wrong, it lives. I suspect, gentlemen, that you are looking at me with compassion; you tell me again that an enlightened and developed man, such, in short,
as the future man will be, cannot consciously desire anything disadvantageous to
himself, that that can be proved mathematically. I thoroughly agree, it can—by
mathematics. But I repeat for the hundredth time, there is one case, one only,
when man may consciously, purposely, desire what is injurious to himself, what is
stupid, very stupid—simply in order to have the right to desire for himself even
what is very stupid and not to be bound by an obligation to desire only what is
sensible. Of course, this very stupid thing, this caprice of ours, may be in reality,
gentlemen, more advantageous for us than anything else on earth, especially in
certain cases. And in particular it may be more advantageous than any advantage
even when it does us obvious harm, and contradicts the soundest conclusions of
our reason concerning our advantage—for in any circumstances it preserves for us
what is most precious and most important—that is, our personality, our individuality. Some, you see, maintain that this really is the most precious thing for mankind; choice can, of course, if it chooses, be in agreement with reason; and especially
if this be not abused but kept within bounds. It is profitable and sometimes even
praiseworthy. But very often, and even most often, choice is utterly and stubbornly
opposed to reason . . . and . . . and . . . do you know that that, too, is profitable,
sometimes even praiseworthy? Gentlemen, let us suppose that man is not stupid.
(Indeed one cannot refuse to suppose that, if only from the one consideration, that,
if man is stupid, then who is wise?) But if he is not stupid, he is monstrously
ungrateful! Phenomenally ungrateful. In fact, I believe that the best definition
of man is the ungrateful biped. But that is not all, that is not his worst defect;
his worst defect is his perpetual moral obliquity, perpetual—from the days of the
Flood to the Schleswig-Holstein period. Moral obliquity and consequently lack of
good sense; for it has long been accepted that lack of good sense is due to no other
cause than moral obliquity. Put it to the test and cast your eyes upon the history
of mankind. What will you see? Is it a grand spectacle? Grand, if you like.
Take the Colossus of Rhodes, for instance, that's worth something. With good
reason Mr. Anaevsky testifies of it that some say that it is the work of man's hands,
while others maintain that it has been created by nature herself. Is it many-
colored? May be it is many-colored, too: if one takes the dress uniforms, military
and civilian, of all peoples in all ages—that alone is worth something, and if you
take the undress uniforms you will never get to the end of it; no historian would
be equal to the job. Is it monotonous? May be it's monotonous too: it's fighting

and fighting; they are fighting now, they fought first and they fought last—you will admit, that it is almost too monotonous.   In short, one may say anything about the history of the world—anything that might enter the most disordered imagination. The only thing one can't say is that it's rational.   The very word sticks in one's throat.   And, indeed, this is the odd thing that is continually happening; there are continually turning up in life moral and rational persons, sages and lovers of humanity who make it their object to live all their lives as morally and rationally as possible, to be, so to speak, a light to their neighbors simply in order to show them that it is possible to live morally and rationally in this world.   And yet we all know that those very people sooner or later have been false to themselves, play-ing some queer trick, often a most unseemly one.   Now I ask you: what can be expected of man since he is a being endowed with such strange qualities?   Shower upon him every earthly blessing, drown him in a sea of happiness, so that nothing but bubbles of bliss can be seen on the surface; give him economic prosperity, such that he should have nothing else to do but sleep, eat cakes and busy himself with the continuation of his species, and even then out of sheer ingratitude, sheer spite, man would play you some nasty trick.   He would even risk his cakes and would deliberately desire the most fatal rubbish, the most uneconomical absurdity, simply to introduce into all this positive good sense his fatal fantastic element.   It is just his fantastic dreams, his vulgar folly that he will desire to retain, simply in order to prove to himself—as though that were so necessary—that men still are men and not the keys of a piano, which the laws of nature threaten to control so com-pletely that soon one will be able to desire nothing but by the calendar.   And that is not all: even if man really were nothing but a piano-key, even if this were proved to him by natural science and mathematics, even then he would not become rea-sonable, but would purposely do something perverse out of simple ingratitude, simply to gain his point.   And if he does not find means he will contrive destruc-tion and chaos, will contrive sufferings of all sorts, only to gain his point.   He will launch a curse upon the world, and as only man can curse (it is his privilege, the primary distinction between him and other animals), may be by his curse alone he will attain his object—that is, convince himself that he is a man and not a piano-key! If you say that all this, too, can be calculated and tabulated—chaos and darkness and curses, so that the mere possibility of calculating it all beforehand would stop it all, and reason would reassert itself, then man would purposely go mad in order to be rid of reason and gain his point!   I believe in it, I answer for it, for the whole work of man really seems to consist in nothing but proving to himself every minute that he is a man and not a piano-key!   It may be at the cost of his skin, it may be by cannibalism!   And this being so, can one help being tempted to rejoice that it has not yet come off, and that desire still depends on something we don't know?

You will scream at me (that is, if you condescend to do so) that no one is touching my free will, that all they are concerned with is that my will should of itself, of its own free will, coincide with my own normal interests, with the laws of nature and arithmetic.

Good Heavens, gentlemen, what sort of free will is left when we come to tabula-tion and arithmetic, when it will all be a case of twice two make four?   Twice two makes four without my will.   As if free will meant that!

(Constance Garnett, tr.)

from THE POSSESSED, III, vi

FYODOR DOSTOEVSKY

"You seem to be boasting to me of your shooting yourself."

"I've always been surprised at every one's going on living," said Kirillov, not hearing his remark.

"H'm! Admitting that's an idea, but . . ."

"You ape, you assent to get the better of me. Hold your tongue; you won't understand anything. If there is no God, then I am God."

"There, I could never understand that point of yours: why are you God?"

"If God exists, all is His will and from His will I cannot escape. If not, it's all my will and I am bound to show self-will."

"Self-will? But why are you bound?"

"Because all will has become mine. Can it be that no one in the whole planet, after making an end of God and believing in his own will, will dare to express his self-will on the most vital point? It's like a beggar inheriting a fortune and being afraid of it and not daring to approach the bag of gold, thinking himself too weak to own it. I want to manifest my self-will. I may be the only one, but I'll do it."

"Do it by all means."

"I am bound to shoot myself because the highest point of my self-will is to kill myself with my own hands."

"But you won't be the only one to kill yourself; there are lots of suicides."

"With good cause. But to do it without any cause at all, simply for self-will, I am the only one."

"He won't shoot himself," flashed across Pyotr Stepanovitch's mind again.

"Do you know," he observed irritably, "if I were in your place I should kill some one else to show my self-will, not myself. You might be of use. I'll tell you whom, if you are not afraid. Then you needn't shoot yourself today, perhaps. We may come to terms."

"To kill some one would be the lowest point of self-will, and you show your whole soul in that. I am not you: I want the highest point and I'll kill myself."

"He's come to it of himself," Pyotr Stepanovitch muttered malignantly.

"I am bound to show my unbelief," said Kirillov, walking about the room. "I have no higher idea than disbelief in God. I have all the history of mankind on my side. Man has done nothing but invent God so as to go on living, and not kill himself; that's the whole of universal history up till now. I am the first one in the whole history of mankind who would not invent God. Let them know it once for all."

"He won't shoot himself," Pyotr Stepanovitch thought anxiously.

"Let whom know it?" he said, egging him on. "It's only you and me here; you mean Liputin?"

"Let every one know; all will know. There is nothing secret that will not be made known. *He* said so."

And he pointed with feverish enthusiasm to the image of the Saviour, before which a lamp was burning. Pyotr Stepanovitch lost his temper completely.

"So you still believe in Him, and you've lighted the lamp; 'to be on the safe side,' I suppose?"

The other did not speak.

"Do you know, to my thinking, you believe perhaps more thoroughly than any priest?"

"Believe in whom? In *Him?* Listen." Kirillov stood still, gazing before him with a fixed and ecstatic look. "Listen to a great idea: there was a day on earth, and in the midst of the earth there stood three crosses. One on the Cross had such faith that he said to another, 'Today thou shalt be with me in Paradise.' The day ended; both died and passed away and found neither Paradise nor resurrection. His words did not come true. Listen: that Man was the loftiest of all on earth, He was that which gave meaning to life. The whole planet, with everything on it, is mere madness without that Man. There has never been any like Him before or since, never, up to a miracle. For that is the miracle, that there never was or never will be another like Him. And if that is so, if the laws of nature did not spare even Him, have not spared even their miracle and made even Him live in a lie and die for a lie, then all the planet is a lie and rests on a lie and on mockery. So then, the very laws of the planet are a lie and the vaudeville of devils. What is there to live for? Answer, if you are a man."

"That's a different matter. It seems to me you've mixed up two different causes, and that's a very unsafe thing to do. But excuse me, if you are God? If the lie were ended and if you realized that all the falsity comes from the belief in that former God?"

"So at last you understand!" cried Kirillov rapturously. "So it can be understood if even a fellow like you understands. Do you understand now that the salvation for all consists in proving this idea to every one? Who will prove it? I! I can't understand how an atheist could know that there is no God and not kill himself on the spot. To recognize that there is no God and not to recognize at the same instant that one is God oneself is an absurdity, else one would certainly kill oneself. If you recognize it you are sovereign, and then you won't kill yourself but will live in the greatest glory. But one, the first, must kill himself, for else who will begin and prove it? So I must certainly kill myself, to begin and prove it. Now I am only a god against my will and I am unhappy, because I am *bound* to assert my will. All are unhappy because all are afraid to express their will. Man has hitherto been so unhappy and so poor because he has been afraid to assert his will in the highest point and has shown his self-will only in little things, like a schoolboy. I am awfully unhappy, for I'm awfully afraid. Terror is the curse of man . . . But I will assert my will, I am bound to believe that I don't believe. I will begin and will make an end of it and open the door, and will save. That's the only thing that will save mankind and will recreate the next generation physically; for with his present physical nature man can't get on without his former God, I believe. For three years I've been seeking for the attribute of my godhead and I've found it; the attribute of my godhead is self-will! That's all I can do to prove in the highest point my independence and my new terrible freedom. For it is very terrible. I am killing myself to prove my independence and my new terrible freedom."

(Constance Garnett, tr.)

THE COMING OF FATE *

LOGAN PEARSALL SMITH

When I seek out the sources of my thoughts, I find they had their beginning in fragile Chance; were born of little moments that shine for me curiously in the past. Slight the impulse that made me take this turning at the crossroads, trivial and fortuitous the meeting, and light as gossamer the thread that first knit me to my

* From: *Trivia* by Logan Pearsall Smith. Copyright 1917 by Doubleday & Company, Inc.

friend. These are full of wonder; more mysterious are the moments that must have brushed me with their wings and passed me by; when Fate beckoned and I did not see it, when new Life trembled for a second at the threshold; but the word was not spoken, the hand was not held out, and the Might-have-been shivered and vanished, dim as a dream, into the waste realms of nonexistence.

So I never lose a sense of the whimsical and perilous charm of daily life, with its meetings and words and accidents. Why, today, perhaps, or next week, I may hear a voice, and, packing up my Gladstone bag, follow it to the ends of the world.

FROM THE MAT-MAKER

In *Moby Dick,* Chapter XLVII

HERMAN MELVILLE

It was a cloudy, sultry afternoon; the seamen were lazily lounging about the decks, or vacantly gazing over into the lead-colored waters. Queequeg and I were mildly employed weaving what is called a sword-mat, for an additional lashing to our boat. So still and subdued and yet somehow preluding was all the scene, and such an incantation of revelry lurked in the air, that each silent sailor seemed resolved into his own invisible self.

I was the attendant or page of Queequeg, while busy at the mat. As I kept passing and repassing the filling or woof of marline between the long yarns of the warp, using my own hand for the shuttle, and as Queequeg, standing sideways, ever and anon slid his heavy oaken sword between the threads, and idly looking off upon the water, carelessly and unthinkingly drove home every yarn: I say so strange a dreaminess did there then reign all over the ship and all over the sea, only broken by the intermitting dull sound of the sword, that it seemed as if this were the Loom of Time, and I myself were a shuttle mechanically weaving and weaving away at the Fates. There lay the fixed threads of the warp subject to but one single, ever returning, unchanging vibration, and that vibration merely enough to admit of the crosswise interblending of other threads with its own. This warp seemed necessity; and here, thought I, with my own hand I ply my own shuttle and weave my own destiny into these unalterable threads. Meantime, Queequeg's impulsive, indifferent sword, sometimes hitting the woof slantingly, or crookedly, or strongly, or weakly, as the case might be; and by this difference in the concluding blow producing a corresponding contrast in the final aspect of the completed fabric; this savage's sword, thought I, which thus finally shapes and fashions both warp and woof; this easy, indifferent sword must be chance—aye, chance, free will, and necessity—no wise incompatible—all interweavingly working together. The straight warp of necessity, not to be swerved from its ultimate course—its every alternating vibration, indeed, only tending to that; free will still free to ply her shuttle between given threads; and chance, though restrained in its play within the right lines of necessity, and sideways in its motions directed by free will, though thus prescribed to by both, chance by turns rules either, and has the last featuring blow at events.

CHAPTER 10

THE PROBLEM OF KNOWLEDGE

> Ah, what a dusty answer gets the soul
> When hot for certainties in this our life!—
> In tragic hints here see what evermore
> Moves dark as yonder midnight ocean's force,
> Thundering like ramping hosts of warrior horse,
> To throw that faint thin line upon the shore!
> —George Meredith, Sonnet L.

In an age "destitute of faith, but terrified at skepticism," it is as imperative to examine theoretically the bases of our knowledge as it is to protect practically the free discussion of what we claim to know.

If indeed philosophy does begin in wonder, as by dint of much echoing since Aristotle we have been led to believe, the supreme wonder may be that aroused by the discovery, made anew by every thoughtful person, "that this so solid-seeming World, after all, may be but an air-image, our Me the only reality." Is there, for that matter, a *real* reality? Do we in truth "clutch at shadows as if they were substances"? Robinson Jeffers offers Carlyle an immediate answer; even "the heart-breaking beauty Will remain when there is no heart to break for it." But he has his answer in Shakespeare and Freneau, the latter asserting that things are concepts in the mind of a superior Being. Berkeleyan subjectivity is pushed through to its *reductio ad absurdum,* Calderón, Wallace Stevens, and George Santayana interpret the theme of the solipsist, "and being's sum Is but the sum of dreams."

Repeatedly in the history of speculation on these matters, man has returned with a kind of small-boyish naiveness, to the immediate clarity and seeming assurance of a reaffirmed realism. The old External World is still there. Seeing is believing. Or is it? The metaphysical and the epistemological problems cannot be separated. Where can we get our evidence except through the senses? But, as W. H. Auden queries, "Are data from the world of Sense, In that case, valid evidence?"

The reader is thus introduced directly to the attitude of skepticism which, he has recognized, has been there in the background all along. Anatole France states the matter plainly: "The same things often assume different appearances. . . . But who shall solve the problem of their true nature?" Though he grounds his skepticism in faith, Pascal agrees with this view in essence: it is "equally impossible to know the parts without knowing the whole and to know the whole without knowing the parts in detail."

There may be many theoretical answers to a complete skepticism; it is certain that there is a profoundly significant practical one. Calderón in *The Dream Called Life* leaves open the question whether we are awake or dreaming; however, if dreaming, he says, man must still walk "as one who knows he soon may wake." Santayana punctuates the whole problem raised by the skeptics with the passionate affirmation:

> I know but this of all I would I knew
> Truth is a dream, unless my dream be true.

It may be, indeed, that an inner source of knowledge can be trusted to yield certainty. There is an inward seeing, says Santayana ("The Psyche"). "Intuition, floods of intuition, have been playing for ages upon human life." Elsewhere, in the classic third sonnet, he is more explicit: "But it is wisdom to believe the heart." Rainer Maria Rilke and Whitman sustain the intuitional position. "Wisdom is of the soul," Whitman contends, "is not susceptible of proof, is its own proof."

Can man return to utter innocence in his perception of nature? Has he failed to achieve knowledge because he has not been free enough of preconceptions? "You must become an ignorant man again," says Wallace Stevens, "and see the sun again with an ignorant eye."

It is in this spirit that Descartes begins his great inquiry: By what methods can we arrive at truth about ourselves and the world? Is there any starting point of established fact? "I think; therefore I am." This axiom has been called the beginning of modern philosophy, though some recent speculation would reverse the sequence of ideas: "I am, therefore I think," declares Unamuno, stating a thesis that lies at the heart of existentialism.

Eddington, representing the scientist at work, suggests broadly the difficulties in the path of those who would regard exact science as the all-sufficient source of knowledge of the universe.

Alfred North Whitehead, in the passage from *Science and the Modern World* calls the conflict of science and religion into the open, pointing to a new theme. "A clash of doctrines," he says, "is not a disaster—it is an opportunity." "It belongs to the self-respect of intellect to pursue every tangle of thought to its final unravelment. The important question is, In what spirit are we going to face the issue?"

FROM THE WORLD OUT OF CLOTHES

In *Sartor Resartus*

THOMAS CARLYLE

"With men of a speculative turn," writes Teufelsdröckh, "there come seasons, meditative, sweet, yet awful hours, when in wonder and fear you ask yourself that unanswerable question: Who am *I*; the thing that can say 'I' *(das Wesen das sich Ich nennt)?* The world, with its loud trafficking, retires into the distance; and, through the paper-hangings, and stone-walls, and thick-plied tissues of Commerce and Polity, and all the living and lifeless integuments (of Society and a Body), wherewith your Existence sits surrounded,—the sight reaches forth into the void Deep, and you are alone with the Universe, and silently commune with it, as one mysterious Presence with another.

"Who am I; what is this ME? A Voice, a Motion, an Appearance;—some embodied, visualized Idea in the Eternal Mind? *Cogito, ergo sum.* Alas, poor Cogitator, this takes us but a little way. Sure enough, I am; and lately was not: but Whence? How? Whereto? The answer lies around, written in all colors and motions, uttered in all tones of jubilee and wail, in thousand-figured, thousand-voiced, harmonious Nature: but where is the cunning eye and ear to whom that God-written Apocalypse will yield articulate meaning? We sit as in a boundless Phantasmagoria and Dream-grotto; boundless, for the faintest star, the remotest century, lies not even nearer the verge thereof: sounds and many-colored visions flit round our sense; but Him, the Unslumbering, whose work both Dream and Dreamer are, we see not; except in rare half-waking moments, suspect not. Creation, says one, lies before us, like a glorious Rainbow; but the Sun that made it lies behind us, hidden from us. Then, in that strange Dream, how we clutch at shadows as if they were substances; and sleep deepest while fancying ourselves most awake! Which of your Philosophical Systems is other than a dream-theorem; a net quotient, confidently given out, where divisor and dividend are both unknown? What are all your national Wars, with their Moscow Retreats, and sanguinary hate-filled Revolutions, but the Somnambulism of uneasy Sleepers? This Dreaming, this Somnambulism is what we on Earth call Life; wherein the most indeed undoubtingly wander, as if they knew right hand from left; yet they only are wise who know that they know nothing.

"Pity that all Metaphysics had hitherto proved so inexpressibly unproductive! The secret of Man's Being is still like the Sphinx's secret: a riddle that he cannot rede; and for ignorance of which he suffers death, the worst death, a spiritual. What are your Axioms, and Categories, and Systems, and Aphorisms? Words, words. High Air-castles are cunningly built of Words, the Words well bedded also in good Logic-mortar, wherein, however, no Knowledge will come to lodge. *The whole is greater than the part:* how exceedingly true! *Nature abhors a vacuum:* how exceedingly false and calumnious! Again, *Nothing can act but where it is:* with all my heart; only, WHERE is it? Be not the slave of Words: is not the Distant, the Dead, while I love it, and long for it, and mourn for it, Here, in the genuine sense, as truly as the floor I stand on? But that same WHERE, with its brother WHEN, are from the first the mastercolors of our Dream-grotto; say rather, the Canvas (the warp and woof thereof) whereon all our Dreams and Life-visions are painted. Nevertheless, has not a deeper meditation taught certain of every climate and age, that the WHERE and WHEN, so mysteriously inseparable from all our thoughts, are but superficial terrestrial adhesions to thought; that the

Seer may discern them where they mount up out of the celestial EVERYWHERE and FOREVER: have not all nations conceived their God as Omnipresent and Eternal; as existing in a universal HERE, an everlasting NOW? Think well, thou too wilt find that Space is but a mode of our human Sense, so likewise Time; there is no Space and no Time: WE are—we know *not* what;—light-sparkles floating in the aether of Deity!

"So that this so solid-seeming World, after all, were but an air-image, our ME the only reality: and Nature, with its thousandfold production and destruction, but the reflex of our own inward Force, the 'phantasy of our Dream'; or what the Earth-Spirit in *Faust* names it, *the living visible Garment of God:*

> 'In Being's floods, in Action's storm,
> I walk and work, above, beneath,
> Work and weave in endless motion!
> > Birth and Death,
> > An infinite ocean;
> > A seizing and giving
> > The fire of Living:
> 'Tis thus at the roaring Loom of Time I ply,
> And weave for God the Garment thou seest Him by.'

Of twenty millions that have read and spouted this thunderspeech of the *Erdgeist,* are there yet twenty units of us that have learned the meaning thereof?

CREDO

ROBINSON JEFFERS

> My friend from Asia has powers and magic, he plucks a blue
> > leaf from the young blue-gum
> And gazing upon it, gathering and quieting
> The God in his mind, creates an ocean more real than the
> > ocean, the salt, the actual
> Appalling presence, the power of the waters.
> He believes that nothing is real except as we make it.   I
> > humbler have found in my blood
> Bred west of Caucasus a harder mysticism.
> Multitude stands in my mind but I think that the ocean in
> > the bone vault is only
> The bone vault's ocean: out there is the ocean's;
> The water is the water, the cliff is the rock, come shocks
> > and flashes of reality.   The mind
> Passes, the eye closes, the spirit is a passage;
> The beauty of things was born before eyes and sufficient
> > to itself; the heart-breaking beauty
> Will remain when there is no heart to break for it.

THE TEMPEST, IV, i, 146-158

WILLIAM SHAKESPEARE

> PROSPERO: You do look, my son, in a moved sort,
> > As if you were dismayed.   Be cheerful, sir,
> > Our revels now are ended.   These our actors,
> > As I foretold you, were all spirits, and

Are melted into air, into thin air;
And, like the baseless fabric of this vision,
The cloud-capped towers, the gorgeous palaces,
The solemn temples, the great globe itself,
Yea, all which it inherit, shall dissolve
And, like this insubstantial pageant faded,
Leave not a rack behind.   We are such stuff
As dreams are made on, and our little life
Is rounded with a sleep.

THE TESTAMENT OF BEAUTY, I, lines 74-87 *

ROBERT BRIDGES

Hast thou then thought that all this ravishing music,
that stirreth so thy heart, making thee dream of things
illimitable unsearchable and of heavenly import,
is but a light disturbance of the atoms of air,
whose jostling ripples, gather'd within the ear, are tuned
to resonant scale, and thence by the enthron'd mind received
on the spiral stairway of her audience chamber
as heralds of high spiritual significance?
and that without thine ear, sound would hav no report,
Nature hav no music nor would ther be for thee
any better melody in the April woods at dawn
than what an old stone-deaf labourer, lying awake
o'night in his comfortless attic, might perchance
be aware of, when the rats run amok in his thatch?

"THERE WAS A YOUNG MAN—"

RONALD KNOX

There was a young man who said, "God
Must think it exceedingly odd
      That this little tree
      Should continue to be
When there is no one about in the quad."

THE REPLY

ANONYMOUS

"Dear Sir, it is not very odd;
I am always about in the quad,
      And that's why this tree
      Will continue to be
Since observed by
                  Yours faithfully,
                        God."

* The author's preferences in spelling and punctuation are observed.

FROM THE POWER OF FANCY

PHILIP FRENEAU

Wakeful, vagrant, restless thing,
Ever wandering on the wing,
Who thy wondrous source can find,
FANCY, regent of the mind;
A spark from Jove's resplendent throne,
But thy nature all unknown.

This spark of bright, celestial flame,
From Jove's seraphic altar came,
And hence alone in man we trace,
Resemblance to the immortal race.

Ah! what is all this mighty WHOLE,
These suns and stars that round us roll!
What are they all, where'er they shine,
But *Fancies* of the Power Divine!
What is this *globe*, these *lands*, and *seas*,
And *heat*, and *cold*, and *flowers*, and *trees*,
And *life*, and *death*, and *beast*, and *man*,
And *time*—that with the *sun* began—
But thoughts on reason's scale combined,
Ideas of the Almighty mind?

FROM LIFE IS A DREAM

PEDRO CALDERÓN DE LA BARCA

We live, while we see the sun,
Where life and dreams are as one;
And living has taught me this,
Man dreams the life that is his,
Until his living is done.
The king dreams he is king, and he lives
In the deceit of a king,
Commanding and governing;
And all the praise he receives
Is written in wind, and leaves
A little dust on the way
When death ends all with a breath.
Where then is the gain of a throne,
That shall perish and not be known
In the other dream that is death?
Dreams the rich man of riches and fears,
The fears that his riches breed;
The poor man dreams of his need,
And all his sorrows and tears;
Dreams he that prospers with years
Dreams he that feigns and foregoes,
Dreams he that rails on his foes;

And in all the world, I see,
Man dreams whatever he be,
And his own dream no man knows.
And I too dream and behold,
I dream and I am bound with chains,
And I dreamed that these present pains
Were fortunate ways of old.
What is life? a tale that is told;
What is life? a frenzy extreme,
A shadow of things that seem;
And the greatest good is but small,
That all life is dream to all
And that dreams themselves are a dream.

(Arthur Symons, tr.)

HOLIDAY IN REALITY *

WALLACE STEVENS

I

It was something to see that their white was different,
Sharp as white paint in the January sun;

Something to feel that they needed another yellow,
Less Aix than Stockholm, hardly a yellow at all,

A vibrancy not to be taken for granted, from
A sun in an almost colorless, cold heaven.

They had known that there was not even a common speech,
Palabra of a common man who did not exist.

Why should they not know they had everything of their own
As each had a particular woman and her touch?

After all, they knew that to be real each had
To find for himself his earth, his sky, his sea.

And the words for them and the colors that they possessed.
It was impossible to breathe at Durand-Ruel's.

II

The flowering Judas grows from the belly or not at all.
The breast is covered with violets.　It is a green leaf.

Spring is umbilical or else it is not spring.
Spring is the truth of spring or nothing, a waste, a fake.

These trees and their argentines, their dark-spiced branches,
Grow out of the spirit or they are fantastic dust.

* Reprinted from *Transport to Summer* by Wallace Stevens by permission of Alfred A. Knopf, Inc.　(Copyright 1942, 1947 by Wallace Stevens.)

The bud of the apple is desire, the down-falling gold,
The catbird's gobble in the morning half-awake—

These are real only if I make them so.   Whistle
For me, grow green for me and, as you whistle and grow green,

Intangible arrows quiver and stick in the skin
And I taste at the root of the tongue the unreal of what is real.

SOLIPSISM *

GEORGE SANTAYANA

I could believe that I am here alone,
    And all the world my dream;
The passion of the scene is all my own,
    And things that seem but seem.

Perchance an exhalation of my sorrow
    Hath raised this vaporous show,
For whence but from my soul should all things borrow
    So deep a tinge of woe?

I keep the secret doubt within my breast
    To be the gods' defense,
To ease the heart by too much ruth oppressed
    And drive the horror hence.

O sorrow that the patient brute should cower
    And die, not having sinned!
O pity that the wild and fragile flower
    Should shiver in the wind!

Then were I dreaming dreams I know not of,
    For that is part of me
That feels the piercing pang of grief and love
    And doubts eternally.

But whether all to me the vision come
    Or break in many beams,
The pageant ever shifts, and being's sum
    Is but the sum of dreams.

THE LABYRINTH

W. H. AUDEN

Anthropos apteros for days
Walked whistling round and round the maze,
Relying happily upon
His temperament for getting on.

* Reprinted from *Poems* by George Santayana; copyright 1923 by Charles Scribner's Sons; used by permission of the publishers.

The hundredth time he sighted, though,
A bush he left an hour ago,
He halted where four alleys crossed,
And recognized that he was lost.

"Where am I?   Metaphysics says
No question can be asked unless
It has an answer, so I can
Assume this maze has got a plan.

If theologians are correct,
A Plan implies an Architect:
A God-built maze would be, I'm sure,
The Universe in miniature.

Are data from the world of Sense,
In that case, valid evidence?
What in the universe I know
Can give directions how to go?

All Mathematics would suggest
A steady straight line as the best,
But left and right alternately
Is consonant with History.

Aesthetics, though, believes all Art
Intends to gratify the Heart:
Rejecting disciplines like these,
Must I, then, go which way I please?

Such reasoning is only true
If we accept the classic view,
Which we have no right to assert,
According to the Introvert.

His absolute presupposition
Is—Man creates his own condition:
This maze was not divinely built,
But is secreted by my guilt.

The center that I cannot find
Is known to my unconscious mind;
I have no reason to despair
Because I am already there.

My problem is how *not* to will;
They move most quickly who stand still;
I'm only lost until I see
I'm lost because I want to be.

If this should fail, perhaps I should,
As certain educators would,
Content myself with the conclusion;
In theory there is no solution.

All statements about what I feel,
Like I-am-lost, are quite unreal:
My knowledge ends where it began;
A hedge is taller than a man."

Anthropos apteros, perplexed
To know which turning to take next,
Looked up and wished he were the bird
To whom such doubts must seem absurd.

from THAÏS, Part I

ANATOLE FRANCE

The old man replied—

"It is useless to act, or to abstain from acting. It matters not whether we live or die."

"Eh, what?" asked Paphnutius. "Do you not desire to live through all eternity? But, tell me, do you not live in a hut in the desert as the hermits do?"

"It seems so."

"Do I not see you naked, and lacking all things?"

"It seems so."

"Do you not feed on roots, and live in chastity?"

"It seems so."

"Have you not renounced all the vanities of this world?"

"I have truly renounced all those vain things for which men commonly care."

"Then you are like me, poor, chaste, and solitary. And you are not so—as I am for the love of God, and with a hope of celestial happiness! That I cannot understand. Why are you virtuous if you do not believe in Jesus Christ? Why deprive yourself of the good things of this world if you do not hope to gain eternal riches in heaven?"

"Stranger, I deprive myself of nothing which is good, and I flatter myself that I have found a life which is satisfactory enough, though—to speak more precisely— there is no such thing as a good or evil life. Nothing is itself either virtuous or shameful, just or unjust, pleasant or painful, good or bad. It is our opinion which gives those qualities to things, as salt gives savor to meats."

"So then, according to you there is no certainty. You deny the truth which the idolaters themselves have sought. You lie in ignorance—like a tired dog sleeping in the mud."

"Stranger, it is equally useless to abuse either dogs or philosophers. We know not what dogs are or what we are. We know nothing."

"Old man, do you belong, then, to the absurd sect of skeptics? Are you one of those miserable fools who alike deny movement and rest, and who know not how to distinguish between the light of the sun and the shadows of night?"

"Friend, I am truly a skeptic, and of a sect which appears praiseworthy to me, though it seems ridiculous to you. For the same things often assume different appearances. The pyramids of Memphis seem at sunrise to be cones of pink light. At sunset they look like black triangles against the illuminated sky. But who shall solve the problem of their true nature? You reproach me with denying appearances, when, in fact, appearances are the only realities I recognize. The sun seems to me illuminous, but its nature is unknown to me. I feel that fire burns—but I know not how or why.   My friend, you understand me badly.   Besides, it is indifferent to me whether I am understood one way or the other."

(Robert B. Douglas, tr.)

FROM PENSÉES, 72

BLAISE PASCAL

Let man then contemplate the whole of nature in her full and grand majesty, and turn his vision from the low objects which surround him.   Let him gaze on that brilliant light, set like an eternal lamp to illumine the universe; let the earth appear to him a point in comparison with the vast circle described by the sun; and let him wonder at the fact that this vast circle is itself but a very fine point in comparison with that described by the stars in their revolution round the firmament. But if our view be arrested there, let our imagination pass beyond; it will sooner exhaust the power of conception than nature that of supplying material for conception.   The whole visible world is only an imperceptible atom in the ample bosom of nature.   No idea approaches it.   We may enlarge our conceptions beyond all imaginable space; we only produce atoms in comparison with the reality of things.   It is an infinite sphere, the center of which is everywhere, the circumference nowhere.   In short it is the greatest sensible mark of the almighty power of God, that imagination loses itself in that thought.

Returning to himself, let man consider what he is in comparison with all existence; let him regard himself as lost in this remote corner of nature; and from the little cell in which he finds himself lodged, I mean the universe, let him estimate at their true value the earth, kingdoms, cities, and himself.   What is a man in the Infinite?

But to show him another prodigy equally astonishing, let him examine the most delicate things he knows.   Let a mite be given him, with its minute body and parts incomparably more minute, limbs with their joints, veins in the limbs, blood in the veins, humors in the blood, drops in the humors, vapors in the drops.   Dividing these last things again, let him exhaust his powers of conception, and let the last object at which he can arrive be now that of our discourse.   Perhaps he will think that here is the smallest point in nature.   I will let him see therein a new abyss.   I will paint for him not only the visible universe, but all that he can conceive of nature's immensity in the womb of this abridged atom.   Let him see therein an infinity of universes, each of which has its firmament, its planets, its earth, in the same proportion as in the visible world; in each earth animals, and in the last mites, in which he will find again all that the first had, finding still in these others the same thing without end and without cessation.   Let him lose himself in wonders as amazing in their littleness as the others in their vastness.   For who will not be astounded at the fact that our body, which a little ago was imperceptible in the universe, itself imperceptible in the bosom of the whole, is now a colossus, a world, or rather a whole, in respect of the nothingness which we cannot reach?   He who regards himself in this light will be afraid of himself, and observing himself sustained in the body given him by nature between those two abysses of the Infinite and Nothing, will tremble at the sight of these marvels; and I think that, as his curiosity changes into admiration, he will be more disposed to contemplate them in silence than to examine them with presumption.

For in fact what is man in nature?   A Nothing in comparison with the Infinite, an All in comparison with the Nothing, a mean between nothing and everything.

Since he is infinitely removed from comprehending the extremes, the end of things and their beginning are hopelessly hidden from him in an impenetrable secret; he is equally incapable of seeing the Nothing from which he was made, and the Infinite in which he is swallowed up.

What will he do then, but perceive the appearance of the middle of things, in an eternal despair of knowing either their beginning or their end? All things proceed from the Nothing, and are borne towards the Infinite. Who will follow these marvelous processes? The Author of these wonders understands them. None other can do so.

Through failure to contemplate these Infinites, men have rashly rushed into the examination of nature, as though they bore some proportion to her. It is strange that they have wished to understand the beginnings of things, and thence to arrive at the knowledge of the whole, with a presumption as infinite as their object. For surely this design cannot be formed without presumption or without a capacity infinite like nature. . . .

Let us then take our compass; we are something, and we are not everything. The nature of our existence hides from us the knowledge of first beginnings which are born of the Nothing; and the littleness of our being conceals from us the sight of the Infinite.

Our intellect holds the same position in the world of thought as our body occupies in the expanse of nature.

Limited as we are in every way, this state which holds the mean between two extremes is present in all our impotence. Our senses perceive no extreme. Too much sound deafens us; too much light dazzles us; too great distance or proximity hinders our view. Too great length and too great brevity of discourse tend to obscurity; too much truth is paralyzing; (I know some who cannot understand that to take four from nothing leaves nothing). First principles are too self-evident for us; too much pleasure disagrees with us. Too many concords are annoying in music; too many benefits irritate us; we wish to have the wherewithal to overpay our debts. . . . We feel neither extreme heat nor extreme cold. Excessive qualities are prejudicial to us and not perceptible by the senses; we do not feel but suffer them. Extreme youth and extreme age hinder the mind, as also too much and too little education. In short, extremes are for us as though they were not, and we are not within their notice. They escape us, or we them.

This is our true state; this is what makes us incapable of certain knowledge and of absolute ignorance. We sail within a vast sphere, ever drifting in uncertainty, driven from end to end. When we think to attach ourselves to any point and to fasten to it, it wavers and leaves us; and if we follow it, it eludes our grasp, slips past us, and vanishes for ever. Nothing stays for us. This is our natural condition, and yet most contrary to our inclination; we burn with desire to find solid ground and an ultimate sure foundation whereon to build a tower reaching to the Infinite. But our whole groundwork cracks, and the earth opens to abysses.

Let us therefore not look for certainty and stability. Our reason is always deceived by fickle shadows; nothing can fix the finite between the two Infinites, which both enclose and fly from it.

If this be well understood, I think that we shall remain at rest, each in the state wherein nature has placed him. As this sphere which has fallen to us as our lot is always distant from either extreme, what matters it that man should have a little more knowledge of the universe? If he has it, he but gets a little higher. Is he not always infinitely removed from the end, and is not the duration of our life equally removed from eternity, even if it lasts ten years longer?

In comparison with these Infinites all finites are equal, and I see no reason for fixing our imagination on one more than on another. The only comparison which we make of ourselves to the finite is painful to us.

If man made himself the first object of study, he would see how incapable he is of going further. How can a part know the whole? But he may perhaps aspire to know at least the parts to which he bears some proportion. But the parts of the world are all so related and linked to one another, that I believe it impossible to know one without the other and without the whole.

Man, for instance, is related to all he knows. He needs a place wherein to abide, time through which to live, motion in order to live, elements to compose him, warmth and food to nourish him, air to breathe. He sees light; he feels bodies; in short, he is in a dependent alliance with everything. To know man, then, it is necessary to know how it happens that he needs air to live, and, to know the air, we must know how it is thus related to the life of man, etc. Flame cannot exist without air; therefore to understand the one, we must understand the other.

Since everything then is cause and effect, dependent and supporting, mediate and immediate, and all is held together by a natural though imperceptible chain, which binds together things most distant and most different, I hold it equally impossible to know the parts without knowing the whole, and to know the whole without knowing the parts in detail.

And what completes our incapability of knowing things, is the fact that they are simple, and that we are composed of two opposite natures, different in kind, soul and body. For it is impossible that our rational part should be other than spiritual; and if any one maintain that we are simply corporeal, this would far more exclude us from the knowledge of things, there being nothing so inconceivable as to say that matter knows itself. It is impossible to imagine how it should know itself. . . .

(W. F. Trotter, tr.)

THE DREAM CALLED LIFE

PEDRO CALDERÓN DE LA BARCA

A dream it was in which I found myself.
And you that hail me now, then hailed me king,
In a brave palace that was all my own,
Within, and all without it, mine; until,
Drunk with excess of majesty and pride,
Methought I towered so big and swelled so wide
That of myself I burst the glittering bubble
Which my ambition had about me blown
And all again was darkness. Such a dream
As this, in which I may be walking now,
Dispensing solemn justice to you shadows,
Who make believe to listen; but anon
Kings, princes, captains, warriors, plume and steel
Ay, even with all your airy theater,
May flit into the air you seem to rend
With acclamations, leaving me to wake
In the dark tower; or dreaming that I wake
From this that waking is; or this and that,
Both waking and both dreaming; such a doubt
Confounds and clouds our mortal life about.

But whether wake or dreaming, this I know
How dreamwise human glories come and go;
Whose momentary tenure not to break,
Walking as one who knows he soon may wake,
So fairly carry the full cup, so well
Disordered insolence and passion quell,
That there be nothing after to upbraid
Dreamer or doer in the part he played;
Whether tomorrow's dawn shall break the spell,
Or the last trumpet of the Eternal Day,
When dreaming, with the night, shall pass away.
(Edward Fitzgerald, tr.)

"DREAMT I TODAY THE DREAM OF YESTERNIGHT" *

GEORGE SANTAYANA

Dreamt I today the dream of yesternight,
Sleep ever feigning one evolving theme,—
Of my two lives which should I call the dream?
Which action vanity? Which vision sight?
Some greater waking must pronounce aright,
If aught abideth of the things that seem,
And with both currents swell the flooded stream
Into an ocean infinite of light.
Even such a dream I dream, and know full well
My waking passeth like a midnight spell,
But know not if my dreaming breaketh through
Into the deeps of heaven and of hell.
I know but this of all I would I knew:
Truth is a dream, unless my dream is true.

FROM THE PSYCHE †

In Soliloquies in England and Later Soliloquies

GEORGE SANTAYANA

There is, then, in every man a Psyche, or inherited nucleus of life, which from its dormant seminal condition expands and awakes anew in each generation, becoming the person recognized in history, law and morals. A man's body is a sort of husk of which his Psyche (itself material) is the kernel; and it is out of the predispositions of this living seed, played upon by circumstances, that his character and his mind are formed. The Psyche's first care is to surround itself with outer organs like a spider with its web; only these organs remain subject to her central control, and are the medium by which she acts upon outer things, and receives, in her patient labor, the solicitations and rebuffs of fortune. The Psyche, being essentially a way of living, a sort of animated code of hygiene and morals, is a very selective principle: she is perpetually distinguishing—in action, if not in words—

between good and bad, right and wrong.   Choice is the breath of her nostrils.   All the senses, instincts, and passions are her scouts.   The further she extends her influence the more she feels how dependent she is on external things, and the more feverishly she tries to modify them, so as to render them more harmonious with her own impulses.

At first, when she was only a vegetative Psyche, she waited in a comparatively peaceful mystical torpor for the rain or the sunshine to foster her, or for the cruel winter or barbarous scythe to cut her down; and she never would have survived at all if breeding had not been her chief preoccupation; but she distributed herself so multitudinously and so fast amongst her children, that she has survived to this day. Later, she found a new means of safety and profit in locomotion; and it was then that she began to perceive distinct objects, to think, and to plan her actions—accomplishments by no means native to her.   Like the Chinese, she is just as busy by night as by day.   Long before the sunrise she is at work in her subterranean kitchen over her pots of stewing herbs, her looms, and her spindles; and with the first dawn, when the first ray of intuition falls through some aperture into those dusky spaces, what does it light up?   The secret springs of her life?   The aims she is so faithfully but blindly pursuing?   Far from it.   Intuition, floods of intuition, have been playing for ages upon human life: poets, painters, men of prayer, scrupulous naturalists innumerable, have been intent on their several visions; yet of the origin and of the end of life we know as little as ever.   And the reason is this: that intuition is not a material organ of the Psyche, like a hand or an antenna; it is a miraculous child far more alive than herself, whose only instinct is play, laughter, and brooding meditation.   This strange child—who could have been his father?—is a poet; absolutely useless and incomprehensible to his poor mother, and only a new burden on her shoulders, because she can't help feeding and loving him.   He *sees;* which to her is a mystery, because although she has always acted as if, in some measure, she felt things at a distance, she has never seen and never can see anything.   Nor are his senses, for all their vivacity, of any use to her.   For what do they reveal to him?   Always something irrelevant: a shaft of dusty light across the rafters, a blue flame dancing on the coals, a hum, a babbling of waters, a breath of heat or of coolness, a mortal weariness, or a groundless joy—all dream-images, of a play world, essences painted on air, such as any poet might invent in idleness. Yet the child cares about them immensely: he is full of sudden tears and of jealous little loves.   "Hush, my child," says good mother Psyche, "it's all nonsense."   It is not for those fantastic visions that she watches: she knits with her eyes shut, and mutters the same old prayers. . . .

"O WORLD, THOU CHOOSEST NOT THE BETTER PART" *

GEORGE SANTAYANA

O world, thou choosest not the better part!
It is not wisdom to be only wise,
And on the inward vision close the eyes,
But it is wisdom to believe the heart.
Columbus found a world, and had no chart,
Save one that faith deciphered in the skies;
To trust the soul's invincible surmise
Was all his science and his only art.
Our knowledge is a torch of smoky pine

* Reprinted from *Poems* by George Santayana; copyright 1923 by Charles Scribner's Sons; used by permission of the publishers.

That lights the pathway but one step ahead
Across a void of mystery and dread.
Bid, then, the tender light of faith to shine
By which alone the mortal heart is led
Unto the thinking of the thought divine.

from DUINO ELEGIES *

RAINER MARIA RILKE

THE THIRD ELEGY

One thing to sing the beloved, another, alas!
that hidden guilty river-god of the blood.
He whom she knows from afar, her lover, what does he know
of that Lord of Pleasure, who often, out of his lonely heart,
before she had soothed him, often as though she did not exist,
streaming from, oh, what unknowable depths would uplift
his god-head, uprousing the night to infinite uproar?
Oh, the Neptune within our blood, oh, his terrible trident!
Oh, the gloomy blast of his breast from the twisted shell!
Hark, how the night grows fluted and hollowed.   You stars,
is it not from you that the lover's delight in the loved one's
face arises?   Does not his intimate insight
into her purest face come from the purest star?

It was not you, alas!   It was not his mother
that bent his brows into such an expectant arch.
Not to meet yours, girl feeling him, not to meet yours
did his lips begin to assume that more fruitful curve.
Do you really suppose your gentle approach could have so
convulsed him, you, that wander like morning-breezes?
You terrified his heart, indeed; but more ancient terrors
rushed into him in that instant of shattering contact.
Call him . . . you can't quite call him away from those somber
        companions.
Truly, he tries to, he does escape them; disburdenedly settles
into your intimate heart, receives and begins himself there.
Did he ever begin himself, though?
Mother, you made him small, it was you that began him;
he was new to you, you arched over those new eyes
the friendly world, averting the one that was strange.
Where, oh where, are the years when you simply displaced
for him, with your slender figure, the surging abyss?
You hid so much from him then; made the nightly-suspected room
harmless, and out of your heart full of refuge
mingled more human space with that of his nights.
Not in the darkness, no, but within your far nearer presence
you placed the light, and it shone as though out of friendship.
Nowhere a creak you could not explain with a smile,
as though you had long known *when* the floor would behave itself
thus . . .

And he listened to you and was soothed. So much it availed,
gently, your coming; his tall cloaked destiny stepped
behind the chest of drawers, and his restless future,
that easily got out of place, conformed to the folds of the curtain.

And he himself as he lay there in such relief,
mingling, under his drowsy eyelids, the sweetness
of your light shaping with foretaste of coming sleep,
seemed to be under protection . . . Within, though: who could avert,
divert, the floods of origin flowing within him?
Alas! there *was* no caution within that sleeper; sleeping,
yes, but dreaming, yes but feverish: what he embarked on!
He, so new, so timorous, how he got tangled
in ever-encroaching roots of inner event,
twisted to primitive patterns, to throttling growths, to bestial
preying forms!   How he gave himself up to it!   Loved.
Loved his interior world, his interior jungle,
that primal forest within, on whose mute overthrownness,
green-lit, his heart stood, Loved.   Left it, continued
into his own roots and out into violent beginning
where his tiny birth was already outlived.   Descended,
lovingly, into the older blood, the ravines
where Frightfulness lurked, still gorged with his fathers.   And every
terror knew him, and winked and quite understood.
Yes, Horror smiled at him . . . Seldom
did you, Mother, smile so tenderly.   How could he help
loving what smiled at him?   Long before you
he loved it, for, even while you bore him,
it was there, dissolved in the water that lightens the seed.

Look, we don't love like flowers, with only a single
season behind us; immemorial sap
mounts in our arms when we love. Oh, maid,
this: that we've loved, *within* us, not one, still to come, but all
the innumerable fermentation; not just a single child,
but the fathers, resting like mountain-ruins
within our depths;—but the dry river-bed
of former mothers;—yes, and the whole of that
soundless landscape under its cloudy or
cloudless destiny:—*this* got the start of you, maid.

And you yourself, how can you tell,—you have conjured up
prehistoric time in your lover. What feelings
whelmed up from beings gone by! What women
hated you in him! What sinister men
you roused in his youthful veins! Dead children
were trying to reach you . . . Oh gently, gently
show him daily a loving, confident task done,—guide him
close to the garden, give him those counter-
balancing nights . . . . . .
                         Withhold him . . . . . .

THE FOURTH ELEGY

. . . . O hours of childhood,
hours when behind the figures there was more
than the mere past, and when what lay before us
was not the future! We were growing, and sometimes
impatient to grow up, half for the sake
of those who'd nothing left but their grown-upness.
Yet, when alone, we entertained ourselves
with everlastingness: there we would stand,
within the gap left between world and toy,
upon a spot which, from the first beginning,
had been established for a pure event.

Who'll show a child just as it is? Who'll place it
within its constellation, with the measure
of distance in its hand? Who'll make its death
from gray bread, that grows hard,—or leave it there,
within the round mouth, like the choking core
of a sweet apple? . . . . . . Minds of murderers
are easily divined. But this, though: death,
the whole of death,—even before life's begun,
to hold it all as gently, and be good:
this is beyond description!
                    (J. B. Leishman and Stephen Spender, trs.)

FROM SONG OF THE OPEN ROAD

WALT WHITMAN

Here is the test of wisdom,
Wisdom is not finally tested in schools,
Wisdom cannot be passed from one having it to another not
          having it,
Wisdom is of the soul, is not susceptible of proof, is its
          own proof,
Applies to all stages and objects and qualities and is content,
Is the certainty of the reality and immortality of things,
          and the excellence of things;
Something there is in the float of the sight of things that
          provokes it out of the soul.
Now I re-examine philosophies and religions,
They may prove well in lecture-rooms, yet not prove at all
          under the spacious clouds and along the landscape and
          flowing currents.
Here is realization,
Here is a man tallied—he realizes here what he has in him,
The past, the future, majesty, love—if they are vacant of
          you, you are vacant of them.

FROM IT MUST BE ABSTRACT *

WALLACE STEVENS

Begin, ephebe, by perceiving the idea
Of this invention, this invented world,
The inconceivable idea of the sun.

You must become an ignorant man again
And see the sun again with an ignorant eye
And see it clearly in the idea of it.

Never suppose an inventing mind as source
Of this idea nor for that mind compose
A voluminous master folded in his fire.

How clean the sun when seen in its idea,
Washed in the remotest cleanliness of a heaven
That has expelled us and our images . . .

The death of one god is the death of all.
Let purple Phoebus lie in umber harvest,
Let Phoebus slumber and die in autumn umber,

Phoebus is dead, ephebe. But Phoebus was
A name for something that never could be named.
There was a project for the sun and is.

There is a project for the sun. The sun
Must bear no name, gold flourisher, but be
In the difficulty of what it is to be.

FROM DISCOURSE ON THE METHOD OF RIGHTLY CONDUCTING THE REASON, AND SEEKING TRUTH IN THE SCIENCES

RENÉ DESCARTES

Good sense is, of all things among men, the most equally distributed; for every one thinks himself so abundantly provided with it, that those even who are the most difficult to satisfy in everything else, do not usually desire a larger measure of this quality than they already possess. And in this it is not likely that all are mistaken: the conviction is rather to be held as testifying that the power of judging aright and of distinguishing Truth from Error, which is properly what is called Good Sense or Reason, is by nature equal in all men; and that the diversity of our opinions, consequently, does not arise from some being endowed with a larger share of Reason than others, but solely from this, that we conduct our thoughts along different ways, and do not fix our attention on the same objects. For to be possessed of a vigorous mind is not enough; the prime requisite is rightly to apply it. The greatest minds, as they are capable of the highest excellencies, are open likewise to the greatest aberrations; and those who travel very slowly may yet make far greater progress, provided they keep always to the straight road, than those who, while they run, forsake it.

For myself, I have never fancied my mind to be in any respect more perfect than those of the generality; on the contrary, I have often wished that I were equal to some others in promptitude of thought, or in clearness and distinctness of imagination, or in fulness and readiness of memory. And besides these, I know of no other qualities that contribute to the perfection of the mind; for as to the Reason or Sense, inasmuch as it is that alone which constitutes us men, and distinguishes us from the brutes, I am disposed to believe that it is to be found complete in each individual; and on this point to adopt the common opinion of philosophers, who say that the difference of greater and less holds only among the *accidents,* and not among the *forms* or *natures* of *individuals* of the same *species.*

I will not hesitate, however, to avow my belief that it has been my singular good fortune to have very early in life fallen in with certain tracks which have conducted me to considerations and maxims, of which I have formed a Method that gives me the means, as I think, of gradually augmenting my knowledge, and of raising it by little and little to the highest point which the mediocrity of my talents and the brief duration of my life will permit me to reach. For I have already reaped from it such fruits that, although I have been accustomed to think lowly enough of myself, and although when I look with the eye of a philosopher at the varied courses and pursuits of mankind at large, I find scarcely one which does not appear vain and useless, I nevertheless derive the highest satisfaction from the progress I conceive myself to have already made in the search after truth, and cannot help entertaining such expectations of the future as to believe that if, among the occupations of men as men, there is any one really excellent and important, it is that which I have chosen.

.   .   .   .

But like one walking alone and in the dark, I resolved to proceed so slowly and with such circumspection, that if I did not advance far, I would at least guard against falling. I did not even choose to dismiss summarily any of the opinions that had crept into my belief without having been introduced by Reason, but first of all took sufficient time carefully to satisfy myself of the general nature of the task I was setting myself, and ascertain the true Method by which to arrive at the knowledge of whatever lay within the compass of my powers.

.   .   .   .

And as a multitude of laws often only hampers justice, so that a state is best governed when, with few laws, these are rigidly administered; in like manner, instead of the great number of precepts of which Logic is composed, I believed that the four following would prove perfectly sufficient for me, provided I took the firm and unwavering resolution never in a single instance to fail in observing them.

The *first* was never to accept anything for true which I did not clearly know to be such; that is to say, carefully to avoid precipitancy and prejudice, and to comprise nothing more in my judgment than what was presented to my mind so clearly and distinctly as to exclude all ground of doubt.

The *second,* to divide each of the difficulties under examination into as many parts as possible, and as might be necessary for its adequate solution.

The *third,* to conduct my thoughts in such order that, by commencing with objects the simplest and easiest to know, I might ascend by little and little, and, as it were, step by step, to the knowledge of the more complex; assigning in thought a certain order even to those objects which in their own nature do not stand in relation of antecedence and sequence.

And the *last,* in every case to make enumerations so complete, and reviews so general, that I might be assured that nothing was omitted.

The long chains of simple and easy reasonings by means of which geometers are accustomed to reach the conclusions of their most difficult demonstrations, had led me to imagine that all things, to the knowledge of which man is competent, are mutually connected in the same way, and that there is nothing so far removed from us as to be beyond our reach, or so hidden that we cannot discover it, provided only we abstain from accepting the false for the true, and always preserve in our thoughts the order necessary for the deduction of one truth from another.

. . . .

I am in doubt as to the propriety of making my first meditations in the place above mentioned matter of discourse; for these are so metaphysical, and so uncommon, as not, perhaps, to be acceptable to every one. And yet, that it may be determined whether the foundations that I have laid are sufficiently secure, I find myself in a measure constrained to advert to them. I had long before remarked that, in relation to practice, it is sometimes necessary to adopt, as if above doubt, opinions which we discern to be highly uncertain, as has been already said; but as I then desired to give my attention solely to the search after truth, I thought that a procedure exactly the opposite was called for, and that I ought to reject as absolutely false all opinions in regard to which I could suppose the least ground for doubt, in order to ascertain whether after that there remained aught in my belief that was wholly indubitable. Accordingly, seeing that our senses sometimes deceive us, I was willing to suppose that there existed nothing really such as they presented to us; and because some men err in reasoning, and fall into paralogisms, even on the simplest matters of Geometry, I, convinced that I was as open to error as any other, rejected as false all the reasonings I had hitherto taken for demonstrations; and finally, when I considered that the very same thoughts (presentations) which we experience when awake may also be experienced when we are asleep, while there is at that time not one of them true, I supposed that all the objects (presentations) that had ever entered into my mind when awake, had in them no more truth than the illusions of my dreams. But immediately upon this I observed that, whilst I thus wished to think that all was false, it was absolutely necessary that I, who thus thought, should be somewhat; and as I observed that this truth, *I think, hence I am,* was so certain and of such evidence, that no ground of doubt, however extravagant, could be alleged by the Skeptics capable of shaking it, I concluded that I might, without scruple, accept it as the first principle of the Philosophy of which I was in search.

In the next place, I attentively examined what I was, and as I observed that I could suppose that I had no body, and that there was no world nor any place in which I might be; but that I could not therefore suppose that I was not; and that, on the contrary, from the very circumstance that I thought to doubt of the truth of other things, it most clearly and certainly followed that I was; while, on the other hand, if I had only ceased to think, although all the other objects which I had ever imagined had been in reality existent, I would have had no reason to believe that I existed; I thence concluded that I was a substance whose whole essence or nature consists only in thinking, and which, that it may exist, has need of no place, nor is dependent on any material thing; so that "I", that is to say, the mind by which I am what I am, is wholly distinct from the body, and is even more easily known than the latter, and is such, that although the latter were not, it would still continue to be all that it is.

After this I inquired in general into what is essential to the truth and certainty of a proposition; for since I had discovered one which I knew to be true, I thought that I must likewise be able to discover the ground of this certitude. And as I observed that in the words *I think, hence I am,* there is nothing at all which gives me assurance of their truth beyond this, that I see very clearly that in order to think it is necessary to exist, I concluded that I might take, as a general rule, the principle, that all the things which we very clearly and distinctly conceive are true, only observing, however, that there is some difficulty in rightly determining the objects which we distinctly conceive.

(John Veitch, tr.)

FROM THE STARTING-POINT

In *The Tragic Sense of Life*

MIGUEL DE UNAMUNO

The defect of Descartes' *Discourse of Method* lies not in the antecedent methodical doubt; not in his beginning by resolving to doubt everything, a merely intellectual device; but in his resolution to begin by emptying himself of himself, of Descartes, of the real man, the man of flesh and bone, the man who does not want to die, in order that he might be a mere thinker—that is, an abstraction. But the real man returned and thrust himself into the philosophy.

"Le bon sens est la chose du monde la mieux partagée." Thus begins the *Discourse of Method,* and this good sense saved him. He continues talking about himself, about the man Descartes, telling us among other things that he greatly esteemed eloquence and loved poetry; that he delighted above all in mathematics because of the evidence and certainty of its reasons, and that he revered our theology and claimed as much as any to attain to heaven—*et prétendais autant qu'aucun autre à gagner le ciel.* And this pretension—a very laudable one, I think, and above all very natural—was what prevented him from deducing all the consequences of his methodical doubt. The man Descartes claimed, as much as any other, to attain to heaven, "but having learned as a thing very sure that the way to it is not less open to the most ignorant than to the most learned, and that the revealed truths which lead thither are beyond our intelligence, I did not dare submit them to my feeble reasonings, and I thought that to undertake to examine them and to succeed therein, I should want some extraordinary help from heaven and need to be more than man." And here we have the man. Here we have the man who "did not feel obliged, thank God, to make a profession (*métier*) of science in order to increase his means, and who did not pretend to play the cynic and despise glory." And afterwards he tells us how he was compelled to make a sojourn in Germany, and there, shut up in a stove (*poêle*) he began to philosophize his method. But in Germany, shut up in a stove! And such his discourse is, a stove-discourse, and the stove a German one, although the philosopher shut up in it was a Frenchman who proposed to himself to attain to heaven.

And he arrives at the *cogito ergo sum,* which St. Augustine had already anticipated; but the *ego* implicit in this enthymeme, *ego cogito, ergo ego sum,* is an unreal—that is, an ideal—*ego* or I, and its *sum,* its existence, something unreal also. "I think, therefore I am," can only mean "I think, therefore I am a thinker"; this being of the "I am," which is deduced from "I think," is merely a knowing; this being is knowledge, but not life. And the primary reality is not that I think, but that I live, for those also live who do not think. Although this living may not be a real living. God! what contradictions when we seek to join in wedlock life and reason!

The truth is *sum, ergo cogito*—I am, therefore I think, although not everything that is thinks. Is not consciousness of thinking above all consciousness of being? Is pure thought possible, without consciousness of self, without personality? Can there exist pure knowledge without feeling, without that species of materiality which feeling lends to it? Do we not perhaps feel thought, and do we not feel ourselves in the act of knowing and willing? Could not the man in the stove have said: "I feel, therefore I am"? or "I will, therefore I am"? and to feel oneself, is it not perhaps to feel oneself imperishable? To will oneself, is it not to wish oneself eternal—that is to say, not to wish to die? What the sorrowful Jew of Amsterdam called the essence of the thing, the effort that it makes to persist indefinitely in its own being, self-love, the longing for immortality, is it not perhaps the primal and fundamental condition of all reflective or human knowledge? And is it not therefore the true base, the real starting-point, of all philosophy, although the philosophers, perverted by intellectualism, may not recognize it?

And, moreover, it was the *cogito* that introduced a distinction which, although fruitful of truths, has been fruitful also of confusions, and this distinction is that between object, *cogito,* and subject, *sum.* There is scarcely any distinction that does not also lead to confusion. But we will return to this later.

For the present let us remain keenly suspecting that the longing not to die, the hunger for personal immortality, the effort whereby we tend to persist indefinitely in our own being, which is, according to the tragic Jew, our very essence, that this is the affective basis of all knowledge and the personal inward starting-point of all human philosophy, wrought by a man and for men. And we shall see how the solution of this inward affective problem, a solution which may be but the despairing renunciation of the attempt at a solution, is that which colors all the rest of philosophy. Underlying even the so-called problem of knowledge there is simply this human feeling, just as underlying the enquiry into the "why," the cause, there is simply the search for the "wherefore," the end. All the rest is either to deceive oneself or to wish to deceive others; and to wish to deceive others in order to deceive oneself.

And this personal and affective starting-point of all philosophy and all religion is the tragic sense of life.

(J. E. Crawford Flitch, tr.)

FROM THE NATURE OF THE PHYSICAL WORLD, INTRODUCTION

ARTHUR S. EDDINGTON

I have settled down to the task of writing these lectures and have drawn up my chairs to my two tables. Two tables! Yes; there are duplicates of every object about me—two tables, two chairs, two pens.

This is not a very profound beginning to a course which ought to reach transcendent levels of scientific philosophy. But we cannot touch bedrock immediately; we must scratch a bit of the surface of things first. And whenever I begin to scratch the first thing I strike is—my two tables.

One of them has been familiar to me from earliest years. It is a commonplace object of that environment which I call the world. How shall I describe it? It has extension; it is comparatively permanent; it is colored; above all it is substantial. By substantial I do not merely mean that it does not collapse when I lean upon it; I mean that it is constituted of "substance" and by that word I am trying to convey to you some conception of its intrinsic nature. It is a *thing;* not like space, which is a mere negation; nor like time, which is—Heaven knows what!

But that will not help you to my meaning because it is the distinctive characteristic of a "thing" to have this substantiality, and I do not think substantiality can be described better than by saying that it is the kind of nature exemplified by an ordinary table. And so we go round in circles. After all if you are a plain common-sense man, not too much worried with scientific scruples, you will be confident that you understand the nature of an ordinary table. I have even heard of plain men who had the idea that they could better understand the mystery of their own nature if scientists would discover a way of explaining it in terms of the easily comprehensible nature of a table.

Table No. 2 is my scientific table. It is a more recent acquaintance and I do not feel so familiar with it. It does not belong to the world previously mentioned— that world which spontaneously appears around me when I open my eyes, though how much of it is objective and how much subjective I do not here consider. It is part of a world which in more devious ways has forced itself on my attention. My scientific table is mostly emptiness. Sparsely scattered in that emptiness are numerous electric charges rushing about with great speed; but their combined bulk amounts to less than a billionth of the bulk of the table itself. Notwithstanding its strange construction it turns out to be an entirely efficient table. It supports my writing paper as satisfactorily as table No. 1; for when I lay the paper on it the little electric particles with their headlong speed keep on hitting the underside, so that the paper is maintained in shuttlecock fashion at a nearly steady level. If I lean upon this table I shall not go through; or, to be strictly accurate, the chance of my scientific elbow going through my scientific table is so excessively small that it can be neglected in practical life. Reviewing their properties one by one, there seems to be nothing to choose between the two tables for ordinary purposes; but when abnormal circumstances befall, then my scientific table shows to advantage. If the house catches fire my scientific table will dissolve quite naturally into scientific smoke, whereas my familiar table undergoes a metamorphosis of its substantial nature which I can only regard as miraculous.

There is nothing substantial about my second table. It is nearly all empty space —space pervaded, it is true, by fields of force, but these are assigned to the category of "influences," not of "things." Even in the minute part which is not empty we must not transfer the old notion of substance. In dissecting matter into electric charges we have traveled far from that picture of it which first gave rise to the conception of substance, and the meaning of that conception—if it ever had any—has been lost by the way. The whole trend of modern scientific views is to break down the separate categories of "things," "influences," "forms," etc., and to substitute a common background of all experience. Whether we are studying a material object, a magnetic field, a geometrical figure, or a duration of time, our scientific information is summed up in measures; neither the apparatus of measurement nor the mode of using it suggests that there is anything essentially different in these problems. The measures themselves afford no ground for a classification by categories. We feel it necessary to concede some background to the measures—an external world; but the attributes of this world, except in so far as they are reflected in the measures, are outside scientific scrutiny. Science has at last revolted against attaching the exact knowledge contained in these measurements to a traditional picture-gallery of conceptions which convey no authentic information of the background and obtrude irrelevancies into the scheme of knowledge.

I will not here stress further the nonsubstantiality of electrons, since it is scarcely necessary to the present line of thought. Conceive them as substantially as you will, there is a vast difference between my scientific table with its substance (if any) thinly scattered in specks in a region mostly empty and the table of every day conception which we regard as the type of solid reality—an incarnate protest against Berkeleian subjectivism. It makes all the difference in the world whether the paper before me is poised as it were on a swarm of flies and sustained in shuttlecock fashion by a series of tiny blows from the swarm underneath, or whether it is supported because there is substance below it, it being the intrinsic nature of substance to occupy space to the exclusion of other substance; all the difference in conception at least, but no difference to my practical task of writing on the paper.

I need not tell you that modern physics has by delicate test and remorseless logic assured me that my second scientific table is the only one which is really there— wherever "there" may be. On the other hand I need not tell you that modern physics will never succeed in exorcising that first table—strange compound of external nature, mental imagery and inherited prejudice—which lies visible to my eyes and tangible to my grasp. We must bid good-bye to it for the present for we are about to turn from the familiar world to the scientific world revealed by physics. This is, or is intended to be, a wholly external world.

"You speak paradoxically of two worlds. Are they not really two aspects or two interpretations of one and the same world?"

Yes, no doubt they are ultimately to be identified after some fashion. But the process by which the external world of physics is transformed into a world of familiar acquaintance in human consciousness is outside the scope of physics. And so the world studied according to the methods of physics remains detached from the world familiar to consciousness, until after the physicist has finished his labors upon it. Provisionally, therefore, we regard the table which is the subject of physical research as altogether separate from the familiar table, without prejudging the question of their ultimate identification. It is true that the whole scientific inquiry starts from the familiar world and in the end it must return to the familiar world; but the part of the journey over which the physicist has charge is in foreign territory.

Until recently there was a much closer linkage; the physicist used to borrow the raw material of his world from the familiar world, but he does so no longer. His raw materials are aether, electrons, quanta, potentials, Hamiltonian functions, etc., and he is nowadays scrupulously careful to guard these from contamination by conceptions borrowed from the other world. There is a familiar table parallel to the scientific table, but there is no familiar electron, quantum or potential parallel to the scientific electron, quantum or potential. We do not even desire to manufacture a familiar counterpart to these things or, as we should commonly say, to "explain" the electron. After the physicist has quite finished his world-building a linkage or identification is allowed; but premature attempts at linkage have been found to be entirely mischievous.

Science aims at constructing a world which shall be symbolic of the world of commonplace experience. It is not at all necessary that every individual symbol that is used should represent something in common experience or even something explicable in terms of common experience. The man in the street is always making this demand for concrete explanation of the things referred to in science; but of necessity he must be disappointed. It is like our experience in learning to read. That which is written in a book is symbolic of a story in real life. The whole intention of the book is that ultimately a reader will identify some symbol, say BREAD, with one of the conceptions of familiar life. But it is mischievous to attempt such identifications prematurely, before the letters are strung into words and the words into sentences. The symbol A is not the counterpart of anything in familiar life. To the child the letter A would seem horribly abstract; so we give him a familiar conception along with it. "A was an Archer who shot at a frog." This tides over his immediate difficulty; but he cannot make serious progress with word-building so long as Archers, Butchers, Captains dance round the letters. The letters are abstract, and sooner or later he has to realize it. In physics we have outgrown archer and apple-pie definitions of the fundamental symbols. To a request to explain what an electron really is supposed to be we can only answer, "It is part of the A B C of physics".

The external world of physics has thus become a world of shadows. In removing our illusions we have removed the substance for indeed we have seen that substance is one of the greatest of our illusions. Later perhaps we may inquire whether in our zeal to cut out all that is unreal we may not have used the knife too ruthlessly. Perhaps, indeed, reality is a child which cannot survive without its nurse illusion. But if so, that is of little concern to the scientist, who has good and sufficient reasons for pursuing his investigations in the world of shadows and is content to leave to the philosopher the determination of its exact status in regard to reality. In the world of physics we watch a shadowgraph performance of the drama of familiar life. The shadow of my elbow rests on the shadow table as the shadow ink flows over the shadow paper. It is all symbolic, and as a symbol the physicist leaves it. Then comes the alchemist Mind who transmutes the symbols. The sparsely spread nuclei of electric force become a tangible solid; their restless agitation becomes the warmth of summer; the octave of aethereal vibrations becomes a gorgeous rainbow. Nor does the alchemy stop here. In the transmuted world new significances arise which are scarcely to be traced in the world of symbols; so that it becomes a world of beauty and purpose—and, alas, suffering and evil.

The frank realization that physical science is concerned with a world of shadows is one of the most significant of recent advances. I do not mean that physicists are to any extent preoccupied with the philosophical implications of this. From their point of view it is not so much a withdrawal of untenable claims as an assertion of freedom for autonomous development. At the moment I am not insisting on the shadowy and symbolic character of the world of physics because of its bearing on philosophy, but because the aloofness from familiar conceptions will be apparent in the scientific theories I have to describe. If you are not prepared for this aloofness you are likely to be out of sympathy with modern scientific theories, and may even think them ridiculous—as, I daresay, many people do.

It is difficult to school ourselves to treat the physical world as purely symbolic. We are always relapsing and mixing with the symbols incongruous conceptions taken from the world of consciousness. Untaught by long experience we stretch a hand to grasp the shadow, instead of accepting its shadowy nature. Indeed, unless we confine ourselves altogether to mathematical symbolism it is hard to avoid dressing our symbols in deceitful clothing. When I think of an electron there rises to my mind a hard, red, tiny ball; the proton similarly is neutral gray. Of course the color is absurd—perhaps not more absurd than the rest of the conception—but I am incorrigible. I can well understand that the younger minds are finding these pictures too concrete and are striving to construct the world out of Hamiltonian functions and symbols so far removed from human preconception that they do not even obey the laws of orthodox arithmetic. For myself I find some difficulty in rising to that plane of thought; but I am convinced that it has got to come. . . .

FROM POINTER READINGS

In *The Nature of the Physical World*

ARTHUR S. EDDINGTON

Let us then examine the kind of knowledge which is handled by exact science. If we search the examination papers in physics and natural philosophy for the more intelligible questions we may come across one beginning something like this: "An elephant slides down a grassy hillside. . . ." The experienced candidate knows that he need not pay much attention to this; it is only put in to give an impression of realism. He reads on: "The mass of the elephant is two tons." Now we are getting down to business; the elephant fades out of the problem and a mass of two tons takes its place. What exactly is this two tons, the real subject-matter of the problem? It refers to some property or condition which we vaguely describe as "ponderosity" occurring in a particular region of the external world. But we shall not get much further that way; the nature of the external world is inscrutable, and we shall only plunge into a quagmire of indescribables. Never mind what two tons *refers* to; what *is* it? How has it actually entered in so definite a way into our experience? Two tons *is* the reading of the pointer when the elephant was placed on a weighing-machine. Let us pass on. "The slope of the hill is 60°." Now the hillside fades out of the problem and an angle of 60° takes its place. What is 60°? There is no need to struggle with mystical conceptions of direction; 60° *is* the reading of a plumb-line against the divisions of a protractor. Similarly for the other data of the problem. The softly yielding turf on which the elephant slid is replaced by a coefficient of friction, which though perhaps not directly a pointer reading is of kindred nature. No doubt there are more round-about ways used in practice for determining the weights of elephants and the slopes of hills, but these are justified, because it is known that they give the same results as direct pointer readings.

And so we see that the poetry fades out of the problem, and by the time the serious application of exact science begins we are left with only pointer readings. If then only pointer readings of their equivalents are put into the machine of scientific calculation, how can we grind out anything but pointer readings? But that is just what we do grind out. The question presumably was to find the time of descent of the elephant, and the answer is a pointer reading on the seconds' dial of our watch.

The triumph of exact science in the foregoing problem consisted in establishing a numerical connection between the pointer reading of the weighing-machine in one experiment on the elephant and the pointer reading of the watch in another experiment. And when we examine critically other problems of physics we find that this is typical. The whole subject-matter of exact science consists of pointer readings and similar indications. We cannot enter here into the definition of what are to be classed as similar indications. The observation of approximate coincidence of the pointer with a scale-division can generally be extended to include the observation of any kind of coincidence—or, as it is usually expressed in the language of the general relativity theory, an intersection of world-lines. The essential point is that, although we seem to have very definite conceptions of objects in the external world, those conceptions do not enter into exact science and are not in any way confirmed by it. Before exact science can begin to handle the problem they must be replaced by quantities representing the results of physical measurement.

Perhaps you will object that although only the pointer readings enter into the actual calculation it would make nonsense of the problem to leave out all reference to anything else. The problem necessarily involves some kind of connecting background. It was not the pointer reading of the weighing-machine that slid down the hill! And yet from the point of view of exact science the thing that really did descend the hill can only be described as a bundle of pointer readings. (It should be remembered that the hill also has been replaced by pointer readings, and the sliding down is no longer an active adventure but a functional relation of space and time measures.) The word elephant calls up a certain association of mental impressions, but it is clear that mental impressions as such cannot be the subject handled in the physical problem. We have, for example, an impression of bulkiness. To this there is presumably some direct counterpart in the external world, but that counterpart must be of a nature beyond our apprehension, and science can make nothing of it. Bulkiness enters into exact science by yet another substitution; we replace it by a series of readings of a pair of calipers. Similarly the grayish black appearance in our mental impressions is replaced in exact science by the readings of a photometer for various wave-lengths of light. And so on until all the characteristics of the elephant are exhausted and it has become reduced to a schedule of measures. There is always the triple correspondence.—

- (a) a mental image, which is in our minds and not in the external world;
- (b) some kind of counterpart in the external world, which is of inscrutable nature;
- (c) a set of pointer readings, which exact science can study and connect with other pointer readings.

And so we have our schedule of pointer readings ready to make the descent. And if you still think that this substitution has taken away all reality from the problem, I am not sorry that you should have a foretaste of the difficulty in store for those who hold that exact science is all-sufficient for the description of the universe and that there is nothing in our experience which cannot be brought within its scope.

FROM RELIGION AND SCIENCE

In *Science and the Modern World*

ALFRED NORTH WHITEHEAD

Science is even more changeable than theology. No man of science could subscribe without qualification to Galileo's beliefs or to Newton's beliefs, or to all his own scientific beliefs of ten years ago.

In both regions of thought, additions, distinctions, and modifications have been introduced. So that now, even when the same assertion is made today as was made a thousand, or fifteen hundred years ago, it is made subject to limitations or expansions of meaning, which were not contemplated at the earlier epoch. We are told by logicians that a proposition must be either true or false, and that there is no middle term. But in practice, we may know that a proposition expresses an important truth, but that it is subject to limitations and qualifications which at present remain undiscovered. It is a general feature of our knowledge, that we are insistently aware of important truths; and yet that the only formulations of these truths which we are able to make presuppose a general standpoint of conceptions which may have to be modified. I will give you two illustrations, both from science: Galileo said that the earth moves and that the sun is fixed; the Inquisition said that the earth is fixed and the sun moves; and Newtonian astronomers, adopting an absolute theory of space, said that both the sun and the earth move. But now we say that any one of these three statements is equally true, provided that you have fixed your sense of "rest" and "motion" in the way required by the statement adopted. At the date of Galileo's controversy with the Inquisition, Galileo's way of stating the facts was, beyond question, the fruitful procedure for the sake of scientific research. But in itself it was not more true than the formulation of the Inquisition. But at that time the modern concepts of relative motion were in nobody's mind; so that the statements were made in ignorance of the qualifications required for their more perfect truth. Yet this question of the motions of the earth and the sun expresses a real fact in the universe; and all sides had got hold of important truths concerning it. But with the knowledge of those times, the truths appeared to be inconsistent.

Again I will give you another example taken from the state of modern physical science. Since the time of Newton and Huyghens in the seventeenth century there have been two theories as to the physical nature of light. Newton's theory was that a beam of light consists of a stream of very minute particles, or corpuscles, and that we have the sensation of light when these corpuscles strike the retinas of our eyes. Huyghens' theory was that light consists of very minute waves of trembling in an all-pervading ether, and that these waves are traveling along a beam of light. The two theories are contradictory. In the eighteenth century Newton's theory was believed, in the nineteenth century Huyghens' theory was believed. Today there is one large group of phenomena which can be explained only on the wave theory, and another large group which can be explained only on the corpuscular theory. Scientists have to leave it at that, and wait for the future, in the hope of attaining some wider vision which reconciles both.

We should apply these same principles to the questions in which there is a variance between science and religion. We would believe nothing in either sphere of thought which does not appear to us to be certified by solid reasons based upon the critical research either of ourselves or of competent authorities. But granting that we have honestly taken this precaution, a clash between the two on points of detail where they overlap should not lead us hastily to abandon doctrines for which we have solid evidence. It may be that we are more interested in one set of doctrines than in the other. But, if we have any sense of perspective and of the history of thought, we shall wait and refrain from mutual anathemas.

We should wait: but we should not wait passively, or in despair. The clash is a sign that there are wider truths and finer perspectives within which a reconciliation of a deeper religion and a more subtle science will be found.

In one sense, therefore, the conflict between science and religion is a slight matter which has been unduly emphasized. A mere logical contradiction cannot in itself point to more than the necessity of some readjustments, possibly of a very minor character on both sides. Remember the widely different aspects of events which are dealt with in science and in religion respectively. Science is concerned with general conditions which are observed to regulate physical phenomena; whereas religion is wholly wrapped up in the contemplation of moral and aesthetic values. On the one side there is the law of gravitation, and on the other the contemplation of the beauty of holiness. What one side sees, the other misses; and vice versa.

Consider, for example, the lives of John Wesley and of Saint Francis of Assisi. For physical science you have in these lives merely ordinary examples of the operation of the principles of physiological chemistry, and of the dynamics of nervous reactions: for religion you have lives of the most profound significance in the history of the world. Can you be surprised that, in the absence of a perfect and complete phrasing of the principles of science and of the principles of religion which apply to these specific cases, the accounts of these lives from these divergent standpoints should involve discrepancies? It would be a miracle if it were not so.

It would, however, be missing the point to think that we need not trouble ourselves about the conflict between science and religion. In an intellectual age there can be no active interest which puts aside all hope of a vision of the harmony of truth. To acquiesce in discrepancy is destructive of candor, and of moral cleanliness. It belongs to the self-respect of intellect to pursue every tangle of thought to its final unravelment. If you check that impulse, you will get no religion and no science from an awakened thoughtfulness. The important question is, In what spirit are we going to face the issue? There we come to something absolutely vital.

A clash of doctrines is not a disaster—it is an opportunity. I will explain my meaning by some illustrations from science. The weight of an atom of nitrogen was well known. Also it was an established scientific doctrine that the average weight of such atoms in any considerable mass will be always the same. Two experimenters, the late Lord Rayleigh and the late Sir William Ramsay, found that if they obtained nitrogen by two different methods, each equally effective for that purpose, they always observed a persistent slight difference between the average weights of the atoms in the two cases. Now I ask you would it have been rational for these men to have despaired because of this conflict between chemical theory and scientific observation? Suppose that for some reason the chemical doctrine had been highly prized throughout some district as the foundation of its social order:—would it have been wise, would it have been candid, would it have been moral, to forbid the disclosure of the fact that the experiments produced discordant results? Or, on the other hand, should Sir William Ramsay and Lord Rayleigh have proclaimed that chemical theory was now a detected delusion? We see at once that either of these ways would have been a method of facing the issue in an entirely wrong spirit. What Rayleigh and Ramsay did was this: They at once perceived that they had hit upon a line of investigation which would disclose some subtlety of chemical theory that had hitherto eluded observation. The discrepancy was not a disaster: it was an opportunity to increase the sweep of chemical knowledge. You all know the end of the story: finally argon was discovered, a new chemical element which had lurked undetected, mixed with the nitrogen. But the story has a sequel which forms my second illustration. This discovery drew attention to the importance of observing accurately minute differences in chemical substances as obtained by different methods. Further researches of the most careful accuracy were undertaken. Finally another physicist, F. W. Aston, working in the Cavendish Laboratory at Cambridge in England, discovered that even the same element might assume two or more distinct forms, termed *isotopes,* and that the law of the constancy of average atomic weight holds for each of these forms, but as between the different isotopes differs slightly. The research has effected a great stride in the power of chemical theory, far transcending in importance the discovery of argon from which it originated. The moral of these stories lies on the surface, and I will leave to you their application to the case of religion and science.

CHAPTER 11

THE ONE AND THE MANY

Glory be to God for dappled things—
    For skies of couple-color as a brinded cow;
      For rose-moles all in stipple upon trout that swim;
Fresh-firecoal chestnut-falls; finches' wings;
    Landscape plotted and pieced—fold, fallow, and plough;
      And áll trádes, their gear and tackle and trim.

All things counter, original, spare, strange;
    Whatever is fickle, freckled (who knows how?)
      With swift, slow; sweet, sour; adazzle, dim;
He fathers-forth whose beauty is past change:
      Praise him.
        —Gerard Manley Hopkins, "Pied Beauty."

What *is* this world? What is the universe made of? Is it, properly speaking, a universe at all? From the beginning of philosophic thought men have asked these questions and meditated the implications of the possible answers. There are three main hypotheses: monism, dualism, and pluralism.

The monist considers the world as entirely of one substance, a substance that may be regarded in religion as God manifesting himself in many ways, and, in modern science, as mass particles in motion or energy, with the differences in things accounted for by different arrangements of these particles in time and space.

The dualist says there is no "universe," no one substance. What we misname the universe is really two substances, mind and matter, each independent of the other. This theory, of course, like all theories of the nature of things, is subject to various modifications. Thus some philosophers deny the existence of mind, others the existence of matter; some think of mind as an efflorescence of matter, and yet others entertain the idea of an ascending scale in nature, with new manifestations at different levels (theory of emergence).

The pluralist maintains that our "universe" is really a pluriverse—many different substances. This theory, like the others, may have a religious cast, visualizing a world of different selves with relative freedom of action under a supreme self or God, or it may be materialistic, visualizing a world without purpose, physical in its manifold nature, without reference to any supernatural power. In this chapter the selections will illustrate only a few of the aspects of these several theories.

Let us begin with monism. In the much-quoted "Flower in the crannied wall," Tennyson gives us one of the central tenets of monism: all the universe is one substance or universal set of relationships; if we could but know any part of that substance, we should know all. It would appear that the universe is mystical and locked away from our finite understanding. Coleridge also sustains this view in greater detail in "Religious Musings." God, he tells us, achieves the unity of all things by means of his diffusion through all. So conceived, everything is a part of God, and fundamentally all things are the same. The universe, truly a universe, becomes figuratively, as Emerson puts it, "a belt of mirrors round a taper's flame."

This theory, appealing from some angles, still leaves something to be desired. If the universe is perfect (as it must be, being God) and our evils only part of God not understood, life loses something in meaning—at least so think Louis MacNeice and others who believe in a pluralistic world. Error and choice must exist, and their existence is not possible to monism. God and the world are not an "All-white Universal." Man is what he is because he is not a beast and because he may hope to be a god. In the eyes of the pluralist, God himself—if the concept is allowed—is the Supreme Self in a society of selves, a hero-God, struggling, like men, and with men, against the ills of the universe. The world, says MacNeice, is "crazier and more of it than we think, Incorrigibly plural." Pluralism commonly tends to be humanistic and naturalistic.

Yet there is order in this "incorrigibly plural" world. How can we explain all the evidence of law except by reference to a Supreme Will or Power of some sort? The materialist, not because he wishes to think so, but from honest conviction agrees with Thomas Wolfe that though things seem "somehow fore-ordered," they are, nevertheless, "accidental as the strings of blind chance."

Walter Pater, interpreting Plato, also argues for a pluralistic world. The process of generalization, developed by Plato, involving the creation, mentally at least, of values, enriches life. Plato's system is essentially dualistic in its main outlines, however, a system of spiritual forms and physical counterparts. Each thing in existence has its ideal pattern or form.

Dualism in its simplest sense is concerned with the differentiation of mind and body, and it often finds literary expression as ethical dualism, as in *Hamlet, Paradise Lost,* and *Faust.* This war between the mind and the body, the flesh and the spirit, is reflected in one or two poems in this chapter. Thus Delmore Schwartz in "The Heavy Bear" calls the body "a stupid clown of the spirit's motive." Hamlet, in one mood, we recall, found instead a beautiful consonance of body and spirit: "What a piece of work is a man! how noble in reason! how infinite in faculties! in form and moving how express and admirable! in action how like an angel! in apprehension how like a god! the beauty of the world, the paragon of animals!" The very image of such a creature should delight us.

A strange fact—if it is a fact—about this simple dualism is that it involves the association of two substances so different that it seems impossible that they should mingle or even meet. The body is material, a concrete thing extended in space. Mind, so dualism holds, is immaterial, without dimensions. How can an immaterial essence control or affect or be affected by the body? As Freda Bond says in "Invisible Kingdom," "How can the brain enfold Fields that five counties are too small to hold?" Our physical world is rich in wonder, but if all the visions of all the minds in the universe could suddenly be made visible to us, what complexity and beauty and ugliness infinitely beyond the scale of our physical world would be seen! Our mental world is a vast one in which each of us, a shimmering entity of glory and darkness, moves at will, relatively unhampered by time and space.

Not only the power of perception of things past and present and the anticipation of events to come, but also the moral sense are attributes of mind, as T. S. Eliot points out in "Animula." How sad that such a miraculous device should live on earth so uncomfortably, finally "Leaving disordered papers in a dusty room, Living first in the silence after the viaticum"! A somewhat happier view of the commingling of flesh and spirit is expressed in the selection by Andrew Marvell.

How is this strange phenomenon called mind accounted for? Is it an extension of matter, not unlike the rays of light from a tungsten filament, as the materialists believe, or should we agree with the dualists who, as we have seen, make an absolute distinction between the conscious and the unconscious? How can the material brain perform the apparently immaterial act of thinking? Such are the questions considered by Dr. Samuel Johnson in *Rasselas*. In this story Imlac asks if qualities and ideas have any existence apart from the mind. He observes that in the mind, as impressions, they certainly have no corporeal extension. Voltaire, on the other hand, though admitting to belief in the existence of mind or intelligence, discredits the idea that there is an essence called the soul.

Despite Wordsworth's distrust of the ability of science to analyze so complex a mystery as the mind ("School-Time," from *The Prelude*), it is fitting for us to inquire what science has to say on these problems. Several of the more important theories regarding the nature of matter and mind are examined briefly by Lord Balfour in his Introduction to *Science, Religion, and Reality*. His arguments, supporting the possibility of the dualism of mind and matter, emphasize the miracle of their apparent interaction.

Scientific theory that all material existence is a mass of energy is the splendid revelation of our time, a revelation seen as through a veil by Democritus and Parmenides and Leibnitz. No less splendid in concept is the possible reality of a separate substance called mind.   Can science prove this theory too, or will it ultimately demonstrate that mind is only a manifestation of energy?   And would this result be less marvelous?

"FLOWER IN THE CRANNIED WALL"
ALFRED LORD TENNYSON

Flower in the crannied wall,
I pluck you out of the crannies,
I hold you here, root and all, in my hand,
Little flower—but *if* I could understand
What you are, root and all, and all in all,
I should know what God and man is.

FROM RELIGIOUS MUSINGS
SAMUEL TAYLOR COLERIDGE

. . . 'Tis the sublime of man,
Our noontide Majesty, to know ourselves
Parts and proportions of one wondrous whole!
This fraternizes man, this constitutes
Our charities and bearings.   But 'tis God
Diffused through all, that doth make all one whole;
This the worst superstition, him except
Aught to desire, Supreme Reality!
The plenitude and permanence of bliss!
O Fiends of Superstition! not that oft
The erring priest hath stained with brother's blood
Your grisly idols, not for this may wrath
Thunder against you from the Holy One!
But o'er some plain that steameth to the sun,
Peopled with Death; or where more hideous Trade
Loud-laughing packs his bales of human anguish;
I will raise up a mourning, O ye Fiends!
And curse your spells that film the eye of Faith,
Hiding the present God; whose presence lost,
The moral world's cohesion, we become
An Anarchy of Spirits!   Toy-bewitched,
Made blind by lusts, disherited of soul,
No common center Man, no common sire
Knoweth!   A sordid solitary thing,
Mid countless brethren with a lonely heart
Through courts and cities the smooth savage roams
Feeling himself, his own low self the whole;
When he by sacred sympathy might make
The whole one Self!   Self, that no alien knows!
Self, far diffused as Fancy's wing can travel!
Self, spreading still!   Oblivious of its own,
Yet all of all possessing!   This is Faith!
This the Messiah's destined victory!

.   .   .   .

Believe thou, O my soul,
Life is a vision shadowy of Truth;
And vice, and anguish, and the wormy grave,
Shapes of a dream!   The veiling clouds retire,
And lo! the Throne of the redeeming God
Forth flashing unimaginable day
Wraps in one blaze earth, heaven, and deepest hell.

Contemplant Spirits! ye that hover o'er
With untired gaze the immeasurable fount
Ebullient with creative Deity!
And ye of plastic power, that interfused
Roll through the grosser and material mass
In organizing surge!   Holies of God!
(And what if Monads of the infinite mind?)
I haply journeying my immortal course
Shall sometime join your mystic choir!

XENOPHANES

RALPH WALDO EMERSON

By fate, not option, frugal nature gave
One scent to hyson and to wallflower,
One sound to pine-groves and to waterfalls,
One aspect to the desert and the lake,
It was her stern necessity.   All things
Are of one pattern made; bird, beast, and flower,
Song, picture, form, space, thought, and character,
Deceive us, seeming to be many things,
And are but one.   Beheld far off, they part
As God and Devil; bring them to the mind,
They dull its edge with their monotony.
To know one element explore another,
And in the second reappears the first.
The specious panorama of a year
But multiplies the image of a day,
A belt of mirrors round a taper's flame,
And universal Nature through her vast
And crowded whole, an infinite paroquet,
Repeats one cricket note.

PLURALITY

LOUIS MacNEICE

It is patent to the eye that cannot face the sun
The smug philosophers lie who say the world is one,
World is other and other, world is here and there,
Parmenides would smother life for lack of air
Precluding birth and death; his crystal never breaks—
No movement and no breath, no progress nor mistakes,

Nothing begins or ends, no one loves or fights,
All your foes are friends and all your days are nights
And all the roads lead round and are not roads at all
And the soul is muscle-bound, the world a wooden ball.
The modern monist too castrates, negates our lives
And nothing that we do, make or become survives,
His terror of confusion freezes the flowing stream
Into mere illusion, his craving for supreme
Completeness means he chokes each orifice with tight
Plaster as he evokes a dead ideal of white
All-white Universal, refusing to allow
Division or dispersal—Eternity is now
And Now is therefore numb, a fact he does not see
Postulating a dumb static identity
Of Essence and Existence which could not fuse without
Banishing to a distance belief along with doubt,
Action along with error, growth along with gaps;
If man is a mere mirror of God, the gods collapse.
No, the formula fails that fails to make it clear
That only change prevails, that the seasons make the year,
That a thing, a beast, a man is what it is because
It is something that began and is not what it was,
Yet is itself throughout, fluttering and unfurled,
Not to be canceled out, not to be merged in world,
Its entity a denial of all that is not it,
Its every move a trial through chaos and the Pit,
An absolute and so defiant of the One
Absolute, the row of noughts where time is done,
Where nothing goes or comes and Is is one with Ought
And all the possible sums alike resolve to nought.
World is not like that, world is full of blind
Gulfs across the flat, jags against the mind,
Swollen or diminished according to the dice,
Foaming, never finished, never the same twice.
You talk of Ultimate Value, universal Form—
Visions, let me tell you, that ride upon the storm
And must be made and sought but cannot be maintained,
Lost as soon as caught, always to be regained,
Mainspring of our striving towards perfection, yet
Would not be worth achieving if the world were set
Fair, if error and choice did not exist, if dumb
World should find its voice for good and God become
Incarnate once for all.   No, perfection means
Something but must fall unless there intervenes
Between that meaning and the matter it should fill
Time's revolving hand that never can be still.
Which being so and life a ferment, you and I
Can only live by strife in that the living die,
And, if we use the word Eternal, stake a claim
Only to what a bird can find within the frame
Of momentary flight (the value will persist
But as event the night sweeps it away in mist).

Man is man because he might have been a beast
And is not what he was and feels himself increased,
Man is man in as much as he is not god and yet
Hankers to see and touch the pantheon and forget
The means within the end and man is truly man
In that he would transcend and flout the human span:
A species become rich by seeing things as wrong
And patching them, to which I am proud that I belong.
Man is surely mad with discontent, he is hurled
By lovely hopes or bad dreams against the world,
Raising a frail scaffold in never-ending flux,
Stubbornly when baffled fumbling the stubborn crux
And so he must continue, raiding the abyss
With aching bone and sinew, conscious of things amiss,
Conscious of guilt and vast inadequacy and the sick
Ego and the broken past and the clock that goes too quick,
Conscious of waste of labor, conscious of spite and hate,
Of dissension with his neighbor, of beggars at the gate,
But conscious also of love and the joy of things and the power
Of going beyond and above the limit of the lagging hour,
Conscious of sunlight, conscious of death's inveigling touch,
Not completely conscious but partly—and that is much.

(August, 1940)

SNOW

LOUIS MacNEICE

The room was suddenly rich and the great bay-window was
Spawning snow and pink roses against it
Soundlessly collateral and incompatible:
World is suddener than we fancy it.

World is crazier and more of it than we think,
Incorrigibly plural. I peel and portion
A tangerine and spit the pips and feel
The drunkenness of things being various.

And the fire flames with a bubbling sound for world
Is more spiteful and gay than one supposes—
On the tongue on the eyes on the ears in the palms of your hands—
There is more than glass between the snow and the huge roses.

THE WAY THINGS ARE *

THOMAS WOLFE

This is the way things are.
Here is the grass,
So green and coarse, so sweet and delicate,
But with some brown rubble in it.

* Reprinted from *The Web and the Rock* by Thomas Wolfe by permission of Harper &
Brothers. Copyright, 1939, by Maxwell Perkins as Executor.

There are the houses all along the street,
The concrete blocks of walls,
Somehow so dreary,
Ugly, yet familiar,
The slate roofs and the shingles,
The lawns, the hedges and the gables,
The backyards with their accidental structures
Of so many little and familiar things
As henhouses, barns.

All common and familiar as my breath,
All accidental as the strings of blind chance,
Yet all somehow foreordered as a destiny:
The way they are,
Because
They are the way they are!
(Arranged in verse by John S. Barnes)

FROM THE THEORY OF IDEAS

In *Plato and Platonism*

WALTER PATER

. . . The Platonic doctrine of "the Many and the One"—the problem with which we are brought face to face in this choice specimen of the humor as well as of the metaphysical power of Plato—is not precisely the question with which the speculative young man of our own day is likely to puzzle himself, or exercise the patience of his neighbor in a railway carriage, of his dog, or even of a Chinese; though the questions we are apt to tear to pieces, organism and environment, or protoplasm perhaps, or evolution, or the *Zeitgeist* and its doings, may, in their turn, come to seem quite as lifeless and unendurable. As the theological heresy of one age sometimes becomes the mere commonplace of the next, so, in matters of philosophic inquiry, it might appear that the all-absorbing novelty of one generation becomes nothing less than the standard of what is uninteresting, as such, to its successor. Still in the discussion even of abstract truths it is not so much what he thinks as the person who is thinking, that after all really tells. Plato and Platonism we shall never understand unless we are patient with him in what he has to tell us about "the Many and the One."

Plato's peculiar view of the matter, then, passes with him into a phase of poetic thought; as indeed all that Plato's genius touched came in contact with poetry. Of course we are not naturally formed to love, or be interested in, or attracted towards, the abstract as such; to notions, we might think, carefully deprived of all the incident, the color and variety, which fits things—this or that—to the constitution and natural habit of our minds, fits them for attachment to what we really are. We cannot love or live upon *genus* and *species,* accident or substance, but for our minds, as for our bodies, need an orchard or a garden, with fruit and roses. Take a seed from the garden. What interest it has for us all lies in our sense of potential differentiation to come: the leaves, leaf upon leaf, the flowers, a thousand new seeds in turn. It is so with animal seed; and with humanity, individually, or as a whole, its expansion into a detailed, ever-changing, parti-colored history of particular facts and persons. Abstraction, the introduction of general ideas, seems to close it up again; to reduce flower and fruit, odor and savor, back again into the dry and worthless seed. We might as well be color-blind at once, and there is not a proper name left! We may contrast generally the mental world we actually live in, where classification, the reduction of all things to common types, has come so far, and where the particular, to a great extent, is known only as the member of a class, with that other world, on the other side of the generalizing movement to which Plato and his master so largely contributed—a world we might describe as being under Homeric conditions, such as we picture to ourselves with regret, for which experience was intuition, and life a continuous surprise, and every object unique, where all knowledge was still of the concrete and the particular, face to face delightfully.

To that gaudy tangle of what gardens, after all, are meant to produce, in the decay of time, as we may think at first sight, the systematic, logical gardener put his meddlesome hand, and straightway all ran to seed; to *genus* and *species* and *differentia*, into formal classes, under general notions, and with—yes! with written labels fluttering on the stalks, instead of blossoms—a botanic or "physic" garden, as they used to say, instead of our flower-garden and orchard. And yet (it must be confessed on the other hand) what we actually see, see and hear, is more interesting than ever; the nineteenth century as compared with the first, with Plato's days or Homer's; the faces, the persons behind those masks which yet express so much, the flowers, or whatever it may happen to be they carry or touch. The concrete, and that even as a visible thing, has gained immeasurably in richness and compass, in fineness, and interest towards us, by the process, of which those acts of generalization, of reduction to class and generic type, have certainly been a part. And holding still to the concrete, the particular, to the visible or sensuous, if you will, last as first, thinking of that as essentially the one vital and lively thing, really worth our while in a short life, we may recognize sincerely what generalization and abstraction have done or may do, are defensible as doing, just for that—for the particular gem or flower—what its proper service is to a mind in search, precisely, of a concrete and intuitive knowledge such as that.

Think, for a moment, of the difference, as regards mental attitude, between the naturalist who deals with things through ideas, and the layman (so to call him) in picking up a shell on the seashore; what it is that the subsumption of the individual into the species, its subsequent alliance to and coordination with other species, really does for the furnishing of the mind of the former. The layman, though we need not suppose him inattentive, or unapt to retain impressions, is in fact still but a child; and the shell, its colors and convolution, no more than a dainty, very easily destructible toy to him. Let him become a schoolboy about it, so to speak. The toy he puts aside; his mind is drilled perforce, to learn *about* it; and thereby is exercised, he may think, with everything except just the thing itself, as he cares for it; with other shells, with some general laws of life, and for a while it might seem that, turning away his eyes from the "vanity" of the particular, he has been made to sacrifice the concrete, the real and living product of nature, to a mere dry and abstract product of the mind. But when he comes out of school, and on the seashore again finds a fellow to his toy, perhaps a finer specimen of it, he may see what the service of that converse with the general has really been towards the concrete, towards what he sees—in regard to the particular thing he actually sees. By its juxtaposition and coördination with what is ever more and more not *it*, by the contrast of its very imperfection, at this point or that, with its own proper and perfect type, this concrete and particular thing has, in fact, been enriched by the whole color and expression of the whole circumjacent world, concentrated upon, or as it were at focus in, it. By a kind of shorthand now, and as if in a single moment of vision, all that, which only a long experience, moving patiently from part to part, could exhaust, its manifold alliance with the entire world of nature, is legible upon it, as it lies there in one's hand.

So it is with the shell, the gem, with a glance of the eye; so it may be with the moral act, with a condition of the mind, or a feeling. You may draw, by use of this coinage (it is Hobbes's figure) this coinage of representative words and thoughts, at your pleasure, upon the accumulative capital of the whole experience of humanity. Generalization, whatever Platonists, or Plato himself at mistaken moments, may have to say about it, is a method, not of obliterating the concrete phenomenon, but of enriching it, with the joint perspective, the significance, the expressiveness, of all other things beside. What broad-cast light he enjoys!—that scholar, confronted with the sea-shell, for instance, or with some enigma of heredity in himself or another, with some condition of a particular soul, in circumstances which may never precisely so occur again; in the contemplation of that single phenomenon, or object, or situation. He not only sees, but understands (thereby only seeing the more) and will, therefore, also remember. The significance of the particular object he will retain, by use of his intellectual apparatus of notion and general law, as, to use Plato's own figure, fluid matter may be retained in vessels, not indeed of unbaked clay, but of alabaster or bronze. So much by way of apology for general ideas—abstruse, or intangible, or dry and seedy and wooden, as we may sometimes think them.

"Two things," says Aristotle, "might rightly be attributed to Socrates: inductive reasoning, and universal definitions." Now when Aristotle says this of Socrates. he is recording the institution of a method, which might be applied in the way just indicated, to natural objects, to such a substance as carbon, or to such natural processes as heat or motion; but which, by Socrates himself, as by Plato after him, was applied almost exclusively to moral phenomena, to the generalization of aesthetic, political, ethical ideas, of the laws of operation (for the essence of every true conception, or definition, or idea, is a law of operation) of the feelings and the will. To get a notion, a definition, or idea, of motion, for example, which shall not exclude the subtler forms of it, heat for instance—to get a notion of carbon, which shall include not common charcoal only, but the diamond, a thing superficially so unlike it, and which shall also exclude, perhaps, some other substance, superficially almost indistinguishable from it: such is the business of physical science, in obedience to rules, outlined by Bacon in the first book of the *Novum Organum*, for securing those acts of "inclusion" and "exclusion," *inclusiones, exclusiones, naturae, debitae,* as he says, "which the nature of things requires," if our thoughts are not to misrepresent them. . . .

THE HEAVY BEAR

DELMORE SCHWARTZ

"the withness of the body"
—Whitehead

The heavy bear who goes with me,
A manifold honey to smear his face,
Clumsy and lumbering here and there,
The central ton of every place,
The hungry beating brutish one
In love with candy, anger, and sleep,

Crazy factotum, disheveling all,
Climbs the building, kicks the football,
Boxes his brother in the hate-ridden city.

Breathing at my side, that heavy animal,
That heavy bear who sleeps with me,
Howls in his sleep for a world of sugar,
A sweetness intimate as the water's clasp,
Howls in his sleep because the tight-rope
Trembles and shows the darkness beneath.
—The strutting show-off is terrified,
Dressed in his dress-suit, bulging his pants,
Trembles to think that his quivering meat
Must finally wince to nothing at all.

That inescapable animal walks with me,
Has followed me since the black womb held,
Moves where I move, distorting my gesture,
A caricature, a swollen shadow,
A stupid clown of the spirit's motive,
Perplexes and affronts with his own darkness,
The secret life of belly and bone,
Opaque, too near, my private, yet unknown,
Stretches to embrace the very dear
With whom I would walk without him near,
Touches her grossly, although a word
Would bare my heart and make me clear,
Stumbles, flounders, and strives to be fed
Dragging me with him in his mouthing care,
Amid the hundred million of his kind,
The scrimmage of appetite everywhere.

INVISIBLE KINGDOM

FREDA C. BOND

Down the long London street the light cut keen
As a knife blade, hard and white: the winter day
Walked shoulder to shoulder with me—but between
Myself and the London noon, the scent of hay
Struck suddenly, as I passed an open stable door,
And the woman, the time, and the hour were there no more.

I was a child, and I felt beneath my knees
The rough boards of the hay cart, saw the painted side
Swaying against the dull sky and the heavy trees;
Thunder purpled the air—and when they cried
"Look out there!" and a truss of hay was flung
Billowing over the side of the cart,
It seemed, a moment, that the heavens hung
Suspended in great waves—that fell apart,

Fell round my knees in strands of grass and clover,
And a lark sang, because fear of the deluge was over.

The light cut keen as a knife between eyes and brain,
And the woman, the time, and the hour were back again.

Until I smelt the hay, I did not know
That I was carrying about with me
A hayfield and a cart—and it must be
That everywhere I go
There goes an unseen realm, unconquered still
By the assault of will,
But yielding up its green and sacred ground
To the random touch of scent and sound.

Time and space can scarce contain
The crowds that throng the unsuspecting brain,
Where every soul assumes a hundred guises,
And the child lives immortal though the man is born,
Where, when the sudden challenge of a questing horn,
Or a bell ringing through the dusk, surprises
The sentries of the unseen realm, its skies appear
All languorous beneath the hand of June, or clear
At the golden fall of the year—
Where winter night goes hand in hand with summer morn.
How can the brain enfold
Fields that five counties are too small to hold?

Down the long London street in the wintry sun
The people walk with less security
Than tight-rope walkers—for each one,
Holding his course in space and time,
Is poised above a gulf, where he
May sink at the sweet bidding of a chime,
Of a tune tinkled on a music box,
Or a bird singing, or may fall
Encountering suddenly the scent of stocks
That weights the air on summer eves,
Wood smoke, or rain-drenched leaves,
Or peaches ripe against the wall.
Of these invisible realms, who can descry
The boundaries, or who can say
Which of the passers-by
Walks down the London street, and which is far away
Under another sky
Whose beams eclipse the winter day?
Kingdom is heaped on kingdom, and the wonder is
How London streets can hold such realms and dynasties.

ANIMULA *

T. S. ELIOT

"Issues from the hand of God, the simple soul"
To a flat world of changing lights and noise,
To light, dark, dry or damp, chilly or warm;
Moving between the legs of tables and of chairs,
Rising or falling, grasping at kisses and toys,
Advancing boldly, sudden to take alarm,
Retreating to the corner of arm and knee,
Eager to be reassured, taking pleasure
In the fragrant brilliance of the Christmas tree,
Pleasure in the wind, the sunlight and the sea;
Studies the sunlit pattern on the floor
And running stags around a silver tray;
Confounds the actual and the fanciful,
Content with playing-cards and kings and queens,
What the fairies do and what the servants say.
The heavy burden of the growing soul
Perplexes and offends more, day by day;
Week by week, offends and perplexes more
With the imperatives of "is and seems"
And may and may not, desire and control.
The pain of living and the drug of dreams
Curl up the small soul in the window seat
Behind the *Encyclopaedia Britannica*.
Issues from the hand of time the simple soul
Irresolute and selfish, misshapen, lame,
Unable to fare forward or retreat,
Fearing the warm reality, the offered good,
Denying the importunity of the blood,
Shadow of its own shadows, specter in its own gloom,
Leaving disordered papers in a dusty room;
Living first in the silence after the viaticum.

Pray for Guiterriez, avid of speed and power,
For Boudin, blown to pieces,
For this one who made a great fortune,
And that one who went his own way.
Pray for Floret, by the boarhound slain between the yew trees,
Pray for us now and at the hour of our birth.

FROM THE GARDEN

ANDREW MARVELL

What wondrous life is this I lead!
Ripe apples drop about my head;
The luscious clusters of the vine
Upon my mouth do crush their wine;

* From *Collected Poems 1909-1935* by T. S. Eliot, copyright, 1936, by Harcourt, Brace and Company, Inc.

The nectarine and curious peach
Into my hands themselves do reach;
Stumbling on melons, as I pass
Ensnared with flowers, I fall on grass.

Meanwhile the mind, from pleasure less,
Withdraws into its happiness;—
The mind, that ocean, where each kind
Does straight its own resemblance find;
Yet it creates, transcending these,
Far other worlds and other seas,
Annihilating all that's made
To a green thought in a green shade.

Here at the fountain's sliding foot
Or at some fruit tree's mossy root,
Casting the body's vest aside,
My soul into the boughs does glide;
There like a bird it sits and sings,
Then whets and combs its silver wings;
And, till prepared for longer flight,
Waves in its plumes the various light.

IMLAC DISCOURSES ON THE NATURE OF THE SOUL

In *Rasselas* (*XLVIII*)

DR. SAMUEL JOHNSON

"What reason," said the prince, "can be given why the Egyptians should thus expensively preserve those carcasses which some nations consume with fire, others lay to mingle with the earth, and all agree to remove from their sight as soon as decent rites can be performed?"

"The original of ancient customs," said Imlac, "is commonly unknown, for the practice often continues when the cause has ceased; and concerning superstitious ceremonies it is vain to conjecture, for what reason did not dictate, reason cannot explain. I have long believed that the practice of embalming arose only from tenderness to the remains of relations or friends, and to this opinion I am more inclined because it seems impossible that this care should have been general. Had all the dead been embalmed, their repositories must in time have been more spacious than the dwellings of the living. I suppose only the rich or honorable were secured from corruption, and the rest left to the course of Nature.

"But it is commonly supposed that the Egyptians believed the soul to live as long as the body continued undissolved, and therefore tried this method of eluding death."

"Could the wise Egyptians," said Nekayah, "think so grossly of the soul? If the soul could once survive its separation, what could it afterwards receive or suffer from the body?"

"The Egyptians would doubtless think erroneously," said the astronomer, "in the darkness of heathenism and the first dawn of philosophy. The nature of the soul is still disputed amidst all our opportunities of clearer knowledge. Some yet say that it may be material, who nevertheless believe it to be immortal."

"Some," answered Imlac, "have indeed said that the soul is material, but I can scarcely believe that any man has thought it who knew how to think; for all the conclusions of reason enforce the immateriality of mind, and all the notices of sense and investigations of science concur to prove the unconsciousness of matter.

"It was never supposed that cogitation is inherent in matter, or that every particle is a thinking being. Yet, if any part of matter be devoid of thought, what part can we suppose to think? Matter can differ from matter only in form, density, bulk, motion, and direction of motion. To which of these, however varied or combined, can consciousness be annexed? To be round or square, to be solid or fluid, to be great or little, to be moved slowly or swiftly one way or another, are modes of material existence, all equally alien from the nature of cogitation. If matter be once without thought, it can only be made to think by some new modification; but all the modifications which it can admit are equally unconnective with cogitative powers."

"But the materialists," said the astronomer, "urge that matter may have qualities with which we are unacquainted."

"He who will determine," returned Imlac, "against that which he knows because there may be something which he knows not; he that can set hypothetical possibility against acknowledged certainty, is not to be admitted among reasonable beings. All that we know of matter is that matter is inert, senseless, and lifeless; and if this conviction cannot be opposed but by referring us to something that we know not, we have all the evidence that human intellect can admit. If that which is known may be overruled by that which is unknown, no being, not omniscient, can arrive at certainty."

"Yet let us not," said the astronomer, "too arrogantly limit the Creator's power."

"It is no limitation of omnipotence," replied the poet, "to suppose that one thing is not consistent with another, that the same proposition cannot be at once true and false, that the same number cannot be even and odd, that cogitation cannot be conferred on that which is created incapable of cogitation."

"I know not," said Nekayah, "any great use of this question. Does that immateriality which, in my opinion, you have sufficiently proved, necessarily include eternal duration?"

"Of immateriality," said Imlac, "our ideas are negative, and therefore obscure. Immateriality seems to imply a natural power of perpetual duration, as a consequence of exemption from all causes of decay. Whatever perishes is destroyed by the solution of its contexture and separation of its parts; nor can we conceive how that which has no parts, and therefore admits no solution, can be naturally corrupted or impaired."

"I know not," said Rasselas, "how to conceive anything without extension. What is extended must have parts, and you allow that whatever has parts may be destroyed."

"Consider your own conceptions," replied Imlac, "and the difficulty will be less. You will find substance without extension. An ideal form is no less real than material bulk; yet an ideal form has no extension. It is no less certain, when you think on a pyramid, that your mind possesses the idea of a pyramid, than that the pyramid itself is standing. What space does the idea of a pyramid occupy more than the idea of a grain of corn; or how can either idea suffer laceration? As is the effect, such is the cause; as thought, such is the power that thinks; a power impassive and indiscerptible."

"But the Being," said Nekayah, "whom I fear to name, the Being which made the soul, can destroy it."

"He surely can destroy it," answered Imlac, "since, however unperishable, it receives from a superior nature its power of duration. That it will not perish by an inherent cause of decay or principle of corruption, may be shown by philosophy; but philosophy can tell no more. That it will not be annihilated by Him that made it, we must humbly learn from higher authority."

The whole assembly stood a while silent and collected. "Let us return," said Rasselas, "from this scene of mortality. How gloomy would be these mansions of the dead to him who did not know that he should never die; that what now acts shall continue its agency, and what now thinks shall think on forever. Those that lie here stretched before us, the wise and the powerful of ancient times, warn us to remember the shortness of our present state; they were, perhaps, snatched away while they were busy like us in the choice of life."

"To me," said the princess, "the choice of life is become less important; I hope hereafter to think only on the choice of eternity."

They then hastened out of the caverns; and, under the protection of their guard, returned to Cairo.

FROM CONVERSATION BETWEEN DR. GOODMAN AND SIDRAC, THE ANATOMIST, CONCERNING THE SOUL

In *Lord Chesterfield's Ears*

VOLTAIRE

GOODMAN: But, my dear Sidrac, why do you always speak of my thinking faculty? Why not just say my soul? It would be done more quickly and I should understand you just as well.

SIDRAC: But I should not understand myself. I feel, I know that God has given me the faculty of thinking and speaking; but I neither feel nor know whether he had given me an entity which is called a soul.

GOODMAN: Really, when I think about it, I perceive I know nothing more about it and that I have long been rash enough to think I did know. I have noticed that the eastern nations call the soul by a name which means life. Following their example, the Romans first meant the life of the animal by the word *anima*. Among the Greeks they spoke of the respiration of the soul. This respiration is a breath. The Latins translated the word breath by *spiritus;* whence comes the word equivalent to "spirit" among nearly all modern nations. Since nobody has ever seen this breath, this spirit, it has been made an entity which no one can see or touch. It has been said to reside in our body without occupying any place there, to move our organs without touching them. What has not been said? It seems to me that all our talk is founded on ambiguities. I see the wise Locke felt that these ambiguities in all languages had plunged human reason into a chaos. He has no chapter on the soul in the only book of reasonable metaphysics ever written. And if he chances to use the word in certain passages, with him it only means our intelligence. Indeed, every one feels he has an intelligence, that he receives ideas, that he associates and dissociates them; but nobody feels he has within him another entity which gives him movement, sensations and thoughts. It is ridiculous to use words we do not understand and to admit entities of which we cannot have the slightest idea.

SIDRAC: We are agreed then about a matter which has been the subject of dispute for so many centuries.

GOODMAN: And I am surprised that we are in agreement.

SIDRAC: It is not surprising, we are honestly searching for truth.   If we were on the benches of the schools, we should argue like the characters of Rabelais.   If we lived in the ages of terrible darkness which so long enveloped England, one of us would perhaps have the other burned.   We live in an age of reason; we easily find what seems to us to be the truth and we dare to express it.

GOODMAN: Yes, but I am afraid this truth is a very paltry affair.   In mathematics we have achieved prodigies which would astonish Apollonius and Archimedes, and would make them our pupils; but what have we discovered in metaphysics?   Our own ignorance.

SIDRAC: And is that nothing?   You admit that the great Being has given you the faculty of feeling and thinking, as he has given your feet the faculty of walking, your hands the power of doing a thousand things, your entrails the power of digesting, your heart the power of urging your blood into your arteries.   We hold everything from him; we could not give ourselves anything, and we shall always be ignorant of the manner which the Master of the universe makes use of to guide us.   For my part, I give him thanks for having taught me that I know nothing of first principles.   Men have always inquired how the soul acts upon the body.   They ought first of all to have found out whether we have one.   Either God has given us this present or he has communicated something which is its equivalent to us.   However he went about it, we are under his hand.   He is our master, that is all I know.

GOODMAN: But tell me at least what you suspect.   You have dissected brains, you have seen embryos and foetuses; have you discovered any sign of the soul in them?

SIDRAC: Not the least, and I have never been able to understand how an immortal, immaterial entity spent nine months uselessly hidden in an evil-smelling membrane between urine and excrement.   It is difficult for me to conceive that this pretended simple soul existed before the formation of its body.   For, if it were not a human simple soul, what use could it have been during the ages?   And then how can we imagine a simple entity, a metaphysical entity, which waits during eternity the moment to animate matter for a few minutes?   What becomes of this unknown entity, if the foetus it should animate dies in the belly of its mother?   It seemed still more ridiculous to me that God should create a soul at the moment a man lies with a woman.   It seems blasphemous that God should await the consummation of an adultery, of an incest, to reward these turpitudes by creating souls in their favor.   It is still worse when I am told that God draws immortal souls from nothingness to make them suffer incredible tortures for eternity.   What!   Burn simple entities, entities which have nothing burnable!   How should we go about burning the sound of a voice, a wind which has passed?   Even then, this sound, and this wind were material during the brief moment of their passage; but a pure spirit, a thought, a doubt?   I am all at sea.   Whichever way I turn, I find nothing but obscurity, contradiction, impossibility, ridiculousness, dreams, extravagance, fables, absurdity, stupidity, charlatanism.

But I am quite easy when I say: God is the Master.   He who causes the innumerable stars to gravitate towards each other, he who made the light, is certainly powerful enough to give us feelings and ideas without our needing a small, foreign, invisible atom called soul.   God has certainly given feeling, memory and industry to all animals.   He has given them life and it is as noble to give life as to give a soul.   It is generally agreed that animals live; it is proved that they have feeling, since they have organs of feeling.   And if they have all that without having a soul, why must we wish to have one at all costs?

GOODMAN: Perhaps from vanity. I am convinced that if a peacock could speak, he would boast of having a soul and he would say his soul is in his tail. I am very much inclined to suspect with you that God made us to eat, to drink, to walk, to sleep, to feel, to think, to be full of passions, pride and misery, without telling us one word of his secret. We do not know any more about this topic than the peacock I speak of; and he who said that we are born, live and die without knowing how, expressed a great truth.

(Richard Aldington, tr.)

FROM SCHOOL-TIME

In *The Prelude*

WILLIAM WORDSWORTH

    . . . But who shall parcel out
His intellect by geometric rules,
Split like a province into round and square?
Who knows the individual hour in which
His habits were first sown, even as a seed?
Who that shall point as with a wand and say
"This portion of the river of my mind
Came from yon fountain?" Thou, my Friend! art one
More deeply read in thy own thoughts; to thee
Science appears but what in truth she is,
Not as our glory and our absolute boast,
But as a succedaneum, and a prop
To our infirmity. No officious slave
Art thou of that false secondary power
By which we multiply distinctions, then
Deem that our puny boundaries are things
That we perceive, and not that we have made.
To thee, unblinded by these formal arts,
The unity of all hath been revealed,
And thou wilt doubt, with me less aptly skilled
Than many are to range the faculties
In scale and order, class the cabinet
Of their sensations, and in voluble phrase
Run through the history and birth of each
As of a single independent thing.
Hard task, vain hope, to analyze the mind,
If each most obvious and particular thought,
Not in a mystical and idle sense,
But in the words of Reason deeply weighed,
Hath no beginning.

FROM SCIENCE, RELIGION, AND REALITY, INTRODUCTION

LORD BALFOUR

VII

Let us then consider, in the first place, some points on which all men are agreed. No one practically doubts that the world in which we live possesses a certain kind and measure of regularity. Every expectation that we entertain, every action that we voluntarily perform, implies the belief. The most fantastic fairy tale requires it as a background; there are traces of it even in our dreams.

Again, we are all at one in treating with suspicion any statement which, in our judgment, is inconsistent with the "sort of way things happen" in the world as we conceive it. It seems to us more probable that this or that witness should be mistaken or mendacious, than that the wonders to which he testified should be true. If we have no antecedent ground for thinking him a liar, we probably accept his statements when he confines his narrative to the familiar or the commonplace; when he deals in marvels we begin to doubt; when his marvels become too marvelous we frankly disbelieve—though well aware (if we be men of sense) that what is exceedingly marvelous may nevertheless be true.

Such, roughly speaking, has been, and is, the general procedure of mankind. But evidently it is ill-suited to satisfy historians, philosophers, or men of science. It lacks precision. It rests on no clear principles. It depends too obviously on personal predilections. We seek a criterion of credibility more objective and more fundamental. We should like to know, for example, whether there is any sort of statement which, without being self-contradictory, may always be pronounced untrue.

This question will, to many high authorities, seem capable of the simplest answer. Unbroken experience (they will tell us) establishes the uniformity of Nature, and it is the uniformity of Nature which makes inferences from experience possible. Were this disturbed by miraculous occurrences the very foundations of science would be shaken. On broad general grounds therefore "miracles" must be treated in this scientific age as intrinsically incredible. They never have happened, and they never can happen. Many excellent people have indeed professed to see them, and we need not doubt their veracity. But illusion is easy, credulity is limitless, and there is nothing in their testimony which can absolve us from the plain duty of purifying or rejecting every narrative in which a taint of the "miraculous" can be detected.

VIII

In spite of its apparent precision all this is very loose talk, raising more questions than it answers.

What, for example, is meant by the uniformity of Nature? About the course of Nature we know little; yet surely we know enough to make us hesitate to call it uniform. Phase follows phase in a perpetual flow; but every phase is unique. Nature, as a whole, neither repeats itself, nor (according to science) can possibly repeat itself. Why, then, when we are considering it as a whole, should we describe it as uniform?

Perhaps it will be said that amidst all this infinite variety some fixed rules are always obeyed. Matter (for example) always gravitates to matter. Energy is never either created or destroyed. May we not—nay must we not—extend yet further this conception of unbroken regularity, and accept the view that nature, if not uniform as a whole, is nevertheless compounded of uniformities, of causal sequences, end-lessly repeated, which collectively illustrate and embody the universal reign of un-alterable law?   Were any of these causal sequences to fail, we should no doubt be faced with a "miracle"; but such an event (it is urged) would violate all experience, and it need not be seriously considered.

IX

Now this has always seemed to me a most unsatisfactory theory.   It throws upon experience a load of responsibility which experience is quite unable to bear.   No doubt, as I have already pointed out, the whole conduct of life depends upon our assuming, instinctively or otherwise, that the kind of thing which has happened once, will, under more or less similar circumstances, be likely to happen again. But this assumption, whether instinctive or reflective, whether wisely acted on or unwisely, supplies a very frail foundation for the speculative structure sometimes based upon it.   Can it be denied, for example, that nature, uncritically observed, seems honeycombed with irregularities, that the wildest excesses of credulity may arise not from ignoring experience, but from refusing to correct it, that the most ruthless editing is required to force the uncensored messages we receive from the external world into the ideal mold which satisfies our individual convictions?

But what is this ideal mold?   We sometimes talk as if by the help of Scientific Method or Inductive Logic we could map out all reality into a scheme of well-defined causes indissolubly connected with well-defined effects, together forming se-quences whose recurrence in different combinations constitutes the changing pat-tern of the universe.

But can such hopes be realized?   In the world of concrete fact nothing occurs through the action of a single cause, nor yet through the simple cooperation of many causes, each adding its own unqualified contribution to the total effect, as we picture horse helping horse to draw a loaded dray.   Our world is a much more complicated affair.   Sequences are never exactly repeated.   Causes can never be completely isolated.   Their operation is never unqualified.   Fence round your lab-oratory experiments with what precautions you will, no two of them will ever be performed under exactly the same conditions.   For the purpose in hand the differ-ences may be negligible.   With skilled observers they commonly are.   But the dif-ferences exist, and they must certainly modify, however imperceptibly, the observed result.

X

It seems evident from considerations like these that no argument directly based on mere experience can be urged either for or against the possibility of "miracles." Common sense looks doubtfully upon anything out of the common; and science follows suit.   But this is very different from the speculative assertion that, since "miracles" are a violation of natural law, their occurrence must be regarded as im-possible.   The intrusion of an unexpected and perhaps anomalous element into the company of more familiar factors in world development may excite suspicion, but it does not of necessity violate anything more important than our preconceived expectations.

I think it will be found that those who most vehemently reject this way of re-garding the world are unconsciously moved not by their knowledge of scientific laws, but by preference for a particular scientific ideal.   They are persuaded that if only we had the right kind of knowledge and adequate powers of calculation, we should be able to explain the whole contents of possible experience by applying mathe-matical methods to certain simple data.   They refuse to believe that this calculable

"Whole" can suffer interference at the hands of any incalculable power. They find no room in the close-knit tissue of the world process, as they conceive it, for any arbitrary element to find lodgment. They have a clear notion of what science ought to be, and that notion is incompatible with the "miraculous."

.   .   .   .

XII

The conception of a material universe, overwhelming in its complexity and its splendor, yet potentially susceptible of complete explanation by the actions and the reactions of two very minute and simple kinds of electrical sub-atom, is, without doubt, extraordinarily fascinating. From the early days of scientific philosophy or (if you prefer it) of philosophical science, thinkers have been hungering after some form of all-embracing atomism. They have now apparently reached it (so far as matter is concerned) by the way of observation and experiment—truly a marvelous performance. Yet the very lucidity of the new conceptions helps to bring home to us their essential insufficiency as a theory of the universe. They may be capable of explaining the constitution and behavior of inanimate objects. They may go some (as yet unmeasured) distance towards explaining organic life. But they certainly cannot explain mind. No man really supposes that he personally is nothing more than a changing group of electrical charges, so distributed that their relative motions enable or compel them in their collective capacity to will, to hope, to love, to think, perhaps to discuss themselves as a physical multiplicity, certainly to treat themselves as a mental unity. No creed of this kind can ever be extracted by valid reasoning from the sort of data which the physics either of the present or the future can possibly supply.

The truth is that the immense advances which in modern times have been made by mechanical or quasi-mechanical explanations of the material world have somewhat upset the mental balance of many thoughtful persons who approach the problems of reality exclusively from the physical side. It is not that they formulate any excessive claims to knowledge. On the contrary, they often describe themselves as agnostics. Nevertheless they are apt unconsciously to assume that they already enjoy a good bird's-eye view of what reality *is,* combined with an unshaken assurance about what it is *not.* They tacitly suppose that every discovery, if genuine, will find its place within the framework of a perfected physics, and, if it does not, may be summarily dismissed as mere superstition.

XIII

After all, however, superstition may be negative as well as positive, and the excesses of unbelief may be as extravagant as those of belief. Doubtless the universe, as conceived by men more primitive than ourselves, was the obscure abode of strange deities. But what are we to say about a universe reduced without remainder to collections of electric charges radiating energy through a hypothetical ether? Thus to set limits to reality must always be the most hazardous of speculative adventures. To do so by eliminating the spiritual is not only hazardous but absurd. For if we are directly aware of anything, it is of ourselves as personal agents; if anything can be proved by direct experiment it is that we can, in however small a measure, vary the "natural" distribution of matter and energy. We can certainly act on our environment, and as certainly our action can never be adequately explained in terms of entities which neither think, nor feel, nor purpose, nor know. It constitutes a spiritual invasion of the physical world:—it is a miracle.

XIV

To me therefore it seems that in the present state of our knowledge or (if you prefer it) of our ignorance, we have no choice but to acquiesce provisionally in an unresolved dualism. Our experience has a double outlook. The first we may call material. It brings us face to face with such subjects as electricity, mass, motion, force, energy, and with such manifestations of energy as ethereal radiation. The second is spiritual. The first deals with objects which are measurable, calculable, capable (up to a point) of precise definition. The second deals with the immeasurable, the incalculable, the indefinable and (let me add) the all-important. The first touches the fundamentals of science; the second is intimately connected with religion. Yet different as they seem, both are real. They belong to the same universe; they influence each other; somewhere and somehow they must be in contact along a common frontier.

But where is that frontier to be drawn? And how are we to describe the relation between these co-terminous provinces of reality? This is perhaps a question for metaphysics rather than for religion or science; and some day, perhaps, metaphysics may provide us with a satisfying answer. In the meanwhile, I may conclude this Introduction at a less ambitious level—concerning myself rather with the relations between religion and science in the practice of life, than with any high problems of speculative philosophy.

XV

I suggest then that in scientific research it is a wise procedure to press "mechanical" theories of the material world to their utmost limits. Were I, for example, a biologist I should endeavor to explain all the phenomena under investigation in terms of matter and motion. I should always be searching for what could be measured and calculated, however confident I might be that in some directions at least the hopeless limitations of such a view would very rapidly become apparent.

In the practice of life, on the other hand, and in the speculation of philosophy, we are free to move within wider horizons. In forming our estimate of the sort of beliefs which may properly be regarded as rationally acceptable, we ought not to be limited by mechanistic presuppositions, however useful these may be in our investigations of Nature. We are spiritual beings, and must take account of spiritual values. The story of man is something more than a mere continuation of the story of matter. It is different in kind. If we cannot calculate the flow of physical events, that is because our knowledge of natural processes is small, and our power of calculation feeble. If we cannot calculate the course of human history, that is because (among other reasons) it is inherently incalculable. No two specimens of humanity exactly resemble each other, or live in circumstances that are exactly comparable. The so-called "repetitions" of history are never more than vague resemblances. The science of history therefore, if there be one, is something quite different from (say) the science of physics. And this is true even when history is wholly divorced from religion. But when it is considered in a different setting, when man is regarded as a spiritual agent in a world under spiritual guidance, events of spiritual significance cannot be wholly judged by canons of criticism which seem sufficient for simpler cases. Unexampled invasions of the physical sphere by the spiritual are not indeed to be lightly believed. But they are certainly not to be rejected merely because historians cannot bring themselves to accept the "miraculous."

XVI

This point of view, for those who are prepared to take it, may help to eliminate some of the chief causes of conflict between science and religion. In times not far distant there were men devoted to religion who blundered ignorantly into science, and men devoted to science who meddled unadvisedly with religion. Theologians found their geology in Genesis; materialists supposed that reality could be identified with the mechanism of matter. Neither procedure is to be commended; nor is it by these paths that the unsolved riddle of the universe can best be approached. A science which declares itself incompatible with religion, a religion which deems itself a substitute for science, may indulge in controversies as interminable as they are barren. . . .

CHAPTER 12

OF TIME AND CHANGE

Like a circle, Time, thou art,
Sourceless, endless, but a chart
Or locus of some point unknown,
Uniform, regular, monotone . . .
Yet pause a moment—curious thought—
A circle symbolizes nought!
—Neville de Caun, "Passing Thought."

All languages reveal man's preoccupation with time. A score of words in any tongue such as *now, then, first, tomorrow, today, tonight,* enter into nearly all our communication with one another; and the concept of time itself, in one form or another, has come to dominate man's life in the Western world. Perhaps our first conscious impression of life, the one impression of our early years that remains sharply with us, is that of the passing of time. How impossibly long those afternoons of infancy and childhood!

A pleasing land of drowsy-head it was,
Of dreams that wave before the half-shut eye:
And of gay castles in the clouds that pass,
Forever flushing round a summer sky.

All our stories then began with that magical phrase, "Once upon a time." One of these stories told of a king in a subterranean castle, enchanted, beyond the power of time—but his beard still grew, flowing white into the table where he sat—where he sits to this day, surrounded by his barons, waiting the hour when he will rise to succor his people. And there was the Israelite leader who achieved the universal dream and stopped the sun: today our best attempt is daylight saving. Perhaps the most treasured of these stories was that of the sleeping princess, immortal beauty hermetically locked away from time, waiting for the kiss that would bring her back to our world of time and change and death. As we grow older, we become more and more conscious of the preciousness of time; and we become aware that everything is subject to the tyranny of time. If we could only grasp one moment, make it surely ours!

Logan Pearsall Smith, in our first selection, finds that this elusiveness of the present is the source of our most profound unhappiness. We are ghosts haunting the past and the future, with no real existence in the present. Carlyle would have time-hats to match the space-hats of Fortunatus. What

441

a world this would be if we could but summon up the poets and sages of the past in flesh and blood instead of relying on what they have bequeathed us of their spirit in song and story! But "the iniquity of oblivion blindly scattereth her poppy." Whatever time may be, it is apparent that our conception of it is highly subjective. In practice we find that time is measured not only by weekday clocks, but also by the flow of experience. This theme attains a noble expression in Ben Jonson's "Pindaric Ode":

> In small proportions we just beauties see,
> And in short measures, life may perfect be.

And in "Cristina," Browning, with a side glance at the doctrine of elective affinities, also urges that life and time should be measured by the intensity of experience. The theme of the subjectivity of time is elaborated extensively by Thomas Mann in the passages from *The Magic Mountain* and St. Augustine in his *Confessions,* discussions in which the interlocking relationship of time, space, motion, and change is emphasized. Reviewing these connections, we appreciate the inspiration of E. E. Cummings' observation: "Time is the autobiography of space."

However opinions may vary about time, on one point all seem agreed: Time is marked by change. Time may be white and tall, Hillyer suggests, but man's road is marked by broken columns, the ravages of time: "It is longer than miles from Olympia to Patras." It is one of the strange illusions of time that we think of ourselves as stable beings in a world of passing time, whereas, as Ronsard remarks, the converse is relatively true: "Alas, Time stays,—we go!"

As change measures time, so change itself is characterized by diversification in the nature of things and alteration in their forms. At first the evolutionary conception of man's origin bred doubt of religion just as the Copernican revolution had done three centuries earlier. But Browning is content with the idea that man is the highest step in evolution ("With Francis Furini"). He marvels rather at the development, apparently not from any earlier source, of moral sense in man, a development that, he argues, deifies man. Tennyson goes a step further, representing man, master of the brute in himself, gazing toward a height that is higher: the "one far-off divine event, to which the whole creation moves."

But man is not the only creature that is evolving. Will man continue to dominate his world, or will he one day become extinct as the plesiosaurus? And how did this process of continuing creation start and how far will it extend—to the evolution of worlds themselves? Such are the questions asked by Clarence Day and Thomas Mann.

What is behind all this struggle, this shaping and unfolding of new forms of life? Do these changes extending infinitely through time proceed blindly or does the apparent design in them argue some great conscient Cause?

Several answers to these questions have already been suggested in various selections remarked above. Heraclitus and many others in early times saw the sufficient cause in fire and the sun. Browning and Tennyson would comfortably find the Hebraic-Christian concept of God the final Cause. Leopardi is frankly agnostic. Finding life evil, he discovers no purpose in the senseless misery of being ("Night-Song of a Nomadic Shepherd of Asia"). Arnold is scarcely more hopeful, while Voltaire's agnosticism finds expression in ridicule. In his famous satire on Leibnitz's doctrine that this is the best of all possible worlds, he makes a farce of the notion that every effect proceeds from a cause in a pre-established harmonious design.

Agnosticism and cynicism are dusty answers, but in one way or another they characterize the comments of many who have inquired about the ultimate Cause. Clough helplessly wonders if our purpose in being is simply to figure out the problem of our being ("Perché Pensa?"). In "New Year's Eve" Hardy apparently is resigned to the "logicless" labors of God. In the splendid conclusion to *The Dynasts*, however, he arrives at the hope that conscience in man will gradually inform the creative energy that shapes all things so that it will ultimately fashion all things fair.

WHAT'S WRONG *

LOGAN PEARSALL SMITH

From their corner of the half-empty drawing-room they could see in a great mirror the other dinner-guests linger and depart. But none of them were going on—what was the good?—to that evening party. They talked of satiety and disenchantment, of the wintry weather, of illness, of age and death.

"But what really frightens me most in life," said one of them, "what gives me a kind of vertigo or shiver, is—it sounds absurd, but it's simply the horror of space, *l'épouvante sidérale*—the dismay of Infinity, the black abysses in the Milky Way, the silence of those eternal spaces."

"But Time," said another of the group, "surely Time is a worse nightmare. Think of it! the Past with never a beginning, the Future going on for ever and ever, and the little Present in which we live, twinkling for a second, between these black abysses."

"What's wrong with me," mused the third speaker, "is that even the Present eludes me. I don't know what it really is; I can never catch the moment as it passes; I am always far ahead or far away behind, and always somewhere else. I am not really here now with you. And why should I go to the party? I shouldn't be there, either, if I went. My life is all reminiscence and anticipation—if you can call it life, if I am not rather a kind of ghost, haunting a past that has ceased to exist, or a future that is still more shadowy and unreal. It's ghastly in a way, this exile and isolation. But why speak of it, after all?"

They rose, and their figures too were reflected in the great mirror, as they passed out of the drawing-room and dispersed, each on his or her way, into the winter night.

FROM NATURAL SUPERNATURALISM

In *Sartor Resartus*

THOMAS CARLYLE

Fortunatus had a wishing Hat, which when he put on, and wished himself Anywhere, behold he was There. By this means had Fortunatus triumphed over Space, he had annihilated Space; for him there was no Where, but all was Here. Were a Hatter to establish himself, in the Wahngasse of Weissnichtwo, and make felts of this sort for all mankind, what a world we should have of it! Still stranger, should, on the opposite side of the street, another Hatter establish himself; and, as his fellow-craftsman made Space-annihilating Hats, make Time-annihilating! Of both would I purchase, were it with my last groschen; but chiefly of this latter. To clap-on your felt, and, simply by wishing that you were Any*where,* straight to be *There!* Next to clap-on your other felt, and, simply by wishing that you were Any*when,* straight-way to be *Then!* This were indeed the grander: shooting at will from the Fire-Creation of the World to its Fire-Consummation; here historically present in the First Century, conversing face to face with Paul and Seneca; there prophetically in the Thirty-first conversing also face to face with other Pauls and Senecas, who as yet stand hidden in the depths of that late Time!

FROM A PINDARIC ODE

BEN JONSON

For what is life, if measured by the space
    Not by the act?
Or maskèd man, if valued by his face,
    Above his fact?
Here's one out-lived his peers,
And told forth fourscore years;
He vexed time, and busied the whole state;
    Troubled both foes and friends;
    But ever to no ends:
What did this stirrer but die late?
How well at twenty had he fallen or stood!
For three of his fourscore he did no good . . .

It is not growing like a tree
In bulk doth make men better be;
Or standing long an oak, three hundred year,
To fall a log at last, dry, bald, and sear:
    A lily of a day,
    Is fairer far in May,
Although it fall and die that night;
It was the plant, and flower of light.
In small proportions we just beauties see;
And in short measures, life may perfect be.

FROM CRISTINA

ROBERT BROWNING

She should never have looked at me
    If she meant I should not love her!
There are plenty . . . men, you call such,
    I suppose . . . she may discover
All her soul to, if she pleases,
    And yet leave much as she found them:
But I'm not so; and she knew it
    When she fixed me, glancing round them.

What? To fix me thus meant nothing?
    But I can't tell (there's my weakness)
What her look said!—no vile cant, sure,
    About "need to strew the bleakness
Of some lone shore with its pearl-seed,
    That the sea feels"—no "strange yearning
That such souls have, most to lavish
    Where there's chance of least returning."

Oh, we're sunk enough here, God knows!
    But not quite so sunk that moments,
Sure tho' seldom, are denied us,
    When the spirit's true endowments
Stand out plainly from its false ones,
    And apprise it if pursuing
Or the right way or the wrong way,
    To its triumph or undoing.

There are flashes struck from midnights,
    There are fire-flames noondays kindle,
Whereby piled-up honors perish,
    Whereby swollen ambitions dwindle,
While just this or that poor impulse,
    Which for once had play unstifled,
Seems the sole work of a life-time
    That away the rest have trifled.

Doubt you if, in some such moment,
    As she fixed me, she felt clearly,
Ages past the soul existed,
    Here an age 'tis resting merely,
And hence fleets again for ages,
    While the true end, sole and single,
It stops here for is, this love-way,
    With some other soul to mingle?

Else it loses what it lived for,
    And eternally must lose it;
Better ends may be in prospect,

> Deeper blisses (if you choose it),
> But this life's end and this love-bliss
> Have been lost here. Doubt you whether
> This she felt as, looking at me,
> Mine and her souls rushed together?

FROM MENTAL GYMNASTIC *

In *The Magic Mountain*

THOMAS MANN

Joachim's reply came impeded and incoherent. He had taken a small thermometer from a red leather, velvet-lined case on his table, and put the mercury-filled end under his tongue on the left side, so that the glass instrument stuck slantingly upwards out of his mouth. Then he changed into indoor clothes, put on shoes and a braided jacket, took a printed form and pencil from his table, also a book, a Russian grammar—for he was studying Russian with the idea that it would be of advantage to him in the service—and, thus equipped, took his place in the reclining-chair on his balcony, throwing his camel's hair rug lightly across his feet.

It was scarcely needed. During the last quarter-hour the layer of cloud had grown steadily thinner, and now the sun broke through in summerlike warmth, so dazzlingly that Joachim protected his head with a white linen shade which was fastened to the arm of his chair, and furnished with a device by means of which it could be adjusted to the position of the sun. Hans Castorp praised this contrivance. He wished to await the result of Joachim's measurement, and meanwhile looked about to see how everything was done: observed the fur-lined sleeping-sack that stood against the wall in a corner of the loggia, for Joachim to use on cold days; and gazed down into the garden, with his elbows on the balustrade. The general rest-hall was populated by reclining patients, reading, writing, or conversing. He could see only a part of the interior, some four or five chairs.

"How long does that go on?" he asked, turning round.

Joachim raised seven fingers.

"Seven minutes! But they must be up!"

Joachim shook his head. A little later he took the thermometer out of his mouth, looked at it, and said: "Yes, when you watch it, the time, it goes very slowly. I quite like the measuring, four times a day; for then you know what a minute—or seven of them—actually amounts to, up here in this place, where the seven days of the week whisk by the way they do!"

"You say 'actually,'" Hans Castorp answered. He sat with one leg flung over the balustrade, and his eyes looked bloodshot. "But after all, time *isn't* 'actual.' When it seems long to you, then it *is* long; when it seems short, why, then it is short. But how long, or how short, it actually is, that nobody knows." He was unaccustomed to philosophize, yet somehow felt an impulse to do so.

Joachim gainsaid him. "How so?—we do measure it. We have watches and calendars for the purpose; and when a month is *up*, why, then up it is, for you, and for me, and for all of us."

"Wait," said Hans Castorp. He held up his forefinger, close to his tired eyes. "A minute, then, is as long as it seems to you when you measure it yourself?"

---

* Reprinted from *The Magic Mountain* by Thomas Mann (translated by H. T. Lowe-Porter), by permission of Alfred A. Knopf, Inc. Copyright 1927 by Alfred A. Knopf, Inc.

"A minute is as long—it *lasts* as long—as it takes the second hand of my watch to complete a circuit."

"But it takes such a varied length of time—to our senses! And as a matter of fact—I say taking it just as a matter of fact," he repeated, pressing his forefinger so hard against his nose that he bent the end of it quite round, "it is motion, isn't it, motion in space? Wait a minute! That means that we measure time by space. But that is no better than measuring space by time, a thing only very unscientific people do. From Hamburg to Davos is twenty hours—that is, by train. But on foot how long is it? And in the mind, how long? Not a second!"

"I say," Joachim said, "what's the matter with you? Seems to me it goes to your head to be up here with us!"

"Keep quiet! I'm very clear-headed today. Well, then, what *is* time?" asked Hans Castorp, and bent the tip of his nose so far round that it became white and bloodless. "Can you answer me that? Space we perceive with our organs, with our senses of sight and touch. Good. But which is our organ of time—tell me that if you can. You see, that's where you stick. But how can we possibly measure anything about which we actually know nothing, not even a single one of its properties? We say of time that it passes. Very good, let it pass. But to be able to measure it—wait a minute: to be susceptible of being measured, time must flow evenly, but who ever said it did that? As far as our consciousness is concerned it doesn't, we only assume that it does, for the sake of convenience; and our units of measurement are purely arbitrary, sheer conventions—"

"Good," Joachim said. "Then perhaps it is pure convention that I have five points too much here on my thermometer. But on account of those lines I have to drool about here instead of joining up, which is a disgusting fact. . . ."

(H. T. Lowe-Porter, tr.)

FROM CHANGES *

In *The Magic Mountain*

THOMAS MANN

What is time? A mystery, a figment—and all-powerful. It conditions the exterior world, it is motion married to and mingled with the existence of bodies in space, and with the motion of these. Would there then be no time if there were no motion? No motion if no time? We fondly ask. Is time a function of space? Or space of time? Or are they identical? Echo answers. Time is functional, it can be referred to as action; we say a thing is "brought about," by time. What sort of thing? Change! Now is not then, here not there, for between them lies motion. But the motion by which one measures time is circular, is in a closed circle; and might almost equally well be described as rest, as cessation of movement—for the there repeats itself constantly in the here, the past in the present. Furthermore, as our utmost effort cannot conceive a final limit either to time or in space, we have settled to think of them as eternal and infinite—apparently in the hope that if this is not very successful, at least it will be more so than the other. But is not this affirmation of the eternal and the infinite the logical-mathematical destruction of every and any limit in time or space, and the reduction of them, more or less, to zero? Is it possible, in eternity, to conceive of a sequence of events, or in the infinite of a succession of space-occupying bodies? Conceptions of distance, move-

---

ment, change, even of the existence of finite bodies in the universe—how do these fare? Are they consistent with the hypothesis of eternity and infinity we have been driven to adopt? Again we ask, and again echo answers. . . .

(H. T. Lowe-Porter, tr.)

FROM BY THE OCEAN OF TIME *

In *The Magic Mountain*

THOMAS MANN

Can one tell—that is to say, narrate—time, time itself, as such, for its own sake? That would surely be an absurd undertaking. A story which read: "Time passed, it ran on, the time flowed onward" and so forth—no one in his senses could consider that a narrative. It would be as though one held a single note or chord for a whole hour, and called it music. For narration resembles music in this, that it *fills up* the time. It "fills it in" and "breaks it up," so that "there's something to it," "something going on"—to quote, with due and mournful piety, those casual phrases of our departed Joachim, all echo of which, so long ago died away. So long ago, indeed, that we wonder if the reader is clear how long ago it was. For time is the medium of narration, as it is the medium of life. Both are inextricably bound up with it, as inextricable as are bodies in space. Similarly, time is the medium of music; music divides, measures, articulates time, and can shorten it, yet enhance its value, both at once. Thus music and narration are alike, in that they can only present themselves as a flowing, as a succession in time, as one thing after another; and both differ from the plastic arts, which are complete in the present, and unrelated to time save as all bodies are, whereas narration—like music—even if it should try to be completely present at any given moment, would need time to do it in.

So much is clear. But it is just as clear that we have also a difference to deal with. For the time element in music is single. Into a section of mortal time music pours itself, thereby inexpressibly enhancing and ennobling what it fills. But a narrative must have two kinds of time: first, its own, like music, actual time, conditioning its presentation and course; and second, the time of its content, which is relative, so extremely relative that the imaginary time of the narrative can either coincide nearly or completely with the actual, or musical, time, or can be a world away. A piece of music called a "Five-minute Waltz" lasts five minutes, and this is its sole relation to the time element. But a narrative which concerned itself with the events of five minutes, might, by extraordinary conscientiousness in the telling, take up a thousand times five minutes, and even then seem very short, though long in relation to its imaginary time. On the other hand, the contentual time of a story can shrink its actual time out of all measure. We put it in this way on purpose, in order to suggest another element, an illusory, even, to speak plainly, a morbid element, which is quite definitely a factor in the situation. I am speaking of cases where the story practices a hermetical magic, a temporal distortion of perspective reminding one of certain abnormal and transcendental experiences in actual life. We have records of opium dreams in which the dreamer, during a brief narcotic sleep, had experiences stretching over a period of ten, thirty, sixty years, or even passing the extreme limit of man's temporal capacity for experience: dreams whose contentual time was enormously greater than their actual or musical

* Reprinted from *The Magic Mountain* by Thomas Mann (translated by H. T. Lowe-Porter), by permission of Alfred A. Knopf, Inc. Copyright 1927 by Alfred A. Knopf, Inc.

time, and in which there obtained an incredible foreshortening of events; the images pressing one upon another with such rapidity that it was as though "something had been taken away, like the spring from a broken watch" from the brain of the sleeper. Such is the description of a hashish eater.

Thus, or in some such way as in these sinister dreams, can the narrative go to work with time; in some such way can time be dealt with in a tale. . . .

Time, however weakened the subjective perception of it has become, has objective reality in that it brings things to pass. It is a question for professional thinkers— Hans Castorp, in his youthful arrogance, had one time been led to consider it— whether the hermetically sealed conserve upon its shelf is outside of time. We know that time does its work, even upon Seven-Sleepers. A physician cites a case of a twelve-year-old girl, who fell asleep and slept thirteen years; assuredly she did not remain thereby a twelve-year-old girl, but bloomed into ripe womanhood while she slept. How could it be otherwise? The dead man—is dead; he has closed his eyes on time. He has plenty of time, or personally speaking, he is timeless. Which does not prevent his hair and nails from growing, or, all in all—but no, we shall not repeat those free-and-easy expressions used once by Joachim, to which Hans Castorp, newly arrived from the flat-land, had taken exception. Hans Castorp's hair and nails grew too, grew rather fast. He sat very often in the barber's chair in the main street of the Dorf, wrapped in a white sheet, and the barber, chatting obsequiously the while, deftly performed upon the fringes of his hair, growing too long behind his ears. First time, then the barber, performed their office upon our hero. When he sat there, or when he stood at the door of his loggia and pared his nails and groomed them, with the accessories from his dainty velvet case, he would suddenly be overpowered by a mixture of terror and eager joy that made him fairly giddy. And this giddiness was in both senses of the word: rendering our hero not only dazed and dizzy, but flighty and light-headed, incapable of distinguishing between "now" and "then," and prone to mingle these together in a timeless eternity.

As we have repeatedly said, we wish to make him out neither better nor worse than he was; accordingly we must report that he often tried to atone for his reprehensible indulgence in attacks of mysticism, by virtuously and painstakingly striving to counteract them. He would sit with his watch open in his hand, his thin gold watch with the engraved monogram on the lid, looking at the porcelain face with the double row of black and red Arabic figures running round it, the two fine and delicately curved gold hands moving in and out over it, and the little second-hand taking its busy ticking course round its own small circle. Hans Castorp, watching the second-hand, essayed to hold time by the tail, to cling to and prolong the passing moments. The little hand tripped on its way, unheeding the figures it reached, passed over, left behind, left far behind, approached, and came on to again. It had no feeling for time limits, divisions, or measurements of time. Should it not pause on the sixty, or give some small sign that this was the end of one thing and the beginning of the next? But the way it passed over the tiny intervening unmarked strokes showed that all the figures and divisions on its path were simply beneath it, that it moved on, and on.—Hans Castorp shoved his product of the Glashütte works back in his waistcoat pocket, and left time to take care of itself.

How make plain to the sober intelligence of the flat-land the changes that took place in the inner economy of our young adventurer? The dizzying problem of identities grew grander in its scale. If today's now—even with decent goodwill— was not easy to distinguish from yesterday's, the day before's or the day before that's, which were all as like each other as the same number of peas, was it not also capable of being confused with the now which had been in force a month or a year ago, was it not also likely to be mingled and rolled round in the course of that other, to blend with it into the always?   However one might still differentiate between the ordinary states of consciousness which we attached to the words "still," "again," "next," there was always the temptation to extend the significance of such descriptive words as "tomorrow," "yesterday," by which "today" holds at bay "the past" and "the future."   It would not be hard to imagine the existence of creatures, perhaps upon smaller planets than ours, practicing a miniature time-economy, in whose brief span and brisk tripping gait of our second-hand would possess the tenacious spatial economy of our hand that marks the hours.   And, contrariwise, one can conceive of a world so spacious that its time system too has a majestic stride, and the distinctions between "still," "in a little while," "yesterday," "tomorrow," are, in its economy, possessed of hugely extended significance.   That, we say, would be not only conceivable, but, viewed in the spirit of a tolerant relativity, and in the light of an already-quoted proverb, might be considered legitimate, sound, even estimable.   Yet what shall one say of a son of earth, and of our time to boot, for whom a day, a week, a month, a semester, ought to play such an important role, and bring so many changes, so much progress in its train, who one day falls into the vicious habit—or perhaps we should say, yields sometimes to the desire —to say "yesterday" when he means a year ago, and "next year" when he means tomorrow?   Certainly we must deem him lost and undone, and the object of our just concern.

There is a state, in our human life, there are certain scenic surroundings—if one may use that adjective to describe the surroundings we have in mind—within which such a confusion and obliteration of distances in time and space is in a measure justified, and temporary submersion in them, say for the term of a holiday, not reprehensible.   Hans Castorp, for his part, could never without the greatest longing think of a stroll along the ocean's edge.   We know how he loved to have the snowy wastes remind him of his native landscape of broad ocean dunes; we hope the reader's recollections will bear us out when we speak of the joys of that straying. You walk, and walk—never will you come home at the right time, for you are of time, and time is vanished.   O ocean, far from thee we sit and spin our tale; we turn toward thee our thoughts, our love, loud and expressly we call on thee, that thou mayst be present in the tale we spin, as in secret thou ever wast and shalt be! —A singing solitude, spanned by a sky of palest gray; full of stinging damp that leaves a salty tang upon the lips.—We walk along the springing floor, strewn with seaweed and tiny mussel-shells.   Our ears are wrapped about by the great mild, ample wind, that comes sweeping untrammeled blandly through space, and gently blunts our senses.   We wander—wander—watching the tongues of foam lick upward toward our feet and sink back again.   The surf is seething; wave after wave, with high, hollow sound, rears up, rebounds, and runs with a silken rustle out over the flat strand: here one, there one, and more beyond, on the bar.   The dull, pervasive, sonorous roar closes our ears against all the sounds of the world.   O deep content, O wilful bliss of sheer forgetfulness!   Let us shut our eyes, safe in eternity!   No— for there in the foaming gray-green waste that stretches with uncanny foreshortening to lose itself in the horizon, look, there is a sail.   There?   Where is there?   How far, how near?   You cannot tell.   Dizzyingly it escapes your measurement.   In order to know how far that ship is from the shore, you would need to know how much room it occupies, as a body in space.   Is it large and far off, or is it small and near?   Your eye grows dim with uncertainty, for in yourself you have no sense-organ to help you judge of time or space.—We walk, walk.   How long, how far? Who knows?   Nothing is changed by our pacing, there is the same as here, once on a time the same as now, or then; time is drowning in the measureless monotony of space, motion from point to point is no motion more, where uniformity rules; and where motion is no more motion, time is no longer time.

The schoolmen of the Middle Ages would have it that time is an illusion; that its flow in sequence and causality is only the result of a sensory device, and the real existence of things in an abiding present. Was he walking by the sea, the philosopher to whom this thought first came, walking by the sea, with the faint bitterness of eternity upon his lips? We must repeat that, as for us, we have been speaking only of the lawful license of a holiday, of fantasies born of leisure, of which the well-conducted mind wearies as quickly as a vigorous man does of lying in the warm sand.

(H. T. Lowe-Porter, tr.)

FROM THE CONFESSIONS OF SAINT AUGUSTINE, Book XI

CHAP. XIII.—*Before the times created by God, times were not.*

15. But if the roving thought of any one should wander through the images of bygone time, and wonder that Thou, the God Almighty, and All-creating, and All-sustaining, the Architect of heaven and earth, didst for innumerable ages refrain from so great a work before Thou wouldst make it, let him awake and consider that he wonders at false things. For whence could innumerable ages pass by which Thou didst not make, since Thou art the Author and Creator of all ages? Or what times should those be which were not made by Thee? Or how should they pass by if they had not been? Since, therefore, Thou art the Creator of all times, if any time was before Thou madest heaven and earth, why is it said that Thou didst refrain from working? For that very time Thou madest, nor could times pass by before Thou madest times. But if before heaven and earth there was no time, why is it asked, What didst Thou then? For there was no "then" when time was not.

16. Nor dost Thou by time precede time; else wouldest not Thou precede all times. But in the excellency of an ever-present eternity, Thou precedest all times past, and survivest all future times, because they are future, and when they have come they will be past; but "Thou art the same, and Thy years shall have no end." Thy years neither go nor come; but ours both go and come, that all may come. All Thy years stand at once, since they do stand; nor were they when departing excluded by coming years, because they pass not away; but all these of ours shall be when all shall cease to be. Thy years are one day, and Thy day is not daily, but today; because Thy today yields not with tomorrow, for neither doth it follow yesterday. Thy today is eternity; therefore didst Thou beget the Co-eternal, to whom Thou saidst, "This day have I begotten Thee." Thou hast made all time; and before all times Thou art, nor in any time was there not time.

CHAP. XIV.—*Neither time past nor future, but the present, only really is.*

17. At no time, therefore, hadst Thou not made anything, because Thou hadst made time itself. And no times are co-eternal with Thee, because Thou remainest for ever; but should these continue, they would not be times. For what is time? Who can easily and briefly explain it? Who even in thought can comprehend it, even to the pronouncing of a word concerning it? But what in speaking do we refer to more familiarly and knowingly than time? And certainly we understand when we speak of it; we understand also when we hear it spoken of by another. What, then, is time? If no one ask of me, I know; if I wish to explain to him who asks, I know not. Yet I say with confidence, that I know that if nothing passed

away, there would not be past time; and if nothing were coming, there would not be future time; and if nothing were, there would not be present time. Those two times, therefore, past and future, how are they, when even the past now is not, and the future is not as yet? But should the present be always present, and should it not pass into time past, time truly it could not be, but eternity. If then, time present—if it be time—only comes into existence because it passes into time past, how do we say that even this is, whose cause of being is that it shall not be—namely, so that we cannot truly say that time is, unless because it tends not to be?

CHAP. XV.—*There is only a moment of present time.*

18. And yet we say that "time is long and time is short"; nor do we speak of this save of time past and future. A long time past, for example, we call a hundred years ago; in like manner a long time to come, a hundred years hence. But a short time past we call, say, ten days ago; and a short time to come, ten days hence. But in what sense is that long or short which is not? For the past is not now, and the future is not yet. Therefore let us not say, "It is long"; but let us say of the past, "It hath been long," and of the future, "It will be long." O my Lord, my light, shall not even here Thy truth deride man? For that past time which was long, was it long when it was already past, or when it was as yet present? For then it might be long when there was that which could be long, but when past it no longer was; wherefore that could not be long which was not at all. Let us not, therefore, say, "Time past hath been long"; for we shall not find what may have been long, seeing that since it was past it is not; but let us say "that present time was long, because when it was present it was long." For it had not as yet passed away so as not to be, and therefore there was that which could be long. But after it passed, that ceased also to be long which ceased to be.

19. Let us therefore see, O human soul, whether present time can be long; for to thee is it given to perceive and to measure periods of time. What wilt thou reply to me? Is a hundred years when present a long time? See, first, whether a hundred years can be present. For if the first year of these is current, that is, present, but the other ninety and nine are future, and therefore they are not as yet. But if the second year is current, one is already past, the other present, the rest future. And thus, if we fix on any middle year of this hundred as present, those before it are past, those after it are future; wherefore a hundred years cannot be present. See at least whether that year itself which is current can be present. For if its first month be current, the rest are future; if the second, the first hath already passed, and the remainder are not yet. Therefore neither is the year which is current as a whole present; and if it is not present as a whole, then the year is not present. For twelve months make the year, of which each individual month which is current is itself present, but the rest are either past or future. Although neither is that month which is current present, but one day only: if the first, the rest being to come, if the last, the rest being past; if any of the middle, then between past and future.

20. Behold, the present time, which alone we found could be called long, is abridged to the space scarcely of one day. But let us discuss even that, for there is not one day present as a whole. For it is made up of four-and-twenty hours of night and day, whereof the first hath the rest future, the last hath them past, but any one of the intervening hath those before it past, those after it future. And that one hour passeth away in fleeting particles. Whatever of it hath flown away is past, whatever remaineth is future. If any portion of time be conceived which cannot now be divided into even the minutest particles of moments, this only is that which may be called present; which, however, flies so rapidly from future to

past, that it cannot be extended by any delay. For if it be extended, it is divided into the past and future; but the present hath no space. Where, therefore, is the time which we may call long? Is it future? Indeed we do not say, "It is long," because it is not yet, so as to be long; but we say, "It will be long." When, then, will it be? For if even then, since as yet it is future, it will not be long, because what may be long is not as yet; but it shall be long, when from the future, which as yet is not, it shall already have begun to be, and will have become present, so that there could be that which may be long; then doth the present time cry out in the words above that it cannot be long.

CHAP. XVI.—*Time can only be perceived or measured while it is passing.*

21. And yet, O Lord, we perceive intervals of times, and we compare them with themselves, and we say some are longer, others shorter. We even measure by how much shorter or longer this time may be than that; and we answer, "That this is double or treble, while that is but once, or only as much as that." But we measure times passing when we measure them by perceiving them; but past times, which now are not, or future times, which as yet are not, who can measure them? Unless, perchance, any one will dare to say, that that can be measured which is not. When, therefore, time is passing, it can be perceived and measured; but when it has passed, it cannot, since it is not.

CHAP. XVII.—*Nevertheless there is time past and future.*

22. I ask, Father, I do not affirm. O my God, rule and guide me. Who is there who can say to me that there are not three times (as we learned when boys, and as we have taught boys), the past, present, and future, but only present, because these two are not? Or are they also; but when from future it becometh present, cometh it forth from some secret place, and when from the present it becometh past, doth it retire into anything secret? For where have they, who have foretold future things, seen these things, if as yet they are not? For that which is not cannot be seen. And they who relate things past could not relate them as true, did they not perceive them in their mind. Which things, if they were not, they could in no wise be discerned. There are therefore things both future and past.

CHAP. XVIII.—*Past and future times cannot be thought of but as present.*

23. Suffer me, O Lord, to seek further; O my Hope, let not my purpose be confounded. For if there are times past and future, I desire to know where they are. But if as yet I do not succeed, I still know, wherever they are, that they are not there as future or past, but as present. For if there also they be future, they are not as yet there; if even there they be past, they are no longer there. Wheresoever, therefore, they are, whatsoever they are, they are only so as present. Although past things are related as true, they are drawn out from the memory,—not the things themselves, which have passed, but the words conceived from the images of the things which they have formed in the mind as footprints in their passage through the senses. My childhood, indeed, which no longer is, is in time past, which now is not; but when I call to mind its image, and speak of it, I behold it in the present, because it is as yet in my memory. Whether there be a like cause of foretelling future things, that of things which as yet are not the images may be perceived as already existing, I confess, my God, I know not. This certainly I know, that we generally think before on our future actions, and that this premeditation is present; but that the action whereon we premeditate is not yet, because it is future; which when we shall have entered upon, and have begun to do that which we were premeditating, then shall that action be, because then it is not future, but present.

24. In whatever manner, therefore, this secret preconception of future things may be, nothing can be seen, save what is. But what now is is not future, but present. When, therefore, they say that things future are seen, it is not themselves, which as yet are not (that is, which are future); but their causes or their signs perhaps are seen, the which already are. Therefore, to those already beholding them, they are not future, but present, from which future things conceived in the mind are foretold. Which conceptions again now are, and they who foretell those things behold these conceptions present before them. Let now so multitudinous a variety of things afford me some example. I behold daybreak; I foretell that the sun is about to rise. That which I behold is present; what I foretell is future,— not that the sun is future, which already is; but his rising, which is not yet. Yet even its rising I could not predict unless I had an image of it in my mind, as now I have while I speak. But that dawn which I see in the sky is not the rising of the sun, although it may go before it, nor that imagination in my mind; which two are seen as present, that the other which is future may be foretold. Future things, therefore, are not as yet; and if they are not as yet, they are not. And if they are not, they cannot be seen at all; but they can be foretold from things present which now are, and are seen. . . .

CHAP. XXI.—*How time may be measured.*

27. I have just now said, then, that we measure times as they pass, that we may be able to say that this time is twice as much as that one, or that this is only as much as that, and so of any other of the parts of time which we are able to tell by measuring. Wherefore, as I said, we measure times as they pass. And if any one should ask me, "Whence dost thou know?" I can answer, "I know, because we measure; nor can we measure things that are not; and things past and future are not." But how do we measure present time, since it hath not space? It is measured while it passeth; but when it shall have passed, it is not measured; for there will not be aught that can be measured. But whence, in what way, and whither doth it pass while it is being measured? Whence, but from the future? Which way, save through the present? Whither, but into the past? From that, therefore, which as yet is not, through that which hath no space, into that which now is not. But what do we measure, unless time in some space? For we say not single, and double, and triple and equal, or in any other way in which we speak of time, unless with respect to the spaces of times. In what space, then, do we measure passing time? Is it in the future, whence it passeth over? But what yet we measure not, is not. Or is it in the present, by which it passeth? But no space, we do not measure. Or in the past, whither it passeth? But that which is not now, we measure not. . . .

CHAP. XXIII.—*That time is a certain extension.*

29. I have heard from a learned man that the motions of the sun, moon, and stars constituted time, and I assented not (28). For why should not rather the motions of all bodies be time? What if the lights of heaven should cease, and a potter's wheel run round, would there be no time by which we might measure those revolutions, and say either that it turned with equal pauses, or, if it were moved at one time more slowly, at another more quickly, that some revolutions were longer, others less so? Or while we were saying this, should we not also be speaking in time? Or should there in our words be some syllables long, others short, but because those sounded in a longer time, these in a shorter? God grant to men to see in a small thing ideas common to things great and small. Both the stars and luminaries of heaven are "for signs and for seasons, and for days and years." No

doubt they are; but neither should I say that the circuit of that wooden wheel was a day, nor yet should he say that therefore there was no time.

30. I desire to know the power and nature of time, by which we measure the motions of bodies, and say (for example) that this motion is twice as long as that. For, I ask, since "day" declares not the stay only of the sun upon the earth, according to which day is one thing, night another, but also its entire circuit from east even to east,—according to which we say, "So many days have passed" (the nights being included when we say "so many days," and their spaces not counted apart), —since, then, the day is finished by the motion of the sun, and by his circuit from east to east, I ask, whether the motion itself is the day, or the period in which that motion is completed, or both? For if the first be the day, then would there be a day although the sun should finish that course in so small a space of time as an hour. If the second, then that would not be a day if from one sunrise to another there were but so short a period as an hour, but the sun must go round four-and-twenty times to complete a day. If both, neither could that be called a day if the sun should run his entire round in the space of an hour; nor that, if, while the sun stood still, so much time should pass as the sun is accustomed to accomplish his whole course in from morning to morning. I shall not therefore now ask, what that is which is called a day, but what time is, by which we, measuring the circuit of the sun, should say that it was accomplished in half the space of time it was wont, if it had been completed in so small a space as twelve hours; and comparing both times, we should call that single, this double time, although the sun should run his course from east to east sometimes in that single, sometimes in that double time. Let no man then tell me that the motions of the heavenly bodies are times, because, when at the prayer of one the sun stood still in order that he might achieve his victorious battle, the sun stood still, but time went on. For in such space of time as was sufficient was that battle fought and ended. I see that time, then, is a certain extension. But do I see it, or do I seem to see it? Thou, O Light and Truth, wilt show me.

CHAP. XXIV—*That time is not a motion of the body which we measure by time.*

31. Dost Thou command that I should assent, if any one should say that time is "the motion of a body"? Thou dost not command me. For I hear that no body is moved but in time. This Thou sayest; but that the very motion of a body is time, I hear not; Thou sayest it not. For when a body is moved, I by time measure how long it may be moving from the time in which it began to be moved till it left off. And if I saw not whence it began, and it continued to be moved, so that I see not when it leaves off, I cannot measure unless, perchance, from the time I began until I cease to see. But if I look long, I only proclaim that the time is long, but not how long it may be; because when we say, "How long," we speak by comparison, as, "This is as long as that," or, "This is double as long as that," or any other thing of the kind. But if we were able to note down the distances of places whence and whither cometh the body which is moved, or its parts, if it moved as in a wheel, we can say in how much time the motion of the body or its part, from this place unto that, was performed. Since, then, the motion of a body is one thing, that by which we measure how long it is another, who cannot see which of these is rather to be called time? For, although a body be sometimes moved, sometimes stand still, we measure not its motion only, but also its standing still, by time; and we say, "It stood still as much as it moved"; or, "It stood still twice or thrice as long as it moved"; and if any other space which our measuring hath either determined or imagined, more or less, as we are accustomed to say. Time, therefore, is not the motion of a body. (J. G. Pilkington, tr.)

FOR EVER *

ROBERT HILLYER

When I say For Ever I think of the temple of Zeus,
The broken drums of the columns buried in grass;
Marble avails not, words are of little use,
It is longer than miles from Olympia to Patras.

For Ever is marble, For Ever is white and tall,
But the road I follow ends in a tangle of weeds
Where lie the drums of the columns, the stones of the wall,
Broken letters of a word that no man reads.

THE PARADOX OF TIME

PIERRE DE RONSARD

Le temps s'en va, le temps s'en va, madame!
Las! le temps non: mais "NOUS nous en allons!

Time goes, you say? Ah, no!
Alas, Time stays, *we* go;
   Or else, were this not so,
What need to chain the hours,
For Youth were always ours?
   Time goes, you say?—ah, no!

Ours is the eyes' deceit
Of men whose flying feet
   Lead through some landscape low;
We pass, and think we see
The earth's fixed surface flee:—
   Alas, Time stays,—we go!

Once in the days of old,
Your locks were curling gold,
   And mine had shamed the crow.
Now, in the self-same stage,
We've reached the silver age;
   Time goes, you say?—ah, no!

Once, when my voice was strong,
I filled the woods with song
   To praise your "rose" and "snow";
My bird, that sang, is dead;
Where are your roses fled?
   Alas, Time stays,—we go!

* Reprinted from *Poems for Music 1917-1947* by Robert Hillyer, by permission of Alfred A. Knopf, Inc. Copyright 1933, 1947 by Robert Hillyer.

See, in what traversed ways,
What backward Fate delays
   The hopes we used to know;
Where are your old desires?—
Ah, where those vanished fires?
   Time goes, you say?—ah, no!

How far, how far, O Sweet,
The past behind our feet
   Lies in the even-glow!
Now, on the forward way,
Let us fold hands, and pray;
   Alas, Time stays, *we* go!
                        (Austin Dobson, tr.)

MUTABILITY

PERCY BYSSHE SHELLEY

We are as clouds that veil the midnight moon;
   How restlessly they speed, and gleam, and quiver,
Streaking the darkness radiantly!—yet soon
   Night closes round, and they are lost for ever:

Or like forgotten lyres, whose dissonant strings
   Give various response to each varying blast,
To whose frail frame no second motion brings
   One mood or modulation like the last.

We rest.—A dream has power to poison sleep;
   We rise.—One wandering thought pollutes the day;
We feel, conceive or reason, laugh or weep;
   Embrace fond woe, or cast our cares away:

It is the same!—For, be it joy or sorrow,
   The path of its departure still is free:
Man's yesterday may ne'er be like his morrow;
   Nought may endure but Mutability.

FROM PARLEYINGS WITH FRANCIS FURINI

ROBERT BROWNING

VII

               ". . . Bounteous God,
Deviser and Dispenser of all gifts
To soul through sense,—in Art the soul uplifts
Men's best of thanks!   What but Thy measuring-rod
Meted forth heaven and earth? more intimate,
Thy very hands were busied with the task
Of making, in this human shape, a mask—

A match for that divine.   Shall love abate
Man's wonder?   Nowise!   True—true—all too true—
No gift but, in the very plenitude
Of its perfection, goes maimed, misconstrued
By wickedness or weakness: still, some few
Have grace to see Thy purpose, strength to mar
Thy work by no admixture of their own,
Limn truth not falsehood, bid us love alone
The type untampered with the naked star!"

VIII

And, prayer done, painter—what if you should preach?
Not as of old when playing pulpiteer
To simple-witted country folk, but here
In actual London try your powers of speech
On us the cultured, therefore skeptical—
What would you?   For, suppose he has his word
In faith's behalf, no matter how absurd,
This painter-theologian?   One and all
We lend an ear—nay, Science takes thereto—
Encourages the meanest who has racked
Nature until he gains from her some fact,
To state what truth is from his point of view,
Mere pin-point though it be: since many such
Conduce to make a whole, she bids our friend
Come forward unabashed and haply lend
His little life-experience to our much
Of modern knowledge.   Since she so insists,
Up stands Furini.

IX

              "Evolutionists!
At truth I glimpse from depths, you glance from heights,
Our stations for discovery opposites,—
How should ensue agreement?   I explain:
'Tis the tip-top of things to which you strain
Your vision, until atoms, protoplasm,
And what and whence and how may be the spasm
Which sets all going, stop you: down perforce
Needs must your observation take its course,
Since there's no moving upwards; link by link
You drop to where the atoms somehow think,
Feel, know themselves to be: the world's begun,
Such as we recognize it.   Have you done
Descending?   Here's ourself,—Man, known today,
Duly evolved at last,—so far, you say,
The sum and seal of being's progress.   Good!
Thus much at least is clearly understood—
Of power does Man possess no particle:
Of knowledge—just so much as shows that still
It ends in ignorance on every side:
But righteousness—ah, Man is deified

Thereby, for compensation!   Make survey
Of Man's surroundings, try creation—nay,
Try emulation of the minimized
Minuteness fancy may conceive!   Surprised
Reason becomes by two defeats for one—
Not only power at each phenomenon
Baffled, but knowledge also in default—
Asking what is minuteness—yonder vault
Speckled with suns, or this the millionth—thing,
How shall I call?—that on some insect's wing
Helps to make out in dyes the mimic star?
Weak, ignorant, accordingly we are:
What then?   The worst for Nature!   Where began
Righteousness, moral sense except in Man?
True, he makes nothing, understands no whit:
Had the initiator-spasm seen fit
Thus doubly to endow him, none the worse
And much the better were the universe.
What does Man see or feel or apprehend
Here, there, and everywhere, but faults to mend,
Omissions to supply,—one wide disease
Of things that are, which Man at once would ease
Had will but power and knowledge?   failing both—
Things must take will for deed—Man, nowise loth,
Accepts pre-eminency: mere blind force—
Mere knowledge undirected in its course
By any care for what is made or marred
In either's operation—*these* award
The crown to?   Rather let it deck thy brows,
Man, whom alone a righteousness endows
Would cure the wide world's ailing.   Who disputes
Thy claim thereto?   Had Spasm more attributes
Than power and knowledge in its gift, before
Man came to pass?   The higher that we soar,
The less of moral sense like Man's we find:
No sign of such before,—what comes behind,
Who guesses?   But until there crown our sight
The quite new—not the old mere infinite
Of changings,—some fresh kind of sun and moon,
Then, not before, shall I expect a boon
Of intuition just as strange, which turns
Evil to good, and wrong to right, unlearns
All Man's experience learned since Man was he.
Accept in Man, advanced to this degree,
The Prime Mind, therefore! neither wise nor strong—
Whose fault? but were he both, then right, not wrong
As now, throughout the world were paramount
According to his will,—which I account
The qualifying faculty.   He stands
Confessed supreme—the monarch whose commands
Could he enforce, how bettered were the world!
He's at the height this moment—to be hurled

Next moment to the bottom by rebound
Of his own peal of laughter. All around
Ignorance wraps him,—whence and how and why
Things are,—yet cloud breaks and lets blink the sky
Just overhead, not elsewhere! What assures
His optics that the very blue which lures
Comes not of black outside it, doubly dense?
Ignorance overwraps his moral sense,
Winds him about, relaxing, as it wraps,
So much and no more than lets through perhaps
The murmured knowledge—'Ignorance exists.'

x

"I at the bottom, Evolutionists,
Advise beginning, rather. I profess
To know just one fact—my self-consciousness,
'Twixt ignorance and ignorance enisled,—
Knowledge: before me was my Cause—that's styled
God: after, in due course succeeds the rest,—
All that my knowledge comprehends—at best—
At worst, conceives about in mild despair.
Light needs must touch on either darkness: where?
Knowledge so far impinges on the Cause
Before me, that I know—by certain laws
Wholly unknown, whate'er I apprehend
Within, without me, had its rise: thus blend
I, and all things perceived, in one Effect.
How far can knowledge any ray project
On what comes after me—the universe?
Well, my attempt to make the cloud disperse
Begins—not from above but underneath:
I climb, you soar,—who soars soon loses breath
And sinks, who climbs keeps one foot firm on fact
Ere hazarding the next step: soul's first act
(Call consciousness the soul—some name we need)
Getting itself aware, through stuff decreed
Thereto (so call the body)—who has stept
So far, there let him stand, become adept
In body ere he shift his station thence
One single hair's breadth. Do I make pretence
To teach, myself unskilled in learning? Lo,
My life's work! Let my pictures prove I know
Somewhat of what this fleshly frame of ours
Or is or should be, how the soul empowers
The body to reveal its every mood
Of love and hate, pour forth its plenitude
Of passion. If my hand attained to give
Thus permanence to truth else fugitive,
Did not I also fix each fleeting grace
Of form and feature—save the beauteous face—
Arrest decay in transitory might
Of bone and muscle—cause the world to bless

Forever each transcendent nakedness
Of man and woman?   Were such feats achieved
By sloth, or strenuous labor unrelieved,
Yet lavished vainly?   Ask that underground
(So may I speak) of all on surface found
Of flesh-perfection!   Depths on depths to probe
Of all-inventive artifice, disrobe
Marvel at hiding under marvel, pluck
Veil after veil from Nature—were the luck
Ours to surprise the secret men so name,
That still eludes the searcher—all the same,
Repays his search with still fresh proof—'Externe,
Not inmost, is the Cause, fool!   Look and learn!'
Thus teach my hundred pictures: firm and fast
There did I plant my first foot.   And the next?
Nowhere!   'Twas put forth and withdrawn, perplexed
At touch of what seemed stable and proved stuff
Such as the colored clouds are: plain enough
There lay the outside universe: try Man—
My most immediate! and the dip began
From safe and solid into that profound
Of ignorance I tell you surges round
My rock-spit of self-knowledge."

from LOCKSLEY HALL

ALFRED LORD TENNYSON

Can I but relive in sadness?   I will turn that earlier page.
Hide me from my deep emotion, O thou wondrous Mother-Age!

Make me feel the wild pulsation that I felt before the strife,
When I heard my days before me, and the tumult of my life;

Yearning for the large excitement that the coming years would yield,
Eager-hearted as a boy when first he leaves his father's field,

And at night along the dusky highway near and nearer drawn,
Sees in heaven the light of London flaring like a dreary dawn;

And his spirit leaps within him to be gone before him then,
Underneath the light he looks at, in among the throngs of men;

Men, my brothers, men the workers, ever reaping something new;
That which they have done but earnest of the things that they
    shall do.

For I dipt into the future, far as human eye could see,
Saw the Vision of the world, and all the wonder that would be;

Saw the heavens fill with commerce, argosies of magic sails,
Pilots of the purple twilight, dropping down with costly bales;

Heard the heavens fill with shouting, and there rained a ghastly dew
From the nations' airy navies grappling in the central blue;

Far along the world-wide whisper of the south-wind rushing warm,
With the standards of the peoples plunging through the thunder-storm;

Till the war-drum throbbed no longer, and the battle-flags were furled
In the Parliament of man, the Federation of the world.

There the common sense of most shall hold a fretful realm in awe,
And the kindly earth shall slumber lapt in universal law.

So I triumphed ere my passion sweeping through me left me dry,
Left me with the palsied heart, and left me with the jaundiced eye;

Eye, to which all order festers, all things here are out of joint.
Science moves, but slowly, slowly, creeping on from point to point;

Slowly comes a hungry people, as a lion, creeping nigher,
Glares at one that nods and winks behind a slowly-dying fire.

Yet I doubt not through the ages one increasing purpose runs,
And the thoughts of men are widened with the process of the suns.

What is that to him that reaps not harvest of his youthful joys,
Though the deep heart of existence beat for ever like a boy's?

Knowledge comes, but wisdom lingers, and I linger on the shore,
And the individual withers, and the world is more and more.

Knowledge comes, but wisdom lingers, and he bears a laden breast,
Full of sad experience, moving toward the stillness of his rest.

.   .   .   .

Or to burst all links of habit—there to wander far away,
On from island unto island at the gateways of the day.

Larger constellations burning, mellow moons and happy skies,
Breadths of tropic shade and palms in cluster, knots of Paradise.

Never comes the trader, never floats an European flag,
Slides the bird o'er lustrous woodland, swings the trailer from the crag;

Droops the heavy blossomed bower, hangs the heavy-fruited tree—
Summer isles of Eden lying in dark-purple spheres of sea.

There methinks would be enjoyment more than in this march of mind,
In the steamship, in the railway, in the thoughts that shake mankind.

There the passions cramped no longer shall have scope and breathing space;
I will take some savage woman, she shall rear my dusky race.

Iron-jointed, supple-sinewed, they shall dive, and they shall run,
Catch the wild goat by the hair, and hurl their lances in the sun;

Whistle back the parrot's call, and leap the rainbows of the brooks,
Not with blinded eyesight poring over miserable books—

Fool, again the dream, the fancy! but I know my words are wild,
But I count the gray barbarian lower than the Christian child.

I, to herd with narrow foreheads, vacant of our glorious gains,
Like a beast with lower pleasures, like a beast with lower pains!

Mated with a squalid savage—what to me were sun or clime?
I the heir of all the ages, in the foremost files of time—

I that rather held it better men should perish one by one,
Than that earth should stand at gaze like Joshua's moon in Ajalon!

Not in vain the distance beacons. Forward, forward let us range,
Let the great world spin for ever down the ringing grooves of change.

Through the shadow of the globe we sweep into the younger day;
Better fifty years of Europe than a cycle of Cathay.

Mother-Age,—for mine I knew not,—help me as when life begun;
Rift the hills, and roll the waters, flash the lightnings, weigh the sun.

O, I see the crescent promise of my spirit hath not set.
Ancient founts of inspiration well through all my fancy yet.

from LOCKSLEY HALL SIXTY YEARS AFTER
ALFRED LORD TENNYSON

Hesper—Venus—were we native to that splendor or in Mars,
We should see the globe we groan in, fairest of their evening stars.

Could we dream of wars and carnage, craft and madness, lust and spite,
Roaring London, raving Paris, in that point of peaceful light?

Might we not in glancing heaven-ward on a star so silver-fair,
Yearn, and clasp the hands and murmur, "Would to God that we were there"?

Forward, backward, backward, forward, in the immeasurable sea,
Swayed by vaster ebbs and flows than can be known to you or me.

All the suns—are these but symbols of innumerable man,
Man or Mind that sees a shadow of the planner or the plan?

Is there evil but on earth? or pain in every peopled sphere?
Well, be grateful for the sounding watch-word "Evolution" here,

Evolution ever climbing after some ideal good,
And Reversion ever dragging Evolution in the mud.

What are men that He should heed us? cried the king of sacred song;
Insects of an hour, that hourly work their brother insect wrong,

While the silent heavens roll, and suns along their fiery way,
All their planets whirling round them, flash a million miles a day.

Many an aeon molded earth before her highest, man, was born,
Many an aeon too may pass when earth is manless and forlorn,

Earth so huge, and yet so bounded—pools of salt, and plots of land—
Shallow skin of green and azure—chains of mountain, grains of sand!

Only That which made us meant us to be mightier by and by,
Set the sphere of all the boundless heavens within the human eye,

Sent the shadow of Himself, the boundless, through the human soul;
Boundless inward in the atom, boundless outward in the Whole.

.   .   .   .

Here is Locksley Hall, my grandson, here the lion-guarded gate.
Not tonight in Locksley Hall—tomorrow—you, you come so late.

Wrecked—your train—or all but wrecked? a shattered wheel? a vicious boy!
Good, this forward, you that preach it, is it well to wish you joy?

Is it well that while we range with Science, glorying in the Time,
City children soak and blacken soul and sense in city slime?

There among the glooming alleys Progress halts on palsied feet,
Crime and hunger cast our maidens by the thousand on the street.

There the master scrimps his haggard sempstress of her daily bread,
There a single sordid attic holds the living and the dead.

There the smoldering fire of fever creeps across the rotted floor,
And the crowded couch of incest in the warrens of the poor.

Nay, your pardon, cry your "Forward," yours are hope and youth, but I—
Eighty winters leave the dog too lame to follow with the cry,

Lame and old, and past his time, and passing now into the night;
Yet I would the rising race were half as eager for the light.

Light the fading gleam of even? light the glimmer of the dawn?
Aged eyes may take the growing glimmer for the gleam withdrawn.

Far away beyond her myriad coming changes earth will be
Something other than the wildest modern guess of you and me.

Earth may reach her earthly-worst, or if she gain her earthly-best,
Would she find her human offspring this ideal man at rest?

Forward then, but still remember how the course of Time will swerve,
Crook and turn upon itself in many a backward streaming curve.

.   .   .   .

Follow you the star that lights a desert pathway, yours or mine.
Forward, till you see the Highest Human Nature is divine.

Follow Light, and do the Right—for man can half-control his doom—
Till you find the deathless Angel seated in the vacant tomb.

THIS SIMIAN WORLD, XIX *

CLARENCE DAY

It has always been a serious matter for men when a civilization decayed. But it may at some future day prove far more serious still. Our hold on the planet is not absolute. Our descendants may lose it.

Germs may do them out of it. A chestnut fungus springs up, defies us, and kills all our chestnuts. The boll weevil very nearly baffles us. The fly seems unconquerable. Only a strong civilization, when such foes are about, can preserve us. And our present efforts to cope with such beings are fumbling and slow.

We haven't the habit of candidly facing this danger. We read our biological history but we don't take it in. We blandly assume we were always "intended" to rule, and that no other outcome could even be considered by Nature. This is one of the remnants of ignorance certain religions have left: but it's odd that men who don't believe in Easter should still believe this. For the facts are of course this is a hard and precarious world, where every mistake and infirmity must be paid for in full.

If mankind ever is swept aside as a failure, however, what a brilliant and enterprising failure he at least will have been. I felt this with a kind of warm suddenness only today, as I finished these dreamings and drove through the gates of the park. I had been shutting my modern surroundings out of my thoughts, so completely, and living as it were in the wild world of ages ago, that when I let myself come back suddenly to the twentieth century, and stare at the park and the people, the change was tremendous. All around me were the well-dressed descendants of primitive animals, whizzing about in bright motors, past tall, soaring buildings. What gifted, energetic achievers they suddenly seemed!

I thought of a photograph I had once seen, of a ship being torpedoed. There it was, the huge, finely made structure, awash in the sea, with tiny black spots hanging on to its side—crew and passengers. The great ship, even while sinking, was so mighty, and those atoms so helpless. Yet, it was those tiny beings that had created that ship. They had planned it and built it and guided its bulk through the waves. They had also invented a torpedo that could rend it asunder.

It is possible that our race may be an accident, in a meaningless universe, living its brief life uncared-for, on this dark, cooling star: but even so—and all the more—what marvelous creatures we are! What fairy story, what tale from the Arabian

* Reprinted from *This Simian World* by Clarence Day, by permission of Alfred A. Knopf, Inc. Copyright 1920, 1948 by Katherine B. Day.

Nights of the jinns, is a hundredth part as wonderful as this true fairy story of simians! It is so much more heartening, too, than the tales we invent. A universe capable of giving birth to many such accidents is—blind or not—a good world to live in, a promising universe.

And if there are no other such accidents, if we stand alone, if all the uncountable armies of planets are empty, or peopled by animals only, with no keys to thought, then we have done something so mighty, what may it not lead to! What powers may we not develop before the Sun dies! We once thought we lived on God's footstool: it may be a throne.

This is no world for pessimists. An amoeba on the beach, blind and helpless, a mere bit of pulp,—that amoeba has grandsons today who read Kant and play symphonies. Will those grandsons in turn have descendants who will sail through the void, discover the foci of forces, the means to control them, and learn how to marshal the planets and grapple with space? Would it after all be any more startling than our rise from the slime?

No sensible amoeba would have ever believed for a minute that any of his most remote children would build and run dynamos. Few sensible men of today stop to feel, in their hearts, that we live in the very same world where that miracle happened.

This world, and our racial adventure, are magical still.

from RESEARCH *

In *The Magic Mountain*

THOMAS MANN

But what was all this ignorance, compared with our utter helplessness in the presence of such a phenomenon as memory, or of that other more prolonged and astounding memory which we called the inheritance of acquired characteristics? Out of the question to get even a glimpse of any mechanical possibility of explication of such performances on the part of the cell-substance. The spermatozoon that conveyed to the egg countless complicated individual and racial characteristics of the father was visible only through a microscope; even the most powerful magnification was not enough to show it as other than a homogeneous body, or to determine its origin; it looked the same in one animal as in another. These factors forced one to the assumption that the cell was in the same case as with the higher form it went to build up: that it too was already a higher form, composed in its turn by the division of living bodies, individual living units. Thus one passed from the supposed smallest unit to a still smaller one; one was driven to separate the elementary into its elements. No doubt at all but just as the animal kingdom was composed of various species of animals, as the human-animal organism was composed of a whole animal kingdom of cell species, so the cell organism was composed of a new and varied animal kingdom of elementary units, far below microscopic size, which grew spontaneously, increased spontaneously according to the law that each could bring forth only after its kind, and, acting on the principle of a division of labor, served together the next higher order of existence.

Those were the genes, the living germs, bioblasts, biophores—lying there in the frosty night, Hans Castorp rejoiced to make acquaintance with them by name. Yet

* Reprinted from *The Magic Mountain* by Thomas Mann (translated by H. T. Lowe-Porter), by permission of Alfred A. Knopf, Inc. Copyright 1927 by Alfred A. Knopf, Inc.

how, he asked himself excitedly, even after more light on the subject was forthcoming, how could their elementary nature be established? If they were living, they must be organic, since life depended upon organization. But if they were organized, then they could not be elementary, since an organism is not single but multiple. They were units within the organic unit of the cell they built up. But if they were, then, however impossibly small they were, they must themselves be built up, organically built up, as a law of their existence; for the conception of a living unit meant by definition that it was built up out of smaller units which were subordinate; that is, organized with reference to a higher form. As long as division yielded organic units possessing the properties of life—assimilation and reproduction—no limits were set to it. As long as one spoke of living units, one could not correctly speak of elementary units, for the concept of unity carried with it in perpetuity the concept of subordinated, upbuilding unity; and there was no such thing as elementary life, in the sense of something that was already life, and yet elementary.

And still, though without logical existence, something of the kind must be eventually the case; for it was not possible to brush aside like that the idea of the original procreation, the rise of life out of what was not life. That gap which in exterior nature we vainly sought to close, that between living and dead matter, had its counterpart in nature's organic existence, and must somehow either be closed up or bridged over. Soon or late, division must yield "units" which, even though in composition, were not organized, and which mediated between life and absence of life; molecular groups, which represented the transition between vitalized organization and mere chemistry. But then, arrived at the molecule, one stood on the brink of another abyss, which yawned yet more mysteriously than that between organic and inorganic nature: the gulf between the material and the immaterial. For the molecule was composed of atoms, and the atom was nowhere near large enough even to be spoken of as extraordinarily small. It was so small, such a tiny, early, transitional mass, a coagulation of the unsubstantial, of the not-yet-substantial and yet substance-like, of energy, that it was scarcely possible yet—or, if it had been, was now no longer possible—to think of it as material, but rather as mean and border-line between material and immaterial. The problem of another original procreation arose, far more wild and mysterious than the organic: the primeval birth of matter out of the immaterial. In fact the abyss between material and immaterial yawned as widely, pressed as importunately—yes, more importunately—to be closed, as that between organic and inorganic nature. There must be a chemistry of the immaterial, there must be combinations of the insubstantial, out of which sprang the material—the atoms might represent protozoa of material, by their nature substance and still not yet quite substance. Yet arrived at the "not even small," the measure slipped out of the hands; for "not even small" meant much the same as "enormously large"; and the step to the atom proved to be without exaggeration portentous in the highest degree. For at the very moment when one had assisted at the final division of matter, when one had divided it into the impossibly small, at that moment there suddenly appeared upon the horizon the astronomical cosmos!

The atom was a cosmic system, laden with energy; in which heavenly bodies rioted rotating about a center like a sun; through whose ethereal space comets drove with the speed of light years, kept in their eccentric orbits by the power of the central body. And that was as little a mere comparison as it would be were one to call the body of any multiple-celled organism a "cell state." The city, the state, the social community regulated according to the principle of division of labor, not only might be compared to organic life, it actually reproduced its conditions. Thus in the inmost recesses of nature, as in an endless succession of mirrors, was reflected the macrocosm of the heavens, whose clusters, throngs, groups, and figures, paled by the brilliant moon, hung over the dazzling, frost-bound valley, above the head of our muffled adept. Was it too bold a thought that among the planets of the atomic solar system—those myriads and milky ways of solar systems which constituted matter—one or other of these inner-worldly heavenly bodies might find itself in a condition corresponding to that which made it possible for our earth to become the abode of life? For a young man already rather befuddled inwardly, suffering from abnormal skin-conditions, who was not without all and any experience in the realm of the illicit, it was a speculation which, far from being absurd, appeared so obvious as to leap to the eyes, highly evident, and bearing the stamp of logical truth. The "smallness" of these inner-worldly heavenly bodies would have been an objection irrelevant to the hypothesis; since the conception of large or small had ceased to be pertinent at the moment when the cosmic character of the "smallest" particle of matter had been revealed; while at the same time, the conceptions of "outside" and "inside" had also been shaken. The atom-world was an "outside" as, very probably, the earthly star on which we dwelt was, organically regarded, deeply "inside". Had not a researcher once, audaciously fanciful, referred to the "beasts of the Milky Way," cosmic monsters whose flesh, bone, and brain were built up out of solar systems? But in that case, Hans Castorp mused, then in the moment when one thought to have come to the end, it all began over again from the beginning! For then, in the very innermost of his nature, and in the inmost of that innermost, perhaps there was just himself, just Hans Castorp, again and a hundred times Hans Castorp, with burning face and stiffening fingers, lying muffled on a balcony, with a view across the moonlit, frost-nighted high valley, and probing, with an interest both humanistic and medical, into the life of the body!

(H. T. Lowe-Porter, tr.)

NIGHT-SONG OF A NOMADIC SHEPHERD OF ASIA

GIACOMO LEOPARDI

What dost thou, Moon, what dost thou there in heaven,
O unresponsive Moon?
I see thee rise at even,
Pass musing o'er the desert, and then set.
Say, wilt thou never tire
Of re-pursuing sempiternal ways?
Dost still not find it irksome, still desire
Upon these vales to gaze?
How like unto thy life
The shepherd's life doth seem,
Rising at day's first beam,
He moves his flock across the plain and sees
Flocks and wells and grass;
Then wearied lays him down at eventide:
Nor hopes for aught beside.
Moon, of what value, pray,
To the shepherd is his life,
Your life to you? To what goal are we tending,
I in brief wanderings, thou
On thine immortal way?

A hoary, weak, old man,
Half-clothed, with naked feet,
A load exceeding heavy on his shoulders,
O'er hill, o'er dale, o'er boulders
Sharp-pointed and deep desert-sand and brambles,
In wind and storm, beneath the raging heat
And later when 'tis chill,
Runs, runs on, never still;
O'er pools and torrents scrambles
Breathless; falls, rises, more and more doth haste,
Without pause, without rest,
Mangled and bleeding; till at length he comes
Where is the limit set
Unto his journey and so great distress:
A gulf, dread, bottomless,
Wherein he plunges and doth all forget.
Moon-maiden, such the way
We mortals live our day.

Man is born with labor,
And birth is but a hazard cast with death.
Even from his earliest breath
He suffers pain; mother and father both
Are from the first intent
To comfort him that he was ever born.
Then, as his years increase,
The twain will never cease by word and deed
To give him day and night
Their strong encouragement
And sympathy in his estate forlorn:
No loving parents scorn
This duty dearest in their children's sight.
But why bring forth to the light,
Why foster, those who then
Must needs on that account be comforted?
If life is evil, why
Endure its misery?
Moon, to no ills a prey,
Such is our mortal way;
But thou, who art not mortal
Heedest perchance but little what I say.

Yet thou, O lone eternal wanderer,
It may be, in my wisdom, thou canst tell
The meaning of our days
Upon this earth, our suffering and woe;
This dying, this last aspect of the face,
When all its color goes,
And the strange vanishing without a trace
From the sweet presence of those that loved us so.
Thou surely knowest full well
The cause of things, thou seest what good or bad

Morning and evening bring,
And the eternal, silent march of time.
Thou knowest, thou knowest well what object sweet
Calls forth the smile of spring,
Who profits by the heat, and what the end
By winter's ice obtained.
To thee a thousand mysteries are clear
Which baffle the poor shepherd's simple wit.
Oft when I gaze on thee
Stationed so silent o'er the prairie wide,
Whose boundary, far descried, is one with heaven's;
Or see thee with my flock
Follow me as I wander, stride for stride;
And when I see in heaven the stars burn bright
Within myself I ponder:
Why all these torches' light?
What makes the ether infinite, that deep
Infinity serene?   What signifies
This immense solitude?   And what am I?
So to myself I cry: and of the vast
Majestical abode,
And of the family innumerable;
Then of the mazy toil, the mazy motions
Of all celestial, all terrestrial things,
Circling in ceaseless rings,
Ever returning whence they took their start:
Of these can I divine
No use, no fruit.   But, Maiden, thou who art
Immortal, knowledge of all is surely thine.
This only I know and feel,
That though eternal cycles
And my frail being may—
Perchance—bring joy or weal
To others, I find life a banal way.

(G. L. Bickersteth, tr.)

SELF-DECEPTION

MATTHEW ARNOLD

Say, what blinds us, that we claim the glory
Of possessing powers not our share?—
Since man woke on earth, he knows his story,
But, before we woke on earth, we were.

Long, long since, undowered yet, our spirit
Roamed, ere birth, the treasuries of God:
Saw the gifts, the powers it might inherit;
Asked an outfit for its earthly road.

Then, as now, this tremulous, eager Being
Strained and longed, and grasped each gift it saw.

Then, as now, a Power beyond our seeing
Staved us back and gave our choice the law.

Ah, whose hand that day through heaven guided
Man's new spirit, since it was not we?
Ah, who swayed our choice, and who decided
What our gifts, and what our wants should be?

For, alas! he left us each retaining
Shreds of gifts which he refused in full.
Still these waste us with their hopeless straining—
Still the attempt to use them proves them null.

And on earth we wander, groping, reeling;
Powers stir in us, stir and disappear.
Ah, and he, who placed our master-feeling,
Failed to place that master-feeling clear.

We but dream we have our wished-for powers.
Ends we seek we never shall attain.
Ah, *some* power exists there, which is ours?
Some end is there, we indeed may gain?

HOW CANDIDE MET HIS OLD MASTER IN PHILOSOPHY, DOCTOR PANGLOSS, AND WHAT HAPPENED

In *Candide*

VOLTAIRE

Candide, moved even more by compassion than by horror, gave this horrible beggar the two crowns he had received from the honest Anabaptist Jacques. The phantom gazed fixedly at him, shed tears and threw its arms round his neck. Candide recoiled in terror.

"Alas!" said the wretch to the other wretch, "don't you recognize your dear Pangloss?"

"What do I hear? You, my dear master! You, in this horrible state! What misfortune has happened to you? Why are you no longer in the noblest of castles? What has become of Miss Cunegonde, the pearl of young ladies, the masterpiece of Nature?"

"I am exhausted," said Pangloss. Candide immediately took him to the Anabaptist's stable where he gave him a little bread to eat; and when Pangloss had recovered:

"Well!" said he, "Cunegonde?"

"Dead," replied the other.

At this word Candide swooned; his friend restored him to his senses with a little bad vinegar which happened to be in the stable. Candide opened his eyes.

"Cunegonde dead! Ah! best of worlds, where are you? But what illness did she die of? Was it because she saw me kicked out of her father's noble castle?"

"No," said Pangloss. "She was disemboweled by Bulgarian soldiers, after having been raped to the limit of possibility; they broke the Baron's head when he tried to defend her; the Baroness was cut to pieces; my poor pupil was treated exactly like his sister; and as to the castle, there is not one stone standing on another, not a barn, not a sheep, not a duck, not a tree; but we were well avenged, for the Abares did exactly the same to a neighboring barony which belonged to a Bulgarian Lord."

At this, Candide swooned again; but, having recovered and having said all that he ought to say, he inquired the cause and effect, the sufficient reason which had reduced Pangloss to so piteous a state.

"Alas!" said Pangloss, " 'tis love; love, the consoler of the human race, the preserver of the universe, the soul of all tender creatures, gentle love."

"Alas!" said Candide, "I am acquainted with this love, this sovereign of hearts, this soul of our soul; it has never brought me anything but one kiss and twenty kicks in the backside. How could this beautiful cause produce in you so abominable an effect?"

Pangloss replied as follows:

"My dear Candide! You remember Paquette, the maid-servant of our august Baroness; in her arms I enjoyed the delights of Paradise which have produced the tortures of Hell by which you see I am devoured; she was infected and perhaps is dead. Paquette received this present from a most learned monk, who had it from the source; for he received it from an old countess, who had it from a cavalry captain, who owed it to a marchioness, who derived it from a page, who had received it from a Jesuit, who, when a novice, had it in a direct line from one of the companions of Christopher Columbus. For my part, I shall not give it to anyone, for I am dying."

"O Pangloss!" exclaimed Candide, "this is a strange genealogy! Wasn't the devil at the root of it?"

"Not at all," replied that great man. "It was something indispensable in this best of worlds, a necessary ingredient; for, if Columbus in an island of America had not caught this disease, which poisons the source of generation, and often indeed prevents generation, we should not have chocolate and cochineal; it must also be noticed that hitherto in our continent this disease is peculiar to us, like theological disputes. The Turks, the Indians, the Persians, the Chinese, the Siamese, and the Japanese are not yet familiar with it; but there is a sufficient reason why they in their turn should become familiar with it in a few centuries. Meanwhile, it has made marvelous progress among us, and especially in those large armies composed of honest, well-bred, stipendiaries who decide the destiny of States; it may be asserted that when thirty thousand men fight a pitched battle against an equal number of troops, there are about twenty thousand with the pox on either side."

"Admirable!" said Candide. "But you must get cured."

"How can I?" said Pangloss. "I haven't a sou, my friend, and in the whole extent of this globe, you cannot be bled or receive an enema without paying or without someone paying for you."

This last speech determined Candide; he went and threw himself at the feet of his charitable Anabaptist, Jacques, and drew so touching a picture of the state to which his friend was reduced that the good easy man did not hesitate to succor Pangloss; he had him cured at his own expense. In this cure, Pangloss only lost one eye and one ear. He could write well and knew arithmetic perfectly. The Anabaptist made him his bookkeeper. At the end of two months, he was compelled to go to Lisbon on business and took his two philosophers on the boat with him. Pangloss explained to him how everything was for the best. Jacques was not of this opinion.

"Men," said he, "must have corrupted Nature a little, for they were not born wolves, and they have become wolves. God did not give them twenty-four-pounder cannons or bayonets, and they have made bayonets and cannons to destroy each other. I might bring bankruptcies into the account and Justice which seizes the goods of bankrupts in order to deprive the creditors of them."

"It was all indispensable," replied the one-eyed doctor, "and private misfortunes make the public good, so that the more private misfortunes there are, the more everything is well."

While he was reasoning, the air grew dark, the winds blew from the four quarters of the globe and the ship was attacked by the most horrible tempest in sight of the port of Lisbon.

(Richard Aldington, tr.)

'PERCHÈ PENSA? PENSANDO S'INVECCHIA'

ARTHUR HUGH CLOUGH

To spend uncounted years of pain,
Again, again, and yet again,
In working out in heart and brain
The problem of our being here;
To gather facts from far and near,
Upon the mind to hold them clear,
And, knowing more may yet appear,
Unto one's latest breath to fear,
The premature result to draw—
Is this the object, end and law,
And purpose of our being here?

MENTAL VICE *

LOGAN PEARSALL SMITH

There are certain hackneyed Thoughts that will force themselves on me; I find my mind, especially in hot weather, buzzed about by moral Platitudes. "That shows—" I say to myself, or "How true it is—" or, "I really ought to have known!" The sight of a large clock sets me off into musings on the flight of Time; a steamer on the Thames or lines of telegraph inevitably suggest the benefits of Civilization, man's triumph over Nature, the heroism of Inventors, the courage amid ridicule and poverty, of Stephenson and Watt. Like faint, rather unpleasant smells, these thoughts lurk about railway stations. I can hardly post a letter without marveling at the excellence and accuracy of the Postal System.

Then the pride in the British Constitution and British Freedom, which comes over me when I see, even in the distance, the Towers of Westminster Palace,—it is not much comfort that this should be chastened, as I walk down the Embankment, by the sight of Cleopatra's Needle, and the Thought that it will no doubt witness the Fall of the British, as it has that of other Empires, remaining to point its Moral, as old as Egypt, to Antipodeans musing on the dilapidated bridges.

I am sometimes afraid of finding that there is a moral for everything; that the whole great frame of the Universe has a key, like a box; has been contrived and set going by a well-meaning but humdrum Eighteenth-century Creator. It would be a kind of Hell, surely, a world in which everything could be at once explained, shown to be obvious and useful. I am sated with Lesson and Allegory; weary of

* From: *Trivia* by Logan Pearsall Smith. Copyright 1917 by Doubleday & Company, Inc.

monitory ants, industrious bees, and preaching animals. The benefits of Civilization cloy me. I have seen enough shining of the didactic Sun.

So gazing up on hot summer nights at the London stars, I cool my thoughts with a vision of the giddy, infinite, meaningless waste of Creation, the blazing Suns, the Planets and frozen Moons, all crashing blindly for ever across the void of space.

NEW YEAR'S EVE

THOMAS HARDY

"I have finished another year," said God,
"In gray, green, white, and brown;
I have strewn the leaf upon the sod,
Sealed up the worm within the clod,
And let the last sun down."

"And what's the good of it?" I said,
"What reasons made you call
From formless void this earth we tread,
When nine-and-ninety can be read
Why nought should be at all?

"Yea, Sire; Why shaped you us, 'who in
This tabernacle groan'—
If ever a joy be found herein,
Such joy no man had wished to win
If he had never known!"

Then he: "My labors—logicless—
You may explain; not I:
Sense-sealed I have wrought, without a guess
That I evolved a Consciousness
To ask for reasons why.

"Strange that ephemeral creatures who
By my own ordering are,
Should see the shortness of my view,
Use ethic tests I never knew,
Or made provision for!"

He sank to raptness as of yore,
And opening New Year's Day
Wove it by rote as theretofore,
And went on working evermore
In his unweeting way.

FROM THE OVERWORLD

In *The Dynasts, After Scene*

THOMAS HARDY

Enter the Spirit and Chorus of the Years, the Spirit and Chorus of the Pities, the Shade of the Earth, the Spirits Sinister and Ironic with their Choruses, Rumors, Spirit-Messengers and Recording Angels.

Europe has now sunk netherward to its far-off position as in the Fore Scene, and it is beheld again as a prone and emaciated figure of which the Alps form the vertebrae, and the branching mountain-chains the ribs, the Spanish Peninsula shaping the head of the écorché. The lowlands look like a gray-green garment half-thrown off, and the sea around like a disturbed bed on which the figure lies.

SPIRIT OF THE YEARS

Thus doth the Great Foresightless mechanize
In blank entrancement now as evermore
Its ceaseless artistries in Circumstance
Of curious stuff and braid, as just forthshown.
  Yet but one flimsy riband of Its web
Have we here watched in weaving—web Enorm,
Whose furthest hem and selvage may extend
To where the roars and plashings of the flames
Of earth-invisible suns swell noisily,
And onwards into ghastly gulfs of sky,
Where hideous presences churn through the dark—
Monsters of magnitude without a shape,
Hanging amid deep wells of nothingness.

Yet seems this vast and singular confection
Wherein our scenery glints of scantest size,
Inutile all—so far as reasonings tell.

SPIRIT OF THE PITIES

Thou arguest still the Inadvertent Mind.—
But, even so, shall blankness be for aye?
Men gained cognition with the flux of time,
And wherefore not the Force informing them,
When far-ranged aeons past all fathoming
Shall have swung by, and stand as backward years?

SPIRIT OF THE YEARS

What wouldst have hoped and had the Will to be?—
How wouldst have paeaned It, if what hadst dreamed
Thereof were truth, and all my showings dream?

SPIRIT OF THE PITIES

The Will that fed my hope was far from thine,
One I would thus have hymned eternally:—

SEMICHORUS I OF THE PITIES (*aerial music*)

To Thee whose eye all Nature owns,
Who hurlest Dynasts from their thrones,
And liftest those of low estate
We sing, with Her men consecrate!

SEMICHORUS II

Yea, Great and Good, Thee, Thee we hail,
Who shak'st the strong, Who shield'st the frail,
Who hadst not shaped such souls as we
If tender mercy lacked in Thee!

SEMICHORUS I

Though times be when the mortal moan
Seems unascending to Thy throne,
Though seers do not as yet explain
Why Suffering sobs to Thee in vain;

SEMICHORUS II

We hold that Thy unscanted scope
Affords a food for final Hope,
That mild-eyed Prescience ponders nigh
Life's loom, to lull it by-and-by.

SEMICHORUS I

Therefore we quire to highest height
The Wellwiller, the kindly Might
That balances the Vast for weal,
That purges as by wounds to heal.

SEMICHORUS II

The systemed suns the skies enscroll
Obey Thee in their rhythmic roll,
Ride radiantly at Thy command,
Are darkened by Thy Masterhand!

SEMICHORUS I

And these pale panting multitudes
Seen surging here, their moils, their moods,
All shall "fulfil their joy" in Thee
In Thee abide eternally!

SEMICHORUS II

Exultant adoration give
The Alone, through Whom all living live,
The Alone, in Whom all dying die,
Whose means the End shall justify!   Amen.

SPIRIT OF THE PITIES

So did we evermore sublimely sing;
So would we now, despite thy forthshowing!

SPIRIT OF THE YEARS

Something of difference animates your quiring,
O half-convinced Compassionates and fond,
From chords consistent with our spectacle!
You almost charm my long philosophy
Out of my strong-built thought, and bear me back
To when I thanksgave thus. . . . Ay, start not, Shades,
In the Foregone I knew what dreaming was,
And could let raptures rule! But not so now.
Yea, I psalmed thus and thus. . . . But not so now.

SEMICHORUS I OF THE YEARS *(aerial music)*

O Immanence, That reasonest not
In putting forth all things begot,
Thou build'st Thy house in space—for what?

SEMICHORUS II

O Loveless, Hateless!—past the sense
Of kindly eyed benevolence,
To what tune danceth this Immense?

SPIRIT IRONIC

For one I cannot answer. But I know
'Tis handsome of our Pities so to sing
The praises of the dreaming, dark, dumb Thing
That turns the handle of this idle Show!

As once a Greek asked I would fain ask too,
Who knows if all the Spectacle be true,
Or an illusion of the gods (the Will,
To wit) some hocus-pocus to fulfil?

SEMICHORUS I OF THE YEARS *(aerial music)*

Last as first the question rings
Of the Will's long travailings;
Why the All-mover,
Why the All-prover
Ever urges on and measures out the chordless chime of Things.

SEMICHORUS II

Heaving dumbly
As we deem,
Molding numbly
As in dream,
Apprehending not how fare the sentient subjects of Its scheme.

SEMICHORUS I OF THE PITIES

Nay;—shall not Its blindness break?
Yea, must not Its heart awake,
Promptly tending
To Its mending
In a genial germing purpose, and for lovingkindness' sake?

SEMICHORUS II

Should It never
Curb or cure
Aught whatever
Those endure
When It quickens, let them darkle to extinction swift and sure.

CHORUS

But—a stirring thrills the air
Like to sounds of joyance there
That the rages
Of the ages
Shall be canceled, and deliverance offered from the darts that
were,
Consciousness the Will informing, till It fashion all things
fair!

CHAPTER 13

NATURALISM: "THE DARK DIVINITY OF EARTH"

Is all this beauty that does inhabit heaven
Trail of a planet's fire? Is all this lust
A chymic means by warring stars contriven
To bring the violets out of Caesar's dust?
—John Masefield, "If all be governed
by the moving stars."

Almost every day brings us added information or conjecture on how our planet, our solar system, and indeed the universe itself came to be. One theory tells us that our universe was once an inconceivably vast sphere of incandescent light, and that after unimaginable time, this light "hardened" into matter. How out of this blazing matter were formed the countless suns that jewel our skies at night has been carefully and wisely debated by our astronomers. Truly, as Santayana says, "The muffled syllables that Nature speaks Fill us with deeper longing for her word." Hence we continue to sift matter and chart the sky and probe into space.

Nothing, it would seem, can long veil itself from our eyes or resist our analysis. We find interminable evidence of natural cause upon cause, until we are almost forced to conclude that the universe is a vast machine, with every motion and every act of every atom determined, a universe of apparently absolute natural law. But neither our farthest-seeing telescope nor our most penetrating microscope brings us any closer to a Final Cause: on this conclusion all naturalists are agreed.

To our steadily increasing knowledge of the nature of the universe there are two possible attitudes. One may regard the universe as the creation of God (whatever his nature may be) or, refusing to accept what cannot be "proved," one may regard the universe as a vast system of energy without conceivable beginning and with a probable end in "frigid chaos and dust." The latter is the basic view of naturalism.

What is the place of man in a naturalistic world? This question is the dismayed concern of Masefield in the sonnet opening this chapter. His attitude here represents fairly the distress of almost everyone when he is first confronted with this hypothesis. If our lives are only a lust contrived by warring stars, we are merely pawns, he says, "ignobler than the grass Cropped by the beast." But naturalism, grim as its facts are, is not a philosophy of despair, as will become increasingly evident as the chapter develops. Its most typical attitude is one of stoical acquiescence, of manly acceptance; and some, indeed, find in it a sufficient challenge to high endeavor. In this connection it merges with humanism.

If our lives have been contrived by the warring stars, what was the process itself by which life itself came to be? This possibly unanswerable question is meditated by Hans Castorp in Thomas Mann's *Magic Mountain*. His answer makes no provision for a soul. Swinburne also discards revealed religion as an answer, but in his acceptance of naturalism he introduces a mysticism of his own: he makes a religion of naturalism. Hertha, the creative principle of growth and change, begets all things, even the concepts of God. In the thinking of many naturalists, nature is thus deified, becoming a substitute for God.

Nature thus conceived may be regarded as either monstrous or beneficent. Swinburne's "Hertha" suggests a large, wholesome reverence. But in "To a Socialist in London," Robert Bridges lays bare the moral hideousness that lies below the bright shows of all earthly creatures. Matthew Arnold also strikes out at the fallacy of a beneficent Nature.

James Thomson and Shelley are specifically interested in the relationship of naturalism and religion. Thomson depicts man as an alien in the family of Nature, an alien who, discontented with her bounty, keeps imagining strange gods. Shelley, on the other hand, distressed with man's wretchedness, is bitter against the conventional ideas of God. "The exterminable spirit it contains," he says, "is nature's only God."

The fate of man is symbolized by Leopardi in a drifting leaf. Nature, "bent on ends that none can know," has no care for our individual hopes and aims. It were better never to have been. But Whitman, constitutionally an optimist, can be counted on to restore the balance: "Nothing is ever really lost, or can be lost, No birth, identity, form—no object of the world." In time and space, in the ample fields of Nature all things will be renewed—a doctrine not far from the natural mysticism of the Orient. Another aspect of this mysticism is frequently encountered in the poetry of A. E., who bows in reverence to the "dark divinity of earth."

It seems a natural consequence of dwelling on such thought as these authors advance that Pater should recommend to us the maxim of "Life as the end of life." Let us heed the testimony of our senses and concentrate on the now. *"America is here and now—here or nowhere."*

Thus man, lonely in an inconscient universe, ponders his destiny, trying with a mind made of matter to solve the mysteries of being. It is a marvelous thing, this mind, as Aldous Huxley reminds us, but "still umbilical to earth, Earth its home and earth its tomb."

But though naturalism may seem a counsel to despair in its renunciation of the hopes of religion, at its best it is instinct with nobleness in regard for conduct. Its ethical meaning in its richest sense is expressed by Bertrand

Russell in *A Free Man's Worship*, a splendid even if somber answer to the dismay of Masefield, with which we began.

"IF ALL BE GOVERNED BY THE MOVING STARS"

JOHN MASEFIELD

If all be governed by the moving stars,
If passing planets bring events to be,
Searing the face of Time with bloody scars,
Drawing men's souls even as the moon the sea;
If as they pass they make a current pass
Across man's life and heap it to a tide,
We are but pawns, ignobler than the grass
Cropped by the beast and crunched and tossed aside.
Is all this beauty that does inhabit heaven
Trail of a planet's fire? Is all this lust
A chymic means by warring stars contriven
To bring the violets out of Caesar's dust?
Better be grass, or in some hedge unknown
The spilling rose whose beauty is its own.

FROM RESEARCH *

In *The Magic Mountain*

THOMAS MANN

What was life? No one knew. It was undoubtedly aware of itself, so soon as it was life; but it did not know what it was. Consciousness, as exhibited by susceptibility to stimulus, was undoubtedly, to a certain degree, present in the lowest, most undeveloped stages of life; it was impossible to fix the first appearance of conscious processes at any point in the history of the individual or the race; impossible to make consciousness contingent upon, say, the presence of a nervous system. The lowest animal forms had no nervous systems, still less a cerebrum; yet no one would venture to deny them the capacity for responding to stimuli. One could suspend life; not merely particular sense-organs, not only nervous reactions, but life itself. One could temporarily suspend the irritability to sensation of every form of living matter in the plant as well as in the animal kingdom; one could narcotize ova and spermatozoa with chloroform, chloral hydrate, or morphine. Consciousness, then, was simply a function of matter organized into life; a function that in higher manifestations turned upon its avatar and became an effort to explore and explain the phenomenon it displayed—a hopeful-hopeless project of life to achieve self-knowledge, nature in recoil—and vainly, in the event, since she cannot be resolved in knowledge, nor life, when all is said, listen to itself.

What was life? No one knew. No one knew the actual point whence it sprang, where it kindled itself. Nothing in the domain of life seemed uncaused, or insufficiently caused, from that point on; but life itself seemed without antecedent.

* Reprinted from *The Magic Mountain* by Thomas Mann (translated by H. T. Lowe-Porter), by permission of Alfred A. Knopf, Inc. Copyright 1927 by Alfred A. Knopf, Inc.

If there was anything that might be said about it, it was this: it must be so highly developed, structurally, that nothing even distantly related to it was present in the inorganic world. Between the protean amoeba and the vertebrate the difference was slight, unessential, as compared to that between the simplest living organism and that nature which did not even deserve to be called dead, because it was inorganic. For death was only the logical negation of life; but between life and inanimate nature yawned a gulf which research strove in vain to bridge. They tried to close it with hypotheses, which it swallowed down without becoming any the less deep or broad. Seeking for a connecting link, they had condescended to the preposterous assumption of structureless living matter, unorganized organisms, which darted together of themselves in the albumen solution, like crystals in the mother-liquor; yet organic differentiation still remained at once condition and expression of all life. One could point to no form of life that did not owe its existence to procreation by parents. They had fished the primeval slime out of the depth of the sea, and great had been the jubilation—but the end of it all had been shame and confusion. For it turned out that they had mistaken a precipitate of sulphate of lime for protoplasm. But then, to avoid giving pause before a miracle —for life that built itself up out of, and fell in decay into, the same sort of matter as inorganic nature, would have been, happening of itself, miraculous—they were driven to believe in a spontaneous generation—that is, in the emergence of the organic from the inorganic—which was just as much of a miracle. Thus they went on, devising intermediate stages and transitions, assuming the existence of organisms which stood lower down than any yet known, but themselves had as forerunners still more primitive efforts of nature to achieve life: primitive forms of which no one would ever catch sight, for they were all of less than microscopic size, and previously to whose hypothetic existence the synthesis of protein compounds must already have taken place.

What then was life? It was warmth, the warmth generated by a form-preserving instability, a fever of matter, which accompanied the process of ceaseless decay and repair of albumen molecules that were too impossibly complicated, too impossibly ingenious in structure. It was the existence of the actually impossible-to-exist, of a half-sweet, half-painful balancing, or scarcely balancing, in this restricted and feverish process of decay and renewal, upon the point of existence. It was not matter and it was not spirit, but something between the two, a phenomenon conveyed by matter, like the rainbow on the waterfall, and like the flame. Yet why not material—it was sentient to the point of desire and disgust, the shamelessness of matter become sensible of itself, the incontinent form of being. It was a secret and ardent stirring in the frozen chastity of the universal; it was a stolen and voluptuous impurity of sucking and secreting; an exhalation of carbonic acid gas and material impurities of mysterious origin and composition. It was a pullulation, an unfolding, a form-building (made possible by the overbalancing of its instability, yet controlled by the laws of growth inherent within it), of something brewed out of water, albumen, salt and fats, which was called flesh, and which became form, beauty, a lofty image, and yet all the time the essence of sensuality and desire. For this form and beauty were not spirit-borne; nor, like the form and beauty of sculpture, conveyed by a neutral and spirit-consumed substance, which could in all purity make beauty perceptible to the senses. Rather was it conveyed and shaped by the somehow awakened voluptuousness of matter, of the organic, dying-living substance itself, the reeking flesh.

(H. T. Lowe-Porter, tr.)

FROM HERTHA

ALGERNON CHARLES SWINBURNE

I am that which began;
   Out of me the years roll;
Out of me God and man;
   I am equal and whole;
God changes, and man, and the form of
   them bodily; I am the soul.

Before ever land was,
   Before ever the sea,
Or soft hair of the grass,
   Or fair limbs of the tree,
Or the flesh-colored fruit of my branches,
   I was, and thy soul was in me.

First life on my sources
   First drifted and swam;
Out of me are the forces
   That save it or damn;
Out of me man and woman, and wild-beast
   and bird; before God was, I am.

Beside or above me
   Nought is there to go;
Love or unlove me,
   Unknow me or know,
I am that which unloves me and loves; I
   am stricken, and I am the blow.

I the mark that is missed
   And the arrows that miss,
I the mouth that is kissed
   And the breath in the kiss,
The search, and the sought, and the seeker,
   the soul and the body that is.

I am the thing which blesses
   My spirit elate;
That which caresses
   With hands uncreate
My limbs unbegotten that measure the
   length of the measure of fate.

But what thing dost thou now,
   Looking Godward, to cry
"I am I, thou art thou,
   I am low, thou art high"?
I am thou, whom thou seekest to find him;
   find thou but thyself, thou art I.

I the grain and the furrow,
　　The plough-cloven clod
And the ploughshare drawn thorough,
　　The germ and the sod,
The deed and the doer, the seed and the
　　sower, the dust which is God.

.　　.　　.　　.　　.　　.　　.　　.

The tree many-rooted
　　That swells to the sky
With frondage red-fruited,
　　The life-tree am I;
In the buds of your lives is the sap of my
　　leaves: ye shall live and not die.

But the Gods of your fashion
　　That take and that give
In their pity and passion
　　That scourge and forgive
That are worms that are bred in the bark
　　that falls off; they shall die and not live.

My own blood is what stanches
　　The wounds in my bark;
Stars caught in my branches
　　Make day of the dark,
And are worshiped as suns till the sunrise
　　shall tread out their fires as a spark.

Where dead ages hide under
　　The live roots of the tree,
In my darkness the thunder
　　Makes utterance of me;
In the clash of my boughs with each other
　　ye hear the waves sound of the sea.

The noise is of Time,
　　As his feathers are spread
And his feet set to climb
　　Through the boughs overhead,
And my foliage rings round him and rustles,
　　and branches are bent with his tread.

The storm-winds of ages
　　Blow through me and cease,
The war-wind that rages,
　　The spring-wind of peace,
Ere the breath of them roughen my tresses,
　　ere one of my blossoms increase.

All sounds of all changes,
　　All shadows and lights
On the world's mountain-ranges
　　And stream-riven heights,

Whose tongue is the wind's tongue and
language of storm-clouds on earth-shaking nights;

All forms of all faces,
All works of all hands
In unsearchable places
Of time-stricken lands,
All death and all life and all reigns and
all ruins, drop through me as sands.

FROM TO A SOCIALIST IN LONDON (Epistle II) *

ROBERT BRIDGES

And what if all Nature ratify this merciless outrage?
If her wonder of arch-wonders, her fair animal life,
Her generate creatures, her motion'd warmblooded offspring,
Haunters of the forest & royal country, her antler'd
Mild-gazers, that keep silvan sabbath idly without end;
Her herded galopers, sleeksided stately careerers
Of trembling nostril; her coy unapproachable estrays,
Stealthy treaders, climbers; her leapers furry, lissom-limb'd;
Her timorous burrowers, and grangers thrifty, the sandy
Playmates of the warren; her clumsy-footed, shaggy roamers;
Her soarers, the feather'd fast-fliers, loftily floating
Sky-sailers, exiles of high solitudinous eyries;
Her perching carolers, twitterers, & sweetly singing birds:
All ocean's finny clans, mute-mouthers, watery breathers,
Furtive arrow-darters, and fan-tail'd easy balancers,
Silvery-scale, gilt-head, thorn-back, frill'd harlequinading
Globe and slimy ribbon: Shell-builders of many-chamber'd
Pearly dwellings, soft shapes mosslike or starry, adorning
With rich floral fancy the gay rock-garden of ebb-tide:
All life, from the massive-bulkt, ivory-tusht, elephantine
Centēnarian, acknowledging with crouching obeisance
Man's will, ev'n to the least petty whiffling ephemeral insect,
Which in a hot sunbeam engend'ring, when summer is high,
Vaunteth an hour his speck of tinsely gaudiness and dies:
Ah! what if all & each of Nature's favorite offspring,
'Mong many distinctions, have this portentous agreement,
MOUTH, STOMACH, INTESTINE?   Question that brute apparatus,
So manifoldly devis'd, set alert with furious instinct:
What doth it interpret but this, that LIFE LIVETH ON LIFE?
That the select creatures, who inherit earth's domination,
Whose happy existence is Nature's intelligent smile,
Are bloody survivors of a mortal combat, a-tweenwhiles
Chanting a brief paean for victory on the battlefield?
Since that of all their kinds most owe their prosperous estate
Unto the art, whereby they more successfully destroy'd
Their weaker brethren, more insatiably devour'd them;

* The author's preferences in spelling are observed.

And all fine qualities, their forms pictorial, admired,
Their symmetries, their grace, & beauty, the loveliness of them,
Were by Murder evolv'd to 'scape from it or to effect it.
   "Surely again (you say) too much is proven, it argues
"Mere horror & despair; unless persuasion avail us
"That the moral virtues are man's idea, awaken'd
"By the spirit's motions; & therefore not to be conceiv'd
"In Nature's outward & mainly material aspect,
"As that is understood. You, since you hold that opinion,
"Run your own ship aground invoking Nature against me."—

TO AN INDEPENDENT PREACHER

(Who preached that we should be "in harmony with nature.")

MATTHEW ARNOLD

"In harmony with Nature?"   Restless fool,
Who with such heat dost preach what were to thee,
When true, the last impossibility;
To be like Nature strong, like Nature cool:—

Know, man hath all which Nature hath, but more,
And in that *more* lie all his hopes of good.
Nature is cruel; man is sick of blood:
Nature is stubborn; man would fain adore:

Nature is fickle; man hath need of rest:
Nature forgives no debt, and fears no grave:
Man would be mild, and with sage conscience blest.

Man must begin, know this, where Nature ends;
Nature and man can never be fast friends.
Fool, if thou canst not pass her, rest her slave!

A VOICE FROM THE NILE

JAMES THOMSON

I come from mountains under other stars
Than those reflected in my waters here;
Athwart broad realms, beneath large skies, I flow,
Between the Libyan and Arabian hills,
And merge at last into the great Mid Sea;
And make this land of Egypt.   All is mine:
The palm-trees and the doves among the palms,
The corn-fields and the flowers among the corn,
The patient oxen and the crocodiles,
The ibis and the heron and the hawk,
The lotus and the thick papyrus reeds,
The slant-sailed boats that flit before the wind
Or up my rapids ropes hale heavily;

Yea, even all the massive temple-fronts
With all their columns and huge effigies,
The pyramids and Memnon and the Sphinx,
This Cairo and the City of the Greek
As Memphis and the hundred-gated Thebes,
Sais and Denderah of Isis queen;
Have grown because I fed them with full life,
And flourish only while I feed them still,
For if I stint my fertilizing flood,
Gaunt famine reaps among the sons of men
Who have not corn to reap for all they sowed,
And blight and languishment are everywhere;
And when I have withdrawn or turned aside
To other realms my ever-flowing streams,
The old realms withered from their old renown,
The sands came over them, the desert-sands
Incessantly encroaching, numberless
Beyond my water-drops, and buried them,
And all is silence, solitude, and death,
Exanimate silence while the waste winds howl
Over the sad immeasurable waste,

Dusk memories haunt me of an infinite past,
Ages and cycles brood above my springs,
Though I remember not my primal birth.
So ancient is my being and august,
I know not anything more venerable;
Unless, perchance, the vaulting skies that hold
The sun and moon and stars that shine on me;
The air that breathes upon me with delight;
And Earth, All-Mother, all beneficent,
Who held her mountains forth like opulent breasts
To cradle me and feed me with their snows,
And hollowed out the great sea to receive
My overplus of flowing energy:
Blessed for ever be our Mother Earth.

Only, the mountains that must feed my springs
Year after year and every year with snows
As they have fed innumerable years,
These mountains they are evermore the same,
Rooted and motionless; the solemn heavens
Are evermore the same in stable rest;
The sun and moon and stars that shine on me
Are evermore the same although they move:
I solely, moving ever without pause,
Am evermore the same and not the same;
Pouring myself away into the sea,
And self-renewing from the farthest heights;
Ever-fresh waters streaming down and down,
The one old Nilus constant through their change.

The creatures also whom I breed and feed
Perpetually perish and dissolve,
And other creatures like them take their place,
To perish in their turn and be no more:
My profluent waters perish not from life,
Absorbed into the ever-living sea
Whose life is in their full replenishment.

Of all these creatures whom I breed and feed,
One only with his works is strange to me,
Is strange and admirable and pitiable,
As homeless where all others are at home.
My crocodiles are happy in my slime,
And bask and seize their prey, each for itself,
And leave their eggs to hatch in the hot sun,
And die, their lives fulfilled, and are no more,
And others bask and prey and leave their eggs.
My doves they build their nests, each pair its own,
And feed their callow young, each pair its own,
None serves another, each one serves itself;
All glean alike about my fields of grain,
And all the nests they build them are alike,
And are the self-same nests they built of old
Before the rearing of the pyramids,
Before great Hekatompylos was reared;
Their cooing is the cooing soft and sweet
That murmured plaintively at evening-tide
In pillared Karnac as its pillars rose;
And they are happy floating through my palms.

But Man, the admirable, the pitiable,
These sad-eyed peoples of the sons of men,
Are as the children of an alien race
Planted among my children, not at home,
Changelings aloof from all my family.
The one is servant and the other lord,
And many myriads serve a single lord:
So was it when the pyramids were reared,
And sphinxes and huge columns and wrought stones
Were haled long lengthening leagues adown my banks
By hundreds groaning with the stress of toil,
And groaning under the taskmaster's scourge,
With many falling foredone by the way,
Half-starved on lentils, onions, and scant bread;
So is it now with these poor fellaheen
To whom my annual bounty brings fierce toil
With scarce enough of food to keep-in life.
They build mud huts and spacious palaces;
And in the huts the moiling millions dwell
And in the palaces their sumptuous lords
Pampered with all the choicest things I yield:
Most admirable, most pitiable Man.

Also their peoples ever are at war,
Slaying and slain, burning, and ravaging,
And one yields to another and they pass,
While I flow evermore the same great Nile,
The ever-young and ever-ancient Nile:
The swarthy is succeeded by the dusk,
The dusky by the pale, the pale again
By sunburned turbaned tribes long-linen-robed:
And with these changes all things change and pass,
All things but Me and this old Land of mine,
Their dwellings, habitudes, and garbs, and tongues:
I hear strange voices: never more the voice
Austere priests chanted to the boat of death
Gliding across the Acherusian lake,
Or satraps parleyed in the Pharaoh's halls;
Never the voice of mad Cambyses' hosts,
Never the voice of Alexander's Greece,
Never the voice of Caesar's haughty Rome:
And with the peoples and the languages,
With the great Empires still the great Creeds change;
They shift, they change, they vanish like thin dreams,
As unsubstantial as the mists that rise
After my overflow from out my fields,
In silver fleeces, golden volumes, rise,
And melt away before the mounting sun;
While I flow onward solely permanent
Amidst their swiftly-passing pageantry.

Poor men, most admirable, most pitiable,
With all their changes all their great Creeds change:
For Man, this alien in my family,
Is alien most in this, to cherish dreams
And brood on visions of eternity,
And build religions in his brooding brain
And in the dark depths awe-full of his soul.
My other children live their little lives,
Are born and reach their prime and slowly fail,
And all their little lives are self-fulfilled;
They die and are no more, content with age
And weary with infirmity.   But Man
Has fear and hope and phantasy and awe,
And wistful yearnings and unsated loves,
That strain beyond the limits of his life,
And therefore Gods and Demons, Heaven and Hell:
This Man, the admirable, the pitiable.

Lo, I look backward some few thousand years,
And see men hewing temples in my rocks
With seated forms gigantic fronting them,
And solemn labyrinthine catacombs
With tombs all pictured with fair scenes of life
And scenes and symbols of mysterious death;

And planting avenues of sphinxes forth,
Sphinxes couched calm, whose passionless regard
Sets timeless riddles to bewildered time,
Forth from my sacred banks to other fanes
Islanded in the boundless sea of air,
Upon whose walls and colonnades are carved
Tremendous hieroglyphs of secret things;
I see embalming of the bodies dead
And judging of the disembodied souls;
I see the sacred animals alive,
And statues of the various-headed gods,
Among them throned a woman and a babe,
The goddess crescent-horned, the babe divine!
Then I flow forward some few thousand years,
And see new temples shining with all grace,
Whose sculptured gods are beautiful human forms.
Then I flow forward not a thousand years,
And see again a woman and a babe,
The woman haloed and the babe divine;
And everywhere that symbol of the cross
I knew aforetime in the ancient days,
The emblem then of life, but now of death.
Then I flow forward some few hundred years,
And see again the crescent, now supreme
On lofty cupolas and minarets
Whence voices sweet and solemn call to prayer.
So the men change along my changeless stream,
And change their faiths; but I yield all alike
Sweet water for their drinking, sweet as wine,
And pure sweet water for their lustral rites:
For thirty generations of my corn
Outlast a generation of my men,
And thirty generations of my men
Outlast a generation of their gods:
O admirable, pitiable Man,
My child yet alien in my family.

And I through all these generations flow
Of corn and men and gods, all-bountiful,
Perennial through their transientness, still fed
By earth with waters in abundancy;
And as I flowed here long before they were,
So may I flow when they no longer are,
Most like the serpent of eternity:
Blessèd for ever be our Mother Earth.

"I PLAY FOR SEASONS; NOT ETERNITIES"

In *Modern Love*

GEORGE MEREDITH

"I play for Seasons; not Eternities!"
Says Nature, laughing on her way.   "So must
All those whose stake is nothing more than dust!"
And so, she wins, and of her harmonies
She is full sure!   Upon her dying rose
She drops a look of fondness, and goes by,
Scarce any retrospection in her eye;
For she the laws of growth most deeply knows,
Whose hands bear, here, a seed-bag; there, an urn.
Pledged she herself to aught, 'twould mark her end!
This lesson of our only visible friend,
Can we not teach our foolish hearts to learn?
Yes! yes!—but oh, our human rose is fair
Surpassingly!   Lose calmly Love's great bliss,
When the renewed forever of a kiss
Sounds through the listless hurricane of hair!

"WHAT ARE WE FIRST? FIRST, ANIMALS, AND NEXT"

In *Modern Love*

GEORGE MEREDITH

What are we first?   First, animals; and next,
Intelligences at a leap; on whom
Pale lies the distant shadow of the tomb,
And all that draweth on the tomb for text.
Into this state comes Love, the crowning sun:
Beneath whose light the shadow loses form.
We are the lords of life, and life is warm.
Intelligence and instinct now are one.
But Nature says: "My children most they seem
When they least know me: therefore I decree
That they shall suffer."   Swift doth young Love flee:
And we stand wakened, shivering from our dream.
Then if we study Nature we are wise.
Thus do the few who live but with the day.
The scientific animals are they.—
Lady, this is my Sonnet to your eyes.

from QUEEN MAB, VI, VII
PERCY BYSSHE SHELLEY

"Spirit of Nature! all-sufficing Power,
Necessity! thou mother of the world!
Unlike the God of human error, thou
Requir'st no prayers or praises; the caprice
Of man's weak will belongs no more to thee
Than do the changeful passions of his breast
To thy unvarying harmony: the slave,
Whose horrible lusts spread misery o'er the world,
And the good man, who lifts, with virtuous pride,
His being, in the sight of happiness,
That springs from his own works; the poison-tree,
Beneath whose shade all life is withered up,
And the fair oak, whose leafy dome affords
A temple where the vows of happy love
Are registered, are equal in thy sight:
No love, no hate thou cherishest; revenge
And favoritism, and worst desire of fame
Thou know'st not: all that the wide world contains
Are but thy passive instruments, and thou
Regard'st them all with an impartial eye,
Whose joy or pain thy nature cannot feel,
    Because thou hast not human sense,
    Because thou art not human mind.

    "Yes! when the sweeping storm of time
Has sung its death-dirge o'er the ruined fanes
And broken altars of the almighty Fiend
Whose name usurps thy honors, and the blood
Through centuries clotted there, has floated down
The tainted flood of ages, shalt thou live
Unchangeable!   A shrine is raised to thee,
    Which, nor the tempest-breath of time,
    Nor the interminable flood,
    Over earth's slight pageant rolling,
        Availeth to destroy,—
The sensitive extension of the world.
    That wondrous and eternal fane,
Where pain and pleasure, good and evil join,
To do the will of strong necessity,
    And life, in multitudinous shapes,
Still pressing forward where no term can be,
    Like hungry and unresting flame
Curls round the eternal columns of its strength."

VII

SPIRIT

"I was an infant when my mother went
To see an atheist burned. She took me there:

The dark-robed priests were met around the pile;
The multitude was gazing silently;
And as the culprit passed with dauntless mien,
Tempered disdain in his unaltering eye,
Mixed with a quiet smile, shone calmly forth:
The thirsty fire crept round his manly limbs;
His resolute eyes were scorched to blindness soon;
His death-pang rent my heart! the insensate mob
Uttered a cry of triumph, and I wept.
'Weep not, child!' cried my mother, 'for that man
Has said, There is no God.' "

FAIRY

       "There is no God!
Nature confirms the faith his death-groan sealed:
Let heaven and earth, let man's revolving race,
His ceaseless generations tell their tale;
Let every part depending on the chain
That links it to the whole, point to the hand
That grasps its term! let every seed that falls
In silent eloquence unfold its store
Of argument; infinity within,
Infinity without, belie creation;
The exterminable spirit it contains
Is nature's only God; but human pride
Is skilful to invent most serious names
To hide its ignorance."

IMITATION

GIACOMO LEOPARDI

Far from the parent bough,
Poor fragile little leaf,
Where goest thou?—I was torn
By a gust from the tall beech where I was born.
From the wood to the meadow now,
As round it eddies, the gale
Whirls me along, then back to the hill from the dale.
With it I must perforce
Drift on forever: that is all I know.
I am going where all else goes,
Whither in Nature's course
The petals of the rose
And the leaves of the laurel go.

(G. L. Bickersteth, tr.)

from ON AN ANCIENT SEPULCHRAL BAS-RELIEF

*(Where a dead maiden is represented in the act of departure,
taking leave of her friends)*

GIACOMO LEOPARDI

Never to see the light
Methinks were best.   But, having once been born,
When beauty on face and limbs
Unfurls its ensign proud,
And afar off the world
Begins to pay her court; when every hope
Hath burst the bud; ere time hath yet allowed
The truth to flash its dismal, pitiless glare
Upon her brow decked for life's festival;
Like vapor formed into a little cloud,
Whose fleeting shapes dissolve into thin air,
To fade away as though she had not been,
And for her radiant future
To exchange the dark, dark silence of the tomb,
This, though the intellect
Pronounce it happiness,
Must none the less the hardest hearts affect.

Mother, bewailed and feared
Since first thy creature-kind was born till now,
Nature, uncommendable monster, thou
Who bringest forth and nurturest but to kill,
If evil it be to die
Untimely, wherefore should these innocent
So perish, and thou consent?
If good, why makest thou
So lamentable, why
So far beyond all comfort such a death
Both to the dying and those who still draw breath?

Wretched in all its aims,
Wretched in all it seeks, in all it shuns,
Is this quick-feeling race!
It pleased thee that the hope
Man cherished in youth
Should be belied by age; that brimmed with woe
His years should flow; from ills his only shield
Be death; ay, this the inevitable end,
This the unchanging law
Imposed on his career.   Ah, why though life
Be run with toil, not let at least life's goal
Bring joy unto the soul?   Why rather clothe
This death we all must die,
That ever-present prospect in our lives,
The very death, by whom

Alone we hope release,
Why clothe it in a gloom
So grim, so fraught with fear?
Why make the port appear
More dreadful to us than the storm-tossed seas?

.   .   .   .

How canst thou, Nature, ah how canst thou have
The heart to tear asunder
Friend from devoted friend,
The brother from the brother,
Father of child bereave,
The lover loveless leave: and bid one die,
The other still live on?   How couldest thou
Constrain our souls to bear
The agony of mortal man surviving
The mortal whom he loves?—But for our woe
Or for our weal no care
Hath Nature, bent on ends that none can know.

(G. L. Bickersteth, tr.)

from RECANTATION

GIACOMO LEOPARDI

Just as a boy, with persevering pains,
From little twigs and leaves of paper, builds
An edifice in shape of church or tower
Or palace; and as soon as he beholds
It finished, straightway turns to knock it down,
Because he stands in need of the same twigs
And paper for some novel building-scheme;
So Nature hath no sooner perfected
Each work of hers, however cunningly
Contrived, than she begins unmaking it,
Elsewhere distributing the separate parts.
And vainly strives mankind to save itself
And others from this wicked game, whereof
The cause is an eternal mystery,
By the ingenious use in countless ways
Of countless means: for, overriding all,
Merciless Nature, incorrigible child,
Persists in her caprice and without pause
For her amusement builds up to destroy.
Hence, infinite in number and in kind,
A swarm of irremediable ills
And pains afflict frail mortals, born to die
Irreparably: hence a power, hostile,
Destructive, on all sides, within, without,
Bludgeons them with unceasing virulence
From the instant of their birth, and wears them down,

Itself unwearying; till, crushed at length
By their unholy Mother, they lie slain.
These, gentle friend, are the last miseries
Of mortal being on earth; old age and death,
Which have begun while yet the infant's lips
Cling to the tender breast which yields him life;
Which state, methinks, the nineteenth century
For all its happiness can no more mend
Than could the ninth or tenth; nor more than ours
Can mend it shall the ages yet to be.

(G. L. Bickersteth, tr.)

CONTINUITIES

(From a talk I had lately with a German spiritualist)

WALT WHITMAN

Nothing is ever really lost, or can be lost,
No birth, identity, form—no object of the world,
Nor life, nor force, nor any visible thing;
Appearance must not foil, nor shifted sphere confuse thy brain.
Ample are time and space—ample the fields of Nature.
The body, sluggish, aged, cold—the embers left from earlier fires,
The light in the eye grown dim, shall duly flame again;
The sun now low in the west rises for mornings and for noons continual;
To frozen clods ever the spring's invisible law returns,
With grass and flowers and summer fruits and corn.

THE VIRGIN MOTHER

A. E.

Who is that goddess to whom men should pray,
But her from whom their hearts have turned away,
Out of whose virgin being they were born,
Whose mother nature they have named with scorn
Calling its holy substance common clay.

Yet from this so despised earth was made
The milky whiteness of those queens who swayed
Their generations with a light caress,
And from some image of whose loveliness
The heart built up high heaven when it prayed.

Lover, your heart, the heart on which it lies,
Your eyes that gaze and those alluring eyes,
Your lips, the lips they kiss, alike had birth
Within that dark divinity of earth,
Within that mother being you despise.

Ah, when I think this earth on which I tread
Hath borne these blossoms of the lovely dead,
And makes the living heart I love to beat,
I look with sudden awe beneath my feet
As you with erring reverence overhead.

EARTH *

JOHN HALL WHEELOCK

Grasshopper, your fairy song
And my poem alike belong
To the dark and silent earth
From which all poetry has birth;
All we say and all we sing
Is but as the murmuring
Of that drowsy heart of hers
When from her deep dream she stirs:
If we sorrow, or rejoice,
You and I are but her voice.

Deftly does the dust express
In mind her hidden loveliness—
And, from her cool silence, stream
The cricket's cry and Dante's dream;
For the earth that breeds the trees
Breeds cities too, and symphonies.
Equally her beauty flows
Into a savior, or a rose—
Looks down in dream, and from above
Smiles at herself in Jesus' love;
Christ's love and Homer's art
Are but the workings of her heart,
Through Leonardo's hand she seeks
Herself, and through Beethoven speaks
In holy thunderings around,
The awful message of the ground.

The serene and humble mold
Does in herself all selves enfold—
Kingdoms, destinies, and creeds,
Proud dreams, heroic deeds,
Science, that probes the firmament,
The high, inflexible intent
Of one, for many, sacrificed;
Plato's brain, the heart of Christ,
All love, all legend, and all lore
Are in the dust forevermore.

* Reprinted from *Dust and Light* by John Hall Wheelock; copyright 1919 by Charles Scribner's Sons, 1947 by John Hall Wheelock; used by permission of the publishers.

Even as the growing grass
Up from the soil religions pass,
And the field that bears the rye
Bears parables and prophecy.
Out of the earth the poem grows
Like the lily, or the rose;
And all man is, or yet may be,
Is but herself in agony
Toiling up the steep ascent
Toward the complete accomplishment
When all dust shall be—the whole
Universe—one conscious soul.

Ah, the quiet and cool sod
Bears in her breast the dream of God.

If you would know what earth is, scan
The intricate, proud heart of man,
Which is the earth articulate,
And learn how holy and how great,
How limitless and how profound
Is the nature of the ground—
How without question or demur
We may entrust ourselves to her
When we are wearied out, and lay
Our faces in the common clay.

For she is pity, she is love,
All wisdom, she, all thoughts that move
About her everlasting breast
Till she gathers them to rest:
All tenderness of all the ages,
Seraphic secrets of the sages,
Vision and hope of all the seers,
All prayer, all anguish, and all tears
Are but the dust, that from her dream
Awakes, and knows herself supreme—
Are but earth, when she reveals
All that her secret heart conceals
Down in the dark and silent loam,
Which is ourselves, asleep, at home.
Yea, and this, my poem, too,
Is part of her as dust and dew—
Wherein herself she doth declare
Through my lips, and say her prayer.

FROM ANIMULA VAGULA

In *Marius the Epicurean*

WALTER PATER

. . . It has been sometimes seen, in the history of the human mind, that when thus translated into terms of sentiment—of sentiment, as lying already half-way towards practice—the abstract ideas of metaphysics for the first time reveal their true significance. The metaphysical principle, in itself, as it were, without hands or feet, becomes impressive, fascinating, of effect, when translated into a precept as to how it were best to feel and act; in other words, under its sentimental or ethical equivalent. The leading idea of the great master of Cyrene, his theory that things are but shadows, and that we, even as they, never continue in one stay, might indeed have taken effect as a languid, enervating, consumptive nihilism, as a precept of "renunciation," which would touch and handle and busy itself with nothing. But in the reception of metaphysical *formulae,* all depends, as regards their actual and ulterior result, on the pre-existent qualities of that soil of human nature into which they fall—the company they find already present there, on their admission into the house of thought; there being at least so much truth as this involves in the theological maxim, that the reception of this or that speculative conclusion is really a matter of will. The persuasion that all is vanity, with this happily constituted Greek, who had been a genuine disciple of Socrates and re-flected, presumably, something of his blitheness in the face of the world, his happy way of taking all chances, generated neither frivolity nor sourness, but induced, rather, an impression, just serious enough, of the call upon men's attention of the crisis in which they find themselves. It became the stimulus towards every kind of activity, and prompted a perpetual, inextinguishable thirst after experience.

With Marius, then, the influence of the philosopher of pleasure depended on this, that in him an abstract doctrine, originally somewhat acrid, had fallen upon a rich and genial nature, well fitted to transform it into a theory of practice, of considerable stimulative power towards a fair life. What Marius saw in him was the spectacle of one of the happiest temperaments coming, so to speak, to an under-standing with the most depressing of theories; accepting the results of a meta-physical system which seemed to concentrate into itself all the weakening trains of thought in earlier Greek speculation, and making the best of it; turning its hard, bare truths, with wonderful tact, into precepts of grace, and delicate wisdom, and a delicate sense of honor. Given the hardest terms, supposing our days are indeed but a shadow, even so, we may well adorn and beautify, in scrupulous self-respect, our souls, and whatever our souls touch upon—these wonderful bodies, these ma-terial dwelling-places through which the shadows pass together for a while, the very raiment we wear, our very pastimes and the intercourse of society. The most discerning judges saw in him something like the graceful "humanities" of the later Roman, and our modern "culture," as it is termed; while Horace recalled his sayings as expressing best his own consummate amenity in the reception of life.

In this way, for Marius, under the guidance of that old master of decorous liv-ing, those eternal doubts as to the *criteria* of truth reduced themselves to a skep-ticism almost drily practical, a skepticism which developed the opposition between things as they are and our impressions and thoughts concerning them—the possi-bility, if an outward world does really exist, of some faultiness in our apprehension of it—the doctrine, in short, of what is termed "the subjectivity of knowledge." That is a consideration, indeed, which lies as an element of weakness, like some admitted fault or flaw, at the very foundation of every philosophical account of the universe; which confronts all philosophies at their starting, but with which none have really dealt conclusively, some perhaps not quite sincerely; which those who are not philosophers dissipate by "common," but unphilosophical, sense, or by religious faith. The peculiar strength of Marius was, to have apprehended this weakness on the threshold of human knowledge, in the whole range of its consequences. Our knowledge is limited to what we feel, he reflected: we need no proof that we feel. But can we be sure that things are at all like our feelings? Mere peculiarities in the instruments of our cognition, like the little knots and waves on the surface of a mirror, may distort the matter they seem but to represent. Of other people we cannot truly know even the feelings, nor how far they would indicate the same modifications, each one of a personality really unique, in using the same terms as ourselves; that "common experience," which is sometimes proposed as a satisfactory basis of certainty, being after all only a fixity of language. But our own impressions!—The light and heat of that blue veil over our heads, the heavens spread out, perhaps *not* like a curtain over anything!—How reassuring, after so long a debate about the rival *criteria* of truth, to fall back upon direct sensation, to limit one's aspirations after knowledge to that! In an age still materially so brilliant, so expert in the artistic handling of material things, with sensible capacities still in undiminished vigor, with the whole world of classic art and poetry outspread before it, and where there was more than eye or ear could well take in—how natural the determination to rely exclusively upon the phenomena of the senses, which certainly never deceive us about themselves, about which alone we can never deceive ourselves!

And so the abstract apprehension that the little point of this present moment alone really is, between a past which has just ceased to be and a future which may never come, became practical with Marius, under the form of a resolve, as far as possible, to exclude regret and desire, and yield himself to the improvement of the present with an absolutely disengaged mind. *America is here and now—here, or nowhere:* as Wilhelm Meister finds out one day, just not too late, after so long looking vaguely across the ocean for the opportunity of the development of his capacities. It was as if, recognizing in perpetual motion the law of nature, Marius identified his own way of life cordially with it, "throwing himself into the stream," so to speak. He too must maintain a harmony with that soul of motion in things, by constantly renewed mobility of character.

Omnis Aristippum decuit color et status et res.—Thus Horace had summed up that perfect manner in the reception of life attained by his old Cyrenaic master; and the first practical consequence of the metaphysic which lay behind that perfect manner, had been a strict limitation, almost the renunciation, of metaphysical enquiry itself. Metaphysic—that art, as it has so often proved, in the words of Michelet, *de s'égarer avec méthode,* of bewildering oneself methodically:—one must spend little time upon that! In the school of Cyrene, great as was its mental incisiveness, logical and physical speculation, theoretic interests generally, had been valued only so far as they served to give a groundwork, an intellectual justification, to that exclusive concern with practical ethics which was a note of the Cyrenaic philosophy. How earnest and enthusiastic, how true to itself, under how many varieties of character, had been the effort of the Greeks after Theory—*Theoria*— that vision of a wholly reasonable world, which, according to the greatest of them, literally makes man like God: how loyally they had still persisted in the quest after that, in spite of how many disappointments! In the Gospel of Saint John, perhaps, some of them might have found the kind of vision they were seeking for; but not in "doubtful disputations" concerning "being" and "not-being," knowledge and appearance. Men's minds, even young men's minds, at that late day, might well seem oppressed by the weariness of systems which had so far outrun positive knowledge; and in the mind of Marius, as in that old school of Cyrene, this sense of *ennui*, combined with appetites so youthfully vigorous, brought about reaction, a sort of suicide (instances of the like have been seen since) by which a great metaphysical *acumen* was devoted to the function of proving metaphysical speculation impossible, or useless. Abstract theory was to be valued only just so far as it might serve to clear the tablet of the mind from suppositions no more than half realizable, or wholly visionary, leaving it in flawless evenness of surface to the impressions of an experience, concrete and direct.

To be absolutely virgin towards such experience, by ridding ourselves of such abstractions as are but the ghosts of by-gone impressions—to be rid of the notions we have made for ourselves, and that so often only misrepresent the experience of which they profess to be the representation—*idola,* idols, false appearances, as Bacon calls them later—to neutralize the distorting influence of metaphysical system by an all-accomplished metaphysic skill: it is this bold, hard, sober recognition, under a very "dry light," of its own proper aim, in union with a habit of feeling which on the practical side may perhaps open a wide doorway to human weakness, that gives to the Cyrenaic doctrine, to reproductions of this doctrine in the time of Marius or in our own, their gravity and importance. It was a school to which the young man might come, eager for truth, expecting much from philosophy, in no ignoble curiosity, aspiring after nothing less than an "initiation." He would be sent back, sooner or later, to experience, to the world of concrete impressions, to things as they may be seen, heard, felt by him; but with a wonderful machinery of observation, and free from the tyranny of mere theories.

So, in intervals of repose, after the agitation which followed the death of Flavian, the thoughts of Marius ran, while he felt himself as if returned to the fine, clear, peaceful light of that pleasant school of healthfully sensuous wisdom, in the brilliant old Greek colony, on its fresh upland by the sea. Not pleasure, but a general completeness of life, was the practical ideal to which this antimetaphysical metaphysic really pointed. And towards such a full or complete life, a life of various yet select sensation, the most direct and effective auxiliary must be, in a word, Insight. Liberty of soul, freedom from all partial and misrepresentative doctrine which does but relieve one element in our experience at the cost of another, freedom from all embarrassment alike of regret for the past and of calculation on the future: this would be but preliminary to the real business of education—insight, insight through culture, into all that the present moment holds in trust for us, as we stand so briefly in its presence. From that maxim of *Life as the end of life,* followed, as a practical consequence, the desirableness of refining all the instruments of inward and outward intuition, of developing all their capacities, of testing and exercising one's self in them, till one's whole nature became one complex medium of reception, towards the vision—the "beatific vision," if we really cared to make it such—of our actual experience in the world. Not the conveyance of an abstract body of truths or principles, would be the aim of the right education of one's self, or of another, but the conveyance of an art—an art in some degree peculiar to each individual character; with the modifications, that is, due to its special constitution, and the peculiar circumstances of its growth, inasmuch as no one of us is "like another, all in all."

FIRST PHILOSOPHER'S SONG *

ALDOUS HUXLEY

A poor degenerate from the ape
Whose hands are four, whose tail's a limb,
I contemplate my flaccid shape
And know I may not rival him,

Save with my mind—a nimbler beast
Possessing a thousand sinewy tails,
A thousand hands, with which it scales,
Greedy of luscious truth, the greased

Poles and the coco palms of thought,
Thrids easily through the mangrove maze
Of metaphysics, walks the taut
Frail dangerous liana ways

That link across wide gulfs remote
Analogies between tree and tree;
Outruns the hare, outhops the goat;
Mind fabulous, mind sublime and free!

But oh, the sound of simian mirth!
Mind, issued from the monkey's womb,
Is still umbilical to earth,
Earth its home and earth its tomb.

A FREE MAN'S WORSHIP †

In *Mysticism and Logic*

BERTRAND RUSSELL

To Dr. Faustus in his study Mephistopheles told the history of the Creation, saying:

"The endless praises of the choirs of angels had begun to grow wearisome; for, after all, did he not deserve their praise? Had he not given them endless joy? Would it not be more amusing to obtain undeserved praise, to be worshiped by beings whom he tortured? He smiled inwardly, and resolved that the great drama should be performed.

"For countless ages the hot nebula whirled aimlessly through space. At length it began to take shape, the central mass threw off planets, the planets cooled, boiling seas and burning mountains heaved and tossed, from black masses of cloud hot sheets of rain deluged the barely solid crust. And now the first germ of life grew in the depths of the ocean, and developed rapidly in the fructifying warmth into vast forest trees, huge ferns springing from the damp mold, sea monsters breeding, fighting, devouring, and passing away. And from the monsters, as the play unfolded itself, Man was born, with the power of thought, the knowledge of good and

* Reprinted from *Leda* by Aldous Huxley, by permission of Harper & Brothers.
† Reprinted from *Sceptical Essays* by Bertrand Russell by permission of W. W. Norton & Company, Inc. Copyright 1928 by Bertrand Russell.

evil, and the cruel thirst for worship. And Man saw that all is passing in this mad, monstrous world, that all is struggling to snatch, at any cost, a few brief moments of life before Death's inexorable decree. And Man said: 'There is a hidden purpose, could we but fathom it, and the purpose is good; for we must reverence something, and in the visible world there is nothing worthy of reverence.' And Man stood aside from the struggle, resolving that God intended harmony to come out of chaos by human efforts. And when he followed the instincts which God had transmitted to him from his ancestry of beasts of prey, he called it Sin, and asked God to forgive him. But he doubted whether he could be justly forgiven, until he invented a divine Plan by which God's wrath was to have been appeased. And seeing the present was bad, he made it yet worse, that thereby the future might be better. And he gave God thanks for the strength that enabled him to forgo even the joys that were possible. And God smiled; and when he saw that Man had become perfect in renunciation and worship he sent another sun through the sky, which crashed into Man's sun; and all returned again to nebula.

" 'Yes,' he murmured, 'it was a good play; I will have it performed again.' "

Such, in outline, but even more purposeless, more void of meaning, is the world which Science presents for our belief. Amid such a world, if anywhere, our ideals henceforward must find a home. That Man is the product of causes which had no prevision of the end they were achieving; that his origin, his growth, his hopes and fears, his loves and his beliefs, are but the outcome of accidental collocations of atoms; that no fire, no heroism, no intensity of thought and feeling, can preserve an individual life beyond the grave; that all the labors of the ages, all the devotion, all the inspiration, all the noonday brightness of human genius, are destined to extinction in the vast death of the solar system, and that the whole temple of Man's achievement must inevitably be buried beneath the debris of a universe in ruins— all these things, if not quite beyond dispute, are yet so nearly certain, that no philosophy which rejects them can hope to stand. Only within the scaffolding of these truths, only on the firm foundation of unyielding despair, can the soul's habitation henceforth be safely built.

How, in such an alien and inhuman world, can so powerless a creature as Man preserve his aspirations untarnished? A strange mystery it is that Nature, omnipotent but blind, in the revolutions of her secular hurryings through the abysses of space, has brought forth at last a child, subject still to her power, but gifted with sight, with knowledge of good and evil, with the capacity of judging all the works of his unthinking Mother. In spite of Death, the mark and seal of the parental control, Man is yet free, during his brief years, to examine, to criticize, to know, and in imagination to create. To him alone, in the world with which he is acquainted, this freedom belongs; and in this lies his superiority to the resistless forces that control his outward life.

The savage, like ourselves, feels the oppression of his impotence before the powers of Nature; but having in himself nothing that he respects more than Power, he is willing to prostrate himself before his gods, without inquiring whether they are worthy of his worship. Pathetic and very terrible is the long history of cruelty and torture, of degradation and human sacrifice, endured in the hope of placating the jealous gods: surely, the trembling believer thinks, when what is most precious has been freely given, their lust for blood must be appeased, and more will not be required. The religion of Moloch—as such creeds may be generically called—is in essence the cringing submission of the slave, who dare not, even in his heart, allow the thought that his master deserves no adulation. Since the independence of ideals is not yet acknowledged, Power may be freely worshiped, and receive an unlimited respect, despite its wanton infliction of pain.

But gradually, as morality grows bolder, the claim of the ideal world begins to be felt; and worship, if it is not to cease, must be given to gods of another kind than those created by the savage. Some, though they feel the demands of the ideal, will still consciously reject them, still urging that naked Power is worthy of worship. Such is the attitude inculcated in God's answer to Job out of the whirlwind: the divine power and knowledge are paraded, but of the divine goodness there is no hint. Such also is the attitude of those who, in our own day, base their morality upon the struggle for survival, maintaining that the survivors are necessarily the fittest. But others, not content with an answer so repugnant to the moral sense, will adopt the position which we have become accustomed to regard as specially religious, maintaining that, in some hidden manner, the world of fact is really harmonious with the world of ideals. Thus Man creates God, all-powerful and all-good, the mystic unity of what is and what should be.

But the world of fact, after all, is not good; and, in submitting our judgment to it, there is an element of slavishness from which our thoughts must be purged. For in all things it is well to exalt the dignity of Man, by freeing him as far as possible from the tyranny of nonhuman Power. When we have realized that Power is largely bad, that man, with his knowledge of good and evil, is but a helpless atom in a world which has no such knowledge, the choice is again presented to us: Shall we worship Force, or shall we worship Goodness? Shall our God exist and be evil, or shall he be recognized as the creation of our own conscience?

The answer to this question is very momentous, and affects profoundly our whole morality. The worship of Force, to which Carlyle and Nietzsche and the creed of Militarism have accustomed us, is the result of failure to maintain our own ideals against a hostile universe: it is itself a prostrate submission to evil, a sacrifice of our best to Moloch. If strength indeed is to be respected, let us respect rather the strength of those who refuse that false "recognition of facts" which fails to recognize that facts are often bad. Let us admit that, in the world we know, there are many things that would be better otherwise, and that the ideals to which we do and must adhere are not realized in the realm of matter. Let us preserve our respect for truth, for beauty, for the ideal of perfection which life does not permit us to attain, though none of these things meet with the approval of the unconscious universe. If Power is bad, as it seems to be, let us reject it from our hearts. In this lies Man's true freedom: in determination to worship only the God created by our own love of the good, to respect only the heaven which inspires the insight of our best moments. In action, in desire, we must submit perpetually to the tyranny of outside forces; but in thought, in aspiration, we are free, free from our fellow-men, free from the petty planet on which our bodies impotently crawl, free even, while we live, from the tyranny of death. Let us learn, then, that energy of faith which enables us to live constantly in the vision of the good; and let us descend, in action, into the world of fact, with that vision always before us.

When first the opposition of fact and ideal grows fully visible, a spirit of fiery revolt, of fierce hatred of the gods, seems necessary to the assertion of freedom. To defy with Promethean constancy a hostile universe, to keep its evil always in view, always actively hated, to refuse no pain that the malice of Power can invent, appears to be the duty of all who will not bow before the inevitable. But indignation is still a bondage, for it compels our thoughts to be occupied with an evil world; and in the fierceness of desire from which rebellion springs there is a kind of self-assertion which it is necessary for the wise to overcome. Indignation is a submission of our thoughts, but not of our desires; the Stoic freedom in which wisdom consists is found in the submission of our desires, but not of our thoughts. From the submission of our desires springs the virtue of resignation; from the freedom of our thoughts springs the whole world of art and philosophy, and the vision of beauty by which, at last, we half reconquer the reluctant world. But the vision of beauty is possible only to unfettered contemplation, to thoughts not weighted by the load of eager wishes; and thus Freedom comes only to those who no longer ask of life that it shall yield them any of those personal goods that are subject to the mutations of Time.

Although the necessity of renunciation is evidence of the existence of evil, yet Christianity, in preaching it, has shown a wisdom exceeding that of the Promethean philosophy of rebellion. It must be admitted that, of the things we desire, some, though they prove impossible, are yet real goods; others, however, as ardently longed for, do not form part of a fully purified ideal. The belief that what must be renounced is bad, though sometimes false, is far less often false than untamed passion supposes; and the creed of religion, by providing a reason for proving that is never false, has been the means of purifying our hopes by the discovery of many austere truths.

But there is in resignation a further good element: even real goods, when they are unattainable, ought not to be fretfully desired. To every man comes, sooner or later, the great renunciation. For the young, there is nothing unattainable; a good thing desired with the whole force of a passionate will, and yet impossible, is to them not credible. Yet, by death, by illness, by poverty, or by the voice of duty, we must learn, each one of us, that the world was not made for us, and that, however beautiful may be the things we crave, Fate may nevertheless forbid them. It is the part of courage, when misfortune comes, to bear without repining the ruin of our hopes, to turn away our thoughts from vain regrets. This degree of submission to Power is not only just and right: it is the very gate of wisdom.

But passive renunciation is not the whole of wisdom; for not by renunciation alone can we build a temple for the worship of our own ideals. Haunting foreshadowings of the temple appear in the realm of imagination, in music, in architecture, in the untroubled kingdom of reason, and in the golden sunset magic of lyrics, where beauty shines and glows, remote from the touch of sorrow, remote from the fear of change, remote from the failures and disenchantments of the world of fact. In the contemplation of these things the vision of heaven will shape itself in our hearts, giving at once a touchstone to judge the world about us, and an inspiration by which to fashion to our needs whatever is incapable of serving as a stone in the sacred temple.

Except for those rare spirits that are born without sin, there is a cavern of darkness to be traversed before that temple can be entered. The gate of the cavern is despair, and its floor is paved with the gravestones of abandoned hopes. There Self must die; there the eagerness, the greed of untamed desire must be slain, for only so can the soul be freed from the empire of Fate. But out of the cavern the Gate of Renunciation leads again to the daylight of wisdom, by whose radiance a new insight, a new joy, a new tenderness, shine forth to gladden the pilgrim's heart.

When, without the bitterness of impotent rebellion, we have learnt both to resign ourselves to the outward rule of Fate and to recognize that the nonhuman world is unworthy of our worship, it becomes possible at last so to transform and refashion the unconscious universe, so to transmute it in the crucible of imagination that a new image of shining gold replaces the old idol of clay. In all the multiform facts of the world—in the visual shapes of trees and mountains and clouds, in the events of the life of man, even in the very omnipotence of Death—the insight of creative idealism can find the reflection of a beauty which its own thoughts first made. In this way mind asserts its subtle mastery over the thoughtless forces of Nature. The more evil the material with which it deals, the more thwarting to untrained desire, the greater is its achievement in inducing the reluctant rock to yield up its hidden treasures, the prouder its victory in compelling the opposing forces to swell the pageant of its triumph.   Of all the arts, Tragedy is the proudest, the most triumphant; for it builds its shining citadel in the very center of the enemy's country, on the very summit of his highest mountain; from its impregnable watch-towers, his camps and arsenals, his columns and forts, are all revealed; within its walls the free life continues, while the legions of Death and Pain and Despair, and all the servile captains of tyrant Fate, afford the burghers of that dauntless city new spectacles of beauty.   Happy those sacred ramparts, thrice happy the dwellers on that all-seeing eminence.   Honor to those brave warriors who, through countless ages of warfare, have preserved for us the priceless heritage of liberty, and have kept undefiled by sacrilegious invaders the home of the unsubdued.

But the beauty of Tragedy does but make visible a quality which, in more or less obvious shapes, is present always and everywhere in life.   In the spectacle of Death, in the endurance of intolerable pain, and in the irrevocableness of a vanished past, there is a sacredness, an overpowering awe, a feeling of the vastness, the depth, the inexhaustible mystery of existence, in which, as by some strange marriage of pain, the sufferer is bound to the world by bonds of sorrow.   In these moments of insight, we lose all eagerness of temporary desire, all struggling and striving for petty ends, all care for the little trivial things that, to a superficial view, make up the common life of day by day; we see, surrounding the narrow raft illumined by the flickering light of human comradeship, the dark ocean on whose rolling waves we toss for a brief hour; from the great night without, a chill blast breaks in upon our refuge; all the loneliness of humanity amid hostile forces is concentrated upon the individual soul, which must struggle alone, with what of courage it can command, against the whole weight of a universe that cares nothing for its hopes and fears. Victory, in this struggle with the powers of darkness, is the true baptism into the glorious company of heroes, the true initiation into the overmastering beauty of human existence.   From that awful encounter of the soul with the outer world, enunciation, wisdom, and charity are born; and with their birth a new life begins. To take into the inmost shrine of the soul the irresistible forces whose puppets we seem to be—Death and change, the irrevocableness of the past, and the powerlessness of man before the blind hurry of the universe from vanity to vanity—to feel these things and know them is to conquer them.

This is the reason why the Past has such magical power.   The beauty of its motionless and silent pictures is like the enchanted purity of late autumn, when the leaves, though one breath would make them fall, still glow against the sky in golden glory.   The Past does not change or strive; like Duncan, after life's fitful fever it sleeps well; what was eager and grasping, what was petty and transitory, has faded away, the things that were beautiful and eternal shine out of it like stars in the night.   Its beauty, to a soul not worthy of it, is unendurable; but to a soul which has conquered Fate it is the key of religion.

The life of Man, viewed outwardly, is but a small thing in comparison with the forces of Nature.   The slave is doomed to worship Time and Fate and Death, because they are greater than anything he finds in himself and because all his thoughts are of things which they devour.   But, great as they are, to think of them greatly, to feel their passionless splendor, is greater still.   And such thought makes us free men; we no longer bow before the inevitable in Oriental subjection, but we absorb it, and make it a part of ourselves.   To abandon the struggle for private happiness, to expel all eagerness of temporary desire, to burn with passion for eternal things— this is emancipation, and this is the free man's worship.   And this liberation is effected by a contemplation of Fate; for Fate itself is subdued by the mind which leaves nothing to be purged by the purifying fire of Time.

United with his fellow-men by the strongest of all ties, the tie of a common doom, the free man finds that a new vision is with him always, shedding over every daily task the light of love.   The life of Man is a long march through the night, surrounded by invisible foes, tortured by weariness and pain, towards a goal that few can hope to reach, and where none may tarry long.   One by one, as they march, our comrades vanish from our sight, seized by the silent orders of omnipotent Death. Very brief is the time in which we can help them, in which their happiness or misery is decided.   Be it ours to shed sunshine on their path, to lighten their sorrows by the balm of sympathy, to give them the pure joy of a never-tiring affection, to strengthen failing courage, to instil faith in hours of despair.   Let us not weigh in grudging scales their merits and demerits, but let us think only of their need—of the sorrows, the difficulties, perhaps the blindnesses, that make the misery of their lives; let us remember that they are fellow-sufferers in the same darkness, actors in the same tragedy with ourselves.   And so, when their day is over, when their good and their evil have become eternal by the immortality of the past, be it ours to feel that, where they suffered, where they failed, no deed of ours was the cause; but wherever a spark of the divine fire kindled in their hearts, we were ready with encouragement, with sympathy, with brave words in which high courage glowed.

Brief and powerless is Man's life; on him and all his race the slow, sure doom falls pitiless and dark.   Blind to good and evil, reckless of destruction, omnipotent matter rolls on its relentless way; for Man, condemned today to lose his dearest, tomorrow himself to pass through the gate of darkness, it remains only to cherish ere yet the blow falls, the lofty thoughts that ennoble his little day; disdaining the coward terrors of the slave of Fate, to worship at the shrine that his own hands have built; undismayed by the empire of chance, to preserve a mind free from the wanton tyranny that rules his outward life; proudly defiant of the irresistible forces that tolerate, for a moment, his knowledge and his condemnation, to sustain alone, a weary but unyielding Atlas, the world that his own ideals have fashioned despite the trampling march of unconscious power.

LINES WRITTEN AFTER CLASS IN PHILOSOPHY 100

CHARLOTTE ROSS

And when the universe is dead,
What then, my brother, can be said
Of Life, of Death, Eternity,
And things when none is left to see?
The light is dimmed; the star grows dark—
And all is ended with a spark.
The universe is cold and bare—
The mind of man, no longer there.
The questing, puzzled strife is gone;
No new tomorrows ever dawn.
Time whirls unlimited through Space,
No thought is left to give it chase.
As on the cooling planet rolls,
Devoid of all its festering souls,
And in the infinite grown cold—
What are the answers left untold?

CHAPTER 14

THE HUMANIST WAY OF LIFE

Know, man hath all which nature hath, but more,
And in that *more* lie all his hopes of good.

—Matthew Arnold, "To an Independent Preacher."

Modern philosophical humanism, sometimes called humanistic naturalism, new humanism, or scientific humanism, must not be confused with Renaissance humanism. Renaissance humanism, though reviving men's interest in the classical values of beauty, order, and reason, was, as Douglas Bush has emphasized, broadly Christian in its central tradition. The new humanism, however, though accepting the values of the Greek and Roman civilization as an important part of its own tradition, is basically anti-theistic.

Aware, as people have long been, of the notable liberalization of man's idea of God from a tribal deity requiring human sacrifice down through the hard, even if magnificent, personal God of Jacob to the gentler concept of the Christian God of mercy, and the further liberalization of that God by many churchmen from an anthropomorphic concept to a beneficent Spirit or mystic Idea (foreshadowed in our thinking by the splendid Anglo-Saxon abstraction of his name—The Good), the humanists have concluded that our concepts of God are man-created. They share with the naturalists the conviction that nature, uncreated and self-perpetuating, is the source of all being, though they would not agree with the mechanistic assumption that all our actions are determined. But the humanist, though discarding the idea of God, does not discard religion. Instead he tends to make a religion of the scientific, social, and aesthetic aspirations of men—a "religion without God," a religion of conduct.

Something of the ferment in men's minds that has produced this way of thinking may be seen in the selections from *Erewhon* that open this chapter. In pointed satire Butler attacks traditional religious views by examining the religion of Erewhon (Nowhere), a land where values are deified and personalized, since, the natives ask, "Who ever heard . . . of such things as kindly training, a good example, an enlightened regard to one's own welfare, being able to keep men straight?" Important in Butler's argument for the humanist way of life is the view that conventional religion tends to "cheapen this present life," is "an impatient cutting, so to speak, of the Gordian knot of life's problems. . . ."

Thus we see, as Masefield remarks, that "man probes for new controls." The old gods are gone, and man, "in his cage of many-millioned pain Burns all to ash to prove if God remain." There is no God, Masefield concludes, but the unity of things: "we, who breathe the air, Are God ourselves and touch God everywhere." Man is alone in the universe; we are our only friends, as Swinburne tells us: "only souls that keep their place By their own light, and watch things roll, And stand, have light for any soul." Moreover, in us, as Humbert Wolfe says, the universe has its growth. Just as the ape (let the symbol stand for the cousin-creature out of whom it is theorized that man developed) aspired to shape man, so man may refashion his idea of God in the image of his own improved being yet to be realized.

Humanism, then, is seen to put heavy stress on conduct. True worship becomes virtuous action—a moral value stressed also by traditional religion, but not equated with itself as it is in humanism. This matter of conduct is also the special concern of literary humanism, a form of humanism (represented by Irving Babbitt and Paul Elmer More) which has its roots in the values of Renaissance humanism and which does not repudiate traditional religion. Correct behavior for a humanist, Babbitt says, must be based on decorum, a sense of proportion. "The virtue that results from a right cultivation of one's humanity, in other words, from moderate and decorous living, is poise."

One of the many questions Babbitt's thoughtful essay elicits is the following: Can humanism be a popular belief (even if limited, as in Babbitt's study, to matters of conduct)? Just how the crowd would feel toward the exclusiveness implied here is visualized by John Davidson in "They Mocked Me." And this exclusiveness of humanism is the concern of Archibald MacLeish, who observes that humanism from this point of view would appear to be anti-democratic, a doctrine opposed to democracy "because excellence, not equality, is its goal and purpose." He insists that if humanism will make itself the "instrument of the renaissance of man, its place, not only in the universities but in the world, is sure." But to make it an effective instrument, humanists must believe in man. "It is necessary to believe in man, not only as the Christians believe in man, out of pity, or as the democrats believe in man, out of loyalty, but also as the Greeks believed in man, out of pride."

Religion also needs the regeneration that humanism can give. In a stimulating appraisal of the functions of philosophy, humanism, science, and religion, Eliot emphasizes the dependence of the four on one another: "Humanism can offer neither the intellectual discipline of philosophy or of science (two different disciplines), nor the emotional discipline of religion. On the other hand, these other activities depend upon humanism to preserve their sanity" (*Religion Without Humanism*). Eliot is dismayed by the tendency of these great motivations of humanity towards flinging away from their interdependence and attempting to serve as the whole meaning of things, whereas they are only parts.   Santayana's reflections prick the bubble of man's pretensions at this point.

"And where are we going?" asks King in *Key Largo*.   And d'Alcala replies, "To a conquest of all there is, whatever there is among the suns and stars." The same person also expresses for Anderson the high hope of humanism: "There'll be a race of men who can face even the stars without despair, and think without going mad."

Whatever humanism may lack as a guide for men, it is a stirring doctrine of faith in the future.   As Yerington, citing Bergson, puts it, "The mightiest of all revolutions in thought is upon us—the idea of the Open Future. . . . God, even God, is just a stupendous becoming: 'he is unceasing life, action, freedom.' . . . Life is a perpetual aspiration, an eternally creative Ongoing, an everlasting Newness."   Particularly appealing is the stress on self-realization: "Man is a brute becoming free spirit.   He is neither bad nor good; he is growing to good.   We think that life is animal in its origin and supernatural in its goal."   Dean Inge tempers our enthusiasm, however, by the sobering reminder that, "It is not certain that there has been much change in our intellectual and moral endowments since pithecanthropus dropped the first half of his name."   H. G. Wells, though acknowledging this gloomy truth, still recalls us to the humanist vision of the "coming City of Mankind."

FROM EREWHON, Chapters 16, 17
SAMUEL BUTLER

They were idolaters, though of a comparatively enlightened kind; but here, as in other things, there was a discrepancy between their professed and actual belief, for they had a genuine and potent faith which existed without recognition alongside of their idol worship.

The gods whom they worship openly are personifications of human qualities, as justice, strength, hope, fear, love, &c., &c.   The people think that prototypes of these have a real objective existence in a region far beyond the clouds, holding, as did the ancients, that they are like men and women both in body and passion, except that they are even comelier and more powerful, and also that they can render themselves invisible to human eyesight.   They are capable of being propitiated by mankind and of coming to the assistance of those who ask their aid.   Their interest in human affairs is keen, and on the whole beneficent; but they become very angry if neglected, and punish rather the first they come upon, than the actual person who has offended them; their fury being blind when it is raised, though never raised without reason.   They will not punish with any less severity when people sin against them from ignorance, and without the chance of having had knowledge; they will take no excuses of this kind, but are even as the English law, which assumes itself to be known to every one.

Thus they have a law that two pieces of matter may not occupy the same space at the same moment, which law is presided over and administered by the gods of time and space jointly, so that if a flying stone and a man's head attempt to outrage these gods, by "arrogating a right which they do not possess" (for so it is written in one of their books), and to occupy the same space simultaneously, a severe punishment, sometimes even death itself, is sure to follow, without any regard to whether the stone knew that the man's head was there, or the head the stone; this at least is their view of the common accidents of life. Moreover, they hold their deities to be quite regardless of motives. With them it is the thing done which is everything, and the motive goes for nothing.

Thus they hold it strictly forbidden for a man to go without common air in his lungs for more than a very few minutes; and if by any chance he gets into the water, the air-god is very angry, and will not suffer it; no matter whether the man got into the water by accident or on purpose, whether through the attempt to save a child or through presumptuous contempt of the air-god, the air-god will kill him, unless he keeps his head high enough out of the water, and thus gives the air-god his due.

This with regard to the deities who manage physical affairs. Over and above these they personify hope, fear, love, and so forth, giving them temples and priests, and carving likenesses of them in stone, which they verily believe to be faithful representations of living beings who are only not human in being more than human. If any one denies the objective existence of these divinities, and says that there is really no such being as a beautiful woman called Justice, with her eyes blinded and a pair of scales, positively living and moving in a remote and ethereal region, but that justice is only the personified expression of certain modes of human thought and action—they say that he denies the existence of justice in denying her personality, and that he is a wanton disturber of men's religious convictions. They detest nothing so much as any attempt to lead them to higher spiritual conceptions of the deities whom they profess to worship. Arowhena and I had a pitched battle on this point, and should have had many more but for my prudence in allowing her to get the better of me.

I am sure that in her heart she was suspicious of her own position for she returned more than once to the subject. "Can you not see," I had exclaimed, "that the fact of justice being admirable will not be affected by the absence of a belief in her being also a living agent? Can you really think that men will be one whit less hopeful, because they no longer believe that hope is an actual person?" She shook her head, and said that with men's belief in the personality all incentive to the reverence of the thing itself, as justice or hope, would cease; men from that hour would never be either just or hopeful again.

I could not move her, nor, indeed, did I seriously wish to do so. She deferred to me in most things, but she never shrank from maintaining her opinions if they were put in question; nor does she to this day abate one jot of her belief in the religion of her childhood, though in compliance with my repeated entreaties she has allowed herself to be baptized into the English Church. She has, however, made a gloss upon her original faith to the effect that her baby and I are the only human beings exempt from the vengeance of the deities for not believing in their personality. She is quite clear that we are exempted. She should never have so strong a conviction of it otherwise. How it has come about she does not know, neither does she wish to know; there are things which it is better not to know and this is one of them; but when I tell her that I believe in her deities as much as she does—and that it is a difference about words, not things, she becomes silent with a slight emphasis.

I own that she very nearly conquered me once; for she asked me what I should think if she were to tell me that my God, whose nature and attributes I had been explaining to her, was but the expression for man's highest conception of goodness, wisdom, and power; that in order to generate a more vivid conception of so great and glorious a thought, man had personified it and called it by a name; that it was an unworthy conception of the Deity to hold Him personal, inasmuch as escape from human contingencies became thus impossible; that the real thing men should worship was the Divine, whereinsoever they could find it; that "God" was but man's way of expressing his sense of the Divine; that as justice, hope, wisdom, &c., were all parts of goodness, so God was the expression which embraced all goodness and all good power; that people would no more cease to love God on ceasing to believe in His objective personality, than they had ceased to love justice on discovering that she was not really personal; nay, that they would never truly love Him till they saw Him thus.

She said all this in her artless way, and with none of the coherence with which I have here written it; her face kindled, and she felt sure that she had convinced me that I was wrong, and that justice was a living person. Indeed I did wince a little; but I recovered myself immediately, and pointed out to her that we had books whose genuineness was beyond all possibility of doubt, as they were certainly none of them less than 1,800 years old; that in these there were the most authentic accounts of men who had been spoken to by the Deity Himself, and of one prophet who had been allowed to see the back parts of God through the hand that was laid over his face.

This was conclusive; and I spoke with such solemnity that she was a little frightened, and only answered that they too had their books, in which their ancestors had seen the gods; on which I saw that further argument was not at all likely to convince her; and fearing that she might tell her mother what I had been saying, and that I might lose the hold upon her affections which I was beginning to feel pretty sure that I was obtaining, I began to let her have her own way, and to convince me; neither till after we were safely married did I show the cloven hoof again.

Nevertheless, her remarks have haunted me, and I have since met with many very godly people who have had a great knowledge of divinity, but no sense of the divine; and again, I have seen a radiance upon the face of those who were worshiping the divine either in art or nature—in picture or statue—in field or cloud or sea—in man, woman, or child—which I have never seen kindled by any talking about the nature and attributes of God. Mention but the word divinity, and our sense of the divine is clouded.

.   .   .   .

I could not conceive why they should not openly acknowledge high Ydgrunism, and discard the objective personality of hope, justice, &c.; but whenever I so much as hinted at this, I found that I was on dangerous ground. They would never have it; returning constantly to the assertion that ages ago the divinities were frequently seen, and that the moment their personality was disbelieved in, men would leave off practicing even those ordinary virtues which the common experience of mankind has agreed on as being the greatest secret of happiness. "Who ever heard," they asked, indignantly, "of such things as kindly training, a good example, and an enlightened regard to one's own welfare, being able to keep men straight?" In my hurry, forgetting things which I ought to have remembered, I answered that if a person could not be kept straight by these things, there was nothing that could straighten him, and that if he were not ruled by the love and fear of men whom he had seen, neither would he be so by that of the gods whom he had not seen.

At one time indeed I came upon a small but growing sect who believed, after a fashion, in the immortality of the soul and the resurrection from the dead; they taught that those who had been born with feeble and diseased bodies and had passed their lives in ailing, would be tortured eternally hereafter; but that those who had been born strong and healthy and handsome would be rewarded for ever and ever. Of moral qualities or conduct they made no mention.

Bad as this was, it was a step in advance, inasmuch as they did hold out a future state of some sort, and I was shocked to find that for the most part they met with opposition, on the score that their doctrine was based upon no sort of foundation, also that it was immoral in its tendency, and not to be desired by any reasonable beings.

When I asked how it could be immoral, I was answered that, if firmly held, it would lead people to cheapen this present life, making it appear to be an affair of only secondary importance; that it would thus distract men's minds from the perfecting of this world's economy, and was an impatient cutting, so to speak, of the Gordian knot of life's problems, whereby some people might gain present satisfaction to themselves at the cost of infinite damage to others; that the doctrine tended to encourage the poor in their improvidence, and in a debasing acquiescence in ills which they might well remedy; that the rewards were illusory and the result, after all, of luck, whose empire should be bounded by the grave; that its terrors were enervating and unjust; and that even the most blessed rising would be but the disturbing of a still more blessed slumber.

To all which I could only say that the thing had been actually known to happen, and that there were several well-authenticated instances of people having died and come to life again—instances which no man in his senses could doubt.

"If this be so," said my opponent, "we must bear it as best we may."

I then translated for him, as well as I could, the noble speech of Hamlet in which he says that it is the fear lest worse evils may befall us after death which alone prevents us from rushing into death's arms.

"Nonsense," he answered, "no man was ever yet stopped from cutting his throat by any such fears as your poet ascribes to him—and your poet probably knew this perfectly well. If a man cuts his throat he is at bay, and thinks of nothing but escape, no matter whither, provided he can shuffle off his present. No. Men are kept at their posts, not by the fear that if they quit them they may quit a frying-pan for a fire, but by the hope that if they hold on, the fire may burn less fiercely. 'The respect,' to quote your poet, 'that makes calamity of so long a life,' is the consideration that though calamity may live long, the sufferer may live longer still."

On this, seeing that there was little probability of our coming to an agreement, I let the argument drop, and my opponent presently left me with as much disapprobation as he could show without being overtly rude.

"NOT THAT THE STARS ARE ALL GONE MAD IN HEAVEN"

In *Sonnets*

JOHN MASEFIELD

Not that the stars are all gone mad in heaven
Plucking the unseen reins upon men's souls,
Not that the law that bound the planets seven
Is discord now; man probes for new controls.
He bends no longer to the circling stars,
New moon and full moon and the living sun,
Love-making Venus, Jove and bloody Mars
Pass from their thrones, their rule of him is done.

And paler gods, made liker men, are past,
Like their sick eras to their funeral urns,
They cannot stand the fire blown by the blast
In which man's soul that measures heaven burns.
Man in his cage of many millioned pain
Burns all to ash to prove if God remain.

There is no God, as I was taught in youth,
Though each, according to his stature, builds
Some covered shrine for what he thinks the truth,
Which day by day his reddest heart-blood gilds.
There is no God; but death, the clasping sea,
In which we move like fish, deep over deep
Made of men's souls that bodies have set free,
Floods to a Justice though it seems asleep.
There is no God, but still, behind the veil,
The hurt thing works, out of its agony.
Still, like a touching of a brimming Grail,
Return the pennies given to passers-by.
There is no God, but we, who breathe the air,
Are God ourselves and touch God everywhere.

FROM PRELUDE

ALGERNON CHARLES SWINBURNE

Because man's soul is man's God still,
What wind soever waft his will
   Across the waves of day and night
   To port or shipwreck, left or right,
By shores and shoals of good and ill;
   And still its flame at mainmast height
Through the rent air that foam-flakes fill
Sustains the indomitable light
Whence only man hath strength to steer
Or helm to handle without fear.

Save his own soul's light overhead,
None leads him, and none ever led,
   Across birth's hidden harbor-bar,
   Past youth where shoreward shallows are,
Through age that drives on toward the red
   Vast void of sunset hailed from far,
To the equal waters of the dead;
   Save his own soul he hath no star,
And sinks, except his own soul guide,
Helmless in middle turn of tide.

No blast of air or fire of sun
Puts out the light whereby we run
   With girded loins our lamplit race,
   And each from each takes heart of grace

And spirit till his turn be done,
   And light of face from each man's face
In whom the light of trust is one;
   Since only souls that keep their place
By their own light, and watch things roll,
And stand, have light for any soul.

FROM THE TEACHER

HUMBERT WOLFE

This I believe:
that if I do not will
the Universe stands still.
I and those of whom I am the part
built it and changed it in our heart,
not out of mud, nor stone, nor seas,
but out of that in which all these
begin, are all, and naught—
the deep desiring thought.

This I believe:
The ape
of which I wear the shape
tumbled in me—his Hell—
a furry archangel,
and, with the only skill he had,
swung with one pitiful blackpad
into the jungle of my will
desiring, till
with a final stroke
he tore his prison-vesture off, and spoke.
He threw aside, because he willed,
the coat that clamped and killed,
and shall he not assume, if he have striven,
when all is done, investiture in heaven?

This I believe:
I am the ape
that God made in His shape,
and who, when he has changed all this,
will at the last refashion God in his.

FROM HUMANISM: AN ESSAY AT DEFINITION *

IRVING BABBITT

As is well known, the word humanist was applied, first in the Italy of the fifteenth century, and later in other European countries, to the type of scholar who was not only proficient in Greek and Latin, but who at the same time inclined to prefer the humanity of the great classical writers to what seemed to him the excess of divinity in the mediaevals. This contrast between humanity and divinity was often con-

* From *Humanism in America*. Edited by Norman Foerster. Copyright, 1930, by Rinehart & Company, Inc. and reprinted with their permission.

ceived very superficially. However, the best of the humanists were not content with opposing a somewhat external imitation of the Ciceronian or Virgilian elegance to the scholastic carelessness of form. They actually caught a glimpse of the fine proportionateness of the ancients at their best. They were thus encouraged to aim at a harmonious development of their faculties in this world rather than at an otherworldly felicity. Each faculty, they held, should be cultivated in due measure without one-sidedness or over-emphasis, whether that of the ascetic or that of the specialist. "Nothing too much" is indeed the central maxim of all genuine humanists, ancient and modern.

In a world of ever-shifting circumstance, this maxim is not always of easy application. Whoever has succeeded in bridging the gap between the general precept and some particular emergency has to that extent achieved the fitting and the decorous. Decorum is simply the law of measure in its more concrete aspects. For every type of humanist decorum is, in Milton's phrase, the "grand masterpiece to observe." Actually this observation may rest on deep insight, as it did in the case of Milton himself, or it may degenerate into empty formalism. The adjustment of which I have spoken between the variable and the permanent elements in human experience requires spiritual effort and most men are spiritually indolent. For genuine adjustment they tend to substitute outer conformity so that decorum itself finally comes to seem a mere veneer, something that has no deep root in the nature of things. Moreover the notions of decent behavior to which men have conformed at any particular period have always been more or less local and relative. It is easy to take the next step and assume that they have been *only* local and relative, an assumption subversive not merely of decorum but of humanism itself. Humanism, one of our modernists has argued, may have done very well for other times and places, but under existing circumstances, it is at best likely to prove only a "noble anachronism." A similar objection to humanism is that it has its source in a psychology of "escape," that it is an attempt to take flight from the present into a past that has for the modern man become impossible. But humanism is not to be identified with this or that body of traditional precepts. The law of measure on which it depends becomes meaningless unless it can be shown to be one of the "laws unwritten in the heavens" of which Antigone had the immediate perception, laws that are "not of today or yesterday," that transcend in short the temporal process. The final appeal of the humanist is not to any historical convention but to intuition.

It does not follow that the humanist is ready to abandon history to the relativist. The main conventions that have prevailed in the past reveal important identities as well as differences. These identities cannot be explained as due to their common derivation from some previous convention. The Chinese made an independent discovery of the law of measure. An important task, indeed, that awaits some properly qualified scholar, preferably a Chinese, is a comparison of Confucian humanism with occidental humanism as it appears, for example, in the *Ethics* of Aristotle. The announcement was made recently in the press that a Harvard astronomer had discovered the "center of the universe" (more strictly the center of our galactic system). In the meanwhile the far more important question is being neglected whether human nature itself has any center. One's faith in the existence of such a center increases when one finds the best commentary on Pascal's dictum that the great man is he who combines in himself opposite virtues and occupies all the space between them, in a Confucian book the very title of which, literally rendered, means the "universal norm" or "center." Here and elsewhere the Confucian books reveal a deep and direct insight into the law of measure. Legge's translation of the Chinese word for decorum (*li*) as "the rules of propriety" has been rightly censured as unduly prim and formalistic; though it must be admitted that a formalistic element is very marked at times even in the older Confucian writings.

Practically the assertion of a "universal center" means the setting up of some pattern or model for imitation. The idea of imitation goes even deeper than that of decorum, but is an idea that humanism shares with religion. Humanism, however, differs from religion in putting at the basis of the pattern it sets up, not man's divinity, but the something in his nature that sets him apart simply as man from other animals and that Cicero defines as a "sense of order and decorum and measure in deeds and words." It dwells on the danger of any attempt to pass too abruptly to the religious level; it holds, if I may be pardoned for quoting myself, that the world would have been a better place if more persons had made sure they were human before setting out to be superhuman. The virtue that results from a right cultivation of one's humanity, in other words from moderate and decorous living, is poise. Perfect poise is no doubt impossible: not even Sophocles succeeded in seeing life steadily and seeing it whole. The difference is none the less marked between the man who is moving towards poise and the man who is moving away from it. Since the break with the somewhat artificial decorum of the eighteenth century most men have been moving away from it. It would not be easy to argue with any plausibility that the typical modernist is greatly concerned with the law of measure; his interest, as a glance at our newspapers should suffice to show, is rather in the doing of stunts and the breaking of records, in "prodigies, feats of strength and crime," the very topics that, according to the traditional report, Confucius banished from his conversation. "Let us confess it," says Nietzsche, speaking not merely for the rank and file but for the leaders, "proportionateness is foreign to us." It is foreign to us because we no longer refer our experience to any center. With the growth of the naturalistic temper, the normal has come to have less appeal than the novel. The pursuit of poise has tended to give way to that of uniqueness, spontaneity, and above all intensity. "The last remnant of God on earth," says Nietzsche himself, "are the men of great longing, of great loathing, of great satiety." Once grant that there is no constant element in life, and one might agree with Walter Pater that a man's highest ambition should be "to burn with a hard gemlike flame," to get "as many pulsations as possible into the given time." Aesthetic perceptiveness is an excellent thing, but thus to set it up as an end in itself is almost at the opposite pole from humanism. Yet Pater has been called a humanist. One might so regard him if one accepted his view that the distinctive humanistic trait is an all-embracing curiosity. Humanism appears primarily, not in the enlargement of comprehension and sympathy, desirable though this enlargement may be, but in the act of selection, in the final imposition on mere multiplicity of a scale of values. Matthew Arnold, with his striving for centrality, has far better claims to be regarded as a humanist than Pater—and that in spite of his inadequacy on the side of religion. The model that Arnold sets up for imitation in the name of culture is a constant corrective of everything that is one-sided and out of proportion. "I hate," he says, speaking not only for himself but for all true humanists, "all over-preponderance of single elements."

.   .   .   .

The reason for the radical clash between the humanist and the purely naturalistic philosopher is that the humanist requires a center to which he may refer the manifold of experience; and this the phenomenal world does not supply. In getting his center the humanist may appeal primarily to tradition, or as I have said, to intuition. In the latter case he will need to submit to a searching Socratic dialectic the word intuition itself—to distinguish between intuitions of the One and intuitions

of the Many.   Otherwise he will run the risk of not being a modern but only a
modernist.   The contrast between modern and modernist is not unlike that between Socrates and the sophists.   Both modern and modernist are under compulsion to accept in some form the ancient maxim that man is the measure of all
things.   Only, the measure of the modern is based on a perception of the something in himself that is set above the flux and that he possesses in common with
other men; whereas the perception with which the modernist is chiefly concerned,
to the subversion of any true measure whatsoever, is of the divergent and the
changeful both within and without himself.   The present menace to humanism,
it has been said, is less from its enemies than from those who profess to be its
friends.   Thus Mr. F. C. S. Schiller of Oxford proclaims himself a humanist, and
at the same time seeks to show that the true humanist was not Socrates but that
precursor of recent "flowing" philosophers, Protagoras.

It should be noted that many of our votaries of change and mobility are more
emotional than Protagoras or any other Greek sophist.   They tend to make, not
their own thoughts, but their own feelings the measure of all things.   This indulgence in feeling has been encouraged by the sentimentalists who have discovered in feeling not only the quintessentially human element, but, as I said in
speaking of Rousseau, the ultimate ground of fraternal union.   In our own time,
partly perhaps as a result of the psychoanalytical probing of the sources of the
emotional life in the subconscious, there is a growing distrust of the sentimentalist.
To be sure, one may, according to the psychoanalyst, turn the emotions to good
account by a process of "sublimation."   Why not escape still more completely
from one's complexes and infantile survivals by adjusting oneself to the cosmic
order that is revealed to the scientific investigator in his laboratory?   One may
thus cease to be egocentric and become truly mature and disinterested.   This is
the attitude that Mr. Walter Lippmann recommends in *A Preface to Morals,* and it
is this attitude that, by a flagrant misuse of the word, he terms "humanism."   It
is well that a man should adjust himself to the reality of the natural order and,
as a preliminary, should strive to be objective in the scientific sense; but humanism
calls for an adjustment to a very different order that is also "real" and "objective"
in its own way.   It insists in short that there is a "law for man" as well as a "law
for thing," and is in this sense dualistic.   Mr. Lippmann's attempt to base ethics
on monistic postulates is, from either a religious or humanistic point of view, a
revival of the stoical error.   Yet he would have us believe that anyone who has
become disinterested after the scientific fashion has got the equivalent not only of
humanism but of "high religion."   By thus dissimulating the gap between the
wisdom of the ages and the wisdom of the laboratory, he is flattering some of the
most dangerous illusions of the present time.   He escapes from the main humani-
tarian tendency to give to feeling a primacy that does not belong to it, only to
encourage its other main tendency to accord to physical science a hegemony to
which it is not entitled.

It is self-evident that humanitarianism of the scientific or utilitarian type, with
its glorification of the specialist who is ready to sacrifice his rounded development,
if only he can contribute his mite to "progress," is at odds with the humanistic ideal
of poise and proportion.   The religious pretensions of humanitarianism of this
type are even more inacceptable, at least if one understands by religion anything
resembling the great traditional faiths.   The Baconian has inclined from the
outset to substitute an outer for an inner working—the effort of the individual
upon himself—that religion has, in some form or other, always required.   The
result has been to encourage the acquisitive life and also the pursuit of material
instead of spiritual "comfort."

FROM THE TESTAMENT OF A MAN FORBID

JOHN DAVIDSON

They mocked me: "Yah!
The fox who lost his tail! Though you are crazed
We have our wits about us."
                          "Nay," I cried;
"There was besides an ape who lost his tail
That he might change to man. Undo the past!
The rainbow reaches Asgard now no more;
Olympus stands untenanted; the dead
Have their serene abode in earth itself,
Our womb, our nurture, and our sepulchre.
Expel the sweet imaginings, profound
Humanities and golden legends, forms
Heroic, beauties, tripping shades, embalmed
Through hallowed ages in the fragrant hearts
And generous blood of men; the climbing thoughts
Whose roots ethereal grope among the stars,
Whose passion-flowers perfume eternity,
Weed out and tear, scatter and tread them down:
Dismantle and dilapidate high heaven.
It has been said: Ye must be born again.
I say to you: Men must be that they are.
Philosophy, the juggling dupe who finds
Astounding meanings in the Universe,
Commodiously secreted by himself;
Religion, that appoints the soul a flight
Empyreal—hoods its vision then and plucks
Its plumes, its arching pinions tethers down
To flap about a laystall; Art sublime,
The ancient harlot of the ages, she
Whose wig of golden tinct, enameled face
And cushioned bosom rivet glowing looks,
Whose scented flatulence diviner seems
Than dulcet breath of girls who keep their trysts
In hawthorn brakes devoutly, when the sap
Bestirs the troubled forest and the winds
Solace the moonlit earth with whispered news:
Religion, Art, Philosophy—this God,
This beauty, this Idea men have filled
The world with, study still, and still adore,
Are only segments of the spirits's tail
We must outgrow, if spirit would ascend
(Let Spirit be the word for body-and-soul!
Will language ne'er be fused and forged anew?)
And quit the withering life of fear and shame,
Of agony and pitiful desire
To reign untailed in heaven hereafter—Laugh!
The changing image seizes you. Or thus:
This Beauty, this Divinity, this Thought,

This hallowed bower and harvest of delight
Whose roots ethereal seemed to clutch the stars,
Whose amaranths perfumed eternity,
Is fixed in earthly soil enriched with bones
Of used-up workers; fattened with the blood
Of prostitutes, the prime manure; and dressed
With brains of madmen and the broken hearts
Of children. Understand it, you at least
Who toil all day and writhe and groan all night
With roots of luxury, a cancer struck
In every muscle; out of you it is
Cathedrals rise and Heaven blossoms fair;
You are the hidden putrefying source
Of beauty and delight, of leisured hours,
Of passionate loves and high imaginings;
You are the dung that keeps the roses sweet.
I say, uproot it; plough the land; and let
A summer-fallow sweeten all the World."

With mud bespattered, bruised with staves, and stoned—
"You called us dung!"—me from their midst they drove.
Alone I went in darkness and in light,
Color and sound attending on my steps,
And life and death, the ministers of men,
My constant company. But in my heart
Of hearts I longed for human neighborhood,
And bent my pride to win men back again.

FROM HUMANISM AND THE BELIEF IN MAN

ARCHIBALD MacLEISH

. . . For there is a definition of humanism by which humanism becomes a belief in the one thing in which man has greatest need now to believe—himself, and the dignity and importance of the place he fills in the world he lives in. There is a definition of humanism by which humanism becomes precisely the belief of man in his own dignity, in his essential worth as a man, in what Ralph Barton Perry calls "his characteristic perfection": a belief not in the potentiality of man, but in the actuality of man; a belief not in the classic perfection of the beautiful letters men have written in the distant past, but in the human perfection of the men who wrote those letters and of others like them, whether writers or others than writers, and whether living in the past or in the present or not yet born; a belief not in the thing a man may become if he reads the right books and develops the right tastes and undergoes the right discipline, but a belief in the thing he is.

No one has put this better than Professor Perry in his superb *Definition of the Humanities.* "The reference to man in the context of the so-called 'humanities,'" he says, "is . . . not descriptive or apologetic, but eulogistic; not 'human—all too human,' or 'only human,' but human in the sense in which one deems it highest praise to be called 'a man.'" The answer humanism has in its power to make to the two great questions, how to govern and how to teach, is the answer of belief in man, "in the sense in which one deems it highest praise to be called 'a man.'"

If the world can be taught to believe in the worth of man, in the dignity of man, in the "characteristic perfection" of man, it can be taught not only to survive but to live. If the world can be governed in belief in the worth of man, in the dignity of man, it can be governed in peace.

These propositions need no proof. They speak for themselves. If government throughout the world were directed by a convinced belief in the dignity of man as man, in the worth of man as man, so that decisions of government were everywhere made in consonance with that belief and in furtherance of it, no one can doubt that the world would be well governed and that peace would be as nearly certain as peace can be in a variable universe. It is lack of faith in the essential dignity and worth of man which corrupts and weakens democratic governments, substituting for a government by the people in the people's interest, which is peace, a government of rulers in the rulers' interest—which may be war. It is doubt of the dignity and worth of man which opens the road to the tyrannies and dictatorships which have no choice but war. It is cynical contempt for the worth and dignity of man which makes the wars of the dictators wars of slavery and subjugation.

If the fundamental proposition upon which the government of the world was based were the proposition that man, because he is man, and in his essential quality as man, has worth and value which governments exist to serve and to protect, regardless of race and regardless of color or religion, there would be little room for the play of international politics which, under color of realism or under color of necessity, puts power first or oil first or gold first, and men second or nowhere, preparing thus for the wars of power or of oil or gold. If the first business of government everywhere were man, the whole man of the humanists; if the first object of government everywhere were the good of man, man "in the sense in which one deems it highest praise to be called 'a man' "; if the first principle of government everywhere were the principle that government exists for man and not man for government, there would be no place for the governments of which the first business is business, or for the governments of which the first object is economic advantage, or for the governments of which the first principle is power.

But to govern in this way it is necessary first of all to believe, and not merely to declare that one believes, in the fundamental worth and value of man and to practice that belief and never to cease to practice it. It is necessary to believe in man, not only as the Christians believe in man, out of pity, or as the democrats believe in man, out of loyalty, but also as the Greeks believed in man, out of pride.

5

The same thing is true of the question how to teach. If education were informed with a belief in the dignity and worth of man; if the purpose of education were an understanding not only of the weaknesses of man and the sicknesses of man and the failures of man but of the essential nobility of man also, of his "characteristic perfection," men would be able again to occupy their lives and to live in the world as the Greeks lived in it, free of the bewilderment and frustration which has sent this generation, like the Gadarene swine, squealing and stumbling and drunk with the longing for immolation, to hurl themselves into the abysses of the sea.

If science were taught, not as something external to man, something belittling of man, but as one of the greatest of the creations of the human spirit; if economics were taught not as a structure of deterministic laws superior to man and controlling his conduct, but as one of the many mirrors man has constructed to observe the things he does; if history and descriptive literature were taught not as peepholes through which the unworthy truth about mankind may be observed but as expressions of man's unique ability and willingness to see and judge himself; if belief in man and in his dignity and worth became the controlling principle of education, so that the people of the world were taught to respect the common principle of humanity in others and in themselves, and to believe that their lives would be shaped and their future determined not by some law of economics, or by some formula of science, or by some regimen of the subconscious, but by their own wills and on their own responsibility—if these things could be accomplished, who will doubt that the sense of irresponsibility and frustration which has driven so many millions of our contemporaries down the blind steep of slavery into war could be corrected?

The task education must accomplish, if free societies are to continue to exist, is the re-creation of the sense of individual responsibility—which means the re-establishment of the belief of men in man. Fascism is only another name for the sickness and desperation which overcome a society when it loses its sense of responsibility for its own life and surrenders its will to a tyrant, it, and it alone, has invented. But the sense of responsibility in a nation is a sense of responsibility in the individuals who compose that nation, for the sense of responsibility is always a charge upon the individual conscience and vanishes when many share it. And to re-create the sense of individual responsibility it is necessary to restore the belief of men in man—the belief that man can direct his destiny if he will.

It is impossible to charge the consciences of men with responsibility for the world they live in without convincing them that they can act upon their world—that the power to decide and act is theirs. No one knew that better than Abraham Lincoln, who knew many things about the human soul. When it became necessary for him, in the terrible December of 1862, to drive home to the Congress a sense of its responsibility, he used these words: "Fellow citizens, we cannot escape history. We of this Congress and this Administration will be remembered in spite of ourselves. No personal significance or insignificance can spare one or another of us. The fiery trial through which we pass will light us down, in honor or dishonor, to the latest generation . . . We—even we here—hold the power and bear the responsibility."

What education in the free countries must drive home, if the free countries are to survive, is the conviction that we—even we here—hold the power and bear the responsibility. The task is in part a task beyond the power of the schools as such, for the sense of individual responsibility and power involves a sense of individual participation, and a sense of individual participation is only possible in a society in which individuals can make themselves felt directly and not through agglomerations of money or people. There must be social changes as well as educational changes. But the educational changes come first. Not until men believe that the responsibility can be theirs to bear, and therefore should be theirs to bear, will they make it theirs. To teach men to believe in themselves therefore is to teach them responsibility and so to assure their freedom.

6

These, as I understand humanism, are the answers the humanists have it in their power to give to their time and to the questions their time has asked of them. They are answers which seem to me to be true and to dispose, once and for all, of the question whether humanism has anything to say to the generation to which we belong. Any school, any philosophy, which can go as close to the root of the essential sickness of our time has a right to be heard, and may claim that right, and may denounce fairly and justly those who deprive it of that right, pretending that other points of view are more practical and therefore more important.

But these answers are not the answers, as I read the record, which the humanists —all the humanists at least—are willing to give. On the contrary, many humanists would reject them, and reject them for a reason which goes very deep. They would reject them because the dignity of man in which they believe is not the dignity implicit in these answers—is not, that is to say, a dignity which men possess because they are men, but only a dignity which men may earn by undergoing certain disciplines and acquiring certain characteristics.

Man, to these humanists, is not born with worth, but may acquire worth. Until he has earned it he has no right or reason to believe in himself, nor should a belief in man determine the attitude in which he is to be ruled. Humanism to these humanists, in other words, is not a democratic doctrine on which a practice of self-government can be founded, but an aristocratic doctrine which, because its concern is inward, has little to say of government of any kind. It is, if anything, a doctrine opposed to democracy and to theories of the universal worth of man, because excellence, not equality, is its goal and purpose.

It would be a mistake to dismiss these humanists as dwellers in towers, or their definitions as definitions of refuge. The passion for excellence can be a sword as well as a sanctuary. Committed to the love of the arts and the great books and the monuments of unaging intellect, as Yeats so wonderfully called them, and the courtesies and graces and perceptions of a civilized and generous life, the worshipers of excellence have waged war, and noble war, against an increasing vulgarity which has won its greatest triumphs in our time, having found the mechanical means at last to intrude its coarseness into every hour, however private, and every chamber, however secret, of our lives.

Those to whom humanism is the worship of excellence do not admit, as they look around them in the streets and trains and hotel lobbies of our world, that all men have dignity and worth. They do not believe, as they look back across the centuries to the world they imagine to have existed in Athens and in Rome, that all men are able to govern themselves or should be allowed to. They do not agree, as they face the crisis of our time, that freedom is the answer to everything. They do not necessarily hold with public freedom. The freedom they seek is inward in the large and lofty world of enlightened intellect where learning paints the various landscape and a trained and delicate taste selects the road. That there must be peace and quiet outside the mind, if a man is to journey within it, they readily admit. But the peace without, they say, is not their business.

7

It is understandable enough that men should love what these men love, and hate what they hate. Their ideal of the truly civilized man is in every way admirable. Their contempt for a world in which taste is determined in advertising agencies, and intelligence is measured by the answers children give to questions on the air, is a contempt which later generations of Americans will not find strange. But what is not understandable is their choice of the word humanism to describe their inward and selective life. Humanism as a word cannot cut itself off from its root or forget its derivation. Humanism, to deserve the *humanitas* from which it comes, must incorporate some notion of things appropriate to every man as man—things worthy of man in every man.

It must incorporate, that is to say, some notion of a universal dignity which men possess as men and by virtue of their manhood. The dignity of man upon which a philosophy of man, a school devoted to man, is based cannot be a rare and sought-for attribute which only the school can teach man to acquire and only the philosophy aid man to deserve. You do not construct out of the airy goal at which you hope to arrive the solid ground from which you depart. You do not derive the dignity of man on which your philosophy is founded from the dignity which those few who practice your philosophy can claim to possess. The dignity of man is either here and now or it is never. It is either in mankind or it is nowhere.

One can no more make an aristocracy of human dignity than one can make an aristocracy of human love or human curiosity, or any other fundamental human characteristic. Some men will develop their manlike qualities farther than others. Some will be more learned, have surer taste, livelier imagination, greater gentility —will be, in brief, more civilized than others. But whatever the degree of their development, the qualities with which the true humanist is concerned are the man-like qualities—the qualities which men possess because they are men; the qualities, therefore, which all men possess to one degree or another. It is man whom the humanist values, and man is in all men—is all men.

To limit humanism, therefore,—to put a narrower construction upon it than this,—is quite literally to deprive it of its fundamental meaning. It is as though a select association of superior and cultivated people were to call themselves the association of mankind. The word mankind, in such a context, would have an ironic meaning or have none at all. So humanism, if its concern is not man, and therefore all men, has only an ironic meaning or has none. But founded on the universal human basis which its root implies, the name becomes a noble and in-telligible word with meanings which our time needs more than any others.

This war is a war against those who, in contempt of man and in despair of man's power to direct his life, have surrendered their lives into the hands of tyrants they themselves have created. It is a war against the philosophy of contempt for man and despair of his future which those who have surrendered their lives have in-vented to justify themselves, or have accepted from their masters. It is a war therefore in which the issue is, in last analysis, the issue of man—of the concept of man which is to shape and control our time; of the idea of man which govern-ments are to reflect and societies to mirror.

We, on our side, have found it easy to put our cause into negative words, into words of resistance. We are opposed to the philosophy of contempt for man and to those who accept that philosophy: we have seen what it does to those who prac-tice it and to those upon whom it is practiced also. But we have not found it easy to put our cause into the affirmative words of our own purpose. And for this reason: that the affirmative statement of our cause is a declaration of belief in man, and we have not been altogether ready and willing to make that declara-tion, since we too have felt the winds of fear and doubt which turned our enemies to disbelievers. More than anything else, we need a rebirth of belief in our-selves as men. If humanism will make itself the instrument of the renaissance of man, its place, not only in the universities but in the world, is sure. For if it will make itself that instrument it will give our time its cause.

FROM RELIGION WITHOUT HUMANISM *

T. S. ELIOT

It is curious that whilst on the one hand the liberal theologian tends to pay homage to an illusory divinity called "science" the advanced scientist tends to pay homage to an equally vague "religion." People seem to suppose that by science

* From *Humanism in America*. Edited by Norman Foerster. Copyright, 1930, by Rine-hart & Company, Inc. and reprinted with their permission.

yielding points to religion, and religion yielding points to science, we shall quite soon arrive at a position of comfortable equilibrium. What will be "real" will be the technical progress of science, and the material organization of the churches: we shall still have professors of physics and we shall still have clergy, and nobody will lose his job. Scientists and clergy alike seem to speak nowadays as if they were in terror of the specter of unemployment: "I will not make exaggerated claims," they both seem to say, "lest I may be discovered to be superfluous."

But this apparent approximation of science and religion, which we discover in such theological works as those I have mentioned, and in such popular scientific works as those of Whitehead and Eddington, is a delusion. The meeting is a mere cancellation to zero. Nothing positive is attained by reciprocal surrender. The theologian says, "of course dogma is not truth," and the scientist says, "of course science is not truth." Everyone is happy together; and possibly both parties turn to *poetry* (about which neither scientist nor theologian knows anything) and say, "there is truth, in the inspiration of the poet." The poet himself, who perhaps knows more about his own inspiration than a psychoanalyst does, is not allowed to reply that poetry is poetry, and not science or religion—unless he or some of his mistaken friends produce a theory that Poetry is Pure Poetry, Pure Poetry turning out to be something else than poetry and thereby securing respect.

Both parties, the liberal theologian and the scientist, are deficient in humanism. But what is more serious, to my mind, is that the humanist is deficient in humanism too, and must take his responsibility with the others. What happens, in the general confusion, is not only that each party abdicates his proper part, but that he interferes with the proper part of the others. The theologian is terrified of science, and the scientist is becoming terrified of religion; whilst the humanist, endeavoring to pay proper, but not excessive due to both, reels from side to side. And the world reels with him.

On the following point I speak with diffidence, recognizing my lack of qualification where qualification is severe and exact. Humanism has much to say of Discipline and Order and Control; and I have parroted these terms myself. I found no discipline in humanism; only a little intellectual discipline from a little study of philosophy. But the difficult discipline is the discipline and training of emotion; this the modern world has great need of; so great need that it hardly understands what the word means; and this I have found is only attainable through dogmatic religion. I do not say that dogmatic religion is justified because it supplies this need—that is just the psychologism and the anthropocentrism that I wish to avoid—but merely state my belief that in no other way can the need be supplied. There is much chatter about mysticism: for the modern world the word means some spattering indulgence of emotion, instead of the most terrible concentration and askesis. But it takes perhaps a lifetime merely to realize that men like the forest sages and the desert sages, and finally the Victorines and John of the Cross and (in his fashion) Ignatius really *mean what they say*. Only those have the right to talk of discipline who have looked into the Abyss. The need of the modern world is the discipline and training of the emotions; which neither the intellectual training of philosophy or science, nor the wisdom of humanism, nor the negative instruction of psychology can give.

In short, we can use the term Humanism in two ways. In the narrower sense, which tends always under emphasis to become narrower still, it is an important part in a larger whole; and humanists, by offering this part as a substitute for the whole, are lessening, instead of increasing, its importance; they offer an excuse to the modern theologian and the modern scientist (only too ready to grasp it) for *not* being humanistic themselves, and for leaving humanism to its own specialists.

Humanism can offer neither the intellectual discipline of philosophy or of science (two different disciplines), nor the emotional discipline of religion. On the other hand, these other activities depend upon humanism to preserve their sanity. Without it, religion tends to become either a sentimental tune, or an emotional debauch; or in theology, a skeleton dance of fleshless dogmas, or in ecclesiasticism, a soulless political club. Without it, science can be merely a process of technical research, bursting out from time to time, and especially in our time, into sentimental monstrosities like the Life Force, or Professor Whitehead's God.

But in the full and complete sense of the word, Humanism is something quite different from a part trying to pretend to be a whole, and something quite different from a "parasite" of religion. It can only be quite actual in the full realization and balance of the disciplined intellectual and emotional life of man. For, as I have said, without humanism both religion and science tend to become other than themselves, and without religion and science—without emotional and intellectual discipline—humanism tends to shrink into an atrophied caricature of itself. It is the spirit of humanism which has operated to reconcile the mystic and the ecclesiastic in one church; having done this in the past, humanism should not set itself up now as another sect, but strive to continue and enlarge its task, laboring to reconcile and unite all the parts into a whole. It is the humanist who could point out to the theologian the absurdities of his repudiation, acceptance, or exploitation of "science," and to the scientist the absurdities of his repudiation, acceptance, or exploitation of religion. For when I say "reconcile," I mean something very different from the dangerous and essentially anti-humanistic adventures of the Bishop of Birmingham or Professor Whitehead. And let us leave Einstein alone, who has his own business to attend to.

As I believe I am writing chiefly for those who know or think they know, what "humanism" means, I have not in this paper attempted any definition of it. I take it that the reader thinks he knows what it means, and that he will understand that I am putting before him the difference between what I think he thinks it means and what I think I think it means.

I have just one note to add, which is the preface to an extensive sequel. I believe that at the present time the problem of the unification of the world and the problem of the unification of the individual, are in the end one and the same problem; and that the solution of one is the solution of the other. Analytical psychology (even if accepted far more enthusiastically than I can accept it) can do little except produce monsters; for it is attempting to produce unified individuals in a world without unity; the social, political, and economic sciences can do little, for they are attempting to produce the great society with an aggregation of human beings who are not units but merely bundles of incoherent impulses and beliefs. The problem of nationalism and the problem of dissociated personalities may turn out to be the same. The relevance of this paragraph to what precedes it will, I hope, appear upon examination.

FROM PIETY *

In *Reason in Religion*

GEORGE SANTAYANA

Mankind at large is also, to some minds, an object of piety. But this religion of humanity is rather a desideratum than a fact: humanity does not actually appear to anybody in a religious light. The *nihil homine homini utilius* remains a signal

---

* Reprinted from *The Life of Reason: Reason in Religion* by George Santayana; copyright 1933 by Charles Scribner's Sons; used by permission of the publishers.

truth, but the collective influence of men and their average nature are far too mixed and ambiguous to fill the soul with veneration. Piety to mankind must be three-fourths pity. There are indeed specific human virtues, but they are those necessary to existence, like patience and courage. Supported on these indispensable habits, mankind always carries an indefinite load of misery and vice. Life spreads rankly in every wrong and impracticable direction as well as in profitable paths, and the slow and groping struggle with its own ignorance, inertia, and folly, leaves it covered in every age of history with filth and blood. It would hardly be possible to exaggerate man's wretchedness if it were not so easy to overestimate his sensibility. There is a *fond* of unhappiness in every bosom, but the depths are seldom probed; and there is no doubt that sometimes frivolity and sometimes sturdy habit helps to keep attention on the surface and to cover up the inner void. Certain moralists, without meaning to be satirical, often say that the sovereign cure for unhappiness is work. Unhappily, the work they recommend is better fitted to dull pain than to remove its cause. It occupies the faculties without rationalizing the life. Before mankind could inspire even moderate satisfaction, not to speak of worship, its whole economy would have to be reformed, its reproduction regulated, its thoughts cleared up, its affections equalized and refined.

To worship mankind as it is would be to deprive it of what alone makes it akin to the divine—its aspiration. For this human dust lives; this misery and crime are dark in contrast to an imagined excellence; they are lighted up by a prospect of good. Man is not adorable, but he adores, and the object of his adoration may be discovered within him and elicited from his own soul. In this sense the religion of humanity is the only religion, all others being sparks and abstracts of the same. The indwelling ideal lends all the gods their divinity. No power, either physical or psychical, has the least moral prerogative nor any just place in religion at all unless it supports and advances the ideal native to the worshiper's soul. Without moral society between the votary and his god religion is pure idolatry; and even idolatry would be impossible but for the suspicion that somehow the brute force exorcised in prayer might help or mar some human undertaking.

There is, finally, a philosophic piety which has the universe for its object. This feeling, common to ancient and modern Stoics, has an obvious justification in man's dependence upon the natural world and in its service to many sides of the mind. Such justification of cosmic piety is rather obscured than supported by the euphemisms and ambiguities in which these philosophers usually indulge in their attempt to preserve the customary religious unction. For the more they personify the universe and give it the name of God the more they turn it into a devil. The universe, so far as we can observe it, is a wonderful and immense engine; its extent, its order, its beauty, its cruelty, makes it alike impressive. If we dramatize its life and conceive its spirit, we are filled with wonder, terror, and amusement, so magnificent is that spirit, so prolific, inexorable, grammatical, and dull. Like all animals and plants, the cosmos has its own way of doing things, not wholly rational nor ideally best, but patient, fatal, and fruitful. Great is this organism of mud and fire, terrible this vast, painful, glorious experiment. Why should we not look on the universe with piety? Is it not our substance? Are we made of other clay? All our possibilities lie from eternity hidden in its bosom. It is the dispenser of all our joys. We may address it without superstitious terrors; it is not wicked. It follows its own habits abstractedly; it can be trusted to be true to its word. Society is not impossible between it and us, and since it is the source all our energies, the home of all our happiness, shall we not cling to it and praise it, seeing that it vegetates so grandly and so sadly, and that it is not for us to blame it for what, doubtless, it never knew that it did? Where there is such infinite and laborious potency there is room for every hope. If we should abstain from judging a father's errors or a mother's foibles, why should we pronounce sentence on the ignorant crimes of the universe, which have passed into our own blood? The universe is the true Adam, the creation the true fall; and as we have never blamed our mythical first parent very much, in spite of the disproportionate consequences of his sin, because we felt that he was but human and that we, in his place, might have sinned too, so we may easily forgive our real ancestor, whose connatural sin we are from moment to moment committing, since it is only the necessary rashness of venturing to be without foreknowing the price or the fruits of existence. . . .

"ALL WILL GROW GREAT AND POWERFUL AGAIN"
In *The Book of Hours*
RAINER MARIA RILKE

ALL WILL GROW GREAT AND POWERFUL AGAIN:
the seas be wrinkled and the land be plain,
the trees gigantic and the walls be low;
and in the valleys, strong and multiform,
a race of herdsmen and of farmers grow.

No churches to encircle God as though
he were a fugitive, and then bewail him
as if he were a captured wounded creature,—
all houses will prove friendly, there will be
a sense of boundless sacrifice prevailing
in dealings between men, in you, in me.

No waiting the beyond, no peering toward it,
but longing to degrade not even death;
we shall learn earthliness, and serve its ends,
to feel its hands about us like a friend's.

(Babette Deutsch, tr.)

FROM KEY LARGO, Act II
MAXWELL ANDERSON

KING: Then we both die—as a sacrifice to the rules.
It would be something to know who it is arranges
these little ironies.
I came here running from a civil war
where madmen and morons tore a continent
apart to share it, where death and rape were common
as flies on a dead soldier, and alien men
were weary of native women. I ran from that storm
of rape and murder, because I couldn't help

and nobody could help, and I wanted at least
to save my life, in any crawling way,
and the great master of the laboratory,
(wearing spectacles, probably) drives me down
to this bloody wharf, where I must choose again
between death and the rape of a woman, between death
and the murder of innocent men.   I made my choice
long ago, and ran, and left them bleeding
there in the field.   And I say it's better to live—
if one could live alone in the Everglades
and fill his stomach with fish, and sleep at night,
and knock his oysters from the mangrove roots,
and let the dead bury their dead, for there's no faith sure,
no magnanimity that won't give way
if you test it often enough, no love of woman
or love of man, that won't dry up in the end
if the drouth lasts long enough, no modesty
that isn't relative.   There's no better than you
among all women—and yet when you envisioned
the choice between Murillo and your death
there was a flash when your mind asked itself,
must it be death?   Is even the man Murillo
worse than death?   And if you can ask the question
then there's more than one answer.
ALEGRE: How did you know that!
KING: Because the mind, the bright, quick-silver mind,
has but one purpose, to defend the body
and ward off death.   Because it's the law of earth
where life was built up from the very first
on rape and murder—where the female takes what she gets
and learns to love it, and must learn to love it,
or the race would die!   Show me one thing secure
among these names of virtues—justice and honor
and love and friendship—and I'll die for it gladly,
but where's justice, and where's honor, and where's friendship,
and what's love, under the rose?
ALEGRE: Then you've never loved.
KING: Not as you've loved, perhaps, for you assume
that it's forever, and I've known, and know,
that it's till the fire burns down, till the stimulant
of something new or something stolen's gone,
till you know all the intimate details
and the girl's with child, and cries.   And if that's true
of love, it's true of all the other doors—
the doors of all the illusions, and one by one
we all jump at them.   We jump first at the door
with Christ upon it, hanging on the cross,
then the door with Lenin, legislating heaven,
then the emblem of social security, representing
eighteen dollars a week, good luck or bad,
jobs or no jobs—then the door with the girl expectant,
the black triangle door, and they all give meaning

to life, and mental sustenance, but then
there comes a day when there's no sustenance,
and you jump, and there's nothing you want to buy with money,
and Christ hangs dead on the cross, as all men die,
and Lenin legislates a fake paradise,
and the girl holds out her arms, and she's made of sawdust,
and there's sawdust in your mouth!

ALEGRE: But if this were true,
then why would one live—woman or man or beast,
or grub in the dark?

KING: To eat and sleep and breed
and creep in the forest.

ALEGRE: Answer him, father, answer,
because it sounds like truth—but if it were true
one couldn't live!   There is something in women
that is as he says, and there is something in men
that merely wants to live, but answer him!
We're not like this!

D'ALCALA: Why, girl, we're all alone,
here on the surface of a turning sphere
of earth and water, cutting a great circle
round the sun, just as the sun itself
cuts a great circle round the central hub
of some great constellation, which in turn
wheels round another.   Where this voyage started
we don't know, nor where it will end, nor whether
it has a meaning, nor whether there is good
or evil, whether man has a destiny
or happened here by chemical accident—
all this we never know.   And that's our challenge—
to find ourselves in this desert of dead light-years,
blind, all of us, in a kingdom of the blind,
living by appetite in a fragile shell
of dust and water; yet to take this dust
and water and our range of appetites
and build them toward some vision of a god
of beauty and unselfishness and truth—
could we ask better of the mud we are
than to accept the challenge, and look up
and search for god-head?   If it's true we came
from the sea-water—and children in the womb
wear gills a certain time in memory
of that first origin—we've come a long way;
so far there's no predicting what we'll be
before we end.   It may be women help
this progress choosing out the men who seem
a fractional step beyond sheer appetite—
and it may be that's sacred, though my values
are hardly Biblical—and perhaps men help
by setting themselves forever, even to the death,
against cruelty and arbitrary power,
for that's the beast—the ancient, belly-foot beast

from which we came, which is strong within us yet,
and tries to drag us back down. Somehow or other,
in some obscure way, it's the love of woman
for man, and a certain freedom in her love
to choose tomorrow's men, and the leverage
in the interplay of choice between men and women,
that's brought us here—to this forking of the roads—
and may take us farther on.

KING: And where are we going?

D'ALCALA: To a conquest of all there is, whatever there is
among the suns and stars.

KING: And what if it's empty—
what if the whole thing's empty here in space
like a vast merry-go-round of eyeless gods
turning without resistance—Jupiter
and Mars and Venus, Saturn and Mercury,
carved out of rock and trailed with cloud and mist,
but nothing, and in all the constellations,
no meaning anywhere, nothing? Then if man gets up
and makes himself a god, and walks alone
among these limitless tensions of the sky,
and finds that he's eternally alone,
and can mean nothing, then what was the use of it,
why climb so high, and set ourselves apart
to look out on a place of skulls?

D'ALCALA: Now you want to know
what will come of us all, and I don't know that.
You should have asked the fish what would come of him
before the earth shrank and the land thrust up
between the oceans. You should have asked the fish
or asked me, or asked yourself, for at that time
we were the fish, you and I, or they were we—
and we, or they, would have known as much about it
as I know now—yet it somehow seems worth while
that the fish were not discouraged, and did keep on—
at least as far as we are.—For conditions
among the fish were quite the opposite
of what you'd call encouraging. They had
big teeth and no compunction. Bigger teeth
than Hitler or Murillo.
Over and over again the human race
climbs up out of the mud, and looks around,
and finds that it's alone here; and the knowledge
hits it like a blight—and down it goes
into the mud again.
Over and over again we have a hope
and make a religion of it—and follow it up
till we're out on the topmost limb of the tallest tree
alone with our stars—and we don't dare to be there,
and climb back down again.
It may be that the blight's on the race once more—
that they're all afraid—and fight their way to the ground.

But it won't end in the dark. Our destiny's
the other way. There'll be a race of men
who can face even the stars without despair,
and think without going mad.

FROM EMERSON AND THE OPEN FUTURE

In *Emerson and Beyond*

WILLIAM YERINGTON

The mightiest of all revolutions in thought is upon us—the idea of the Open Future. From of old, to be sure, there have been lonely seers who knew that all things are a metamorphosis. Heraclitus the Greek called the world a flux. Protagoras announced the doctrine of Becoming. Lucretius put God and the Golden Age in the future. Hegel said that all being is becoming. Schelling saw a universe that was alive and rushing continually from form to form. To Schopenhauer the deepest reality was a cosmic Will that was always going on to incalculable futures. Goethe and Lamarck were evolutionists long before the Darwinians. Spencer, with his universal evolutionism, was a spokesman of the age. Nietzsche conceived man as a stage toward Superman. Browning, with his doctrine of the unattainable ideal (Ah, but a man's reach must exceed his grasp, Or what's a heaven for) was a radical futurist. "What's come to perfection perishes," he said of Greek art, and he preferred the imperfect art of Florence because there was more future in it. Whitman would give no duties or dogmas; he would give living impulses. "After me, vista," he cried. Ibsen declared all orthodoxies wrong because they represent truths of yesterday, which are no longer truths.

To William James the world was the unfinished work of a finite God who labored mightily to build primordial chaos into law. Bernard Shaw believes that all things, from the atom to man's brain, are experiments which some developing Life-Force makes in its effort toward self-expression. Bertrand Russell sees man making for himself a spiritual home in a brute universe that is indifferent to his values and his ideals. Croce says: "Reality shows itself as a continuous growing upon itself. The plant dreams of the animal, the animal of man, man of superman. With every historical movement man surpasses himself." But mankind generally has been a worshiper of yesterday; his gods, his paradise, his revelations and inspirations were all in the past. He has progressed rather blunderingly to larger futures, with eyes backward turned continually. But we are becoming futurists: God and Paradise are in the making; revelation is the deeper insight, the larger horizon we are growing toward; inspiration is from an ideal that beckons ahead, not a memory that vanishes behind. The best miracles, the best religions are to come. Another revolution in our habits of thought is involved. We must see that goings are more significant than goals, that everything is to be judged by its tendency. We must see that the spiritual enrichment resulting from our progress toward insights and ideals is far more precious than any service that possessed ideals and insights may give. 'Tis not belief that counts, but the mental process undergone in arriving at belief.

The great prophet of an Open Future is Bergson. To Bergson the only being is Becoming. Even what we call a thing is but the snapshot view of a transition, like a photograph of lightning taken by an instantaneous camera. And God— even God is just a stupendous Becoming: "he is unceasing life, action, freedom." The whole of things is a perpetual going-on like the going-on of human consciousness. The world advances incessantly to unpredictable futures; it creates as it goes; genuine novelties are always upspringing. Because Life is creative its action is incalculable; not even Omniscience could predict its tomorrows. Evolution is not the realization of powers latent in the primordial stuff of existence, for then the world would be a mechanical system, and with Bergson the world is a spiritual system. Neither is evolution the unrolling of a plan, for a plan would close and determine it. Life is a perpetual aspiration; its futures do not merely actualize a potentiality or plan of today: they transcend the present; there is genuine creation. Everything is tendency. With Bergson the one enemy to life is fixedness, material or mental fixedness. See how lower life forms run into blind alleys. The shell that the mollusc built closed forever the evolutionary road he had been traveling. The fixedness in the nervous system of brutes, the unchangeability of their habits, shunted from them the evolutionary impetus: their journey upward came to an end. Man's brain tends continually toward automatism; but it retains some little plasticity; and that is man's only hope: that makes him unique among all creatures; that gives The Life a passage through an impeded channel; otherwise, man would fall back into immobility and sleep; and the story of evolution in this corner of the universe would come to an end.

I do not pretend that the masses have this vision of life today, more than in Greece two thousand years ago: the thought of the masses is always anachronism. But among people of insight it is frequently to be met with. So when I say that the conception of Being as Becoming is a characteristic twentieth-century insight, I can hardly be accused of giving prejudiced testimony. Even the world that science envisages is a metamorphosis. We used to regard atoms as static things; now we know an atom is a process. Matter—what is it? Crude, hard stuff—a wayfaring man, though a fool, need not err therein: a changeable aggregate of changeless units. That is the answer of yesterday. But now the units have melted to flowing shadows. A dust-mote is only a bundle of bundles of inconceivable energy.

Our fathers lived in a little prison-like three-story world, with a celestial autocrat upon the third floor. But we inhabit a universe that stretches on all sides to infinity, pervaded by a Will to whom we are becoming eyesight and intelligence. Yesterday, the God of philosophers was the Absolute, who could not have a history because he had no past or future; past and future were an Eternal Now, as Tennyson phrased it. That which we call history was but the fictitious enacting in fictitious time of what was everlastingly present to God. Our God today can have genuine experience; he can blunder; he can get new insights; he can be surprised. His life is a Romance.

Likewise ethics. Absolute moralities; categorical imperatives; inflexible decalogs; right is right because the divine despot commands—from these we have passed to the forward-looking ethic of pragmatism, that says right is right because it best meets the spiritual needs of today; and a good man is not he who keeps all the commandments, but the man whose life is directed by an enlightened good will. The Age has mothered a whole brood of forward-looking ideals—democracy, socialism, anarchism, bolshevism. . . .

Since there are no finalities, we cannot properly speak of a goal. But, though the Power has no plan, it seems to have a purpose. A program is complete and closed; a purpose is endlessly adaptable, and suggestive merely. Life must change its plans, like a growing boy. It learns, it gets new insights. The universe is indeed a spiritual adventure; the doors of the future are wide open. But being controlled by a purpose is not destructive of adventure. Most men after maturity have an abiding aspiration; but their lives are not planned like a program: the purpose may be achieved in numberless ways; it may lead us into innumerable surprises and perils. Why should the cosmical life be different? The purpose apparently is to spiritualize matter: witness a rose petal, a beautiful face. That, in its highest form, would be the development of free personalities.

Automatism is the Arch Foe. Theologies strangle religion; codes smother the enthusiasms that created them. Society grows by institutionalizing the visions of genius—and then the institution kills the vision. Morality is the keeping life alert, spontaneous, creative. To let a mechanical system of any kind do our choosing is immorality, is damnation, because it is spiritual paralysis. We do feel, with James, that the Universe needs our loyalties, our idealisms; otherwise it may fail. But the finest faithfulness is loyalty to selfhood, a brave effort toward spontaneousness of spirit. That is our part in The Drama. When we looked at life instead of reports about it, we made another discovery. We found that life is something immenser than our formulas. Our rational philosophies have about the same relation to life that a puddle has to the wonder and majesty of Niagara. Experience is fluid; before you have written your formula it has flowed on and changed. So intellectualism crumbled. Modern spirits no longer think to chase Truth and capture it at the walled end of the road. There is no end; and the road widens as we go. Then the idea struck them—the glory, the stimulation is not in possessing truth, but in seeking. Suppose we did arrive: what then? To possess final truth—that would be a tragedy. For it would paralyze growth. Progress toward a religion is more valuable than a religion possessed. Not *what* you believe, but *how* you believe, is the significant thing—the enthusiasm, the reality, the direction of your belief. Enthusiasm is what counts. Reality—not the dead-alive assent to inherited opinions: what Carlyle called sincerity. Men are damnably at ease in Zion. And tendency is not in the world of idea but in the world of will. So the modern man became a Pragmatist. He turned right-about-face: we must construe life no longer in terms of Idea, but in terms of Will. By their fruits shall ye know truths. Religions are tools. Whatever in the largest way is successful, whatever most vitalizes your will, whether demonstrable or not, is for you at this moment the truth. At this moment: you must not make a fetish of it, as men have always done; for it may not be significant at all tomorrow. Our forefathers sought to indoctrinate people, to teach them creeds. We know that is not the way of life, but the way of death. Our forefathers hungered and thirsted for final truth. We would keep men from final truth as we would keep their bodies from stagnation. Certitude kills inquiry; it kills adventure. Therefore it paralyzes both mind and will. It destroys faith at the roots. No; we would not house people in truths; we would release them to the eternal process of life. The old faith was directed toward what was established and sure; the new faith is directed toward what ought to be and is uncertain. So far as we do not venture, have we lapsed from life. All creation involves danger, for it is a reliance upon the Untried. At the risk of paradox, I will say that doubt is an ally of faith. Faith is in the building temple, not the built. It is trust in the Untried. Reality is Aspiration. It is the courage that faces the peril of going on. . . .

But Emerson and Bergson are in harmony concerning the life of the soul. Whether the ultimate reality be an Over-Soul or a Great Life flowing through time, man is a becoming; the essence of him is growth. The supreme good of existence is self-realization; and, because we are gods potentially, self-realization is an eternal process. In his exaltation of spirit over machinery; in his spiritual anarchism, the protest against an overinstitutionalized life, the demand for the release of the individual; in his unconquerable idealism, sometimes perhaps overstressing inwardness as opposed to the centrifugal forces of society; in his deprecation of exterior helps on behalf of spiritual enrichment; in his protest against repetition and habit; in

his revolt from all the static elements, the automatisms, of society—traditions, orthodoxies, idols, sacred forms; in his gospel of enthusiasm as the proper state of
man; in his demand for spontaneousness—in these things he is our contemporary.
The championship of genuine persons, souls that are not fed on vicarious revelation but on realities, souls that stand foursquare, is now a commonplace. We demand, at least in theory, that a man be genuine, a living spirit. We will not have
him abdicate his godhood by absconding to some sheltered wall of Opinion or
Custom crumbling into decay. We know, with Emerson, that wherever life is,
there is peril. Yesterday is always afraid of Tomorrow; the Old is intimate and
warm with memories; the New cold and bleak. Emerson was not afraid of Tomorrow. His championship of doubt is distinctively modern. We know too that
"the ground occupied by the skeptic is the vestibule of the temple." We know
too that skepticism is a greater religion in the making.

But to our thought the world is an adventure in a more thoroughgoing sense
than Emerson could imagine. God is the constructive principle of things pain-
fully building an aboriginal chaos into law. The cataclysms of nature, the dis-
orders of society, individual sin—are survivals of that primal lawlessness. Evolution is the slow evoking of order, the shaping of chaos into cosmos. It is the spirit
of God moving upon a world without form, and void, trying to fashion its crude
stuff into beauty. And here is the staggering thought: the Universe may fail. The
contrast between Emerson's Meliorism and James' Moralism is plain enough. To
the first, the redemptive principle in the world is omnipotent; nature is predestined
to be perfected. To James, a limited Power at the heart of things is doing its
utmost to conquer the aboriginal Disorder; but the task is gigantic; more God does
not because more he cannot. The actual world is neither moral nor immoral, divine nor undivine. The keynote of our whole thought about the universe today
is that no values are given; all must be achieved. Not even the eternal heavens
can have any divineness except what they achieve. Man must cooperate; we must
do our part toward spiritualizing the Universe by building into its huge Indifference the values we most cherish, just as we have fashioned the crude earth to
habitable cities. We must create a moral world in this immense uncaring universe.
God may not be sufficient to the task: I must help. Emerson thought the world
would surely be saved through God's will; we think the world will perhaps be saved
through man's will. . . .

. . . Life can only be experienced; it cannot be stated. The only absolute truth
is that Existence is wonderful. The miracle asks to be tasted, not to be explained.
Perhaps all philosophies and religions are true—true of their little areas. They become false when they arrogate to themselves any other region; and most of them
have presumed to be universal. System-making is precarious business, anyway; our
philosophy is our temperament writ large. Syllogistically minded people will have
a completely reasonable world. Card-index souls (to use James Oppenheim's
phrase) will believe in a planned-out universe. Folk who are intensely personal are
Theists; impersonal souls (like Shelley) are Atheists. Immature spirits want a universe neat and compact and expressible in a little formula; they want a home.
Virile souls will be infatuated with the very Outdoors character, the homelessness,
of their world. To mechanical folk the world is a huge machine; to the spiritual
anarchist it is Disorder; to vagabonds it is an Adventure; to children and to the
Afraid it is Father. Not that people are one-sided or fragmentary in their knowledge of the arguments; they are one-sided in their sensitiveness. Most intelligent
folk know all the arguments; but some reasons do not weigh as much as others on
the scales of their temperament. The main theistic argument makes no appeal
whatever to the constitutional pluralist. He sees it as the effort of a mind that

lusts after simplicity to bring into oneness the discordant elements of the world. The same argument is overwhelming to a man whose soul desires unity. It is, after all, an emotional thing. The trouble with philosophy is, it assumes Life to be rational. But Life is superbly unrational. The universe is probably varied enough to fulfil all the definitions—with an unguessed plus that is infinite. As I have shown, Emerson was not blind to this truth. He despised systems; then, very human-like, turned and made a system of his own. It had this advantage over most philosophies: it was the informal, rather rhapsodical, utterance of a poet about the Wonder of Existence. And it did see life as an eternally creative Ongoing, an everlasting Newness.

FROM OUR PRESENT DISCONTENTS

In *Outspoken Essays*

WILLIAM RALPH INGE

The myth of progress is our form of apocalyptism. In France it began with sentimentalism, developing normally into homicidal mania. In England it took the form of a kind of Deuteronomic religion. As a reward for our national virtues, our population expanded, our exports and imports went up by leaps and bounds, and our empire received additions every decade. It was plain that when Christ said "Blessed are the meek, for they shall inherit the earth," He was thinking of the British Empire. The whole structure of our social order encouraged the measurement of everything by quantitative standards. Everyone could understand that a generation which travels sixty miles an hour must be five times as civilized as one which only traveled twelve. Thus the beneficent "law of progress" was exemplified in that nation which had best deserved to be its exponent. The myth in question is that there is a natural law of improvement, manifested by greater complexity of structure, by increase of wants and the means to satisfy them. A nation advances in civilization by increasing in wealth and population, and by multiplying the accessories and paraphernalia of life.

Belief in this alleged law has vitiated our natural science, our political science, our history, our philosophy, and even our religion. Science declared that "the survival of the fittest" was a law of Nature, though Nature has condemned to extinction the majestic animals of the saurian era, and has carefully preserved the bug, the louse, and the *spirochaeta pallida*.

> We dined as a rule on each other;
> What matter?   the toughest survived,

is a fair parody of this doctrine. In political science, by a portentous snobbery, the actual evolution of European government was assumed to be in the line of upward progress. Our histories contrasted the benighted condition of past ages with the high morality and general enlightenment of the present. In philosophy, the problem of evil was met by the theory that though the Deity is not omnipotent yet, He is on His way to become so. He means well, and if we give Him time, He will make a real success of His creation. Human beings, too, commonly make a very poor thing of their lives here. But continue their training after they are dead and they will all come to perfection. We have been living on this secularized idealism for a hundred and fifty years. It has driven out the true idealism, of which it is a caricature, and has made the deeper and higher kind of religious faith abnormally

difficult. Even the hope of immortality has degenerated into a belief in apparitions and voices from the dead.

Nature knows nothing of this precious law. Her figure is not the vertical line,
nor even the spiral, but the circle—the vicious circle, according to Samuel Butler.
"Men eat birds, birds eat worms, worms eat men again." Some stars are getting
hotter, others cooler. Life appears at a certain temperature and is extinguished at
another temperature. Evolution and involution balance each other and go on
concurrently. The normal condition of every species on this planet is not progress
but stationariness. "Progress," so-called, is an incident of adaptation to new conditions. Bees and ants must have spent millennia in perfecting their organization;
now that they have reached a stable equilibrium, no more changes are perceptible.
The "progress" of humanity has consisted almost entirely in the transformation of
the wild man of the woods, not into *homo sapiens,* but into *homo faber,* man the
tool-maker, a process of which Nature expresses her partial disapproval by plaguing
us with diverse diseases and taking away our teeth and claws. It is not certain that
there has been much change in our intellectual and moral endowments since *pithecanthropus* dropped the first half of his name. I should be sorry to have to maintain that the Germans of today are morally superior to the army which defeated
Quintilius Varus, or that the modern Turks are more humane than the hordes of
Timour the Tartar. If there is to be any improvement in human nature itself we
must look to the infant science of eugenics to help us.

It is not easy to say how this myth of progress came to take hold of the imagination, in the teeth of science and experience. Quinet speaks of the "fatalistic optimism" of historians, of which there have certainly been some strange examples.
We can only say that secularism, like other religions, needs an eschatology, and has
produced one. A more energetic generation than ours looked forward to a gradual
extension of busy industrialism over the whole planet; the present ideal of the
masses seems to be the greatest idleness of the greatest number, or a Fabian farm-
yard of tame fowls, or (in America) an ice-water-drinking gynecocracy. But the superstition cannot flourish much longer. The period of expansion is over, and we
must adjust our view of earthly providence to a state of decline. For no nation
can flourish when it is the ambition of the large majority to put in fourpence and
take out ninepence. The middle class will be the first victims; then the privileged
aristocracy of labor will exploit the poor. But trade will take wings and migrate
to some other country where labor is good and comparatively cheap.

The dethronement of a fetish may give a sounder faith its chance. In the time
of decay and disintegration which lies before us, more persons will seek consolation where it can be found. "Happiness and unhappiness," says Spinoza, "depend
on the nature of the object which we love. When a thing is not loved, no quarrels
will arise concerning it, no sadness will be felt if it perishes, no envy if it is possessed by another; no fear, no hatred, no disturbance of the mind. All these things
arise from the love of the perishable. But love for a thing eternal and infinite feeds
the mind wholly with joy, and is itself untainted with any sadness; wherefore it is
greatly to be desired and sought for with our whole strength." It is well known
that these noble words were not only sincere, but the expression of the working
faith of the philosopher; and we may hope that many who are doomed to suffer
hardship and spoliation in the evil days that are coming will find the same path to
a happiness which cannot be taken from them. Spinoza's words, of course, do not
point only to religious exercises and meditation. The spiritual world includes art
and science in all their branches, when these are studied with a genuine devotion to
the Good, the True, and the Beautiful for their own sakes. We shall need "a remnant" to save Europe from relapsing into barbarism; for the new forces are almost

wholly cut off from the precious traditions which link our civilization with the great eras of the past. The possibility of another dark age is not remote; but there must be enough who value our best traditions to preserve them till the next springtime of civilization. We must take long views, and think of our great-grandchildren.

It is tempting to dream of a new Renaissance, under which the life of reason will at last be the life of mankind. Though there is little sign of improvement in human nature, a favorable conjunction of circumstances may bring about a civilization very much better than ours today. For a time, at any rate, war may be practically abolished, and the military qualities may find another and a less pernicious outlet. "Sport," as Santayana says, "is a liberal form of war stripped of its compulsions and malignity; a rational art and the expression of a civilized instinct." The art of living may be taken in hand seriously. Some of the ingenuity which has lately been lavished on engines of destruction may be devoted to improvements in our houses, which should be easily and cheaply put together and able to be carried about in sections; on labor-saving devices which would make servants unnecessary; and on international campaigns against diseases, some of the worst of which could be extinguished forever by twenty years of concerted effort. A scientific civilization is not impossible, though we are not likely to live to see it. And, if science and humanism can work together, it will be a great age for mankind. Such hopes as these must be allowed to float before our minds: they are not unreasonable, and they will help us to get through the twentieth century, which is not likely to be a pleasant time to live in.

—

FROM THE GOOD WILL IN MAN

In *New Worlds for Old*

H. G. WELLS

It seems to me that the whole spirit and quality of both the evil and the good of our time, and of the attitude not simply of the Socialist but of every sane reformer toward these questions, was summarized in a walk I had a little while ago with a friend along the Thames Embankment, from Blackfriars Bridge to Westminster. We had dined together and we went there because we thought that with a fitful moon and clouds adrift, on a night when the air was a crystal air that gladdened and brightened, that crescent of great buildings and steely, soft-hurrying water must needs be altogether beautiful. And indeed it was beautiful: the mysteries and mounting masses of the buildings to the right of us, the blurs of this colored light or that, blue-white, green-white, amber or warmer orange, the rich black archings of Waterloo Bridge, the rippled lights upon the silent flowing river, the lattice of girders, and the shifting trains of Charing Cross Bridge—their funnels pouring a sort of hot-edged moonlight by way of smoke—and then the sweeping line of lamps, the accelerated run and diminuendo of the Embankment lamps as one came into sight of Westminster. The big hotels were very fine, huge swelling shapes of dun dark-gray and brown, huge shapes seamed and bursting and fenestrated with illumination, tattered at a thousand windows with light and the indistinct glowing suggestions of feasting and pleasure. And dim and faint above it all and very remote was the moon's dead wan face veiled and then displayed.

But we were dashed by an unanticipated refrain to this succession of magnificent things, and we did not cry, as we had meant to cry, how good it was to be alive! We found something else, something we had forgotten.

Along the Embankment, you see, there are iron seats at regular intervals, seats you cannot lie upon because iron arm-rests prevent that, and each seat, one saw by the lamplight, was filled with crouching and drooping figures. Not a vacant place remained, not one vacant place. These were the homeless, and they had come to sleep here. Now one noted a poor old woman with a shameful battered straw hat awry over her drowsing face, now a young clerk staring before him at despair; now a filthy tramp, and now a bearded, frock-coated, collarless respectability; I remember particularly one ghastly long white neck and white face that lopped backward, choked in some nightmare, awakened, clutched with a bony hand at the bony throat, and sat up and stared angrily as we passed. The wind had a keen edge that night, even for us who had dined and were well-clad. One crumpled figure coughed and went on coughing—damnably.

"It's fine," said I, trying to keep hold of the effects to which this line of poor wretches was but the selvage; "it's fine! But I can't stand this."

"It changes all that we expected," admitted my friend, after a silence.

"Must we go on—past them all?"

"Yes. I think we ought to do that. It's a lesson perhaps—for trying to get too much beauty out of life as it is, and forgetting. Don't shirk it!"

"Great God!" cried I. "But must life always be like this? I could die, indeed, I would willingly jump into this cold and muddy river now, if by so doing I could stick a stiff dead hand through all these things into the future,—a dead commanding hand insisting with a silent irresistible gesture that this waste and failure of life should cease, and cease forever."

"But it does cease! Each year in its proportions it is a little less."

I walked in silence, and my companion talked by my side.

"We go on. Here is a good thing done, and there is a good thing done. The Good Will in man—"

"Not fast enough. It goes so slowly—and in a little while we too must die."

"It can be done," said my companion.

"It could be avoided," said I.

"It shall be in the days to come. There is food enough for all, shelter for all, wealth enough for all. Men need only know it and will it. And yet we have this!"

"And so much like this!" said I.

So we talked and were tormented.

And I remember how later we found ourselves on Westminster Bridge, looking back upon the long sweep of wrinkled black water that reflected lights and palaces and the flitting glow of steamboats, and by that time we had talked ourselves past our despair. We perceived that what was splendid remained splendid, that what was mysterious remained insoluble for all our pain and impatience. But it was clear to us: the thing for us two to go upon was not the good of the present nor the evil, but the effort and the dream of the finer order, the fuller life, the banishment of suffering, to come.

"We want all the beauty that is here," said my friend, "and more also. And none of these distresses. We are here—we know not whence nor why—to want that and to struggle to get it, you and I and ten thousand others thinly hidden from us by these luminous darknesses. We work, we pass—whither I know not, but out of our knowing. But we work—we are spurred to work. That yonder—those people are the spur for us who cannot answer to any finer appeal. Each in our measure must do. And our reward? Our reward is our faith. Here is my creed tonight. I believe out of me and the Good Will in me and my kind there comes a regenerate world—cleansed of suffering and sorrow. That is our purpose here—to forward that. It gives us work for all our lives. Why should we ask to know more? Our errors—our sins—tonight they seem to matter very little. If we stumble and roll in the mud, if we blunder against each other and hurt one another."

"We have to go on," said my friend after a pause.

We stood for a time in silence.

One's own personal problems came and went like a ripple in the water. Even that whiskey dealer's advertisement upon the southern bank became through some fantastic transformation a promise, an enigmatical promise, flashed up the river reach in letters of fire. London was indeed very beautiful that night. Without hope she would have seemed not only as beautiful but as terrible as a black panther crouching on her prey. Our hope redeemed her. Beyond her dark and meretricious splendors, beyond her throned presence, jeweled with links and points and cressets of fire, crowned with stars, robed in the night, hiding cruelties, I caught a moment's vision of the coming City of Mankind, of a city more wonderful than all my dreaming, full of life, full of youth, full of the spirit of creation.

THE BASE OF ALL METAPHYSICS

WALT WHITMAN

And now gentlemen,
A word I give to remain in your memories and minds,
As base and finale too for all metaphysics.

(So to the students the old professor,
At the close of his crowded course.)

Having studied the new and antique, the Greek and Germanic systems,
Kant having studied and stated, Fichte and Schelling and Hegel,
Stated the lore of Plato, and Socrates greater than Plato.
And greater than Socrates sought and stated, Christ divine
    having studied long,
I see reminiscent today those Greek and Germanic systems,
See the philosophies all, Christian churches and tenets see,
Yet underneath Socrates clearly see, and underneath Christ
    the divine I see,
The dear love of man for his comrade, the attraction of friend
    to friend,
Of the well-married husband and wife, of children and parents,
Of city for city and land for land.

CHAPTER 15

SOME ASPECTS OF PRAGMATISM

Now our research is done, measured the shadow,
The plains mapped out, the hills a natural bound'ry.
Such and such is our country. There remains to
Plough up the meadowland, reclaim the marshes.
—C. Day Lewis, *From Feathers to Iron*, 1.

Pragmatism, William James tells us, is a "looking away from first things, principles, 'categories,' supposed necessities; . . . [a] looking towards last things, fruits, consequences, facts." It does not admit the existence of absolutes. Truth, beauty, duty, all the virtues, have no separate existence from human experience. The impulse to good is what it is—no more. It does not imply the existence of some supernatural value, since there is nothing beyond nature: nature comprehends all that man can know—it comprehends man himself. In limiting knowledge to experience, pragmatism agrees with naturalism; in applying method to the evaluation of experience, it qualifies humanism (most humanists are pragmatists in their approach to life).

In pragmatism there is no gold standard of truth. Truth depends upon the results of action. If an idea, or plan of action as pragmatism interprets the term, works effectively, achieves a good end, it is true. If it fails, it is false. Thus no doctor who was a pragmatist would ever feel twinges of conscience in concealing harmful facts from his patient, and no true pragmatist would ever be misled by the fictive ideal of personal liberty to ignore the rights of others. On the other hand, this philosophy of satisfactory action is dangerous in that its ideals may be perverted by the asocial. Always to act wisely and impartially with expediency as a standard would hardly be possible to the best of us.

Toward religion, always consistent, pragmatism maintains the same attitude as it does to all experience. Though disallowing any knowledge of an absolute, it admits of higher aspiration in man's nature, and makes much of the will to believe. A belief that makes for more effective living justifies itself, is a "true" belief. Certain pragmatists regard supernaturalism as a primitive tool by which men hoped to propitiate the forces of Nature. Modern man, they believe, should look instead to science and learning in general to solve his problems. Following this bent, pragmatism has come more and more to emphasize the scientific method, the measuring of all

541

things by experience. But it shares with humanism a belief in the high potentialities of humanity.

In our first selection, "Transitional Poem," C. Day Lewis suggests the central thesis of pragmatism. Man should content himself with experience. If there is truth beyond experience, it is beyond our comprehension. And this is the burden of Oliver Wendell Holmes's letter to William James. Conventional philosophies, he tells us, with their attempts to interpret absolutes, "sin through arrogance." The "only promising activity is to make my universe coherent and livable, not to babble about the universe."

James, in the selection from "What Pragmatism Means," graphically illustrates and defends pragmatic method. "Theories thus become instruments, not answers to enigmas, in which we can rest." As Oliver Wendell Holmes puts it, "the best test of truth is the power of the thought to get itself accepted in the competition of the market" (Perry, *The Thought and Character of William James* II, pp. 458-59). If these consequences cannot be demonstrated, the idea is invalid and meaningless. This thesis is sustained in detail by F. C. S. Schiller in his essay entitled *Humanism,* an enjoyable imaginary conversation between himself and Plato and Aristotle. Both Schiller and James are in complete agreement that knowledge must be useful to be valid or true, and both conclude that the so-called knowledge of the absolute is useless and without meaning. Dewey further extends this discussion of the pragmatic method by an inquiry into its nature and the value of "authority." In *The Varieties of Religious Experience* James anticipates, and, as he thinks, refutes these arguments.

Matthew Arnold accepts the pragmatic argument that experience is all that we can know: "Once read thy own breast right, and thou hast done with fears; Man gets no other light, Search he a thousand years." Our "own acts, for good or ill, are mightier powers" than the false powers our minds invent and ascribe to the absolute. But, Arnold concludes, men need not despair: "Fear not! Life still leaves human effort scope." This sentiment is the most important lesson of pragmatism: Let us make the best of this, our only life. Here we can plan a useful world for our children. It is the whimsical but serious conclusion of Voltaire: " ' 'Tis well said,' replied Candide, 'but we must cultivate our gardens.' " Like the old Turk, we should not inquire what is going on in Constantinople (the inaccessible or unreality).

Pragmatism, then, is pre-eminently the philosophy of living, but not ignoble living. We should live to learn, without fear of the future—"follow knowledge," as Tennyson says, "like a sinking star Beyond the utmost bound of human thought"—or to the limits of human thought, rather; to think of going further leads into the pragmatically inconceivable realm of another world.

Pragmatism as James sees it, however, entertains the possibility of the will to believe, and Pater urges this doctrine on us in the selection from *Marius the Epicurean*: " 'Tis in thy power to think as thou wilt." Is the will itself, he asks, an organ of vision? If so, the vision desired may exist. But which, we may ask, of the many religions offers us the possible truth? Before pragmatism was recognized as a formal philosophy, Lessing gave us the pragmatic answer to this question in his delightful *Nathan the Wise*: The true faith will show itself by its works.

But this is a side excursion. As C. Day Lewis says, the Hereafter is "a land which later we may tell of, Here-now we know." This is our country. Let us "Plough up the meadowland, reclaim the marshes."

TRANSITIONAL POEM, 17

C. DAY LEWIS

When nature plays hedge-schoolmaster,
Shakes out the gaudy map of summer
And shows me charabanc, rose, barley-ear
And every bright-winged hummer,

He only would require of me
To be the sponge of natural laws
And learn no more of that cosmography
Than passes through the pores.

Why must I then unleash my brain
To sweat after some revelation
Behind the rose, heedless if truth maintain
On the rose-bloom her station?

When bullying April bruised mine eyes
With sleet-bound appetites and crude
Experiments of green, I still was wise
And kissed the blossoming rod.

Now summer brings what April took,
Riding with fanfares from the south,
And I should be no Solomon to look
My Sheba in the mouth.

Charabancs shout along the lane
And summer gales bay in the wood
No less superbly because I can't explain
What I have understood.

Let logic analyze the hive,
Wisdom's content to have the honey:
So I'll go bite the crust of things and thrive
While hedgerows still are sunny.

LETTER TO WILLIAM JAMES
OLIVER WENDELL HOLMES

Washington, March 24, 1907

Dear Bill,—

I have read your two pieces about pragmatism (pedantic name) and am curious to hear the rest. Meantime I will fire off a reflection or two. For a good many years I have had a formula for truth which seems humbler than those you give . . . but I don't know whether it is pragmatic or not. I have been in the habit of saying that all I mean by truth is what I can't help thinking. The assumption of the validity of the thinking process seems to mean no more than that: I am up against it—I have gone as far as I can go—just as when I like a glass of beer. But I have learned to surmise that my *can't helps* are not necessarily cosmic can't helps—that the universe may not be subject to my limitations; and philosophy generally seems to me to sin through arrogance. It is like the old knight-errants who proposed to knock your head off if you didn't admit that their girl was not only a nice girl but the most beautiful and best of all possible girls. I can't help preferring champagne to ditch water,—I doubt if the universe does.

But a reference to the universe seems to let in the Absolute that in form I was expelling. To that I answer that I admit it to be but a guess. I think the despised *ding an sich* is all right. It stands on faith or a bet. The great act of faith is when a man decides that he is not God. But when I admit that you are not my dream, I seem to myself to have admitted the universe and the *ding an sich*,—unpredicable and only guessed at, as somewhat out of which I come rather than coming out of me. But if I did come out of it, or rather, if I am in it, I see no wonder that I can't swallow it. If it fixed my bounds, as it gives me my powers, I have nothing to say about its possibilities or characteristics except that it is a kind of thing (using this phraseology skeptically and under protest) that has me in its belly and so is bigger than I. It seems to me that the only promising activity is to make *my* universe coherent and livable, not to babble about *the* universe. Truth then, as one, I agree with you, is only an ideal—an assumption that if everyone was as educated and clever as I he would feel the same compulsions that I do. To a limited extent only do men feel so in fact, so that in fact there are as many truths as there are men. But if we all agreed, we should only have formulated our limitations . . . I think the attempt to make these limitations compulsory on anything outside our dream—to demand significance, etc., of the universe—absurd. I simply say it contains them, and bow my head. To defy it would be equally absurd, as it would furnish me the energy with which to shake my fist. Most of us retain enough of the theological attitude to think that we are little gods. It is the regular position of skeptical French heroes,—like the scientific man in Maeterlinck's "Bees."

I have written more of a letter than I have time to write, but I add that I don't think fundamental doubt at all inconsistent with practical idealizing. As long as man's food produces extra energy he will have to let it off, i.e., to act. To act affirms, for the moment at least, the worth of an end; idealizing seems to be simply the generalized and permanent affirmation of the worth of ends. One may make that affirmation for purposes of conduct, and leave to the universe the care of deciding how much it cares about them. Again I bow my head and try to fulfil what seems to me my manifest destiny. . . . As to pain, suicide, etc., I think you make too much row about them, and have had thoughts on the need of a society for the promotion of hard-heartedness. It is as absurd for me to be spearing my old commonplaces at you as it would be for an outsider to instruct me in the theory of legal responsibility, but you see, *mon vieux*, although it is years since we have had any real talk together, I am rather obstinate in my adherence to ancient sympathies and enjoy letting out a little slack to you.

I think your "Defense of Pragmatism" an admirable piece of writing. Also it commands my full sympathy so far as I see. Its classification reminded me (in the freedom merely) of Patten's *Development of English Thought*—a most amusing and suggestive book—one of those that like your piece makes me say, "Give me the literature of the last twenty-five years and you may destroy the rest" (when I want to horrify the cultured). In general nowadays I would rather read sociology than philosophy; though I was interested by Santayana's four volumes, spite of their slight tendency to improvise; and though I devoted a certain time, the summer before last, to enough study of Hegel's *Logic* to enable me for the moment to say specifically what I thought the fallacies, and then dismissed it from my mind. Adieu. Yours ever,

O. W. Holmes

P.S. I have just read your other paper, also good. Your general line of thought has been used by protectionists—that protection unlocks energies and gets more out of men. . . .

FROM WHAT PRAGMATISM MEANS

In *Pragmatism*

WILLIAM JAMES

Some years ago, being with a camping party in the mountains, I returned from a solitary ramble to find every one engaged in a ferocious metaphysical dispute. The *corpus* of the dispute was a squirrel—a live squirrel supposed to be clinging to one side of a tree-trunk; while over against the tree's opposite side a human being was imagined to stand. This human witness tries to get sight of the squirrel by moving rapidly round the tree, but no matter how fast he goes, the squirrel moves as fast in the opposition direction, and always keeps the tree between himself and the man, so that never a glimpse of him is caught. The resultant metaphysical problem now is this: *Does the man go round the squirrel or not?* He goes round the tree, sure enough, and the squirrel is on the tree; but does he go round the squirrel? In the unlimited leisure of the wilderness, discussion had been worn threadbare. Everyone had taken sides, and was obstinate; and the numbers on both sides were even. Each side, when I appeared therefore appealed to me to make it a majority. Mindful of the scholastic adage that whenever you meet a contradiction you must make a distinction, I immediately sought and found one, as follows: "Which party is right," I said, "depends on what you *practically mean* by 'going round' the squirrel. If you mean passing from the north of him to the east, then to the south, then to the west, and then to the north of him again, obviously the man does go round him, for he occupies these successive positions. But if on the contrary you mean being first in front of him, then on the right of him, then behind him, then on his left, and finally in front again, it is quite as obvious that the man fails to go round him, for by the compensating movements the squirrel makes, he keeps his belly turned towards the man all the time, and his back turned away. Make the distinction, and there is no occasion for any farther dispute. You are both right and both wrong according as you conceive the verb 'to go round' in one practical fashion or the other."

Although one or two of the hotter disputants called my speech a shuffling evasion, saying they wanted no quibbling or scholastic hairsplitting, but meant just plain honest English "round," the majority seemed to think that the distinction had assuaged the dispute.

I tell this trivial anecdote because it is a peculiarly simple example of what I wish now to speak of as *the pragmatic method*. The pragmatic method is primarily a method of settling metaphysical disputes that otherwise might be interminable. Is the world one or many?—fated or free?—material or spiritual?—here are notions either of which may or may not hold good of the world; and disputes over such notions are unending. The pragmatic method in such cases is to try to interpret each notion by tracing its respective practical consequences. What difference would it practically make to any one if this notion rather than that notion were true? If no practical difference whatever can be traced, then the alternatives mean practically the same thing, and all dispute is idle. Whenever a dispute is serious, we ought to be able to show some practical difference that must follow from one side or the other's being right.

.   .   .   .

It is astonishing to see how many philosophical disputes collapse into insignificance the moment you subject them to this simple test of tracing a concrete consequence. There can *be* no difference anywhere that doesn't *make* a difference elsewhere—no difference in abstract truth that doesn't express itself in a difference in concrete fact and in conduct consequent upon that fact, imposed on somebody, somehow, somewhere, and somewhen. The whole function of philosophy ought to be to find out what definite difference it will make to you and me, at definite instants of our life, if this world-formula or that world-formula be the true one.

There is absolutely nothing new in the pragmatic method. Socrates was an adept at it. Aristotle used it methodically. Locke, Berkeley, and Hume made momentous contributions to truth by its means. Shadworth Hodgson keeps insisting that realities are only what they are "known as." But these forerunners of pragmatism used it in fragments: they were preluders only. Not until in our time has it generalized itself, become conscious of a universal mission, pretended to a conquering destiny. I believe in that destiny, and I hope I may end by inspiring you with my belief.

Pragmatism represents a perfectly familiar attitude in philosophy, the empiricist attitude, but it represents it, as it seems to me, both in a more radical and in a less objectionable form than it has ever yet assumed. A pragmatist turns his back resolutely and once for all upon a lot of inveterate habits dear to professional philosophers. He turns away from abstraction and insufficiency, from verbal solutions, from bad *a priori* reasons, from fixed principles, closed systems, and pretended absolutes and origins. He turns towards concreteness and adequacy, towards facts, towards action and towards power. That means the empiricist temper regnant and the rationalist temper sincerely given up. It means the open air and possibilities of nature, as against dogma, artificiality, and the pretense of finality in truth.

At the same time it does not stand for any special results. It is a method only. But the general triumph of that method would mean an enormous change in what I called in my last lecture the "temperament" of philosophy. Teachers of the ultra-rationalistic type would be frozen out, much as the courtier type is frozen out in republics, as the ultramontane type of priest is frozen out in protestant lands. Science and metaphysics would come much nearer together, would in fact work absolutely hand in hand.

Metaphysics has usually followed a very primitive kind of quest. You know how men have always hankered after unlawful magic, and you know what a great part in magic *words* have always played. If you have his name, or the formula of incantation that binds him, you can control the spirit, genie, afrite, or whatever the power may be. Solomon knew the names of all the spirits, and having their names, he held them subject to his will. So the universe has always appeared to the natural mind as a kind of enigma, of which the key must be sought in the shape of some illuminating or power-bringing word or name. That word names the universes's *principle,* and to possess it is after a fashion to possess the universe itself. "God," "Matter," "Reason," "the Absolute," "Energy," are so many solving names. You can rest when you have them. You are at the end of your metaphysical quest.

But if you follow the pragmatic method, you cannot look on any such word as closing your quest. You must bring out of each word its practical cash-value, set it at work within the stream of your experience. It appears less as a solution, then, than as a program for more work, and more particularly as an indication of the ways in which existing realities may be *changed.*

Theories thus become instruments, not answers to enigmas, in which we can rest. We don't lie back upon them, we move forward, and, on occasion, make nature over again by their aid. Pragmatism unstiffens all our theories, limbers them up and sets each one at work. Being nothing essentially new, it harmonizes with many ancient philosophic tendencies. It agrees with nominalism for instance, in always appealing to particulars; with utilitarianism in emphasizing practical aspects; with positivism in its disdain for verbal solutions, useless questions and metaphysical abstractions.

All these, you see, are *anti-intellectualist* tendencies. Against rationalism as a pretension and a method pragmatism is fully armed and militant. But, at the outset, at least, it stands for no particular results. It has no dogmas, and no doctrines save its method. As the young Italian pragmatist Papini has well said, it lies in the midst of our theories, like a corridor in a hotel. Innumerable chambers open out of it. In one you may find a man writing an atheistic volume; in the next some one on his knees praying for faith and strength; in a third a chemist investigating a body's properties. In a fourth a system of idealistic metaphysics is being excogitated; in a fifth the impossibility of metaphysics is being shown. But they all own the corridor, and all must pass through it if they want a practicable way of getting into or out of their respective rooms.

No particular results then, so far, but only an attitude of orientation, is what pragmatic method means. *The attitude of looking away from first things, principles, "categories," supposed necessities; and of looking towards last things, fruits, consequences, facts.*

. . . .

A new opinion counts as "true" just in proportion as it gratifies the individual's desire to assimilate the novel in his experience to his beliefs in stock. It must both lean on old truth and grasp new fact; and its success (as I said a moment ago) in doing this, is a matter for the individual's appreciation. When old truth grows, then, by new truth's addition, it is for subjective reasons. We are in the process and obey the reasons. That new idea is truest which performs most felicitously its function of satisfying our double urgency. It makes itself true, gets itself classed as true, by the way it works; grafting itself then upon the ancient body of truth, which thus grows much as a tree grows by the activity of a new layer of cambium.

Now Dewey and Schiller proceed to generalize this observation and to apply it to the most ancient parts of truth. They also once were plastic. They also were called true for human reasons. They also mediated between still earlier truths and what in those days were novel observations. Purely objective truth, truth in whose establishment the function of giving human satisfaction in marrying previous parts of experience with newer parts played no role whatever, is nowhere to be found. The reasons why we call things true is the reason why they *are* true, for "to be true" *means* only to perform this marriage-function.

The trail of the human serpent is thus over everything. Truth independent; truth that we *find* merely; truth no longer malleable to human need; truth incorrigible, in a word; such truth exists indeed superabundantly—or is supposed to exist by rationalistically minded thinkers; but then it means only the dead heart of the living tree, and its being there means only that truth also has its paleontology, and its "prescription," and may grow stiff with years of veteran service and petrified in men's regard by sheer antiquity. But how plastic even the oldest truths nevertheless really are has been vividly shown in our day by the transformation of logical and mathematical ideas, a transformation which seems even to be invading physics. The ancient formulas are reinterpreted as special expressions of much wider principles, principles that our ancestors never got a glimpse of in their present shape and formulation.

FROM USELESS KNOWLEDGE

In *Humanism*

F. C. S. SCHILLER

It will readily be understood that once the idealistic art of waking oneself up out of our world of appearances and thereby passing into one of higher reality is fully mastered, the temptation to exercise it becomes practically irresistible. Nevertheless, it was not until nearly two years (as men reckon time) after the first memorable occasion when he discoursed to me concerning the adaptation of the Ideal State to our present circumstances that I succeeded in sufficiently arousing my soul to raise it once again to that supernal Academe where the divine Plato meditates in holy groves beside a fuller and more limpid stream than the Attic Ilissus.

When I was breathlessly projected into his world, Plato was reclining gracefully beside a moss-grown boulder and listening attentively to a lively little man who was discoursing with an abundance of animation and gesticulation. When he observed me, he stopped his companion, who immediately came hurrying towards me, and after politely greeting me, amiably declared that the Master would be delighted to converse with me. I noticed that he was a dapper little man, apparently in the prime of life, though beginning to grow rather bald about the temples. He was carefully robed, and his beard and his hair, such as it was, were scented. One could not help being struck by his refined, intelligent countenance, and his quick, observant eyes.

As soon as Plato had welcomed me, his companion went off to get, he said, a garden chair from a gleaming marble temple (it turned out to be a shrine of the Muses) at a little distance, and I naturally inquired of Plato who the obliging little man was.

"Why, don't you know?" he replied. "Don't you recognize my famous pupil, Aristotle?"

"Aristotle! No, I should never have supposed he was like that."

"What then would you have expected?"

"Well, I should have expected a bigger man for one thing, and one far less agreeable. To tell the truth, I should have expected Aristotle to be very bumptious and conceited."

"You are not quite wrong," said Plato with an indulgent smile, "he *was* all you say, when he first came hither. But this is Aristotle *with the conceit taken out of him,* so that you now behold him reduced to his true proportions and can see his real worth."

"Ah! that explains much. I now see why *you* are even greater and more impressive than I expected, and why he appears to be on such good terms with you once more."

.   .   .   .

" . . . The world and the truth and the good we were discussing are those *relative to us,*" [said I].

"I see that I was wrong in basing my argument for absolute truth on the perceptions of the senses. But of the eternal truths of mathematics and the like one may surely affirm that they necessarily exist for all intelligences?" [said Aristotle].

"Even this is more than I can grant you."

"How so?"

"They seem to me to be also relative to us; nay, human institutions of the plainest kind."

"Is it not self-evident and absolutely certain that the straight line is the shortest between two points?"

"That is *our* definition of distance. It will do in the sense in which you use it, if I may add, 'for one living in a spatial world which behaves like ours, and apparently yours, once he has succeeded in postulating a system of geometry which suits his world.'"

"I really do not understand you."

"I fear I have not the space to explain myself, and to show you the practical aim of our assumptions concerning 'Space,' even if I dared to discuss the foundations of geometry in the presence of Plato. But it really does not affect my point. What I desire to maintain is that the eternal truths are at bottom postulates, demands we make upon our experience because we need them in order that it may become a cosmos fit to live in."

"But I do not find myself postulating them at all. They are plainly self-evident and axiomatic."

"That is only because your axioms are postulates so ancient and so, firmly rooted that no one now thinks of disputing them."

"Your doctrine seems as monstrous as it is unfamiliar."

"I can neither help that nor establish it fully at this juncture. Perhaps, if the gods are willing, I shall find another occasion to expound to you the proofs of this doctrine, and even, if the gods are gracious, to convince you. For it seems to me that in a manner you already admit the principle of my doctrine."

"It would greatly surprise me if I did."

"You contend, do you not, that concerning ethical matters it is impossible to have the right opinion without, at the same time or before, having the right habit of action, so that, as Roger Ascham has said, 'ill-doings breed ill-thinkings, and of corrupted manners spring perverted judgments'?"

"And do I not contend rightly?"

"I am not denying that your view is right, though perhaps you overstate the impossibility of separating ethical theory from ethical practice. What I should like you to see, however, is that this same doctrine may be extended also to speculative matters. Why should we not contend that the true meaning and right understanding of theoretical principles also appears only to him who is proposing to use them practically? Can we not say that the Scythian was both prudent and wise who would not grant that 2 and 2 made 4 until he knew what *use* was to be made of the admission? Just as the wicked man destroys his intellectual insight into ethical truth by his action, so the mere theorist destroys his insight and understanding of 'theoretical' truth by refusing to use that truth and to apply it practically, failing to see that, both in origin and intention, it is a mass of thoroughly practical devices to enable us to live better."

"I cannot admit that the two cases are at all parallel. In practical matters indeed I rightly hold that action and insight are so conjoined as not to admit of separation, but to extend this doctrine to the apprehension of theoretic truth would lead to many absurdities."

"For instance?"

"Well, for one thing, you would have to go into training for the attainment of philosophic insight after the fashion of an Indian Gymnosophist whom I once met in Asia and who wished to convert me to the pernicious doctrine that all things were one."

"How did he propose to effect this?"

"Well, in the first place he declared that truths could not be implanted in the soul by argument, but must grow out of its essence by its own action. So he refused to give any rational account of his opinions, but told me that if I submitted to his discipline, I should infallibly come to see for myself what he knew to be true. I asked him how, and was amused to find that he wanted me to sit in the sun all day in a stiff and upright posture, breathing in a peculiar way, stopping the right nostril with the thumb, and then slowly drawing in the breath through the left, and breathing it out through the right. By doing this and ejaculating the sacred word *Om* ten thousand times daily, he assured me I should become a god, nay, greater than all gods. I asked him how soon this fate was likely to befall me, if I tried. He thought enlightenment might come to me in one year, or ten, or more. It all depended on me. I replied that even if I failed to get a sunstroke I should be more likely to become an idiot than a god, but that I should already be one if I tried anything so silly. You, however, seem to me to be committing yourself to the same absurdity when you try to extend to contemplation the method which is appropriate only to action."

"But that, Aristotle, is just the point to be proved. My contention is that Pragmatism extends to the acquisition of theoretical principles a method as appropriate to them as to practice. As for Gymnosophistic, I think that your Indian friend's method was really quite different. For though he professed to reach truth by training, there was no rational connection between the truths he aimed at and the methods he advocated, which indeed could only produce self-deception. In moral matters, on the other hand, it is, as you say, necessary to dispose the mind for the perception of truth by appropriate action. If we declined to do this we should not start with a mind free from bias and impartially open to every belief— for that is impossible—but with one biased by different action in a different direction. So that really the training you demand is only what is needed to clear away the antimoral prejudices to which our character would otherwise predispose us. Is this not so?"

"Certainly; you speak well so far."

"Thank you.   May I point out next that the method of Pragmatism is precisely the same in theoretic as in practical matters?   In neither can the truth or false-hood of a conception be decided in the abstract and without experience of the manner of its working.   It gets its real *meaning* only in, from, and by, its use: apart from its use the meaning of any 'Truth' remains potential.   And you can use it only if you desire to use it.   And the desire to use it can only arise if it makes a difference to you whether or not you conceive it, and, if so, how.   You must, therefore, desire, or, as I should say, postulate it, if you are to have it at all.   If, on the other hand, your practical experience suggests to you that a certain conception would be useful, *if it were true,* you will reasonably give it a trial to see whether it is not 'true,' and if thus you discover it and find that you can work with it, you will certainly call it 'true' and believe that it *is* 'true,' and has been so from all eternity, and all this the more confidently and profoundly, the more extensively useful it appears.   Thus it is by hypothetically postulating what we desire to be true because we expect it to be useful, and accepting it as true if we can in any way render it useful, that we seem to me manifestly to come by our principles.   Nor do I see how we could really come by them in any other way, or that we should be prudent if we admitted their claims to truth on any other ground."

"Might they not be self-evident?"

"Self-evidence only seems an accident of our state of mind and in no way a complete guarantee of truth.   To none do so many things seem so strongly self-evident as to the insane.   Much that was false has been accepted as self-evident and no doubt still is.   Its self-evidence only means that we have *ceased* to question a principle or not yet *begun* to do so."

"And can you not see that there are intrinsically necessary truths?"

"Not a bit.   Unless by necessary you mean needful, an intrinsic necessity seems to me a contradiction.   Necessity is always dependence, and so hypothetical."

"You blaspheme horribly against the highest beings in the universe, the Deity and the Triangle!"

"Even though you should threaten to impale me on the acutest angle of the most acute-angled specimen of the latter you can find in your world of 'necessary matter' (μὴ ἐνδεχομένων ἄλλως ἔχειν), I should not refrain from speaking thus.   For I want you to see the exact point of my doctrine, and where it diverges from your own."

"Of course—I see that.   If you can prove your derivation of the Axioms and show that the necessary is only the needful, the speculative reason must say a long farewell to its independence."

"Perhaps it will be none the worse for that."

At this point Plato interposed a question.

"Have I understood you rightly, most astonishing young man, to affirm that theoretic truth was wholly derivative and subservient to practical purposes?"

"You have."

"In that case would you not have to regard theoretic falsehood as, in the last resort, practical uselessness?"

"You are very nearly right, Plato; the practical uselessness of the theoretic 'truth' which turns out to be false is what convinces us.   I am glad I have made my point so clear to you."

"And would you contend generally that the 'useless' and the 'false' were not two things but one, doubly named?"

"Not quite.   For the useless is not always dismissed as 'false.'   It may also be rejected as 'unreal,' as is done by those who, deeming dreams to be useless, account them *unreal*. And perhaps it might be most accurate to call the 'useless' 'unmeaning' rather than 'false.' But that hardly matters, for the unmeaning will be called 'false' or 'unreal' as suits our purpose."

"It seems however that you do *not* say that *the false is useless*?"

"Not until you see that when you can call it false you must *already* have discovered the limits of its use. And certainly I would not deprive you, Plato, of all men, of your *'noble lies.'* "

"Nor would you say that the *useful* and the *true* were quite the same?"

"Not, except in the ideal state, in which no use could be found but for the whole truth, and all were too reasonable and too well educated to desire to pursue seeming 'truths' which were useless and therefore to be judged false. But might we not ask Aristotle to tell us all that logically follows from the two propositions which I am maintaining, viz., that *whatever is true is useful* and that *whatever is useless is false?*"

"Yes. I think you could assist us greatly, Aristotle, by doing this."

"I shall do so with the greatest pleasure, that, to wit, of logical contemplation. If *whatever is true is useful* it follows that (1) *nothing true is useless,* and (2) that *nothing useless is true,* that (3) *whatever is useless is false,* that (4) *some things useful are true,* and (5) *not false,* while (6) *some things false are useless* and (7) *not useful.* But since your second proposition that *whatever is useless is false,* is the third of those which follow from your first, that *whatever is true is useful,* being indeed its 'obverted contrapositive,' it is clear that in this also all the others are implied."

"What a thing it is to be a formal logician and conversant with the forms of immediate inference! I myself have never been able to break myself of the habit of trying to convert an universal affirmative simply, and I suppose I ought now to be able to guess how far you are from agreeing with a statement which I found lately in a book by one of your Oxford sophists, who seemed to be discussing much the same questions, that 'the false is the same as the theoretically untenable'? *You* would rather say that it was 'the same as the practically untenable'?"

"Yes, the false is that which *fails* us, and causes us to fail. For I would go on to say that the theoretically untenable always turns out to be so called because it is practically untenable."

"The sophist whom, with difficulty, I read seemed to see no way from the one to the other."

"I don't suppose he wished to. It would have upset his whole philosophy, and you know how ready philosophers are to declare inexplicable and not to be grasped by man whatever 'difficulty' reveals the errors into which they have plunged."

"Yes, there is no Tartaros to which they would not willingly descend rather than confess that they have started on the wrong track. But even you have asserted the existence of a better way rather than shown it to us."

"I must confess, Plato, that much as I should have wished to show you that my way is both practical and practicable I have not had the time to do this. But if I had, I feel sure that I could do so."

"Say on; there is no limit but life itself to the search for Truth."

"That is all very well for *you,* whose abode has been in these pleasant places for so long, and to whom, it seems, there comes neither death nor change. But I have to go back."

"To your pupils?"

"Yes, and already I feel the premonitory heaviness in my feet. It will slowly creep upwards, and when it reaches the head I shall go to sleep and wake again in another world far from you."

"I am sorry; though it will interest us to see how you vanish. But before you pass away, will you not, seeing that all truth you say is practical, tell us what in this case is the practical application of the 'truths' you have championed?"

"With the greatest pleasure, Plato, that is what I was coming back to. They form my excellent excuse for neglecting to tell men about your ideas."

"I do not quite see how."

"Why, so long as my knowledge of your world is useless to them, it is for them, literally and in the completest way, false!"

"But surely both they and you must admit that there is much useless knowledge?"

"There is much, of course, which is so called, and actually is useless for certain purposes, but nothing which can be so for all. Much that is 'useless' is so because certain persons refuse to use it or are unable to do so. Pearls are useless to swine, and, as Herakleitos said, gold to asses. And so neither ass nor hog could truly call them precious. Or, again, often what is called useless is that which is *indirectly* useful. It is useful as *logically completing* a system of knowledge which is useful in other parts and as a whole. Or perhaps in some cases the use is prospective and has not yet been discovered. A great deal of mathematics would be in this position. But if no use could be found for mathematics, they would sink into the position of difficult *games,* and then their only use would be to amuse those who liked to play with them. Or lastly, there is a good deal of knowledge which is comparatively, or as Aristotle would say, accidentally, useless, because the time spent in acquiring it might be more usefully employed otherwise. For instance, you might count the hairs on Aristotle's head, and the knowledge might enable you to win a bet that their number was less than a myriad. But ordinarily such knowledge would be deemed useless, seeing that you might have been better employed."

"But would these explanations cover all the facts?"

"Not perhaps quite all in our world, in which there is also seeming 'useless knowledge,' which is not really knowledge at all, but falsely so called; being as it were a parasitic growth upon the real and useful knowledge, or even a perversion thereof, a sort of harmless tumor or malignant cancer, which would not arise in a healthy state and should be extirpated wherever it appears."

"Still it exists."

"As evil exists; indeed it seems to be merely one aspect of the evil that exists."

"Are you not now extending your explanations so far that your paradox is in danger of becoming a truism? Can you any longer give me an instance of really useless knowledge?"

"Of course not, Plato, seeing that my contention is that whatever is truly knowledge is useful, and whatever is not useful is not truly knowledge, while in proportion as any alleged knowledge is seen to be useless it is in danger of being declared false! The only illustration I can give, therefore, is of knowledge falsely so-called, which is thought to be useful, but is really useless, and therefore false or, if you prefer, unmeaning."

"Even of that we should like an example."

"I see, Plato, that you are willing to embroil me with most of the philosophers in my world. For if I am to speak what is in my mind, I must say that knowledge of the Absolute or, what comes to the same, of the Unknowable, seems to me to be of the kind you require...."

FROM THEORIES OF KNOWLEDGE

In *Democracy and Education*

JOHN DEWEY

The development of the experimental method as the method of getting knowledge and of making sure it *is* knowledge, and not mere opinion—the method of both discovery and proof—is the remaining great force in bringing about a transformation in the theory of knowledge. The experimental method has two sides. (i) On one hand, it means that we have no right to call anything knowledge except where our activity has actually produced certain physical changes in things, which agree with and confirm the conception entertained. Short of such specific changes, our beliefs are only hypotheses, theories, suggestions, guesses, and are to be entertained tentatively and to be utilized as indications of experiments to be tried. (ii) On the other hand, the experimental method of thinking signifies that thinking is of avail; that it is of avail in just the degree in which the anticipation of future consequences is made on the basis of thorough observation of present conditions. Experimentation, in other words, is not equivalent to blind reacting. Such surplus activity—a surplus with reference to what has been observed and is now anticipated—is indeed an unescapable factor in all our behavior, but it is not experiment save as consequences are noted and are used to make predictions and plans in similar situations in the future. The more the meaning of the experimental method is perceived, the more our trying out of a certain way of treating the material resources and obstacles which confront us embodies a prior use of intelligence. What we call magic was with respect to many things the experimental method of the savage; but for him to try was to try his luck, not his ideas. The scientific experimental method is, on the contrary, a trial of ideas; hence even when practically—or immediately—unsuccessful, it is intellectual, fruitful; for we learn from our failures when our endeavors are seriously thoughtful.

The experimental method is new as a scientific resource—as a systematized means of making knowledge, though as old as life as a practical device. Hence it is not surprising that men have not recognized its full scope. For the most part, its significance is regarded as belonging to certain technical and merely physical matters. It will doubtless take a long time to secure the perception that it holds equally as to the forming and testing of ideas in social and moral matters. Men still want the crutch of dogma, of beliefs fixed by authority, to relieve them of the trouble of thinking and the responsibility of directing their activity by thought. They tend to confine their own thinking to a consideration of which one among the rival systems of dogma they will accept. Hence the schools are better adapted, as John Stuart Mill said, to make disciples than inquirers. But every advance in the influence of the experimental method is sure to aid in outlawing the literary, dialectic, and authoritative methods of forming beliefs which have governed the schools of the past, and to transfer their prestige to methods which will procure an active concern with things and persons, directed by aims of increasing temporal reach and deploying greater range of things in space. In time the theory of knowing must be derived from the practice which is most successful in making knowledge; and then that theory will be employed to improve the methods which are less successful.

THE PROBLEM OF METHOD

In *Ethics*

JOHN DEWEY

The attempt to settle these issues in our discussion of ethics would obviously involve an exhibition of partisanship. But, what is more important, it would involve the adoption of a method which has been expressly criticized and repudiated. It would assume the existence of final and unquestionable knowledge upon which we can fall back in order to settle automatically every moral problem. It would involve the commitment to a dogmatic theory of morals. The alternative method may be called experimental. It implies that reflective morality demands observation of particular situations, rather than fixed adherence to *a priori* principles; that free inquiry and freedom of publication and discussion must be encouraged and not merely grudgingly tolerated; that opportunity at different times and places must be given for trying different measures so that their effects may be capable of observation and of comparison with one another. It is, in short, the method of democracy, of a positive toleration which amounts to sympathetic regard for the intelligence and personality of others, even if they hold views opposed to ours, and of scientific inquiry into facts and testing of ideas.

The opposed method, even when we free it from the extreme traits of forcible suppression, censorship, and intolerant persecution which have often historically accompanied it, is the method of appeal to authority and to precedent. The will of divine beings, supernaturally revealed; of divinely ordained rulers; of so-called natural law, philosophically interpreted; of private conscience; of the commands of the state, or the constitution; of common consent; of a majority; of received conventions; of traditions coming from a hoary past; of the wisdom of ancestors; of precedents set up in the past, have at different times been the authority appealed to. The common feature of the appeal is that there is some voice so authoritative as to preclude the need of inquiry. The logic of the various positions is that while an open mind may be desirable in respect to physical truths, a completely settled and closed mind is needed in moral matters.

Adoption of the experimental method does not signify that there is no place for authority and precedent. On the contrary, precedent is, as we noted in another connection, a valuable *instrumentality* (p. 304). But precedents are to be *used* rather than to be implicitly followed; they are to be used as tools of analysis of present situations, suggesting points to be looked into and hypotheses to be tried. They are of much the same worth as are personal memories in individual crises; a storehouse to be drawn upon for suggestion. There is also a place for the use of authorities. Even in free scientific inquiry, present investigators rely upon the findings of investigators of the past. They employ theories and principles which are identified with scientific inquirers of the past. They do so, however, only as long as *no evidence is presented calling for a re-examination of their findings and theories.* They never assume that these findings are so final that under no circumstances can they be questioned and modified. Because of partisanship, love of certainty, and devotion to routine, accepted points of view gain a momentum which for long periods even in science may restrict observation and reflection. But this limitation is recognized to be a weakness of human nature and not a desirable use of the principle of authority.

In moral matters there is also a presumption in favor of principles that have had a long career in the past and that have been endorsed by men of insight;

the presumption is especially strong when all that opposes them is the will of some individual for exemption because of an impulse or passion which is temporarily urgent. Such principles are no more to be lightly discarded than are scientific principles worked out in the past. But in one as in the other, newly discovered facts or newly instituted conditions may give rise to doubts and indicate the inapplicability of accepted doctrines. In questions of social morality more fundamental than any particular principle held or decision reached is the attitude of *willingness to re-examine and if necessary to revise current convictions, even if that course entails the effort to change by concerted effort existing institutions, and to direct existing tendencies to new ends.*

It is a caricature to suppose that emphasis upon the social character of morality leads to glorification of contemporary conditions just as they are. The position does insist that morals, to have vitality, must be related to these conditions or be up in the air. But there is nothing in the bare position which indicates whether the relation is to be one of favor or of opposition. A man walking in a bog must pay even more heed to his surroundings than a man walking on smooth pavement, but this fact does not mean that he is to surrender to these surroundings. The alternative is not between abdication and acquiescence on one side, and neglect and ignoring on the other; it is between a morals which is effective because related to what is, and a morality which is futile and empty because framed in disregard of actual conditions. Against the social consequences generated by existing conditions there always stands the idea of other and better social consequences which a change would bring into being.

FROM CONCLUSIONS

In *The Varieties of Religious Experience*

WILLIAM JAMES

Knowledge about a thing is not the thing itself. You remember what Al-Ghazzali told us in the Lecture on Mysticism,—that to understand the causes of drunkenness, as a physician understands them, is not to be drunk. A science might come to understand everything about the causes and elements of religion, and might even decide which elements were qualified, by their general harmony with other branches of knowledge, to be considered true; and yet the best man at this science might be the man who found it hardest to be personally devout. *Tout savoir c'est tout pardonner.* The name of Renan would doubtless occur to many persons as an example of the way in which breadth of knowledge may make one only a dilettante in possibilities, and blunt the acuteness of one's living faith. If religion be a function by which either God's cause or man's cause is to be really advanced, then he who lives the life of it, however narrowly, is a better servant than he who merely knows about it, however much. Knowledge about life is one thing; effective occupation of a place in life, with its dynamic currents passing through your being, is another.

For this reason, the science of religions may not be an equivalent for living religion; and if we turn to the inner difficulties of such a science, we see that a point comes when she must drop the purely theoretic attitude, and either let her knots remain uncut, or have them cut by active faith. To see this, suppose that we have our science of religions constituted as a matter of fact. Suppose that she has assimilated all the necessary historical material and distilled out of it as its essence the same conclusions which I myself a few moments ago pronounced.

Suppose that she agrees that religion, wherever it is an active thing, involves a belief in ideal presences, and a belief that in our prayerful communion with them, work is done, and something real comes to pass. She has now to exert her critical activity, and to decide how far, in the light of other sciences and in that of general philosophy, such beliefs can be considered *true*.

Dogmatically to decide this is an impossible task. Not only are the other sciences and the philosophy still far from being completed, but in their present state we find them full of conflicts. The sciences of nature know nothing of spiritual presences, and on the whole hold no practical commerce whatever with the idealistic conceptions towards which general philosophy inclines. The scientist, so-called, is, during his scientific hours at least, so materialistic that one may well say that on the whole the influence of science goes against the notion that religion should be recognized at all. And this antipathy to religion finds an echo within the very science of religions itself. The cultivator of this science has to become acquainted with so many groveling and horrible superstitions that a presumption easily arises in his mind that any belief that is religious probably is false. In the "prayerful communion" of savages with such mumbo-jumbos of deities as they acknowledge, it is hard for us to see what genuine spiritual work—even though it were work relative only to their dark savage obligations—can possibly be done.

The consequence is that the conclusions of the science of religions are as likely to be adverse as they are to be favorable to the claim that the essence of religion is true. There is a notion in the air about us that religion is probably only an anachronism, a case of "survival," an atavistic relapse into a mode of thought which humanity in its more enlightened examples has outgrown; and this notion our religious anthropologists at present do little to counteract.

This view is so widespread at the present day that I must consider it with some explicitness before I pass to my own conclusions. Let me call it the "Survival theory" for brevity's sake.

The pivot round which the religious life, as we have traced it, revolves, is the interest of the individual in his private personal destiny. Religion, in short, is a monumental chapter in the history of human egotism. The gods believed in— whether by crude savages or by men disciplined intellectually—agree with each other in recognizing personal calls. Religious thought is carried on in terms of personality, this being, in the world of religion, the one fundamental fact. Today, quite as much as at any previous age, the religious individual tells you that the divine meets him on the basis of his personal concerns.

Science, on the other hand, has ended by utterly repudiating the personal point of view. She catalogues her elements and records her laws indifferent as to what purpose may be shown forth by them, and constructs her theories quite careless of their bearing on human anxieties and fates. Though the scientist may individually nourish a religion, and be a theist in his irresponsible hours, the days are over when it could be said that for Science herself the heavens declare the glory of God and the firmament showeth his handiwork. Our solar system, with its harmonies, is seen now as but one passing case of a certain sort of moving equilibrium in the heavens, realized by a local accident in an appalling wilderness of worlds where no life can exist. In a span of time which as a cosmic interval will count but as an hour, it will have ceased to be. The Darwinian notion of chance production, and subsequent destruction, speedy or deferred, applies to the largest as well as to the smallest facts. It is impossible, in the present temper of the scientific imagination, to find in the driftings of the cosmic atoms, whether they work on the universal or on the particular scale, anything but a kind of aimless weather, doing and undoing, achieving no proper history, and leaving no result. Nature has no one distinguishable ultimate tendency with which it is possible to feel a sympathy. In the vast rhythm of her processes, as the scientific mind now follows them, she appears to cancel herself. The books of natural theology which satisfied the intellects of our grandfathers seem to us quite grotesque, representing, as they did, a God who conformed the largest things of nature to the paltriest of our private wants. The God whom science recognizes must be a God of universal laws exclusively, a God who does a wholesale, not a retail business. He cannot accommodate his processes to the convenience of individuals. The bubbles on the foam which coats a stormy sea are floating episodes, made and unmade by the forces of the wind and water. Our private selves are like those bubbles,—epiphenomena, as Clifford, I believe, ingeniously called them; their destinies weigh nothing and determine nothing in the world's irremediable currents of events.

You see how natural it is, from this point of view, to treat religion as a mere survival, for religion does in fact perpetuate the traditions of the most primeval thought. To coerce the spiritual powers, or to square them and get them on our side, was, during enormous tracts of time, the one great object in our dealings with the natural world. For our ancestors, dreams, hallucinations, revelations, and cock-and-bull stories were inextricably mixed with facts. Up to a comparatively recent date such distinctions as those between what has been verified and what is only conjectured, between the impersonal and the personal aspects of existence, were hardly suspected or conceived. Whatever you imagined in a lively manner, whatever you thought fit to be true, you affirmed confidently; and whatever you affirmed, your comrades believed. Truth was what had not yet been contradicted, most things were taken into the mind from the point of view of their human suggestiveness, and the attention confined itself exclusively to the aesthetic and dramatic aspects of events.

How indeed could it be otherwise? The extraordinary value, for explanation and prevision, of those mathematical and mechanical modes of conception which science uses, was a result that could not possibly have been expected in advance. Weight, movement, velocity, direction, position, what thin, pallid, uninteresting ideas! How could the richer animistic aspects of Nature, the peculiarities and oddities that make phenomena picturesquely striking or expressive, fail to have been first singled out and followed by philosophy as the more promising avenue to the knowledge of Nature's life? Well, it is still in these richer animistic and dramatic aspects that religion delights to dwell. It is the terror and beauty of phenomena, the "promise" of the dawn and of the rainbow, the "voice" of the thunder, the "gentleness" of the summer rain, the "sublimity" of the stars, and not the physical laws which these things follow, by which the religious mind still continues to be most impressed; and just as of yore, the devout man tells you that in the solitude of his room or of the fields he still feels the divine presence, that inflowings of help come in reply to his prayers, and that sacrifices to this unseen reality fill him with security and peace.

Pure anachronism! says the survival-theory;—anachronism for which deanthropomorphization of the imagination is the remedy required. The less we mix the private with the cosmic, the more we dwell in universal and impersonal terms, the truer heirs of Science we become.

In spite of the appeal which this impersonality of the scientific attitude makes to a certain magnanimity of temper, I believe it to be shallow, and I can now state my reason in comparatively few words. That reason is that, so long as we deal with the cosmic and the general, we deal only with the symbols of reality, but *as soon as we deal with private and personal phenomena as such, we deal with realities in the completest sense of the term.* I think I can easily make clear what I mean by these words.

The world of our experience consists at all times of two parts, an objective and a subjective part, of which the former may be incalculably more extensive than the latter, and yet the latter can never be omitted or suppressed. The objective part is the sum total of whatsoever at any given time we may be thinking of, the subjective part is the inner "state" in which the thinking comes to pass. What we think of may be enormous,—the cosmic times and spaces, for example,—whereas the inner state may be the most fugitive and paltry activity of mind. Yet the cosmic objects, so far as the experience yields them are but ideal pictures of something whose existence we do not inwardly possess but only point at outwardly, while the inner state is our very experience itself; its reality and that of our experience are one. A conscious field *plus* its object as felt or thought of *plus* an attitude towards the object *plus* the sense of a self to whom the attitude belongs—such a concrete bit of personal experience may be a small bit, but it is a solid bit as long as it lasts; not hollow, not a mere abstract element of experience, such as the "object" is when taken all alone. It is a *full* fact, even though it be an insignificant fact; it is of the *kind* to which all realities whatsoever must belong; the motor currents of the world run through the like of it; it is on the line connecting real events with real events. That unsharable feeling which each one of us has of the pinch of his individual destiny as he privately feels it rolling out on fortune's wheel may be disparaged for its egotism, may be sneered at as unscientific, but it is the one thing that fills up the measure of our concrete actuality, and any would-be existent that should lack such a feeling, or its analogue, would be a piece of reality only half made up.

If this be true, it is absurd for science to say that the egotistic elements of experience should be suppressed. The axis of reality runs solely through the egotistic places,—they are strung upon it like so many beads. To describe the world with all the various feelings of the individual pinch of destiny, all the various spiritual attitudes, left out from the description—they being as describable as anything else—would be something like offering a printed bill of fare as the equivalent for a solid meal. Religion makes no such blunder. The individual's religion may be egotistic, and those private realities which it keeps in touch with may be narrow enough; but at any rate it always remains infinitely less hollow and abstract, as far as it goes, than a science which prides itself on taking no account of anything private at all.

A bill of fare with one real raisin on it instead of the word "raisin," with one real egg instead of the word "egg," might be an inadequate meal, but it would at least be a commencement of reality. The contention of the survival-theory that we ought to stick to nonpersonal elements exclusively seems like saying that we ought to be satisfied forever with reading the naked bill of fare. I think, therefore, that however particular questions connected with our individual destinies may be answered, it is only by acknowledging them as genuine questions, and living in the sphere of thought which they open up, that we become profound. But to live thus is to be religious; so I unhesitatingly repudiate the survival-theory of religion, as being founded on an egregious mistake. It does not follow, because our ancestors made so many errors of fact and mixed them with their religion, that we should therefore leave off being religious at all. By being religious we establish ourselves in possession of ultimate reality at the only points at which reality is given us to guard. Our responsible concern is with our private destiny, after all.

You see now why I have been so individualistic throughout these lectures, and why I have seemed so bent on rehabilitating the element of feeling in religion and subordinating its intellectual part. Individuality is founded in feeling; and the recesses of feeling, the darker, blinder strata of character, are the only places in the world in which we catch real fact in the making, and directly perceive how events happen, and how work is actually done. Compared with this world of living individualized feelings, the world of generalized objects which the intellect contemplates is without solidity or life. As in stereoscopic or kinetoscopic pictures seen outside the instrument, the third dimension, the movement, the vital element, are not there. We get a beautiful picture of an express train supposed to be moving, but where in the picture, as I have heard a friend say, is the energy or the fifty miles an hour?

Let us agree, then, that Religion, occupying herself with personal destinies and keeping thus in contact with the only absolute realities which we know, must necessarily play an eternal part in human history. The next thing to decide is what she reveals about those destinies, or whether indeed she reveals anything distinct enough to be considered a general message to mankind. We have done as you see, with our preliminaries, and our final summing up can now begin.

I am well aware that after all the palpitating documents which I have quoted, and all the perspectives of emotion-inspiring institution and belief that my previous lectures have opened, the dry analysis to which I now advance may appear to many of you like an anticlimax, a tapering-off and flattening out of the subject, instead of a crescendo of interest and result. I said awhile ago that the religious attitude of Protestants appears poverty-stricken to the Catholic imagination. Still more poverty-stricken, I fear, may my final summing up of the subject appear at first to some of you. On which account I pray you now to bear this point in mind, that in the present part of it I am expressly trying to reduce religion to its lowest admissible terms, to that minimum, free from individualistic excrescences, which all religions contain as their nucleus, and on which it may be hoped that all religious persons may agree. That established, we should have a result which might be small, but would at least be solid; and on it and round it the ruddier additional beliefs on which the different individuals make their venture might be grafted, and flourish as richly as you please. I shall add my own over-belief (which will be, I confess, of somewhat pallid kind, as befits a critical philosopher), and you will, I hope, also add your over-beliefs, and we shall soon be in the varied world of concrete religious constructions once more.

FROM EMPEDOCLES ON ETNA, I, ii

MATTHEW ARNOLD

The outspread world to span
A cord the Gods first slung,
And then the soul of man
There like a mirror, hung,
And bade the winds through space impel the gusty toy.

Hither and thither spins
The wind-borne, mirroring soul,
A thousand glimpses wins,
And never sees a whole;
Looks once, and drives elsewhere, and leaves its last employ.

The Gods laugh in their sleeve
To watch man doubt and fear,
Who knows not what to believe
Since he sees nothing clear,
And dares stamp nothing false where he finds nothing sure.

Is this, Pausanias, so?
And can our souls not strive,
But with the winds must go,
And hurry where they drive?
Is fate indeed so strong, man's strength indeed so poor?

I will not judge. That man,
Howbeit, I judge as lost,
Whose mind allows a plan,
Which would degrade it most;
And he treats doubt the best who tries to see least ill.

Be not, then, fear's blind slave!
Thou art my friend; to thee,
All knowledge that I have,
All skill I wield, are free.
Ask not the latest news of the last miracle,

Ask not what days and nights
In trance Pantheia lay,
But ask how thou such sights
May'st see without dismay;
Ask what most helps when known, thou son of Anchitus!

What! hate, and awe, and shame
Fill thee to see our time;
Thou feelest thy soul's frame
Shaken and out of chime?
What! life and chance go hard with thee too, as with us;

Thy citizens, 'tis said,
Envy thee and oppress,
Thy goodness no men aid,
All strive to make it less;
Tyranny, pride, and lust, fill Sicily's abodes;

Heaven is with earth at strife,
Signs make thy soul afraid,
The dead return to life,
Rivers are dried, winds stayed;
Scarce can one think in calm, so threatening are the Gods;

And we feel, day and night,
The burden of ourselves—
Well, then, the wiser wight
In his own bosom delves,
And asks what ails him so, and gets what cure he can.

The sophist sneers: "Fool, take
Thy pleasure, right or wrong."
The pious wail: "Forsake
A world these sophists throng."
Be neither Saint nor Sophist led, but be a man!

These hundred doctors try
To preach thee to their school.
"We have the truth!" they cry;
And yet their oracle,
Trumpet it as they will, is but the same as thine.

Once read thy own breast right,
And thou hast done with fears;
Man gets no other light,
Search he a thousand years.
Sink in thyself! there ask what ails thee, at that shrine.

What makes thee struggle and rave?
Why are men ill at ease?—
'Tis that the lot they have
Fails their own will to please,
For man would make no murmuring, were his will obeyed.

And why is it, that still
Man with his lot thus fights?—
'Tis that he makes this *will*
The measure of his *rights,*
And believes Nature outraged if his will's gainsaid.

Couldst thou, Pausanias, learn
How deep a fault is this;
Couldst thou but once discern
Thou hast no *right* to bliss,
No title from the Gods to welfare and repose;

Then thou wouldst look less mazed
Whene'er of bliss debarred,
Nor think the Gods were crazed
When thy own lot went hard.
But we are all the same—the fools of our own woes!

For, from the first faint morn
Of life, the thirst for bliss
Deep in man's heart is born;
And skeptic as he is,
He fails not to judge clear if this be quenched or no.

Nor is the thirst to blame.
Man errs not that he deems
His welfare his true aim,
He errs because he dreams
The world does but exist that welfare to bestow.

We mortals are no kings
For each of whom to sway
A new-made world up-springs,
Meant merely for his play;
No, we are strangers here; the world is from of old.

In vain our pent wills fret,
And would the world subdue.
Limits we did not set
Condition all we do;
Born into life we are, and life must be our mold.

Born into life!—man grows
Forth from his parents' stem,
And blends their bloods, as those
Of theirs are blent in them;
So each new man strikes root into a far foretime.

Born into life!—we bring
A bias with us here,
And, when here, each new thing
Affects us we come near;
To tunes we did not call our being must keep chime.

Born into life!—in vain,
Opinions, those or these,
Unaltered to retain
The obstinate mind decrees;
Experience, like a sea, soaks all-effacing in.

Born into life!—who lists
May what is false hold dear,
And for himself make mists
Through which to see less clear;
The world is what it is, for all our dust and din.

Born into life!—'tis we,
And not the world, are new;
Our cry for bliss, our plea,
Others have urged it too—
Our wants have all been felt, our errors made before.

No eye could be too sound
To observe a world so vast,
No patience too profound
To sort what's here amassed;
How man may here best live no care too great to explore.

But we—as some rude guest
Would change, where'er he roam,
The manners there professed
To those he brings from home—
We mark not the world's course, but would have *it* take *ours*.

The world's course proves the terms
On which man wins content;
Reason the proof confirms—
We spurn it, and invent
A false course for the world, and for ourselves, false powers.

Riches we wish to get,
Yet remain spendthrifts still;
We would have health, and yet
Still use our bodies ill:
Bafflers of our own prayers, from youth to life's last scenes.

We would have inward peace,
Yet will not look within;
We would have misery cease,
Yet will not cease from sin;
We want all pleasant ends, but will use no harsh means;

We do not what we ought,
What we ought not, we do,
And lean upon the thought
That chance will bring us through;
But our own acts, for good or ill, are mightier powers.

Yet, even when man forsakes
All sin,—is just, is pure,
Abandons all which makes
His welfare insecure,—
Other existences there are, that clash with ours.

Like us, the lightning-fires
Love to have scope and play;
The stream, like us, desires
An unimpeded way;
Like us, the Libyan wind delights to roam at large.

Streams will not curb their pride
The just man not to entomb,
Nor lightnings go aside
To give his virtues room;
Nor is that wind less rough which blows a good man's barge.

Nature, with equal mind,
Sees all her sons at play;
Sees man control the wind,
The wind sweep man away;
Allows the proudly riding and the foundering bark.

And, lastly, though of ours
No weakness spoil our lot,
Though the nonhuman powers
Of Nature harm us not,
The ill deeds of other men make often *our* life dark.

.   .   .   .

Yet still, in spite of truth,
In spite of hopes entombed,
That longing of our youth
Burns ever unconsumed,
Still hungrier for delight as delights grow more rare.

We pause; we hush our heart,
And thus address the Gods:
"The world hath failed to impart
The joy our youth forbodes,
Failed to fill up the void which in our breasts we bear.

"Changeful till now, we still
Looked on to something new:
Let us, with changeless will,
Henceforth look on to you,
To find with you the joys we in vain here require!"

Fools! That so often here
Happiness mocked our prayer,
I think, might make us fear
A like event elsewhere;
Make us, not fly to dreams, but moderate desire.

And yet, for those who know
Themselves, who wisely take
Their way through life, and bow
To what they cannot break,
Why should I say that life need yield but *moderate* bliss?

Shall we, with temper spoiled,
Health sapped by living ill,
And judgment all embroiled
By sadness and self-will,
Shall *we* judge what for man is not true bliss or is?

Is it so small a thing
To have enjoyed the sun,
To have lived light in the spring,
To have loved, to have thought, to have done;
To have advanced true friends, and beat down baffling foes—

That we must feign a bliss
Of doubtful future date,
And while we dream on this,
Lose all our present state,
And relegate to worlds yet distant our repose?

Not much, I know, you prize
That pleasure may be had,
Who look on life with eyes
Estranged, like mine, and sad;
And yet the village-churl feels the truth more than you,

Who's loath to leave this life
Which to him little yields—
His hard-tasked sunburnt wife,
His often-labored fields,
The boors with whom he talked, the country-spots he knew.

But thou, because thou hear'st
Men scoff at Heaven and Fate,
Because the Gods thou fear'st
Fail to make blest thy state,
Tremblest, and wilt not dare to trust the joys there are!

I say: Fear not! Life still
Leaves human efforts scope.
But, since life teems with ill,
Nurse no extravagant hope;
Because thou must not dream, thou need'st not then despair!

FROM CANDIDE, Conclusion

VOLTAIRE

As for Martin, he was firmly convinced that people are equally uncomfortable everywhere; he accepted things patiently. Candide, Martin and Pangloss sometimes argued about metaphysics and morals. From the windows of the farm they often watched the ships going by, filled with effendis, pashas, and cadis, who were being exiled to Lemnos, to Mitylene and Erzerum. They saw other cadis, other pashas and other effendis coming back to take the place of the exiles and to be exiled in their turn. They saw the neatly impaled heads which were taken to the Sublime Porte. These sights redoubled their discussions; and when they were not arguing, the boredom was so excessive that one day the old woman dared to say to them:

"I should like to know which is worse, to be raped a hundred times by Negro pirates, to have a buttock cut off, to run the gauntlet among the Bulgarians, to be whipped and flogged in an auto-da-fé, to be dissected, to row in a galley, in short to endure all the miseries through which we have passed, or to remain here doing nothing?"

" 'Tis a great question," said Candide.

These remarks led to new reflections, and Martin especially concluded that man was born to live in the convulsions of distress or in the lethargy of boredom. Candide did not agree, but he asserted nothing. Pangloss confessed that he had always suffered horribly; but, having once maintained that everything was for the best, he had continued to maintain it without believing it.

One thing confirmed Martin in his detestable principles, made Candide hesitate more than ever, and embarrassed Pangloss. And it was this. One day, there came to their farm Paquette and Friar Giroflée who were in the most extreme misery; they had soon wasted their three thousand piastres, had left each other, made it up, quarreled again, been put in prison, escaped, and finally Friar Giroflée had turned Turk. Paquette continued her occupation everywhere and now earned nothing by it.

"I foresaw," said Martin to Candide, "that your gifts would soon be wasted and would only make them the more miserable. You and Cacambo were once bloated with millions of piastres and you are no happier than Friar Giroflée and Paquette."

"Ah! Ha!" said Pangloss to Paquette, "so Heaven brings you back to us, my dear child? Do you know that you cost me the end of my nose, an eye, and an ear! What a plight you are in! Ah! What a world this is!"

This new occurrence caused them to philosophize more than ever.

In the neighborhood there lived a very famous Dervish, who was supposed to be the best philosopher in Turkey; they went to consult him; Pangloss was the spokesman and said:

"Master, we have come to beg you to tell us why so strange an animal as man was ever created."

"What has it to do with you?" said the Dervish. "Is it your business?"

"But, reverend father," said Candide, "there is a horrible amount of evil in the world."

"What does it matter," said the Dervish, "whether there is evil or good? When his highness sends a ship to Egypt, does he worry about the comfort or discomfort of the rats in the ship?"

"Then what should we do?" said Pangloss.

"Hold your tongue," said the Dervish.

"I flattered myself," said Pangloss, "that I should discuss with you effects and causes, this best of all possible worlds, the origin of evil, the nature of the soul and pre-established harmony."

At these words the Dervish slammed the door in their faces.

During this conversation the news went round that at Constantinople two viziers and the mufti had been strangled and several of their friends impaled. This catastrophe made a prodigious noise everywhere for several hours. As Pangloss, Candide and Martin were returning to their little farm, they came upon an old man who was taking the air under a bower of orange-trees at his door. Pangloss, who was as curious as he was argumentative, asked him what was the name of the mufti who had just been strangled.

"I do not know," replied the old man, "I have never known the name of any mufti or of any vizier. I am entirely ignorant of the occurrence you mention; I presume that in general those who meddle with public affairs sometimes perish miserably and that they deserve it; but I never inquire what is going on in Constantinople; I content myself with sending there for sale the produce of the garden I cultivate."

Having spoken thus, he took the strangers into his house. His two daughters and his two sons presented them with several kinds of sherbet which they made themselves, caymac flavored with candied citron peel, oranges, lemons, limes, pineapples, dates, pistachios and Mocha coffee which had not been mixed with the bad coffee of Batavia and the Isles. After which this good Mussulman's two daughters perfumed the beards of Candide, Pangloss and Martin.

"You must have a vast and magnificent estate?" said Candide to the Turk.

"I have only twenty acres," replied the Turk. "I cultivate them with my children; and work keeps at bay three great evils: Boredom, vice and need."

As Candide returned to his farm he reflected deeply on the Turk's remarks. He said to Pangloss and Martin:

"That good old man seems to me to have chosen an existence preferable by far to that of the six kings with whom we had the honor to sup."

"Exalted rank," said Pangloss, "is very dangerous, according to the testimony of all philosophers; for Eglon, King of the Moabites, was murdered by Ehud; Absalom was hanged by the hair and pierced by three darts; King Nadab, son of Jeroboam, was killed by Baasha; King Elah by Zimri; Ahaziah by Jehu; Athaliah by Jehoiada; the Kings Jehoiakim, Jeconiah and Zedekiah were made slaves. You know in what manner died Croesus, Astyages, Darius, Denys of Syracuse, Pyrrhus, Perseus, Hannibal, Jugurtha, Ariovistus, Caesar, Pompey, Nero, Otho, Vitellius, Domitian, Richard II of England, Edward II, Henry VI, Richard III, Mary Stuart, Charles I, the three Henrys of France, the Emperor Henry IV. You know . . ."

"I also know," said Candide, "that we should cultivate our gardens."

"You are right," said Pangloss, "for when man was placed in the Garden of Eden, he was placed there *ut operaratur eum,* to dress it and to keep it; which proves that man was not born for idleness."

"Let us work without arguing," said Martin; " 'tis the only way to make life endurable."

The whole small fraternity entered into this praiseworthy plan, and each started to make use of his talents. The little farm yielded well. Cunegonde was indeed very ugly, but she became an excellent pastry-cook; Paquette embroidered; the old woman took care of the linen. Even Friar Giroflée performed some service; he was a very good carpenter and even became a man of honor; and Pangloss sometimes said to Candide:

"All events are linked up in this best of all possible worlds; for, if you had not been expelled from the noble castle, by hard kicks in your backside for love of Miss Cunegonde, if you had not been clapped into the Inquisition, if you had not wandered about America on foot, if you had not stuck your sword in the Baron, if you had not lost all your sheep from the land of Eldorado, you would not be eating candied citrons and pistachios here."

" 'Tis well said," replied Candide, "but we must cultivate our gardens."

(Richard Aldington, tr.)

ULYSSES

ALFRED LORD TENNYSON

It little profits that an idle king,
By this still hearth, among these barren crags,
Matched with an aged wife, I mete and dole
Unequal laws unto a savage race,
That hoard, and sleep, and feed, and know not me.
I cannot rest from travel; I will drink
Life to the lees. All times I have enjoyed
Greatly, have suffered greatly, both with those
That love me, and alone; on shore, and when
Through scudding drifts the rainy Hyades
Vext the dim sea. I am become a name;
For always roaming with a hungry heart
Much have I seen and known,—cities of men
And manners, climates, councils, governments,
Myself not least, but honored of them all,—
And drunk delight of battle with my peers,
Far on the ringing plains of windy Troy.
I am a part of all that I have met;

Yet all experience is an arch wherethro'
Gleams that untraveled world whose margin fades
Forever and forever when I move.
How dull it is to pause, to make an end,
To rust unburnished, not to shine in use!
As though to breathe were life! Life piled on life
Were all too little, and of one to me
Little remains; but every hour is saved
From that eternal silence, something more,
A bringer of new things; and vile it were
For some three suns to store and hoard myself,
And this gray spirit yearning in desire
To follow knowledge like a sinking star
Beyond the utmost bound of human thought.
This is my son, mine own Telemachus,
To whom I leave the scepter and the isle,—
Well-loved of me, discerning to fulfil
This labor, by slow prudence to make mild
A rugged people, and through soft degrees
Subdue them to the useful and the good.
Most blameless is he, centered in the sphere
Of common duties, decent not to fail
In offices of tenderness, and pay
Meet adoration to my household gods,
When I am gone. He works his work, I mine.
There lies the port; the vessel puffs her sail;
There gloom the dark, broad seas. My mariners,
Souls that have toiled, and wrought, and thought with me,
That ever with a frolic welcome took
The thunder and the sunshine, and opposed
Free hearts, free foreheads,—you and I are old;
Old age hath yet his honor and his toil.
Death closes all; but something ere the end,
Some work of noble note, may yet be done,
Not unbecoming men that strove with Gods.
The lights begin to twinkle from the rocks;
The long day wanes; the slow moon climbs, the deep
Moans round with many voices. Come, my friends,
'Tis not too late to seek a newer world.
Push off, and sitting well in order smite
The sounding furrows; for my purpose holds
To sail beyond the sunset, and the baths
Of all the western stars, until I die.
It may be that the gulfs will wash us down;
It may be we shall touch the Happy Isles,
And see the great Achilles, whom we knew.
Though much is taken, much abides; and though
We are not now that strength which in old days
Moved earth and heaven; that which we are, we are,—
One equal temper of heroic hearts,
Made weak by time and fate, but strong in will
To strive, to seek, to find, and not to yield.

WHAT IS TO COME

WILLIAM ERNEST HENLEY

What is to come we know not. But we know
That what has been was good—was good to show,
Better to hide, and best of all to bear.
We are the masters of the days that were:
We have lived, we have loved, we have suffered
   . . . even so.

Shall we not take the ebb who had the flow?
Life was our friend. Now, if it be our foe—
Dear, though it spoil and break us!—need we care
   What is to come?

Let the great winds their worst and wildest blow,
Or the gold weather round us mellow slow:
We have fulfilled ourselves, and we can dare
And we can conquer, though we may not share
In the rich quiet of the afterglow
   What is to come.

FROM THE WILL AS VISION

In *Marius the Epicurean*

WALTER PATER

That flawless serenity, better than the most pleasurable excitement, yet so easily ruffled by chance collision even with the things and persons he had come to value as the greatest treasure in life, was to be wholly his today, he thought, as he rode towards Tibur, under the early sunshine; the marble of its villas glistening all the way before him on the hillside. And why could he not hold such serenity of spirit ever at command? he asked, expert as he was at last become in the art of setting the house of his thoughts in order. " 'Tis in thy power to think as thou wilt": he repeated to himself: it was the most serviceable of all the lessons enforced on him by those imperial *conversations.*—" 'Tis in thy power to think as thou wilt." And were the cheerful, sociable, restorative beliefs, of which he had there read so much, that bold adhesion, for instance, to the hypothesis of an eternal friend to man, just hidden behind the veil of a mechanical and material order, but only just behind it, ready perhaps even now to break through:—were they, after all, really a matter of choice, dependent on some deliberate act of volition on his part? Were they doctrines one might take for granted, generously take for granted, and led on by them, at first as but well-defined objects of hope, come at last into the region of a corresponding certitude of the intellect? "It is the truth I seek," he had read, "the truth, by which no one," gray and depressing though it might seem, "was ever really injured." And yet, on the other hand, the imperial wayfarer, he had been able to go along with so far on his intellectual pilgrimage, let fall many things concerning the practicability of a methodical and self-forced assent to certain principles or presuppositions "one could not do without." Were there, as the expression *one could not do without* seemed to hint, beliefs, without which life itself must be almost impossible, principles which had their sufficient ground of evidence in that very fact? Experience certainly taught that, as regarding the sensible world he could attend or not, almost at will, to this or that color, this or that train of sounds, in the whole tumultuous concourse of color and sound, so it was also, for the well-trained intelligence, in regard to that hum of voices which besiege the inward no less than the outward ear. Might it be not otherwise with those various and competing hypotheses, the permissible hypotheses, which, in that open field for hypothesis—one's own actual ignorance of the origin and tendency of our being—present themselves so importunately, some of them with so emphatic a reiteration, through all the mental changes of successive ages? Might the will itself be an organ of knowledge, of vision?

FROM NATHAN THE WISE

GOTTHOLD EPHRAIM LESSING

NATHAN: In days of yore, there dwelt in the East a man
 Who from a valued hand received a ring
 Of endless worth; the stone of it an opal,
 That shot an ever-changing tint; moreover,
 It had the hidden virtue him to render
 Of God and man beloved, who, in this view,
 And this persuasion, wore it. Was it strange
 The Eastern man ne'er drew it off his finger,
 And studiously provided to secure it
 For ever to his house? Thus he bequeathed it,
 First, to the most beloved of his sons—
 Ordained that he again should leave the ring
 To the most dear among his children—and,
 That without heeding birth, the favorite son,
 In virtue of the ring alone, should always
 Remain the lord o' th' house. You hear me, Sultan?
SALADIN: I understand thee—on.
NATHAN: From son to son,
 At length this ring descended to a father
 Who had three sons alike obedient to him;
 Whom, therefore, he could not but love alike.
 At times seemed this, now that, at times the third
 (Accordingly as each apart received
 The overflowings of his heart) most worthy
 To heir the ring, which, with good-natured weakness,
 He privately to each in turn had promised.
 This went on for a while. But death approached;
 The father now embarrassed, could not bear
 To disappoint two sons, who trusted him.
 What's to be done? In secret he commands
 The jeweler to come, that from the form
 Of the true ring, he may bespeak two more.
 Nor cost nor pains are to be spared, to make
 The rings alike—quite like the true one. This
 The artist managed. When the rings were brought

The father's eye could not distinguish which
Had been the model.   Overjoyed, he calls
His sons, takes leave of each apart—bestows
His blessing and his ring on each—and dies.
You hear me?

SALADIN: (*who has turned away in perplexity*):   Ay! I hear.
Conclude the tale.

NATHAN: 'Tis ended, Sultan!   All that follows next
May well be guessed.   Scarce is the father dead,
When with his ring each separate son appears,
And claims to be the lord of all the house.
Question arises, tumult and debate;
For the true ring could no more be distinguished
Than now can—the true faith.

SALADIN: How, how?—is that
To be the answer to my query?

NATHAN: No,
But it may serve as my apology;
If I can't venture to decide between
Rings which the father got expressly made,
That they might not be known from one another.

SALADIN: The rings—don't trifle with me; I must think
That the religions which I named can be
Distinguished, e'en to raiment, drink, and food.

NATHAN: And only not as to their grounds of proof.
Are not all built alike on history,
Traditional, or written?   History
Must be received on trust—is it not so?
In whom now are we likeliest to put trust?
In our own people surely, in those men
Whose blood we are, in them who from our childhood
Have given us proofs of love, who ne'er deceived us,
Unless 'twere wholesomer to be deceived.
How can I less believe in my forefathers
Than thou in thine?   How can I ask of thee
To own that thy forefathers falsified,
In order to yield mine the praise of truth?

SALADIN: By the living God!
The man is in the right—I must be silent.

NATHAN: Now let us to our rings return once more.
As said, the sons complained.   Each to the judge
Swore from his father's hand immediately
To have received the ring, as was the case,
After he had long obtained the father's promise
One day to have the ring, as also was.
The father, each asserted, could to him
Not have been false; rather than so suspect
Of such a father, willing as he might be
With charity to judge his brethren, he
Of treacherous forgery was bold to accuse them.

SALADIN: Well, and the judge—I'm eager now to hear
What thou wilt make him say.   Go on, go on.

NATHAN: The judge said, "If ye summon not the father
  Before my seat, I can not give a sentence.
  Am I to guess enigmas? Or expect ye
  That the true ring should here unseal its lips?
  But hold—you tell me that the real ring
  Enjoys the hidden power to make the wearer
  Of God and man beloved: let that decide.
  Which of you do two brothers love the best?
  You're silent. Do these love-exciting rings
  Act inward only, not without? Does each
  Love but himself? Ye're all deceived deceivers—
  None of your rings is true. The real ring,
  Perhaps, is gone. To hide or to supply
  Its loss, your father ordered three for one."
SALADIN: Oh, charming, charming!
NATHAN: "And," the judge continued,
  "If you will take advice, in lieu of sentence,
  This is my counsel to you—to take up
  The matter where it stands. If each of you
  Has had a ring presented by his father,
  Let each believe his own the real ring.
  'Tis possible the father chose no longer
  To tolerate the one ring's tyranny;
  And certainly, as he much loved you all,
  And loved you all alike, it could not please him,
  By favoring one, to be of two the oppressor.
  Let each feel honored by this free affection
  Unwarped of prejudice; let each endeavor
  To vie with both his brothers in displaying
  The virtue of his ring; assist its might
  With gentleness, benevolence, forbearance,
  With inward resignation to the Godhead;
  And if the virtues of the ring continue
  To show themselves among your children's children
  After a thousand thousand years, appear
  Before this judgment-seat—a greater one
  Than I shall sit upon it, and decide."—
  So spake the modest judge.
SALADIN: God!
NATHAN: Saladin?
  Feel'st thou thyself this wiser, promised man?
SALADIN: I, dust—I, nothing—God?
NATHAN: What moves thee, Sultan?
SALADIN: Nathan, my dearest Nathan, 'tis not yet
  The judge's thousand thousand years are past—
  His judgment seat's not mine. Go, go, but love me. . . .

(William Taylor, tr.)

FROM FEATHERS TO IRON, 1

C. DAY LEWIS

Suppose that we, tomorrow or the next day,
Came to an end—in storm the shafting broken,
Or mistaken signal, the flange lifting—
Would that be premature, a text for sorrow?

Say what endurance gives or death denies us.
Love's proved in its creation, not eternity:
Like leaf or linnet the true heart's affection
Is born, dies later, asks no reassurance.

Over dark wood rises one dawn felicitous,
Bright through awakened shadows fall her crystal
Cadenzas, and once for all the wood is quickened.
So our joys visit us, and it suffices.

Nor fear we now to live who in the valley
Of the shadow of life have found a causeway;
For love restores the nerve and love is under
Our feet resilient.   Shall we be weary?

Some say we walk out of Time altogether
This way into a region where the primrose
Shows an immortal dew, sun at meridian
Stands up for ever and in scent the lime tree.

This is a land which later we may tell of.
Here-now we know, what death cannot diminish
Needs no replenishing; yet certain are, though
Dying were well enough, to live is better.

Passion has grown full man by his first birthday.
Running across the bean-fields in a south wind,
Fording the river mouth to feel the tide-race—
Child's play that was, though proof of our possessions.

Now our research is done, measured the shadow,
The plains mapped out, the hills a natural bound'ry.
Such and such is our country.   There remains to
Plough up the meadowland, reclaim the marshes.

POSTSCRIPT

THE SONG OF THE ETERNAL WATERS *

MIGUEL DE UNAMUNO

The narrow road, hewn out of the naked rock, goes winding along above the abyss. On one side rise high tors and crags, on the other side is heard the ceaseless murmur of waters in the dark depths of the ravine, deeper than eye can reach. At intervals the track widens so as to form a kind of refuge, just large enough to hold about a dozen people, a resting-place, screened by leafy branches, for those who travel along the road above the ravine. In the distance, crowning the summit of a jutting crag, a castle stands out against the sky. The clouds passing over it are torn by the pinnacles of its tall towers.

With the pilgrims goes Maquetas. He walks hurriedly, sweating, seeing nothing but the road in front of his eyes, except when from time to time he raises them towards the castle. As he walks he sings an old wailing song that his grandmother taught him when he was a child, and he sings it so that he shall not hear the ominous murmur of the torrent flowing unseen in the depths of the abyss.

As he approaches one of the resting-places, a maiden who is sitting inside on a bank of turf calls to him:

"Maquetas, come here and stop awhile. Come and rest by my side, with your back to the abyss, and let us talk a little. Nothing heartens us for this journey like a few words spoken in love and companionship. Stay awhile here with me. Afterwards you will go on your way again refreshed and renewed."

"I cannot, my girl," Maquetas replied, slowing his pace but without halting. "I cannot. The castle is still a great way off and I must reach it before the sun sets behind its towers."

"You will lose nothing by staying here awhile, young man, for afterwards you will take the road again with more mettle and with new strength. Are you not tired?"

"That I am, lass."

"Then stay awhile and rest. Here you have this turf for your couch and my lap for your pillow. Come, stay!"

And she opened her arms, offering him her bosom.

Maquetas paused for a moment, and as he did so there came to his ears the voice of the invisible torrent flowing in the depths of the abyss. He quitted the road, stretched himself on the turf and laid his head on the girl's lap. With her fresh rosy hands she wiped the sweat from his brow, while his eyes gazed up at the morning sky overhead, a sky that was as young as the eyes of the girl.

"What is it you are singing, lass?"

" 'Tis not I singing—it is the water that flows down there, behind us."

"And what is it that it sings?"

"It sings the song of eternal rest. But now rest yourself."

"Eternal, did you say?"

"Yes, that is what the torrent sings. But now rest."

* Reprinted from *Essays and Soliloquies* by Miguel de Unamuno, by permission of Alfred A. Knopf, Inc. Copyright 1924 by Alfred A. Knopf, Inc.

"And afterwards . . ."

"Rest, Maquetas, and don't say 'afterwards.' "

The girl put her lips to his lips and kissed him. Maquetas felt the kiss melt and flow through all his body, and so sweet it was that it seemed as if all the sky poured itself down over him. His senses swooned. He dreamed that he was falling endlessly down into the bottomless abyss . . .

When he awoke and opened his eyes he saw above him the sky of evening.

"O lass, how late it is! Now I shall not have time to reach the castle. Let me go, let me go."

"Go then, and God guide and companion you. And don't forget me, Maquetas."

"Give me one kiss more."

"Take it, and may it strengthen you."

With the kiss Maquetas felt that his strength was increased a hundredfold and he began to run along the road, the lilt of his song keeping time with his strides. And he ran and ran, leaving the other pilgrims behind him. One of them shouted to him as he passed:

"You'll stop, Maquetas."

Then he saw that the sun was beginning to set behind the towers of the castle and Maquetas felt a chill strike his heart. The fires of the sunset lasted but for a moment. He heard the grating of the chains of the drawbridge. And Maquetas said to himself:

"They are shutting the castle-gate."

Night began to fall, an impenetrable night. Very soon Maquetas had to halt, for he could see nothing, absolutely nothing. Blackness enveloped everything. Maquetas stood still, silent, and in the impenetrability of the darkness he heard only the murmur of the waters of the torrent in the abyss. The cold grew denser.

Maquetas stooped down, felt the road with his numb hands, and began to creep along on all fours, warily, like a fox. He kept edging away from the abyss.

He went forward like this for a long, long time. And he said to himself:

"Ah, that lass deceived me! Why did I heed her?"

The cold became horrible. It penetrated everywhere, like a thousand-edged sword. Maquetas no longer felt the touch of the ground, he no longer felt his own hands; he was benumbed. He stopped still. Or rather he scarcely knew whether he was stopping or crawling.

Maquetas felt himself suspended in the midst of the darkness, black night all around him. He heard nothing but the ceaseless murmur of the waters of the abyss.

"I will call out," Maquetas said to himself, and he made an effort to shout. But no sound was heard; his voice did not come forth out of his chest. It was as if it were frozen within him.

Then Maquetas thought:

"Can I be dead?"

And as the thought took hold of him, it seemed as if the darkness and the cold fused together and eternalized themselves round about him.

"Can this be death?" Maquetas went on thinking. "Shall I have to live henceforward like this, in pure thought, in memory? And the castle? And the abyss? What do the waters say? What a dream, what an appalling dream! And not to be able to sleep! . . . To die like this, dreaming, dying little by little, and not to be able to sleep! . . . And now what am I going to do? What shall I do tomorrow?

"Tomorrow? What is tomorrow? What does tomorrow mean? What is this idea of tomorrow that seems to come to me out of the depth of the darkness, where the waters are singing? Tomorrow? For me there is now no tomorrow. Everything is now, everything is blackness and cold. Even this song of the eternal waters seems like a song of ice—just one prolonged note.

"But can I really have died? How long the dawn is in coming! But I don't even know how long it is since the sun set behind the towers of the castle . . .

"Once upon a time," he went on thinking, "there was a man who was called Maquetas, a great wayfarer, and he walked for days and days journeying to a castle, where a good dinner awaited him and a warm fire and a good bed to rest in, and in the bed a good bedmate. And there in the castle he was going to live days without end, listening to stories that went on for ever, joying in his sweet companion, a life of perpetual youth. And those days would be all alike and all peaceful. And as they passed, oblivion would fall on them. And all those days would be thus one eternal day, one same day eternally renewed, a perpetual today overflowing with a whole infinity of yesterdays and with a whole infinity of tomorrows.

"And Maquetas believed that that was life, and set out on his journey. And he journeyed on, stopping at inns where he slept, and when the sun rose he went on his way again. And once, as he was leaving an inn, he met an aged beggar who was sitting on the trunk of a tree by the door, and the beggar said to him: 'Maquetas, what meaning have things?' And that Maquetas answered him, shrugging his shoulders: 'What does that matter to me?' And the aged beggar asked him again: 'Maquetas, what does this road mean?' And that Maquetas, now somewhat irritated, answered him: 'Why do you ask me what the road means? How should I know? Does anybody know? Does the road mean anything? Leave me in peace, and God be with you.' And the aged beggar knitted his brows and smiled sadly, gazing on the ground.

"And then Maquetas came to a very rugged country and had to cross a wild mountain range by a precipitous footpath hewn out of the rock, high up over an abyss, in the depths of which sang the waters of an invisible torrent. And thence he discerned afar the castle that he had to reach before the sun set, and when he discerned it his heart leaped for joy in his breast, and he quickened his steps. But a lass, sweet as a vision, compelled him to stop and rest awhile on a bank of turf, and that Maquetas rested his head on her lap and stopped. And when he left her the lass gave him a kiss, the kiss of death, and as soon as the sun set behind the towers of the castle the cold and the darkness closed in all round him and the darkness and the cold grew denser and merged into one. And there fell a silence from which only that song of the eternal waters emerged. Yonder, in life, sounds, songs, murmurs, used to issue out of a vague murmurous background, out of a kind of mist of sound; but here this song emerged out of the profound silence, the silence of darkness and cold, the silence of death.

"Of death? Yes, of death, for that Maquetas, that valiant wayfarer, died. . . .

"How sweet the story is, and how sad! It is sweeter, far sweeter, sadder, far sadder, than that old song my grandmother taught me. Let me see, how does it go? I will repeat it over again.

"Once upon a time there was a man who was called Maquetas, a great wayfarer, and he walked for days and days journeying to a castle. . . .' "

And Maquetas repeated to himself again and again and again and again the story of that other Maquetas, and he continues repeating it and so he will go on repeating it as long as the waters of the invisible torrent go on singing, and the waters will sing for ever, ever, ever, without a yesterday and without a tomorrow, for ever, ever, ever. . . .

(J. E. Crawford Flitch, tr.)

INDEX OF TITLES

579

INDEX OF NAMES

INDEX OF SUBJECTS